Palgrave Studies in Prisons and Penology

Series Editors
Ben Crewe
Institute of Criminology
University of Cambridge
Cambridge, UK

Yvonne Jewkes
Social & Policy Sciences
University of Bath
Bath, UK

Thomas Ugelvik
Faculty of Law
University of Oslo
Oslo, Norway

This is a unique and innovative series, the first of its kind dedicated entirely to prison scholarship. At a historical point in which the prison population has reached an all-time high, the series seeks to analyse the form, nature and consequences of incarceration and related forms of punishment. Palgrave Studies in Prisons and Penology provides an important forum for burgeoning prison research across the world.

Series Advisory Board:
Anna Eriksson (Monash University)
Andrew M. Jefferson (DIGNITY - Danish Institute Against Torture)
Shadd Maruna (Rutgers University)
Jonathon Simon (Berkeley Law, University of California)
Michael Welch (Rutgers University).

More information about this series at
http://www.palgrave.com/gp/series/14596

Alexandra Cox • Laura S. Abrams
Editors

The Palgrave International Handbook of Youth Imprisonment

palgrave
macmillan

Editors
Alexandra Cox
Department of Sociology
University of Essex
Colchester, UK

Laura S. Abrams
Luskin School of Public Affairs
University of California Los Angeles
Los Angeles, CA, USA

Palgrave Studies in Prisons and Penology
ISBN 978-3-030-68758-8   ISBN 978-3-030-68759-5   (eBook)
https://doi.org/10.1007/978-3-030-68759-5

© The Editor(s) (if applicable) and The Author(s) 2021
This work is subject to copyright. All rights are solely and exclusively licensed by the Publisher, whether the whole or part of the material is concerned, specifically the rights of translation, reprinting, reuse of illustrations, recitation, broadcasting, reproduction on microfilms or in any other physical way, and transmission or information storage and retrieval, electronic adaptation, computer software, or by similar or dissimilar methodology now known or hereafter developed.
The use of general descriptive names, registered names, trademarks, service marks, etc. in this publication does not imply, even in the absence of a specific statement, that such names are exempt from the relevant protective laws and regulations and therefore free for general use.
The publisher, the authors and the editors are safe to assume that the advice and information in this book are believed to be true and accurate at the date of publication. Neither the publisher nor the authors or the editors give a warranty, expressed or implied, with respect to the material contained herein or for any errors or omissions that may have been made. The publisher remains neutral with regard to jurisdictional claims in published maps and institutional affiliations.

Cover illustration: Klaus Vedfelt

This Palgrave Macmillan imprint is published by the registered company Springer Nature Switzerland AG.
The registered company address is: Gewerbestrasse 11, 6330 Cham, Switzerland

Foreword

The United Nations Global Study on Children Deprived of Liberty concludes that more than seven million children (under 18 years of age) are deprived of liberty per year worldwide. Most of them are kept in institutions of all kinds, including special facilities for children with disabilities, others are placed in migration-related detention, and more than 1.5 million children are held in justice-related detention, that is, in police custody, pre-trial detention facilities and prisons. These are still conservative estimates, based upon a broad variety of data submitted by governments, the United Nations and other inter-governmental organizations, civil society and academia. In 2014, the UN General Assembly had invited the Secretary General to commission this Global Study. In 2016 I was requested to lead the Global Study research process as an independent expert, and in 2019 I submitted the results of our comprehensive and inclusive research and data collection to the General Assembly.

The high number of children deprived of liberty stands in direct contrast to the requirement of the Convention on the Rights of the Child, the UN human rights treaty with the highest number of States parties (196), which clearly states that the detention of children shall be used only as a measure of last resort. This means that children shall be deprived of liberty only in exceptional circumstances on a case-by-case basis if non-custodial solutions are really not available or appropriate. Although some progress has been achieved in recent years, it is evident that much more needs to be done in terms of deinstitutionalization, diversion, ending migration-related detention, strengthening child welfare systems and similar measures. This is crucial since children have to be protected from the traumatic experiences detention settings inevitably create. Depriving children of their liberty means depriving them of their childhood. It is our responsibility to give children in detention back their childhood. Children have a right to grow up safe and surrounded by love—if not in their family, then in a family-type setting. States have a corresponding obligation to support the family, which is the natural and fundamental group unit of society responsible for the upbringing, care and education of children. Where children are unable to remain with their families, States must invest in effective child welfare systems that provide non-custodial alternatives to the deprivation of liberty in numerous settings including institutions, migration detention or in the context of the administration of justice. Children deprived of liberty are invisible to the large majority of society and their fate constitutes the most overlooked violation of the Convention on the Rights of the Child.

The Palgrave International Handbook of Youth Imprisonment deals with one important aspect of deprivation of liberty which is related to the administration of justice. In addition to case studies in Europe, the United States and other world regions, the Handbook raises important issues, such as whether to reform or abolish the current practice of youth prisons altogether. It points at the disproportionate confinement of poor and socially, economically and politically marginalized children across the globe. It describes the bitter experiences and emotions of children behind bars and the long-lasting detrimental impact of detention on their physical and mental health.

I congratulate the editors of the Palgrave Handbook, Alexandra Cox and Laura Abrams, for having compiled such a rich variety of academic contributions which confirm the findings of the Global Study and the need for far-reaching institutional reforms in the field of child justice and youth imprisonment. Governments shall stop "tough on crime policies" against children; decriminalize the behaviour of children and abolish status offences; establish specialized child justice systems; raise the minimum age of criminal responsibility to at least 14 years; abolish life sentences and other excessive prison sentences for children; apply diversion at every stage of the criminal justice process and empower police officers, prosecutors, judges and prison personnel to involve the families and transfer children to their families or family-type settings within the child protection system; replace punitive and repressive child justice systems by restorative justice approaches; keep police custody to a maximum of 24 hours and pre-trial detention never longer than 30 days until formal charges are laid; provide children with effective procedural safeguards and complaints mechanisms at every stage of the child justice proceedings; develop an effective system of independent and unannounced monitoring of all places of child detention; treat children in detention with humanity, dignity and full respect for their human rights; abolish corporal punishment, other forms of physical and psychological violence as well as solitary confinement; and make widely available early release and post-release programmes, such as mentoring programmes, community service work and group/family counselling.

I sincerely hope that the Palgrave International Handbook on Youth Imprisonment will have an impact on making the invisible visible and help to start a process of liberating children from detention in the context of the administration of justice. Children behind bars constitute a practice of structural violence. By drastically reducing the number of children in detention, the Palgrave Handbook, together with the Global Study, will foster the aims of the "Agenda 2030", which strives to end violence against children and to leave no one behind, and in particular no child behind bars.

Vienna and Venice, November 2020

Manfred Nowak is Professor of International Human Rights at Vienna University and Secretary General of the Global Campus of Human Rights, based in Venice. In 2016, he was appointed as Independent Expert leading the UN Global Study on Children Deprived of Liberty.

The United Nations Global Study on Children Deprived of Liberty was published in November 2019 and in a slightly corrected version in June 2020 online and in print. Since October 2020, an Executive Summary is also available in English and will be translated into the other five UN languages. Download the Executive Summary (68 pages) as well as the entire Global Study (768 pages) in PDF or consult the interactive version on omnibook: https://omnibook.com/Global-Study-2019.

Manfred Nowak
Professor of International Human Rights
Vienna University

Acknowledgements

This volume would not be possible without the work of so many scholars and activists who have dedicated their careers to the cause of youth imprisonment. We also thank the many, many young people who took part in these studies, and whose stories filled these chapters. Without you, we would not be any closer to understanding youth imprisonment on this global scale.

To Palgrave editor Josie Taylor, editorial assistant Liam Inscoe-Jones, and series editors, Ben Crewe, Yvonne Jewkes, and Thomas Ugelvik, thank you for ushering this project through from start to finish and for believing in the value of this work. Much appreciation to University of California, Los Angeles (UCLA) graduate student Kaylyn Canlione for her dedication and assistance with this project, editorial work, and overall organization.

Finally, we wish to thank our families and friends for your support to complete this project during the COVID-19 pandemic.

Contents

1 **Introduction**   1
 Alexandra Cox and Laura S. Abrams

Part I   Violated: Children's Rights are Human Rights   17

2 **Self-Isolation May Feel Like Jail: It's Nothing Compared to Youth Prison**   19
 Hernán Carvente-Martinez

3 **Children and Young People in Custody in England and Wales: Rights and Wrongs**   23
 Laura Janes

4 **Everyday Violence in *El Redentor* Specialized Care Center in Bogotá, Colombia**   51
 Laura Liévano-Karim and Amy E. Ritterbusch

5 **Doing Time: Young People and the Rhetoric of Juvenile Justice in Ghana**   77
 Kofi E. Boakye and Thomas D. Akoensi

Part II	Socio-Legal Contexts of Youth Imprisonment	105
6	The Rebirth of Delinquent 'Adult-Children': Criminal Capacity, Socio-economic Systems, and the Malleability of Penality of Child Delinquency in India *Shailesh Kumar*	107
7	Juvenile Deprivation of Liberty in Brazil: Discretion, Expansion and Deterioration *Rafael Barreto Souza*	141
8	"I Wanna Be Somebody by the Time I Turn 25": Narratives of Pathways into Crime and Reentry Expectations Among Young Men in Germany and the United States *Michaela Soyer and Janina L. Selzer*	165
Part III	Regulating Emotions and Relationships Behind Bars	183
9	State Property *Jim St. Germain*	185
10	Boredom: A Key Experience of Youth Imprisonment *Tea Torbenfeldt Bengtsson*	205
11	Friendship in the Juvenile Correctional Institution *Anne M. Nurse*	225
12	Juvenile Facility Staff: Research, Policy, and Practice *Alexandra Cox*	243
Part IV	Gendering Justice	265
13	Straight and Narrow: Girls, Sexualities, and the Youth Justice System *Lisa Pasko*	267
14	"This Place Saved My Life": The Limits of Christian Redemption Narratives at a Juvenile Detention Facility for Girls *Mary E. Thomas*	285

15	Horizontal Surveillance and Therapeutic Governance of Institutionalized Girls *Carla P. Davis*	305
16	'Hypermasculinity' in Interaction: Affective Practices, Resistance and Vulnerability in a Swedish Youth Prison *Anna G. Franzén*	333
17	Incarcerated Young Men and Boys: Trauma, Masculinity and the Need for Trauma-Informed, Gender-Sensitive Correctional Care *Nina Vaswani, Carla Cesaroni, and Matthew Maycock*	355

Part V	Coming Home: Life After Youth Imprisonment	377
18	The Expectations and Challenges of Youth Reentry *Elizabeth Panuccio*	379
19	Nothing's Changed but Me: Reintegration Plans Meet the Inner City *Jamie J. Fader*	413
20	Young Women and Desistance: Finding a Net to Fall Back On *Laura S. Abrams and Diane J. Terry*	437

Part VI	Young Adulthood and Long-Term Confinement	461
21	My Shame *Christian Branscombe*	463
22	The Pains of Life Imprisonment During Late Adolescence and Emerging Adulthood *Serena Wright, Susie Hulley, and Ben Crewe*	479
23	Surviving Life: How Youth Adapt to Life Sentences in Adult Prisons *Kaylyn C. Canlione and Laura S. Abrams*	503

24 Experiencing the Death Penalty as a Child in Malawi: The Story of Henry Dickson 525
Linda Kitenge and Alexious Emmanuel Silombela Kamangila

Part VII Abolition and the Future of Youth Justice 537

25 The Pitfalls of Separating Youth in Prison: A Critique of Age-Segregated Incarceration 539
Hedi Viterbo

26 Toward Transformation: The Youth Justice Movement in the United States on Ending the Youth Prison Model 563
Liz Ryan

27 Critical Reflections on Education for Children in Youth Justice Custody 593
Caroline Lanskey

28 Transforming Youth Justice Inside and Out 615
Vincent Schiraldi and Alexander Schneider

Index 635

Notes on Contributors

Laura S. Abrams is Professor of Social Welfare at UCLA Luskin School of Public Affairs, USA. She holds an MSW and a PhD from the University of California, Berkeley, USA. Her scholarship has examined experiences of youth in the US justice system, through reentry and the transition to adulthood. She is pursuing research in the area of youth justice policy and cross-national comparative studies. She is the author of two award-winning books: *Compassionate Confinement: A Year in the Life of Unit C* (2013) and *Everyday Desistance: The Transition to Adulthood Among Formerly Incarcerated Youth* (2017) and over 80 peer-reviewed articles. She is the lead editor of *The Voluntary Sector in Prisons: Encouraging Personal and Institutional Change* (Palgrave Macmillan, 2016) and the co-editor of this volume.

Thomas D. Akoensi is Senior Lecturer in Criminology and Criminal Justice at the School of Social Policy, Sociology and Social Research, University of Kent, UK. His research interests are in the fields of penology, legitimacy and criminal justice, comparative criminology, and organizational behavior.

Tea Torbenfeldt Bengtsson is a Senior Researcher at VIVE, the Danish National Centre for Social Science Research. Her research includes qualitative studies of youth in out-of-home care and locked secure care facilities, with a focus on risk-taking, marginalization, and social interventions. Her research explores violence in youths' everyday lives and their encounters with criminal court.

Kofi E. Boakye is Senior Lecturer in Criminology at Anglia Ruskin University and an affiliated fellow of the Violence Research Centre, Institute of Criminology, University of Cambridge, UK. His research interests include youth justice, youth violence, comparative criminology, and violence prevention.

Christian Branscombe is a restorative justice advocate and healing facilitator between survivors of violent crimes and their offenders. At the age of 19, Branscombe committed first-degree murder and received a sentence of Life Without the Possibility of Parole. While incarcerated, he built a direct amends program, used art to develop his and others' voices, and was deeply impacted by Healing Dialogue and Action, a restorative justice program. Through their work, Christian was given the opportunity to extend an amends to the direct survivor of his crime, Gunner Johnson. The face-to-face conversation (healing dialogue)—documented on CNN's Redemption Project—led to a remarkable and unexpected friendship. After 25 years in prison, Branscombe's sentence was commuted by the California Governor. He is dedicated to sharing his healing journey.

Kaylyn C. Canlione is a graduate student (2021) in the Social Welfare and Public Policy Departments in the UCLA Luskin School of Public Affairs, USA.

Hernán Carvente-Martinez is the Founder and CEO of Healing Ninjas, a health and wellness company using technology to build and deepen community between people on their respective healing journeys. He is a Chicano social entrepreneur, community organizer, and leader in the fight to end youth incarceration. He is also the National Youth Partnership Strategist at the Youth First Initiative, a national campaign in the USA focused on closing youth prisons and reinvesting that money into community alternatives. He is an advisor to the Credible Messenger Justice Center, serves on the board of Community Connection for Youth, and is a grant-making committee member for the New Youth Program of the Prospect Hill Foundation. He was awarded the "Spirit of Youth Award" by the Coalition for Juvenile Justice and the "Next Generation Champion for Change" award by the John D. and Catherine T. MacArthur Foundation. He holds a BS from John Jay College, USA.

Carla Cesaroni is an Associate Professor at Ontario Tech University in Canada and an associate researcher at the Scottish Centre of Crime and Justice Research, UK. For the past two decades, Cesaroni has researched the experiences and adjustment of incarcerated adolescent boys and young adult men. She has recently concluded a comparative study of 190 incarcerated young men in Canadian and Scottish prisons. Her work includes a study of young people's perceptions of their interactions with police.

Alexandra Cox is a Senior Lecturer in the Department of Sociology at the University of Essex, UK. She has served as Assistant Professor of Sociology at State University of New York (SUNY) New Paltz and, and as a research scholar in law at Yale University Law School. She holds a PhD in Criminology from the University of Cambridge and her undergraduate degree from Yale University. Her book, *Trapped in a Vice: the Consequences of Confinement for Young People* (Rutgers University Press, 2018) received the American Society of Criminology Critical Criminology book award. Prior to receiving her PhD, she worked at the Neighborhood Defender Service of Harlem and Drug Policy Alliance's Office of Legal Affairs. She is a former Gates Cambridge scholar and a Soros Justice Advocacy fellow.

Ben Crewe is Professor of Penology and Criminal Justice, and Deputy Director of the Prions Research Centre, at the Institute of Criminology, University of Cambridge, UK. His books include *The Prisoner Society and Life Imprisonment from Young Adulthood: Adaptation, Identity and Time* (Palgrave Macmillan, 2020). He is one of the co-editors of the Palgrave Studies in Prisons and Penology book series, and one of the launch editors of the journal *Incarceration*.

Carla P. Davis is Associate Professor of Sociology at Beloit College, USA. Her research and teaching focus on social inequalities (race, ethnicity, gender, class) and the ways these hierarchies are reflected and reproduced in institutional structures, policies, programs, and practices. Her most recent publication is *Girls and Juvenile Justice: Power, Status, and the Social Construction of Delinquency* (Palgrave Macmillan, 2017).

Jamie J. Fader is an Associate Professor in the Department of Criminal Justice at Temple University, USA. She is an expert in youth justice, transitions to adulthood among vulnerable youth, and qualitative research methods. Her book, *Falling Back: Incarceration and Transitions to Adulthood Among Urban Youth* (2013) won the 2016 American Society of Criminology Michael J. Hindelang book award for the "most outstanding contribution to research in criminology" and the Academy of Criminal Justice Sciences book award for an "extraordinary contribution to the study of crime and criminal justice." She serves as a member of the Columbia University Emerging Adult Justice Learning Community, a partnership of researchers, practitioners, and policy makers focused on improving justice outcomes for emerging adults.

Anna G. Franzén is an Assistant Professor at the Department of Child and Youth Studies, Stockholm University, Sweden. Drawing mainly on discursive, narrative, and interactional frameworks, her research at large centers on young men and boys and questions of identity, violence, humor, and masculinity. She has conducted several video-ethnographic studies in institutions such as detention homes, prisons, and schools, analyzing issues such as subjectivity, affect, power, and resistance in interaction.

Susie Hulley is a Senior Research Associate at the Institute of Criminology, University of Cambridge. Hulley's recent work has focused on the experiences of men and women serving long life sentences, which they received when they were young, and the application of the legal doctrine of "joint enterprise" in practice. Hulley is co-author of the book *Life Imprisonment from Young Adulthood: Adaptation, Identity and Time* (Palgrave Macmillan, 2020) and has published papers in international journals on topics including anti-social behavior, respect in prison, the experience of long-term imprisonment, and issues of legitimacy associated with joint enterprise.

Laura Janes was admitted as a solicitor in 2006 and has oversight of the Howard League (UK) legal service for people under 21 in prison. She has a professional doctorate in Youth Justice. Laura has developed an expertise in advising and representing children and young people in penal detention in relation to prison law, public law, and criminal appeal matters. Janes is a committee member of the Association of Prison Lawyers and the Legal Aid Practitioners' Group. She is also a visiting fellow at the London South Bank University and Chair of Legal Action Group. In 2019, Janes was awarded Solicitor of the Year by the First 100 years' Inspirational Women in Law Awards.

Linda Kitenge joined Reprieve in 2020 as a Caseworker in the Africa team. She has worked as a Parliamentary Assistant for an MP in the House of Commons. Prior to that, she has spent two years working for NGOs in Burundi and New York City. Linda holds an MA in International Politics and Security Studies from the University of Bradford and a Bachelor of Laws from the University of Birmingham.

Shailesh Kumar is a Commonwealth scholar, funded by the UK government, and a PhD student at the School of Law, Birkbeck College, University of London, UK. He is conducting an empirical study of the reforms brought by the POCSO (Protection of Children from Sexual Offences) Act 2012 that deals with sexual violence against children in India. He has published articles in *International Journal for the Semiotics of Law* and *Contexto Internacional*, and most recently a chapter in *The Routledge International Handbook of Penal Abolition*.

Caroline Lanskey is a University Lecturer in Criminology and Criminal Justice at the University of Cambridge Institute of Criminology and a deputy director of the Institute's Research Centre for Community, Gender and Social Justice, UK. Her research interests stem from her cross-disciplinary experience of education and criminology and include youth justice and young people affected by the criminal justice system, youth voice and participation, the experiences of prisoners' families and children, citizenship and migration, and education and the arts in criminal justice and research methodologies. At the Institute of Criminology, she has worked on several research projects related to education in criminal justice settings, including an evaluation of a training intervention for staff in secure settings for young people; an Economic and Social Research Council (ESRC) postdoctoral research fellowship on the education of young people in custody; a study of the education pathways of young people in the youth justice system; an evaluation of the Ormiston Families "Breaking Barriers" program in schools for children with imprisoned parents; and a historical review of safeguarding children in the secure estate. She is co-Principal Investigator (PI) of Inspiring Futures, a cross-disciplinary evaluation study of arts programs in criminal justice settings.

Laura Liévano-Karim is a Fulbright fellow and PhD student in the UCLA Luskin School of Public Affairs in the Department of Social Welfare, USA. She holds a Bachelor of Science in Psychology from Carleton University in Ottawa, Canada, and a Master in Public Policy from Universidad de los Andes in Bogotá, Colombia. Before joining the PhD program at the Department of Social Welfare, she has worked as a researcher on diverse projects, both quantitative and qualitative, addressing multiple social justice dilemmas in Colombia including violence targeting populations of young people experiencing basic needs instability, throughout rural and urban zones of Colombia. Liévano-Karim has also worked as a lecturer at Universidad de los Andes.

Matthew Maycock is a Baxter fellow in the School of Education and Social Work at the University of Dundee, Scotland, and a visiting fellow at the Centre for Gender Studies, Karlstad University, Sweden. He has worked at the Scottish Prison Service undertaking research often on gender and transgender issues in prison as well as facilitating staff development across a range of areas. He was previously an Investigator Scientist within the Settings and Organisations Team at Social and Public Health Sciences Unit (SPHSU), University of Glasgow. He holds a PhD from the University of East Anglia that analyzed modern slavery through the theoretical lens of masculinity.

Manfred Nowak is Professor of International Human Rights at Vienna University and Director of the Vienna Master of Arts in Human Rights. He has been appointed as Secretary General of the Global Campus of Human Rights (formerly European Inter-University Centre for Human Rights (EIUC)) in January 2016. He has served in various expert functions, such as UN Expert on Enforced Disappearances (1993–2006), UN Special Rapporteur on Torture (2004–2010), Judge at the Human Rights Chamber for Bosnia and Herzegovina (1996–2003) and Vice Chairperson of the EU

Fundamental Rights Agency (2013–2018). In 2016, he was appointed Independent Expert leading the UN Global Study on Children Deprived of Liberty. He was Director of the Netherlands Institute of Human Rights at Utrecht University (SIM, 1987–1989) and of the Ludwig Boltzmann Institute of Human Rights at Vienna University (BIM, 1992–2019) as well as a visiting professor at the University of Lund (2002–2003), the Graduate Institute of International and Development Studies in Geneva (2008–2009) and Stanford University in Palo Alto (2014). He is the author of more than 600 publications in the fields of public international law and human rights.

Anne M. Nurse is Professor of Sociology at the College of Wooster in Ohio, USA. She holds a PhD from the University of California, Davis, and she specializes in criminology, inequality, and research methods. She is the author of numerous articles in the areas of juvenile corrections and child sexual abuse prevention and she has authored two books: *Fatherhood Arrested: Parenting from Within the Juvenile Justice System* and *Locked Up, Locked Out: Young Men in the Juvenile Justice System* (2002 and 2010). Additionally, Nurse is a co-author of the popular textbook *Social Inequality: Forms, Causes, and Consequences* (2019). Her newest book, *Confronting Child Sexual Abuse: Knowledge to Action* is forthcoming from Lever Press.

Elizabeth Panuccio is Assistant Professor of Criminal Justice at Fairleigh Dickinson University's Metropolitan Campus, USA. Panuccio holds a PhD in Criminal Justice from Rutgers University-Newark. Prior to that, she received an MA in Criminal Justice from Rutgers-Newark, an MA in Sociology from Fordham University, and a BA in Sociology from Drew University. She has worked as a research associate on program evaluations and community research projects in partnership with both nonprofits and criminal justice agencies. Her areas of interest are prisoner reentry, families in the criminal justice system, emerging adulthood, developmental criminology, and qualitative research.

Lisa Pasko is Associate Professor of Sociology and Criminology and affiliated faculty in Gender and Women's Studies Program at the University of Denver, USA. In addition to numerous articles, book chapters, and technical reports, she is the co-author of *The Female Offender: Girls, Women, and Crime* and *Girls, Women, and Crime: Selected Readings* (2013). Pasko's research examines the intersectionality of race, gender, and sexualities in the lives of justice-involved girls. She recently finished an Office of Juvenile Justice and Delinquency Prevention grant entitled "Characteristics and Predictors of Juvenile Diversion Program Success for Girls: A Focus on the Latina First-Time Offender." With Vera Lopez, she is completing an edited volume entitled *Violando la Ley: Latinas in the Justice System* (NYU Press, 2020).

Amy E. Ritterbusch is Assistant Professor of Social Welfare at the UCLA Luskin School of Public Affairs, USA. She has led social justice-oriented participatory action research (PAR) initiatives with street-connected communities in Colombia for the last decade and recently in Uganda. Her work involves the documentation of human rights violations and forms of violence exerted against homeless individuals, sex workers, drug users, and street-connected children and youth and subsequent community-driven mobilizations to catalyze social justice outcomes within these communities. Throughout her research and teaching career, she has explored different approaches to engaging students and community leaders through critical and responsible interaction between classroom and street spaces in Colombia and Uganda through the lens of social justice-oriented PAR. Her research has been funded by the Open Society Foundations, the National Science Foundation, the Fulbright U.S. Program, and other networks promoting global social justice.

Liz Ryan is a campaign strategist, youth justice policy expert, and civil and human rights advocate on issues impacting children, youth and their families. Ryan directs the Youth First initiative, a national campaign to end youth incarceration and invest in youth in their communities, where she is responsible for overall strategy, management, and resource development. Previously, she founded the Campaign for Youth Justice (CFYJ) and has worked at several national nonprofits, including the Center on Budget & Policy Priorities, the Youth Law Center, and the Children's Defense Fund. She has held senior legislative and policy positions on Capitol Hill. Ryan is an Adjunct Faculty member at the American University and holds a Master's degree from the George Washington University and a BA from Dickinson College, USA.

Vincent Schiraldi is a Senior Research Scientist at the Columbia University School of Social Work and co-Director of the Columbia University Justice Lab, USA. He has extensive experience in public life, founding the policy think tank, the Justice Policy Institute, then moving to government as Director of the Juvenile Corrections in Washington DC, as Commissioner of the New York City Department of Probation, and Senior Policy Adviser to the NYC Mayor's Office of Criminal Justice. Schiraldi gained national reputation as a fearless reformer who emphasized the humane and decent treatment of men, women, and children under his correctional supervision. He pioneered efforts at community-based alternatives to incarceration in NYC and Washington DC. Schiraldi holds an MSW from New York University and a Bachelor of Arts from Binghamton University.

Alexander Schneider is a project manager for Youth Justice Initiatives at the Columbia University Justice Lab, USA. His past work included managing programs for a number of nonprofits, and his volunteer work included teaching in jails and as a United States Peace Corps volunteer in Ukraine. Schneider holds a Master's in Nonprofit Management from the New School and a BA from the University of Toronto.

Janina L. Selzer is a doctoral candidate in sociology at the City University of New York Graduate Center at Hunter College in the USA. She is writing her mixed-method dissertation about Iraqi immigration in Germany and the USA.

Alexious Emmanuel Silombela Kamangila graduated from the University of Malawi, Chancellor College. He was admitted to the bar in 2016 and has continued practice, with a focus in criminal law. In 2018, he attained a certificate in capital defense and became a Makwanyane Institute Fellow upon completing an Attorney Against the Death Penalty Training offered by Cornell University. He enrolled at National University of Ireland, Galway (NUIG) to research "Access to Justice for persons with Cognitive Disability; the Right to Fair Trial in Thin Air." He was awarded a First Class LLM in International Comparative Disability Law and Policy in 2019. For more than a decade, he has and continues to volunteer for the Community of Sant' Egidio Malawi. He initiated the *Justice for All* project through which he offers free legal service to those that cannot afford it in the criminal justice system especially those facing homicide trials. A Reprieve Fellow based in Malawi, he is an abolitionist who leads the advocacy strategies for the abolition of the death penalty and elimination of torture in Malawi.

Rafael Barreto Souza is a lawyer and researcher at the Laboratory of Penal Policy Management of the University of Brasilia (LabGEPEN/UnB); Member of the Advisory Committee of the international initiative to create a Universal Protocol for Non-coercive Investigative Interviewing; and Professor of Law at the University IESB in Brasilia, Brazil (on leave). He has worked as an expert and coordinator of the Brazilian National Preventive Mechanism Against Torture (MNPCT). Souza has also worked as a legal consultant to the International Bar Association (IBAHRI), as a fellow for the Inter-American Rapporteurship on the Rights of the Child (IACHR/OAS), among other UN bodies and civil society organizations. Souza holds a master's degree in development studies from the Graduate Institute of International and Development Studies (IHEID) in Geneva, and a master's degree in law from the Federal University of Ceará in Brazil. He works for the UNDP in a criminal justice reform initiative with the Brazilian National Justice Council (CNJ).

Michaela Soyer is an Assistant Professor in the Sociology Department at Hunter College, City University of New York, USA. She is the author of two books: *A Dream Denied – Incarceration, Recidivism and Young Minority Men* and *Lost Childhoods: Poverty, Trauma, and Violent Crime in the Post-Welfare Era*.

Jim St. Germain is the co-founder of Preparing Leaders of Tomorrow (PLOT), a youth mentoring program in the USA. St. Germain holds an associate degree in human services from the Borough of Manhattan Community College and a bachelor of arts degree in political science from John Jay College of Criminal Justice, USA. He serves on the Board of the National Juvenile Defender Center and was appointed by President Barack Obama to the Coordinator Council on Juvenile and Justice Delinquency Prevention (CCJJ). St. Germain is an author, storyteller, and motivational speaker whose work encompasses issues related to criminal justice, mentoring, mental health, substance abuse, education, and poverty. St. Germain is the co-author of a newly released book, *The Good Immigrant*, and a memoir, *A Stone of Hope*. St. Germain has written and co-directed "Every9Hours," which tackles police shootings in the USA.

Diane J. Terry is a Senior Research Associate in the Psychology Applied Research Center at Loyola Marymount University, USA. She has over ten years of experience in the field of social welfare and program evaluation research. Her research focuses on mental health disparities among communities of color, permanency, and well-being outcomes for youth and families involved with the child welfare system, and criminal desistance among formerly incarcerated young adults. As a program evaluator, she has specialized in mixed-methods, multi-year evaluation studies where she has played a key role in evaluation implementation, mixed-methods data collection, and project management.

Mary E. Thomas is Associate Professor of Women's, Gender & Sexuality Studies at Ohio State University, USA. She is the author of *Multicultural Girlhood: Racism, Sexuality, and the Conflicted Spaces of American Education* (2011).

Nina Vaswani is a research fellow and the research lead at the Centre for Youth & Criminal Justice (CYCJ), hosted by the University of Strathclyde, Scotland. Vaswani oversees the varied research program at CYCJ, which aims to conduct and use research to help support practice and policy development in youth justice and related fields. Vaswani's main research interest is in the experiences of loss, bereavement, and trauma in children and young people, especially those who are marginalized or who are in conflict with the law, as well as the vulnerabilities of young men in contact with the justice system, in addition to organizational and system responses to trauma and how the "system" interacts with childhood adversity and trauma.

Hedi Viterbo is Lecturer in Law at Queen Mary University of London, UK. Previously, he was Lecturer in Law at the University of Essex, a Leverhulme Early Career Fellow at SOAS, University of London, a visiting scholar at Harvard Law School, and a visiting researcher at Columbia University. He holds a PhD in Law from London School of Economics (LSE) and an LLM (summa cum laude) from Tel Aviv University; he is also a graduate of the latter's four-year Interdisciplinary Program for Outstanding Students. His research examines legal issues concerning childhood, state violence, and sexuality from an interdisciplinary and global perspective. His publications include *Problematizing Law, Rights, and Childhood in Israel/Palestine* (Cambridge University Press, forthcoming) and *The ABC of the OPT: A Legal Lexicon of the Israeli Control over the Palestinian Territory* (2018), co-authored with Orna Ben-Naftali and Michael Sfard.

Serena Wright is Lecturer in Criminology at the Department of Law and Criminology, Royal Holloway, University of London (RHUL), UK. She is also the departmental lead for LearningTogether@RHUL. Her research interests include the gendered experience of penal sanctions within the life course, encompassing both short-term and life imprisonment. She has recently published her first monograph, *Life Imprisonment from Young Adulthood: Adaptation, Identity and Time* (Palgrave Macmillan, 2020), and is co-editing a special issue of the *Prison Service Journal* focused on life imprisonment with Susie Hulley.

List of Figures

Fig. 5.1	Detention of young people at the Swedru Industrial Home (now Junior Boys' Correctional Centre) 1947–1989	82
Fig. 5.2	Young people in Senior Correctional Centre 2014–2019	92
Fig. 5.3	Age distribution of young people in Senior Correctional Centre 2014–2019	94
Fig. 7.1	Growth rate of detention measures	152
Fig. 7.2	Semi-liberty share of custodial measures	155
Fig. 17.1	Complicating factors and outcomes arising from the interaction of trauma, masculinity, youth and prison	365
Fig. 27.1	A multi-layered perspective on education in custody	599

List of Tables

Table 3.1	The rules that apply to young people in detention	28
Table 3.2	Key rights and rules affecting young people's lives in custody	29
Table 3.3	Oversight and monitoring of secure establishments holding young people	33
Table 4.1	Participants table	59
Table 5.1	Swedru Boys' Junior Correctional Centre, Central Region 2015–2019	87
Table 5.2	Accra Girls Junior Correctional Centre, Greater Accra 2015–2019	87
Table 6.1	Key legislations with year of enactment, MACR, ACM, and detention conditions (1860–1946)	113
Table 6.2	Key legislations with year of enactment, MACR, ACM, and trial and detention conditions (1947–present)	117
Table 6.3	Year-wise breakup of data on Juvenile Delinquency (arrest data)	126
Table 6.4	Year-wise breakup of total incidences of four 'heinous' offences under the IPC and crimes under the POCSO Act by delinquent children (arrest data)	126
Table 6.5	Year-wise breakup of 'Disposal of Juveniles Arrested and Sent to Courts'	127
Table 6.6	Education and family background of juveniles arrested	128
Table 6.7	Annual family income of juveniles apprehended	128
Table 7.1	Growth rate per measure	153
Table 7.2	Criminal offenses by adolescents subject to custodial measures (%)	156
Table 8.1	American respondents	171

List of Tables

Table 8.2	German respondents	172
Table 10.1	Details about the five youth presented in the following analysis. All information shared by the youth	211
Table 12.1	Interview sample demographics	251
Table 13.1	Summary background of girls	272
Table 18.1	Descriptive characteristics of participants	387
Table 19.1	Reoffending, reincarceration, and other criminal justice outcomes, three years after release	429
Table 20.1	Sample characteristics	440
Table 22.1	Frequencies and means for key demographic variables: Survey participants and interviewees aged 18–25 years at the time of the study	486
Table 22.2	Mean averages, standard deviation, and range for key demographic variables: Survey participants and interviewees aged 18–25 years at the time of the study	487
Table 22.3	Ranked (top 10 of 39 "problems") mean severity scores comparing survey respondents aged 18–25 years and ≥26 years at the time of study	488
Table 23.1	Participant characteristics	510

1

Introduction

Alexandra Cox and Laura S. Abrams

Numerous children are imprisoned across the globe in deplorable conditions, despite international legal conventions which suggest that children should be detained only as a last resort. In 2014, the United Nations commissioned a global study of children deprived of liberty; using a broad range of data, researchers in this study estimated that across the globe, there were 1.5 million children detained in criminal justice-related matters throughout 2018 (Nowak 2019: 41). This handbook brings together the perspectives of researchers, advocates, and young people themselves on the shape, experiences, and challenges to the imprisonment of young people.

Article 37b of The United Nations Convention on the Rights of the Child (UNCRC), of which 196 countries are signatories, requires that detention should only be used as a last resort and for the shortest appropriate period of time (United Nations 1989). The UNCRC set standards for the treatment of children in care, including protection from violence and degrading punishment. However, there is a substantial gap between policy, international law,

---

A. Cox (✉)
Department of Sociology, University of Essex, Colchester, UK
e-mail: alexandra.cox@essex.ac.uk

L. S. Abrams
Luskin School of Public Affairs, University of California Los Angeles, Los Angeles, CA, USA
e-mail: abrams@luskin.ucla.edu

© The Author(s), under exclusive license to Springer Nature Switzerland AG 2021
A. Cox, L. S. Abrams (eds.), *The Palgrave International Handbook of Youth Imprisonment*, Palgrave Studies in Prisons and Penology, https://doi.org/10.1007/978-3-030-68759-5_1

and practice (Nowak 2019: 260). Not only are a substantial number of children around the world subjected to lengthy terms of imprisonment, but they are frequently exposed to abuse and violence in custody, poor health and mental health care, and a lack of access to educational, vocational, and training options (Nowak 2019). Systems of confinement globally also reflect intersectional patterns of criminalization by race, ethnicity, immigration status, class, caste, gender, and sexuality: impoverished children, particularly boys, face systemic racism in the processes of arrest and confinement across the globe, raising considerable questions about the uses and abuses of confinement for the purposes of social control. Finally, the UNCRC prohibits the incarceration of children with adults, but in a number of nations around the world, children are routinely placed into detention with adults and sentenced to adult terms of imprisonment. As many as 1000 children across the globe are estimated to be on death row for crimes that they committed when they were children (Nowak 2019: 292).

The incarceration of young people raises significant questions about the state's role in the development and care of its youngest citizens and has particular consequences for children's ability to thrive, grow, and make political, social, and economic contributions to the nation state. It also has consequences for the establishment of trust between young citizens and states and the role of care and control more generally in the lives of citizens. A state's decision to incarcerate a young person, and the conditions which they subject them to, often reflect a broader set of commitments—to the rule of law, to equity and fairness, and to human rights more generally. Thus, institutions used to imprison young people reflect a state's broader set of commitments to the dignity and worth of its citizens.

Despite the large numbers of children in confinement globally, a number of nations have engaged in substantial reforms toward decarceration. These reforms have resulted in a considerable decrease in the numbers of confined children in several high-incarceration nations around the world, including the United States and the United Kingdom (National Juvenile Justice Network 2018; Youth Justice Board/Ministry of Justice 2019). As the number of children in detention and residential facilities has declined, some advocates have pushed for non-custodial solutions, such as the use of small group home facilities and foster homes. This has opened the door for discussions about the appropriate shape of care for young people in placements outside of their homes and families and raises questions about the deprivation of liberty, appropriate oversight, and conditions of confinement for children separated from their families. In the UN Global Study on Children Deprived of Liberty, researchers found that there are 5.4 million children globally in institutions, separated from their families, and at risk of the deprivation of liberty (Nowak 2019).

Despite the evidence of rampant abuse and violence, institutions that house children in conflict with the law are notoriously difficult to access and study. Indeed, there is often much to hide from the outsider's lens. Yet it remains critically important to study the contours of imprisonment, not only to understand the effects of imprisonment on young people but also to contribute to our understanding of proposals for reform, restructuring, and abolition. Fortunately, researchers around the globe have centered their attention on juvenile imprisonment, and there is an emerging research literature, particularly critical qualitative and ethnographic studies in this field that this volume aims to highlight.

A note on language: we have titled this book *The Palgrave International Handbook of Youth Imprisonment* in part because we believe that it is critical to recognize the relevance of the term 'imprisonment' for describing the conditions which young people find themselves in across the globe, even though the terminology may differ locally. In fact, there are often quite politically charged debates about the terminology used to describe these institutions for children, with many state and local governments insisting that these are in fact 'treatment facilities,' 'residential centers,' or 'youth offender institutions,' *not* prisons (see also Vaught 2017: 58). However, we assert that the term 'imprisonment' more adequately captures the transnational experience of incarceration that young people face and which has important commonalities in terms of the experiences related to the deprivation of liberty.

One common feature of juvenile facility life across the globe is an emphasis on behavioral change, and in particular, the uses of cognitive behavioral change programming to 'reform' the youth in their care. A number of researchers have identified how young people often perform change in the face of a demanding set of program expectations and interventions (Sankofa et al. 2017; Fader 2013; Abrams and Anderson-Nathe 2013; Inderbitzin 2007). There is also remarkable global consistency in the practices of what has been termed *responsibilization*, whereby young people's actions are often individualized and considerable demands are placed on them to take responsibility for their own future selves, from child welfare-oriented facilities in Sweden (Franzén 2014; Gradin Franzén 2014) to more traditional punitive facilities in Canada (Gray and Salole 2005), Australia (Halsey 2008), Ghana (Ayete-Nyampong 2013), and the United States (Cox 2011; Kramer et al. 2013). Young people's individual selves and autonomy are often emphasized in this process, yet many researchers have noted the contradictions inherent in stressing such autonomy in the lives of children who are still dependent on the state and their families for their well-being, from Portugal (Zoettl 2018) to the United States (Myers 2013). They have also pointed to the ways that treatment programming often gets sacrificed in the face of demands of 'paperwork' and bureaucratic measures (Drybread 2016; Cox 2018).

Closely related to the behavioral demands of facility life are concerns over the emotional landscape of juvenile imprisonment. A number of scholars have addressed the deep demands placed on young people in custody not only to express their emotions but also to police them through the demands of self-control in the custodial landscape (Abrams and Anderson-Nathe 2013; Tilton 2020). The stress of confinement and toll that this takes on young people's emotional well-being has been explored in participatory action research and projects which focus on youth voice in particular (Desai 2019). The experience of confinement also produces a range of emotions for young people, and one of the particularly salient emotions is boredom, explored in this volume by Tea Bengtsson and elsewhere (2012; Henriksen and Refsgaard 2020). They have also examined the role that a young person's early life experiences, particularly their exposure to emotional and physical abuse and violence, may play in their negative adaptation to confinement (Zhao 2020) and the role that emotions about crime itself plays in shaping young people's experiences of custody (Hosser et al. 2008; Crewe et al. 2020).

Other scholars have focused on young people's relationships to authority in custody, and the ways that those relationships may mediate their engagement with correctional programs. In a study of a therapeutic program for young offenders in Arizona (USA), for example, Bortner and Williams (1997: 120) found that young people desired stability, fairness, and consistency. They conferred legitimacy on the program at its beginning stages, and generally complied with its rules, when they felt that the rules and enforcement of rules were clear and that they were treated with respect. The young people withdrew their support for the program when they felt that staff made up rules arbitrarily and "unjustly rationalized their actions" (Bortner and Williams 1997: 122). Their study usefully points to the ways that young people place value on the principles of perceived legitimacy, ethicality, and fairness within institutions that are often riddled with inconsistencies (see also Van der Laan and Eichelsheim 2013; Zhao et al. 2020).

Often, young people find that even despite having 'graduated' from or aging out of juvenile facilities, their lives continue to be shaped by systems of control—from child welfare to the police and probation that they experience as oppressive and stifling. Jerry Flores, in his study of the experiences of a group of girls moving in and out of custody in California, terms the constant surveillance of girls in and out of confinement "wraparound incarceration"

(2016). Jamie Fader (2013), whose seminal work on juvenile incarceration is reprinted in this volume, similarly found that young people in Philadelphia struggled as they sought to navigate their lives outside of confinement without adequate social support and facing constant scrutiny by agents of the state (see also Abrams and Terry 2014, 2017; Halsey 2007). Others have examined the ways that young people continue to experience the stigma of their experiences in confinement, such as work by Chui and Cheng (2013), about young people who have left custody in Hong Kong. Across the globe, studies find that reentry and community reintegration present a host of challenges as well as opportunities, much of which are contextualized by youth serving systems, policies, and practices.

Juvenile facilities can be an important site to study the performances and policing of gender, as individual-level engagement in crime has been a rich terrain in which to understand how gender performances can be made and re-made. Institutions may play a role in entrenching those identities as young people seek out ways to find acceptance within often-precarious institutional circumstances. Researchers have also critically examined the gendered dimensions of juvenile facility life, and in particular, the ways that hegemonic forms of masculinity and femininity are both resisted and reproduced in facility life (Cesaroni and Alvi 2010; Reich 2010; Harvey 2007; Bengtsson 2015). They have also studied the ways that gender norms are policed and enforced within the facilities, and the pathways and experiences that shape gendered forms of detention (Flores and Pamplona 2020). In her study of the experiences of young men in Young Offender Institutions in the United Kingdom, Kate Gooch examined the ways that aggression by young men enabled them to perform a form of adulthood and set themselves apart from childhood vulnerabilities (2017). In her study of young people's expressions of manhood in a juvenile detention center in northeastern Brazil, Kristin Drybread (2014) argued that young people shored up their sense of manhood in order to resist their definition as 'children' by the state.

Scholars across the globe have studied the lives and experiences of girls in custody in particular, primarily because girls often make up such a small percentage of children in confinement. Studies of girls have also identified the unique array of vulnerabilities that they have experienced in their pathways to the system, which may also play a role in shaping their experiences of institutionalization. Researchers from Denmark (Henriksen 2017), to England (Sharpe 2009), to the United States have examined the ways that girls are often pathologized, sexualized (Thomas 2019), and framed as more 'difficult' than boys and treated through a welfarist approach that often reproduces their marginality.

As identified in the Global study, the disproportionate confinement of children of color, migrant youth, and socially and politically marginalized children across the globe is a consistent feature of local systems. Juvenile imprisonment often becomes a mechanism through which state and local authorities separate and control children who are deemed to be unruly, threatening, and 'wayward,' and these ideas are arguably deeply shaped by racialized social understandings. In their studies of the interior life of facilities, scholars have explored the racialized dimensions of behavioral control (Cox 2015; Tilton 2020; Wilson 2003; Vaught 2017), as well as young people's experiences of racism in custody (Holley and van Vleet 2006; Barn et al. 2018; Rolnick 2016). In Canada, the United States, and Australia, the policing and incarceration of indigenous youth, from the history of boarding schools to the present-day practices of discipline and over incarceration, have been explored in depth (Cesaroni et al. 2019; Corrado et al. 2014; White 2015; Arya and Rolnick 2008; Hill 2007). The British 'borstal' model is one that was exported to its colonial subject-states and has left ongoing dynamics of coloniality as Boakye and Akoensi explore in this volume.

The adultification of young people who commit crimes is a thread that links a number of studies in this field, both via the law and through the construction of children who commit crimes as 'thugs not children,' 'unchildlike,' and deserving of harsh punishment in the context of the United States (Tilton 2013; Brown 2011), Israel, and Palestine (Shalhoub-Kevorkian 2019), and other places across the globe. This adultification is also deeply racialized. Several additional studies have examined the legal processes and consequences of adultification, as reflected in individuals incarcerated in adult prisons who were sentenced as children. These scholars have examined the ways that young people age behind bars, how they navigate the complicated terrain of familial and personal relationships with others, express agency and reflect on their actions, and manage external social and legal constructions of them as irredeemable (see Crewe et al. 2017; Tyanan 2019; and Abrams and Canlione, this volume).

While there is a wealth of rich scholarly work on the nature and experience of juvenile imprisonment, rarely has this work been brought together, and little is known globally about cross-cutting themes surrounding youth confinement. Countries can most certainly learn more in conversation with one another. In this volume, we bring together views from a wide variety of countries and contexts to present the most recent, cutting edge research on youth imprisonment that has the potential to shape how the field can create better systems of care for all young people in conflict with the law.

This Volume

This volume tackles some key questions surrounding youth imprisonment for the twenty-first century and beyond. For example, what is the purpose of youth prisons? Should the goal be to reform or abolish these institutions altogether? Who is deserving of imprisonment and who is exempt? Is there any 'justice' remaining in 'youth justice'? With recent calls to abolish youth prisons altogether (Bernstein 2014; Goldson 2005; Ryan, this volume), we must ask ourselves if there is a continuing purpose to youth imprisonment and what the future might hold.

To ground the reader in these important questions, we start this volume by examining human rights and children's rights in the context of global youth imprisonment. The range of data, policy, and the historical and contemporary review of the conditions of confinement in these chapters touches on philosophical questions about the nature and function of youth imprisonment, beginning with a personal exposé by Hernán Carvente-Martinez, detailing his imprisonment in the United States, and implications for thinking about confinement in the context of COVID-19. Fundamentally, as Laura Janes writes in her chapter on youth imprisonment in the United Kingdom, youth imprisonment, while governed by the law, continues to deprive children of their rights, is marred by the overrepresentation of poor and ethnic minority youth, and has consistently failed to pass even the basic standards of human care. Next, Laura Liévano-Karim and Amy Ritterbusch reveal how conditions of violence and deprivation are consistently challenged and brought to public attention but fail to produce meaningful changes in human rights violations in Columbia. This piece dovetails with Kofi Boakye and Thomas Akoensi's study of youth imprisonment systems in Ghana, which illustrates how these systems are historically and currently driven by state and/or colonial control over those who are poor. These chapters beg the question of how we can continue to try to 'reform' youth justice systems when continual reports show us that the system itself is set up to fail our most vulnerable young people. These themes are then continued in Part VII of this volume which tackles fundamental questions surrounding reform or abolition of the system as we look toward the future.

Next, we turn to a group of chapters that focus on the socio-legal constructions of youth imprisonment. These chapters span four continents as they examine the legal regulations and institutions that surround youth delinquency and imprisonment in the United States, Germany, Brazil, and India. In chapters by Shailesh Kumar (India) and Rafael Baretto Souza (Brazil), we find that ongoing attempts to 'reform' youth justice, whether changing the age range for the system, setting a minimum age, or uses of 'diversion' do little to change the numbers of children, and particularly those from the poorest and most marginalized groups, to being reached by systems of law, probation, and government control through detention. In fact, at times, reforms tend to produce unintended effects of net widening or shifting custody and control to other populations. Following this argument, in Michaela Soyer and Janine Selzer's comparative study between Germany and the United States, we find that youth sentencing laws and those connections to a state's education and welfare policies construct young people's abilities to see pathways toward a successful future.

In Part III of this volume, the authors examine some of the most overlooked aspects of youth imprisonment—the dimensions and range of emotions that are experienced as a young person living behind bars. Although it is often assumed that the pains of imprisonment are related to the overt physical harms and deprivations associated with custody, it is often the everyday life of confinement, and in particular, the emotional life of confinement, which can reveal a great deal about the pains of imprisonment. This set of chapters covers scholarly investigations on such issues as boredom, friendships, and relationships with facility staff. These chapters draw from research spanning the United States, Denmark, Canada, and the United Kingdom. In this section, we come to understand that the emotional landscape of youth justice represents more than custody and control: living behind bars is also subject to developmentally significant experiences that are common among youth, such as 'boredom' and filling time, as Tea Bengtsson writes. This set of unique empirical studies also highlights the importance of friendships, as Anne Nurse writes, and relationships with facility staff, that Alexandra Cox examines. The interplay between institutional conditions and interpersonal experiences is an overlooked layer of confinement, but nonetheless one that youth who are imprisoned may mark their experiences inside youth facilities. Jim St. Germain, who was incarcerated in New York's juvenile justice system, details his experiences as a young man sent from detention to a residential facility, where he was confronted with the demands of a point-based behavioral change system that had little relevance for the challenges he was facing in his young life.

The emotional and relational dimensions of imprisonment lay a foundation to consider key questions surrounding the construction of gender and sexuality in youth facilities. Each chapter in Part IV digs deeply into youths' experiences of confinement in gendered ways. For young women, chapters by Mary Thomas, Lisa Pasko, and Carla Davis qualitatively tackle different aspects of incarceration of young (cis)women in the United States and Canada, including regulation of sexuality, morality, and spirituality and reinforcing gender and racialized hierarchies. The settings explored are unique in their composition as faith based, gender segregated, and co-educational institutions, respectively, but all settings have a way of enforcing gendered and often marginalized positions as women due to the combination of therapeutic and institutional narratives.

For young (cis) men, institutions construct identities with similar mechanisms, but different norms. Anna Gradin Franzén's research in Sweden finds that the emotional labor of youth prisons takes a particular form when intertwined with the experience of masculinities. In her ethnographic study and in contrast to prior literature, she finds that a particular form of vulnerability emerges that not only reinforces hegemonic, traditional masculinity but offers other possibilities as well. As Vaswani et al. writes, the forms of masculinities constructed in youth facilities coexist with alternative narratives, such as trauma and vulnerability, due to the unique nature of 'rehabilitation' for young men behind bars. Along with the three chapters on young women, this part of the volume reveals youth incarceration not just as a site of containment and control but also one with distinct messaging and implications for gender, sexuality, and the pursuit of a 'transformed' self.

In Part V, we examine what happens to young people once they are released from incarceration. Different from the stories and insights learned regarding long-term imprisonment, nearly all young people who are sentenced within the youth justice system will return to society. But how are they prepared for this transition? What happens in the transition to adulthood? Both Elisabeth Panuccio and Jamie Fader's works ethnographically examine the lives of young men who are released from youth confinement and expected to step into adulthood roles and responsibilities. Panuccio shows how the expectations of those around them, their families and loved ones, are mismatched with what they were prepared to handle. Another mismatch identified in Fader's chapter shows the clash between the personal transformation emphasized in youth prisons versus the reality of unchanged structural conditions. Laura Abrams and Diane Terry's chapter, also set in the United States, unearths similar processes for young women, yet emphasizes the gender-based violence and absence of safety nets that characterize young women's reentry experiences. All of this work takes a deep dive into reentry based on the identities and expectations of youth corrections, the lack of preparation for the realities of life outside, and the harsh structural conditions that surround young people when they find themselves in conditions where crime may be their best opportunity for survival.

'Youth justice' and 'youth imprisonment' are socially constructed terms with evolving meanings (Abrams et al. 2018). Recently, the concept of youth imprisonment has been applied to young adults (e.g., ages 18–24) who are also sometimes sentenced as in a youth court, in specific courts for 'young adults,' or otherwise sentenced in adult court, with adult penalties for crimes committed as minors. In Part VI of this volume, we consider what it means for young people to grow up behind bars. We begin this section with a personal exposé written by Christian Branscombe, who was sentenced to life without the possibility of parole in the United States and was released after he appealed his sentence. He reflects on the meaning of shame, the major crime he committed at age 19, and his healing through restorative justice and connection with the family of his victim.

The next two chapters tackle the major themes of the pains of imprisonment and the pathway toward healing during a life sentence. Based on a mixed-methods study conducted in the United Kingdom, Serena Wright, Susie Hulley, and Ben Crewe argue that the losses associated with long-term imprisonment are particularly acute for young adults. Kaylyn Canlione and Laura Abrams present research with a similar population in the United States, former youth lifers who are now free, reflecting that even during the transition to long-term incarceration, these young people experienced a core process in choosing to live, rather than just survive, in violent prisons. These themes of survival, long-term punishment, and loss are then examined in the nation of Malawi through a story of Henry Dickson, a young person's journey from death row to freedom. As Linda Kitenge and Alexious Kamaglia attest, gross human rights violations occur when all people—but particularly young people—are condemned to life in prison or death.

In the last section of this volume, 'Abolition and the Future of Youth Justice' these concluding chapters leave open the possibility of imagining a very different future for youth imprisonment. Here we present varied opinions about what we should do with what scholars generally typically agree is a broken system with human rights violations across the globe. These violations are not a result of aberrations, but rather are part of systemic injustice itself. But the question remains: what to do about youth in conflict with the law? In the first chapter of this section, Hedi Viterbo argues for an end to age-segregated incarceration, meaning that the long-held, defining feature of youth prisons (i.e., separate from adults) no longer serves any meaningful purpose. While imprisoning youth with adults is a controversial opinion, Liz Ryan goes a step further to argue for the abolition of youth prisons altogether. She argues as youth imprisonment in the United States is a failed experiment regardless of reforms, no young person should ever be subject to any form of imprisonment moving forward. Caroline Lanskey's chapter broadens the discussion about what youth confinement might contribute in the future by presenting a model education for youth who are imprisoned. Finally, in our last chapter, Vincent Shiraldi and Alex Schneider write about how reform is achieved from within and how to make youth justice a better system through various means, including less reliance on incarceration and more humane facilities that are closer to home. While these chapters do not point to any one solution, they provocatively challenge us to think about the future (if any) of youth imprisonment and how to get there.

Conclusion

As co-editors, we are excited to introduce readers to the global and diverse perspectives included in this volume. We recognize that our volume is more Western-centric than is optimal and that key parts of the globe are not well represented. There remains a dearth of research knowledge and funding support for research done on and about institutions in Eastern Europe and Russia, Southeast Asia, Central America, and the Middle East in particular. Hence, we hope that this volume is a launching point for future studies that critically examine how youth imprisonment takes shape in different contexts, cultures, and socio-legal systems. While there is much work to be done to end the harmful and abusive practices of youth imprisonment, we remain hopeful that scholarship, advocacy, and testimony will continue to lead us toward justice as a guiding principle in the care and protection of youth.

References

Abrams, L. S., & Anderson-Nathe, B. (2013). *Compassionate confinement: A year in the life of unit C.* New Brunswick, NJ: Rutgers University Press.

Abrams, L. S., Jordan, S. P., & Montero, L. A. (2018). What is a juvenile? A cross-national comparison of youth justice systems. *Youth Justice, 18*(2), 111–130.

Abrams, L. S., & Terry, D. (2017). *Everyday desistance: The transition to adulthood among formerly incarcerated youth.* Rutgers University Press.

Abrams, L. S., & Terry, D. L. (2014). "You can run but you can't hide": How formerly incarcerated young men navigate neighborhood risks. *Children and Youth Services Review, 47*, 61–69.

Arya, N., & Rolnick, A. (2008, July 1). A tangled web of justice: American Indian and Alaska native youth in federal, state, and tribal justice systems. Campaign for Youth Justice Policy Brief, Vol. 5, 2009. Available at SSRN. Retrieved from https://ssrn.com/abstract=1892959

Ayete-Nyampong, L. (2013). *Entangled realities and the underlife of a total institution: An ethnography of correctional centres for juvenile and young offenders in Accra, Ghana*. PhD thesis, Wageningen University, The Netherlands.

Barn, R., Feilzer, M., & Hardwick, N. (2018). Black and minority ethnic boys and custody in England and Wales: Understanding subjective experiences through an analysis of official data. *Social Sciences, 7*, 226.

Bengtsson, T. T. (2012). Boredom and action-experiences from youth confinement. *Journal of Contemporary Ethnography, 41*(5), 526–553.

Bengtsson, T. T. (2015). Performing hypermasculinity: Experiences with confined young offenders. *Men and Masculinities, 19*, 410–428.

Bernstein, N. (2014). *Burning down the house: The end of juvenile prison*. The New Press.

Bortner, M. A., & Williams, L. M. (1997). *Youth in prison*. New York: Routledge.

Brown, E. (2011). The 'unchildlike child': Making and marking the child/adult divide in the juvenile court. *Children's Geographies, 9*(3–4), 361–377.

Cesaroni, C., & Alvi, S. (2010). Masculinity and resistance in adolescent carceral settings. *Canadian Journal of Criminology and Criminal Justice, 52*, 303–320.

Cesaroni, C., Grol, C., & Fredericks, K. (2019). Overrepresentation of Indigenous youth in Canada's criminal justice system: Perspectives of Indigenous young people. *Australian & New Zealand Journal of Criminology, 52*(1), 111–128.

Chui, W. H., & cheng, K. K.-Y. (2013). The mark of an ex-prisoner: Perceived discrimination and self-stigma of young men after prison in Hong Kong. *Deviant Behavior, 34*, 671–684.

Corrado, R. R., Kuehn, S., & Margaritescu, I. (2014). Policy issues regarding the overrepresentation of incarcerated Aboriginal young offenders in a Canadian context. *Youth Justice, 14*, 40–62.

Cox, A. (2011). Doing the programme or doing me? The pains of youth imprisonment. *Punishment & Society, 13*, 592–610.

Cox, A. (2015). Responsible Submission: The Racialized Consequences of Neoliberal Juvenile Justice Practices. *Social Justice, 41*.

Cox, A. (2018). *Trapped in a Vice: the Consequences of Confinement for Young People*. New Brunswick, NJ: Rutgers University Press.

Crewe, B., Hulley, S. & Wright, S. (2017). Swimming with the Tide: Adapting to Long-Term Imprisonment. *Justice Quarterly, 34*, 517–541.

Crewe, B., Hulley, S. & Wright, S. (2020). *Life Imprisonment from Young Adulthood: Adaptation, Identity and Time*. London.

Desai, S. R. (2019). "Hurt people, hurt people": The trauma of juvenile incarceration. *Urban Review, 51*, 638–658.

Drybread, K. (2014). Murder and the making of man-subjects in a Brazilian juvenile prison. *American Anthropologist, 116*, 752–764.

Drybread, K. (2016). Documents of indiscipline and indifference: The violence of bureaucracy in a Brazilian juvenile prison. *American Ethnologist, 43*, 411–423.

Fader, J. (2013). *Falling back: Incarceration and transitions to adulthood among urban youth*. New Brunswick: Rutgers University Press.

Flores, J. (2016). *Caught up: Girls, surveillance, and wraparound incarceration*. Berkeley: University of California Press.

Flores, J., & Pamplona, R. S. (2020). Young women's intimate partner relationships and institutional responses inside a California Juvenile Detention Centre. *Culture, Health & Sexuality*. https://doi.org/10.1080/13691058.2020.1776398.

Franzén, A. G. (2014). Responsibilization and discipline: Subject positioning at a youth detention home. *Journal of Contemporary Ethnography, 44*, 1–29.

Goldson, B. (2005). Child imprisonment: A case for abolition. *Youth Justice, 5*(2), 77–90.

Gooch, K. (2017). 'Kidulthood': Ethnography, juvenile prison violence and the transition from 'boys' to 'men'. *Criminology & Criminal Justice, 19*, 80–97.

Gradin Franzén, A. (2014). Responsibilization and discipline: Subject positioning at a youth detention home. *Journal of Contemporary Ethnography, 44*, 251–279.

Gray, G. C., & Salole, A. T. (2005). The local culture of punishment: An ethnography of criminal justice worker discourse. *The British Journal of Criminology, 46*, 661–679.

Halsey, M. J. (2007). Negotiating conditional release: Juvenile narratives of repeat incarceration. *Punishment and Society, 8*, 147–181.

Halsey, M. J. (2008). Risking desistance: Respect and responsibility in the custodial and post-release contexts. In P. Calen (Ed.), *Imaginary penalities*. Cullompton: Willan.

Harvey, J. (2007). *Young men in prison*. Cullompton: Willan.

Henriksen, A.-K. (2017). Confined to care: Girls' gendered vulnerabilities in secure institutions. *Gender & Society, 31*, 677–698.

Henriksen, A.-K., & Refsgaard, R. C. B. (2020, August). Temporal experiences of confinement: Exploring young people's experiences in Danish secure institutions. *Young*.

Hill, J. (2007). Daring to dream: Towards an understanding of young black people's reflections post-custody. *Youth Justice, 7*(1), 37–51.

Holley, L. C., & van Vleet, R. K. (2006). Racism and classism in the youth justice system: Perspectives of youth and staff. *Journal of Poverty, 10*(1), 45–67.

Hosser, D., Windzio, M., & Greve, W. (2008). Guilt and shame as predictors of recidivism: A longitudinal study with young prisoners. *Criminal Justice and Behavior, 35*(1), 138–152.

Inderbitzin, M. (2007). A look from the inside: Balancing custody and treatment in a juvenile maximum-security facility. *International Journal of Offender Therapy and Comparative Criminology, 51*, 348–362.

Kramer, R., Rajah, V., & Sung, H.-E. (2013). Neoliberal prisons and cognitive treatment: Calibrating the subjectivity of incarcerated young men to economic inequalities. *Theoretical Criminology, 17*(4), 535–556.

Myers, R. (2013). The biographical and psychic consequences of 'welfare inaction' for young women in trouble with the law. *Youth Justice, 13*, 218–233.

National Juvenile Justice Network. (2018). *2017 NJJN member youth justice advances.* Washington, DC: National Juvenile Justice Network.

Nowak, M. (2019). *The United Nations global study on children deprived of liberty.* Geneva: United Nations.

Reich, A. (2010). *Hidden truth: Young men navigating lives in and out of juvenile prison.* Berkeley: University of California Press.

Rolnick, A. C. (2016). Locked up: Fear, racism, prison economics, and the incarceration of native youth. *American Indian Culture and Research Journal, 40*(1), 55–92.

Sankofa, J., Cox, A., Fader, J., Inderbitzin, M., Abrams, L., & Nurse, A. (2017). Juvenile corrections in the era of reform: A meta-synthesis of qualitative studies. *International Journal of Offender Therapy and Comparative Criminology, 62*, 1763–1786.

Shalhoub-Kevorkian, N. (2019). *Incarcerated childhood and the politics of unchilding.* Cambridge: Cambridge University Press.

Sharpe, G. (2009). The trouble with girls today: Professional perspectives on young women's offending. *Youth Justice, 9*, 254–269.

Thomas, M. E. (2019). "Y'all trying to make a mockery out of me." The confined sexualities of girls in a US juvenile detention facility. *Emotion, Space and Society, 32*, 100533.

Tilton, J. (2013). Rethinking youth voice and institutional power: Reflections from inside a service learning partnership in a California juvenile hall. *Children and Youth Services Review, 35*, 1189–1196.

Tilton, J. (2020). Race, rage and emotional suspects: Ideologies of social mobility confront the racial contours of mass incarceration. *Children & Society, 34*, 291–304.

Tyanan, R. (2019). *Young Men's Experiences of Long-Term Imprisonment: Living Life.* London: Routledge.

United Nations. (1989). *United Nations Convention of the Rights of the Child.* New York: United Nations.

Van der Laan, A., & Eichelsheim, V. (2013). Juvenile adaptation to imprisonment: Feelings of safety, autonomy and well-being, and behaviour in prison. *European Journal of Criminology, 10*, 424–443.

Vaught, S. (2017). *Compulsory: Education and the dispossession of youth in a prison school.* Minneapolis, MN: University of Minnesota Press.

White, R. (2015). Indigenous young people and hyperincarceration in Australia. *Youth Justice, 15*(3), 256–270.

Wilson, D. (2003). Keeping quiet' or 'going nuts': Some emerging strategies used by young black people in custody at a time of childhood being re-constructed. *The Howard Journal of Criminal Justice, 42*, 411–425.

Youth Justice Board/Ministry of Justice. (2019). Youth justice statistics 2017/8. London: Ministry of Justice via: https://assets.publishing.service.gov.uk/government/uploads/system/uploads/attachment_data/file/774866/youth_justice_statistics_bulletin_2017_2018.pdf

Zhao, J. (Solomon), Wang, X., & Zhang, H. (2020). The role of perceived legitimacy and its effect on prison adaptation: A longitudinal study on a Chinese juvenile prison. *International Journal of Offender Therapy and Comparative Criminology, 64*(1), 100–123.

Zhao, R. (2020). Child maltreatment and adjustment to confinement: An exploratory study of male juvenile offenders in China. *Journal of Family Violence.* Published online 01 August 2020.

Zoettl, P. A. (2018). Rules, skills and autonomy: Pathological concepts of youth offending in Portuguese juvenile justice and custody. *International Journal of Law, Crime and Justice, 52*, 1–9.

Part I

Violated: Children's Rights are Human Rights

Epigraph to Section I

"Untitled"

> Jail is not life's gate
> It is a place for horrible days
> A number for company rates
> Murder to robbers name the date
>
> Ephemeral demands
> Made by my own hands
> Tear stained grass
> All out blast
>
> No second chances
> No lucky breaks
> Years to be served
> For simple mistakes
>
> March 4, 2020
> Central Juvenile Hall, Los Angeles, CA, USA

2

Self-Isolation May Feel Like Jail: It's Nothing Compared to Youth Prison

Hernán Carvente-Martinez

I still can't quite shake the claustrophobia.

Although I now live in my own home, sometimes I wake up and feel like the walls are closing in around me. I try to push down the feelings of panic.

Seven years have passed since I spent four years in a youth prison, but I'm still working through the trauma.

You'd think I'd be prepared for the self-isolation required of all of us during the COVID-19 pandemic. After all, I'm used to being asked to remain in one place. I'm used to watching the United States' fragile social support system fail people, and I'm used to having to survive with whatever I have—which is often very little. But this time of crisis is bringing back painful personal memories.

I remember sitting in a cell for hours on end, isolated from the rest of the world. I remember the brownish water we were sometimes given to drink. I remember how creative I had to get to occupy my mind since I had the same routine every single day.

While many people have jokingly made the comparison, self-isolation is not like jail. On the outside, we have work, and classes, television, and relatively easy access to family or friends via virtual tools.

I get it. We're all struggling with the new world order now. But the sad reality that I hope everyone can see as a result of this crisis is that young people all

---

H. Carvente-Martinez (✉)
Youth First Initiative and Healing Ninjas, Inc., New York, NY, USA

© The Author(s), under exclusive license to Springer Nature Switzerland AG 2021
A. Cox, L. S. Abrams (eds.), *The Palgrave International Handbook of Youth Imprisonment*, Palgrave Studies in Prisons and Penology, https://doi.org/10.1007/978-3-030-68759-5_2

over the country are, at this very moment, locked up in juvenile prisons and detention centers during the worst public health crisis of our lifetimes (Meyer and Madrigal 2020). Incarcerated young people must be feeling an unimaginable amount of fear and anxiety today.

They can't take the steps necessary to protect themselves from the virus. Living in such close proximity with other people, there's no ability to socially distance. They don't have easy access to cleaning and sanitizing equipment, let alone soap to wash their hands. There's a reason why the virus is thriving in these facilities—it's a breeding ground for this highly contagious virus (Ellis 2020).

What's more, the minimal steps some states have taken to reduce the spread of the virus have monumental consequences on the mental health of these young people. Many facilities have canceled visitation from families and support systems, including teachers for educational programming. I've heard stories of parents unable to reach their children at all, and young people are scared of how the virus is affecting their community back home.

With activities canceled, young people are stuck in their cells alone day in and day out, with little to keep them occupied (Green 2020). Can you imagine the effects on a child, especially right now?

It honestly boggles my mind that people think this is okay.

Yet while attention has rightly been given to adult populations in prisons and detention centers, young people are largely being left out of the conversation.

Following my release, I struggled to find a job, adjust to the wide range of technology now available to me, afford food, or take care of my family. But I made it because of the support I received from my community.

But I remain angry. I remain frustrated. No person, whether locked up or free, should ever have to experience what I once had to survive while incarcerated, especially not during a global health crisis. COVID-19 should be a reminder to us that prisons were never designed to protect people, but to warehouse them and remove them from our communities with very little support.

I now work for the Youth First Initiative, which fights against youth incarceration across the country and advocates for community-based alternatives. Tens of thousands of young people still sit in prisons all over the United States and countless taxpayer dollars are being spent to keep them behind bars and vulnerable to COVID-19 (Mason and McDowell 2020). That money should be redirected to alternatives to incarceration and to programs that will help youth released from juvenile facilities receive schooling and job training.

A society is judged by how it treats the most vulnerable among them and, in this moment, we are failing incarcerated young people. I'm hoping we take this opportunity to listen to and learn from those who are hurting the most. I want to see a world where every young person has the opportunity to live out their full potential, free from prisons and this deadly virus.

References

Ellis, E. G. (2020). Covid-19 poses a heightened threat in jails and prisons. Wired. Retrieved from https://www.wired.com/story/coronavirus-covid-19-jails-prisons/.

Green, E. L. (2020). 'Pacing and Praying': Jailed youths seek release as virus spreads. *New York Times*. Retrieved from https://www.nytimes.com/2020/04/14/us/politics/coronavirus-juvenile-detention.html.

Mason, M., & McDowell, R. (2020). 3 takeaways of AP review of COVID-19 in youth detention. *The Associated Press*. Retrieved from https://apnews.com/fa118e4e6ad02e5b5007192ec7fa3e9d.

Meyer, R., & Madrigal, A. (2020). A new statistic reveals why america's covid-19 numbers are flat. *The Atlantic*. Retrieved from https://www.theatlantic.com/technology/archive/2020/04/us-coronavirus-outbreak-out-control-test-positivity-rate/610132/.

3

Children and Young People in Custody in England and Wales: Rights and Wrongs

Laura Janes

Children and young adults in custody have an array of rights, complemented by an extensive system of monitoring compliance with corresponding duties that such rights imply for criminal justice agencies (through the National Preventive Mechanism). Despite their well-defined rights and the monitoring arrangements in place, the treatment of young people in penal custody continues to be so egregious that prisons holding children in England and Wales are widely accepted as not fit for purpose (Independent Improvement Board 2017). The author, a practising lawyer in an English penal charity, has found that the stigma attached to young people who offend, combined with their lack of visibility, facilitates a continued gap between young people's rights in theory and the extent to which they are realised in practice.

The difficulties faced by young people in prison suggest that the rights framework is insufficient to render them "practical and effective" (*Airey v Ireland* [1979] 2 E.H.R.R. 305, §24). In response to the problems faced by young people in prison in enforcing their rights, the Howard League developed a specialist legal service in 2002 (Howard League 2017). The legal work reveals that even when rights arguments are raised by specialist lawyers on behalf of young people, it remains extremely difficult to improve their situations.

L. Janes (✉)
Howard League for Penal Reform, London, UK
e-mail: laura.janes@howardleague.org

This chapter examines the potential and challenges for a rights-based approach to ameliorate treatment of children in custody.

The author suggests that so long as the criminal justice system continues to be underpinned by a punitive approach to young people who offend, making rights practical and effective will remain a significant challenge.

Young People in Custody: A Falling Number of Highly Vulnerable Young People, Disproportionately from Minority Backgrounds and Care

Custody is the most serious penal sanction available in the UK. It is recognised in law as such a serious measure that it should only ever be imposed on any person, regardless of age, as a last resort (Saadi v United Kingdom [2006] ECHR 732; Criminal Justice Act 2003, section 152(2)). In the case of children, there is an additional duty to ensure custody is imposed for the shortest appropriate period of time (Sentencing Council 2017; United Nations Convention on the Rights of the Child ("UNCRC"), Article 37).

In this chapter the term "children" refers to those aged 10–17, "young adults" to those aged 18–21 and "young people" to both groups. Although there is a growing consensus that young adulthood should extend to 25, as the brain typically continues to mature until the mid-twenties for the purposes of prison placement, young adults are defined as those aged 18–21 (Justice Committee 2016). Most of the information in this chapter deals with the situation in England and Wales as they share a legal system. Northern Ireland and Scotland have distinct systems.

Over and above the deprivation of liberty, the incarceration of children and young adults is recognised as particularly damaging to children's physical and mental well-being as young people are still developing until well into their mid-twenties (Sawyer et al. 2018; Willow 2015). Bateman et al. (2013, p. 2) conclude that the "custodial experience itself can exacerbate problems, severing positive ties with the family and wider community and bringing additional trauma". The additional trauma that young people experience in custody ranges from self-harm, violence and, in extreme cases, death (Gooch 2016; Harris 2015).

Research on the impact of incarceration on children in New Zealand from a psychological perspective concludes that as the "sentence time progresses, adolescents become more deeply immersed in the criminal justice system and move further from prosocial involvement in society, thus limiting opportunity for the individual to 'age out' of their delinquent behaviour" (Lambie and Randell 2013, p. 451).

The largest longitudinal study of patterns of offending by children in the UK found that the most effective way to avoid further offending is to keep children's contact with the criminal justice system to as low a level as possible (McAra and McVie 2010).

In recent years, the number of children and young adults in custody in England and Wales has declined significantly (Bateman 2015). As of June 2019, there were 812 children in the penal system, compared with 2596 children in June 2009—a reduction of two-thirds (Ministry of Justice 2019a). This has followed a significant reduction in the number of child arrests, which reduced by two-thirds between 2010 and 2017 (Howard League 2018).

Despite this drop, the number of children relative to the child population detained is still high for a Western European country (World Prison Brief n.d.). It is even higher if one includes the children detained on welfare orders and in secure mental hospitals (Hales et al. 2018). Children from Black, Asian and Minority Ethnic ("BAME") backgrounds have not benefited from the decline in the use of custody to the same extent as their white peers, and as a consequence there has been a dramatic increase in the proportion of the detained child population from a BAME background (Bateman 2017; Lammy 2017). Of the 812 children in penal detention in June 2019, 470 (58 per cent) were from BAME backgrounds (Ministry of Justice 2019a, Tables 2.1 and 2.6). Black children are seven-and-a-half times more likely to receive a long-term custodial sentence than would be anticipated from their representation in the general 10–17 population (Bateman 2017). Between a third and half of children in custody report having been in the care of their local authority for their own welfare prior to custody (HMIP 2019a).

The number of young adults in custody has also decreased sharply in recent years, although not as dramatically as in the case of children (Bateman 2015). Despite this decline, a significant number of young adults remain in prison (Justice Committee 2016, p. 6). According to the Ministry of Justice, as of 30 June 2019, the total prison population was 82,710. There were 4188 young adults aged 18–20 and 9297 young adults aged 21–24 in prison (Ministry of Justice 2019b, Table 1.3). Young adults account for 16 per cent of the prison population but less than 8 per cent of the general population (Office for National Statistics 2019). Although young adults classified other than "White" only constitute 18.5 per cent of the general population aged 18–24 in England and Wales, 39 per cent of 18–20 year-olds and 34 per cent of 21–24 year-olds in prison self-report as "Black", "Asian", "Mixed" or "Chinese or Other"

(Office for National Statistics 2011; Ministry of Justice 2016a). Nearly half of young men and two-thirds of young women in custody aged between 16 and 21 have recently been in local authority care (T2A 2016).

Notwithstanding the vulnerabilities of young people entering custody and the high number of young people owed a duty of care by local authorities, it was only in 2002 that, following a legal challenge brought by the Howard League for Penal Reform, the government was forced to accept that the rights and protections of the Children Act 1989 did not fall away on entry to prison (*R (Howard League for Penal Reform) v Secretary of State for the Home Department & Anor* [2003] 1 FLR 484). The analysis of the characteristics of children in prison in the judgement remains sadly relevant:

> [Children in custody] are, on any view, vulnerable and needy children. Disproportionately they come from chaotic backgrounds. Many have suffered abuse or neglect….Over half of the children in YOIs have been in care. Significant percentages report having suffered or experienced abuse of a violent, sexual or emotional nature. A very large percentage have run away from home at some time or another. Very significant percentages were not living with either parent prior to coming into custody and were either homeless or living in insecure accommodation. Over half were not attending school, either because they had been permanently excluded or because of long-term non-attendance. Over three-quarters had no educational qualifications. Two-thirds of those who could be employed were in fact unemployed. Many reported problems relating to drug or alcohol use. Many had a history of treatment for mental health problems. Disturbingly high percentages had considered or even attempted suicide. (§§10–11)

Youth Justice Board ("YJB") statistics for children entering custody between April 2014 and March 2016 show that Youth Offending Team workers had concerns about the mental health of one-third of children, two-thirds were not engaging in education and almost half had substance misuse concerns (Ministry of Justice 2017a). Many young adults in custody were previously children in custody and share the same characteristics as that cohort. A Ministry of Justice survey (2015) conducted in 2005–2006 found that 18–20 year-olds were more likely than older prisoners to report issues with schooling; to link their offending to alcohol use; and state that having a job on release would stop them from reoffending.

Proven reoffending rates, measured as the imposition of a further caution or conviction for an offence committed within 12 months of release, for young people released from custody are higher than those for adults aged 21 and over and, in the case of children, as high as over 64 per cent for children within a 12-month period (Justice Committee 2016; Ministry of Justice 2019d).

Children and young adults are detained in establishments that are officially designated to hold them, although the spread of accommodation varies from distinct child-focused units in the case of younger children to cells in adult prisons designated for young adults aged 18–20.

Children, defined by law as anyone under the age of 18 (Children Act 1989, section 105), can be detained in secure children's homes ("SCHs"), secure training centres ("STCs") and Young Offender Institutions ("YOIs") (Defence for Children International 2018). There are around nine SCHs and they tend to be reserved for younger children: they are small local authority-run units staffed by professionals who are usually skilled youth and social care workers. These establishments are expensive by comparison with other forms of custodial provision and the places available in such establishments for children in the penal system have been reduced by half in the last decade (YJB 2010; Argar 2019). There are three STCs: two are privately run and a third has been taken into public management from a private company after an undercover documentary revealed widespread abuse (Panorama 2016). They are larger than SCHs and are less likely to have all staff trained to work specifically with children. YOIs can only take boys aged 15 and over and tend to be staffed by prison officers and have low staff-to-child ratios: most children in custody are detained in these institutions (Ministry of Justice 2019c). There are three designated YOIs for young adults only, although most adult prisons tend to have cells and wings designated for young adults.

In 2016, a government-commissioned review of youth justice resulted in a new policy to replace YOIs and STCs with "secure schools" (Ministry of Justice 2016b, §§121–122). Despite accepting the notion that YOIs and STCs should be closed, as of March 2021, the Government had only announced a single pilot secure school, which will be on the site of Medway STC (Argar 2018).

The Rights Framework and Inspection Regime

The lives of young people in custody are heavily regulated by rules and guidance that determine their rights, entitlements and what can be done to them. The type of establishment pre-determines the rules that apply to the child's daily life while in custody. This framework is complemented by an extensive system of monitoring compliance with those duties.

The rules and guidance, whether statutory or policy documents, structure the lives and experiences of young people in custody and differ according to the institution the young person is held in. Table 3.1 provides an overview of the statutory regulations that apply to each of the type of institution in which young people in custody are held.

The rules contain a number of key common features, many of which are also underpinned by English and Welsh law, and in the case of children, the UNCRC (Table 3.2). The law acknowledges that children have enhanced rights, many of which are enshrined in the UNCRC. While the UNCRC, which has been signed by all states in the world except the USA, has not been formally incorporated into English law (it has been incorporated into Welsh and Scottish law, although the UK government referred the recent Scottish decision to incorporate the UNCRC into Scottish law to the Supreme Court), the courts have repeatedly said that it can "properly be consulted insofar as they proclaim, reaffirm or elucidate the content of those human rights that are generally recognised throughout the European family of nations, in particular the nature and scope of those fundamental rights that are guaranteed by the European Convention" (*R (Howard League for Penal Reform) v Secretary of State for the Home Department & Anor* [2003] 1 FLR 484, §51). The provisions that are most relevant to children in prison include Article 12, which provides for children to have the right to express their views freely in all matters affecting the child, with support if necessary; Article 37, which states that children should only be detained as a last resort and for the shortest appropriate period of time, and Article 40, which requires that children in conflict with the law be treated in a way which promotes their sense of "dignity and worth".

Table 3.2 summarises the main rights, in the UNCRC or statute, that apply to children in custody and matches these to the corresponding rules and guidance that govern practice in various parts of the children's custodial estate.

Table 3.1 The rules that apply to young people in detention

Penal institution	The rules and guidance that apply
Secure Children's Homes (SCHs) (from ten years old)	Children's Home (England) Regulations 2015 (CH Regs)
Secure Training Centres (STCs) (from 12 years old)	Secure Training Centre Rules 1998 (STC Rules)
Young Offender Institutions (YOIs) (15–18 year-olds)	Young Offender Institution Rules 2000 (YOI Rules) Prison Service Instructions 08/2012 (Care and management of young people)
Young Offender Institutions (18–20 year-olds)	Young Offender Institution Rules 2000
Secure Schools (to be rolled out from 2022)	Children's Homes (England) Regulations 2015, and regulations under the Academies Act 2000

Table 3.2 Key rights and rules affecting young people's lives in custody

Action	Free-standing rights/law	Rules
Purposeful activity including gym and education	Article 2 of the first protocol to the Convention for the Protection of Human Rights and Fundamental Freedoms ("ECHR") and Article 28 UNCRC provide for the right to education. Article 8 ECHR provides for the right to personal development. Article 40 of the UNCRC says children should be treated in a way that reinforces the desirability of promoting the child's reintegration, Article 29 provides for the right to an education which develops personality, respect for others' rights and the environment.	All young people must be provided with purposeful activity, including minimum amounts of access to education and gym (YOI Rule 3, STC Rule 3, CH Regs 9). It is the policy of the Ministry of Justice that all children in any custodial setting should have 30 hours of education (YJB 2015). In YOIs, children of statutory school age are only entitled to a minimum of 15 hours a week of education and two hours a week of physical education (YOI Rules 38 and 41). In STCs, children must be given at least 25 education hours per week (STC Rule 28(2)). In SCHs, children must be supported to make measurable progress towards achieving their educational potential (CH Reg 8).
Healthcare	Article 8 ECHR provides for the right to physical and psychological development. Access to health care in custody should be equivalent to that in the community (*R (Brooks) v Secretary of State for Justice & Anor* [2008] EWHC 3041).	Young people must be able to access healthcare (YOI Rule 27(1), STC Rule 22(1), CH Reg 10). Staff in YOIs and STCs must promptly pass requests for medical help to a medical officer (YOI Rule 27(2), STC Rule 22(2)).

(continued)

Table 3.2 (continued)

Action	Free-standing rights/law	Rules
Contact with the outside world	Article 8 ECHR provides for the right to a private and family life.	The rules provide for some contact with the outside world through letters (PSI 08/2012 §4.62, STC Rule 11(1)(a), CH Reg 22(3)(b)), phone calls (PSI 49/2011 §6.10, STC Rule 11(2), CH Reg 22(3)(a)) and social visits (YOI Rule 10, STC Rule 11 and CH Reg 22(1)). In a YOI, young people are entitled to send and receive letters once a week (YOI Rule 10(1)(a)) and have access to a telephone for at least two hours a day (PSI 49/2011 §6.10). They may have two one-hour social visits in every four-week period (YOI Rule 10(1)(b)). In STCs, a child is entitled to send three letters per week and one one-hour visit per week (STC Rule 11). In SCHs, children are entitled to send and receive letters, access a telephone and have private visits at any reasonable time (CH Reg 22(3)(b), 22(3)(a) and 22(1)). Depending on the sentence and risk assessment, temporary releases under supervision are possible (YOI Rule 5, STC Rule 5, CH Reg 9).
A response to (suspected) abuse	Section 47 of the Children Act 1989 requires child protection concerns to be investigated. Article 3 ECHR protects people from inhuman and degrading treatment and Article 8 ECHR provides for personal development, including physical and psychological integrity.	Staff must deal promptly with any abuse or impropriety which comes to their knowledge (YOI Rule 67(2), STC Rule 39(2), CH Reg 34). In SCHs there is an additional duty to "help each child to understand and manage the impact of any experience of abuse or neglect" (CH Reg 6(2)(b)(v)) and to operate a disciplinary process in respect of employees who fail to report an incident of abuse, or suspected abuse, whether past or present (CH Reg 33(2)(b)).
The right to complain	Article 13 ECHR protects the right to a remedy. Article 12 UNCRC requires children's voices to be heard.	Children and young people must be given information about their rights (YOI Rule 7, STC Rule 7, CH Reg 7(d)) and a system of complaints must exist (YOI Rule 8, STC Rule 8, CH Reg 7). The Ministry of Justice provides advocacy support to children in custody but not young adults, and this is required for children in SCHs (CH Reg 7(d)(iii), Ministry of Justice n.d.).

(continued)

Table 3.2 (continued)

Action	Free-standing rights/law	Rules
A system of behaviour management including punishment	Behaviour management must be fair as a matter of common law and, when it may result in an action such as the deprivation of liberty, Article 6 ECHR requires that the procedure must be fair. Article 12 UNCRC requires for children's voices to be heard in matters affecting them.	All establishments holding young people may have a system for behaviour management (YOI Rule 6 and 44 to 66, STC Rule 6, CH Reg 35). In YOIs children and young adults may face a formal disciplinary process for breaking YOI rules, which can result in a range of sanctions from loss of privileges to additional days in prison (YOI Rules 60 and 60A). Children must not be punished with cellular confinement (YOI Rule 61).
Removal/ separation from association with other children	The isolation of a child is governed by Article 8 ECHR and therefore must be in accordance with the law, necessary and proportionate. Article 37 as interpreted by the UN Committee on the Rights of the Child prohibits a child being kept alone in a room without meaningful human contact for 22 or more hours a day.	Children should be permitted to socialise with each other. In YOIs and STCs, a child or young person may only be removed from association in exceptional circumstances where it is in the interests of the young person or others (YOI Rule 49(1), STC Rule 36(1)). In YOIs, the maximum amount of time of removal is three days (YOI Rule 49(2)). The approval of the Board of Visitors or Secretary of State is required if the period is longer than three days and may be renewed from time to time (YOI Rule 49(2)). It can be imposed for a maximum of 21 days in a governor's adjudication (YOI Rule 60(g)). In STCs, the child should not be left alone for more than three continuous hours or for more than three hours in any 24-hour period (STC Rule 36). In SCHs, children should only be separated when necessary to prevent injury to any person or to prevent serious damage to property. A record should be made and kept of all uses of single separation in SCHs and children should be offered the opportunity to read and add a comment to the record of their separation (Department for Education 2015, §9.65).

(continued)

Table 3.2 (continued)

Action	Free-standing rights/law	Rules
Authorised force on children by staff in prescribed circumstances	Article 3 ECHR prohibits inhuman and degrading treatment, as recognised in *R (C) v Secretary of State for Justice* [2009] QB 657.	Force must not be more than is reasonable, necessary and proportionate (PSO 1600 §2.2, STC Rule 37, CH Reg 20(2)) such as to prevent escape, injury or damage to property (PSO 1600 §4.33, STC Rule 38, CH Reg 20(1)). In YOIs, restraint may be used as a response to non-compliance in exceptional circumstances (PSI 06/2014 §4.3.7).

There are some significant omissions in the rules. For example, the YOI Rules do not refer to the need to have regard to the welfare of the child or the best interests of the child as a primary consideration in matters affecting them, even though the welfare principle is well established in English law and the best interests' principle underpins much international law.

There are a number of bodies that scrutinise and test the extent to which institutions that hold children and young adults in penal custody are doing as they should. These range from organisations that routinely inspect establishments to those that oversee complaints or provide oversight and monitoring inside establishments (Table 3.3).

Table 3.3 provides a summary of the various agencies that are responsible for monitoring custodial establishments where young people in custody are detained. It distinguishes those with a specific responsibility for establishments where children reside and those which have oversight for places of detention more broadly including those where children and young adults are detained.

The intense scrutiny of the conditions of detention for young people and in particular children has resulted in a series of damning findings. Reports by Her Majesty's Inspectorate of Prisons (HMIP), which inspects children's YOIs and STCs every year, illustrate the nature of the concerns echoed by many other bodies. The Inspectorate's expectations are based on and referenced against international human rights standards, with the aim of promoting treatment and conditions in detention which at least meet recognised international human rights standards. In recent years, the Inspectorate and other bodies have found a significant number of shortfalls in the performance of establishments holding children and young adults, some of which reveal a system-wide lack of regard for the human rights that underpin the inspection

Table 3.3 Oversight and monitoring of secure establishments holding young people

Body	Remit
Children	
Children's Rights Advocates	Work on the ground in all places of penal detention for children (Ministry of Justice n.d.).
Youth Custody Service Monitors	Originally designed as the eyes and ears of the Home Office in STCs to determine contractual compliance and provided by the Youth Justice Board; now monitors from the Youth Custody Service regularly visit all places of penal detention for children.
Youth Justice Board ("YJB")	Statutory body with oversight of the entire youth justice system for children. The Board monitors the system, advises the Secretary of State for Justice, ministers and professionals, commission research, award grants and promotes good practice. Its priorities include the resettlement and safety in custody of children (YJB 2019).
Local authorities	Safeguarding mechanisms, serious case reviews, Local Authority Designated Officers ("LADO") who are responsible for investigating abuse of children in custody.
Office of the Children's Commissioner	Can visit all places detaining children unannounced and do reports, has a child-rights advocacy service and co-ordinates the children and young people's subgroup of the National Preventive Mechanism (Children's Commissioner n.d.).
Child safeguarding practice review panel	This panel includes representatives from the police and children's social, education and health sectors. The aim of this group is to improve the welfare of children around the country, in particular identifying and reviewing serious safeguarding cases (Ministry of Justice 2018).
Office for Standards in Education, Children's Services and Skills ("Ofsted")	Inspects STCs and SCHs, and YOIs holding children at the invitation of Her Majesty's Inspectorate of Prisons (Ofsted 2015).
General oversight including places where children and young adults are detained	
Her Majesty's Inspectorate of Prisons ("HMIP")	Inspects STCs and children's YOIs once a year, at least, and produces reports, as well as an annual thematic report. Young adult prisons are inspected less regularly. Since 30 November 2017, the Chief Inspector has had the power to issue an urgent notification which requires the Secretary of State to report back with a plan of remedial action within 28 days (HMIP 2017a).

(continued)

Table 3.3 (continued)

Body	Remit
National Preventive Mechanism ("NPM")	Established in March 2009, the NPM is made up of the 21 statutory bodies that independently monitor all places of detention. It prepares an annual report laid before Parliament. Coordinated by HMIP, it receives technical assistance from the UN Subcommittee on Prevention of Torture and Other Cruel, Inhuman or Degrading Treatment or Punishment and the UK government must account for the NPM's ability to perform its functions to the SPT and other UN bodies (NPM n.d.).
European Committee for the Prevention of Torture and Inhuman or Degrading Treatment or Punishment ("CPT")	The CPT organises visits to places of detention in order to assess how persons, including young people, deprived of their liberty are treated. CPT delegations have unlimited access to places of detention and a right to move inside such places without restriction. After each visit, the CPT sends a detailed report to the State concerned. This report includes the CPT's findings, recommendations, comments and requests for information. The CPT also requests a detailed response to the issues raised in its report (Council of Europe n.d.).
The UN Subcommittee on Prevention of Torture and Other Cruel, Inhuman or Degrading Treatment or Punishment ("SPT")	The SPT is composed of 25 independent experts elected by States Parties to the Optional Protocol to the Convention against Torture. The Committee may undertake visits to States Parties, during the course of which it may visit any place where persons may be deprived of their liberty and has an advisory function which involves providing assistance and advice to States Parties on the establishment and operation of National Preventive Mechanisms. The SPT produces a public annual report on its activities which it presents to the Committee against Torture and the UN General Assembly in New York and convenes three times a year for one-week-long sessions at the United Nations Office at Geneva (OHCHR n.d.).
Ad hoc inquiries	Parliamentary Committees such as the Justice Committee and the Joint Committee on Human Rights may from time to time consider the situation of young people in custody (Joint Committee on Human Rights 2019; Justice Committee 2019, 2021). Other inquiries may be commissioned by Government or independent bodies.
Independent Monitoring Board ("IMB")	Appointed by the Secretary of State and provided for under the YOI Rules the IMB has a presence in all YOIs so that young people can raise concerns directly. Boards prepare annual reports for each establishment that are published (IMB n.d.).
Prisons and Probation Ombudsman ("PPO")	Responds to complaints in YOIs and STCs, but only where the complaint has not been resolved internally and passes its assessment criteria—can produce learning lessons bulletins and can make recommendations (PPO n.d.).

criteria. Bodies such as HMIP make recommendations designed to remedy or reduce human rights infringements. Yet the latest annual report shows that less than half of its recommendations are implemented (HMIP 2019b).

The Wrongs Young People in Custody Face

Children and young adults face a wide range of difficulties in custody, including exposure to higher levels of violence, self-harm, restraint and punishment than the general population. There is a sharp contrast between extensive rights and monitoring arrangements, outlined above, and the evidence of the unpalatable experiences of young people in custody explored in this section.

It has been argued that the continuing wrongs faced by young people in custody may be explained by a deep rooted punitive stance towards young people who break the law in England and Wales, manifested by the low age of criminal responsibility (ten years old) in a system based on retribution (Muncie 2008). Muncie (2008) argues that these values have achieved a political legitimacy. The punitive discourse may explain why the principles of juvenile protection and support that govern the legal rights and entitlements of young people in custody are far less prominent in the political narrative surrounding young people in conflict with the law.

Due to the different establishments and regimes in place for children and young adults, the problems they face are different. Each group is considered in turn.

Children

Children aged 17 and under in custody face high levels of violence and harm and a significant number of children have died in penal custody in England and Wales since 1990 (Gooch 2016). According to data from the Ministry of Justice (2017b), the use of force on children in prison increased by 36 per cent, assaults increased by 95 per cent and self-harm increased by 120 per cent in the five years leading up to 2015/2016.

The risk of routine abuse while in prison was demonstrated by the exposé of Medway STC in which the BBC filmed officers abusing children (Panorama 2016). The Medway Improvement Board (2016), set up by the British Government in response to the BBC programme, conceded that the revelations of abuse in the programme "were, by common consent, deeply shocking" (Medway Improvement Board 2016, p. 3). The Improvement Board described the broadcast as showing highly vulnerable children, "being physically and emotionally abused by those who were employed to protect and care for them" (Medway Improvement Board 2016, p. 3).

Abuse at Medway occurred despite child protection measures, strict safeguarding procedures and regular scrutiny from external bodies including HMIP, Ofsted and the YJB, who had monitors permanently on site. In fact, the joint report by HMIP and Ofsted published prior to the BBC broadcast found that the "overall effectiveness of Medway … STC … to meet the needs of young people is judged good with outstanding features" (HMIP and Ofsted 2014, p. 4). Exposure to, let alone experience of, the level of violence shown in the *Panorama* broadcast would give rise to a child protection referral in the community.

The contrast between the reality of children's lives at Medway as demonstrated by the undercover journalist and the approval of the same institution by the official monitoring body for protecting children's welfare provides stark confirmation that the existence of rights, regulations and oversight are not in themselves adequate to safeguard young people from abuse. Indeed, the processes that are intended to protect children in custody can—as demonstrated in this case—not only fail to uncover abuse where it happens but also provide a false sense of security. This in turn may encourage complacency and contribute to a narrative that conditions in custody are better than they in fact are.

In response to the abuse at Medway and the findings of the Improvement Board, the Ministry of Justice commissioned an independent review of the whole secure estate. The Youth Custody Improvement Board (YCIB) published a report in February 2017. It noted that:

> the YJB itself has acknowledged that the YSE [Youth Secure Estate] is not fit for the purpose of caring for or rehabilitating children and young people. The YCIB believe this is correct, and is an astonishing analysis by the YJB, given that it has been in operation for over a decade. This inevitably raises a question as to why the YJB and MoJ have not been able to intervene in the YSE to ensure that it was fit for purpose and keeping children and staff safe. (Independent Improvement Board 2017, p. 2)

In his annual report published in July 2017, the Chief Inspector of Prisons said that "by February 2017, we concluded that there was not a single establishment that we inspected in England and Wales in which it was safe to hold children and young people" (HMIP 2017b, p. 9). It should be noted that the Chief Inspector does not inspect SCHs and that the standard of care in such establishments is significantly better than in other parts of the secure estate (Bateman 2016).

In September 2017, the Local Government Association (LGA) called for urgent action to improve safety in YOIs following HMIP's damning report about unsafe conditions in all YOIs. Richard Watts, Chair of the LGA's Children and Young People Board, stated: "There is no other situation in which children and young people would be placed into environments that are known to be unsafe, and youth custody should be no exception" (LGA 2017). He called upon the government to take urgent remedial action. The government did not publish a response to this.

The Chief Inspector has presented a slightly less depressing picture in subsequent reports. Nonetheless, the number of children who report feeling unsafe has remained consistently high. In 2019, HMIP published an analysis of 12- to 18-year-olds' perceptions of their experiences in STCs and YOIs between 1 April 2017 and 31 March 2018. Forty per cent of the boys in YOIs and over a third (34 per cent) of the children in STCs did not feel safe at some point (HMIP 2019a).

The Independent Inquiry into Child Sexual Abuse (IICSA 2019, p. vi) found that:

> information obtained directly from the relevant custodial institutions and related authorities has found 1070 reported incidents of alleged sexual abuse in the period 2009–2017, despite the significant drop in numbers of detained children over that time and the relatively low number overall. These allegations were mostly against staff and were often alleged to have taken place during restraint or body searches.

The United Nations Subcommittee on Prevention of Torture raised serious concerns about these findings in its report in May 2019 (United Nations 2019). In April 2019 a Parliamentary committee found children's rights were being breached in respect of the widespread use of solitary confinement and restraint (Joint Committee on Human Rights 2019). In July 2019 the Chief Inspector of Prisons issued the first urgent notification in respect of a children's prison—Feltham prison in West London (HMIP 2019c).

Young Adults

The failures outlined in the reports about children in detention continue for young adults in custody, although this age group receives less scrutiny than children. Between 2007 and 2014, 97 young adults aged 18–24 took their own lives in custody (Harris 2015). The Chief Inspector of Prisons has repeatedly reported that around 40 per cent of young adults state that they are routinely kept in their cells 22 hours a day or more (HMIP 2018, 2019b). In his annual report for 2018–2019, the Chief Inspector noted that "[a]s of 31 December 2018, 13,474 young adult men aged 18–24 were held in adult male prisons (17 per cent of all male prisoners)" and "generally reported a less positive experience of prison life than their older peers. They were often over-represented on the lowest level of the incentives scheme and in disciplinary proceedings, and prisons were not investigating the underlying reasons for this sufficiently" (HMIP 2019b, p. 30). These findings echo concerns by the Justice Committee about "punitive and restrictive measures to prevent violence, including shockingly long hours of being restricted to cells and high levels of adjudications are short-term means of managing a risky and vulnerable population" (Justice Committee 2016, p. 51). The Justice Committee (2018) has commented on the lack of robust evidence in this area.

The data that is available shows concerning levels of self-harm by, and assaults on, young adult prisoners. In 2018, there were 3270 recorded incidents of self-harm amongst 18–24 year-olds. This represents an increase of 60 per cent since 2004 (from 2040 incidents). The biggest increases are seen in the male 21–24 age group, where self-harm incidents have gone up by 156 per cent over that period (from 782 to 1999 incidents). There were 4403 assaults on prisoners in the 18–24 age group in 2018, an increase of 143 per cent since 2004, when 1809 assaults were recorded against this age group (Ministry of Justice 2019e). These increases are even more worrying when viewed against the significant reductions in the number of young adults in prison over the same period (Ministry of Justice 2019b).

In spite of the clear framework governing the treatment of young people in custody and the extensive monitoring arrangements, it is evident that very vulnerable children and young adults routinely have their rights breached.

The Howard League's Legal Work

In response to young people's difficulties in enforcing their rights, the Howard League for Penal Reform developed a specialist legal service in 2002 (Howard League 2017). This service was designed to meet the need of young people to access a legal service that could mount challenges to breaches of rights that the system had been unable to rectify or prevent from occurring. The charity's lawyers advise and represent young people aged 21 and under in prison or at risk of going to prison.

Calls to the Howard League advice line reflect the concerns outlined in the reports and illustrate the extent of breaches of rights that persist in places where young people are detained.

Between May 2014 and June 2019, the Howard League dealt with over 5500 discrete issues for almost 4000 individuals on its confidential legal telephone advice line for young people. The demographics of callers to the Howard League broadly reflect the composition of young people in custody. Over 90 per cent of callers in this period were male and just under half were white. The Howard League received more requests for help on treatment and conditions in custody than any other issue.

On a daily basis, the Howard League advises young people of their rights and challenges unfair treatment that appears to flout those rights. This service provides an opportunity for young people to access legal mechanisms to uphold their rights in circumstances where the regulatory framework has failed to do so. While in some cases this results in improvements in the treatment of young people, it remains an uphill struggle despite the legal framework that exists to protect young people's rights, even where experienced lawyers advocate on a young person's behalf.

Two case studies illustrate the reluctance of the courts and authorities to adopt a rights-based approach, along with the benefits of legal challenges in raising the profile of the rights narrative and influencing key actors in the criminal justice system. The legal framework allows challenges to be brought, but the hurdles faced along the way reflect the extent to which the culture of rights is still the exception rather than the norm. Those making rights-based arguments are often seen as trouble-making and difficult. Both case studies below concern the separation of young people from their peers, often resulting in them spending 22 hours or more a day locked up alone without meaningful human contact—a practice that has been found by a parliamentary committee to be widespread and in breach of children's rights (Joint Committee on Human Rights 2019).

The Case of AB: A Child Isolated in a Young Offenders' Institution

AB, represented by the Howard League, was kept in solitary confinement at Feltham when he was 15 years old. The widely accepted international definition of solitary confinement is: being kept for 22 or more hours a day alone in a cell without meaningful contact and available stimuli reduced to a minimum (International Psychological Trauma Symposium 2007). AB was held in these conditions for at least 55 days. He was locked alone in his cell for over 23 hours a day. He received no education and had no access to gym, psychological interventions or any purposeful activity. He was permitted no contact with other children and had limited contact with adults. AB was just one of many children who told the Howard League that they had been isolated in this way without any proper safeguards in place, resulting in no clear plan as to how or when the isolation might come to an end. The Howard League issued a judicial review challenging AB's treatment (*R (AB) v Secretary of State for Justice* [2017] 4 WLR 153).

The High Court found that AB's isolation did not comply with the requirements of the YOI Rules regarding children being removed from associating with others or guidance issued by the Secretary of State for Justice. His treatment was therefore not in accordance with the law and in breach of his human rights. As a result of this decision, prison staff are more aware of the legal requirement to properly record all instances of isolation and go through the correct procedures designed to safeguard against its prolonged use. However, the High Court and later the Court of Appeal did not accept that AB's treatment was inhuman and degrading and found that it did not amount to a breach of his right to personal and psychological development (*R (AB) v Secretary of State for Justice* [2019] 4 WLR 42). In both the High Court and the Court of Appeal, a detailed analysis of AB's behaviour was made and it was found that his behaviour "made integration impossible". The Court of Appeal found his isolation was justified for the purpose of Article 8 of the European Convention on Human Rights on grounds of "safety" which arose, in part, "in response to his very challenging and abusive behaviour" (*R (AB) v Secretary of State for Justice* [2019] 4 WLR 42, §70). The Court of Appeal also examined the relevance of the UNCRC and the interpretation of the UN Committee on the Rights of the Child and found these provisions only prohibited the use of solitary confinement to punish a child as part of a disciplinary process. AB has petitioned the Supreme Court to be allowed to appeal the decision.

Despite the refusal of the courts to rule that solitary confinement can never be justified in the case of children, the publicity around this challenge going to court resulted in some significant developments. It has triggered a number of reports in national media, raising the profile of the issue (see, e.g., "Feltham boy's solitary confinement breached human rights", BBC 2017 and Travis 2017). It also prompted a statement from the British Medical Association, the Royal College of Psychiatrists and the Royal College of Paediatrics and Child Health condemning the use of solitary confinement on children in custody and raising ethical concerns around medics being involved in the process

(BMA 2018). It may also have prompted a parliamentary inquiry on the subject, which found that its use is widespread and a breach of human rights (Joint Committee on Human Rights 2019).

Aylesbury: Young Adults in Isolation

A similar concern about the inappropriate and prolonged use of segregation emerged from calls to the Howard League advice line from young adults at Aylesbury prison, a YOI for 18–20 year-olds. Between March 2018 and February 2019, the Howard League received 178 calls from young adults at Aylesbury, 19 per cent of whom said they were spending over 22 hours a day in their cells. Howard League lawyers made dozens of complaints to the prison, arguing that keeping a young adult in conditions of solitary confinement was unlawful and a breach of the prison rules. Several of the complaints were escalated to the Prisons and Probation Ombudsman (PPO) (PPO 2019). Initially the complaints were not upheld by the Ombudsman, finding that the prison had "no option" but to behave as it did and noting the poor behaviour of the young people resulting in the need for them to be isolated from their peers. It is difficult to square this finding with regulations and legal framework designed to safeguard young adults from being kept in solitary confinement.

The Howard League continued to submit complaints to the PPO, and some of these were upheld, resulting in a string of recommendations to HMYOI Aylesbury in at least three cases. In these cases, the PPO found that the initial decision to place the young adult in the segregation unit was valid, but criticised the lack of effort made to give the young people stimulating activities while on the unit. The Ombudsman was not satisfied that the authority for the young adults' continuing segregation was valid or that staff acted quickly enough to bring their isolation to an end. Concerns were also raised about the lack of an adequate regime in the segregation unit over sustained periods and the failure by staff to record information or respond to the Ombudsman's requests for information in a timely manner.

In each of the cases, the Ombudsman called on the governor of Aylesbury prison to write a letter of apology to the young adult concerned, to take steps to bring his isolation to an end (if that had not already occurred) and to review the segregation regime. These recommendations were accepted.

Following these reports, the prison was put into "special measures" in February 2019. Special measures is a process whereby prisons are provided with additional resources to deal with identified problems. In the case of Aylesbury the number of young adults held there had reduced by around half in Spring 2019. Between March and July 2019 the number of calls from young adults at Aylesbury has declined and only seven per cent of calls concerned isolation.

Making Rights Practical and Effective: A Work in Progress

The case studies from the Howard League's legal work illustrate both the potential for rights to be used to make a difference and the challenges inherent in this attempt. It is clear from the plethora of reports that violations continue to occur until challenged and that the process of challenging rights violations can be prolonged and difficult. Rights are intended to be "practical and effective", but it would appear that for many young people they remain "theoretical or illusory" (*Airey v Ireland* [1979] 2 E.H.R.R. 305, §24).

The AB case did not succeed in the High Court and Court of Appeal in establishing that solitary confinement can never be acceptable, and AB's behaviour was regarded as justifying his treatment. However, the case triggered strong moral responses from a range of bodies such as the BMA (2018) and the Joint Committee on Human Rights (2019), highlighting human rights breaches and ethical concerns around placing children in solitary confinement. There is also no doubt that staff, professionals, young people and their families are much more aware of the likelihood that keeping a child in his or her cell for 22 hours or more a day may violate human rights.

AB and the young people at Aylesbury had the benefit of specialist independent legal advice to challenge their solitary confinement. Despite this expert support and advocacy, challenges have been difficult, lengthy and in the case of AB only partially successful. The number of complaints to the PPO from people under 21 is disproportionately small: according to the Ombudsman's annual report published in 2019, they accounted for just 26 of the 2569 that were investigated (PPO 2019). The Ombudsman has suggested that this is because young people find the complaints process overly bureaucratic or complicated.[1]

This suggests that legal challenges may not be sufficient to make children's rights practical and effective. The language of rights in custody in England and Wales is not commonplace and the prison environment is characterised by an imbalance of power affecting every aspect of the detained person's life. Empowering young people in custody by providing them with information about their universal rights can therefore be a challenge.

There is still a long way to go until a rights-based culture has been fully embraced, despite the UK's advanced monitoring structures and child protection measures. The only way to create a penal landscape in which rights are respected and protected is for them to become embedded. That requires a culture shift in which those working in the criminal justice system do not see rights as a threat but as an asset or completely normal. It is only in the last few years that specific courses have been available for prison officers working with children and only very recently that the course had included a specific focus on children's rights (Unitas n.d.). There are no equivalent training opportunities for officers working with young adults or adult prisoners.

Complaints tend to be met with resistance and challenges rarely result in systemic change, often using the "poor behaviour" of young people to rebut allegations that rights have been infringed. This is in keeping with punitive values that Muncie (2008) suggests have gained political legitimacy in the USA, England and Wales and much of Western Europe. These dynamics at play in the system suggest young people who offend are deemed to be underserving of rights, over and above the right to liberty, to which others are entitled. So long as the criminal justice system continues to be underpinned by a punitive approach to young people who offend, making rights practical and effective will remain extremely difficult.

Note

1. Many of the young people that contact the Howard League do so on the recommendation of professionals or other people in prison and the initial contact often begins with a request for practical assistance about a pressing matter such as representation for a disciplinary matter or the need for support on release—also they can call us on a free number.

Bibliography

Argar, E. (2018, October 2). *Letter to Bob Neill MP* [online]. Retrieved September 2019, from https://www.parliament.uk/documents/commons-committees/Justice/correspondence/Edward-Argar-secure-schools.pdf.

Argar, E. (2019, July 18). *Youth custody*. UK Parliament: Written question, HC 277224 [online]. Retrieved October 15, 2019, from https://www.parliament.uk/business/publications/written-questions-answers-statements/written-question/Commons/2019-07-15/277224/.

Bateman, T. (2015). *Resettlement of young people leaving custody – Lessons from the literature, Updated 2015* [online]. Retrieved September 1, 2019, from http://www.beyondyouthcustody.net/wp-content/uploads/Resettlement-of-young-people-leaving-custody-lessons-from-the-literature-March-2015.pdf.

Bateman, T. (2016). *The state of youth custody* [online]. Retrieved October 27, 2019, from http://thenayj.org.uk/wp-content/uploads/2016/10/NAYJ-Briefing-State-of-Youth-Custody-2016.pdf.

Bateman, T. (2017). *The state of youth justice 2017* [online]. Retrieved October 27, 2019, from http://thenayj.org.uk/wp-content/uploads/2019/02/State-of-Youth-Justice-report-for-web-Sep17.pdf.

Bateman, T., Hazel, N., & Wright, S. (2013). *Resettlement of young people leaving custody – Lessons from the literature* [online]. Retrieved September 1, 2019, from http://www.beyondyouthcustody.net/wp-content/uploads/Resettlement-of-Young-People-Leaving-Custody-Lessons-from-the-literature.pdf.

BBC. (2017, July 4). *Feltham boy's solitary confinement breached human rights* [online]. Retrieved October 23, 2019, from https://www.bbc.co.uk/news/uk-40491331.

BMA. (2018). *Joint position statement on solitary confinement of children and young people* [online]. Retrieved September 1, 2019, from https://www.bma.org.uk/collective-voice/policy-and-research/equality/the-medical-role-in-solitary-confinement/our-joint-position-statement-on-the-medical-role-in-solitary-confinement.

Children's Commissioner. (n.d.). *Behind closed doors* [online]. Retrieved October 15, 2019, from https://www.childrenscommissioner.gov.uk/our-work/behind-closed-doors/.

Council of Europe. (n.d.). [online]. Retrieved October 15, 2019, from https://www.coe.int/en/web/cpt/about-the-cpt.

Defence for Children International. (2018). *Children's rights behind bars – Reintegration and rights from a participatory perspective* [online]. Retrieved September 1, 2019, from http://www.childrensrightsbehindbars.eu/outputs/crbb-2-0-outputs/eu-handbook.

Department for Education. (2015). *Guide to the children's homes regulations including the quality standards* [online]. Retrieved October 15, 2019, from https://assets.publishing.service.gov.uk/government/uploads/system/uploads/attachment_data/file/463220/Guide_to_Children_s_Home_Standards_inc_quality_standards_Version__1.17_FINAL.pdf.

Gooch, K. (2016). A childhood cut short: Child deaths in penal custody and the pains of child imprisonment. *The Howard Journal of Crime and Justice, 55*: 278–294 [online]. Retrieved September 1, 2019, from https://onlinelibrary.wiley.com/doi/abs/10.1111/hojo.12170.

Hales, H., Warner, L., Smith, J., & Bartlett, A. (2018). *Census of young people in secure settings on 14 September 2016: Characteristics, needs and pathways of care* [online]. Retrieved September 1, 2019, from https://www.england.nhs.uk/publication/secure-settings-for-young-people-a-national-scoping-exercise/.

Harris, T., & The Harris Review Panel. (2015). *Changing prisons, saving lives – Report of the independent review into self-inflicted deaths in custody of 18–24 year olds* [online]. Retrieved September 1, 2019, from http://iapdeathsincustody.independent.gov.uk/wp-content/uploads/2015/07/Harris-Review-Report2.pdf.

HMIP. (2017a). *HM Chief Inspector of Prisons welcomes new 'Urgent Notification' agreement with potential to strengthen the impact of inspections in failing jails* [online]. Retrieved October 15, 2019, from https://www.justiceinspectorates.gov.uk/hmiprisons/media/press-releases/2017/11/hm-chief-inspector-of-prisons-welcomes-new-urgent-notification-agreement-with-potential-to-strengthen-the-impact-of-inspections-in-failing-jails/.

HMIP. (2017b). *Annual report 2016–2017* [online]. Retrieved September 1, 2019, from https://www.gov.uk/government/uploads/system/uploads/attachment_data/file/629719/hmip-annual-report-2016-17.pdf.

HMIP. (2018). *Annual report 2017–2018* [online]. Retrieved September 1, 2019, from https://www.justiceinspectorates.gov.uk/hmiprisons/inspections/annual-report-2017-18/.

HMIP. (2019a). *Children in custody 2017–18* [online]. Retrieved September 1, 2019, from https://www.justiceinspectorates.gov.uk/hmiprisons/wp-content/uploads/sites/4/2019/01/6.5164_HMI_Children-in-Custody-2017-18_A4_v10_web.pdf.

HMIP. (2019b). *Annual report 2018–2019* [online]. Retrieved September 1, 2019, from https://www.justiceinspectorates.gov.uk/hmiprisons/wp-content/uploads/sites/4/2019/07/6.5563_HMI-Prisons-AR_2018-19_WEB_FINAL_040719.pdf.

HMIP. (2019c). *Urgent notification for HMYOI Feltham 'A'* [online]. Retrieved October 15, 2019, from https://www.gov.uk/government/publications/urgent-notification-for-hmyoi-feltham-a.

HMIP, & Ofsted. (2014). *Inspection of Medway Secure Training Centre* [online]. Retrieved September 1, 2019, from https://reports.ofsted.gov.uk/provider/11/1027076.

Howard League. (2017). *Justice for young people: 15 years of successful legal work* [online]. Retrieved September 1, 2019, from https://howardleague.org/publications/justice-for-young-people-2/.

Howard League. (2018, September 10). *Child arrests in England and Wales reduced by more than two-thirds in seven years* [online]. Retrieved September 1, 2019, from https://howardleague.org/news/child-arrests-in-england-and-wales-reduced-by-more-than-two-thirds-in-seven-years/.

Independent Improvement Board. (2017). *Findings and recommendations of the Youth Custody Improvement Board* [online]. Retrieved September 1, 2019, from https://assets.publishing.service.gov.uk/government/uploads/system/uploads/attachment_data/file/594448/findings-and-recommendations-of-the-ycib.pdf.

Independent Inquiry into Child Sexual Abuse (IICSA). (2019). *Sexual abuse of children in custodial institutions: 2009–2017 investigation report* [online]. Retrieved

September 1, 2019, from https://www.iicsa.org.uk/publications/investigation/custodial.

Independent Monitoring Board. (n.d.). *About us* [online]. Retrieved October 15, 2019, from https://www.imb.org.uk/about-us/.

International Psychological Trauma Symposium. (2007). *The Istanbul statement on the use and effects of solitary confinement* [online]. Retrieved October 23, 2019, from http://solitaryconfinement.org/uploads/Istanbul_expert_statement_on_sc.pdf.

Joint Committee on Human Rights. (2019). Youth detention: Solitary confinement and restraint. *Nineteenth Report of Session 2017–19*, HC 994, HL 343 [online]. Retrieved October 15, 2019, from https://www.parliament.uk/business/committees/committees-a-z/joint-select/human-rights-committee/inquiries/parliament-2017/youth-detention-solitary-confinement-17-19/.

Justice Committee. (2016). The treatment of young adults in the criminal justice system. *Seventh Report of Session 2016–17*, HC 169 [online]. Retrieved September 1, 2019, from https://publications.parliament.uk/pa/cm201617/cmselect/cmjust/169/169.pdf.

Justice Committee. (2018). Young adults in the criminal justice system. *Eighth Report of Session 2017–19*, HC 419 [online]. Retrieved September 1, 2019, from https://publications.parliament.uk/pa/cm201719/cmselect/cmjust/419/41902.htm.

Justice Committee. (2019). *MPs to investigate children and young people in custody* [online]. Retrieved October 15, 2019, from https://www.parliament.uk/business/committees/committees-a-z/commons-select/justice-committee/news-parliament-2017/children-young-people-custody-launch-17-29/.

Justice Committee. (2021). Children and Young People in Custody (part 2): The Youth Secure Estate and Resettlement. Sixteenth Report of Session 2019–21, HC 922 [online]. Retrieved March 28, 2021, from https://committees.parliament.uk/publications/4637/documents/46888/default/.

Lambie, I., & Randell, I. (2013). The impact of incarceration on juvenile offenders. *Clinical Psychology Review, 33*(3), 448–459.

Lammy, D. (2017). *Lammy review: Final report* [online]. Retrieved September 1, 2019, from https://www.gov.uk/government/publications/lammy-review-final-report.

Local Government Association (LGA). (2017). *Councils call for urgent action to improve safety in youth offending institutions* [online]. Retrieved September 1, 2019, from https://www.local.gov.uk/about/news/councils-call-urgent-action-improve-safety-youth-offending-institutions.

McAra, L., & McVie, S. (2010). Youth crime and justice: Key messages from the Edinburgh study of youth transitions and crime. *Criminology & Criminal Justice, 10*(2), 179–209 [online]. Retrieved September 1, 2019, from http://journals.sagepub.com/doi/pdf/10.1177/1748895809360971.

Medway Improvement Board. (2016). *Final report of the Board's Advice to Secretary of State for Justice* [online]. Retrieved September 1, 2019, from https://www.gov.uk/government/uploads/system/uploads/attachment_data/file/523167/medway-report.pdf.

Ministry of Justice. (2015). *Needs and characteristics of young adults in custody: Results from the Surveying Prisoner Crime Reduction (SPCR) survey* [online]. Retrieved September 1, 2019, from https://assets.publishing.service.gov.uk/government/uploads/system/uploads/attachment_data/file/449586/Young-adults-in-custody.pdf.

Ministry of Justice. (2016a). *Race and the criminal justice system – Chapter 7: Offenders under supervision or in custody tables*, table 7.01 [online]. Retrieved September 1, 2019, from https://www.gov.uk/government/statistics/race-and-the-criminal-justice-system-2016.

Ministry of Justice. (2016b). *The government response to Charlie Taylor's review of the youth justice system* [online]. Retrieved September 1, 2019, from https://assets.publishing.service.gov.uk/government/uploads/system/uploads/attachment_data/file/576553/youth-justice-review-government-response.pdf.

Ministry of Justice. (2017a). *Key characteristics of admissions to youth custody April 2014 to March 2016* [online]. Retrieved September 1, 2019, from https://www.gov.uk/government/uploads/system/uploads/attachment_data/file/585991/key-characteristics-of-admissions-april-2014-to-march-2016.pdf.

Ministry of Justice. (2017b). *Youth justice statistics 2015/2016 England and Wales* [online]. Retrieved September 1, 2019, from https://www.gov.uk/government/uploads/system/uploads/attachment_data/file/585897/youth-justice-statistics-2015-2016.pdf.

Ministry of Justice. (2018). *Members announced for new Child Safeguarding Practice Review Panel* [online]. Retrieved October 15, 2019, from https://www.gov.uk/government/news/members-announced-for-new-child-safeguarding-practice-review-panel.

Ministry of Justice. (2019a). *Youth custody data June 2019* [online]. Retrieved October 13, 2019, from https://assets.publishing.service.gov.uk/government/uploads/system/uploads/attachment_data/file/823750/youth-custody-report-june-2019.xlsx.

Ministry of Justice. (2019b). *Prison population: 30 June 2019* [online]. Retrieved October 13, 2019, from https://assets.publishing.service.gov.uk/government/uploads/system/uploads/attachment_data/file/820162/population-30June2019-quarterly.ods.

Ministry of Justice. (2019c). *Youth justice statistics 2017/2018 England and Wales* [online]. Retrieved September 1, 2019, from https://www.gov.uk/government/statistics/youth-justice-statistics-2017-to-2018.

Ministry of Justice. (2019d). *Proven reoffending statistics: July to September 2017, Proven reoffending tables (annual average), January 2017 to March 2017*, table C1b. Retrieved October 27, 2019, from https://assets.publishing.service.gov.uk/government/uploads/system/uploads/attachment_data/file/832664/proven-reoffending-jul17-sep17-annual.ods.

Ministry of Justice. (2019e). *Safety in custody quarterly: Update to March 2019* [online]. Retrieved September 1, 2019, from https://www.gov.uk/government/statistics/safety-in-custody-quarterly-update-to-march-2019.

Ministry of Justice. (n.d.). *Young people in custody – Advocacy service* [online]. Retrieved October 15, 2019, from https://www.gov.uk/young-people-in-custody/advocacy-services.

Muncie, J. (2008). The 'Punitive Turn' in Juvenile Justice: Cultures of control and rights compliance in Western Europe and the USA. *Youth Justice, 8*(2), 107–121.

National Preventative Mechanism. (n.d.). *Background* [online]. Retrieved October 15, 2019, from https://www.nationalpreventivemechanism.org.uk/about/background/.

Office for National Statistics. (2011). *Census 2011, Ethnic group by sex by age* [online]. Retrieved September 1, 2019, from https://www.nomisweb.co.uk/census/2011/dc2101ew.

Office for National Statistics. (2019). *Population estimates for the UK, England and Wales, Scotland and Northern Ireland: Mid-2018.* Retrieved January 3, 2020, from https://www.ons.gov.uk/peoplepopulationandcommunity/populationandmigration/populationestimates/bulletins/annualmidyearpopulationestimates/mid2018.

Office of the United Nations High Commissioner for Human Rights (OHCHR). (n.d.). *Introduction* [online]. Retrieved October 15, 2019, from https://www.ohchr.org/EN/HRBodies/OPCAT/Pages/OPCATIntro.aspx.

Ofsted. (2015). *Handbook for the inspection of learning and skills and work activities in prisons and young offender institutions* [online]. Retrieved October 15, 2019, from https://assets.publishing.service.gov.uk/government/uploads/system/uploads/attachment_data/file/455107/Handbook_for_the_inspection_of_learning_and_skills_and_work_activities_in_prisons_and_young_offender_institutions_from_1_September_2015.pdf.

Panorama. (2016, January 11). *BBC One Television* (Previously retrieved from https://www.bbc.co.uk/programmes/b06ymzly).

Prisons and Probation Ombudsman (PPO). (2019). *Annual report 2018–19* [online]. Retrieved October 23, 2019, from https://s3-eu-west-2.amazonaws.com/ppo-prod-storage-1g9rkhjhkjmgw/uploads/2019/10/PPO_Annual-Report-2018-19_WEB-final-1.pdf.

Prisons and Probation Ombudsman (PPO). (n.d.). *How to submit a complaint* [online]. Retrieved October 15, 2019, from https://www.ppo.gov.uk/investigations/make-complaint/how-to-make-a-complaint-dvd/.

Sawyer, S. M., Azzopardi, P. S., Wickremarathne, D., & Patton, G. C. (2018). The age of adolescence. *The Lancet Child & Adolescent Health, 2*(3), 223–228.

Sentencing Council. (2017). *Sentencing children and young people: Overarching principles and offence specific guidelines for sexual offences and robbery – Definitive guideline* [online]. Retrieved September 1, 2019, from https://www.sentencingcouncil.org.uk/wp-content/uploads/Sentencing-Children-and-Young-People-definitive-guideline-Web.pdf.

Transition to Adulthood (T2A) Alliance. (2016). *Written evidence to the House of Commons Justice Select Committee Inquiry on Young Adult Offenders* [online]. Retrieved September 1, 2019, from http://data.parliament.uk/WrittenEvidence/

CommitteeEvidence.svc/EvidenceDocument/Justice/Young%20adult%20 offenders/written/21967.html.
Travis, A. (2017, July 4). 'Prolonged solitary confinement' of boy at Feltham YOI 'breached human rights'. *The Guardian* [online]. Retrieved October 23, 2019, from https://www.theguardian.com/society/2017/jul/04/feltham-yoi-high-court-human-rights.
Unitas. (n.d.). *About* [online]. Retrieved October 23, 2019, from https://www.unitas.uk.net/about/.
United Nations. (2019). *Concluding observations on the sixth periodic report of the United Kingdom of Great Britain and Northern Ireland. Convention against torture and other cruel, inhuman or degrading treatment or punishment* [online]. Retrieved October 15, 2019, from https://tbinternet.ohchr.org/_layouts/15/treatybodyexternal/Download.aspx?symbolno=CAT%2fC%2fGBR%2fCO%2f6&Lang=en.
Willow, C. (2015). *Children behind bars: Why the abuse of child imprisonment must end*. Bristol: Policy Press.
World Prison Brief. (n.d.). *World prison brief data for Europe* [online]. Retrieved September 1, 2019, from https://www.prisonstudies.org/map/europe.
Youth Justice Board (YJB). (2010). *Youth justice annual workload data 2008/09* [online]. Retrieved October 15, 2019, from https://assets.publishing.service.gov.uk/government/uploads/system/uploads/attachment_data/file/279875/yjb-workload-data-2008-09.pdf.
Youth Justice Board (YJB). (2015). *Protected education – 60/40 split* [online]. Retrieved October 15, 2019, from https://assets.publishing.service.gov.uk/government/uploads/system/uploads/attachment_data/file/465531/Protected_Education_60-40_split_definition_and_guidance.PDF.
Youth Justice Board (YJB). (2019). *Annual report and accounts 2018/19* [online]. Retrieved October 21, 2019, from https://assets.publishing.service.gov.uk/government/uploads/system/uploads/attachment_data/file/820763/YJB_Annual_Report_and_Accounts_2018-19_pages_web.pdf.

Statute, Regulations and Codes of Practice

Academies Act 2000
Children Act 1989
Children Act 2004
Children and Young Persons Act 1933
Children's Homes (England) Regulations 2015
Criminal Justice Act 2003
European Convention on Human Rights (ECHR) (formally the Convention for the Protection of Human Rights and Fundamental Freedoms)
Prison Service Instructions (PSI) 49/2011 (Prisoner communication services)
Prison Service Instructions (PSI) 08/2012 (Care and management of young people)

Prison Service Instructions (PSI) 06/2014 (Use of force in the young people's estate)
Prison Service Order (PSO) 1600 (Use of force)
Secure Training Centre Rules 1998
United Nations Convention Rights of the Child
Young Offender Institution Rules 2000

Cases

Airey v Ireland [1979] 2 E.H.R.R. 305
R (AB) v Secretary of State for Justice [2017] 4 WLR 153
R (AB) v Secretary of State for Justice [2019] 4 WLR 42
R (C) v Secretary of State for Justice [2009] QB 657
R (Howard League for Penal Reform) v Secretary of State for the Home Department & Anor [2003] 1 FLR 484
R (Brooks) v (1) Secretary of State for Justice, (2) Isle of Wight Primary Care Trust [2008] EWHC 3041
Saadi v United Kingdom [2006] ECHR 732

4

Everyday Violence in *El Redentor* Specialized Care Center in Bogotá, Colombia

Laura Liévano-Karim and Amy E. Ritterbusch

The Context of Juvenile Detention Centers in Colombia

> It is torture that you have to be here [at *El Redentor*], and that they beat you hard, that the detention facility officials mistreat you. That is common here, even the food is bad and everything else here is as if it were for animals—Pedro.[1]

Colombia is a country that has endured one of the longest internal armed conflicts in the world. Almost nine million people are registered as victims of the armed conflict (Unidad para la Atención y Reparación Integral a las Víctimas 2019) having experienced diverse forms of violence such as forced displacement, kidnapping or sexual violence, among others (Unidad para la Atención y Reparación Integral a las Víctimas 2019). Moreover, Colombia has been a drug-producing country throughout its contemporary history (Colombia Reports 2019). Reports have found that approximately 70% of the drugs that are consumed globally are produced in Colombia, which is a social dilemma affecting communities throughout the country (Colombia Reports 2019). Additionally, Colombia faces diverse social challenges, including a 12.2% incidence of multidimensional poverty in 2017 (Departamento

---

L. Liévano-Karim (✉) • A. E. Ritterbusch
University of California Los Angeles, Los Angeles, CA, USA
e-mail: lauralievanok@g.ucla.edu

© The Author(s), under exclusive license to Springer Nature Switzerland AG 2021
A. Cox, L. S. Abrams (eds.), *The Palgrave International Handbook of Youth Imprisonment*, Palgrave Studies in Prisons and Penology, https://doi.org/10.1007/978-3-030-68759-5_4

Nacional de Estadística 2019a), structural inequality, lack of access to opportunities, an unemployment rate of 9.8% (Departamento Nacional de Estadística 2019b) and a lifetime intimate partner violence prevalence of 33.3% (United Nations Women n.d.), among other social ills. This context of multilevel violence and inequality throughout the country is important to keep in mind as we consider the stories of the nine young men highlighted in this chapter (Instituto Colombiano de Bienestar Familiar 2015; Villanueva-Congote et al. 2018).

Juvenile justice in Colombia is governed by the Code on Children and Adolescents established by the 1098 National Law of 2006. It is defined as a system of norms, guidelines and specialized judicial and administrative institutions that govern or intervene in the investigation and prosecution of punishable acts committed by adolescents between the ages of 14 and 18 years old. The Code on Children and Adolescents of Colombia can be seen as a model of progressive thinking because it enacts United Nations standards by being one of the few countries that have ratified 18 as the official minimum age for a person to be prosecuted as an adult (Human Rights Watch 1994; Zalkind and Simon 2004). Therefore, system-affected youth in Colombia (between the ages of 14 and 18 years old) are criminally punishable and sanctioned by law but are prosecuted in juvenile courts rather than in adult criminal courts (Zalkind and Simon 2004).

Moreover, the policies governing juvenile justice in Colombia theoretically serve a protective, educational and restorative purpose and must be applied with the support of family and specialists (Instituto Colombiano de Bienestar Familiar 2019). These also seek to restore the violated rights of both the victims and the adolescents who committed the criminal offense (Instituto Colombiano de Bienestar Familiar 2019). According to this logic, law and society recognizes system-affected youth as individuals who are simultaneously exercising their fundamental rights as children and adolescents by being prosecuted in a different system following a process that must—presumably—guarantee restorative justice, truth and reparation as stated in article 140 of The Code on Children and Adolescents (2006).

However, the infrastructure of the facilities, which was observed during fieldwork in the institutional context in Bogotá, does not adhere to the expectations presented by the law. All youth remain inside closed spaces throughout the majority of the day (except one or two hours weekly when they have time to play sports in the outside), moving from the dormitories to the cafeteria and into the classrooms. Moreover, the institutional management does not adhere to the minimum living conditions stipulated by the law (Red de Coaliciones Sur 2014). The state seems to have abandoned system-affected youth and has overlooked violence perpetrated against them (Human Rights Watch 1994; Red de Coaliciones Sur 2014). While acts of violence within the facilities have been documented by local media sources, this is the first investigation to assess the context of adversity from the perspective of young people themselves. The experiences of violence told in the media frequently come from their caregivers all in an effort to achieve changes for the youth's living conditions inside *El Redentor* (Las 2 Orillas 2018; Rodríguez 2018). This abandonment is indicative of the criminalization of poverty in Colombia and how children and adolescents involved in juvenile justice are banished from society, from childhood and from personhood in general. A report released by the National Ombudsman Office found that[2] 90% of the system-affected youth living in confinement at *El Redentor* came from the lowest socioeconomic levels in the country (Defensoría del Pueblo 2015). Thus, the most marginalized youth in society are those who end up confined (Defensoría del Pueblo 2015). Moreover, the International Catholic Child Bureau (n.d.) indicates that of the 15,474 children and adolescents who were sanctioned to confinement in 2004 in Colombia, 99% of them were living below the poverty line (Fernández Díaz 2014; International Catholic Child Bureau n.d.) which as mentioned suggests a criminalization of those with fewer opportunities in society. Furthermore, the Colombian Institute for Family Welfare has identified poverty as one of the macro risk factors for youth in Colombia to commit offenses (Instituto Colombiano de Bienestar Familiar 2015).

The 2006 Code on Children and Adolescents, which holds that no youth involved in criminal activity can be incarcerated in an adult prison under any circumstances, changed the formerly named 'Centers for the Protection of the Youth Offender'[3] to 'Specialized Care Centers'[4] (CAE). This name change symbolized a paradigm shift and an administrative innovation for the juvenile justice system in the country. Adolescents were now seen as subjects of rights and active citizens (Instituto Colombiano de Bienestar Familiar 2013). Therefore, in compliance with the 2006 legal standard, adolescents between the ages of 14 and 18 years old who have been sanctioned must be admitted to a Specialized Care Center (Instituto Colombiano de Bienestar Familiar 2019). These facilities are thus expected to enable the adolescent to complete the imposed sanction following the restorative process delineated by the law as well as to guarantee their rights and ensure their full development.

The main child welfare institution in the country is the Colombian Family Welfare Institute (ICBF, for the acronym in Spanish). This entity, which works at the national level, is in charge of preventing and promoting the welfare of Colombian families by focusing on marginalized and vulnerable infants, children and youth across the country (Instituto Colombiano de

Bienestar Familiar 2020). ICBF was established under Law 75 of 1968, reorganized by Law 7 of 1979 and recently ascribed by the Decree number 4156 of 2011, to be under the Administrative Department for Social Prosperity of Colombia (DPS, according to the acronym in Spanish). The DPS governs four other national entities all of which, as the ICBF, are part of the social inclusion and reconciliation sector in the country.

In 2012, under the Decree number 0987, the structure of the Colombian Family Welfare Institute was modified and the functions of its sub-divisions were redefined. This reorganization established the sub-division of criminal responsibility, under the General Management Division of ICBF, to be in charge of defining the specific guidelines and processes in terms of the juvenile justice system in the country. Following the institutional definition of the technical and administrative guidelines and processes by the sub-division of criminal responsibility, each of the 33 regional divisions of the Colombian Family Welfare Institute were delegated implementation power in the particular regions where these operate in the country.

In Bogotá, the capital city of Colombia, there are three youth detention centers. All facilities are situated side by side in the south of the city, which is an area where multidimensional poverty is most highly concentrated in the city (Bogotá Cómo Vamos 2015). Two centers are for males and one is for females. *El Redentor Centro de Atención Especializada*, which in English is interpreted as 'The Redeemer, Specialized Care Center', is one of the two centers exclusively for male system-affected youth. The differences between the two facilities depend on the organizations that are managing them. Thus, older adolescents are sometimes located in one or the other facility. At the present time, the context of care of *El Redentor* is highly problematic for multiple reasons. First, there have been multiple shifts in operational management between different organizations, foundations and religious communities under contract with the Colombian Institute for Family Welfare (ICBF) over the last decade (Las 2 Orillas 2018; Rubio Serrano 2018). Second, the organizations that have been granted contracts with ICBF to operate the facility lack specialized training in working with this community within a restorative and protective framework (Rubio Serrano 2018). Lastly, although grave human rights violations are known to occur inside the correctional facility, state officials have not taken restorative action.

In this chapter, we examine violence and other forms of abuse occurring within *El Redentor*. This underscores contradictions between the principles of juvenile justice in Colombia aligned with a restorative justice approach and the reality of how system-affected youth are treated within the system. As mentioned, the juvenile justice system in Colombia seeks to restore justice in the lives of young person involved in criminal activity and those who have been affected by this criminal activity (Instituto Colombiano de Bienestar Familiar 2019). The legal framework guiding the juvenile justice system considers the criminal offense committed by the system-affected youth as a social problem resulting from the absence of the state coupled with a lack of protective factors for families living in multidimensional poverty (Instituto Colombiano de Bienestar Familiar 2015; Villanueva-Congote et al. 2018). This indicates that the perspective of the juvenile justice system is that the criminal offense is the result of the ideal conditions being created for the young adult to commit the crime (Fernández Díaz 2014; Villanueva-Congote et al. 2018). Therefore, in theory, as seen in article 140 of the 2006 Code of Children and Adolescents the juvenile justice systems seek to restore the rights of systems-affected adolescents through education in an effort to intervene any factors that would result in additional crimes being committed (Villanueva-Congote et al. 2018). Thus, the system seeks to protect society from additional crimes being committed by system-affected youth through restorative and preventative means rather than punitive measures (Villanueva-Congote et al. 2018). The system processes and measures are all meant to have a pedagogical approach that is differentiated from the punitive systems of adults. It should guarantee restorative justice, truth and reparation.

Violence in Juvenile Detention Centers

In the global North and global South, scholars have drawn attention to the juvenile justice system as a space of adversity where multiple acts of violence occur (Davidson-Arad et al. 2009; Hodge and Yoder 2017; Matthews 2018; Mountz 2016; Office of the SRSG on Violence Against Children 2012; Peterson-Badali and Koegl 2002). Among these reflections are the mental health and structural consequences of adverse institutional experiences in the juvenile justice system (Kramer et al. 2013) and also the need for improved training mechanisms for state officials working with youth in the system (Peterson-Badali and Koegl 2002; Galardi and Settersten 2018; Gardner 2010). As Abrams and Terry (2017) mention in *Everyday Desistance*, there has been increasing public commotion surrounding the "economic, social and psychological consequences of youth incarceration" (p. 1) in the United States that has led to several broad sweeping efforts for system reform and/or improvement, varying by local political contexts and movements.

Violence Documented by a Video Recorded in the Specialized Care Center El Redentor

In Colombia, however, there has been little media attention or public outcry related to youth incarceration until a recent video, released to the press in September 2018, depicted the brutal treatment of system-affected youth by state officials in one of the male-serving facilities in Bogotá. What can be seen in the video, which lasts less than one minute, is that around 6:00 pm on Friday, September 28, 2018, a group of seven police officers surrounded a group of youth, wearing only their underwear, and began beating them with wooden sticks (El Espectador 2018). It is unknown how many youths were forced to get on the ground; however, in the video there seems to be at least 13 young men lying face down on the cement floor of the institution. The video also displays the physical wounds the adolescents had on their backs from the beating and also shows how an officer keeps beating a young boy even after he pleads for him to stop (El Espectador 2018).

In addition to the physical violence that occurred during the event, the video reveals verbal and psychological violence against the youth as officers insulted them while beating them. For example, during the first ten seconds of the video, we see a young man looking upward toward the officers who were hitting him and his peers, crying out loudly in pain. An officer then yells at the young man, "face down, face down[5]" and keeps on beating him as another officer says, "face down faggot, or is it that you can't hear?[6]" During the following seconds of the video we hear the young men saying something to the officer while on the floor but it is not clear enough to understand what they are saying. While this happens, another officer says: "shut up you triple son of a bitch pig".[7] These and many more insults can be heard in the video (El Espectador 2018).

Although the video highlights crude forms of violence toward adolescents, the viewer responses in social media include statements that reveal societal indifference or even normalization of these forms of violence. The following are examples of social media responses to the video: "I do not know why people are outraged [with the video] when that is what that herd of corrupt children need, [they need] to be hit with batons and shot if necessary, unruly kids!"[8] and "Excellent! Although we still need more whipping and bullets in order to heal the moral rot that corrodes Colombia (…) [come down] hard on those rats [referring to the system-affected youth]".[9] We include these reactions from the popular media as a means of illustrating the stigmatization against system-affected youth in the Colombian context beyond the institutions created to support their wellbeing.

Public figures and politicians also reacted to the video. The attorney general in charge of crimes against children and adolescents mentioned the following: "The country is in total outrage given events [of police violence at *El* Redentor]. Events that can be described as cruel and inhumane and are completely contrary to the care and treatment system-affected youth should receive. Moreover, these can be classified as a type of torture"[10] (La FM 2018). Additionally, the Former Director of the Colombian Institute for Family Welfare (ICBF) made the following statement: "My dream is to close the Specialized Care Center because I believe that its infrastructure is not adequate. Specialized Care Centers must be made with the purpose of re-socialization of youth and the last thing we need is for the centers to become schools for crime" (Vargas Ovalle 2018). With similar indignation, a local representative issued the following response: "We cannot tolerate that the public official in charge of guaranteeing the security of *El Redentor* (…) are the same ones who beat young half-naked men lying on the ground at mercy of the blows and insults of police officers" (Bastidas 2018).

The video depicts the severe perpetration of violence against adolescents inside a facility that has the responsibility to protect them and provide a context of restorative justice in their lives. Juvenile detention facilities must strengthen their efforts to prevent and respond to violence against system-affected youth. Aiming to achieve a non-violent atmosphere for all system-affected children and adolescents has been slowly recognized as a priority in Colombia that will contribute to that transition to a post-conflict society.[11]

Research Questions

In the absence of evidence regarding violence perpetrated within the juvenile justice system, the research team employed qualitative methods to conduct a qualitative assessment of violence occurring in *El Redentor*. The overarching aim of the study was to document the violence perpetrated against the young men as described and contextualized by them. Thus, our main research objective was to understand and describe their experiences of violence inside the institution for justice-seeking purposes. Moreover, we seek to answer the following research questions:

1. What is the context of violence in *El Redentor*, occurring on and around September 2018 (date of incident made public through a video), and beyond?
2. Who are the perpetrators of violence in *El Redentor*?

3. What protective factors do young men experience while at *El Redentor*?
4. What are the specific forms of violence perpetrated against adolescents and young people in *El Redentor*?
5. Do young men have suggestions for institutional change in *El Redentor*? If so, what are these suggestions?

Methodology

In order to document youth perceptions of violence in the context of *El Redentor*, the research team conducted nine semi-structured interviews with system-affected youth in this facility between the ages of 18 and 20 years old during the month of June in 2019. The research team employed purposive sampling based on the following inclusion criteria: (1) 18 years old or older at the time of interview (2) confined inside *El Redentor* on or before September 2018 (which was when the video of police violence was recorded). We obtained official access to *El Redentor* by a formal institutional collaboration with the now former Deputy Prosecutor for Children and Adolescents Dr. Mario Gómez Jiménez of the Attorney General's Office of Colombia. Dr. Gómez Jiménez granted us the access to *El Redentor* by sending an official letter to the Family Welfare Institute of Colombia (ICBF) asking for authorization for us to enter the facility.

However, given safety and privacy considerations of the institutions we did not have access to the list of institutionalized youth, thus we were not permitted to do direct recruitment of the participants and we were limited to interview the participants who were referred to us from the gatekeepers in the institution. The gatekeepers, who were all institutional staff at *El Redentor*, assert that they connected us with the totality of the young men who fulfilled the inclusion criteria. Moreover, we had no access to the different buildings, after entering the institution we were only allowed to walk directly into a boardroom where the interviews took place, so although additional interviews would be optimal in methodological terms, we were not permitted further access. The following table includes the pseudonyms used for each of the nine participants in the study, their age at the time of the interview, the number of months of the sanction they were given and their age of entry to *El Redentor* (see Table 4.1). *El Redentor* was selected as the study site because the acts of violence were perpetrated within this institution, as per abovementioned video leaked to mainstream media.

4 Everyday Violence in *El Redentor* Specialized Care Center... 59

Table 4.1 Participants table

Pseudonym[a]	Age (the day of the interview)	Action[b]	Sanction (in months)	Age of entry to *El Redentor*
Daniel	18	Aggravated and qualified theft	10	16
Juan	19	Qualified theft	12	17
Pablo	18	Domestic violence	16	17
Sebastián	18	Qualified theft	12	17
Felipe	18	Aggravated and qualified theft	13	17
Guillermo	20	Aggravated murder	84	19
David	18	Carnal access with a person who is incapable of resisting	24	17
Diego	18	Qualified theft	10	17
Pedro	18	Qualified theft	15	17
Means	18.33		21.78	17.11

[a]For confidentiality purposes the names, last names, exact dates of entry to the institution and birth dates of the participants have not been included
[b]While weary of the stigmatizing risks of labeling these acts, we include this categorical information according to English interpretation of the terminology in Spanish

The interviews were conducted by a Colombian doctoral researcher of the UCLA Department of Social Welfare who was granted access to the institution by the Division of Children and Adolescent Welfare of the Attorney General's office after a process of in-country approval within the Colombian Family Welfare institution. Institutional review board approval was granted by the University of California, Los Angeles, and informed consent was completed with each of the nine participants by the doctoral researcher.

The interview instrument contained the concepts we aimed to explore in the form of the following sections: (1) general perceptions of the detention center; (2) perceptions of protective factors; (3) perceptions of violence and safety in the institutional context; (4) experiences of police violence and (5) suggestions for institutional change in the Specialized Care Center. After the interviews and the transcriptions were done NVIVO12 was used to codify the data set according to the following overarching topics: (1) life in *El Redentor*, which includes perceptions of system-affected youth in relation to their daily activities inside the facility and (2) violence in *El Redentor*, which includes descriptions of situations of violence they have either experienced or witnessed. Two coding cycles were conducted including an exploratory first cycle on violence and protective factors in the institution and a second coding cycle focusing on the practices of dehumanization and the effects of stigma by authority figures and educators in juvenile detention centers.

Throughout the coding process, violence was conceptualized as any form of aggressive physical or psychological behavior exerted against the youth either coming from state officials or their peers. Physical violence included kicking, punching, using tear gas and stabbing while psychological or emotional violence included insults, yelling or using degrading or dehumanizing language intended to make the youth feel insufficient, incomplete or sad, among other negative emotions. Overall, all analytic categories (codes) included in the codebook were related to different forms of violence. These were (1) 'daily life at *El Redentor*', which included descriptions of the regular daily activities held while at *El Redentor*; (2) 'violence in *El Redentor*', which included any form of violence experienced, witnessed or heard about from the interviewee; (3) 'escape attempts', which are common at *El Redentor* and are usually the situations where police officers get involved were also coded; (4) 'police violence against youth living at *El Redentor*', which was a node specifically focused on descriptions related to the incident that had occurred in September 2018; (5) 'Peer advice', which included any advice, from the perspective of youth, related to how to stay safe when living at *El Redentor*; and (6) 'suggestions and recommendations for improving the everyday experiences at *El Redentor*' (see Appendix for the codebook). The overarching theme that emerged from the analysis was the idea of 'everyday violence' described by the young men who participated in the study. In the following section we describe the findings the analysis revealed by focusing on three particular themes, which are (1) the relationship youth in the specialized care center *El Redentor* have with the detention facility officials, (2) the everyday emotions of system-affected youth in *El Redentor* as described by the nine participants of the study and 3) the hiding of the violence that occurs within the facility from child welfare officials.

Youth Perceptions of Life in *El Redentor*

The coding process revealed more than 400 mentions of violent acts against youth in *El Redentor* in multiple contexts including the daily life of the institution, escape attempts and acts of violence perpetrated by police external to the formal institutional structure. The perpetrators of violence against youth mentioned in the interviews include detention facility officials, night guards (*los nocturnos*) and those who manage the surveillance and security structure of the detention center, known as *los paleros* (the baton men).

Everyday Violence in the Institutional Context of Youth Incarceration in Colombia

Overall, the participants perceived life in *El Redentor* as violent and lonely. David, for example, mentioned that the first days are particularly challenging at the center. He defines life as being very hard in particular throughout those first days at the institution, where, according to him, you are expected by your peers to pronounce your masculinity by trying to run away from the center, by getting involved in violent fights with your peers often involving weapons made of pieces of glass from broken windows or parts of nail clippers.[12]

Some examples of the descriptions given by the participants in terms of life at the center include:[13]

> the truth is that life here [at *El Redentor*] is a little hard because when you get here for the first time, you have to get into fights in order to show others that you can stand up for yourself and "...when I was new here I tried to escape various times and there were some people [detention facility official] who would try to beat me because you would be trying to escape and they would hit you with batons." (Juan)[14]

Moreover, new incoming youth are expected by other young men in the institution to try and escape from confinement, as one participant described:

> About 20 days ago they [peers] got out of control. It was a Sunday (...) all of them where on top of the roof and all were completely out of control. All the different sections [at the center] were uprooted, and there were people on the roofs and everything. I went to my section and realize the roof was all broken and I thought 'oh they escaped from here [through the roof]' and in fact they had. (Sebastián)[15]

When asked about life at *El Redentor*, Felipe mentioned it was very hard and that treatment from detention facility officials was often violent: "Well, here [at the center] life is very hard. There's a lot of abuse and it is all the time for no reason. The [detention facility officials] spray tear gas and beat [us] with batons".[16] Furthermore, the same participant mentioned it was common to see fights among different actors at the center: "Oh yeah. Well, you see fights all the time, that is not unusual here since one has already seen them before".[17]

The Relationship with Detention Facility Officials

Overall, the relationship with detention facility officials is not considered positive. Youth share with the officials only what is strictly necessary, and moreover, caring relationships between the youth and the institutional staff are not developed. One of the young men who participated in the study mentioned how detention facility officials at *El Redentor* did not build any strong relationships with him or his peers. He notes that detention facility officials barely interact with youth at the center: "Yes, the detention facility officials… they don't get involved with us. They only ask you to be helpful with waking up, making your bed, and getting showered and brushing your teeth. You see? There is some kind of schedule" (Sebastián).[18] Another participant indicated that there were times when the detention facility officials were friendly. However, whenever there was any kind of problem, the detention facility officials would not even let them talk. The detention facility officials would simply storm in and start kicking and beating the young men and sometimes would use tear gas. This may indicate a lack of specialized training received by the detention facility officials at the center as well as a contradiction between the mission of the center (restore the offenders rights) and the reality system-affected youth experience when sentenced to confinement.

Detention facility officials regularly beat the young men. In the words of Daniel: "It is common [to be hit], what I mean is, that it is common that they [detention facility officials] hit you, slap your face, punch and kick you".[19] In addition, Pedro mentioned living at the center as something filthy and described *El Redentor* (including the interaction with detention facility officials) as abusive and harsh.[20] The following excerpt contains this participant's point of view about living at *El Redentor* and the interactions between him and his peers with the detention facility officials: "… [*El Redentor*] is grotesque, this place is bad because here you get mistreated. Here it's a torment to live. Here you get beaten hard. When they beat you badly and *Bienestar* [child welfare officials] come [here] they [the detention facility officials] will hide, hide the tear gas, and hide the batons".[21]

Two participants mentioned detention facility officials made them and their peers feel belittle. Oscar said he felt like being treated as a dog while at the center.[22] These narratives of violence inside the institution demonstrate how these youth are stripped of their personhood and are denied basic rights within the juvenile justice system.

The Everyday Emotions of System-Affected Youth

The instrument used for the data collection included questions that pertained to the participants' emotions in a regular day at *El Redentor*. Participants highlighted that they are constantly fearful of being beat to death by their peers and detention facility officials, in particular those who work during the night shift. For example, Daniel mentioned he was sometimes frightened or felt fear of having to be in a fight that would injure him badly or might even kill him. He continued mentioning that it is common to have to fight while at the center, which agrees with what another participant had mentioned in relation to having to show yourself as a 'real strong man'.

> [Here, at *El Redentor*] you are always with the fear that one day you are going to have to fight hard or get killed or that they might [other peers] do something to you. But well, that is normal, to get here and hit someone or fight with handmade daggers, it is normal, here that is normal. (David)[23]

Another participant mentioned fear as the only constant in his daily life: "everyday [I feel fear or anguish], because [while being at *El Redentor*] you do not know who is going to pick a fight [with you]" (Pedro).[24] Moreover, a 20-year-old participant said he was particularly fearful during the first days at the institution because he did not know how the social system worked and he expected that others would try to break him down:

> When I arrived [I felt fear], because when I arrived [the first time to *El Redentor*] I did not know how things worked here and when you have just arrived is when [your peers] are trying hardest to find how to break you down. They will start bullying you because you are new [at the center]. (Oscar)[25]

In terms of feeling fear, Felipe mentioned he felt fear at night when the detention facility officials for the night shift arrive. According to this participant, the night shift detention facility officials are more violent than those who work during the daytime. He describes the following: "Clearly [I have felt fear] when the detention facility officials for the night shift arrive, they aren't doubtful or anything, [they will arrive] and beat you right away wherever the tube [they use to hit us] hits you [they don't care]".[26] Again, this is an example where we identify the contradiction between the detention facility officials being a place of protection with detention facility officials who nurture the development of the young adults and the reality of how they feel, which includes, as mentioned, feelings of fear for their physical safety.

Hiding Violence from Child Welfare Officials

Even with the frequent violence at *El Redentor*, three out of the nine participants mentioned how the violence exerted by the detention facility staff was intentionally hidden from child welfare officials. Two of these mentions are as follows:

> Here [in *El Redentor*] the detention facility officials are always beating you and there is a lot of abuse all the time, they take advantage when [child welfare officials] are not here to hit you (…) and when you tell someone from *Bienestar* [Colombian Institute of Family Welfare] what is happening, they [the detention facility officials] will say you are gossiping and lock you in *Perse* [a small cell without any windows, nor bathroom or beds], hit you and take away your possibility of having family visits. (Felipe)[27]

> Living here [at *El Redentor*] is a torment because here they are always beating you hard and when they beat you and someone from *Bienestar* [Colombian Institute of Family Welfare] comes, they [the detention facility officials] will hide themselves and hide the tear gas and hide the batons [they used to hit us]. (Pedro)[28]

This current scenario therefore calls for a multifaceted response and requires a range of strategies to strengthen the efforts to respond to violence against system-affected youth. The Institute of Family Welfare needs to demonstrate greater diligence and commitment to the investigation and prosecution of state officials that perpetrate violence against adolescents living in the Specialized Care Centers (such as *El Redentor*).

In summary, the voices of the system-affected youth in Colombia reveal inconsistencies between daily institutional practice and the legal guidelines that are stipulated in the (2006) Code of Childhood and Adolescence. The voices of the nine system-affected youth revealed various forms of violence exerted against them while in *El Redentor*, highlighting the particular high risk of having to face violence when in conflict with the law. These findings suggest Specialized Care Centers, such as *El Redentor* in Bogotá, Colombia, should play a more effective role in preventing and responding to the various forms of violence occurring within the system. Institutions involved with the juvenile justice system, in particular all foundations and organizations that administer and operate Specialized Care Centers around the country (including *El Redentor*), should respond against the perpetration of violence rather than exerting and reproducing it.

Recommendations

Violence against system-affected youth takes a variety of forms and is influenced by a range of factors, from the political and socioeconomic context of where it occurs to the personal characteristics of the different actors involved. In a general sense, regarding the acts of violence and covering up violence as mentioned above, we call for a multifaceted response including a range of strategies to strengthen the efforts to respond to violence against system-affected youth. The Institute of Family Welfare needs to demonstrate greater diligence and commitment to the investigation and prosecution of state officials that perpetrate violence against adolescents living in the Specialized Care Centers (such as *El Redentor*). The findings also suggest that the realities lived by system-affected youth in *El Redentor* Specialized Care Center do not reflect the alternative, restorative and educational justice suggested by law in Colombia. This system is expected to contribute to the human development of the youth, but their voices indicate that this is not the case (ICBF 2015). Moreover, the system should align with a restorative justice approach that seeks to support the development and wellbeing of the adolescents in conflict with the law and not to punish them or impose punitive measures (Villanueva-Congote et al. 2018).

Drawing from the voices of the participants, one principal concern is the need to improve their relationship with detention facility officials. For example, an 18-year-old system-affected youth suggested:

> Detention facility officials should not be as explosive as they currently are, they should treat us better. So instead of saying 'hey motherfucker go and do that' (…) they should not have to yell at us but rather in a simple proper manner talk to us and we do the things they ask us to. (Sebastián, male, 18 years of age)[29]

Moreover, the same participant suggested there should be more education (could be in the form of workshops of community-building activities) in relation to how to build respectful relationships between peers and between the system-affected youth and XDetentionfacility officials.

Overall, the elimination of violence from the detention facility officials against the system-affected youth was what the majority of participants recommended (seven out of the nine participants). From their perspective, the unjustified and frequent violent treatment is what leads to the majority of the problems inside *El Redentor*. Youth participants also recommend the following:

That [the detention facility officials] do not beat us that much. This is the only way [to make things better]. They [the detention facility officials] should be gentlemen, because they are rude so we [system-affected youth] become rude too and that is the problem here [in *El Redentor*]. (Oscar, male, 20 years of age)[30]

That [the detention facility officials] don't be violent, because that makes us [system-affected youth] feel anger. (Daniel, male, 18 years of age)[31]

Structural changes are therefore needed for the system to improve. In order to prevent offenses to occur there is the need to reduce poverty rates that as mentioned have been associated with risk factors for youth to commit crimes in the first place (ICBF 2015). Moreover, family structure support is necessary for the children in impoverished neighborhoods to have their caregivers' acts as protective factors. As mentioned in a recent policy recommendation document issued by the National Institute of Family Welfare (ICBF), substance use and abuse by children and adolescents should also be prioritized in order to reduce criminality and reentry (ICBF 2015). Specific to *El Redentor* there is an urgent need for training of the administrative staff that as told by the young adults confined there tends to be abusive and to rely overly in violence to get the individuals to fulfill their daily activities. Additional to these, the initiatives inside the institutions should focus on enabling these young male adults to consolidate their life project. Therefore, offer them formative educational options, relevant to their needs and health care. Lastly, a need for changes in the infrastructure of the specialized care center is also needed, given it currently does not seem to fulfill its role of being a space for truth and restoration rather than a place to punish the adolescents.

In order to promote institutional change that works against institutional cultures of violence, we suggest the design of specialized training for detention facility officials. Drawing from the United Nations framework, 'Model Strategies and Practical Measures on the Elimination of Violence against Children in the Field of Crime Prevention and Criminal Justice' (2015), it is considered necessary to "prohibit and effectively prevent the use of corporal punishment as a disciplinary measure [and] to adopt clear and transparent disciplinary policies and procedures that encourage the use of positive and educational forms of discipline" (p. 17). There is also the need for closer and stronger communication between system-affected youth and detention facility officials in *El Redentor* given the participants mentioned these relationships were distant and weak. Additional to this, youth participation and perspectives should be central to any of the reform processes and there should be spaces for the young offender's voices to be heard throughout their trajectories within the system. It is also important to keep in mind system-affected youth are also subject to violence from their peers, therefore overcrowding should be prevented and lack of supervision from detention facility officials (UNODC 2015).

Conclusion

The experiences of system-affected youth we have shared throughout the chapter demonstrate that violence against system-affected youth perpetrated by state officials exists and currently occurs in Colombia without consequences at the institutional level. Therefore, state officials should receive adequate training to work with system-affected youth within the juvenile justice system in Colombia and strict measures that prevent this kind of impunity should be ensured.

The voices and perspectives of the young men who participated in the interviews contribute to a better understanding of how they are treated within this particular specialized care center. Although the results cannot be generalized to all specialized care centers in Colombia, these findings indicate young men do not necessarily feel protected or cared for by the personnel in the institution or society. In fact, they feel constant abuse. Therefore, legislation and policies that can be considered innovative and in line with the principles of human rights and children's rights are not necessarily being implemented. At least not from the point of view of the participants who feel constant fear for their physical integrity and life within the center and were also frequent witnesses and victims of violence. Moreover, the fact that the majority of young men in conflict with the law in Colombia comes from impoverished background indicates that there is a need for targeted intervention to neighborhoods with concentrated disadvantages in the city, this in order to mediate the risk of having children and adolescents committing crimes because they do not see other options to succeed or fulfill their dreams. We continue to explore pathways for justice seeking through allies in human rights organizations and other social justice initiatives in Colombia.

Building on findings presented in this chapter, future research should examine effective, social justice-aligned mechanisms for the prevention and response to incidents of violence perpetrated by state officials against system-affected youth in the juvenile justice system. Ways to strengthen the efforts to prevent violence in specialized care centers such as *El Redentor* should also be explored in order to identify how to eliminate violence against children and adolescents and how to identify, investigate and prosecute the state officials who perpetrate these violent acts. Moreover, future research should seek ways to ensure that the practices in Specialized Care Centers in Colombia do not further abuses against children and adolescents involved within the juvenile detention center.

Acknowledgments We would like to express our gratitude for the work of Camila Delgadillo Chacón, María José Valencia Garzón, Geraldine Villamizar Torres and María José Castro Galeano who transcribed the nine audios of the interviews. We would also like to thank the attorney Mario Gómez Jiménez for authorizing our entrance to the specialized care center and ultimately enabling this work to be done. Moreover, we are grateful to the School of Government Alberto Lleras Camargo at Universidad de los Andes that was an institutional home to both authors for many years prior to transitioning to the University of California, Los Angeles.

Appendix: Codebook

Código	Definición	Ejemplo
Un día en el Redentor	Percepciones de los jóvenes sobre el lugar donde residen privados de su libertad, y las experiencias que viven. Descripción de un día típico en el Redentor.	"Pues la verdad acá la vida es un poquito dura porque uno cuando es nuevo le toca llegar digamos a darse traques, a plantarse, ¿si me entiende?" "Pues por el momento ha sido buena porque he aprendido (.) cosas que no aprendí en la calle ni (.) ni mucho menos"
Violencia en el Redentor	Descripciones de situaciones de violencia que hayan sido vividas, conocidas, o vistas por los jóvenes. Violencia física o emocional. *seguramente habrá *overlap* entre el nodo de violencia y el de fugas.	"…hay veces que los los cuchos dentran a pegarle a uno y entonces uno no tiene en ese momento una punta, entonces qué hace uno, uno coge una toalla se se la pone en el brazo y rompe el vidrio y ahí ya tiene para defenderse" "Acá a uno lo tienen cómo un secuestro es- esto es tort- esto es tortura estar acá"

Código	Definición	Ejemplo
Fugas	Descripción de intentos o fugas logradas, por el joven, sus amigos o sus compañeros. Descripción o explicación de por qué los jóvenes intentan fugarse de la institución.	"porque uno digamos uno corre. Uno así en la fila y uno sale a correr, y los educadores le pegan a uno con los palos. Si lo alcanzan, le dan duro y si se puede volar, se voló y ya" "Ahh si, yo si me intenten- una vez yo iba así por el muro de al frente y salte a la calle y pues un policía salió a correr detras mío y yo ya iba por la avenida Boyacá y casi me vuelo. Y otra vez, salté por atrás y me cogieron la policía, la policía me cogió"
Caso de violencia policial (sept 2018)	Todo lo relacionado con el caso de violencia policial que se llevó a cabo en el CIPA a finales de Septiembre de 2018. ¿cómo se enteraron? ¿de qué se enteraron? ¿qué opinan sobre eso?	"hmm pues en ese tiempo pues yo todavía corría y pues yo fui uno, pues no fui uno de los que me pegaron, pero fui uno de los que me subí al muro y me di de cuenta cómo les pegaban entonces lo que hice yo fue devolverme, inmediatamente devolverme pa la sección, pero aun así me alcanzaron a coger, me alcanzaron a pillar, lo que hicieron es encerrarme a Perse. Pero si pues ese día me di de cuenta, mal acto mal acto de los tombos, mal hecho" "Pues, los policías dentraron así todo esto estaba así descontrolado y pues ya después cuando los cogieron les daban palo, les daban bolillo, los gaseaban, les pegaban cachetadas así en las manos"
Factores de Protección	Cómo se protegen los jóvenes, entre ellos o individualmente.	"Pues para asegurar acá mi vida adentro pues ahí si como dice el dicho "tengo que ser sordo, ciego y mudo" porque si me preguntaron algo no lo se, que vi algo: no no se, que si algo: no nada. Vivo la mía y todo lo mío y ya. Lo que quedo fue tranquilo. Pero si pero si digo algo tengo el riesgo que de pronto em apuñaleen, que me casquen o algo ¿si me entiende?" "Nada, acá a uno nadie lo puede proteger"

Código	Definición	Ejemplo
Sugerencias o cambios	Descripciones de propuestas de cambios en la institución en *pro* del mejoramiento de las condiciones de vida de los jóvenes en el Redentor.	"Ni coordinadores así tan explosivos, sino que les den un mejor trato a los chinos (.) hacia uno mismo ¿si ve? (ni) que ah que malparido que vaya y haga eso. Que agh que mire que no le- que no tenga necesidad de gritarlo sino sopla- simplemente con una con una buena palabra los chinos entiendan y y hagan las cosas bien" "Pues que no den tanto palo. Es la única forma y que sean señores por que ellos también son groseros y nosotros también. Entonces, ese es el dilema entre todos"

Notes

1. Original interview excerpt in Spanish: "Acá la tortura es que a uno lo tengan y le den duro. Lo tengan menospreciado. Y siempre hacen eso acá. La comida todo eso acá es cómo pa' animales".
2. Defensoría del Pueblo.
3. In Spanish: Centros de Protección del Menor Infractor.
4. In Spanish: Centros de Atención Especializada.
5. Original interview excerpt in Spanish: "Boca abajo! Boca abajo!"
6. Original interview excerpt in Spanish: "Boca abajo marica, ¿es qué no escucha?"
7. Original interview excerpt in Spanish: "callese marrano triplehijueputa".
8. Original interview excerpt in Spanish: "No sé por qué se indigna la gente con toda esa manada de menores corruptos eso es lo que les hace falta. Que les den más duro palo y plomo cuando sea necesario. Muchachos revoltosos gamines".
9. Original interview excerpt in Spanish: "Excelente! Falta más rejo y más bala para sanar la podredumbre moral que corroe a Colombia. La educación es una medida necesaria al largo plazo, pero como medidas inmediatas el estado y la sociedad deben ser implacables e inflexibles contra violadores, ladrones, asesinos, narcos y secuestradores. Duro con las ratas".
10. Original interview excerpt in Spanish: "Es una indignación total la que tiene el país frente a eventos que pueden ser calificados como tratos crueles e inhumanos, contrarios a cualquier tipo de atención o tratamiento y puede ser calificados como de tipo penal de tortura" (La FM 2018).
11. Aiming to achieve a non-violent atmosphere for all system-affected children and adolescents has been slowly recognized as a priority in Colombia that will

contribute to the peace building process in the country. Moreover, Colombia is currently in the nascent state of implementing the peace accords signed between the Government and FARC (the largest guerrilla group in the country) in September 2016. Additionally, the priorities established in the peace agreement align with the priorities defined by the juvenile justice system. In particular, both frameworks highlight the value of justice, clarification of the truth and reparation (Gobierno Nacional Colombia & FARC EP 2016).

12. Original interview excerpt in Spanish: "pues la verdad acá [en el Redentor] la vida es un poquito dura porque uno cuando es nuevo le toca llegar digamos a darse traques a plantarse".
13. For the following extracts that will be presented, it is important to note that in some cases the cultural and political meaning may be lost in the interpretation process. For this reason, we include the verbatim Spanish version representing these youth voices and experiences of violence as footnotes throughout the text.
14. Original interview excerpt in Spanish: "recién nuevo pues tenía intentos de evasiones, me intentaba evadir y pues había ahí algunas personas que intentaban agredirme y pues porque uno se intenta volar [los educadores] le sacaban palo, tambos".
15. Original interview excerpt in Spanish: "Hace como veinte días más o menos se des- se descontrolaron, fue un domingo (…) todos los chinos estaban subidos así encima del techo y eso. Ya estaban re-descontrolados los chinos (…) todas las secciones se alborotaron y eso habían chinos subidos en el techo y todo. Yo me fui pa' la sección y miré y todo el techo de la sección estaba roto, y yo [pensé] 'uy estos maricas se salieron de acá' y claro, se habían salido por todo el techo ese".
16. Original interview excerpt in Spanish: "Qué cómo es [la vida en El Redentor]? Pues que no esto acá es re perro, pues acá el trato y todo eso es mucho menosprecio y todo además por todo gasean, dan palo".
17. Original interview excerpt in Spanish: "Si ya, pues uno a cada rato ve las peleas cada rato, no es raro ya como que uno ya las ha visto antes".
18. Original interview excerpt in Spanish: "Si los educadores [en El Redentor], ellos con uno no se meten. Solamente le piden a uno que le colaboren con la levantada, tendiendo la cama y vaya y báñese, cepíllese ¿si ve? y hay cierto horario".
19. Original interview excerpt in Spanish: "Es común [que nos peguen] o sea es común que le peguen a uno así cachetadas, puños, patadas, así".
20. Original interview excerpt in Spanish: "[El Redentor] es una porquería, esto [El Redentor] es malo, porque acá a uno lo maltratan. Acá [en el Redentor] es un tormento uno vivir. Porque acá a uno le dan duro. Cuando le dan duro a uno y viene Bienestar [ICBF], ellos [staff institucional] se esconden, esconden el gas, el palo".

21. Original interview excerpt in Spanish: "[El Redentor] es una porquería, esto [El Redentor] es malo, porque acá a uno lo maltratan. Acá [en el Redentor] es un tormento uno vivir. Porque acá a uno le dan duro. Cuando le dan duro a uno y viene Bienestar [ICBF], ellos [staff institucional] se esconden, esconden el gas, el palo".
22. Original interview excerpt in Spanish: "es como un perro, estar acá encerrado y estar menospreciado acá".
23. Original interview excerpt in Spanish: "Usted corre con el miedo de que no, de que pronto llegue y me toque duro o me maten o me hagan algo y, pero pues es <u>normal</u> acá llegar y darse traques o darse o cogerse o pararse con puntas, es normal ya acá, eso ya es normal".
24. Original interview excerpt in Spanish: "puff todos los días [siento miedo], porque uno no sabe quién le va a tirar a uno".
25. Original interview excerpt in Spanish: "Cuando llegue, porque cuando llegue yo no sabía cómo eran las cosas y [a] uno cuando llega es donde más le buscan el quiebre. Se la comienzan es a montar a uno por que es nuevo".
26. Original interview excerpt in Spanish: "Claro [que he sentido miedo], cuando se llegan los nocturnos en la noche, que ellos, ellos si no copean ni nada, [llegan] es a darle a uno donde le caiga el tubaso".
27. Original interview excerpt in Spanish: "Que acá dan mucho palo y que todo el menosprecio a toda hora que, que ellos se aprovechan cuando no está bienestar pa' pegarle, y cuando llega el bienestar ahí si lo sacan a uno ahí de Perse pa' que no lo vean las de bienestar y si uno les dice a las de bienestar le empiezan a uno a decir que sapo y entonces a toda hora lo quieren guardar y pegarle a uno cuando no está bienestar y le quitan la visita se la (friegan) a uno para todo".
28. Original interview excerpt in Spanish: "¿Acá? (0.4) acá es un <u>tormento</u> uno vivir. Porque acá a uno le dan duro. Cuando le dan duro a uno y viene bienestar, ellos se esconden. Esconden el <u>gas</u>, el <u>palo</u>".
29. Original interview excerpt in Spanish: "Ni coordinadores así tan explosivos, sino que les den un mejor trato a los chinos (.) hacia uno mismo ¿si ve? (ni) que ah que malparido que vaya y haga eso. Que agh que mire que no le- que no tenga necesidad de gritarlo sino sopla- simplemente con una con una buena palabra los chinos entiendan y y hagan las cosas bien".
30. Original interview excerpt in Spanish: "<u>Pues que no den tanto palo</u>. (Es la única forma) y que sean señores por que ellos también son groseros y nosotros también. Entonces, ese es el dilema entre todos".
31. Original interview excerpt in Spanish: "Como que no sean más vio- que no sean violentos los educadores ¿no? Porque lo que le da rabia a uno es eso".

References

Abrams, L. S., & Terry, D. J. (2017). *Everyday desistance: The transition to adulthood among formerly incarcerated youth*. New Brunswick, NJ: Rutgers University Press.

Bastidas, L. (2018). *Se requiere el máximo castigo de policías que apalearon a jóvenes en El Redentor*. Retrieved September 4, 2020, from http://concejodebogota.gov.co/se-requiere-el-maximo-castigo-de-policias-que-apalearon-a-jovenes-en-el/cbogota/2018-10-09/095044.php

Bogotá Cómo Vamos. (2015). *Informe de Calidad de Vida de Bogotá*. Retrieved September 4, 2020, from http://www.bogotacomovamos.org/app/uploads/static/files/informe_localidades2015/pobreza-y-desigualdad.html

Colombia Reports. (2019). *Colombia's drug trade*. Retrieved September 4, 2020, from https://colombiareports.com/colombia-drug-trafficking/

Davidson-Arad, B., Benbenishty, R., & Golan, M. (2009). Comparison of violence and abuse in juvenile correctional facilities and schools. *Journal of Interpersonal Violence, 24*(2), 259–279. https://doi.org/10.1177/0886260508317183.

Defensoría del Pueblo. (2015). Violaciones a los Derechos Humanos de Adolescentes privados de la libertad: Recomendaciones para enfrentar la crisis del sistema de responsabilidad penal para adolescentes. Retrieved from: https://www.defensoria.gov.co/public/pdf/ViolacionesDDHHadolescentesprivadoslibertad.pdf.

Departamento Nacional de Estadística. (2019a). *Comunicado de Prensa: Pobreza Multidimensional en Colombia, año 2017*. Retrieved September 4, 2020, from https://www.dane.gov.co/files/investigaciones/condiciones_vida/pobreza/cp_pobreza_multidimensional_17_v2.pdf

Departamento Nacional de Estadística. (2019b). *Gran encuesta integrada de hogares (GEIH) Mercado Laboral*. Retrieved September 4, 2020, from https://www.dane.gov.co/index.php/estadisticas-por-tema/mercado-laboral/empleo-y-desempleo

El Espectador. (2018, September 8). El Redentor: así fue la represión de la policía a los jóvenes detenidos. *El Espectador* [Video File]. Retrieved September 4, 2020, from https://www.youtube.com/watch?v=2WuL-O0LAco

Fernández Díaz, L. (2014). *Análisis de las Estrategias de Reintegración del Adolescente Infractor en el Centro de Atención Especializada El Redentor de Bogotá*. Retrieved September 4, 2020, from https://repository.unilibre.edu.co/bitstream/handle/10901/7703/FernandezDiazLizeth2014.pdf?sequence=1&isAllowed=y

Galardi, T. R., & Settersten, R. A. (2018). "They're just made up different": Juvenile correctional staff perceptions of incarcerated boys and girls. *Children and Youth Services Review, 95*, 200–208. https://doi.org/10.1016/j.childyouth.2018.10.040.

Gardner, J. (2010). Democracy's orphans: Rights, responsibility, and the role of the state in the lives of incarcerated youth. *Youth & Society, 42*(1), 81–103. https://doi.org/10.1177/0044118X09336268.

Gobierno Nacional Colombia & FARC EP. (2016). Acuerdo Final para la Terminación del Conflicto y la Construcción de una Paz Estable y Duradera. Retrieved from:

http://www.altocomisionadoparalapaz.gov.co/procesos-y-conversaciones/Paginas/Texto-completo-del-Acuerdo-Final-para-la-Terminacion-del-conflicto.aspx.

Hodge, A. I., & Yoder, J. R. (2017). The relationship between abusive experiences and staff controls in juvenile correctional facilities: The mediating effects of externalizing behavior. *Criminal Justice and Behavior, 44*(10), 1281–1299. https://doi.org/10.1177/0093854817727796.

Human Rights Watch. (1994). *Code for minors*. Retrieved September 4, 2020, from https://www.hrw.org/reports/1994/colombia/gener3.htm

Instituto Colombiano de Bienestar Familiar. (2013). *El ABC del Sistema de Responsabilidad Penal para Adolescentes (SRPA)*. Retrieved September 4, 2020, from https://repository.oim.org.co/bitstream/handle/20.500.11788/785/COL-OIM%200433-1.pdf?sequence=2&isAllowed=y

Instituto Colombiano de Bienestar Familiar. (2015). *ADOLESCENTES, JÓVENES Y DELITOS: "Elementos para la comprensión de la delincuencia juvenil en Colombia"*. Retrieved September 4, 2020, from https://repository.oim.org.co/bitstream/handle/20.500.11788/1647/95.%20Boletin%20ICBF%20Delincuencia%20Juvenil.pdf?sequence=1&isAllowed=y

Instituto Colombiano de Bienestar Familiar. (2019). *Sistema de Responsabilidad Penal para Adolescentes*. Retrieved September 4, 2020, from https://www.icbf.gov.co/bienestar/proteccion/responsabilidad-penal

Instituto Colombiano de Bienestar Familiar. (2020). *El Instituto*. Retrieved September 4, 2020, from https://www.icbf.gov.co/instituto

International Catholic Child Bureau. (n.d.). *Juvenile Justice in Colombia*. Retrieved September 4, 2020, from https://bice.org/en/juvenile-justice-in-colombia/

Kramer, R., Rajah, V., & Sung, H. (2013). Neoliberal prisons and cognitive treatment: Calibrating the subjectivity of incarcerated young men to economic inequalities. *Theoretical Criminology, 17*(4), 535–556. https://doi.org/10.1177/1362480613497780.

La FM. (2018). *Tras golpiza de policías a menores en El Redentor, Fiscalía investiga al ICBF*. Retrieved September 4, 2020, from https://www.lafm.com.co/judicial/tras-golpiza-de-policias-menores-en-el-redentor-fiscalia-investiga-al-icbf

Las 2 Orillas. (2018). *El Redentor, manejado por psicólogos, pero con policías controlando a garrote*. Retrieved September 4, 2020, from https://www.las2orillas.co/el-redentor-manejado-por-psicologos-pero-con-policias-controlando-garrote/

Matthews, S. (2018). *The institutionalized abuse of incarcerated girls*. Retrieved September 4, 2020, from https://ksr.hkspublications.org/2018/08/13/the-institutionalized-abuse-of-incarcerated-girls/

Mountz, S. E. (2016). That's the sound of the police: State-sanctioned violence and resistance among LGBT young people previously incarcerated in girls' juvenile justice facilities. *Affilia, 31*(3), 287–302. https://doi.org/10.1177/0886109916641161.

Office of the SRSG on Violence against Children. (2012). *Prevention of and responses to violence against children within the juvenile justice system*. Retrieved September 4, 2020, from https://violenceagainstchildren.un.org/sites/violenceagainstchildren.

un.org/files/documents/publications/8._prevention_of_and_responses_to_violence_against_children_within_the_juvenile_justice_system.pdf

Peterson-Badali, M., & Koegl, C. J. (2002). Juveniles' experiences of incarceration: The role of correctional staff in peer violence. *Journal of Criminal Justice, 30*, 41–49.

Red de Coaliciones Sur. (2014). *Regional juvenile justice observatory: Monitoring report on juvenile justice systems in Latin America*. Retrieved September 4, 2020, from https://defenceforchildren.org/wp-content/uploads/2015/02/Monitoring-Report-Regional-Observatory_AS.pdf

Rodríguez, J. (2018). *Procuraduría advierte que violencia en El Redentor es algo sistemático*. Retrieved September 4, 2020, from https://www.rcnradio.com/judicial/procuraduria-advierte-que-violencia-en-el-redentor-es-un-acto-sistematico

Rubio Serrano, R. (2018). *El Redentor: Evidencia de una crisis profunda en la Justicia Juvenil en Colombia*. Retrieved September 4, 2020, from https://www.razonpublica.com/index.php/econom-y-sociedad-temas-29/11490-el-redentor-evidencia-de-una-crisis-profunda-en-la-justicia-juvenil-en-colombia.html

Unidad para la Atención y Reparación Integral a las Víctimas. (2019). *Registro Único de Víctimas*. Retrieved September 4, 2020, from https://www.unidadvictimas.gov.co/es/registro-unico-de-victimas-ruv/37394

United Nations Women. (n.d.). *Global database on violence against women. Country profile: Colombia*. Retrieved September 4, 2020, from https://colombiareports.com/colombia-drug-trafficking/

United Nations Office on Drugs and Crime (UNODC). (2015). *Introducing the United Nations Model Strategies and Practical Measures on the Elimination of Violence against Children in the Field of Crime Prevention and Criminal Justice: A New Tool for Policymakers, Criminal Justice Officials and Practitioners*. Retrieved from: https://www.unodc.org/documents/justice-and-prison-reform/14-08451_Strategy_eBook.pdf.

Vargas Ovalle, J. M. (2018). *ICBF propuso cerrar 'El Redentor'*. Retrieved September 4, 2020, from https://www.lafm.com.co/judicial/icbf-propuso-cerrar-el-redentor

Villanueva-Congote, J., Jaramillo-Bernal, M. C., Sotomayor-Carreño, E., Gutiérrez-Congote, C., & Torres-Quintero, A. (2018). La salud mental en los modelos de atención de adolescentes infractores. Los casos de Colombia, Argentina, Estados Unidos y Canadá. *Universitas Medica, 59*(4). Retrieved September 4, 2020, from https://www.redalyc.org/articulo.oa?id=231056644004

Zalkind, P., & Simon, R. J. (2004). *Global perspectives on social issues: Juvenile justice systems*. Lanham, MD: Lexington Books.

5

Doing Time: Young People and the Rhetoric of Juvenile Justice in Ghana

Kofi E. Boakye and Thomas D. Akoensi

Introduction

As with colonisation, globalisation has had a significant impact on virtually all aspects of life in Ghana and Africa more broadly (Meagher 2003; Opoku 2010; Yaro 2013). Although increased interconnectedness and integration have brought several advantages (Giddens 1990; Muncie 2005), the neoliberal globalisation that encourages resource exploitation and trade imbalances has resulted in weak economies, high levels of illiteracy, unemployment and poverty in Africa (Meagher 2003; Opoku 2010; Yaro 2013). Furthermore, colonial rule and globalisation have encouraged the transfer of neoliberal penal policies from western countries and global institutions to the global south (Sloth-Nielsen 2001; Wacquant 2001; Muncie 2005; Goldson and Muncie 2015; Ame 2018). Thus, the effect of neoliberal penality, specifically western conceptions of justice, is seen in the punishment of young people involved with the juvenile system in Ghana and many countries in Africa (Sloth-Nielsen 2001; Mensa-Bonsu 2017; Odongo 2017; Ame 2018). And yet, as Muncie (2005, p. 47) observed, little attention has "been given to the

K. E. Boakye (✉)
Anglia Ruskin University, Cambridge, UK
e-mail: kofi.boakye@anglia.ac.uk

T. D. Akoensi
University of Kent, Medway, UK

extent to which legal globalization itself is a concept driven by western notions of 'civilized' human rights" and how this, in practice, may undermine the rights and treatment of young people in conflict with the law.

This chapter examines the juvenile justice system in Ghana and its treatment of young people in custody. The chapter begins with a brief background context to Ghana. This is followed by an overview of the juvenile justice system in Ghana beginning with the colonial period. Contemporary juvenile justice processes are then outlined focusing on the legal regime underpinning juvenile justice, arrest, investigation and detention conditions of young people caught up in the justice system. At each of these stages, we highlight the tensions and contradictions in juvenile justice administration in Ghana, with a particular emphasis on the treatment of incarcerated young people. We note that although the current system of juvenile justice in Ghana emphasises a welfare and rights-based approach to young people in conflict with the law that purports to prioritise their best interests, in reality the system appears to be based on an amalgam of welfare, justice, crime control and diversion paradigms. We contend that the tensions and contradictions in the philosophy and administration of juvenile justice in Ghana undermine the rights and treatment of young people in custody. These tensions and contradictions are, in part, a consequence of the cultural dislocation caused by the imposition or uncritical adoption of colonial and neoliberal policies. Such uncritical policy transfers have engendered underdevelopment, increased poverty and hindered the state's ability to protect and provide for the majority of its citizens, especially the young and most vulnerable who come into contact with the justice system. We conclude with reflections on how the juvenile justice system can improve its treatment of young people in conflict with the law.

Our focus in this chapter is on young persons from age 12 to 21. This focus is consistent with the legal definition of young people in Ghana. The Juvenile Justice Act of Ghana (Act 653) makes a distinction between a "juvenile" and a "young person" with a "juvenile" defined as a person under 18 years in conflict with the law and a "young person" referring to persons between ages 18 and 21. Also, it is important to note from the outset that, in many ways, our analysis is constrained by the lack of research and the paucity of official data on young people in the juvenile justice system in Ghana.

Children in Context

The family in Ghana is recognised as an important safety net for children. The family is responsible for instilling discipline by teaching social roles and standards, exercising social control, protection, socialisation, policing and care and ensuring a seamless transition to adulthood (Arthur 1996; Nukunya 2003). Brown (1996, p. 21) defines family in Ghana as typically "male-headed units of extended families consisting of one or several wives and their children and often extended with unmarried or elderly relatives." Heterosexual marriage is a near universal institution in Ghana to realise a family and offers couples with a status of adulthood, ancestral linkages, economic and social support resources and completeness of life (Oppong and Abu 1987; Aryee 1997; Annor 2014; Akoensi 2017). Children are further valued in Ghanaian society as they provide economic, spiritual and psychological worth for parents (Nukunya 2003; Teye 2013). In old age, children are even more important as they serve as a permanent source of social security as responsibilities for the care of the elderly are traditionally entrusted in the offspring (Nukunya 2003; Teye 2013). This is more so in a context where formal welfare support structures are "either absent or ineffective" (Boakye 2020, p. 9). Large family sizes are thus desired and achieved in families. Ghana's total fertility rate (TFR), despite declining from 6.4 children per woman in 1988, to 4.4 in 2003, is still relatively high at 4.3 in 2008 and 3.8 in 2019 with estimated average household size of 4.4 (Demographic and Health Survey, 2015, 2020). The inability of marriages to bring forth children poses serious challenges for the sustainability of such marriages and fulfilment for the couples, especially married women who are the subject of societal opprobrium and are often reported to experience psychological distress and depression due to infertility (Alhassan et al. 2014; Donkor et al. 2017).

Recently, female participation in the labour force has increased in both the formal and informal sectors of Ghana's economy. Whilst females represent 53.8 per cent of the employed population, males represent 46.2 per cent. This is in addition to women's supposed traditional roles in the home, which involve childcare and undertaking household chores such as cooking and cleaning, have barely changed despite increasing male participation in household chores (Ghana Statistical Service 2015, 2016). Despite these changing labour force dynamics (women's domination amongst employed adults and increasingly female-headed households) and the emphasis on marriage and procreation in Ghana as the dominant familial structure, a stringent economic outlook underpinned by stagnant wages, high cost of living and high levels of youth unemployment, families and children have become more vulnerable to exploitation, abuse and antisocial behaviour (Weinberg 1965; Arthur 1996; Boakye 2013, 2020; Oduro 2012). For example, 21 per cent of children and adolescents (5–17 years) are working in hazardous conditions beyond household chores and economic activities; 19 per cent of adolescent girls are married before 18 years (an adolescent birth rate of 75 per 1000 adolescent girls 15–19 years, with the poor and those living in rural areas at greater risk of child bearing) and only a handful—40 per cent of the adolescent population (15–19 years)—are enrolled in secondary school education in Ghana (Ghana Statistical Service 2018). Official figures from the Commission on Human Rights and Administrative Justice (CHRAJ) shows a significant number of petitions from mothers seeking resolutions to human rights violations concerning their children (CHRAJ 2013). Among the major concerns are failure of fathers to provide maintenance allowance, unlawful custody, denial of paternity and deprivation of education (CHRAJ 2013; also see Laird 2011). The consequences of these exposures to vulnerabilities are most evident in the metropolis, and especially among "street children" (i.e. homeless children and children sent to by their parents to hawk on the street) in the form of interpersonal violence and sexual victimisation (Boakye 2013, 2020; Oduro 2012).

Juvenile Justice System: A Brief History

Prior to colonial rule, Ghana (formerly known as the Gold Coast) had its own traditional justice system which had deterrence and restoration as its core principles. In this system, there was no distinction between young persons and adults on the basis of chronological age in justice administration (Ame 2018). Offences were thought to disrupt individual and group harmony and ancestral spirits. The teaching of moral codes and standards and the exercise of social control through conformity was the bedrock of crime control and the responsibility of the extended family (Abotchie 1997; Nukunya 2003).

A young person's delinquency (e.g. petty theft) was typically dealt with in the family through adjudications led by the family head. When the delinquent act is more serious and transcends the family (e.g. sexual offence, murder, manslaughter, etc.), such issues are brought before the Chief of the town or village and his elders for adjudication. Appropriate sanctions are imposed on the young person after careful deliberations to establish the facts of the case and its seriousness. What must be emphasised, however, is that the entire family, clan and lineage of the young person bear the brunt of such punishment which often was aimed at restoring the social harmony that existed prior to the commission of the offence and pacifying the ancestral spirits. In traditional justice administration, Sarbah (1968, p. 30) observes in the *Fanti National Constitution* that:

> Fines are paid for accidental homicide; such as carelessly wounding a person taking part in a chase. A person found guilty of criminal intercourse with a married woman is liable to pay to the injured husband a fine… In case of theft, the guilty offender is made to restore to the owner the stolen article or its value and to his ruler he pays a fine.

Crime and punishment are thus a collective responsibility and ensured communal harmony. Formal justice institutions such as detention centres and welfare structures such as orphanages are not indigenous to Ghana. The same traditional justice set up had handled issues of child welfare in everyday—and crises—times including child custody and child maintenance following divorce, kinship fostering and adoption following the demise or unavailability of parent(s) among others (Goody 1982; Oppong 1973; Ansah-Koi 2006; Nachinab et al. 2018). The entire community including the extended family network and other community network of benefactors ensured the welfare and provided guardianship of at-risk children which personified the saying that "it takes a village to raise a child" (Abdullah et al. 2018, p. 450). The "obligations of communities, sympathy, altruism, or religious beliefs" are the core values that ensure and sustain continuity of care for young persons in the community in Ghana (Ansah-Koi 2006, p. 558).

Like many countries in Africa (see Clifford 1974; Sloth-Nielsen 2001; Fourchard 2006; Odongo 2017), Ghana's current juvenile justice system is a vestige of colonial rule (Arthur 1991; Mensa-Bonsu 2017; Ame 2018). In many ways, the colonial experience has also been part of the reason for the disconnect between theory and practice of juvenile justice in Ghana, especially the condition and treatment of incarcerated young people. The first juvenile detention facility in Ghana was established in 1928 by the Salvation Army (Ame 2018). Prior to this period, the criminal code in Ghana operated by the British did not make a legal distinction between adults and children or young people, nor did the code distinguish between young people in conflict with the law and those in need of care and protection (Mensa-Bonsu 2017;

Ame 2018). Young people caught up in the justice system therefore received similar treatment as adults.

Several important pieces of legislation were passed between 1944 and 1946 in an effort to formally establish a juvenile justice system in Ghana. Important among these were the Court (Amendment) Ordinance (1944) which began the separation of the juvenile and adult justice system, and the Industrial Schools and Institutions Ordinance (1945), which mandated the establishment of juvenile detention facilities and regulated the conduct of staff and training at these facilities (see de Graft-Johnson 1965; Ame 2018). These efforts were a direct response to increasing urbanisation and its attendant consequences including a high rate of urban unemployment and neglected children (Weinberg 1965; Mensa-Bonsu 2017). According to Mensa-Bonsu (2017, p. 5) the combined effect of urbanisation in the early period of the twentieth century and the second world war was that "[A]s people abandoned their traditional homes and family support for life in urban areas, children in need of care grew in such numbers that the establishment of institutions of juvenile justice to deal with the problem became necessary." These detention facilities were a direct replica of the Industrial Schools and Borstal Institutions in Britain and ordinances that reflect the English Children's Act of 1908. The emphasis was therefore on custody and custodial institutions to address a problem caused by decades of economic exploitation and exacerbated by the Second World War which created a paternal void due to many young men fighting in the war alongside British forces in other colonies such as Burma (Arthur 1991; Mensa-Bonsu 2017; Ame 2018). For example, records from the Swedru Junior Correctional Centre (JCC) show evidence of the welfare paternalism principle that governed the running of these detention facilities for young people. As Fig. 5.1 shows, very high numbers of

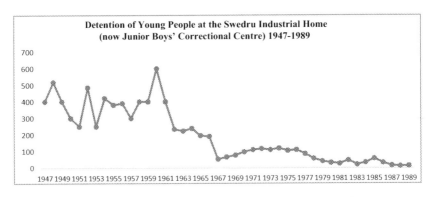

Fig. 5.1 Detention of young people at the Swedru Industrial Home (now Junior Boys' Correctional Centre) 1947–1989

young people were detained in the correctional facility during the period of colonial rule from 1947 to the early years of independence in 1957. The figures began to drop precipitously from the 1960s to present. The records show that the majority of children in these facilities were there for minor theft, but mostly because they were viewed as children in moral danger, and hence in need of care and protection.

Juvenile Justice Reform in Ghana

Ghana's juvenile justice system remained largely unchanged even after independence from Britain in 1957 until the 1990s. These reforms were driven by the United Nations and international obligations, and endorsed by the Ghanaian government, which required enactment of domestic laws to be consistent with its international commitments. For example, Ghana was the first country in the world to ratify the United Nation Convention on the Rights of the Child (UNCRC) on February 5, 1990 (UNTC 2020). Ghana also played a key role in the enactment of the Organisation of Africa Union (OAU), now Africa Union (AU), Charter on the Rights and Duties of the African Child. Importantly, the country has adapted international standards and guidelines on the detention and treatment of young people in conflict with the law, including the UN Standard Minimum Rules for the Administration of Juvenile Justice (United Nations 1986, the Beijing Rules), the UN Rules for the Protection of Juveniles Deprived of their Liberties (United Nations 1990a) and the UN Guidelines for the Prevention of Delinquency (United Nations 1990b, the Riyadh Guidelines).

As a consequence of these international commitments, Ghana made successive legislative changes on juvenile justice and imprisonment. The first is the amendment to provisions of the Criminal Offences Act, 1960 (Act 29) that increased the age of criminal responsibility to 12 years from 7 years (based on the British common law standard); the enactment of the Children's Act 560, of 1998, which increased the upper limit of childhood from 17 to 18 years, and the Juvenile Justice Act, 2003 (Act 563, hereafter, JJA), which replaced the provisions in the Criminal Procedure Code, 1960 (Act 30), and introduced separate legal regimes for children at risk of offending from those who have actually committed crimes, as well as the introduction of institutions (e.g. probation services) for dealing with children in conflict with the law. The Criminal Code (Amendment) Act, 1998 (Act 554), also raised the age of sexual consent from 14 years to 16 years. The Human Trafficking Act, 2005 (Act 694), prohibits and punishes the trafficking of people including children whilst making provision for their rescue, rehabilitation and reintegration. The Domestic Violence Act, 2007 (Act 732), also penalises violence against spouses and children (see Child Frontiers 2011; UNICEF 2016 for further analysis of legal framework for children rights in Ghana).

With the enactment of these laws, the language of juvenile justice shifted from purely welfare paternalism to a rights-based approach that emphasised the "best interests" of the child (Mensa-Bonsu 2017, p. 7). The best interests of the child, a rather vague and complicated concept (see, e.g. Morris and Gelsthorpe 2006, p. 32), were interpreted broadly in the JJA to mean various things including an emphasis on diversion and use of detention as a last resort, minimum and maximum term limit of 3 to 36 months depending on the age of the child and the seriousness of the offence, and adoption of western-style restorative justice practices, in particular victim-offender mediation.

This rights-based approach that appears to underpin the JJA demands heavy financial commitments for the stated objectives to be realised. We contend that the financial and policy commitment required for these goals to be realised has not been forthcoming and progress realised thus far has been mainly attributable to sponsorship from civil society groups in Ghana, especially the UNICEF Ghana office that has collaborated with the Ghana Police Service, Judicial Service of Ghana, Ministry of Gender and Children's Affairs, Department of Social Welfare to conduct research and build the capacity of various statutory stakeholders to achieve their goals under the JJA. As such, there is a major gap between the JJA provisions and what happens in practice. The vulnerability of young people is arguably further exacerbated when they come into contact with the formal juvenile justice system. In the ensuing sections, we outline various provisions of the JJA for arrest, prosecution and sentencing of children in conflict with the law and the extent to which these provisions are being met by statutory organisations such as the Ghana Police Service, Judicial Service of Ghana, Department of Social Welfare and the Ghana Prisons Service.

Arrest, Investigations and Diversions

As in all jurisdictions, the police are likely young people's first contact with the criminal justice system in Ghana. The police have the mandate to effect a juvenile arrest with or without a warrant. The magistrate of a juvenile court must issue such a warrant. Conditions under which a police officer can arrest a juvenile without a warrant include a crime being committed in the presence of the officer; the possession of implements for further crime commission;

and obstructing an officer from performing his/her duties and finally if the young person escapes lawful custody. Following arrest, the police can either formally caution a young person with conditions or informally caution the young person if the alleged crime is not serious and thus divert the juvenile from the formal criminal justice system. When cautions are not used, a young person can be held in custody for not more than 48 hours and should be released on bail unless substantial danger is posed to himself or herself or the community (s.21). The condition for bail should be determined in such a way that it is not harsh and excessive and takes the young person's circumstances into account. Young people must also be held in detention conditions separate from adults and must have the right to food, medical treatment, and reasonable visits from parents/guardians and a lawyer.

Evidence from a research collaboration between the Ghana Police Service, the International Bureau for Children's Rights, and UNICEF Ghana office involving interviews with police officers ($n = 65$), visits to police training schools and informal chats with 165 police officers and 1002 police recruits, focus group discussions with 39 children in conflict with the law and other institutions and stakeholders involved with justice delivery in Ghana concerning children reveals a divergence between legal and policy aspirations and implementation of these standards in practice (Ghana Police Service 2016). Findings show that police rarely exercise the use of caution when young people are arrested (Ghana Police Service 2016). In addition, there is also the lack of designated holding cells for young people resulting in the police taking arrested youth to their homes, seating them at the police back office, handcuffing them to a chair in the station or holding them with adults in cells are the norm (Ghana Police Service 2016). The general lack of police training on the contents of the JJA is arguably a major barrier to child-friendly policing. Although specialised police units, such as the Domestic Violence and Victim Support Unit (hereafter, DOVVSU), and Anti-Human Trafficking Unit (AHTU), are knowledgeable about the JJA and other child protection policies, the lack of logistics and facilities hinder implementation. For instance, there is a lack of budgetary allocation for the feeding and medical expenses of young people in detention, and police officers have had to provide for the welfare needs of juveniles in detention from their personal resource (Ghana Police Service 2016). Although it is commonly understood that young people who are apprehended must be processed by DOVVSU police personnel, because the Unit has no presence especially at rural district police stations around the country, that means young people tend to be processed similarly as adults.

During investigations, reports have noted that police dealings with children in conflict with the law fall short of legal requirements:

> Police investigators are neither trained in, nor provided with special procedures for, handling children in conflict with the law. Consequently, some are unaware of the child's right to family accompaniment (or lawyer or probation officer if family/guardians are unavailable). Interviews with police officers revealed only few of them advised children of their right to legal counsel. (Ghana Police Service 2016, p. 14)

Indeed, a prior survey conducted in 588 adult police cells and 318 adult prison cells found 10,488 young people held in adult police cells across the country between 1993 and 2003 (Department of Social Welfare 2005). This contravenes provisions of the JJA, UNCRC (Article 3 and 40), the Beijing Rules (Rule 13) and Article 17 and 18 of the UN Rules for the Protection of Juveniles Deprived of their Liberties.

The Children's Act (1998) emphasises and requires the establishment of child panels in all the district assemblies in Ghana. Child panels are local groups established to facilitate the diversion process for children involving victim-offender mediation in civil and minor criminal issues. Child panels, as currently constituted, do not appear to reflect the traditional justice setup; that is a more decentralised system where the locals are allowed to select members from the family unit and elders of the communities in consultation with the chiefs and queen mothers. Instead, child panels comprised seven members appointed by the Minister from relevant stakeholders in the local community: representative from a women's organisation, a representative from the traditional council, a district social worker, a member of the Justice and Security Subcommittee of the District Assembly, two persons from the community with high moral standing and the Chairperson of the Social Services Subcommittee of the District Assembly, who chairs the panel. This composition means child panels often involve unconnected persons drawn from artificial boundary demarcation systems that districts represent, which often weakens their effectiveness.

The role of the child panel is reflected in section 24 (4) of JJA (2003) which states that a Social Enquiry Report (SER) may make a recommendation that a matter before a juvenile court be referred to a child panel in respect of a minor offence. The JJA emphasises the principles of restorative justice involving accountability for crimes committed, reconciliation, restoration, preventing stigmatisation and restitution between offender and victim (s. 25).

In an assessment of the child panels in Ghana, Adu-Gyamfi (2019) identified a number of challenges affecting their operations. Through

5 Doing Time: Young People and the Rhetoric of Juvenile Justice…

Table 5.1 Swedru Boys' Junior Correctional Centre, Central Region 2015–2019

Correctional facility/year	Total number of juveniles in detention	Number of juveniles aged 12–14	Number of juveniles aged 15–17	Number sentenced for minor crimes	Number sentenced for serious crime	Number of first-time offenders	Length of Sentence/Months
2019	20	10	10	12	8	11	3–36
2018	29	18	11	17	12	21	3–36
2017	22	10	12	15	7	10	3–36
2016	14	6	8	7	7	12	3–36
2015	30	16	14	19	11	14	3–36

Table 5.2 Accra Girls Junior Correctional Centre, Greater Accra 2015–2019

Correctional facility/year	Total number of juveniles in detention	Number of juveniles aged 12–14	Number of juveniles aged 15–17	Number sentenced for minor crimes	Number sentenced for serious crime	Number of first-time offenders	Length of sentence/months
2019	9	3	6	7	2	8	3–36
2018	14	1	14	14	1	10	3–36
2017	15	6	9	10	5	13	3–36
2016	15	4	11	14	1	13	3–36
2015	16	7	9	12	4	14	3–36

semi-structured interviews with stakeholders, he identified administrative challenges involving excessive political influence affecting the competence and calibre of panel members; structural issues involving the duplication of roles of the DOVVSU of the Ghana Police Service, the Juvenile Court and Family Tribunal; financial constraints related to the lack of funds to remunerate panel members by the various district assemblies; and development challenges involving mainly incompetent members without requisite training in child welfare issues as undermining the effectiveness of child panels in Ghana. Consequently, the few child panels established by some district assemblies never really took off (Mensa-Bonsu 2017).

The Child Frontiers (2011) report, an analysis of child protection systems in Ghana, showed that only a handful of district assemblies have established child panels mainly because of difficulties associated in establishing them. In their survey, only 70 districts out of a possible 216 have established child panels. These functional child panels are also replete with a variety of challenges. Ame (2017), in an overview of the juvenile justice system in Ghana, concluded that "very few child panels have actually been established, and of those, very few are functioning as envisioned by the law makers" (p. 21).

On account of the above challenges, it is not surprising that the Government of Ghana (2015) acknowledge that child panel system needs reform in view of the constraints under the law in the composition and mode of appointment of panel members, as well as their lack of resources. It is also not surprising that the majority of young people in detention are serving time for less serious offences (see Tables 5.1 and 5.2; also Boakye 2013). The Ghana police service, however, has been known to also divert young people from the formal criminal justice system when it can, although there is no consistency or guidance for police departments to utilise their discretion in diverting young people who engage in minor offences. In a survey of juvenile justice in Ghana, the Department of Social Welfare (2005) found that the majority of youth who were cautioned and discharged from police stations were mostly for cases of petty theft, minor assault and family squabbles.

Court Appearance and Prosecution/Defence

The juvenile court is the only court with the right to try criminal cases involving young people. However, when a young person is on trial with an adult as a co-defendant, or charged with an offence that attracts the death penalty for an adult (e.g. first degree murder), or a juvenile court is not constituted in the area where the crime was committed, the young person's case will be held in an adult court although the young person has to be remitted to the juvenile court for sentence (s.17). Young people also have a right to a lawyer and free legal aid, although these are often unavailable and young people are generally unaware of this statutory provision (Osei 2013).

The juvenile court is composed of a panel of three members: the presiding magistrate of a district court and two lay panel members one of whom must be a social welfare officer (Judicial Service of Ghana 2018). Juvenile courts are held in private with only parties to the case, their lawyers, witnesses and persons invited by the courts allowed to be present. Proceedings of the juvenile court are not open to the media and anonymity is granted to those making an appearance before the court. The setting of the juvenile court is informal and police officers are not permitted to appear in juvenile courts in their police uniforms. The JJA requires that in order to facilitate the work of the juvenile court, in every case a social enquiry report must be prepared for each young person by a probation officer (social worker) after investigations into the family, school and young person's living conditions. The SER is to help the court understand the young person's background and the antecedents of their offence and also to make recommendations as to the appropriate disposition order.

The JJA requires that Court hearings of juveniles be conducted within six months. Within this period, disposal avenues available to the juvenile court include conditional or unconditional discharge; release on probation; commit to the care of a relative or fit person; commit to a correctional centre; order payment of fine or damages or costs and finally, order parent, guardian or close relative of the offender to give security for the good behaviour of the young person. However, if a case travels beyond the mandatory six-month period, the court is supposed to release the young person unconditionally and they will no longer be held liable for the offence.

The duration of detention should this be used is detailed in the JJA: three months for a person under 16 years old; six months for person at 16 years or above but below 18 years old; 24 months for a person of 18 years old or above and a maximum sentence of three years for serious offence: murder, rape, indecent assault involving unlawful harm, robbery with aggravated circumstance, drug offences and offences related to firearms. However, conditions on the ground paint a different picture. Probation officers are few and under resourced. There are 175 probation officers and 138 social welfare officers sitting as child panel members throughout Ghana (Judicial Service of Ghana 2018). Probation officers sometimes have to bear their own transport costs, and families of children have been noted to contribute—this provides opportunity for corruption and potential abuse of office. Despite the centralisation of SERs to the juvenile court, probation officers lack computers to assist with their work and have been reported to hand over hand-written notes to judges who are unable to decipher their handwriting (Ghana Police Service 2016). Cases of conflict of interest have also been reported against probation officers who sit on the juvenile court panel and at the same time, act as authors of the SER for the same juvenile. This phenomenon is pervasive in districts with only one welfare officer (Judicial Service of Ghana 2018). Magistrates have bemoaned the quality of some SERs, and there have been concerns expressed about the impartiality of probation officers and a lack of research on factors that explain young people's offending behaviour and effective rehabilitation programmes for young people (Boakye 2013; Judicial Service of Ghana 2018).

Ghana lacks designated and dedicated juvenile courts. Out of the 185 district courts in Ghana, only three are designated as family and juvenile courts and these are all located in Accra, the capital of Ghana (Judicial Service of Ghana 2018). Thus, all the other district courts run juvenile courts on a temporary basis with the risk of revealing young people's identity to the public and the media who often report such cases with their names or images (Judicial Service of Ghana 2018). The existing juvenile courts are also known to sit irregularly, resulting in long delays beyond the mandatory six-month trial period and the attendant long stay of young persons in remand detention centres sometimes for seven months (Ayete-Nyampong 2017a). Irregular sitting of juvenile courts and frequent adjournments is caused by lack of panel members, low motivation and poor remuneration (Department of Social Welfare 2005). The majority of young people appear in court without legal counsel (Hoffmann and Baerg 2011; Judicial Service of Ghana 2018). With no "duty counsel" system attached to juvenile courts, legal aid lawyers hardly appear in juvenile courts (Judicial Service of Ghana 2018).

Detention Conditions

Young people who are convicted in the juvenile court are to be committed to institutions for a period as a last resort when all forms of disposal have been considered. Currently, there are five institutions officially available for the committal of young people and all these facilities were inherited from the colonial period (and these facilities continue to be used for the same purpose of incarceration of young people). These are the Junior Correctional Centre in Swedru for boys for those aged 14–16 years; Pong Tamale Industrial School for those aged between 14 and 17 years; the Senior Correctional Centre (SCC, formerly the Borstal Institute) in Accra for young persons aged 17–21 years; the Junior Correctional Centre in Sekondi for boys between the ages of 12–14 years and the Junior Correctional Centre in Accra for girls, which is the only detention facility for young females in Ghana. The Junior Correctional Centre for girls also doubles as a senior correctional centre for girls, remand centre for girls, a shelter for abused children and a vocational school for girls. The remand facility for boys is also located within the same premises as the correctional centre for girls. The close proximity of these facilities and the mixing of children with different needs in these facilities raises serious concerns about effective management and being responsive to the specific needs of these different groups (see Bosiakoh and Andoh 2010). Besides the general lack of funding for these centres, security at the facility is porous, with just a day and night security officer, insufficient staffing and a virtual absence of skills training for young people of the remand homes because the young people are kept in the remand facilities on a temporary basis (Hoffmann and Baerg 2011).

Young Persons in Custody: Some Issues and Concerns

The Department of Social Welfare (2005) observed several issues associated with institutionalisation as the least effective method of rehabilitation. These include the enduring stigmatisation and rejection of young people by society, the learning of institutional culture, negative influences by their peers in institutional setting and the disruption of the education for the children. Also, the evidence shows that the majority of young people committed to detention facilities are first-time offenders (see Tables 5.1 and 5.2). Although the lack of a proper police recording system raises doubt about the accuracy of this evidence (e.g. young people have been known to give false information including date of birth and names upon arrest, see Ayete-Nyampong 2017a), the disproportionate number of first-time offenders in custody contradicts provisions of the JJA and raises concerns about the punitive attitudes of judges.

An even more insidious problem is revealed in previous research which confirmed that 2164 young people were held in adult prisons in Ghana between 1993 and 2003 (Department of Social Welfare 2005). This high figure is both a consequence of the old paternalistic regime that abolished the juvenile courts (Mensa-Bonsu 2006, p. 7) and the tendency for police officers to ask children to inflate their age in order to be processed as adult offenders (Mensa-Bonsu 2017, p. 12). Influencing young persons to inflate their age allowed the police to avoid the safeguard requirements for children contained in the JJA including prohibition to hold children in adult police cells, requirements to be handled by officer of the same gender and to inform a parent or guardian of the young person as soon as arrest is made. A police officer cannot question or interview a young person without the presence of a parent, guardian or lawyer and an officer must be familiar with the special court processes and requirements for young people which is often a challenge because of lack of training. The poor but improving birth registration rate in Ghana (currently at 71 per cent) partly accounts for this situation as many children are without birth certificates or other reliable ways of determining their age (Ghana Statistical Service 2018). Although this problem of sending young people to adult prisons appears to have been addressed with the coming into effect of the JJA, there is no evidence to suggest that this is indeed the case.

Infrastructural Provisions and Conditions of Detainment

While the JJA emphasises the best interests of the child and the importance of rehabilitation, in practice the condition of these correctional facilities hardly

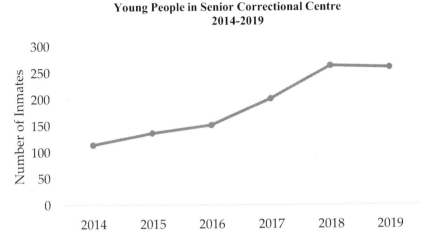

Fig. 5.2 Young people in Senior Correctional Centre 2014–2019

meets these requirements. First there is the poor physical condition of the facilities. As all the detention facilities in Ghana were inherited from British colonial rule and virtually neglected by successive governments; the physical structures are weak and in a deplorable condition (Ayete-Nyampong 2017a). Of the five juvenile detention facilities remaining, only three are effectively in use. These are the Boys' Junior Correctional Centre in Swedru, the Girls' Junior Correctional Centre in Accra and the Boys' Senior Correctional Centre in Accra. Tables 5.1 and 5.2 show the number of young people detained in the two junior correctional facilities over the last five years (2015–2019), and Fig. 5.2 shows similar data for the Senior Correctional Centre from 2014 to 2019. Even with the considerable decline in the number of young people detained in these facilities compared with the colonial period, the general neglect means several buildings within the facilities are rendered unusable. Although it is difficult to obtain accurate data on the number of young people who escape from detention, there have been reports of frequent escape of young people from detention facilities in the country (Daily Graphic 2015; Ghanaweb 2016; Ayete-Nyampong 2017b).

Virtually all the detention centres for young people are located in the regional capitals of Ghana. This affects the mobility of the police in transporting young people between juvenile courts and places of detention. It is no surprise that most young people are kept in police custody for the sake of convenience rather than designated juvenile detention centres (see Department of Social Welfare 2005). On one of its inspections of police cells in the Central Region of Ghana, the Commission for Human Rights and Administrative

Justice discovered that three young people had been held for five months in two police stations although the court had directed that the young people be sent to a juvenile detention facility (Ghana News Agency 2005). This was in clear contravention of the welfare and best interests' principle underpinning the JJA and other legislative instruments (e.g. Article 28(3) of the 1992 constitution that prohibits damage to the mental wellbeing of children).

Education and Rehabilitation of Young Persons

In order to facilitate reform and rehabilitation at these institutions, young people are encouraged to learn a trade including carpentry, tailoring, basket weaving, masonry and dressmaking among others. There also appears to be a gender gap in the quality of these vocational provisions. Young people at the SCC for boys are trained to sit the National Vocational Training Institute (NVTI) qualifications, providing them with better job prospects and further educational qualifications at various polytechnic institutions. However, vocational provisions for girls incarcerated at the JCC are not certified (Ayete-Nyampong 2017a). As another example of gender disparities, the SCC has an additional education school block for Junior High School which follows the national curriculum and syllabus and thus facilitates the education of young people, as well as an information communication and technology (ICT) centre to equip the young people with computer literacy. However, educational facilities are lacking in the only JCC for girls. Girls who were participating in formal education prior to their detention have their educational aspirations truncated (Osei 2013).

Despite the provision of vocational education, just a handful of young people in both JCC and SCC are enrolled due to different sentences. In a survey of 66 young people at the SCC and 10 young people at the detention facility for girls, Osei (2013) found that whilst 46 per cent of the total sample were enrolled in a vocation, 40 per cent were yet to be enrolled, 8 per cent were not eligible and 6 per cent had expressed no desire to learn a vocation. The sentencing regime (maximum sentence of three years) negatively impacts on the young person's education and career aspirations. Ayete-Nyampong (2017b) also observed a general lack of interest in formal education by young people of the SCC. Whilst some young people showed little interest in formal classes and had to be coaxed to attend, others slept during lessons by placing their heads on the desk. These results are consistent with the evidence from previous studies which showed that young people who end up in detention are more likely compared with those in school to exhibit negative attitudes to school, admit having academic problems and have histories of truancy (Boakye 2013). Such observed relationship have implications for the reintegration of young people into the society after detention. For example, the relationship underscores the importance of working with young people to identify their needs, interests and potential and adopting a collaborative approach to address them rather than the top-down approach that fails to reflect their underlying needs and interests.

Spotlight on the Senior Correctional Centre (SCC)

When a young person is sentenced to the SCC, a valid detention order, the SER prepared for the court, police removal form (that details the young person's possessions on arrest) and a medical report that confirms the young person's age and general health condition must be presented to enable the young person to undergo admission formalities. The JJA further prescribes that the juvenile court satisfied itself via consultation with the detention centre to ensure that adequate space and facilities are available to address the needs of the young person. However, it appears these provisions are not adequately observed. For example, as Fig. 5.3 shows, the number of young people in custody at the Senior Correctional Centre more than doubled from 114 in 2014 to 260 in 2019. Children of different ages (12–21) who should be

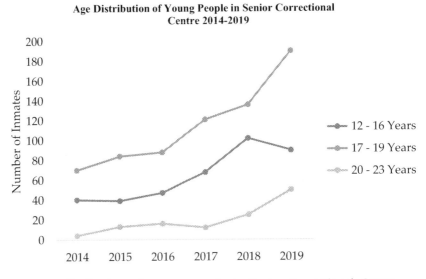

Fig. 5.3 Age distribution of young people in Senior Correctional Centre 2014–2019

separated are sometimes held together in large dormitories. This practice violates the international principle, contained in the UN Convention on the Rights of the Child, of holding young children separately from older children and young adults (see Fig. 5.3). The SCC relies on a largely ineffective age classification system to hold young people in their care (12–15 and 16–20 expected to be held together in the same dormitory) instead of considering other more robust criteria such as the type of offence and length of sentence (Ghana Police Service 2016).

The SCC is severely underfunded by the state. For example, the government feeding allocation for incarcerated people is 1.80 Ghana cedis per day (equivalent to 27 pence or 33 dollar cents) and about 95 per cent of people incarcerated in the SCC have complained about the quality of their meals (Osei 2013). Thus, the quality of nourishment is in doubt given the pittance of government's allocation. The SCC is thus heavily reliant on donations from religious, civil society and other benevolent organisations for its survival and sustenance. This inadequate provisions could affect the health of young people incarcerated in the centre given that there is no physician stationed at the SCC. The situation constitutes a violation of the young people's fundamental rights and key provisions of the UN standard minimum rules for the administration of juvenile justice.

The SCC also lacks an effective monitoring system to assist secondary school students who attend classes beyond the confines of the institution. The centre relies on the daily goodwill of students to return to the facility after lessons at nearby high schools and a technical training college. The various workshops for trade training in carpentry, tailoring, auto-mechanics and masonry among others at the SCC all lack materials and equipment to facilitate learning and the rehabilitation of the young people. Also, being the only senior correctional centre for boys in the country, there is enormous pressure on the limited facilities available (Adzewodah 2019).

The SCC regime is tightly controlled in a disciplined military-like manner similar to adult open camp prisons. Mendez (2014, p. 12)—the UN special rapporteur—"clinically documented traumatic physical injuries on seven juvenile inmates, resulting from a severe caning incident that had taken place within the 48 hours prior to the visit of his team" as a disciplinary measure against inmates by prison officials. At the instigation of the Special Rapporteur to the Director-General of the Ghana Prisons Service, a formal enquiry and disciplinary proceedings initiated against three prison officers, with the main perpetrator a Chief Officer, dismissed from the prison service for violating agreed procedures against corporal punishment and torture of incarcerated people.

A recent riot involving incarcerated people in the SCC chasing officers out of the centre and subsequently resulting in the escape of 14 incarcerated young persons and the recapturing of 9 escaped youth raises questions about the extent to which individuals experience the weight of the SCC regime (Ghanaian Times 2015; Ghana Prisons Service 2015). On the heavy-light continuum where "heavy" regimes are experienced as oppressive, confrontational and intimidating and "light" regimes characterised by an atmosphere of relaxation, approachability and cooperativeness of prison staff (Crewe et al. 2014), it appears that the punitive or "heavy" prison regime at the SCC might have contributed to the riot (Ayete-Nyampong 2013; Osei 2013; Mendez 2014). The response to the riot also appears very heavy-handed and a violation of the rights of the young people with supposedly difficult ones sent to the neighbouring James Camp prison—a facility for holding adult men (Ghanaian Times 2015; also see Egozy and Cox 2017).

Release and Reintegration of Offenders

The juvenile courts can release a young person on probation. The function of the probation officer is mainly to supervise the young person to comply with the conditions of the probation order including visiting the home, school and workplace of the offender who, for example, might be undergoing trade training (Department of Social Welfare 2005). Support services that facilitate reintegration of children in conflict with the law with their family and community are lacking and, where the law exists, they are rarely used. For instance, the law makes provisions for early release and empowers officers-in-charge of correctional facilities to supervise this arrangement and prepare a report on the young person. However, due to the lack of awareness and resources and understaffing, such measures are rarely used (Ghana Police Service 2016). Also, although convicted young people in detention and due for release are entitled to home visits in order to prepare them, their families and the community at large for reintegration, this happens irregularly. The Ghana Police Service (2016, p. 21) observes "children are discharged without any preparation, psychological or otherwise, potentially making them more likely to reoffend." In fact, very little research exists in Ghana on factors that contribute to young people's risk of offending and evidence about effectiveness of rehabilitation programmes for young people (see Boakye 2013, 2020).

Another major challenge is the stigmatising effect of institutionalisation. For example, it has been noted that parents of young people usually fail to turn up to collect their wards on release dates (Ayete-Nyampong 2013). Some of the reasons suggested for such parental failure are shame and stigma that is associated with the offence and custody (personal communication, April 2019). The SCC sometimes holds sessions with some family members prior to the release of the young person in order to facilitate family reunion and reintegration (Ayete-Nyampong 2013; Adzewodah 2019). Section 37 (1) of the JJA also demands that the young person, probation officer or close relative applies to the juvenile court where the young person was sentenced to expunge the conviction or order. This provision is part of the effort to give the young person a fresh start at life and facilitate their reintegration into society. However, the provision limits expunging of criminal records of low level offences but not serious offences which raises questions about the effectiveness of this provision. Also, with the lack of family involvement with less than 50 per cent of young people receiving family visits during incarceration (Osei 2013), the extent to which families will know and take advantage of this provision and support reintegration is doubtful.

Conclusion

The question of how to respond to young people in conflict with the law is a particularly difficult one. It requires a delicate balance between protecting the rights of the young person and ensuring public safety (Morris and Gelsthorpe 2006; Mensa-Bonsu 2017). This complexity is further exacerbated in the case of Ghana and Africa where a "bifurcated" justice system has emerged. As shown in this chapter, on hand there is a "formal" juvenile justice system, a consequence of colonial history and neoliberal globalisation, and on the other hand is an "informal" traditional juvenile justice system that is emasculated but not completely eliminated. This bifurcated juvenile justice system exists because of the imposition of a foreign justice system and penal policies that either ignore or undermine the traditional structures and institutions for responding to crime and justice delivery (Busia 1968; Abotchie 1997; Ame 2018). The challenges confronting the juvenile justice system in Ghana and Africa can, therefore, be understood, in part, against this backdrop. Although in theory the current juvenile justice system of Ghana is consistent with provisions of international requirements on how to treat young people in conflict with the law, in practice the country struggles to fulfil many of these provisions. From the outlook Ghana's juvenile justice system appears to balance welfare paternalism with a rights-based approach that emphasise the best interests of the child. In reality, the justice system struggles to define precisely what constitutes the child's best interests (see also Kelly 1997; Morris and

Gelsthorpe 2006). Even, where some clarity exists, like in many postcolonial jurisdictions (e.g. Sloth-Nielsen 2001; Fourchard 2006; Cox 2012), the system has been unable to protect the rights of young people. This is especially the case for young people in custody.

Thus, the progressive juvenile justice legal framework that consolidates provisions contained in international conventions simply does not correspond with implementation in arrest, investigations, prosecution and sentencing and the detention conditions and reintegration of children in conflict with the law. Like many African countries, the current juvenile justice system in Ghana lack clarity on its underlying philosophy on how to treat young people. The system is blighted with several challenges which make it not particularly child-friendly despite the rhetoric and political gestures (Sloth-Nielsen 2001; Mensa-Bonsu 2017; Odongo 2017). Police corruption, lack of training on JJA provisions for criminal justice stakeholders, lack of specialist training for police officers, judicial staff especially magistrates and prison officers to adequately address the needs of young people caught up in the justice system constrains the realisation of the JJA provisions. These realities make children and young people a doubly vulnerable population in Ghana when they come into conflict with the law.

To address the challenges confronting the juvenile justice system in Ghana it is tempting to assume that investment in the existing juvenile justice system in terms of infrastructural upgrade, improved conditions of service and intervention programmes is all that is required. Such important steps may help improve the experiences of young people in the justice system. However, we contend that a more fundamental issue that requires attention is a critical re-examination of the very foundation of the juvenile justice system in Ghana and the penal philosophy that underpins it. Research is urgently needed in Ghana and Africa more generally on the conception of the child (e.g. Twum-Danso Imoh 2019), traditional notions of punishment (e.g. Arthur 1991; Abotchie 1997) and on the question of what factors explain young people's offending and effective ways to respond (Boakye 2013, 2020). It is important to adopt a youth justice approach that begins with the local; that is, an approach that first recognises, interrogates and adapts the positives from the traditional justice system (Abotchie 1997; Twum-Danso Imoh 2019). The lessons from a critical analysis of the local context and system of justice could help inform the global discourse about youth justice and best practices (see Cox 2012; Abram et al. 2018). This approach would be a useful way to address some of the tensions and contradictions that characterise the juvenile justice system and how it treats especially young people in custody in Ghana and Africa generally.

References

Abdullah, A., Cudjoe, E., & Manful, E. (2018). Barriers to childcare in children's homes in Ghana: Caregivers' solutions. *Children and Youth Services Review, 88*, 450–456.

Abotchie, C. (1997). *Social control in traditional Southern Eweland of Ghana: Relevance for crime prevention.* Accra: Ghana Universities Press.

Abram, L. S., Jordan, S. P., & Montero, L. A. (2018). What is a juvenile? A cross-national comparison of youth justice systems. *Youth Justice, 18*(2), 111–130.

Adu-Gyamfi, J. (2019). Ghana's child Panels: Effective child protection and juvenile justice system or superfluous creation? *The British Journal of Social Work, 49*, 2059–2072.

Adzewodah, V. (2019). Juvenile justice system in Ghana: The case of the Senior Correctional Centre, Accra-Ghana. In *Juvenile justice system in Ghana: Meeting the objectives of Ghana's correctional centres.* Accra: Centre for Democratic Development.

Akoensi, T. D. (2017). In this job, you cannot have time for family': Work–family conflict among prison officers in Ghana. *Criminology & Criminal Justice, 18*(2), 207–225.

Alhassan, A., Ziblim, A. R., & Muntaka, S. (2014). A survey on depression among infertile women in Ghana. *BMC Women's Health, 14*(1). https://doi.org/10.1186/1472-6874-14-42.

Ame, R. (2017). The juvenile justice system in Ghana. *Ghana Social Science Journal, 14*, 1–30.

Ame, R. K. (2018). The origins of the contemporary juvenile justice system in Ghana. *Journal of Family History, 43*(4), 394–408.

Annor, F. (2014). Managing work and family demands: The perspectives of employed parents in Ghana. In Z. Mokomane (Ed.), *Work-family interface in sub-Saharan Africa: International perspectives on social policy, administration and practice* (pp. 17–36). Springer International Publishing.

Ansah-Koi, A. A. (2006). Care of orphans: Fostering interventions for children whose parents die of AIDS in Ghana. *Families in Society: The Journal of Contemporary Social Services, 87*(4), 555–564.

Aryee, A. F. (1997). The African family and changing nuptiality patterns. In A. Adepoju (Ed.), Family, population and development in Africa (pp. 78–96). London: Zed Books.

Arthur, J. A. (1991). Development of penal policy in British West Africa: Exploring the colonial dimension. *International Journal of Comparative and Applied Criminal Justice, 15*(1–2), 187–206.

Arthur, J. (1996). Rehabilitation of juvenile offenders in Ghana. *Journal of Offender Rehabilitation, 24*, 23–37.

Ayete-Nyampong, L. (2013). *Entangled realities and the underlife of a total institution: An ethnography of correctional centres for juvenile and young offenders in Accra, Ghana*. PhD thesis, Wageningen University, The Netherlands.

Ayete-Nyampong, L. (2017a). Insider insights about education provisions for children in conflict with the law in Correctional centres in Ghana. In *1st Asia Pacific Conference on Contemporary Education (APCCE)*. Adelaide: Asia Pacific Institute of Advanced Research.

Ayete-Nyampong, L. (2017b). Practicalities and complexities surrounding escape occurrences in Ghana's correctional centres for children in conflict with the Law. *International Journal of Research in Sociology and Anthropology, 3*, 1–7.

Boakye, K. E. (2013). Correlates and predictors of juvenile delinquency in Ghana. *International Journal of Comparative and Applied Criminal Justice, 37*(4), 257–278.

Boakye, K. E. (2020). Juvenile sexual offending in Ghana: Prevalence, risks and correlates. *Child Abuse and Neglect, 101*. https://doi.org/10.1016/j.chiabu.2019.104318.

Bosiakoh, T. A., & Andoh, P. (2010). Differential association theory and juvenile delinquency in Ghana's capital city – Accra: The case of Ghana Borstal Institute. *International Journal of Sociology and Anthropology, 2*, 199–205.

Brown, C. K. (1996). Gender roles and household allocation of resources and decision-making in Ghana. In E. Ardayfio-Schandorf (Ed.), *The changing family in Ghana* (pp. 21–41). Accra: Ghana Universities Press.

Busia, K. A. (1968). *The position of the chief in the modern political system of Ashanti: A Study of the influence of contemporary changes on Ashanti Political Institutions*. London: Cass.

CHRAJ. (2013). *Annual reports*. Accra: Commission for Human Rights and Administrative Justice (CHRAJ).

Clifford, W. (1974). *An introduction to African criminology. Nairobi*. Oxford University Press.

Cox, P. (2012). History of global criminology: (Re)inventing delinquency in Vietnam. *British Journal of Criminology, 52*, 17–31.

Crewe, B., Liebling, A., & Hulley, S. (2014). Heavy-light, absent-present: re-thinking the 'weight' of imprisonment. *British Journal of Sociology, 65*, 388–410.

Daily Graphic. (2015). *Strengthen security at Osu Remand Home*. Retrieved August 6, 2020, from https://www.graphic.com.gh/news/general-news/strengthen-security-at-osu-remand-home.html.

de Graft-Johnson, K. (1965). Social control in a changing society. *Ghana Journal of Sociology, 1*, 47–55.

Demographic and Health Survey. (2015). Ghana Demographic and Health Survey 2014. Accra: Ghana Statistical Service. Available at https://statsghana.gov.gh/gssmain/fileUpload/pressrelease/2014%20GDHS%20%20Report.pdf (accessed 2 July 2020).

Demographic and Health Survey. (2020). Ghana. The DHS Program. Statcompiler: USAID. Available at https://www.statcompiler.com/en/ (accessed 2 July 2020).

Department of Social Welfare. (2005). *A report on the state of juvenile justice administration in Ghana (A decade assessment: 1993–2003)*. Accra: Government of Ghana.

Donkor, E. S., Naab, F., & Kussiwaah, D. Y. (2017). "I am anxious and desperate": Psychological experiences of women with infertility in The Greater Accra Region, Ghana. *Fertility Research and Practice, 3*(1), 1–6.

Egozy, O., & Cox, A. (2017). Youth facilities and violence: An overview. In P. Sturmey (Ed.), *The Wiley handbook on violence and aggression*. London: Wiley.

Fourchard, L. (2006). Lagos and the invention of juvenile delinquency in Nigeria, 1920–60. *The Journal of African History, 47*(1), 115–137.

Frontiers, C. (2011). *Report on the mapping and analysis of Ghana's Child Protection system*. Kowloon.

Ghana News Agency. (2005). *Three Juveniles kept in police cells instead of Borstal Home*. Retrieved February 2, 2020, from https://www.ghanaweb.com/GhanaHomePage/NewsArchive/Three-Juvenals-kept-in-police-cells-instead-Borstal-Home-79947.

Ghana Police Service. (2016). *Integrating child-friendly policing into the Ghana Police Service: Mapping report summary*. Accra: Government of Ghana.

Ghana Prisons Service, 2015. Annual Report. Accra.

Ghana Statistical Service. (2015). *Demographic and health survey: Key findings*. Accra: GSS.

Ghana Statistical Service. (2016). *2015 Labour force report*. Retrieved February 2, 2020, from https://www2.statsghana.gov.gh/docfiles/publications/Labour_Force/LFS%20REPORT_fianl_21-3-17.pdf.

Ghana Statistical Service. (2018). *Ghana multiple indicator cluster survey (MICS 2017/18), snapshots on key survey findings report*. Accra: GSS.

Ghanaian Times. (2015). *Riot: Juveniles chase prison officers at Borstal Institute*. Retrieved February 2, 2020, from https://www.myjoyonline.com/news/riot-juveniles-chase-prison-officers-at-borstal-institute/.

Ghanaweb. (2016). *6 escape from Osu Remand Home*. Retrieved August 6, 2020, from https://www.ghanaweb.com/GhanaHomePage/NewsArchive/6-escape-from-Osu-remand-home-417816.

Giddens, A. (1990). *The consequences of modernity*. Cambridge: Polity Press.

Goldson, B., & Muncie, J. (2015). Juvenile justice: International law and children's rights. In *International encyclopedia of the social & behavioral sciences* (pp. 956–962). Elsevier. https://doi.org/10.1016/b978-0-08-097086-8.86045-6.

Goody, E. (1982). *Parenthood and social reproduction: Fostering and occupational roles in West Africa*. Cambridge: Cambridge University Press.

Government of Ghana. (2015). *Justice for children policy*. Accra. Retrieved February 2, 2020, from http://www.mogcsp.gov.gh/index.php/mdocs-posts/justice-for-children-policy/.

Hoffmann, S., & Baerg, C. (2011). *Juvenile justice in Ghana: A study to assess the status of juvenile justice in Ghana*. Accra. Retrieved February 2, 2020, from http://www.humanrightsinitiative.org/publications/ghana/JuvenileJusticeinGhana.pdf.

Judicial Service of Ghana. (2018). *Children before the courts in Ghana: Towards child-friendly justice*. Accra.

Kelly, J. B. (1997). The best interests of the child: A concept in search of meaning. *Family and Conciliation Courts Review, 35*(4), 377–387.

Laird, S. E. (2011). Enforcing the law on child maintenance in sub-Saharan Africa: A case study of Ghana. *International Journal of Law, Policy and the Family, 25*(2), 220–243.

Meagher, K. (2003). A back door to globalisation? Structural adjustment, globalisation and transborder trade in West Africa. *Review of African Political Economy, 30*(95), 57–75.

Mendez, J. E. (2014). *Report of the special rapporteur on torture and other cruel, inhuman or degrading treatment or punishment: Mission to Ghana*. New York.

Mensa-Bonsu, H. J. A. N. (2006). *Ghana's juvenile justice system on probation ... making progress with painful steps and slow*. Accra: Ghana Academy of Arts and Sciences.

Mensa-Bonsu, H. J. A. N. (2017). Ghana. In S. Decker & N. Marteache (Eds.), *International handbook of juvenile justice* (pp. 3–28). Cham: Springer. https://doi.org/10.1007/978-3-319-45090-2_1.

Morris, A., & Gelsthorpe, L. (2006). Towards good practice in juvenile justice policy in the commonwealth. *Commonwealth Law Bulletin, 32*(1), 27–58.

Muncie, J. (2005). The globalization of crime control—The case of youth and juvenile justice: Neo-liberalism, policy convergence and international conventions. *Theoretical Criminology, 9*(1), 35–64.

Nachinab, G. T., Donkor, E., & Naab, F. (2018). Child adoption as a management alternative for infertility: A qualitative study in rural northern Ghana. *International Journal of Caring Sciences, 11*(3), 1763–1770.

Nukunya, G. (2003). *Tradition and change in Ghana*. Accra: Ghana Universities Press.

Odongo, G. O. (2017). Kenya. In S. Decker & N. Marteache (Eds.), *International handbook of juvenile justice* (pp. 29–43). Cham: Springer International Publishing. https://doi.org/10.1007/978-3-319-45090-2_2.

Oduro, G. Y. (2012). 'Children of the street': Sexual citizenship and the unprotected lives of Ghanaian street youth. *Comparative Education, 48*(1), 41–56.

Opoku, D. K. (2010). From a 'success' story to a highly indebted poor country: Ghana and neoliberal reforms. *Journal of Contemporary African Studies, 28*(2), 155–175.

Oppong, C. (1973). *Growing up in Dagbon*. Accra: Ghana Publishing Corporation.

Oppong, C., & Abu, K. (1987). *Seven roles of women: Impact of education, migration and employment on Ghanaian mothers*. Geneva: International Labour Office.

Osei, B. A. (2013). *Evaluating the effectiveness of Ghana's juvenile justice system in rehabilitating the offender*. Ghana: Aseshi University College.

Sarbah, J. M. (1968). *Fanti national constitution* (2nd ed.). London: Frank Cass & Co. Ltd.

Sloth-Nielsen, J. (2001). The role of international human rights law in the development of South Africa's legislation on juvenile justice. *Law, Democracy and Development, 5*(1), 59–83.

Teye, J. K. (2013). Economic value of children and fertility preferences in a fishing community in Ghana. *GeoJournal, 78*(4), 697–708.

Twum-Danso Imoh, A. T. D. (2019). Terminating childhood: Dissonance and synergy between global children's rights norms and local discourses about the transition from childhood to adulthood in Ghana. *Human Rights Quarterly, 41*(1), 160–182.

United Nations. (1986). *Standard Minimum Rules for the Administration of Justice*. New York, United Nations.

United Nations. (1990a). *The Protection of Juveniles Deprived of their Liberty*. New York, United Nations.

United Nations. (1990b). *Guidelines for the Prevention of Delinquency*. New York, United Nations.

UNICEF. (2016). *Creating an ideal legal framework for child protection in Ghana: Legal analysis report*. Accra.

UNTC. (2020). *Convention of the rights of the child*. United Nations Treaty Collection. Retrieved February 2, 2020, from https://treaties.un.org/pages/ViewDetails.aspx?src=IND&mtdsg_no=IV 11&chapter=4&lang=en.

Wacquant, L. (2001). The penalization of poverty and the rise of neoliberalism. *European Journal of Criminal Policy and Research, 9*, 401–412.

Weinberg, S. K. (1965). Urbanization and male delinquency in Ghana. *Journal of Research in Crime and Delinquency, 2*(2), 85–94.

Yaro, J. A. (2013). Neoliberal globalisation and evolving local traditional institutions: Implications for access to resources in rural Northern Ghana. *Review of African Political Economy, 40*(137), 410–427.

Part II

Socio-Legal Contexts of Youth Imprisonment

Epigraph to Section II

"If"

If I grew up with good parents, maybe I wouldn't be like this.
If I grew up with loving parents, maybe I would show love.
If I grew up with caring parents, maybe I would be more caring.
If I grew up with role models, maybe I would be a better person.
If I grew up with fairness, maybe I would learn fairness.
If I grew up with my parents, maybe i wouldn't feel alone and be proud of myself.

March 29, 2020
Barry J. Nidorf Juvenile Hall, Sylmar, CA, USA

6

The Rebirth of Delinquent 'Adult-Children': Criminal Capacity, Socio-economic Systems, and the Malleability of Penality of Child Delinquency in India

Shailesh Kumar

Introduction

It was a British summer afternoon and while eating my lunch from the *Hare Krishna* stall,[1] a childhood memory visited me. One evening when I was around ten years old, in my hometown Barh, I thought of saving three rupees by not paying for a plate of *Chaat* I had from a street-side *Chaatwala*. After I finished eating, I looked around, and finding him busy with other customers, I left back for home without paying. I was welcomed with a scolding by my mother and was sent back to pay the sum. I was scared, but the *Chaatwala* happily took the money without any trouble. Perhaps he thought that I was a child, after all, and such acts deserve mercy. This memory was followed by one of the 2012 Delhi gang rape incidents which sparked public rage when a child in conflict with the law in the case was not punished on par with the adults punished for this incident. Although these two instances are obviously not comparable, I sought to explore the relationship between the nature of children's behaviour and the responses to it by social systems and the state from a socio-historical perspective in India.

In the Indian subcontinent's socio-cultural history, which predominantly relates to Hinduism,[2] the concept and conceptions of child and childhood have had a peculiar social and religious significance, since the Vedic period

---

S. Kumar (✉)
School of Law, Birkbeck College, University of London, London, UK

until today. The relationship between children's capacities, understandings, and accountability laid the foundation for children's behaviours to be treated differently than those of adults. Intriguingly, in India, caste and gender are social identities so rigidly attached to one's birth in a particular family and being born in a particular sex, respectively, that they leave an indelible imprint on children, shaping the birth, life, and death of their childhood (Ghose 2003; Kumar 2016). Alongside class, the two identities act as barriers or facilitators to a child's growth.[3] These socio-economic systems, together with the changing nature of the state, have affected how India, since the Vedic period, has dealt with children and their behaviours.

This chapter's focus is juvenile imprisonment,[4] which involves the state taking the recourse of prison to fulfil the conservative agenda of 'retribution' or the liberal agenda of 'reform' of delinquent children. In this chapter, I examine the shifting age boundaries of the legal definition of juvenile, which relate to the Minimum Age of Criminal Responsibility (MACR)[5] and the Age of Criminal Majority (ACM)[6] (Abrams et al. 2018), from the Vedic era through the colonial period to the present time. I analyse the malleability of state and societal responses to children's behaviours.

The first section devoted to historical inquiry traces the status of children and childhood in the Hindu legal texts and legal systems in ancient India to reflect how that may have influenced the present response to children's behaviours both by the Indian society and the Indian state. With a discussion on the function of the integrating mechanisms of culture and labour as institutions of control and punishment that shapes childhood differentially for different children, the second section explores 'colonial childhoods', exploring the vested interests of the British and the native Indians. The third section delves into the changing responses of the postcolonial neoliberal Indian state to children's behaviour and the birth of delinquent 'adult-children'.

In the fourth section, I examine the legal reforms brought in to improve the policy and procedures for the administration of juvenile justice at the turn of the twenty-first century. The fifth section considers the telos of the institution of juvenile justice and offers evidence-based arguments as to why and how the latest legislation, the Juvenile Justice (Care and Protection of Children) Act 2015 (JJ-II), has high potential to result in juvenile (in)justice. I argue that it has led to the rebirth of delinquent 'adult-children' thus contributing to the state's current response anti-child and anti-social behaviour. Ultimately, I finish with conclusions and recommendations in my attempt to present novel junctions between scholarship and public policy.

Childhood, Delinquency, Gender, and *Varna* in the Precolonial Indian Subcontinent

A comprehensive historical study of child delinquency in the Indian context demands recourse to a methodological dialogue between history and socio-legal studies (Gittins 2008). In a historical materialist framework, ancient Indian history can be organised into four phases—beginning with the pastoral society (early Vedic: c. 1500–1200 BC), to agrarian (later Vedic: c. 1200–600 BC), to one of revolt and a period of questioning (ascetic antiritualism: c. 600–300 BC), to a feudal one with the emergence of Empires (Kumar 2021).[7] As multiple faiths and beliefs have coexisted in India, religion[8] continues to play a vital role when it comes to the country's social-economic-political significance. Since the early Vedic period, children have always possessed a very important place for Hindus, particularly sons, as per the Vedic texts.

Manava Dharmasastra, in this regard, mentions the etymology of the word *putra* (son) as "he who rescues (tra) his father from the hell named 'Put'" (Davis Jr. 2017, p. 151). Highlighting further a son's importance to his family and father in the Hindu culture, Davis Jr. (2017, p. 151) states that "Without a son, the family line and the soul after death both perish. With a son, a father gains immortality and everlasting worlds." No doubt such an understanding of the male child and its continuity in the Indian social culture translates into a gender-biased socio-legal understanding of childhood and treatment of children's behaviour.

The Dharmasastra[9] recognises two important stages in a child's development—one relates to ritual capacity (initiation) and the other to legal capacity. Exploring this further, Davis Jr. (2017) notes that until his eighth year a child (*sisu*) is considered the same as an embryo (*garbha*) and attains the capacity to perform rituals at the age of eight. Until the sixteenth year he is a youth (*bala*) or adolescent (*poganda*), and upon turning 16 he acquires legal capacity and is competent in commerce (Davis Jr. 2017). At this age he is independent if his parents are dead, or else, he is dependent irrespective of his age, that is, even after turning 16 (Davis Jr. 2017). Its impact can be seen even today in the form of a joint or extended family system that I will discuss in the next section. Thus, Rocher (2012) argues, the *bala or poganda* may not enter into contracts and is afforded some protections like reduced guilt and liability for both religious and legal offences. After turning 16, according to Davis Jr. (2017), he obtains legal majority and becomes capable to enter into legal transactions of all kinds. However, for female children, Rocher (2012, p. 237) contends that "majority occurs at age twelve and relates not to legal capacity but eligibility and fitness for marriage and childbearing."

The distinction between minority and majority in terms of age can also be looked at from what Davis Jr. (2017) calls the pejorative connotations of childhood expressed in the Dharmasastra. Not only does it say that a man ignorant of the Veda and *Dharma* is to be called a child, but also children are disqualified as witnesses, and childishness has very often been equated with foolishness. Regarding responses to children's behaviour in precolonial times, scholars have argued that the recognition of child delinquency as different from adult criminality existed prior to the advent of British laws (Kumari 2004). Manusmriti,[10] written between c. 185 BC and AD 200, for example, mentions that a child littering on a public road was not liable for punishment but only an admonition and made to clean it, while an adult in similar circumstances was required to pay a fine and made to clean the filth (Kumari 2015).

The Vedic rituals were restricted to the three privileged Varnas, that is, social classes,[11] while the Sudras, the fourth underprivileged class, alongside the lowest so-called untouchable castes were disentitled to rituals and altogether from studying and using Vedic texts (Aktor 2017).[12] Though such evidence does offer a picture of childhood and children's rights in the Vedic era in the Indian subcontinent, Davis Jr. (2017) contends that until recently, no broad scale study of the idea and history of childhood has been undertaken for ancient or medieval India. It is noteworthy that classifying a child into a sex and a caste had a religious, legal, and social function. The Hindu child, therefore, borrowing from Gittins (2008, p. 37), defined "not just physiological immaturity but also…dependency, powerlessness and inferiority."

With the gradual entry of Islam in the late first millennium AD in the Indian subcontinent, the precolonial society's socio-religious culture became more pluralistic. Transitioning from a pastoral to agrarian to a feudal society, the socio-familial relations were carved in a manner that Indian subcontinental children in their early years were predominantly in the care of female members of the joint or extended family, rather than in the men's world (Kakar 2012). So, even after reaching eight years of age, Savarna children might have been either under the control of teachers or at home mostly with caretakers. 'Other' children might have been under parental-familial control. Actions of children classified as 'deviant' within the culture were either ignored at home or might have been met with responses like scolding or some form of corporal punishment at the hands of teachers and parents. Further, the silence of the Dharmasastra on child delinquency implies that such behaviours were dealt with by an informal agency such as the family or community (Kethineni and Klosky 2005), rather than the formal institutional agencies like Kings, their agents, or the formal criminal legal system.

Children, Responsibility, and Criminal Law: The Social, Economic, and Political Dimensions of Childhood, Child Delinquency, and Punishment in Colonial India

'Child' has never been a monolithic term in India. After the entry of the British colonial rule, the term became more complicated. The naturally and socially constructed power-hierarchical notions of age, caste, class, ethnicity, gender, race, religion, sex, and other such notions engendered multiple categorisations of child and childhood. Along with these identities, what also generally shaped the childhood in the Indian society during the precolonial and into the colonial times were motherhood and the joint or extended family (Kakar 2012). The extended family is a familial unit wherein two or more brothers remain together post-marriage and bring their wives to the parental household. They continue to live together with all of their children thereafter and remain devoted and obedient to their parents. At the root of the extended family lie the principles of filial loyalty and fraternal solidarity, which demands common residence and common socio-economic-ritual activities (Kakar 2012).

Changing cultural milieu and socio-economic material conditions have also contributed to the construction of childhood in India, particularly in the wake of British imperialism. These conditions, through the institutions of culture and labour, socially controlled a child by non-punitive measures of informal non-state agencies. Children also experienced punitive measures through the institution of extra-legal physical punishment, and their inclusion or exclusion from the unskilled labour market led to the shortening or lengthening of the period of adolescence (Hartjen 1982).

In its journey from a collective of independent princely states to a British colony, a new notion of sovereignty was infused through the ideology of criminal justice in India (Singha 1998). The diversified precolonial judicial administration system of a highly developed civilisation was gradually replaced by the English common law (Galanter 1968) in the garb of oriental despotism.[13] Such an approach to transplant the presumed 'superior' British legal system to replace the indigenous one did not conform with the individualised and community-based justice delivery of the precolonial Indian society (Galanter 1978; Skuy 1998) and the responses to children's behaviour in particular.

The enactment of criminal laws and juvenile laws by the British in the second half of the nineteenth century in India reflected the needs and ideas appropriate to England's criminal justice system, rather than those of India. Such policy-making did not represent Britain's attempt to modernise India's criminal justice system, but rather the use of India as an experimental site to test out improvements in its own primitive criminal justice system (Magarey 1978; Skuy 1998; Emsley 2005). As Magarey (1978) puts it, "the invention of juvenile delinquency" had already taken place in England in the early nineteenth century.

The British system rationalised the confinement of youth in reformatory ideals. Reformers such as Mary Carpenter argued, "juvenile offenders were especially amenable to correct socialization if they could be removed from criminalizing influences, equipped with basic literacy skills, exposed to religious influence, trained to work, and given an interest in their own obedience" (Sen 2004, p. 83). However, Sen (1969–2018), a historian who studied childhood and the institutionalisation of discipline and punishment during colonial regimes in South Asia and in the Indian Ocean world, contends that the idea of institutionalisation emerging in England was a disciplinary apparatus (Sen 2004). It was, he argues, inspired by the class-bias of the middle-class Victorians, targeting not only the children of the working poor and the 'dangerous classes' but also homeless and street children whose status were equated with 'savages', 'stray animals', and 'Arabs'. He further argues that the colonial reformatory project in India was more about experiments rather than reformed children (Sen 2005).

In 1843, a Ragged School was established in the industrial city of Calcutta (Kumari 2004). It was based on the idea of John Pounds (1766–1839), the crippled cobbler who went on to become a teacher and altruist and the brain behind England's Ragged School form of free education for destitute and working-class children in the early nineteenth century. The British then enacted the Apprentices Act 1850, the Indian Penal Code 1860 (IPC), the Code of Criminal Procedure 1861, and the Reformatory Schools Acts of 1876 and 1897. Together they laid down a landscape for the differential treatment of orphans, poor and vagrant children, and CCL.

The 1850 Act empowered father or guardian or Magistrate in the capacity of a guardian to apprentice children above 10 and under 18 years to learn trade, crafts, and employments to their 'masters'. The term of contract had to be maximum of seven years and not to prolong beyond the time when such a child is of the age of 21 years, or in the case of a female, beyond the time of her marriage.[14] The first nationwide criminal code, IPC 1860, implemented soon after the 1857–1858 Rebellion, fixed the MACR to below the age of 7 years (Table 6.1). This MACR is still in force, despite India being a signatory state of the UN Convention on the Rights of the Child 1989 (CRC) that says an MACR below age 12 would be unacceptable by international standards (Abrams et al. 2018). There is a presumption of *doli incapax* for children above 7 and under 12 years of age. So, the IPC fixed the ACM at 12.

6 The Rebirth of Delinquent 'Adult-Children': Criminal Capacity...

Table 6.1 Key legislations with year of enactment, MACR, ACM, and detention conditions (1860–1946)

Year	Legislation	MACR	ACM	Detention conditions
1860	Indian Penal Code (IPC)	7 years[15]	12[16]	N/A
1861	Code of Criminal Procedure (CrPC)	N/A	16 years (only male)[17]	– Judicial discretion to send children under age 16 to reformatories rather than prisons.
1864	Whipping Act (WA)	N/A	16 years (only male)[18]	– Whipping for males in lieu of any other punishment for offences not punishable by death.
1876	Reformatory Schools Act (RSA- I)	7 years	16 years (only male)[19]	– Male youthful offenders to be sent to and detained in a reformatory school for minimum 2 to maximum 7 years, only if a Magistrate thought the boy a proper person to be an inmate of a Reformatory school. – Boys above 18 years not to be detained in reformatory school.
1897	Reformatory Schools Act (RSA- II)	7 years	15 years	– Male youthful offenders to be sent to and detained in a reformatory school for minimum 3 to maximum 7 years, as opposed to imprisonment or transportation, only if a Magistrate thought the boy a proper person to be an inmate of a reformatory school. – Female youthful offenders to be discharged after due admonition or to be delivered to a parent or guardian or nearest adult relative.[20] – Persons above 18 years not to be detained in reformatory school.
1920–1946	Children Act of Madras (1920), Bengal (1922), Bombay (1924), Andhra (adopted the Madras Children Act 1920), Delhi (1941), Mysore (1943), Travancore (1945), and Cochin (1946).	7 years	Varied between 16 and 21 years and also varied with regard to sex of the person	– Prohibition on death sentence, transportation, or imprisonment. – Person to be sent to a certified school, except where the court certifies that the person is of so unruly or of so depraved a character that he is not a fit person to be sent to a certified school. – Person not to be kept in school beyond 18 years of age.

Thus, from 1860, for all persons, except those under 7, and those above 7 and under 12 years of age who could not be proved by the state to be *doli capax*, the regular courts and prisons were used alongside all the punishments prescribed in the IPC. The 1861 Code prescribed judicial discretion to confine children under age 16 in a reformatory rather than to imprison them in a jail.[21] Thereafter, the corporal punishment of whipping was introduced as a judicial punishment through the Whipping Act of 1864. Motivated by the colonial question of finance, the whip was more fiscally prudent than prison sentences (McClure 2020). This helped decrease children's increasing population in prisons and catered to the fear of the Prison Committee 1864 that unworthy parents would encourage their children to commit offenses to receive government education (Kumari 2015). Whipping, which showcased colonial political authority wrapped in legal violence and signalled a deterrent orientation of colonial penology (Sen 2005), was employed for males for offences not punishable with death.[22] So, this means that some children might have even faced the death penalty.

The 1876 Act kept the ACM at 16 years. ACM was brought back to 15 years under the 1897 Act with the rationale that a male above 15 is unamenable to reform (Kumar 2019). The 1876 Act did not have any provision for female CCL. Later, the 1897 Act did mention the "power to deal in other ways with youthful offenders including girls."[23] Under this provision a Court was directed to discharge a girl after due admonition or to be delivered to a parent or guardian or nearest adult relative, instead of sentencing her to transportation or imprisonment or detention in a reformatory school. The 1897 Act prescribed confinement of boys, convicted of even serious crimes, in reformatories, as opposed to imprisonment or transportation (Hartjen 1995). Nonetheless, the reformatories were, unlike in Europe, "run by makeshift personnel with uneven levels of commitment to modern ideas of punishment and rehabilitation" (Sen 2004, p. 84).

Female juvenile delinquency was a bigger headache for the colonial administrators. The administrators were cautious about institutionalisation of native girls, despite elite native Indian's indifference or support towards colonial state intervention in the lives of marginal natives (Sen 2005). British administrators were driven by the assumptions that girls' detention would damage their marriageability as they would be detained beyond their marriageable age. This would further damage their economic dependence on males and transition into adulthood. Administrators also thought that keeping girls from different castes together may lead to contamination (Sen 2005).[24] These measures they believed would pose a threat to their prioritisation of protection of structures of patriarchy and caste within the native family (Sen 2005). Thus, the girls in conflict with law were, rather, punished with varying prison terms on conviction, put into asylums, sentenced to life in penal transportation, and were even sent to the Andaman Islands (Sen 2005). It is important to understand here that the children of the colony were valuable to both the colonial and national projects, and "Indians who sought to decolonize the institutions of childhood had to reclaim the native child from institutional and disciplinary spaces" (Sen 2005, p. 2). For the colonial project, the children were potential tools for empire-making, while for the national project, they were significant for building nationhood.

The first half of the twentieth century saw a further attitudinal shift in the state response to children across the globe. After the First World War, there was a universal movement for having special laws and institutions for CCL. Upon the recommendations of the Indian Jail Committee (1919–1920), the Children Acts were enacted in the industrial provinces of Madras, Bengal, and Bombay in 1920, 1922, and 1924, respectively. Other Indian provinces failed either to enact or to fully enforce separate legislation for children, and even separate children's courts could not be much of a reality (Kethineni and Klosky 2005). These Acts and their later versions granted more state control and had different cut-off ages[25] to define child or youthful offenders and therefore there was regional variation in the treatment of children (Kumari 2015). Imprisonment and the death penalty continued as penal measures to control child delinquency in jurisdictions with no or poorly enforced children legislations.

The Geneva Declaration of the Rights of the Child 1924 and the Second World War stressed the idea of child victimhood globally, and thus, lead to a transformation in the ideologies of childhood and state response to children's behaviour in India (Kumar 2019). Nevertheless, there seems to be a dearth of broad scale scholarship on child delinquency in Colonial India from a theoretical perspective of intersectionality along the lines of caste and religion. This could be because the scholars have been perhaps more invested in colonialist and nationalist explorations, rather than an in-depth investigation through social hierarchies of caste and religion, of children and childhood in colonial India.

Child Delinquency, Socio-economic-Political Settings in the Postcolonial India, and the Birth of Delinquent 'Adult-Children'

Upon attainment of independence from the British rule in 1947, India became a democracy with the vote extended to people above 21 years[26] of age. With severe poverty, illiteracy, and inequality, and a predominantly agrarian economy, India had to recover and rebuild herself from the colonial disaster.

It had also to wrestle with the violence of caste, class, gender, and religion to make its diversity an enabler rather than a barrier to egalitarianism. However, the postcolonial Indian state not only inherited a colonial criminal justice system, penal structures, and punishments, but also arguably continued to use it in a ruthless manner against the 'new' marginalised people with inhumane prison environments (Banerjee 2005; Mathur 2005; Murali 2006; Karnam 2009; Kumar 2021). Child delinquency in the post-colony, therefore, needs to be framed not only at the intersection of colonial modernity and postcolonial developmental anxieties, but also the embedded precolonial social culture.

Independent Indian states and union territories were, unlike for adults, free to enact their own laws for child delinquency and juvenile justice systems, which thereby led to what Hartjen (1995, p. 2) called, "a diverse patchwork of fully implemented, partially implemented, unimplemented, and nonexistent legislation for juveniles in India." So, the IPC did nationalise the adult criminal justice system, but there was no nationalisation of child justice systems. Both the neglected and delinquent children, most likely, as Hartjen (1995, p. 6) argues, "were handled by the all-purpose children's courts established under the central government and various state governments since 1920." Thus, even the poor children likely went through these courts under charges so as to get them into the system of care (Hartjen 1995).

Hartjen (1982, p. 471) claims that "the delinquency rate is a function of the socio-economic forces that affect the society's capacity to integrate young people." Thus, except in some industrial former presidencies like Madras, Bengal, and Bombay, childhood delinquency might not have become a serious nationwide law and order problem for the postcolonial state. The reason for this was the prevalent protective net of the extended familial and socio-economic structure of the then agrarian India. As Beteille (1974) has pointed out, in agrarian, as opposed to industrial societies, social life is governed more by persons than by abstract rules or laws. Thus, "Indian children (and their behavior) were traditionally circumscribed by the bonds of family and its *jati* (caste) and community embeddedness" (Hartjen 1995, p. 13) through a mechanism of informal social controls without much state intervention.

The collection of former British dominions and princely states that came together as a country had to locate a sense of nationhood. Alongside its embarkment on a developmental path of economic transformation initially through nationalisation and then through economic liberalisation post 1991, India's legal framework had to reflect nationalisation as per the new ruling political class. In line with this thought, the gradual nationalisation of child justice systems was carried out. The Children Act of 1960 (CA) brought uniformity in law to the Union Territories (UTs)[27] under the direct rule of the

6 The Rebirth of Delinquent 'Adult-Children': Criminal Capacity...

central government, while later on the Juvenile Justice Act of 1986 (JJA) extended the CA to Indian states, except Jammu & Kashmir, standardising large multi-ethnic multi-cultural societies of India. JJA had profound repercussions for young people charged with crimes, which I will discuss as we proceed further (Table 6.2).

The CA of 1960 discontinued the use of death penalty or imprisonment as sentencing options for children in the UTs. The CA also brought a sex-based definition of child according to gender and age: a male below 16 years and a female below 18 years. It further established two adjudicatory bodies, that is, the Child Welfare Board and Children's Courts, to deal with neglected and

Table 6.2 Key legislations with year of enactment, MACR, ACM, and trial and detention conditions (1947–present)

Year	Legislation	MACR	ACM	Detention conditions
1947–1986	Children Act in different Indian states	7 years	16–21 years	– Prohibition on death sentence, transportation, or imprisonment. – Person to be sent to a certified school, except where the court certifies that the person is of so unruly or of so depraved a character that he is not a fit person to be sent to a certified school. – Person not to be kept in school beyond 18 years of age.
1960	Children Act (CA) (only for UTs)	7 years	16 (male)/18 (female)	– Prohibition on death sentence or imprisonment.
1986	Juvenile Justice Act (JJA)	7 years	16 (male)/18 (female)	– Prohibition on death sentence or imprisonment or committal to prison in default of payment of fine or furnishing security.
2000	Juvenile Justice (Care and Protection of Children) Act (JJ- I)	7 years	18 years	– Prohibition on death sentence or imprisonment or committal to prison in default of payment of fine or furnishing security.
2015	Juvenile Justice (Care and Protection of Children) Act (JJ- II)	7 years	18 years	– Children in the age-group of 16–18 years may be diverted to the adult criminal justice system for committing 'heinous' offences under certain circumstances and maybe punished like an adult.

delinquent children, respectively. It also had provisions for residential institutions for such children, which included the Observation Home (during trial) and Special Home (after conviction). However, these were limited to the Union Territories. For the rest of India, that is, the Indian states, as the juvenile delinquency statistics of the Indian government[28] suggest, juveniles included persons from age 7 up to age 21 regardless of difference in the cut-off ages in the Children's Act of different states and UTs. This may mean that 21 years was the ACM under some of the legislations.

From the year 1961[29] to 1987, the year in which the JJA was enforced, the number of apprehended youths went up from 53,776 to 179,962, with the highest being 190,567 in 1981. As there were no Child Welfare Boards except in the Union Territories, most of the apprehended children were sent to courts (Hartjen 1995), and this number increased from 47,852 in 1961 to 154,399 in 1986. Girls accounted for an average of 6–7% of the apprehended children up to 1987. Until 1987, there were different forms of final orders that could be passed in such cases after non-acquittal. These were releasing the child with advice, admonition, or fine, or restoring them to guardians, or releasing them on probation, or sending them to schools and institutions, or to reformatories and borstals, or to prisons. The data appears silent about the awarding of the death sentence.[30]

If we look at the number of juveniles imprisoned from the year 1971[31] to the year 1987, we find that an average of 16.65% of juveniles sent to courts were incarcerated each year, with a maximum of 34,256 juveniles incarcerated in the year 1982. If we look at the socio-economic-educational profiles of these juveniles from 1971 to 1987, they were mostly very poor, and on an average, around 50% were illiterate and a meagre 5.1% had classed the Tenth class. In the same duration, out of those apprehended, on an average 12.6% were homeless and 40% belonged to the Scheduled Castes and Scheduled Tribes. This suggests an overlap of social, economic, and educational status as well as who actually were being apprehended and then incarcerated. However, the juveniles in UTs and some states were still within the protective net of the juvenile justice system.

Averaging the recorded crimes over the three decades from 1958 to 1987, a majority of those apprehended were involved in property crimes, particularly theft and burglary. Many times, only these two offences together crossed the 40% of the total offences recorded. Crimes affecting the human body or life, which included rape, kidnapping and abduction, and homicide, were a meagre 3–4%. The percentage of total cognisable[32] crimes under IPC committed by juveniles to total cognisable crimes under IPC committed in India was a meagre 2–5%. And the percentage of juveniles apprehended was extremely low, that is, less than 1% of the total arrests (Verma 1997). Moreover, the majority of juveniles were apprehended from industrialised states like Maharashtra, West Bengal, Tamil Nadu, and Gujarat, suggesting that these children could mostly be the urban poor.[33]

Actual children's social deviance, however, as the qualitative research on it suggests, was much more pervasive in India than what the official statistics speak, and the reason could be the reporting or enforcement discretion and reluctance of police and Indian adults to treat child delinquency through formal legal means (Hartjen 1995; Steffensmeier et al. 2018).[34] In his multifaceted study of delinquent behaviour and its control in the Indian state of Tamil Nadu during 1970s, Hartjen (1982, p. 469) argues that "the apparent reluctance of Indian adults and legal authorities to control juvenile misconduct by formal, legal means is also partially explained by the network of role relationships." By role relationship, Hartjen (1982, p. 468) means "a variety of obligations toward kin, *jati*, and community," which form social life in agrarian societies. He contends that "because social life occurs within the domains of family and locality, norm violations and interpersonal disputes are perceived as family, *jati*, or village concerns (Hartjen 1982, p. 469)," and state agencies have minimal contact with matters of social control.

He further notes that "a majority of the children that judicial or correctional officials deal with are either involved in activities such as begging or carrying illegal alcohol or have turned to petty crime because they lost family relationships and were thus severed from economic support" (Hartjen 1982, p. 470). Hartjen (1982) also records that there were no stories or reports on delinquency or youth crime in the crime news in Tamil Nadu. Further, as his research reveals, the public imagination was dominated by the belief that not only for the status-offence delinquent behaviour but also in cases of serious criminal cases informal agents like the family should deal with the matter rather than formal agents such as the police (Hartjen 1982).

Socio-economic Changes in 1980s, Adultification, and JJA: The Birth of Delinquent 'Adult-Children'

As stated earlier, the juvenile delinquency statistics until 1987 included persons in the age-group of 7–21 years, though already the definition of child and thus the ACM was fixed to 16 for males and 18 for females under the CA 1960 and children's act of some other states, thereby criminalising the behaviour of males above 16 and females above 18 in those parts of India where such legislations were in force. So, India's approach, while framing the new juvenile legislation for the entire country, which it did in 1986, should have been to provide a wider net of juvenility of 21 years and to make the juvenile justice system more effective by completely disengaging carceral measures and improving the educational and thereby the economic capacities of CCL for social reintegration. Further, the sex-differentiated definition of child in the CA should have been rationalised to have 21 years as cut-off age for all children irrespective of sex for two reasons. First, males in 16–18 would have been legally treated at par with females of the same age. Second, all young persons in the age-group of 18–21 years would have become subject to the child justice system. The CII reports, however, stressed that youth in the age-group of 16 to 21 years formed 60% of the total apprehended juveniles in the 1960s and crossed 80% in the 1980s, while being highest at 91.3% in the year 1987. The postcolonial state bogged down under the pressure of this 'rising' juvenile crime rates by this age-group, and in 1986, the JJA followed the CA, and an exclusionary child justice system was nationalised.

The JJA defined a 'Juvenile' as a male below 16 years of age or a female below 18 years of age. The postcolonial state, thus, fixed a low ACM for males, who constituted around 94% of total apprehended juveniles until 1987, for the whole of India. It excluded entire groups of males in the 16–21 age-group and females in the 18–21 age-group from the protective net of the juvenile justice system through one legal act, thereby formally criminalising them, which it could easily have avoided. The state threw all these young people into the adult court and punishment system in the name of criminal justice. The result was, what I call, the birth of delinquent 'adult-children'. This happened despite the fact that "a hefty proportion of the youths who were sentenced to correctional facilities for juveniles in the early 1980s were 'dependent or neglected' youths, not delinquents" (Hartjen 1995, p. 6).

One could imagine the horrifying implications of JJA by thinking that, if we employ the JJA's definition of child to the 1987 CII juvenile delinquency statistics, 91.3% (16–21 years) and 72.3% (18–21 years) of male and female juvenile delinquents, respectively, would have legally become adults in the eyes of criminal law. So, from 1988 onwards, the volume of delinquent 'adult-children' in India might have been similar. Such changes occurred despite the fact that until the 1990s, there was no delinquency problem of any discernible proportion in India and it could have been sufficiently tackled by improving the existing hodgepodge of local legal control (Hartjen 1995). One needs to investigate the factors and identify specific interest groups behind such legal changes that must have led to production of so many criminalised adult-children since 1988. Such an investigative approach has been taken to study certain rights-based legislation (Nilsen 2018).

Even Hartjen himself has not explored this in detail, arguing that it requires an extensive socio-historical analysis, but speculates reasons behind this legal reform. He says that "significant socioeconomic changes were taking place in India during the mid-1980s and one area in which these changes were felt was the way that Indian society viewed and reared its young and the way that it believed (as exemplified in the law) that miscreants should be treated" (Hartjen 1995, p. 3). Another reason he gives is India's attempt towards showcasing unitary control in federalism. The latter reason, however, does not give much idea of legislature's motive behind fixing the ACM at as low as 16 for male and 18 for female. The United States adopted a similar approach in 1970s and 1980s, where the proliferation of such transfer regimes, applied in some states to young children even of age 14, was questioned. Scholars have argued that transferring adolescents to the criminal court exposes them to harsh and sometimes toxic forms of punishment that have the perverse effect of increasing criminal activity (Fagan 2008). Even the empirical evidence is too limited to be definitive of such an approach achieving greater incapacitation and providing more effective deterrence (Bishop 2000).

The JJA established 'Juvenile Courts' and 'Juvenile Welfare Boards'. The law mandated that the Boards and Juvenile Courts, as far as practicable, are to be held in a different building or room than the usual court building/courtroom, or on different days or at times if the sitting is to be held in regular adult courts.[35] The JJA abolished the death sentence or imprisonment or committal to prison in default of payment of fine or furnishing security for delinquent juveniles.[36] Even in the cases where a serious offence has been committed by a young person above 14 years old, the JJA prescribed that such a young person is to be kept in safe custody in such place and manner as the juvenile court thinks fit and not to be kept in a Special Home.[37]

A major economic change in India Hartjen hinted at came in the form of the 1991 economic liberalisation policy. Indian society went through a gradual small-scale shift from an agrarian to an industrial society with urbanisation and industrialisation leading to the exponential growth of the Indian middle class. The social integrative features and structures prevalent in the pre-industrial Indian society were gradually waning, thereby weakening the traditional familial, social, economic, and emotional ties in the post-industrial Indian society. As Hartjen (1982) asserts, post-industrial development generates disintegrative structures which alienate children (and adolescents), thereby stimulating more youth crime. Urban-centric development a neoliberal mindset and more economic inequality could have led to growth of urban poverty and child delinquency. However, statistics on juvenile delinquency did not reflect this change largely due to the fact that the figures from 1988 onwards excluded older youths, that is, males in 16–21 age-group and females in 18–21 age-group, who were most likely to be found in conflict with law by the juvenile justice system.

The JJA led to a major decline in the percentage of juvenile crimes to the total IPC crimes. This percentage suddenly went down from 3.7% in 1987 to 1.7% in 1988 and then steadily to 1.2% in 1989, 0.9% in 1990, 0.8% in 1991, 0.7% in 1992, 0.6% in 1993, and remained at 0.5% till 2000. JJA also altered the share of girls as apprehended juveniles. Up to 1987, such girls were less than 8%. It rose to 13.4% in 1988 and 31.9% in 1989 and came down to 18% in 1990. It remained around an average of 22% till 2000. Thus, notwithstanding adults and law enforcers' continued reluctance to put children into formal legal systems and socio-economic changes, the data does not speak of development of a youth subculture of violence.

Towards a Better Treatment of Children's Behaviours in the Twenty-First Century: Widening the Juvenility Net and Correcting Other Discrepancies

In 2000, the Indian parliament enacted the Juvenile Justice (Care and Protection of Children) Act 2000 (JJ-I). The Act removed the sex-discriminatory definition of child by including all children below 18 years of age within its ambit. It continued the prohibition of death sentence[38] and imprisonment as sentencing options for CCL.[39] For the serious nature of offences committed by youth, JJ-I improved upon the JJA and raised the age to 16 years from the previous 14 years for such CCL to be kept in safe custody.

A destigmatised corpus of terms like 'Juvenile in conflict with law' (JCL), 'adjudication', and 'children in need of care and protection' (CNCP) were formulated. Moreover, JJ-I "emphasised the social reintegration of children without resorting to judicial proceedings, and by adopting a child-friendly approach in the adjudication and disposition of matters in the best interest of children" (Kumar 2019, p. 121). A progressive understanding permeated the legislature, that to prevent child delinquency, the formal sanctions of state should be non-punitive in nature. It was also the result of the hard work of the child rights activists and organisations who convinced the state that CCL, irrespective of their nature of crime, are victims of the social systems and institutions and should be reformed by employing non-punitive techniques.

Two issues that remained vague in the JJ-I were the stage of the case at which the age of the accused child shall be determined and whether the serious offences under special statutes shall invite different punishment. Both of these issues were settled by the Supreme Court of India in the favour of children. The Court held that the age of the accused child shall be the age on the date of incident, and responses for serious offences under special statutes shall be non-penal and within the juvenile justice system. These were later incorporated into law through the amendment of JJ-I in 2006 (Kumar 2019). Practically, however, the poor infrastructural and personnel training support (Snehi 2004) was as big a problem as the evidence for age. Evidence of age was a problem because of widespread illiteracy and poor documentation of births. Thus, the demand of documentary evidence for birth or other proof of age by court to prevent an accused from punishment has always acted against marginalised children.

The Juvenile Justice Rules of 2001 and 2007 attempted to tackle this through a set of documents issued by local authority or the school from where the juvenile has passed Matric, that is, their tenth year, and in case of their absence, by a medical opinion of a Medical Board. Further, the continuity of prohibition of the death sentence and incarceration for CCL, irrespective of the nature of their crime, reinforced the Parliament's belief that incarcerating children with adults would impose far more social costs than their institutionalisation through reformatories. Irrespective of the nature of crime, the Indian delinquent children in the 7–18 age-group were neither to be tried by the criminal justice system nor to be incarcerated as adults.

However, this legal protection was short-lived. The gang rape and homicide of a 23-year-old girl *Nirbhaya* (name in popular discourse) in Delhi on 16 December 2012 by six persons, including a boy just short of 18 years led to a huge countrywide mass protest. It further translated into penal populism leading to the enhancement of punishment and its age-based gradation for sexual violence against women and children.[40] Such a punitive response by the state is actually an unintended product of a never-seen-before social movement and public protests cutting across sexual identity, an unprecedented democratisation of participation in policing (Shakil 2013), and feminist engagement with criminal law (Kotiswaran 2018).

As one accused in the *Nirbhaya* case was a minor, and the JJ-I prescribed only treatment-based sentences for CCL, he was sent to a correction home for three years and was released thereafter. There were some more sexual violence incidents during this period (Kumar 2019), and this culminated into a continuous public rage. Questions such as whether age should matter in serious offences, including rape, and why a juvenile should not be treated and punished as an adult in serious offences were raised (Kumari 2015).[41] The social reaction to child delinquency in such circumstances took the populist punitive form. Even the constitutionality of definition of child under JJ-I[42] and for lowering of cut-off age for defining child[43] were challenged before the Supreme Court. But the Court remained unmoved and upheld it, defending 18 years as the ACM irrespective of the nature of offence committed by the teenager (Kumar 2019). Nonetheless, under the public pressure and media panic, the state succumbed and altered its non-punitive stance towards children by the passage of the Juvenile Justice (Care and Protection of Children) Act 2015 (JJ-II).

The JJ-II and the Rebirth of Delinquent 'Adult-Children': Incarceration of 'Heinous' Child 'Offender' and Juvenile (In)justice

"Law itself may not only punish crime, but improvise it," said Marx (1859). In 2015, the Indian government, riding on the wave of penal populism and neoliberal political rationality under the façade of women's safety and security, hastily passed the JJ-II (Kapur 2013; Pande 2014; Kumari 2015, 2016). It was arguably more of an emotion-based policy-making than an evidence-based policy-making (Sait 2016), as punitive responses to CCL by their transfer to adult court and incarceration on conviction have neither reduced the juvenile crime rate nor have they prevented recidivism in other jurisdictions of the world (Feld 1993; Bishop 2000; 'For the Good of the Child, for the Good of Society: Using Scotland and Jamaica as Models to Reform U.S. Juvenile Justice Policy', 2002; Fagan 2008). It appears, then, that JJ-II is the law improvising crime by pushing children into the criminal justice system.

The JJ-II has an option to deny bail and prescribe harsher punishment in the form of imprisonment to CCL in the age-group of 16–18. In cases where a child from this age-group is alleged to commit a heinous offence(s),[44] a preliminary assessment would be carried out by the Juvenile Justice Board (JJB) to be completed within three months from the date of first production of the child before it.[45] The assessment is not a trial but is to assess the capacity of the child to commit and understand consequences of the alleged offence.[46] After the age determination, and by this assessment, the JJB would look at the child's mental and physical capacity to commit the offence, ability to understand the consequences of the offence, and circumstances in which the child allegedly committed the offence.[47] If JJB passes an order of need for trial of child as an adult, then it may order transfer of trial to Children's Court.[48]

6 The Rebirth of Delinquent 'Adult-Children': Criminal Capacity... 125

Now, the Court will do an assessment and if it also thinks that the child has to be tried as an adult as per the Code of Criminal Procedure 1973, a regular trial would take place.[49] A final order with an individual care plan for the rehabilitation of the child, including follow-up by the probation officer or the District Child Protection Unit or a social worker to evaluate the child's progress, would be passed.[50] The child found to be in conflict with law would be sent to a place of safety and will stay there until they are 21 years old.[51] Then, it would be decided by the Court if the child has undergone reformative changes while being in place of safety and can be a contributing member of the society.[52] If not, then such a child shall complete the remainder of his term in a jail.[53] The data on CCL awarded imprisonment in 2017 and 2018 clearly shows this punitive provision in action (Table 6.5). With judicial discretion at so many levels, these laws may translate into juvenile (in)justice rather than justice.

Such a recategorisation of child delinquents on the basis of age, capacity, understanding, and nature of offence goes against the international development and CRC's directions. It has reproduced delinquent 'adult-children' in a subtle way, in order to satiate the public anger. The state justified its populist punitive approach based on the myths of an exponential rise in numbers of crimes by the children of this age-group, which I have critiqued elsewhere through statistics that speak otherwise (Kumar 2019). Further, the state has also emphasised the very high percentage of CCL in the 16–18 age-group to that of total CCL to weave narratives of evil around these children. They were demonised by the state to co-opt the social movements on women and children safety and gender justice to expand its own punitive power and strengthen its sexual security apparatus (Kapur 2013). Such an expansion in the scope of carceral politics has been carried out through the modalities and language of penal populism, the rise of neoliberalism, and by implicating 'carceral' feminism (Kapur 2013; Kumar 2019).

Statistical Investigation: Locating the Apprehended Juveniles

This subsection presents statistics on the apprehended juveniles as well as CCL. There are various reasons to do so. First is to study the impact of JJ-II on the numbers of apprehended juveniles, the frequency of incidents, and the nature of charges against them, just before and after the passage of JJ-II. Second is to examine the nature of court orders for CCL. Third is to locate the apprehended juveniles through their socio-economic-educational background.

Table 6.3 Year-wise breakup of data on Juvenile Delinquency (arrest data)

Year	Total incidences of juvenile crime	Total number of juveniles apprehended	Crime rate[54]	Numbers (percentage) of juveniles in 16–18 years age-group
2013	35,861 (34,225)[55]	43,506	N/A	28,830 (66.3 %)
2014	38,565	48,230	N/A	36,138 (74.9 %)
2015	33,433	41,385	N/A	29,731 (71.8 %)
2016	35,849	44,171	8.0	32,577 (73.8 %)
2017	33,606	40,420	7.5	29,194 (72.2 %)
2018	31,591	38,256	7.1	28,867 (75.5 %)

Table 6.4 Year-wise breakup of total incidences of four 'heinous' offences under the IPC and crimes under the POCSO Act by delinquent children (arrest data)

Year	Murder	Kidnapping and abduction	Rape	Crime under POCSO Act	Dacoity
2013	845	933	1388	N/A	190
2014	841	1455	1989	N/A	182
2015	853	1630	1688	N/A	193
2016	892	1538	1903	N/A	218
2017	727	919	1614	794	155
2018	767	893	1547	1165	160

The percentage of borderline CCL has always been in a substantial majority. From 2013–2018, there is clear fluctuation, rather an exponential growth, in the number of CCL in the 16–18 age-group (Table 6.3), as well as the heinous crimes committed by them (Table 6.4).

Moreover, the rise in rape and kidnapping/abduction cases, post 2013, though fluctuating, could also be due to the passage of the Protection of Children from Sexual Offences Act 2012 (POCSO). POCSO has increased the age of consent to sexual activity from 16 to 18 years, thereby criminalising consensual sexual activity between children in the 16 to 18 years age-group. This has led to an upsurge in the reporting of rape and kidnapping/abduction cases against children mostly in the 16–18 age-group. Further, if we look at the share of juvenile crimes in total IPC crimes registered in the country between 2005 and 2015, it has varied between 1.0% and 1.2%, which is a negligible change from the range of 0.5% to 1.0% in the 1990s. The implications of JJ-II and its complex criminal process are already visible in the numbers of incarcerated children and the huge percentage of cases pending disposal in 2017 and 2018 (Table 6.5).

Further, some statistics on juvenile delinquency from the CII-2017 report are important. The report says that juveniles apprehended in the 19 Indian metropolitan cities (with a population of over 2 million) amounts to 23.9%

Table 6.5 Year-wise breakup of 'Disposal of Juveniles Arrested and Sent to Courts'[56]

| Year | Total number of juveniles apprehended[57] | Disposal of juveniles held guilty ||||||| Percentage of juveniles acquitted or otherwise disposed of[58] |
		Sent to home after advice or admonition	Released on probation and placed under the care of parents/guardians/child care institutions	Sent to special homes or fit institute	Dealt with fine	Awarded imprisonment	
2015	56,501	13.0%	19.0%	17.1%	4.6%	None	8.1%
2016	65,659	15.3%	18.2%	15.6%	3.9%	None	8.6%
2017	65,485	12.3%	3.3%	11.4%	3.6%	0.6% (422)	5.5%
2018	76,185	18.4%	6.8%	11.4%	3.1%	0.6% (482)	5%

Table 6.6 Education and family background of juveniles arrested[59]

	Education			Family background			
Year	Illiterate	Up to primary	Above primary but below Matric/H. Sec.	Matric/H. Sec. and above	Living with parents	Living with guardians	Homeless
2015	11.5%	34.4%	N/A	N/A	85.6%	N/A	3.9%
2016	12.2%	32.8%	45.3%	9.6%	86.2%	10.3%	3.5%
2017	10.7%	26.7%	43.5%	19.1%	83.4%	8.7%	8%
2018	9.4%	27.9%	44.5%	18.2%	84.8%	9.0%	6.3%

Table 6.7 Annual family income of juveniles apprehended[60]

Year	Up to ₹25,000	Between ₹25,000 and ₹50,000	Between ₹50,000 and ₹200,000	From ₹2 lakh to ₹3 lakh	Above ₹3 lakh
2013	50.2%	27.3%	20.2%	1.4%	0.6%
2014	55.6%	22.4%	19.5%	1.6%	0.9%
2015	42.4%	28.2%	25.9%	2.3%	1.1%

of the total juveniles apprehended in the entire India. Similarly, 22.6% of crimes committed by juveniles across India took place in these 19 cities only. Also, in 2017, where the all India juvenile crime rate was as low as 7.5, in metropolitan cities like Delhi and Chandigarh it was very high—52.9 and 39.8, respectively.

Another important factor to be noted here is the profile of JCLs who are at the risk of being separated from their family and have a high chance to end up behind bars. Approximately one-third to half of the apprehended juveniles do not even cross the primary level of education (Table 6.6). If such juveniles are in the 16–18 age-group and proven to commit heinous offences, alongside unfavourable judicial decisions after their time in place of safety, certainly such children would end up in the 'no-school-but-prison' pipeline. Most of them live with their families, half of which are very poor (much below the minimum wages) and most are poor (Tables 6.6 and 6.7). Even the rising percentage in the column of apprehended juveniles with Matric and above level of education in 2017–2018 (Table 6.6) could be because of the POCSO.

So, looking at Tables 6.6 and 6.7, a general understanding can be formed about the location of the apprehended child delinquents on the societal map of education, family background, and class. The connection between poverty and criminality is not only framed in terms of production of criminogenic circumstances and inevitability of indulgence in social deviance but it also produces a psychology of 'paupers ought to be criminals' in the minds of the executive and the judiciary. Such a bias may many a times not only tilt the scale of justice towards conviction for poor accused children from the very time of their arrest but may put them in the line of fire of abusive behaviour of the personnel involved at each stage of even the juvenile justice system. And after JJ-II, this sphere has extended to the criminal justice system too.

Conclusions and Recommendations: Non-punitive State Response as a Public Good

This chapter showcases the messy realities of the malleable nature of not only the penalty of child delinquency, but of child delinquency and childhood as well. I have shown how legal boundaries of childhood have been drawn and redrawn from time to time due to different socio-political-economic factors. Since the ancient times through the colonial era to the postcolonial times leading into the twenty-first century, childhood and children's behaviour have remained amorphous. Moulded by caste, gender, class, race, and religion, I have examined how the making and unmaking of children through canon law and state law define children's rights, obligations, privileges, and exclusion.

It is evident that traditional institutions like caste, extended family, and community continue to play a vital role in the Indian subcontinent in dealing with children's behaviour and keeping the state agencies away from children whose behaviour may have come in conflict with law, though perhaps at the cost of corporal punishment by parents and teachers. The profound impact of British colonialism on the Indian subcontinent in terms of experimenting with colonial institutions and punishments with the native children has also been discussed. The impact of the postcolonial neoliberal state and the waning of traditional institutions of social control on severance of support structure for children has also been discovered. Therefore, identification and revitalisation of traditional institutions in the lives of teenagers and young adults may help to attenuate youth crime (Steffensmeier et al. 2018).

This chapter has also revealed the active role played by social systems, particularly caste, gender, and race, in the marginalisation of children from certain social and political communities and their high probability of getting trapped in the state institutionalisation project and their victimisation by state violence. The adverse effects of historical injustice meted out to the members of lower castes continued to reflect in the social location of CCL even in the late twentieth-century India. The logical incompatibility of a welfare state and penal state in independent India rooted in its criminal law has also been exposed by showing how a very low MACR combined with lowering of ACM produced delinquent 'adult-children' through JJA. However, the motives behind this approach of JJA need further investigation.

I have also narrated the progressive journey of juvenile jurisprudence in India based on a reformative model at the turn of the twenty-first century, where it ratified the CRC in 1992 and enacted and amended JJ-I. However, this journey was halted and reversed by the internal pressures like public outrage, and moral and media panics the national level in the wake of the 2012 *Nirbhaya* case. The state misutilised the spectre of this case to tilt the scale of 'heinous' child delinquency from being an offspring of socio-economic marginalities and lack of understanding of gender justice to the construction of socially disgusted evils leading to the rebirth of delinquent 'adult-children'.

It may be argued that the Indian state has failed to respond to and invest in the children (and their parents and families), and various social and state institutions that shape their everyday lives, and thus their experiences and actions. Looking at the significance of sexual violence in tilting the scale of state response towards penal populism, feminists and child rights activists need to engage with criminal legal reform in a way that does not lead to expansion of the penal state and enforcement of sexual security regime. CRC calls on those involved in the operation of juvenile justice to act in accordance with the general principles of non-discrimination (including gender sensitivity), the best interests of the child, the child's right to life, survival and development, and respect for the views of the child (Van Bueren 2006).

The very low MACR of 7 years since 1860, which must be increased to 12, and the adultification of children and criminalisation of their behaviour by JJ-II, clearly violates these principles. Juvenile justice jurisprudence must operate on the philosophy of employment of non-punitive state response to prevent the child from stigma, fear, and pain of the criminal justice system in order to reintegrate the child in the society. The JJ-II has the potential of more delays, more violence, and further exclusion of children from their families and society through criminalisation and incarceration. I have presented data of child delinquents who are poor, illiterate and either without parents or with broken families, and thus are themselves victims of harm and violence. Notable also is the huge imbalance between the penal state, with all its might of police and prosecution, and a child—weak, minor, and marginalised. In such circumstances, there is too much risk for an apprehended juvenile to be proven innocent and be saved from incarceration.

Furthermore, no other law in India considers a person under age 18 as possessor of capacity to understand his or her actions. All these concerns vouch for the argument that a non-punitive state response would serve the Indian children and the Indian society as a public good. The focus of the state should be to gradually find alternatives to the carceral infrastructure and to invest in child welfare, public education, public and mental healthcare, and social housing systems, particularly for the urban poor. An abolitionist attempt should be, what Cox (2019, p. 555) suggests, to "begin with the goal of eliminating the social disgust that is aimed at the most hated among us—the people deemed to be the least reformable—the child who sexually offends, the gang member who murders, the chronic and violent child 'offender'—and envision a strategy that does not rely upon custody as a mechanism to effect change."

It is also not useful to take recourse in the argument of low child delinquency in India, for I myself have been a child in conflict with law, and there could be many like me, who either do not come under the radar of law due to certain discretion or buy their way out of this justice system. We should think, based on empiricism and anthropological studies, whether JJ-II caters to the best interests of a child. Quite paradoxically, when we have more evidence of failure of the retributive and deterrent approach in dealing with the CCL, we are moving in that direction of fooling and failing ourselves collectively as a society.

Notes

1. A stall run by ISCKON (the Hare Krishna movement) near the SOAS building in the Bloomsbury area of London that offers voluntary donation-based food to any person who wishes for it.
2. Historically, Hinduism is a pluralistic ethno-geographic category. In this chapter, it has both a religious connotation for my discussion of ancient Vedic texts, as well as the ethno-geographic connotation to invoke the Indian subcontinental social culture that transcends all religions and beliefs. See Lorenzen (1999).
3. It can generally be observed in the Indian society, across religions, that a favourable location in all the three social systems, that is, an 'upper caste-upper class-male' identity, might offer a far more potential to children to grow holistically, and navigate easily through their childhood and post-childhood lives, that too sometime with comparatively lesser efforts than those who do not fall in this 'accidentally privileged' category. As such, subject to some amount of subaltern penetration in the socio-cultural capital of the accidentally privileged, the essence of one's existence in the Indian society arguably continues to be, as Hartjen (1982: 468) says, "dictated by ascribed rather than achieved attributes."

4. Another dimension of juvenile imprisonment could possibly be the 'circumstantial incarceration' of those children whose mothers have been incarcerated and who out of biological or socio-economic necessities need to stay with their mothers who are incarcerated. Many childhoods are destroyed and lost behind those iron bars. As per the National Crime Records Bureau's report, approximately 1866 children lived in prison with their mothers at the end of 2015 in India. See http://indiatogether.org/prison-children and http://blogs.cuit.columbia.edu/rightsviews/2018/09/06/children-languishing-behind-bars-a-grim-reality-of-indian-prisons/. This chapter does not deal with this aspect.
5. It refers to the youngest age in which a person may be prosecuted for a crime, and in the case of a system with a designated juvenile court, it also refers to the minimum age of its jurisdiction (Abrams et al. 2018).
6. It refers to the age at which a person becomes subject to adult criminal charges and penalties with the full force of the law (Abrams et al. 2018).
7. There is no authoritative answer on the exact duration of each of these natures of societies but there is a consensus among Marxist historians on their temporal order. See Thapar (2002).
8. Only 0.1% of the total Indian population did not state their religion. Census Data, 2001, Religion, available at: http://censusindia.gov.in/Census_And_You/religion.aspx.
9. It is a collection of treatises on Dharma originally written in Sanskrit. It was influential in the colonial Indian history. The British made it a part of the Anglo-Hindu jurisprudence, particularly for all suits regarding Inheritance, Marriage, Caste and other religious Usages or Institutions, for all the non-Muslims (Gentoos) of the Indian subcontinent, but gradually displaced it by laws that were foreign in origin or inspiration (Rocher 1972).
10. A religio-legal text ascribed to Manu, which presents a detailed caste code and duties of different social groups, particularly the conduct of Brahmins, the polluting nature of women and devaluation of lower caste groups. It arguably came after 185 BC (Ambedkar 1948).
11. The three privileged Varnas are, namely, Brahmins, Kshatriyas, and Vaishyas (Kumar 2016). Colloquially, they are referred as the 'Savarnas', 'upper castes' or 'higher castes.'
12. The Sudras and untouchables are legally categorised as the OBCs (Other Backward Classes) and the SCs (Scheduled Castes), respectively.
13. It is a theory often associated with the utilitarian view of Asian civilizations. It visualized a system of government consisting of a despotic ruler with absolute power, said to be characteristic of Asian societies. Generally, this theory characterised empires outside Europe as autocratic and backward. See Thapar (2002).
14. S. 1, the Apprentices Act, 1850.
15. See S. 82, IPC.

6 The Rebirth of Delinquent 'Adult-Children': Criminal Capacity... 133

16. See S. 83, IPC.
17. British administrators did not use reformatories for female CCL.
18. No female was to be punished by whipping. S. 7, WA 1864.
19. The Act defined 'Youthful offender' only in terms of a 'boy'. S. 3, RSA- I.
20. S. 31, RSA- II.
21. S. 433, CrPC.
22. S. 8, WA.
23. S. 31, RSA- II.
24. Sen is silent about the implications of religion and caste on the probability of institutionalisation of native male children and the nature of their associations among themselves within the reformatories. However, he does reflect on the linkage between caste, 'intellectual capacity', profession, and social hierarchy by mentioning the operation of caste within reformatory whereby certain incarcerated young people appeared 'unsuited' for book learning and how caste acted as an erasure of punishment for certain released children from higher castes (Sen 2004).
25. The Madras Children Act 1920 defined 'youthful offender' as anyone younger than 18 guilty of an offense, Bombay Children Act 1924 defined child as under 16, and Bengal defined it as under 18 (Kumari 2015). Interestingly, these laws included non-criminal acts of juveniles too, on the line of delinquency legislation in American states and European countries, so as to give the state legal guardianship over uncontrollable, homeless, dependent, neglected, or destitute children as well (Hartjen 1995).
26. Later on, the Constitution (Sixty-first Amendment) Act, 1988, lowered the voting age of elections to the Lok Sabha and to the Legislative Assemblies of States from 21 years to 18 years.
27. During the passage of this Act in 1960, there were following Union Territories: Delhi, Andaman and Nicobar Islands, Lakshadweep, Himachal Pradesh, Manipur, Nagaland, and Tripura. The Act was extended to newly formed Union Territories of Goa and Daman and Diu in 1962, to Dadra and Nagar Haveli in 1963, and to Pondicherry in 1963.
28. This entire chapter uses the data furnished by the government agency NCRB (National Crime Records Bureau) in the form of annual reports called CII (Crime in India). The 'Juvenile Delinquency Statistics' is available from the year 1958 onwards. Sometimes it appears that the NCRB itself fails to read its previous years' reports.
29. The age categorisations recorded in the juvenile delinquency statistics in the CII reports from 1958 to 1960 was 7–12, 12–17, and 17–21 years, which became uniform from 1961 to 1987 as 7–12, 12–16, and 16–21 years.
30. The state does not maintain this data properly. There is some data available, though privately, about the age of the prisoners executed in India since independence. I could trace eight male persons whose age at the time of execution was between 18 and under 21 years. They were executed between 1947 and

1988. See State-wise List of Prisoners Executed in India Since 1947 (n.d.), Death Penalty Research Project, National Law University, Delhi. I would like to thank Anup Surendranath for sharing this list with me.
31. The data on incarceration of juveniles and on the socio-economic background of the juveniles apprehended is available from the year 1971 onwards.
32. Crimes under the IPC have been divided into cognisable and non-cognisable. "Cognizable offence" means an offence for which, and "cognizable case" means a case in which, a police officer may, in accordance with the First Schedule or under any other law for the time being in force, arrest without warrant. S. 2(c), the Code of Criminal Procedure 1973.
33. Madhya Pradesh also contributed significantly despite the fact that it cannot be categorised as an industrialised state. But, as it has a big population of Scheduled Tribes, I can speculate that it became a prominent contributor because a large number of tribal children might have been apprehended.
34. To see this phenomenon in popular culture, see the Bollywood movie *Singham* (2011).
35. Section 27(2), JJA.
36. Section 22(1), JJA.
37. Proviso, section 22(1), JJA.
38. However, there is a report from 2016 that offers data through interviews of death row prisoners and their families. It says that out of 310 prisoners on the death row and whose age information was available, 18 and 54 prisoners claimed to have been below 18 years (juveniles) and between 18 and 21 years (young adults) of age, respectively, at the time of the incident. An analysis of the decisions sentencing the 18 juveniles shows that the claim of juvenility was not addressed in the trial court decisions in 12 cases. In the remaining six decisions where arguments on juvenility were raised, the trial court summarily dismissed those claims without even ordering a further investigation. See Chapter 4, Socio-Economic Profile, Vol. 1, Death Penalty Report (2016). I would like to thank Anup Surendranath for sharing this report with me.
39. Section 16, JJ-I.
40. Sections 376 AB and 376 DB have been inserted in the Indian Penal Code through the Criminal Law (Amendment) Act 2018 prescribing *death* as one of the sentencing options for rape and gang rape, respectively, on children under 12 years of age. Also, section 6(1) has been inserted in the Protection of Children from Sexual Offences (POCSO) Act 2012 through the POCSO (Amendment) Act 2019 prescribing *death* as one of the sentencing options for aggravated penetrative sexual assault against a child.
41. To see this phenomenon in popular culture, see the Bollywood movie Mardaani 2 (2019).
42. *Salil Bali v. Union of India* (2013) 7 SCC 705.
43. *Subramanian Swami v. Raju through the Juvenile Justice Board* (2013) 10 SCC 465.

44. It includes the offences for which the minimum punishment under the Indian Penal Code or any other law for the time being in force is imprisonment for seven years or more. See section 2(33), the JJ-II. There are 20 offences under the IPC 1860 and 26 offences under Special & Local Laws that can be categorised as 'heinous offences' under the JJ-II.
45. S. 15 and S. 14(3), JJ-II.
46. Explanation, S. 15(1), JJ-II.
47. S. 15(1), JJ-II.
48. S. 18(3), JJ-II.
49. S. 19(1)(i), JJ-II.
50. S. 19(2), JJ-II.
51. S. 19(3), JJ-II.
52. S. 20(1), JJ-II.
53. S. 20(2)(ii), JJ-II.
54. Crime rate is calculated as crime per one lakh of population.
55. The numbers in brackets are from CII report 2015, which do not match with those mentioned in CII reports 2013 and 2014. It appears that the NCRB did not read its own reports from the previous years.
56. The CII reports from 2016 onwards use this phrase. See Table 5A.5 of the CII 2016, 2017, and 2018. The CII report 2015 has used the phrase, "Final Order of Apprehended Children in Conflict with Law during 2015," and also mentions that all the apprehended juveniles were produced before various 'juvenile boards' rather than being sent to courts. See Chapter 10, Juveniles in Conflict with Law, CII 2015.
57. This includes the number of juveniles whose cases were pending disposal at the beginning of the year and the juveniles apprehended during the year.
58. The percentage left after the addition of the guilty and acquittal percentages is the percentage of the cases pending disposal. So, for the years 2015, 2016, 2017, and 2018, percentages of cases pending disposal were 38.2%, 38.4%, 63.3%, and 54.7%, respectively.
59. See Chapter 10, Juveniles in Conflict with Law, CII 2015 and Table 5A.6 of the CII 2016, 2017, and 2018.
60. This data is not available from the year 2016 onwards in the respective CII reports.

References

Abrams, L. S., et al. (2018). What is a juvenile? A cross-national comparison of youth justice systems. *Youth Justice, 18*(2), 111–130.

Aktor, M. (2017). Social classes (varṇa). In P. Olivelle & D. Davis (Eds.), *The Oxford history of Hinduism: Hindu law: A new history of Dharmaśāstra*. New York: Oxford University Press.

Ambedkar, B. R. (1948). *The untouchables: Who were they and why they became untouchables?* New Delhi: Amrit Book Co.
Apprentices Act 1850.
Banerjee, S. (2005). Indian jails: Turned upside down. *Economic and Political Weekly, 40*(50), 5226–5228.
Beteille, A. (1974). *Studies in Agrarian social structure*. Delhi: Oxford University Press.
Bishop, D. M. (2000). Juvenile offenders in the adult criminal justice system. *Crime and Justice, 27*, 81–167. https://doi.org/10.1086/652199.
Bombay Children Act 1924.
Children Act 1960.
Code of Criminal Procedure 1861.
Code of Criminal Procedure 1973.
Constitution (Sixty-first Amendment) Act 1988.
Cox, A. (2019). Challenging the logics of reformism and humanism in juvenile justice rhetoric. *Critical Criminology, 27*(4), 543–558. https://doi.org/10.1007/s10612-019-09474-4.
Criminal Law (Amendment) Act 2018.
Davis, D. R., Jr. (2017). Children. In P. Olivelle & D. R. Davis Jr. (Eds.), *The Oxford History of Hinduism: Hindu Law: A New History of Dharmaśāstra*. New York: Oxford University Press.
Death Penalty Report. (2016). Vol. 1, National Law University, Delhi.
Emsley, C. (2005). *Crime and Society in England, 1750–1900*. Great Britain: Pearson Education Limited.
Fagan, J. (2008). Juvenile crime and criminal justice: Resolving border disputes. *The Future of Children, 18*(2), 81–118. https://doi.org/10.1353/foc.0.0014.
Feld, B. C. (1993). Criminalizing the American juvenile court. *Crime and Justice, 17*, 197–280. https://doi.org/10.1086/449214.
For the good of the child, for the good of society: Using Scotland and Jamaica as models to reform U.S. Juvenile Justice Policy. (2002). *Harvard Law Review, 115*(7), 1964–1987.
Galanter, M. (1968). The displacement of traditional law in modern India. *Journal of Social Issues, 24*, 65–91.
Galanter, M. (1978). Indian law as an Indigenous conceptual system. *Social Science Research Council, 32*, 42–46.
Ghose, S. (2003). The dalit in India. *Social Research, 70*(1), 83–109.
Gittins, D. (2008). The historical construction of childhood. In M. J. Kehily (Ed.), *Introduction to childhood studies*. McGraw-Hill Education.
Hartjen, C. A. (1982). Delinquency, development, and social integration in India. *Social Problems, 29*(5), 464–473.
Hartjen, C. A. (1995). Legal change and juvenile justice in India. *International Criminal Justice Review, 5*, 1–16. https://doi.org/10.3366/ajicl.2011.0005.
Indian Penal Code 1860.
Juvenile Justice (Care and Protection of Children) Act 2000.

Juvenile Justice (Care and Protection of Children) Act 2015.
Juvenile Justice Act 1986.
Kakar, S. (2012). *The inner world: A psychoanalytical study of childhood and society in India*. Oxford University Press.
Kapur, R. (2013). Gender, sovereignty and the rise of sexual security regime in international law and postcolonial India. *Melbourne Journal of International Law, 14*, 317–345. https://doi.org/10.3366/ajicl.2011.0005.
Karnam, M. (2009). Deaths in prisons in Andhra Pradesh. *Economic and Political Weekly, 44*(11), 19–23.
Kethineni, S., & Klosky, T. (2005). Juvenile justice and due process rights of children in India and the United States. *International Criminal Justice Review, 15*(2), 131–146.
Kotiswaran, P. (2018). Governance feminism in the postcolony: Reforming India's rape laws. In J. Halley et al. (Eds.), *Governance feminism: An introduction*. University of Minnesota Press.
Kumar, V. (2016). Caste, contemporaneity and assertion. *Economic & Political Weekly, 51*(50), 84–86.
Kumar, S. (2019). Shifting epistemology of juvenile justice in India. *Contexto Internacional, 41*(1), 113–140. https://doi.org/10.1590/s0102-8529.2019410100006.
Kumar, S. (2021). Thinking beyond penal reform in India: Questioning the logic of Colonial punishments. In M. J. Coyle & D. Scott (Eds.), *The Routledge international handbook of penal abolitionism*. Oxon and New York: Routledge.
Kumari, V. (2004). *The juvenile justice system in India: From welfare to rights*. New Delhi: Oxford University Press.
Kumari, V. (2015). Juvenile justice in India. In F. E. Zimring, M. Langer, & D. S. Tanenhaus (Eds.), *Juvenile justice in global perspective* (pp. 145–197). New York University Press.
Kumari, V. (2016). The Juvenile Justice Act 2015: Critical understanding. *Journal of the Indian Law Institute, 58*(1), 83–103. Retrieved from http://cara.nic.in/PDF/JJ%20act%202015.pdf.
Lorenzen, D. N. (1999). Who invented Hinduism? *Comparative Studies in Society and History, 41*(4), 630–659. https://doi.org/10.1017/S0010417599003084.
Madras Children Act 1920.
Magarey, S. (1978). The invention of juvenile delinquency in early nineteenth-century England. *Labour History, 34*, 11–27.
Marx, K. (1859). *Population, crime, and pauperism, Marx and Engels collected works*. Retrieved from http://marxengels.public-archive.net/en/ME1167en.html#N368.
Mathur, S. (2005). Torture, empire and nation. *Economic and Political Weekly, 40*(10), 993–995.
McClure, A. (2020). Archaic Sovereignty and Colonial Law: The reintroduction of corporal punishment in Colonial India, 1864–1909. *Modern Asian Studies, 54*(5), 1712–1747.

Murali, K. (2006). Institutional apathy towards undertrial prisoners. *Economic and Political Weekly, 41*(37), 3936–3938.

Nilsen, A. G. (2018). India's turn to rights-based legislation (2004–2014): A critical review of the literature. *Social Change, 48*(4), 653–665. https://doi.org/10.1177/0049085718800861.

Pande, B. B. (2014). In the name of Delhi gang rape: The proposed tough juvenile justice law reform initiative. *Journal of National Law University, Delhi, 2*, 145–166. https://doi.org/10.3366/ajicl.2011.0005.

Protection of Children from Sexual Offences (Amendment) Act 2019.

Protection of Children from Sexual Offences (POCSO) Act 2012.

Reformatory Schools Act 1876.

Reformatory Schools Act 1897.

Rocher, L. (1972). Indian response to Anglo-Hindu law. *Journal of the American Oriental Society, 92*(3), 419–424.

Rocher, L. (2012). *Studies in Hindu Law and Dharmaśāstra*. Ed. D. R. Davis Jr. London and New York: Anthem Press.

Sait, N. A. (2016). *Juvenile Justice Act 2015; An emotional aftermath of the dreaded 'Nirbhaya Incident'; A step backward, live law*. Retrieved December 23, 2017, from http://www.livelaw.in/juvenile-justice-act-2015-emotional-aftermath-dreaded-nirbhaya-incident-step-backward/.

Sen, S. (2004). A separate punishment: Juvenile offenders in Colonial India. *The Journal of Asian Studies, 63*(1), 81–104. https://doi.org/10.1017/S0021911804000075.

Sen, S. (2005). *Colonial Childhoods: The Juvenile Periphery of India, 1850–1945*. London: Anthem Press.

Shakil, A. (2013). Protests, the justice Verma committee and the government ordinance. *Economic & Political Weekly, 48*(06).

Singha, R. (1998). *A Despotism of Law: Crime and Justice in Early Colonial India*. Delhi: Oxford University Press.

Skuy, D. (1998). Macaulay and the Indian Penal Code of 1862: The myth of the inherent superiority and modernity of the English legal system compared to India's legal system in the nineteenth century. *Modern Asian Studies, 32*(3), 513–557.

Snehi, Y. (2004). State and child justice: Stories of delinquent juveniles. *Economic and Political Weekly, 39*(41), 4512–4515.

State-wise List of Prisoners Executed in India Since 1947. (n.d.). *Death penalty research project*. Delhi: National Law University.

Steffensmeier, D., Lu, Y., & Kumar, S. (2018). Age–crime relation in India: Similarity or divergence vs. hirschi/gottfredson inverted J-shaped projection? *British Journal of Criminology, 59*(1), 144–165. https://doi.org/10.1093/bjc/azy011.

Thapar, R. (2002). *The Penguin History of Early India: From the Origins to AD 1300*. London: Penguin Books.

Van Bueren, G. (2006). *A commentary on the United Nations convention on the rights of the child (Article 40: Child criminal justice)*. Leiden and Boston: Martinus Nijhoff Publishers.

Verma, A. (1997). Book review: Comparative delinquency: India and the United States. *Criminal Justice Review*. https://doi.org/10.1177/073998638700092005.

Whipping Act 1864.

7

Juvenile Deprivation of Liberty in Brazil: Discretion, Expansion and Deterioration

Rafael Barreto Souza

Introduction

Juvenile detention is not systematically studied, and worldwide statistics are seldom available due to the lack of accurate record keeping and the wide array of institutions that are used to deprive children of liberty. Hence, it is extremely challenging to know how many children and adolescents are deprived of liberty in the world (Human Rights Watch 2016). A decade ago, UNICEF broadly estimated that around one million children were held in detention globally. It was only in the early 2010s that the United Nations addressed this information gap and conducted a Global Study on Children Deprived of Liberty.

The research team published in June 2019 a summary report presenting estimates varying from 160,000 to 250,000 children in remand centers and detention facilities worldwide on any given day. This means that the Brazilian youth detention system represents from 10.3% to 16.2% of all adolescents around the globe who are deprived of liberty. This number is staggeringly high considering that the Brazilian population corresponds to just 2.7% of the world's population (Worldometers n.d.).

The detained youth population in Brazil has risen 510% over just 20 years, from 4245 young people in 1996 to 25,929 in 2016.[1] This rate is higher than the growth rate of adult incarceration in Brazil—approximately 350% in the same period—which has the third highest gross prison population globally,

R. Barreto Souza (✉)
University of Brasilia (LabGEPEN/UnB), Brasília, Brazil

only behind the US and China (World Prison Brief 2019). They are both part of the same phenomenon, connected by the similarities in criminal law enforcement dynamics, though separate in terms of legal standards and institutions.

Contrary to the trend in many Western countries' criminal justice such as the US, ideologies in Brazil have not been shifting away from law-and-order approaches (Cox 2018). Though the Brazilian law emphasizes family-based interventions and community inclusion, practice does not. Media and public opinion have been growing amenable to tough approaches on adolescent offenders and the political scene has adjusted accordingly. The federal legislature is currently debating a controversial constitutional amendment to lower the age of criminal majority from 18 to 16 years old, at the same time that bills are also under consideration to establish longer detention and harsher treatment for youth. The literature has characterized these developments as part of a *moral panic* surrounding youth crime (Budó and Cappi 2018).

Based in this paradigm, this chapter aims to provide an overview of the juvenile justice system in Brazil in order to understand the potential and challenges of the Brazilian system. The study adopted a descriptive methodology, seeking to analyze existing legal theories to justify and refute the approaches to justice in the Brazilian juvenile system and its legal and practical consequences. It also analyzes data published over the last 11 years by the federal government (2006 to 2016) and uses it to examine growth and decline among three measures of deprivation of liberty: pre-trial detention, post-trial detention and semi-liberty.[2]

This chapter is divided in two main sections. First, the legal framework is discussed depicting the 1990 Statute of the Child and Adolescent and the Law of National System of Socio-Educational Assistance (SINASE, Portuguese acronym) passed in 2012, with an analytical focus on the discretionary powers within the juvenile justice system. Second, the chapter delves into federal data on socio-education detention.

Legal Framework

Statute of the Child and Adolescent (ECA)

In 1990, Brazil was the first country in Latin America to incorporate the Convention on the Rights of the Child into its national legislation. The Statute of the Child and Adolescent (ECA, Portuguese acronym) has been internationally acclaimed as one of the most progressive laws in the world on the matter, providing broad protections to children and becoming a model for other countries in the region (Canineu 2017). This was spearheaded by the progressive movement that drafted the 1988 Constitution after a 40-year period of military dictatorship responsible for thousands of deaths and enforced disappearances and suppression of human rights. The Constitution was the first-ever to inscribe an article on children with strong protective principles.

ECA quashed the former Minors Code, reformed the Childhood and Youth Courts, created a number of civil society-based councils and monitoring institutions, as well as inaugurated a paradigm shift on the Brazilian view on how to understand and deal with children's rights. Children became subjects of rights with integral protections, grounded on family-based interventions, instead of subordinated persons under the *irregular situation doctrine*, an institution-based intervention system (Maciel and Carneiro 2013, p. 53). Moreover, ECA laid out a systemic approach to child policies, setting the groundwork for structured care agencies, directing child-specific funds to be run by mixed civil society/government councils and demanding "absolute priority" to fulfilling children's and adolescents' rights (art. 4).

One of the highlights of this reform was the abolition of the institutionalization model centered on the State Foundation for the Welfare of Minors (FEBEM, Portuguese acronym). FEBEM reformatories held all sorts of children and adolescents that were considered to in a so-called *irregular situation*—what the research literature has characterized as the "needy and delinquent" (Maciel and Carneiro 2013). There was no differentiation in facilities between adolescents who committed criminal offenses and those in need of care due to abandonment, neglect or abuse. The 1990 Statute broke off this logic, by advocating for family and community living as central to any intervention and separate institutions for vulnerable children in foster care homes, and, on the other hand, adolescents in conflict with the law, based on non-custodial measures and exceptional use of detention.

ECA also gave a stronger role to the Judiciary, especially to the Childhood and Youth Courts. They became the only competent decision-maker in all children's matters and were granted largely discretionary powers in deciding over adolescent criminal charges. These specialized courts emerged late in Brazil compared to the US. The first juvenile court was founded in Chicago in 1899, and, by 1925, 48 US states had juvenile courts. In contrast, the first Brazilian specialized court was established in 1927 in the then capital Rio de Janeiro (Liazos 1974, p. 4; Zanella and Lara 2015).

The new law drew a clear line based on age for different legal subsystems. For all legal purposes, the concept of *child* applies to anyone 11 years old or younger, including newborns and infants. *Adolescent*, on the other hand, is someone who is aged from 12 to 17 years old. ECA created two subsystems when it concerns criminal offenses and penalties. Regarding trouble with the law, children (0 to 11 years old) hold no criminal responsibility, whereas adolescents do.[3] However, criminal responsibility at the age of 12 is very low vis-à-vis international standards and recommendations that suggest a minimum age at 14 years old (United Nations 2019, para. 109).

It is important to stress, however, that criminal responsibility for adolescents is dealt with through a different system than adults, who are treated in a penal system based on penitentiaries and a retributive rationale. For adolescents, the ECA created the *socio-education system* which attempts to provide a combination of care and punishment through a pedagogical rationale.

Discretionary Socio-educational Measures

Though the ECA ended prosecution for status offenses for adolescents, which were the norm under the repealed Minors Code, it kept a long leash for judicial discretion on how to sentence adolescents. Legal proceedings are embedded with discretion at every stage. Police officials, upon arresting an adolescent for any wrongful act, are required to bring him or her before a police chief.[4] This authority is then obligated to process the case, establish the charges under criminal legislation and keep the adolescent in temporary detention. In the next 24 hours, ECA dictates that the adolescent, along with police records, be brought before a prosecutor for an *informal hearing*. The law also asserts that "if possible, his/her parents or guardian, victim and witnesses"[5] should be present to the hearing. There is no mention of a lawyer though. Following this hearing, the prosecutor can either close the police report, grant remission (pardon), or press charges before court.

Filing a case in court inaugurates a proceeding in which a lawyer finally has to be present, due process safeguards are considered and written petitions registered. Sentencing is similarly discretionary, resulting in either acquittal or conviction. In case of conviction, a judge can apply six socio-educational measures[6] or none of them, as remission is always an option to judges at any stage of the proceedings. Emphasis should be placed on the word *can*. Prosecutors and judges *can* chose to give remission or press charges in any case, for any criminal offense (Machado 2006, p. 112). Ideally, such discretion should be applied in benefit of the accused adolescent, based on the exceptionality principle for the use of punitive prerogatives by the state. For instance, if a youth is accused of a violent or serious crime, it is possible to pardon or charge him/her by asking for softer penalties and non-custodial measures. Yet that rarely happens. Discretion has contributed to a disproportionate use of the deprivation of liberty and subsequent overcrowding and human rights violations within units.

The system sets flexibility for prosecutors and judges, which is arguably worsened by non-mandatory legal assistance by lawyers or public defenders in pre-judicial stages. This allows for the selectivity of state punitive powers through wide problems in police work that include racial profiling, biases in stop and frisk operations toward marginalized youths and other mechanisms for discrimination (MNPCT 2018).

Contemporaneous legislation in other countries went in a different direction. The 1989 New Zealand Children Young Persons and Their Families Act, for example, set up warnings and formal police cautions to be carried out by police authorities as a diversion strategy and an alternative to prosecution. There is also a mandatory procedure to consult with a Youth Justice Coordinator before instituting proceedings against an adolescent, as well as the necessity of family group conferences carried out based on restorative justice principles and practices, aiming at reaching an agreement (New Zealand 1989). The Brazilian Statute has no provisions of this kind. The first legal mention of restorative justice came in 2012.

Restorative justice initiatives have grown significantly in Brazil in the last few years. The 2019 research from the National Justice Council indicated that 25 out of the 31 Brazilian courts—state and federal—reported hosting some kind of program or project that implements restorative practices and that 75% of all the practices were carried out by Childhood and Youth Courts. Despite this growth, restorative justice is still small in scale and limited in scope. Only 20% of courts surveyed had personnel dedicated exclusively to restorative justice, thus most initiatives have been based on volunteering, isolated and on-and-off ventures (CNJ 2019a). Notwithstanding, strengthening restorative justice may have positive impacts in curbing discretion, increasing the sense of justice among victims and reducing detention of adolescents.

The two custodial measures in ECA—semi-liberty and detention—deserve a closer analysis. Detention is the harshest penalty under the law for adolescents. It requires segregation in closed facilities with a substantial security component for 24 hours a day, 7 days a week. Schooling, sports and counseling are undertaken within the walls of the facility. Contacts with the outside world are allowed only through family visitation and scarce outside activities. Semi-liberty, however, is a lighter form of deprivation of liberty, conceived as an alternative to detention or as part of the process of existing on a detention unit (Martins and Peixoto 2010). It allows for external activities, such as school and professional training attendance, regardless of judicial authorization. Enrollment in school and professionalization programs should be primarily in outside community institutions, according to the law. Family contact happens mostly in the adolescent's house, usually during weekends. Still it restricts liberty substantially and segregates adolescents from their household and family for most of the time, and it can result in re-incarceration in the case of not abiding by semi-liberty rules.

Detention, the toughest measure, is the only socio-educational measure subject to legal limitations to discretion, which is inscribed in ECA's art. 121:

> Art. 122. The internment measure can only be applied when:
> I—it is a criminal offense committed through serious threat or violence to the person;
> II—there is reiteration of other serious offenses;
> III—there is repeated and unjustifiable non-compliance with a measure previously imposed.

"Serious threat or violence to the person" is the key criterion for the maximum method of deprivation of liberty. It includes crimes such as robbery, rape and homicide. It does not include other offenses like drug trafficking and possession of a firearm, which are not violent acts against persons. Most adolescents are detained due to this provision (CNJ 2019b, p. 31).

Under the second and third clauses of art. 121, these offenses may nonetheless result in detention if it is a case of a reoffending adolescent that has committed "serious offenses". The seriousness of the offense is subject to the judge's discretion. This second clause has also been the basis for a significant number of adolescents being detained. This second clause of detention is executed after conviction and is not timebound. Judges do not sentence adolescents for a specific amount of time to be served in socio-educational units; they are deprived of liberty *for an indeterminate period of time*. Detention can last a month, six months, a year, two years, up until the maximum of three years established in ECA or until they turn age 21. The third clause in art. 121 is known in the literature as *sanction-internment*, since it emanates as a penalty for not abiding by conditions of a previous socio-educational measure, whether semi-liberty or a non-custodial one. Sanction-internment is restricted to a maximum of 90 days.

Lastly, detention is also possible as a post-arrest measure operating as a form of pre-trial detention, for a maximum of 45 days. It is important to highlight that ECA allowed pre-trial detention as the only precautionary measure available for youths, with application limited to extremely serious and necessary situations, in light of the presumption of innocence. Indeterminate detention raises a number of questions on the legal nature of socio-educational measures. Teixeira and Da Costa (2006) place them precisely: What is the purpose of socio-educational measures? To punish or to educate? Or would it be both? If so, how is it possible to guarantee the prevalence of the pedagogical objectives while avoiding the logic of the adult penal system? If their nature is penal, how can criminal defendants' constitutional safeguards be assured for youths?

SINASE Law: Deterred Discretion

The balance between discretion and due process protections has been on the agenda of legal practitioners and academia since ECA's inception, yet little consensus has been reached. In 2012, federal Law 12.594 established the National System of Socio-Educational Assistance (SINASE)—spearheading a systemic approach for inter-sectorial policies and integration between government agencies (education, health, etc.) and the justice system. The SINASE Law regulates the implementation of socio-educational measures after a judge's sentence and sets out standards for articulating the purposes of these measures, which are applicable. These standards set the responsibility of the adolescent for the harmful consequences of the criminal offense, whenever possible encouraging its reparation; social integration of the adolescent and the guarantee of his/her individual and social rights; disapproval of the criminal conduct, making effective the provisions of the sentence as a maximum standard of deprivation of liberty, observed the limits in law.

Additionally, the SINASE Law pins down several principles in its art. 35: minimum intervention, exceptionality of judicial intervention and the imposition of socio-educational measures. These principles favor restorative justice and, whenever possible, meeting the needs of victims; proportionality in relation to the offense committed; the brevity of the measure; and the principle that an adolescent cannot receive more serious treatment than that granted to an adult.

Procedurally, the 2012 law strengthened rules regarding the violation of non-custodial measures and semi-liberty conditions. Before ruling on detention, for example, courts must hold a revocation hearing with defense lawyers. It also instituted a six-month due date to reevaluate every socio-educational measure by Childhood and Youth Courts, as a periodic review to be based on a psychosocial report on the adolescent's progress. Moreover, the new legislation prohibited the sentencing of an adolescent in a more severe measure (e.g.

detention) solely considering "the seriousness of the infraction, the priors and the duration of the measure" (art. 42, §2°). In other words, the pedagogical aspects are expected to be the main compass in judicial decision-making after sentencing, as opposed to the offence *per se* and personal criminal records.

However, the reform brought about with the SINASE Law built up criminal law-based safeguards, on the one hand, while reinforcing the role of psychosocial expertise in determining the State's right to punish, on the other. Shecaira (2014) asserts that procedures created by this criminal subsystem must obey the fundamental rights and procedural guarantees and the right to a fair trial. This has not happened; Brazil was late in adopting guarantees that were settled in 1967 by the US Supreme Court on the *Gault* case, for example, upholding that the primary due process clause of the 14th Amendment also applies to adolescent defendants (US Supreme Court 1967).

Before 2012, children's rights experts and advocates denounced serious problems with the absence of regulations regarding the execution of socio-educational measures. Complaints involved loose definitions on the degree of restriction of freedom allowed, non-specification of disciplinary infractions and administrative penalties, as well as a vacuum over the indeterminate period of socio-educational measures proceedings (Machado 2006). After the SINASE Law entered into force, these issues were supposed to have been solved.

However, the law on paper differs from the law in practice. The Brazilian National Preventive Mechanism against Torture (NPM)[7] has systematically reported the lack of internal procedural regulations in detention units, causing severe "legal insecurity, since there are no disciplinary rules foreseen, demonstrating the complete illegality that reigns in detention units" (MNPCT 2018, p. 97). Disciplinary sanctions are imposed without express and prior legal provisions and without a guarantee of basic rights, such as due process and access to legal defense. Since there seldom are disciplinary commissions, which handle cases of disciplinary infractions in units by youths—such as insulting employees, possessing drugs and rioting—the procedure and application of sanctions are carried out by the guards instead of facility directors and psychosocial staff.

Despite setbacks in implementation, the SINASE Law addressed several of these issues and seriously curbed *de jure* judicial discretionary powers. Still, these powers were not extinguished. They were transferred, to a large extent, to psychologists, social workers and teachers working in detention and semi-liberty units, known as making up the *psychosocial teams*.

Psychosocial teams are in charge of formulating an individual assistance plan (PIA, Portuguese acronym) for each adolescent, engaging in its formulation process both the adolescent and his or her family. According to the law,

7 Juvenile Deprivation of Liberty in Brazil: Discretion, Expansion...

these plans must include, inter alia, an interdisciplinary evaluation, with the objectives and goals chosen by the adolescent, an indication of social integration and professional training activities and forms of family participation. Every PIA has to be written up within 45 days.

First, the 45-day deadline implicitly ensures that no one in pre-trial detention will have a plan of his or her own, since the precautionary measure of pre-trial detention itself is up to 45 days, and this is too short of a deadline to get the plan completed. Psychosocial teams mostly cannot—and are not required to—formulate PIA plans for pre-trial detained youths, which undermines the care/assistance component of any pre-trial detention.

For those who are in post-sentence detention, PIAs can be an important instrument for drafting life plans and future paths, fostering new abilities and useful outside-world skills, if they are adequately devised and followed up. However, this is rarely the case, as independent monitors and NGOs have continuously reported (MNPCT 2016, 2019; Fórum DCA-CE 2017).

There are no national standardized guidelines for PIA formulation. Every socio-education state agency is its own experimental laboratory for the development of PIAs, with worrisome results. The Brazilian NPM reports that PIAs are often non-existent or bluntly flawed in practically all units inspected in over 20 states. Psychosocial teams are understaffed, overworked, negligent or sometimes complicit with torture and ill-treatment. Through NPM monitoring, PIAs have been characterized in Roraima state as "an example of merely filling out a form with basic information, only to comply with a legal requirement" (MNPCT 2018, pp. 88–89). In Mato Grosso state, the unit monitored did not prepare PIAs for any of the adolescents detained. In a female socio-educational unit in Natal, "it was not possible to identify the participation of the adolescents themselves and their families in the elaboration of PIAs" (MNPCT 2018, pp. 88–89). In the state of Tocantins, the NPM assessed the psychosocial team as having "very conservative models of family structures, with cases where the fact of a separation between father and mother of the adolescent implies a record of *unstructured family*" (MNPCT 2018, pp. 88–89).

As mentioned, PIAs have become a source of power for psychosocial technical teams. SINASE Law sets out that judges' evaluation of socio-educational measures "will depend on the Individual Assistance Plan (PIA), instrument of foresight, registry and management of the activities to be developed by the adolescent" (art. 52). Hence, PIAs are now a cornerstone of the socio-education system, pinning down subjective evaluation criteria and often issuing recommendations on whether youths should remain incarcerated or eventually recede to a harsher regime (e.g. detention) at every six-month judicial review. All this is carried out by professionals with an ethical duty to "base their work in respecting and promoting *freedom, dignity, equality* and the integrity of the human being" (CFP 2005). So why do they do it?

In a world of indeterminate detention, imprecise information, long confinement periods, precarious schooling and lack of activities, the report from the psychosocial team is all adolescents dream of, think and ask about, together with their court reevaluation date. This affliction has been documented in several academic studies and also by NGOs and independent monitors, such as the Brazilian NPM. They also highlight how in many states, the ratio between the number of adolescents and the number of psychosocial staff is below standards, leading to infrequent counseling, fewer activities, as well as heightened distress among those detained (Costa 2015; Fórum DCA-CE 2017; MNPCT 2018). The power of *the report* is huge. It creates a realm of symbolic power, as understood by Bourdieu (1999), with grave repercussions on freedom and detention of youths.

Technical knowledge in the fields of psychology, social work or teaching constitutes a set of power relations, as there is not "any knowledge that does not presuppose and constitute at the same time power relations" (Foucault 1995, p. 27). In the context of deprivation of liberty, particularly among adolescents, knowledge-based power becomes all the more apparent. As young persons in a human development stage, they are particularly exposed to narratives constructed around pedagogical purposes, the benefits of strict discipline and social control. Hence, in Brazilian socio-educational units, psychosocial knowledge expands systems of administration and social control, defining youths and producing realities of compliance or non-compliance based on PIA goals defined by the subjects themselves. It is indeed puzzling how one can subsidize punishment—i.e. the continuance of the deprivation of liberty—based on the punished's self-designed plan of individual assistance (Sarup 1993; Gečienė 2002).

Perceptions of the risks that young people present are heightened vis-à-vis historical moral preconceptions and danger-based perspectives in Brazilian culture, which psychosocial teams are also privy to. These are often governed by conservative notions of family, labor and housing. *Favelas*,[8] non-nuclear families and informal jobs tend to be perceived as inadequate and hotbeds of criminal activity, particularly by adolescents. Coupled with the criminalization of young people by race and class, these features are common to most, if not all, youths deprived of liberty.

As Batista (2003, pp. 118; 84) stresses in an analysis on drug charges against adolescents, "to the youngster from middle classes who consumes it, it is applied the medical stereotype. To the poor youngster who trades it, the criminal stereotype". Similarly, Cox (2018), in a study on the US juvenile system, concluded that the punitive philosophy is applied to impoverished and 'risky' youth who are considered ungovernable (therefore in need of court intervention), unworthy and individually responsible—moral categories that lead to the criminalization of poverty.

Lastly, Teixeira and Da Costa (2006, p. 478) raise a fundamental question: is it possible to solve the mysterious enigma of combining such contradictory ingredients (discipline and affection, assistance and control, punishment and education)? On every invocation of the idea of the 'pedagogical proposal of the socio-educational measure', the idea remains veiled as one of the main unfulfilled promises of the ECA law.

All of these dilemmas have implications for the detention data of adolescents in the last decade, when ECA has been put in practice and more recently when the SINASE Law passed. The discretion in the law has correlated to increased incarceration and overcrowding.

Deprivation of Liberty: Data Analysis

The federal government of Brazil collects and publishes official data yearly, under the auspices of the Ministry of Women, Family and Human Rights. Data collection is performed through a questionnaire-based survey applied to state government agencies that run socio-educational units. The survey inquires how many adolescents are detained in a *snapshot* date—namely late November—and not an annual average, or daily/monthly statistics. Hence, seasonal fluctuations during the year or within that particular month are not captured in the data.

Despite methodological setbacks, the data proves to be useful. The number of adolescents detained in socio-education facilities grew by 57% from 2006 to 2015 (SDH/PR 2010, 2011, 2014, 2015, 2017, 2018; MDS and SDH/PR 2012; MDH 2018). If before ECA came into force, more than 80% of children and adolescents were not deprived of liberty due to criminal charges, today that is no longer the case (Machado 2006, p. 114). The trend has reversed (Fig. 7.1).

Looking at this graph, it is noticeable that detention rates have mostly risen during this period. There are more than 10,000 youths incarcerated now than there were 11 years ago. The system has expanded profoundly. But it has not happened uniformly. There have been variations according to the different detention measures—pre-trial detention, detention and semi-liberty.

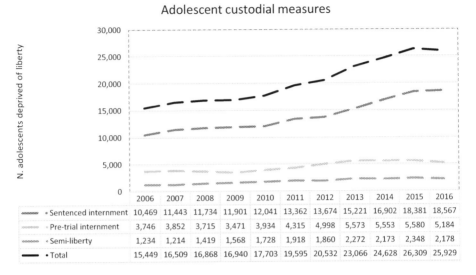

Fig. 7.1 Growth rate of detention measures

Detention and Pre-trial Detention

Pre-trial detention rates grew and shrank on and off during the period of 2006 to 2016, which resulted in a 38.4% increase in pre-trial youth detainees in Brazil over 11 years. Through the time span, pre-trial detention rates actually fell proportionally as a share of overall deprivation of liberty, going from a 35.8% share in 2006 to 28% in 2016. Pre-trial detention has then receded nearly eight percentage points, indicating an important reduction in its uses by judges as compared to other measures (Table 7.1).

In a year-to-year growth rate analysis, 2015 to 2016 saw the sharpest drop in the period, at 7.1% in pre-trial detention. However yearly growth variation reached a peak of 15.8% in 2012 and a bottom decline of 7.1% in 2016. Thus, the last year's falling rate cannot yet be perceived as part of a continuous process, rather as an unstable variation.

Pre-trial detention then grew nearly half of overall detention in the period—38.4% compared to 67.8%. That may indicate that it has been less adopted than other measures, and there are a few hypotheses to explain the phenomenon.

Considering due process, the data may indicate a stronger consideration of the exceptionality principle in post-arrest decisions by judges. And on the pedagogical perspective, the less pre-trial detention the better, bearing in mind that pre-trial adolescents do not even have a PIA to orientate schooling,

7 Juvenile Deprivation of Liberty in Brazil: Discretion, Expansion...

Table 7.1 Growth rate per measure

	Detention	Growth (%)	Pre-trial detention	Growth (%)	Semi-liberty	Growth (%)	Total	Growth (%)
2006	10,469		3746		1234		15,449	
2007	11,443	9.30	3852	2.83	1214	−1.62	16,509	6.86
2008	11,734	2.54	3715	−3.56	1419	16.89	16,868	2.17
2009	11,901	1.42	3471	−6.57	1568	10.50	16,940	0.43
2010	12,041	1.18	3934	13.34	1728	10.20	17,703	4.51
2011	13,362	10.97	4315	9.68	1918	11.00	19,595	10.69
2012	13,674	2.33	4998	15.83	1860	−3.02	20,532	4.78
2013	15,221	11.31	5573	11.50	2272	22.15	23,066	12.34
2014	16,902	11.04	5553	−0.36	2173	−4.36	24,628	6.77
2015	18,381	8.75	5580	0.49	2348	8.05	26,309	6.83
2016	18,567	1.01	5184	−7.10	2178	−7.24	25,922	−1.47
Average	13,972	5.99	4538	−66.65	1810	6.25	20,320	5.39
Growth in period		77.35		38.39		76.50		67.79

counseling and other activities. This can also be correlated to an expanding judicial implementation of deterred discretion sparked by the SINASE Law. Another hypothesis is that this reduced use of pre-trial detention may have resulted from local task force initiatives to review cases pending trial in some states (DPE/RS 2016; TJES 2016; Nascimento 2019).

On the other hand, this reduction can also be associated with the legal limits *per se*, which dictate that pre-trial detention cannot surpass the maximum of 45 days—fewer days detained would lead to fewer youths detained. It may also be credited to speeder pre-trial procedures, as it can be the case in some states that have instituted integrated post-arrest socio-educational centers, known by the accronym NAI (*núcleo de atendimento inicial*) (GDF 2019; Prefeitura de São Carlos 2019; SEJUSP-MG 2019). These faster proceedings however do not necessarily result in non-custodial measures after trial. Rather, they can result in speedier trials determining post-sentence detention, which can cut down pre-trial detention in the data while stepping up post-sentence detention correspondingly.

In any case, it is hard to attribute these variations to a particular policy, legal reform or caselaw modification in High Courts as their direct cause. There are several localized events in different states that could provide reasons for these variations in combination with national policies. All measures can have timebound effects and not necessarily reflect structural change. Further research is needed.

Unlike the decline in pre-trial detention, post-sentencing detention increased unimpeded every year, despite some fluctuation in rates. In the end, there was a 77.3% increase in post-sentencing incarceration over 11 years. Considering total numbers, the only drop displayed since data started being collected happened between 2015 and 2016: a 1.5% decline (MDH 2018, p. 6). Again, this small reduction cannot yet be perceived as a trend in adolescent de-incarceration.

Several factors may be associated with this continuous increase. First, as mentioned, it may indicate that efforts to reduce pre-trial detention may have speeded up convictions culminating in higher post-trial detention rates during the whole period. Another possibility is that the entry into force of SINASE Law in 2012 slowly shifted discretion toward psychosocial teams leading to late releases of adolescents, as teams have been poorly staffed and inadequately trained, and progress reports could have been filed late and often comprising punitive analysis, recommendations and rationale.

The data seems to show a judicial preference toward post-trial detention throughout the time span. The preference is further demonstrated by the deficient adoption of semi-liberty, the less-onerous custodial measure also applicable for violent criminal offenses and for early release from detention.

Semi-liberty

Semi-liberty growth and decline were similarly intermittent, but altogether represented a 76.5% growth rate from 2006 to 2016. It grew consistently from 2008 to 2011 (16.8% to 11%), then had a swift drop and then a large hike of 22.15% in 2013, followed by new ups and downs. Youths subject to semi-liberty detention grew irregularly year after year and then faced a significant fall in 2016, corresponding to a 7.2% reduction. As opposed to the unobstructed growth in detention, semi-liberty did not face the same preference among judges.

Proportionally, semi-liberty showed a slightly increased participation in overall detention numbers, from 8% in 2016 to 8.4% in 2016. This can almost be seeing as negative, since semi-liberty is a lighter form of detention which should by law be adopted preferably to detention, and in 11 years it has not had a substitution effect over the harshest regime of detention.

Semi-liberty spiked in 2013 (9.8%) but then dropped more than one percentage point. Its proportional representation in socio-education detention measures is characterized by ups and downs as seen in the graph below, never reaching two-digit percentage points (Fig. 7.2).

If overcrowding and institution closures characterized detention units in the period, the opposite has happened to semi-liberty. Semi-liberty units are

7 Juvenile Deprivation of Liberty in Brazil: Discretion, Expansion... 155

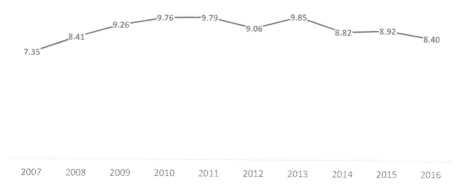

Fig. 7.2 Semi-liberty share of custodial measures

seldom fully occupied in the country. While responsible for around 13% of available beds in the system, semi-liberty on average represented 8.8% of all youths detained in Brazil. In 2013, the occupancy rate for semi-liberty was merely 67.3%. In 2014, it even fell a little to 67%. All the while, detention overcrowding soared. Often states with the highest overcrowding rates present the lowest semi-liberty occupancy rates—for example, Mato Grosso do Sul state in 2014 had 365.5% rate of detention occupancy against 27.5% in semi-liberty, and Ceará state had 243.4% occupancy in detention and 69% in semi-liberty facilities.

Moreover, there is a lack of use of semi-liberty as an alternative to detention when ruling in criminal cases. This scenario is particularly worrisome considering the Brazilian discretion-based system which should prioritize non-custodial measures.

As presented in Table 7.2, criminal typology in official federal data is even more alarming in presenting evidence of detention overuse. Analyzing four years—2013 to 2016—criminal offenses that objectively fall within the "serious threat or violence to the person" standard represented on average 61% of all youths detained. That means that approximately 39% of adolescents detained were at least a priori eligible to milder non-custodial measures or semi-liberty.

The data points to semi-liberty being severely underused when there is a lot of legal leeway to use it. This can be associated with judges, prosecutors and lawyers not knowing or fully understanding what semi-liberty is and what is

Table 7.2 Criminal offenses by adolescents subject to custodial measures (%)

Offense	2013 (%)	2014 (%)	2015 (%)	2016 (%)	Average (%)
Robbery	42.03	44.41	46.00	47.00	
Homicide	9.23	9.47	10.00	10.00	
Attempted homicide	3.12	3.46	3.00	3.00	
Death ensuing robbery	2.03	2.13	2.00	3.00	
Rape	1.20	1.28	1.00	1.00	
Violent offenses	*57.61*	*60.75*	*62.00*	*64.00*	*61.09*
Drug charge	24.81	24.24	24.00	22.00	
Possession of firearm	2.39	1.88	2.00	2.00	
Theft	3.58	3.30	3.00	3.00	
Other	11.61	9.83	9.00	9.00	
Non-violent offenses	*42.39*	*39.25*	*38.00*	*36.00*	*38.91*

its role, but it can also be related to punitivism and retributionism. Anything less the detention can often be perceived as a "soft on crime" approach, something unpopular in Brazilian sentiment nowadays.

Overcrowding

Parallel to increased detention and semi-liberty, overcrowding in custodial units skyrocketed during the same period. The National Prosecution Council (CNMP, Portuguese acronym)—the federal regulatory body for all prosecutors—in a 2014 study calculated that out of 434 socio-educational detention facilities throughout the 27 states, 317 were detention facilities (73%) with a capacity of 18,072 (87%) and 117 were semi-liberty units (27%) with a capacity of 2739 (13%) (CNMP 2015). From 2013 to 2014, the maximum capacity of detention units (both pre-trial and sentenced) was reduced in 14 out of the 27 Brazilian states, that is, the number of available beds was cut short. In Piauí state, for example, the number available of accommodations for youths was reduced by 55% over this time period. However, neither in these states nor in Brazil as whole the occupancy rates dropped, hence the reduction of detention beds culminated in an even higher overcrowding rate, which reached 121% in 2014 (CNMP 2015).

Reduction in capacity can be related with two main factors: changes in architectural regulations and improvement in monitoring to socio-educational units by independent bodies. Physical infrastructure reform in socio-educational units traces back to 2006. This was when the National Council on the Rights of the Child and Adolescent (CONANDA, Portuguese acronym) approved Resolution n. 119, a 100-page guideline publication on everything from government institutional setting to architectural design standards for detention and semi-liberty facilities. Among these guidelines, the Resolution established as standards a maximum of 40 beds for detention units and 20 beds for semi-liberty. These guidelines gained traction with the 2008 Inter-American Court of Human Rights ruling on detention of adolescents in FEBEM Tatuapé Complex, in São Paulo state (Teixeira and Da Costa 2006, p. 434).

In 2010, the federal government did a survey on all 27 states and found that only 8% of all units had been built before ECA (1990), 92% of units built after the ECA, of which 15% were built after the SINASE Resolution (2006) (SDH/PR 2010). In 2015, the Inter-American Commission on Human Rights ordered Brazil to adopt several measures to reduce overcrowding in the state of Ceará (IACHR 2015) and Espírito Santo (Nitahara 2014). Nonetheless, according to a 2014 survey, more than 63% of detention units still did not comply with the 40-bed standard for detention and 22.2% were not in accordance with the standard of 20 beds in semi-liberty (CNMP 2015, pp. 30–37).

On the other hand, state-specialized Prosecutorial bodies and Public Defender Offices from all over the country began a legal battle for halting overcrowding by banning newly detained adolescents from being admitted into overcrowded detention units and, in some cases, determining that precarious units be closed all together. There have been hundreds of lawsuits that resulted in limited occupancy of certain units and closure of others (PR 2014; CE 2015; GO 2015; Melo 2017). This enhanced conditions in a few detention units while worsened overcrowding in many others. This helps explain the drop in capacity and worsened conditions through the system as a whole.

This scenario may change after the Supreme Court ruled in 2018 on the limitation of occupancy not for a specific detention unit but for an entire state-level system, thus imposing effective occupancy standards to curtail overcrowding—in 2019 the ruling had affected five states (RBS TV 2019). Thus state governments and courts have been ordered to control the influx of adolescents based on the exact number of beds. Perhaps this will shed light on underused semi-liberty and non-custodial measures as alternatives to detention.

Concluding Remarks

Police profiling and rigid processing rules, coupled with high levels of judicial discretionary powers, have led to the expansion of youth in detention in Brazil over the last three decades. Expansion, paired with reduction in capacity, produced overcrowding, which then led to the aggravated deterioration of detention conditions. These worsened conditions feature greater confinement time, raised internal conflicts, torture, ill-treatment and more frequently than ever: deaths. In 2015 alone, 53 adolescents died inside the socio-educational units, a number higher than the previous year—48 deaths (MDH 2018; MNPCT 2018).

In November 2017, a group of armed men broke into a semi-liberty unit in Ceará state, subdued guards, shot and killed four adolescents held in the facility. Investigations remain open, and it is suspected that it was a gang-related account setting (O Lagoa 2017). In May 2018, in a detention unit in the state of Goiás, a riot was set off protesting a decision to transfer an adolescent to a different unit. A mattress was burnt; guards sat back and watched as dormitories were set in flames and took a long time before getting fire extinguishers. Ten adolescents were burned to death (Pires 2019). Reports of adolescents dying in detention are varied throughout the country, some due to lax security, others due to flat-out negligence and active violence.

Release from youth detention has been somewhat affected by SINASE reform, gently diverting discretion from judges to psychosocial teams and individual plans. Despite being too early to draw conclusions on how this reform will play out, there remains considerable cultural and political barriers hindering the de-incarceration of adolescents.

However, modest changes in incarceration trends, such as a drop in overall detention rates, a bit more robust adoption of semi-liberty measures and a sharp decrease in pre-trial detention are indications of positive change. Also, a new Supreme Court ruling on limited occupancy may produce positive results on overcrowding. This however must come together with strong incentives for adequate, accessible and high-quality diversion and non-custodial solutions at all stages, particularly restorative justice (United Nations 2019, paras 107–113). Curbing youth detention in Brazil is a systemic problem to which only an actual paradigm shift can address.

Notes

1. For the purposes of this chapter the term "detention" will be used as a synonym for "deprivation of liberty", which under Brazilian Law is composed of three circumstances: pre-trial internment, internment and semi-liberty; typology discussed in this chapter.
2. In this article, "detention" is used as the English translation for the term "*internação*", which is the most restrictive form of deprivation of liberty under Brazilian law.

3. The author will use the terminology of criminal *responsibility* instead of *liability* or others because it would entail detailed translating efforts to communicate the exact same meaning. This discussion, though important, is beyond the domain of this chapter.
4. The author has translated the police authority called *delegado de polícia* as *police chief*. The Brazilian police is divided in two main forces: Military Police (responsible for street-level policing) and Civil Police (in charge of crime investigation and processing the prisoners' arrests by the Military Police). The *delegado de polícia* is part of the Civil Police and heads police stations.
5. Article 179, ECA (1990).
6. The socio-education system is based on individual responsibility laid out through six socio-educational measures: (1) warning; (2) obligation to repair the damage; (3) provision of services to the community; (4) assisted freedom; (5) semi-liberty and (6) internment. The latter two are custodial measures that amount to deprivation of liberty under the law.
7. The NPM is an independent government body internationally mandated under the Optional Protocol to the Convention against Torture and Other Cruel, Inhuman or Degrading Treatment or Punishment (OPCAT) to carry out visit to places of deprivation of liberty. Since its creation in 2015, the NPM has worked closely on internment units.
8. *Favela* is what slum-like dwellings are commonly referred to in Brazil.

References

Batista, V. M. (2003). *Difíceis Ganhos Fáceis. Drogas e Juventude Pobre no Rio de Janeiro*. Edição: 2ª. Rio de Janeiro: Revan

Bourdieu, P. (1999). *Language and symbolic power*. Reprint edition (J. Thompson, Ed.; G. Raymond & M. Adamson, Trans.). Cambridge: Harvard University Press

Budó, M. de N., & Cappi, R. (2018). *Punir os Jovens? A centralidade do castigo nos discursos midiáticos e parlamentares sobre o ato infracional*. Belo Horizonte: Letramento. Retrieved August 24, 2019, from https://www.academia.edu/37234757/Punir_os_Jovens_A_centralidade_do_castigo_nos_discursos_midi%C3%A1ticos_e_parlamentares_sobre_o_ato_infracional.

Canineu, M. L. (2017). Brazil: Reject trying children as adults. *Human Rights Watch*. Retrieved September 3, 2019, from https://www.hrw.org/news/2017/09/26/brazil-reject-trying-children-adults-0.

CE, D. G. (2015). *Justiça determina interdição de três centros para adolescentes infratores, Ceará*. Retrieved December 15, 2019, from http://g1.globo.com/ceara/noticia/2015/05/justica-determina-interdicao-de-tres-centros-para-adolescentes-infratores.html.

CFP, C. F. de P. (2005). *Código de Ética Profissional do Psicólogo*. Brasília: Conselho Federal de Psicologia, p. 20. Retrieved from https://site.cfp.org.br/wp-content/uploads/2012/07/codigo-de-etica-psicologia.pdf.

CNJ, C. N. de J. (2019a). *Mapeamento dos Programas de Justiça Restaurativa*. Brasília: Conselho Nacional de Justiça, p. 51. Retrieved from https://www.cnj.jus.br/wp-content/uploads/conteudo/arquivo/2019/06/8e6cf55c06c5593974bfb880 3a8697f3.pdf.

CNJ, C. N. de J. (2019b). *Reentradas e reinterações infracionais: um olhar sobre os sistemas socioeducativo e prisional brasileiros*. Brasília: Conselho Nacional de Justiça, p. 64. Retrieved from https://www.cnj.jus.br/wp-content/uploads/2020/03/Panorama-das-Reentradas-no-Sistema-Socioeducativo.pdf.

CNMP, C. N. do M. P. (2015). *Relatório da Infância e Juventude—Resolução nº 67/2011: Um olhar mais atento às unidades de internação e semiliberdade para adolescentes*. Brasília: CNMP. Retrieved October 9, 2016, from http://www.cnmp.mp.br/portal/images/Um_Olhar_mais_Atento_09.06_WEB.pdf.

Costa, D. L. P. C. de O. (2015). As adolescentes e a medida socioeducativa de internação : rompendo o silêncio. https://doi.org/10.26512/2015.03.D.18108.

Cox, A. (2018). *Trapped in a vice: The consequences of confinement for young people*. None Edition. New Brunswick, Camden: Rutgers University Press.

DPE/RS, D. P. do E. do R. G. do S. (2016). *CASE Novo Hamburgo recebeu mutirão da Defensoria Pública, Defensoria Pública do Estado do Rio Grande do Sul*. Retrieved September 1, 2019, from http://www.defensoria.rs.def.br/case-novo-hamburgo-recebeu-mutirao-da-defensoria-publica.

Fórum DCA-CE, F. P. das Ong. de D. dos D. de C. e A. (2017). *4º Relatório de Monitoramento do Sistema Socioeducativo do Ceará Meio Fechado, Meio Aberto e Sistema de Justiça Juvenil*. Fortaleza: Fórum DCA-CE. Retrieved from http://cedecaceara.hospedagemdesites.ws/site/wp-content/uploads/2018/12/4-Monitoramento-SSE-final.pdf.

Foucault, M. (1995). *Discipline & punish: The birth of the prison* (A. Sheridan, Trans.). New York: Vintage Books

GDF, G. do D. F. (2019). NAI. Retrieved December 15, 2019, from http://www.crianca.df.gov.br/nai/.

Gečienė, I. (2002). The notion of power in the theories of Bourdieu, Foucault and Baudrillard. *Sociologija. Mintis ir veiksmas, 10*, 116–124. https://doi.org/10.15388/SocMintVei.2002.2.6171.

GO, P. R. G. (2015). *Justiça determina a interdição de parte de centro de internação em GO, Goiás*. Retrieved December 15, 2019, from http://g1.globo.com/goias/noticia/2015/09/justica-determina-interdicao-de-parte-de-centro-de-internacao-em-go.html.

Human Rights Watch, 34th Floor | New. (2016). *World report 2016: Rights trends in children behind bars*. New York: Human Rights Watch. Retrieved August 25, 2019, from https://www.hrw.org/world-report/2016/children-behind-bars.

IACHR, I.-A. C. on H. R. (2015). *PM 60/15—Adolescents deprived of freedom in facilities of juvenile detention reform for men in the state of Ceará, Brasil*. Retrieved from http://www.oas.org/es/cidh/decisiones/pdf/2015/MC60-15-PT.pdf.

Liazos, A. (1974). Class oppression: The functions of juvenile justice. *Insurgent Sociologist, 5*(1), 2–24. https://doi.org/10.1177/089692057400500101.

Machado, M. d. T. (2006). Sistema especial de proteção da liberdade do adolescente na Constituição Brasileira de 1988 e no Estado da Criança e do Adolescente. In *Justiça, adolescente e ato infracional: socioeducação e responsabilização* (pp. 87–121). São Paulo: ILANUD.

Maciel, K. R. F. L. A., & Carneiro, R. M. X. G. (2013). *Curso de Direito da Criança e do Adolescente: Aspectos Teóricos e Práticos* (6th ed.). São Paulo: SARAIVA EDITORA.

Martins, D. T., & Peixoto, R. B. (2010). *Semiliberdade: Cadernos de Socioeducação*. Curitiba: Secretaria de Estado da Criança e da Juventude.

MDH, M. d. D. H. (2018). *Levantamento Anual SINASE 2016* (p. 26). Brasília: Ministério dos Direitos Humanos—MDH.

MDS, M. do D. S. e C. à F. and SDH/PR, S. E. de D. H. da P. da R. (2012). *Atendimento Socioeducativo ao Adolescente em Conflito com a Lei—Levantamento Nacional 2011*. Brasília: Ministério do Desenvolvimento Social e Combate à Fome e Secretaria Especial de Direitos Humanos. Retrieved May 17, 2015, from http://www.sdh.gov.br/assuntos/criancas-e-adolescentes/pdf/SinaseLevantamento2011.pdf.

Melo, Q. (2017). *Justiça alega irregularidades e determina interdição temporária e afastamento de diretora de Cento Socioeducativo em Feijó, G1*. Retrieved December 15, 2019, from https://g1.globo.com/ac/acre/noticia/justica-alega-irregularidades-e-determina-interdicao-temporaria-e-afastamento-de-diretora-de-cento-socioeducativo-em-feijo.ghtml.

MNPCT, M. N. de P. e C. à T. (2016). *Relatório de visita a unidades de privação de liberdade do Mato Grosso do Sul*. Brasília: MNPCT. Retrieved from http://www.sdh.gov.br/sobre/participacao-social/sistema-nacional-de-prevencao-e-combate-a-tortura-snpct/mecanismo/file.2016-11-01.7083488762.

MNPCT, M. N. de P. e C. à T. (2018). *Relatório Anual 2017*. Brasília: MNPCT. Retrieved from https://www.mdh.gov.br/informacao-ao-cidadao/participacao-social/mecanismo-nacional-de-prevencao-e-combate-a-tortura-mnpct/relatorios-1/RelatrioAnual20172018.pdf.

MNPCT, M. N. de P. e C. à T. (2019). *Relatório de visita a unidades de privação de liberdade do Estado de Goiás*. Brasília: MNPCT. Retrieved from http://www.mdh.gov.br/sobre/participacao-social/sistema-nacional-de-prevencao-e-combate-a-tortura-snpct/mecanismo/relatorio-de-visita-tocantins/.

Nascimento, I. C. (2019, July 31). Equilíbrio no número de vagas e população do sistema socioeducativo. *TV Jornal*. Retrieved September 1, 2019, from https://tvjornal.ne10.uol.com.br/por-dentro-com-cardinot/2019/07/31/equilibrio-no-numero-de-vagas-e-populacao-do-sistema-socioeducativo-%C2%A0-173767.

New Zealand. (1989). *Children, Young Persons, and Their Families Act 1989 No 24*. Retrieved August 31, 2019, from http://www.legislation.govt.nz/act/public/1989/0024/65.0/DLM147088.html.

Nitahara, A. (2014, September 30). OEA condena tortura a menores no Espírito Santo. *EBC*. Retrieved September 1, 2019, from http://www.ebc.com.br/cidadania/2014/09/oea-condena-tortura-a-socioeducandos-no-espirito-santo.

O Lagoa. (2017, November 15). Polícia prende envolvido na morte de internos de Centro de Semiliberdade. *O Lagoa—Notícias sobre Fortaleza, Ceará, Brasil e Mundo*. Retrieved April 26, 2020, from https://olagoa.com.br/policia-prende-envolvido-na-morte-de-internos-de-centro-de-semiliberdade/.

Pires, F. B., Toni. (2019). *Goiás reconhece responsabilidade na morte de 10 menores carbonizados, EL PAÍS*. Retrieved April 26, 2020, from https://brasil.elpais.com/brasil/2019/06/17/politica/1560808150_918606.html.

PR, D. G. (2014). *Justiça determina fechamento de unidade socioeducativa de Cascavel, Oeste e Sudoeste*. Retrieved December 15, 2019, from http://g1.globo.com/pr/oeste-sudoeste/noticia/2014/09/justica-determina-fechamento-de-da-unidade-socioeducativa-de-cascavel.html.

Prefeitura de São Carlos. (2019). *NAI*. Retrieved December 15, 2019, from http://www.saocarlos.sp.gov.br/index.php/prefeitura/utilidade-publica/nucleo-de-atendimento-integrado-nai.html.

RBS TV. (2019, June 13). Quase 200 menores infratores podem ser liberados no RS se STF decidir por habeas corpus coletivo. *G1*. Retrieved December 15, 2019, from https://g1.globo.com/rs/rio-grande-do-sul/noticia/2019/06/13/quase-200-menores-infratores-podem-ser-liberados-no-rs-se-stf-decidir-por-habeas-corpus-coletivo.ghtml.

Sarup, M. (1993). *An Introductory Guide to Post-Structuralism and Postmodernism* (2nd ed.). Athens: University of Georgia Press.

SDH/PR, S. E. de D. H. (2010). *Levantamento Nacional do Atendimento Socioeducativo ao Adolescente em Conflito com a Lei—2009* (p. 13). Brasília: Secretaria de Direitos Humanos da Presidência da República.

SDH/PR, S. E. de D. H. da P. da R. (2011). *Levantamento Anual Oficial: Atendimento Socioeducativo ao Adolescente em Conflito com a Lei—2010*. Brasília: Secretaria Especial de Direitos Humanos da Presidência da República.

SDH/PR, S. E. de D. H. da P. da R. (2014). *Levantamento Anual dos/as Adolescente em Cumprimento de Medida Socioeducativa—2012*. Brasília: Secretaria Especial de Direitos Humanos da Presidência da República.

SDH/PR, S. E. de D. H. da P. da R. (2015). *Levantamento Anual SINASE 2013: Privação e restrição de liberdade*. Brasília: Secretaria Especial de Direitos Humanos da Presidência da República.

SDH/PR, S. E. de D. H. da P. da R. (2017). *Levantamento Anual SINASE 2014*. Brasília: Secretaria Especial de Direitos Humanos da Presidência da República.

SDH/PR, S. E. de D. H. da P. da R. (2018). *Levantamento Anual SINASE 2015*. Brasília: Secretaria Especial de Direitos Humanos da Presidência da República.

SEJUSP-MG, S. de E. de J. e S. P. (2019). *CIA-BH*. Retrieved December 15, 2019, from http://www.seguranca.mg.gov.br/socioeducativo/cia-bh.

Shecaira, S. S. (2014). *Sistema de Garantias e o Direito Penal Juvenil*. Edição: 2ª. São Paulo: Revista dos Tribunais.

Teixeira, M. d. L. T., & Da Costa, A. C. G. (2006). Sócio-educação. In ILANUD, I. L. A. das N. U. para P. do D. e T. do D (Ed.), *Justiça, adolescente e ato infracional: socioeducação e responsabilização* (pp. 427–468). San José de Costa Rica: ILANUD.

TJES, T. de J. do E. S. (2016, November 29). Seminário que marca os dois anos de implantação do Ciase em Vitória terá a participação do presidente do TJES. Retrieved September 1, 2019, from http://www.tjes.jus.br/seminario-que-marca-os-dois-anos-de-implantacao-do-ciase-em-vitoria-tera-a-participacao-do-presidente-do-tjes/.

United Nations, G. A. (2019). *Report on the global study on children deprived of liberty*. A/74/136. New York: United Nations. Retrieved from https://undocs.org/A/74/136.

US Supreme Court. (1967). *In re Gault, 387 U.S. 1, Justia Law*. Retrieved August 25, 2019, from https://supreme.justia.com/cases/federal/us/387/1/.

World Prison Brief. (2019). *Highest to lowest—Prison population total*. https://prisonstudies.org/highest-to-lowest/prison-population-total.

Worldometers. (n.d.). *Brazil population (2019)—Worldometers*. Retrieved August 25, 2019, from https://www.worldometers.info/world-population/brazil-population/.

Zanella, M. N., & Lara, A. M. d. B. (2015). O Código de Menores de 1927, o direito penal do menor e os congressos internacionais: o nascimento da justiça juvenil. *Angelus Novus*, 105–128.

8

"I Wanna Be Somebody by the Time I Turn 25": Narratives of Pathways into Crime and Reentry Expectations Among Young Men in Germany and the United States

Michaela Soyer and Janina L. Selzer

Introduction

In this chapter we compare the narratives of young men in Pennsylvania and Baden-Württemberg, Germany, about their pathways into crime and their expectations for their future. We explore how the young men's perspectives reflect the different structural conditions and cultural assumptions of both countries. Our analysis relies on interviews with thirty incarcerated young men in Pennsylvania who were adjudicated as adults for crimes they committed when they were still under the age of majority (i.e., under age eighteen in the United States and under the age of twenty in Germany).[1] The German sample consists of seventeen male respondents who participated in interviews over the course of three years in and Baden-Württemberg's only youth prison, the *Justiz Vollzugsanstalt* (JVA) Adelsheim. Using an exploratory comparative approach we show the different ways social institutions impact how young men at the margins of society narrativize their past and imagine their future. Building on prior comparative work (Abrams et al. 2018; Hart 2015; Hazel 2008), this chapter engages with an alternative, less punitive penal regime and accounts for the growing political desire to understand youth justice models on a global scale.

M. Soyer • J. L. Selzer (✉)
The City University of New York, New York, NY, USA
e-mail: jselzer@gradcenter.cuny.edu

Structural Differences Between the United States and Germany

Comparing the United States to Germany, the size of both countries may be the most obvious difference that comes to mind. With a population of 83 million people, Germany has about 1/4th of the population of the United States. While it takes about seven hours to drive from the Southern German city of Munich to the northern city of Hamburg, a trip by car from NYC to LA is at least a forty-one-hour undertaking.

The differences in social and cultural dynamics of both countries go far beyond the apparent demographic and geographic distinctions. During the second half of the twentieth century, Germany and the United States have evolved in different directions as their governments managed punishment, citizenship, education, and the welfare state. The following overview of the structural conditions and cultural contingencies in countries is not meant to be exhaustive and focuses on the justice and educational systems.

Criminal and Juvenile Justice Context

Journalists who have visited German prisons consider Germany a model for humane punishment and successful rehabilitation akin to the Nordic systems (cf. Turner and Travis 2015). In 2015, Germany incarcerated 76.2 people per 100,000 inhabitants (Aebi et al. 2017). Incarceration rates in the United States have hovered around 600 people per 100,000 inhabitants over the last few years (Carson 2020). In Germany a prisoner sentenced to life imprisonment will not complete the entire life sentence; they will likely leave prison after fifteen years. The age of criminal responsibility is fourteen—which is on the higher end compared to other Western European nations (Hazel 2008), and the juvenile justice system may be applicable to youths as old as twenty years of age if a judge deems that his or her cognitive maturation is delayed.

This rehabilitation-focused penal regime in Germany developed in opposition to the atrocities of the Third Reich. In 1949, when Germany received its new constitution, Allied Forces, particularly the United States, ensured the creation of a political structure that prevented a reoccurrence of an inhumane dictatorship. The German Basic Law introduced the concept of inviolable human dignity that has to be protected by all state authority. The German criminal justice system is therefore bound to protect the "human dignity" of its imprisoned people—a much stronger mandate than the protection from cruel and unusual punishment the US constitution provides (Whitman 2003).

While the Southern German justice system seems to be a safe haven for rehabilitation and treatment in the justice system, it is not without problems. The influx of refugees from Syria has given rise to an anti-immigrant political rhetoric. The so-called *Alternative für Deutschland* (AfD), a party explicitly running on a law and order, anti-immigrant platform, has been elected by a large margin to the state parliament in Baden-Württemberg.[2] As the legacy of the atrocities committed during the Third Reich recede into the background, demands for harsher punishments, especially for immigrants and their children, have become more socially acceptable (Walter 2003). Similar to policies in the United States, the political demands for harsher punishments have coincided with a steady decline in crime rates in Germany (Höynck and Ernst 2014).

The first juvenile court in the United States was founded in 1899 in Cook County, IL. A little less than one hundred years after its establishment, state governments began to undermine the separation between the juvenile and adult court systems. Within the framework of so-called transfer laws, cases involving children accused of serious crimes could be moved from the juvenile to the adult court system. Such a transfer enabled the imposition of long sentences regardless of the defendant's age.

The Pennsylvania legislature introduced Act 33 into the judicial code in 1995. This amendment allowed for an automatic transfer of juveniles fifteen or older who have committed certain felonies. Additionally, teenagers who have committed a felony may be transferred to the adult criminal justice system if the judge finds that sending the defendant to criminal court is in the public interest. This may also be the case for repeat offenders who have failed to respond to prior interventions within the juvenile justice system.

Educational Context

The educational systems in the United States and Germany are structured very differently and impact opportunities young people have once they are released from prison. Germany has a long tradition of a dual educational system that offers less academically inclined youth the opportunity to receive formal training in trade (i.e., as a mechanic, hairdresser, or plumber). In several southern German states decisions about a child's future are made in fourth grade, when students aged nine or ten are sent to either vocational or high schools. Though it is possible to switch between tracks, it is very rare that students move from the vocational school system into the high school system (Bernhard 2017).

To enter a German university, students have to pass the *Abitur*, a degree that is roughly equivalent to the American high school diploma or the British A-levels. According to data collected by the German ministry of education (Bundesministerium für Bildung und Forschung 2019), 40.1 percent of the 2018 cohort finished their education with an Abitur. Those who come from immigrant families, as about 70 percent of the young men held at the JVA located in Adelsheim, one of the field sites for this research, do, are less likely to achieve this educational milestone than children of native German families, who are growing up under more affluent circumstances (Maaz et al. 2010).

Germany also lacks easily accessible alternative pathways—such as the GED (high school equivalency diploma) in the United States—to obtaining a high school diploma (Bernhard 2017). While those who did not finish high school have many opportunities to find gainful employment, their earning potential and upward mobility are nevertheless curtailed (Aybek 2008).

In the United States, African-American and Latinx students are more likely to attend underfunded schools in high crime neighborhoods with low graduation rates (Shedd 2015). German students who do not finish the Abitur may be able to enter apprenticeship programs that offer viable perspectives for stable employment. Individuals who do not complete high school in the United States are more likely to be unemployed than high school graduates. If they find work, they tend to get paid lower salaries than those who finished their high school diploma (McCaul et al. 1992). American workers who were twenty-five years old in 2016 and had not earned a high school diploma earned a median wage of $25,400. In comparison, workers of the same age group who had finished high school earned a median wage of $32,800 (McFarland et al. 2018).

The relationship between diminished earnings and young people's decisions to leave high school before graduating is particularly relevant for the formerly incarcerated. Forty percent of people incarcerated in American state prisons have neither a high school diploma nor a GED (Harlow 2003). The lack of a formal education in combination with the stigma of a criminal record reduces employment opportunities after release, especially for African-American men (Western 2018; Pager 2003).

Almost paradoxically, while someone who has been recently released from prison may struggle to find gainful employment, his or her opportunities to obtain a four-year college degree are better than for a young person in Germany who has been tracked into vocational training. Obtaining a GED offers a clear path to community college and eventually a four-year degree. While the community college pathway to a college degree may be shaped by resource scarcity and longer pathways to graduation, community colleges open doors to higher education especially for economically disadvantaged students of color (Goldrick-Rab 2010).

Methodology and Field Sites

Data collection proceeded differently at both field sites given the specificity of each criminal justice system. The young men in Pennsylvania faced long prison sentences, while the young men in Germany were released within the time frame of this study. As a result, Soyer was able to interview seven of the German respondents again after their release. Depending on their release date, the community interviews in Germany took place between six months to a year after the young men had left prison.

At the Pennsylvania field site, Soyer interviewed thirty young men aged between eighteen and twenty-one over the course of three months between April and June 2014. All respondents were incarcerated at the State Correctional Institution (SCI) Pine Grove in Central Pennsylvania.[3] They were housed in a unit that is specifically designed for young men who are adjudicated for crimes they committed before they had turned eighteen.[4] In 2014, approximately 300 young people were held there. According to the Pennsylvania Juvenile Act, adults remain incarcerated at Pine Grove until they are twenty-two. If they have not finished their sentences by then, they are relocated to adult prisons across the state for the remainder of their time.[5] Soyer recruited participants through an internal communication system that sent a digital call for participation to those people who had a TV in their cell. Thirty people aged between eighteen and twenty-one agreed to be interviewed and Soyer met with all but one participant three times over the course of three months.[6] A majority of the respondents from Pennsylvania grew up in abject poverty and experienced a high level of childhood trauma. Housing instability, hunger, parental drug use, and being exposed to violence in their home as well as in their neighborhood were an integral part of the young men's upbringing (Soyer 2018).

The second field site for this project is the JVA located in Adelsheim, a small town in Baden-Württemberg, Germany. In 2017 the German prison housed on average 340 youths aged between fourteen and twenty-four years of age.[7] Thirteen out of the seventeen German youths who enrolled in this study had a so-called migration background (*Migrationshintergrund*), and four considered themselves to be ethnically German.[8] The setup of the juvenile prison as well as the limited number of long-term prisoners prevented an exact replication of the recruitment strategies utilized in Pennsylvania.

With the support of Wolfgang Stelly, researcher at the Criminological Institute at the University of Tübingen and member of the *Kriminologischer Dienst* in Baden-Württemberg, Soyer approached potential respondents individually and presented the research project to them.[9]

The young men recruited into the study had a comparable criminal record and similar age range as the Pennsylvania group. Their case files indicated that a majority of the group was not able to complete even the most remedial school work, and several respondents were diagnosed with ADHD. The German young men who participated in the study served between one and five years at the JVA. Like their counterparts in Pennsylvania, the young people who participated had been convicted of serious crimes, such as armed robbery or rape, or attempted murder. They were considered to be among the most serious cases in the state. The final number of respondents Soyer interviewed at the prison in Adelsheim was seventeen. Interviews at both field sites were transcribed and inductively coded in a word processing program. For this chapter we draw on the part of the interviews that cover the young men's pathway into criminal behavior and their reentry expectations. The demographic characteristics of the respondents are detailed below (Tables 8.1 and 8.2).

Life-Course Histories

Despite these important similarities, the life-course histories of the German and US respondents diverge from each other in meaningful ways due to the contexts described above. For example, although the German and American respondents had been sentenced for very similar crimes, the German respondents served much shorter sentences. The discrepancy in sentencing arose because the German respondents were adjudicated in juvenile court, while the respondents in Pennsylvania were sentenced in criminal court proceedings. The level of poverty the young men experienced during their childhood differed significantly as well. The extreme resource scarcity the Pennsylvania respondents lived through shaped their pathways into crime (Soyer 2018). The German participants grew up poor in relation to their middle-class peers; however, their families' struggles never reached the level of desperation the American respondents recalled. The young men in Germany explain their pathways into criminal behavior by pointing to psychological strain caused by familial dysfunctions or unexpected personal tragedies, such as parental death or illness. In contrast to the American group, they do not rationalize their

8 "I Wanna Be Somebody by the Time I Turn 25": Narratives...

Table 8.1 American respondents

Name[a]	Race	Year of birth	Conviction	Sentence[b]
Alexander	Latino	1993	Theft	2–4 years
Andrew	Mixed	1993	Burglary	2–6 years
Austin	Black	1994	Arson	1–5 years
Blake	Black	1992	Drug manufacture/ sale/ deliver	1–5 years
Bryan	Black	1993	Carrying firearm w/o license	2–5 years
Connor	Mixed	1994	Robbery	3–10 years
Dylan	Black	1993	Murder third degree	25–50 years
Elijah	Black	1992	Drug manufacture/ sale/ deliver	3–7 years
Gabriel	Black	1993	Robbery	4–8 years
Henry	White	1994	Theft	2–4 years
Issac	Black	1994	Murder third degree	20–40 years
Jaxon	Black	1994	Robbery	2–8 years
Jeremiah	Black	1993	Aggravated assault	4–8 years
Jesus	Latino	1994	Aggravated harassment	2–4 years
John	Mixed	1994	Robbery	2–3 years
Jordan	Black	1993	Robbery	4–8 years
Joshua	Black	1993	Robbery	2–5 years
Josiah	Black	1993	Burglary	3–6 years
Julian	White	1992	Aggravated assault	4–17 years
Kayden	Black	1994	Aggravated assault	2–4 years
Luke	White	1994	Robbery	3–10 years
Marc	Black	1994	Aggravated assault	9–20 years
Mateo	Latino	1993	Aggravated assault	2–5 years
Miguel	Latino	1992	Robbery	5–10 years
Nate	Asian	1993	Robbery of motor vehicles	4–8 years
Oliver	White	1994	Receiving stolen property	9 months–3 years
Robert	White	1993	Sale or transfer of firearms	15–30 years
Samuel	Black	1994	Robbery	2–4 years
Tyler	Black	1992	Robbery	5–12 years
William	White	1994	Aggravated assault	4–8 years

[a]Names are anonymized
[b]Numbers are rounded

criminal behavior as way of providing for their family. As we present the data from both field sites, we show how these economic and social contexts shape the young men's narrative about pathways into crime and reentry expectations.

Poverty and Pathways into Crime

Jordan, a young man serving four to eight years for robbery in Pennsylvania, describes his childhood home as a "crack house." […] "I'd open the door, and people were like […] watch out! Running, hide guns under the couch, and coke, and friends smoking in there." Another participant, Gabriel, who by the time of the interview had already spent two of his four- to eight-year sentence

Table 8.2 German respondents

Name[a]	Parental country of origin	Year of birth	Conviction	Sentence[b]
Carlo	Italy/Togo	1999	Aggravated assault	3 years
Conrad	Germany	1995	Theft, property damage	2 years
Burat	Turkey	1999	Robbery and extortion	4 years
Miro	Kosovo	1996	Aggravated sexual abuse of minors, theft	3 years and 3 months
Thaman	Sri Lanka	~1996	Rape and extortion	3 years
Sahib	India	1996	Attempted murder	6 years
Arslan	Turkey	1994	Attempted murder	5 years and 6 months
Marcel	German	1998	Robbery, theft, aggravated assault	2 years and 2 months
Jens	Croatia/Germany	2000	Extortion, aggravated theft	2 years
Martin	Germany	1996	Receiving of stolen property	1 year and 1 month
Achim	Germany	1997	Assault and battery	1 year and 6 months
Johannes	Germany/USA	1997	Assault and battery	1 year and 5 months
Eren	Turkey	1996	Assault, driving while drunk, driving without a license, resisting arrest	3 years and 9 months
Armend	Kosovo	1999	Harassment, theft, trespassing, damage to property	1 year and 6 months
Alexander	Uzbekistan	1997	Aggravated robbery, carrying of a firearm	2 years and 9 months
Marko	Roma from Serbia	1995	Assault, driving while drunk, driving without a license, resisting arrest	1 year and 6 months
Adam	Poland	1997	Aggravated assault with a weapon	2 years and 5 months

[a]Names are anonymized
[b]Numbers are rounded

for robbery at Pine Grove, recalls moving homes frequently as a child. His family regularly lived in homeless shelters. He remembers seeing things "you shouldn't see when you're young." He further explains: "The shelter we was staying at was right in the middle of the hood. Like so, you got, you got crackheads up here, like it wasn't where children should have been at." Gabriel's pathway into crime is closely connected to the extreme poverty and trauma he experienced growing up. In the end, the drug dealers on the corner did for Gabriel what his mother couldn't do: "I know it's cliché," he explains, "but people selling drugs probably took care of us more than my mom when I was young. Give us money, do stuff." He remembers people in fancy cars giving him money. "They see you messed up, dirty, wearing the same clothes, out all day … so, they know what type of situation you're in."

Several young people interviewed in Pennsylvania remember days when they went hungry because there was not enough food for them to eat at home. Bryan, who had already served two of his two- to five-year sentence he received for carrying a firearm, remembers the extreme poverty he grew up in: "[…] It'd be hard like when, one week there'd be food on the table for all of us. Then the next day, it'd be a certain amount of food on the table for a number of us. And we ugh, damn. We ate, but not as much as everybody else, you know? We had to take turns on like, on who was gonna get a certain amount this week."

Early on, Bryan committed crimes to take care of himself while his mother struggled to feed the family. During his teenage years, his criminal behavior reached a new level. He committed his first armed robbery at fourteen and began selling drugs. At that point, he did not commit crimes anymore to feed his brothers or help out his mother. He readily admits that he was drawn to the lifestyle and excitement that came with committing crimes. Economic pressures and opportunities for crime may have provided the first incentive for criminal behavior, but having money to spend, the freedom to get high, and most importantly feeling in charge of his own destiny propelled Bryan's criminal behavior beyond meeting his immediate needs. When Soyer asked Bryan if he had any positive memories from his childhood he would like to share, he simply replies: "I wish I had some." Like Bryan, Gabriel struggled to recall any happy childhood memories. Gabriel states that he has never been to an amusement or a water park. He adds: "I [have] only been to the zoo one time, that's when I took my son to the zoo."

In contrast to the childhood narratives of the US respondents, none of the German youth report experiencing housing insecurity or food scarcity. Martin, who spent two years at Adelsheim, distinctly felt that he had less than the other children around him. He and his siblings did not wear expensive brand name clothes. There were days when the portions that his mother served were smaller than usual. Yet, Martin and his two sisters never knew hunger. He and his siblings could always go to his grandparents who lived close by to get something to eat. Other than Gabriel, he also did not have to worry about having a safe place to live. He grew up in a three-bedroom apartment and always had his own room.

Martin's childhood was by no means easy. His little sister was sexually abused by his mother's boyfriend. His older sister became addicted to heroin. However, he does not hesitate to recall happy childhood memories. He remembers going on vacation to the Baltic Sea. The German government subsidizes these kinds of trips for families with children as a preventive or rehabilitative measure to address mental and chronic physical health problems of parents and children.[10] Martin refers to his trip as his favorite childhood memory. "We took a boat and when we went for walks, my mom pushed me and my sister around in a little cart. I played a lot with my big sister. She did not want play with cars so we played *Barbie*."

When asked why he believes he ended up in prison, Martin responds unequivocally that he wanted to be noticed by the adults around him. He believes that he committed crimes, such as breaking and entering or drug dealing, to get his mother's attention. His mother, he remembers, worked a lot and was focused on his two sisters. When I asked what his family would have needed as he was growing up he replies: "More government support would have helped." As a single mother she had to work and take care of three children alone. As the middle child who seemed to function relatively well, he felt overlooked. According to his case summary file Martin is emotionally fragile. He has been addicted to drugs and tried to commit suicide.

Arslan, who defines himself as German-Turkish, has spent six years in various locked facilities. While he was initially sent to Adelsheim for armed robbery, his latest charge was for an attempted second-degree murder. He fractured the skull of another person incarcerated at Adelsheim because he called Arslan the 'son of a whore' [*Hurensohn*]. When asked about his childhood, Arslan responded that his parents did everything right. He felt loved and never lacked anything. He happily recalls car rides with his father through the snowy streets of Stuttgart. He remembers going sledding at the park surrounding Solitude castle that sits on a hill on the edge of the city. Afterwards, they usually went out to eat and drink to warm themselves up.

Arslan says that he committed crimes because he wanted to have money to party and buy himself expensive clothes. He was twelve years old when his father died of lung cancer. After that, he remembers spiraling out of control. According to his own assessment he did not respect or listen to anyone anymore. At the same time his mother fell ill and had a heart attack. She has been unable to work and the family moved into government housing. His mother was overwhelmed by her son's behavioral problems. Arslan recalls with some pride that the police in Stuttgart knew him and that he was classified as a high-level juvenile offender.

Parental addiction and the connected parentification of children were an important part of the narrative the young American men developed in relation to their behavioral choices (Soyer 2018). In the narratives of the German respondents, parental drug addiction took on different forms. Rather than crack or heroin addiction, the young men in Germany remembered their fathers' alcohol abuse and related violent outbursts. Two respondents described that their fathers' gambling addiction squandered the family's resources and led to emotional stress and financial hardship.

Armend, for example, has been deeply affected by his father's addiction to playing slot machines. He was born in Germany after his parents fled Kosovo during the war. His father's addiction led the family into poverty and further displacement. Even though his father was working every day the family couldn't pay rent. Armend remembers his father seizing his sister's salary she had earned working as a nurse aid in a psychiatric hospital. When she refused to hand the money over, he became violent. Armend's family lived under very difficult circumstances. After Armend's release, the family was housed in a container like dwelling. They had to share kitchen and bathroom with several single men who according to Armend struggled with drug and alcohol addiction as well. Despite the relative deprivation he experienced, he never had to worry about food and shelter. Growing up without the fear of homelessness and hunger may explain why the German respondents do not frame their criminal behavior in terms of providing for their family's basics needs. Armend, for example, believes that his criminal behavior is driven by his addiction. He plainly stated that he committed theft because he needs the money to buy drugs and alcohol.

According to his case file Armend was sentenced for grand larceny, damage to property, and harassment and remained in Adelsheim for about a year and six months. The social workers at the JVA were aware of his difficult home life, and Armend was offered a place in a non-punitive group home. He refused the offer because he did not want to be away from his mother any longer.

Post-Release Plans and Educational Opportunities

Another notable difference between the two groups is that the German respondents were considered juveniles with their socio-legal context, while the American young men had entered the adult criminal justice system even though they were under age eighteen. This is relevant to what programs they were offered in prison, as legislation in Germany mandates that education not punishment is the main tool to instill youths with a sense of responsibility for their actions.[11] Job training offered at Adelsheim operates according to the principles of the dual educational system. The German apprenticeship system connects the job training under the guidance of a certified master craftsman with a continued basic education at trade schools. The prison in Adelsheim offers eighteen of these apprenticeship programs such as metal worker, electrician, baker, butcher, gardener, as well as painter and carpenter.[12] Youth who have finished at least nine years of schooling and passed final examinations are eligible to enroll in job training at the prison. According to Stelly and Thomas (2015), 68 percent of the young people who were held at Adelsheim in 2014 actually participated in these job training programs in prison. Approximately a third of the remaining 32 percent were enrolled in educational support programs designed to help them finish the minimum amount of schooling necessary to become an apprentice.

Participation in an apprenticeship program offered the young men opportunities for continued training after their release. Victor, who was sentenced to two years and nine months for armed robbery, started his apprenticeship as a fitter in prison. With the help of his supervisor he secured a position on the outside allowing him to continue his training there and thereby facilitating an early release. As a result, his plans for his post-incarceration life have taken on concrete forms: he wants to finish his apprenticeship, become a master of the trade, and get his driver's license. According to this own assessment, his biggest challenge will be to live on the rather limited apprenticeship salary. He is certain though that he will be able to make due and finish his education. His motivation, he says, is his desire to provide for his fiancé. "Her family expects that, he explains, and I expect that from myself as well."

Johannes, who served a two-year sentence for robbery at the time of the interview, is acutely aware that his desired lifestyle will be impossible with the limited salary of an apprentice. He is afraid that he may become "greedy" and start committing crimes again. "If I get an apprenticeship I'll make 800 Euros a month and I have to work. I could make the same amount in three to four hours, while sitting in a car with my friends driving around." Rather than learning a hands-on trade, he would like to enroll in program that prepares him for jobs such as insurance broker or bank teller. He believes that positions like this are out of reach for him because of his criminal record. Johannes is likely correct about his job prospects. But his criminal record is not the main hurdle. Even if he had never committed a crime, he would not be able to land a white-collar apprenticeship. He simply lacks the necessary educational credentials. Employers hiring for white-collar apprenticeships prefer students with the German high school diploma (*Abitur*) obtained after twelve years in school (Baethge 2006). Johannes has only finished nine years of schooling.

Martin is enrolled in educational support programs and participates in yard work at the prison. He has not finished the basic examination that usually takes place after a student attended school for nine years. Passing this exam is necessary for becoming an apprentice. Martin struggles with learning disabilities. His plans for the outside are nevertheless well formed: he wants to begin an apprenticeship as a gardener, one of the few programs that would allow him to finish his schooling while already being an apprentice. Martin's case probes the limits of the dual educational system and its ability to integrate students who do not fulfill the minimum entry requirements. Even educational pathways like gardening require parallel attendance of classes that may be too advanced for students who have failed to succeed even at the most remedial form of schooling (Protsch 2014). Indeed, as Martin confirms in one of the interviews that took place after his release, he was not able to enroll in a gardening apprenticeship but instead finished another year of pre-professional training supposed to ready him for actual employment.

Pennsylvania prisons usually offer vocational training in HVAC (Heating, Ventilation and Air Conditioning), carpentry, and custodial maintenance. However, due to their status and the context of the laws that sentenced them, the young men participating in the Young Adult Offender program are not eligible to enroll in these programs, since they are reserved for the general adult prison population. The Pennsylvania group received some educational support such as GED classes, but they did not participate in any job training that could lead directly to employment after their release. As a result, their plans for life after prison were vague. Joshua, sentenced to two to five years for robbery, says that he plans to get a job and go to school after he is released. He wants to take care of his family. Joshua is hopeful that he will be able to secure a job right away. "Some companies hire people first outta jail, know what I'm saying? They [former inmates] got more to lose," he says.

Jesus is at the end of his two- to four-year sentence for aggravated harassment during his interview. He plans to move in with his grandmother and explains he anticipates needing a certain amount of time to get settled: "I just need to […] get a little job real quick and an apartment, re-register my cars, and I'm cool." He also knows that it will be very difficult for him to live a self-sustaining life. Jesus wants to have a house and a family, possibly his own business. "I wanna be somebody by the time I turn 25," he says and admits: "I just don't know how to go about it right now."

Robert is serving a fifteen- to thirty-year sentence for sale or transfer of stolen firearms. Like two other respondents that are held as Young Adult Offenders at Pine Grove, he will be a middle-aged man by the time he is eligible for parole. For youths like him, plans for the future seem futile. He is worried that he will not be able to adjust to life without supervision after more than a decade of imprisonment. He is particularly anxious about violating his parole and being immediately sent back to state prison. As he puts it: "When I'm in here so long and you put me in a halfway house with that freedom, am I really going to be able to stay there for six months […] Like no fences, no locked doors nothing like that. And, abide by their rules? Or, would I rather just walk away and say hey, come find me." Since his earliest possible release date is so far in the future, he does not participate in any rehabilitative programs. He has been interested in working with cars but Robert's outlook on his employment perspectives after his release is bleak: "The world is going to be changed so much. I'm not going to know what's going on. […] If I try to get back into auto tech I'm going to be so far behind."

Conclusion

The data presented in this chapter show how cultural and structural conditions shape the respondents' narratives about criminal behavior and reentry. The young men incarcerated in Pennsylvania experienced an excess of suffering during their childhood (Soyer 2018). The material and other hardships they endured were extreme and provided the backdrop for the abuse and dysfunction they witnessed as children.

The German welfare state appeared to prevent the most severe poverty, even among this group of largely immigrants. The young men interviewed in Germany did not have to endure hunger and homelessness. They were able to recall happy childhood memories, despite the abuse they experienced in their homes. In comparison to the US participants, the German respondents received more concrete support for a successful reentry process while they were incarcerated. As they look back, they explain their juvenile offending in terms of the psychological burden caused by the lack of attention, familial tragedies, and dysfunctions.

The young men from Pennsylvania experienced much harsher punishments than the German participants. Rehabilitation becomes an irrelevant concept for those who serve sentences that will span decades. At the time of this writing, five years after the initial interviews took place, thirteen of the original thirty respondents continue to linger in state prison. Comparing both groups emphasizes the retributive nature of the American criminal justice system despite slowly declining incarceration rates (Carson 2020; Garland 2001). Structurally, the absence of a generous welfare system in combination with long sentences in the adult criminal justice system maximizes the suffering of the American respondents. Being incarcerated for decades will hamper their ability to reenter society successfully. Left without any immediate government-funded support services, they are likely to rely on family to rebuild their lives. Their material deprivation will be exacerbated by the psychological burden of having to rely on friends and relatives for material support (Western et al. 2015).

In the United States, the marginalization of the young men is overt, while in Germany exclusionary mechanisms operate more subtlety. The German participants are relegated to manual labor and, in consequence, to low-paying professions. Their educational deficits are so large that they fail to find the kind of employment that would secure a comfortable middle-class life style. The interviews highlight the strength of the apprenticeship system. It allows the incarcerated teenagers to conceive concrete career goals rather than holding on to the vague idea of "finding a job." On the other hand, the interviews also reveal an important shortcoming of the system: those who struggle with the most remedial form of schooling—as a majority of the Adelsheim respondents did—have difficulties finding an apprenticeship. The German youths can draw on social services and financial support of the government. The government will pay their rent and they will never have to worry about food. Nevertheless, those who are not able to enroll in an apprenticeship represent the lowest socio-economic strata of German society.

The young men interviewed for this project are outsiders. They do not measure up to the behavioral and occupational standards of German society. Like the Young Adult Offender Program in Pine Grove, the juvenile prison in Adelsheim manages the children of those whose families fail to measure up to mainstream social standards. Most are not ethnically German. They may never find the same kind of success and professional fulfillment many middle-class children in Germany expect to achieve as adults. In both systems, the young men face an uphill battle trying to become self-sufficient members of their societies.

In contrast to the American respondents, the German young men will always have an apartment to call their own that is paid for by the government. They will have furniture, clothes, and food. Their human dignity, as it is ensured in the first article of the German Basic Law, will remain intact. The respondents from Pennsylvania have no such guarantee. They may—at least theoretically—be constitutionally protected from cruel and unusual punishment while they are in prison. Yet once they are released, there is no protection from the cruel and unusual poverty that already shaped their childhood and teenage years.

Notes

1. The data collected in Pennsylvania forms the basis for Michaela Soyer's book *Lost Childhoods Poverty, Trauma, and Violent Crime in the Post-Welfare* (2018).
2. See Landeszentrale für politische Bildung Baden-Württemberg (2016).

3. Because of IRB stipulation and limited resources Soyer had to exclude those incarcerated young people who are under eighteen. She would have needed to get parental consent to secure their participation in the study.
4. In addition to the Young Adult Offender Program, SCI Pine Grove also houses adults serving time as part of the general population. As of May 2016, 926 people were incarcerated there. Approximately 300 young men usually were part of the Young Adult Offender Program. Information based on conference call with superintendent of Pine Grove on March 27, 2014 (Department of Corrections 2016).
5. See Pennsylvania Juvenile Court Judges' Commission (2008).
6. One participant was sent to the restricted housing unit after Soyer conducted the first interview and could not be re-interviewed over the course of the study.
7. Those older than twenty-one may have had their juvenile probation revoked but could still serve their juvenile sentence at the JVA Adelsheim despite their advanced age.
8. Having a "migration background" indicates that one or both of the youths' parents are not ethnically German.
9. "Kriminologischer Dienst" is part of the research branch of the ministry of justice in Baden-Württemberg. This particular research group is located at the prison in Adelsheim and focuses on young people held at this institution.
10. For more information about this opportunity see, for example, AOK (2019).
11. See "Der Vollzug des Jugendarrestes soll das Ehrgefühl des Jugendlichen wecken und ihm eindringlich zum Bewußtsein bringen, daß er für das von ihm begangene Unrecht einzustehen hat. Der Vollzug des Jugendarrestes soll erzieherisch gestaltet werden. Er soll dem Jugendlichen helfen, die Schwierigkeiten zu bewältigen, die zur Begehung der Straftat beigetragen haben" (Jugendgerichtsgesetz 2019).
12. See VAW (2019).

References

Abrams, L. S., Jordan, S. P., & Montero, L. A. (2018). What is a juvenile? A cross-national comparison of youth justice systems. *Youth Justice, 18*(2), 111–130. https://doi.org/10.1177/1473225418779850.

Aebi, M. F., Tiago, M. M., Berger-Kolopp, L., & Burkhardt, C. (2017). *SPACE I—Annual penal statistics: Prison populations*. Strasbourg: Council of Europe.

AOK. (2019). *Mutter-Kind-Kur und Vater-Kind-Kur*. Retrieved August 26, 2019, from https://www.aok.de/pk/uni/inhalt/mutter-kind-kur-und-vater-kind-kur/.

Aybek, C. M. (2008). Jugendliche aus Zuwandererfamilien im Übergang von der Schule in den Beruf—Perspektiven der Lebenslauf- und Integrationsforschung. In U. Hunger, C. M. Aybek, A. Ette, & I. Michalowski (Eds.), *Migrations- und Integrationsprozesse in Europa*. Wiesbaden: VS Verlag für Sozialwissenschaften.

Baethge, M. (2006). Das deutsche Bildungs-Schisma: welche Probleme ein vorindustrielles Bildungssystem in einer nachindustriellen Gesellschaft hat. *SOFI-Mitteilungen*, (34), 13–27.

Bernhard, N. (2017). *Durch Europäisierung zu mehr Durchlässigkeit?* Leverkusen: Budrich Verlag.

Bundesministerium für Bildung und Forschung. (2019). *Bildung*. Retrieved December 15, 2019, from https://www.datenportal.bmbf.de/portal/de/K233.html.

Carson, E. A. (2020). Prisoners in 2018. *Bureau of Justice*. Retrieved May 3, 2020, from https://www.bjs.gov/content/pub/pdf/p18.pdf.

Department of Corrections. (2016). *SCI Pine Grove*. Retrieved June 18, 2016, from http://www.cor.pa.gov/Facilities/StatePrisons/Pages/Pine-Grove.aspx#.V2U9nI4m9aX.

Garland, D. (2001). *The culture of control: Crime and social order in contemporary society*. Chicago, IL: University of Chicago Press.

Goldrick-Rab, S. (2010). Challenges and opportunities for improving community college student success. *Review of Educational Research, 80*(3), 437–469.

Harlow, C. W. (2003). *Education and correctional populations*. Washington, DC: Bureau of Justice Statistics.

Hart, D. (2015). *Corrections or care? The use of custody for children in trouble*. London: Prisoners Education Trust.

Hazel, N. (2008). *Cross-national comparison of youth justice*. London: Youth Justice Board.

Höynck, T., & Ernst, S. (2014). Jugendstrafrecht: ein Vierteljahrhundert—schlechte Zeiten für rationale Kriminalpolitik. *Kritische Justiz, 47*(3), 249–260.

Jugendgerichtsgesetz. (2019). Jugendarrest. Sec. 90. Retrieved September 1, 2019, from https://www.gesetze-im-internet.de/jgg/__90.html.

Landeszentrale für politische Bildung Baden-Württemberg. (2016). *Ergebnis der Landtagswahlen 2016 in Baden-Württemberg*. Retrieved June 30, 2016, from http://www.landtagswahl-bw.de/ergebnis_landtagswahl_2016_bw.html.

Maaz, K., Baumert, J., & Trautwein, U. (2010). Genese sozialer Ungleichheit im institutionellen Kontext der Schule: wo entsteht und vergrößert sich soziale Ungleichheit? In J. Baumert, K. Maaz, & U. Trautwein (Eds.), *Bildungsentscheidungen* (pp. 11–46). Wiesbaden: VS Verlag für Sozialwissenschaften.

McCaul, E. J., Donaldson, G. A., Jr., Coladarci, T., & Davis, W. E. (1992). Consequences of dropping out of school: Findings from high school and beyond. *The Journal of Educational Research, 85*(4), 198–207.

McFarland, J., Cui, J., Rathbun, A., & Holmes, J. (2018). *Trends in high school dropout and completion rates in the United States: 2018*. Washington, DC: National Center for Education Statistics.

Pager, D. (2003). The mark of a criminal record. *American Journal of Sociology, 108*(5), 937–975.

Pennsylvania Juvenile Court Judges' Commission. (2008). *The Juvenile Act. 42 PA C.S. Sec. 6301 et seq*. Harrisburg, PA: Juvenile Court Judges' Commission.

Protsch, P. (2014). *Segmentierte Ausbildungsmärkte: berufliche Chancen von Hauptschülerinnen und Hauptschülern im Wandel*. Berlin: Budrich UniPress. Retrieved September 3, 2019, from https://doi.org/10.3224/86388050.

Shedd, C. (2015). *Unequal city: Race, schools and perceptions of injustice*. New York, NY: Russell Sage Foundation.

Soyer, M. (2018). *Lost childhoods: poverty, trauma, and violent crime in the post-welfare era*. Berkeley, CA: University of California Press.

Stelly, W., & Thomas, J. (2015). *Evaluation des Jugendstrafvollzuge in Baden-Württemberg*. Stuttgart: Kriminologischer Dienst Baden-Württemberg.

Turner, N., & Travis, J. (2015, August 6). What we learned from German prisons. *New York Times*. Retrieved December 12, 2015, from www.nytimes.com/2015/08/07/opinion/what-we-learned-from-german-prisons.html?_r = 0.

VAW. (2019). *Produkte und Ideen der JVA Adelsheim*. Retrieved August 29, 2019, from http://www.jva-adelsheim.de/pb/site/jum2/get/documents/jum1/JuM/Justizvollzugsanstalt%20Adelsheim/PDF/VAW_Darstellungsbroschuere_Adelsheim_160708_RZ_WEB.pdf.

Walter, J. (2003). Aktuelle Entwicklungen und Herausforderungen im deutschen Jugendstrafvollzug. *Neue Kriminalpolitik, 15*(1), 10–14.

Western, B. (2018). *Homeward: Life in the year after prison*. New York, NY: Russell Sage Foundation.

Western, B., Bragga, A., Davis, J., & Sioris, C. (2015). Stress and hardship after prison. *American Journal of Sociology, 120*(5), 1512–1547.

Whitman, J. Q. (2003). *Harsh justice: Criminal punishment and the widening divide between America and Europe*. Oxford: Oxford University Press.

Part III

Regulating Emotions and Relationships Behind Bars

I'm Tired

I'm tired of these people in here.
I'm tired of these staffs.
I'm tired of being in here.
I'm tired of being in a jail cell.
I'm tired of being told what to do
Of being told when to shower.
I wanna be able to do anything whenever.
But my actions took me to this spot where I'm at right now.
Now I know how it is, how it'll go, so I wouldn't be surprised what's next if I was in here.

March 7, 2020
Central Juvenile Hall, Los Angeles, CA, USA

9

State Property

Jim St. Germain

Reprinted from
A Stone of Hope: A Memoir
New York: Harper Collins

J. St. Germain (✉)
Preparing Leaders of Tomorrow, New York, NY, USA

When we make mistakes, meander, slip, and sometimes fall, we find means to gather ourselves, reset our compasses, and continue the journey.—Desmond Tutu

"I was hoping to never see you again."

I had been staring at the dead brown floor for hours. Then, without a word, a heavy clanging and the door opening. A uniformed staff member, handcuffs dangling from his waist, silently took me into a visiting room. There sat Christine Bella, head tilted, slight smile pushing through. "Hi. Remember me?"

It was a relief; I had just about given up on seeing a kind face. "What happened?" she asked.

The Spofford Juvenile Center in the Bronx was one of the few lock-up detention facilities in New York for juveniles. Also known as Bridges, it was a notorious intake place for troubled teens. Word was that lots of guys from the area who rose up and became something— Mike Tyson, Fat Joe—went through Spofford. It was a twisted rite of passage for black and Latino teens in New York, but an awful institution. No matter how much credibility it earned you back home.

For juveniles, this place was the real deal: heavy, locked doors; thick cement and cinder block; high walls with barbed wire; stoic staff; group showers. We were constantly being searched: forced to take off our shoes, which staff would bang upside down; our socks turned inside out; our pockets emptied; our collars padded; our pants taken off and shaken. Staff would enter our rooms randomly and turn everything upside down—as if I could've received something to stash, though I hadn't moved.

My room was a small locked box with a metal sink, so I couldn't hurt anyone or myself. A rickety bed was covered with a slice-thin mattress. There was a window up high but the glass was frosted, maybe because they didn't want us to get any thoughts about the outside world. The hours eked out like a slowly dripping faucet. There was nothing to do but go over how I got here and where I'd be going.

I'd had run-ins with the police before and they were routine: a ride to the precinct, maybe fingerprinting, and a call home. But a Class D felony meant I was headed deeper into the system. Maybe too far for any light to shine through. I would have to adapt quickly, hurt anyone who tried to make me a target. I would just go off on the first person to look at me funny. The heavy metal door and thick walls told me I had no choice but to adapt and survive. *Adapt and survive.* It was like a mantra that I repeated to myself. I just had to keep my head above water as the levels rose and the waves came crashing down.

The law treats crack more severely than cocaine. At the time, crack sentencing was literally a hundred times more severe than powder cocaine. The irony is that crack is actually more diluted than powder cocaine; it can be stretched out with baking soda and cooked up, which is what makes it cheap. The harsher penalties reveal racial bias and embedded systemic issues: it's much easier to arrest crack dealers on street corners than suburban kids or Wall Street brokers. It was only a matter of time before I got caught. As far as Brooklyn police were concerned, I was fish in a barrel.

Before Christine showed up, I had been running through everything in my head, alternating between the small and the large: How did the cops find the product so fast? How long were they going to put me away for? Was being sent away actually better for me? Was someone going to take my spot on the corner? What was my father going to say? Does my family even care enough to visit me?

I thought about the day we left for America, four years earlier. Everyone from the neighborhood knew where we were going so they congregated out in front of the house. I met up with my family on the main road and got on the back of the tap tap to the airport. Neighbors were waving good-bye, yelling things like "Don't forget us!" as the tap tap kicked up rocks on the dusty road. I remember carrying only a small bag, which didn't hold much of anything. I had my plane ticket, I had my visa, and I had the clothes on my back. I was so young, I assumed America was going to take care of the rest.

Spofford was the gateway, the first step into the system. There's a reason it's called the system; it's a well-oiled machine that takes in troubled kids and churns out hardened men. I was on my way.

"You're moving up in the world," Christine said jokingly. "Two D felonies."

We sat in a sparse room, two wooden chairs and a phone. "What, one wasn't enough?"

"But I didn't do it." "Really?"

"Really," I said. "I swear."

"Okay, then this will be easy," she said, half-joking. "It wasn't even my bike—"

"And the drugs?"

"It was like a dime bag of weed—just to smoke. For me." "And the crack?"

"Not mine," I muttered.

"All right," she said, exhaling as she opened my file.

I couldn't make eye contact with her; I felt like I'd let her down. But even as I avoided the truth and her look, having her there calmed me. The system is cold and faceless, an entity that towers over you and seems to exist to make you feel small. Christine made me feel like me again, even if just during the length of our conversation. She laid out my sentencing options. If I lost the case, she could try to convince the judge that I would benefit from a structured environment.

I was conflicted. Ignoring rules and running wild was the only childhood I'd ever known. From six years old I had been fending for myself for basic needs. In Brooklyn, that expanded. I had a powerful thirst for the streets: the block, my homies, the money, marijuana, and alcohol. Lockup would bring withdrawals—both physical and psychological. It was all toxic but my body needed it to function. I'd also heard horror stories about drug hustlers who got traumatized while incarcerated, beaten up or thrown in solitary or kept way past their release date.

I also knew I'd be guaranteed a meal, a bed, medical care, and, hopefully, adults who had a stake in my welfare. I felt guilty and wanted to give my family some peace of mind. Now at least they'd know where I was.

There was a drop of foresight in me too, a voice saying there had to be another way. I knew that my life back on Crown Street had a short clock and I wouldn't make it out. Even then, I recognized the opportunity brought by my arrest.

But all this didn't even really matter because where I went wasn't up to me. It was a Hobson's choice—the illusion of free will. The truth is I had no choice at all.

Christine always complimented me on being a good listener, but often I couldn't comprehend what she was saying regarding my case. I didn't understand the ins and outs of the juvenile justice system or the various services and options being presented to me. The legal terms were beyond my comprehension. I was polite and nodded a lot; most teenage boys aren't too expressive anyway, so I could hide what I didn't understand. But her level of attention and interest mattered more. She would regularly check back, ask if I understood; even when I pretended I did, she would still go over it again more simply. She was caring like that, not forcing me to reveal how little I understood.

The level of compassion I felt from Christine was more important to me at that moment than any details about the legal process. All that felt abstract. The law has to be more than an intellectual exercise. Being seen as a person in that fragile moment can change a child's life, help him feel a basic sense of security in a terrifying world. I don't know how much attorneys understand this: a child about to lose his freedom is looking at this adult as maybe his only hope.

For our rides out to court, or medical appointments, juvenile offenders were transported like dangerous criminals, searched yet again and marched outside. Staff clinked tight metal cuffs around our wrists and ankles and escorted us single file into a white government van, with "Department of Juvenile Justice" in bold on the side. I accepted that I was state property. But I wasn't afraid to ask questions; that's always been my way. We were always in the custody of black or Latino males in their late twenties and thirties, many of whom had been in the streets or had kids in the streets. One time while they were preparing to transport me to Family Court I asked one, "You really need to do this? Cuff my arms and legs like I'm a murderer or something?"

As he clicked the ankle cuffs closed he eyed up at me, a visible sneer, like, *Who does this kid think he is?*

"This is my job, man. I didn't make the rules," he said. "You don't like it, don't get locked up. You thought this was Boy Scouts or some shit? You want to get milk and cookies? Get tucked in to bed?"

He laughed as he got into the passenger seat, but I could see his partner, the driver, looking at me through the rearview mirror during the drive. Old-school hip-hop played through the speakers and all the kids in the back were bopping their heads and mouthing the words. Their eyes were unfocused, the music taking them somewhere else. Music was a luxury and the van was the only time we got to hear any. It was like a satellite back to Earth, as far as we were concerned. Inside those vans, rusted white metal gates ran horizontally in rows, separating the driver from the kids and the kids from each other.

"Hey, son, what's your name?" the driver asked over the music. "Hey you, Mister Question Man. What's your name?"

"Me?" I asked. "Jim."

"I been where you at, Jim."

"Yeah?" Just hearing my first name out of his mouth sounded strange because we were rarely called by name like that. It was usually our full name bellowed in some official way—or a docket number.

"Yeah, a few times," he said. "And my boy's going through it now. And you looking at this wrong. What are you, sixteen?"

"Fifteen."

"Well, shit. This'll be over soon. This is like a crystal ball."

"Huh?"

"The future. If you don't leave the street alone, this will be the rest of your life. What you have left of it."

He wasn't trying to scare me. It was more like he was leveling with me. "Yeah," I said, "maybe, but why do you gotta—"

"Yo," a kid yelled from the back. "Shut the fuck up! We're not trying to hear you. Tryn'a hear the radio, man, not your dumb-ass questions."

"Word up," another voice said.

I turned my face into the gate behind me. "Mind your own fucking business, pussy," I yelled at him.

"Fuck out of here!" he said, kicking the seat.

"Hey, hey. Enough! Quiet!" the driver yelled. He killed the radio and we rode in silence the rest of the way to the courthouse. I could feel the kid in the back stewing.

The van pulled up to a separate entrance area behind the Brooklyn courthouse. We were taken out one by one, lined up, and escorted to a back elevator, then into a dark and depressing room. And there we sat, all day among the faded cinder block and hard lighting, on heavy lockdown. There were cheap plastic chairs bound together and then to the wall so nothing could be moved. A thick metal door with a small square window buzzed every thirty seconds as lawyers, social workers, and probation and court officers came in and out. A phone connected to the courtroom let the guard know whose case was up.

There was an old TV in the corner and since we'd be waiting eight hours, the staff would throw in VHS tapes, usually old boring movies that served as a distraction. Sometimes they'd play "smack" DVDs, homemade videos of underground rappers waving guns, boasting about selling drugs and pimping women, showing off their cars and jewelry. Smack DVDs were the purest form of a familiar impulse: showing off what pieces of the pie we were able to get for ourselves. When a lawyer would come in and catch sight of the movie, a staff member would run up and shut it off.

Some of the juvenile justice staff members weren't that far removed from the kids they were watching. Most were from the same neighborhoods and had similar perspectives. It's true they put in those videos because it kept us content and quiet, but looking back, it's disturbing. Why were they showing us these movies? Didn't they just reinforce some of the reasons why we were there?

The kids were only allowed brief communication with each other; if you encountered someone you had an issue with, this wasn't the place to settle it. But we were kids, and fights were inevitable. If a kid already had been sentenced and there were no longer any incentives to behave, something often went down.

They'd bring in boxes of squashed bologna sandwiches at lunch and if anyone complained, they'd get another version of the "this is why your ass shouldn't get locked up" speech. We'd elbow one another and scramble for ketchup, mustard, and mayo packets, squeeze them onto the sandwiches, and devour them, hoping there'd be extras. Sometimes when I sat there scarfing my food, I thought of the lunch line at school. How we didn't want to show our hunger if it meant showing our poverty. In juvie, that equation went right out the window. Everyone was equal, eating as if our life depended on it. When the phone from the courtroom rang everyone got extremely quiet to hear who was up to see the judge. When a kid's case was called, he'd stand up and take a deep breath; his face would instantly transform from youthful disregard to fear, the tough-guy façade left on that chair. He'd go down the line and everyone would give him a dap, wish him luck: maybe he'd get to go back to the world that led us here in the first place. Since we were all from the same community, we'd also send messages through that kid, things like "Yo, tell my dude Rae I say what's up!" or "Tell B-One I'm holding it down in here." We wanted to send word of ourselves back out there, hoping it would only be a matter of time before we returned too.

Kids who lost their case would be escorted back into that room crying or keeping quietly to themselves, holding in their anger. Others returned beaming, a little bounce in their step, knowing they were getting out soon. And then sometimes a kid didn't come back at all, which meant he got to walk out the door and go home. "Lucky dude," we'd say sometimes. More often we'd say, "He'll be back."

Though it was comforting to see Christine, who always brought a smile and support, my three-minute appearance in front of the judge was just a formality. Most decisions were made before we got there. We were pawns in the larger moves made by invisible hands. It's a strange feeling, having your life decided as if you weren't even there. Most judges wouldn't address us, and prosecutors and defense attorneys talked about us in the third person, and in legal jargon that we didn't have a prayer of understanding. It seemed like we didn't even need to be there. Most kids leave their day in court feeling as unreal and small as they do in the cell.

I got moved from Spofford to a nonsecure detention facility (NSD) on Beach Avenue in the Bronx, right alongside a public housing complex. It was freer, though still far from free. At no time can a kid be alone at an NSD; you are under constant watch, even while you sleep. My room had a lower window, one I could see out of, and even curtains. A thin wooden desk was pushed against the wall with a stool. Security was looser and we could leave our rooms with permission.

Beach Avenue was a blur of faces and forms and questions. Of judges and lawyers, social workers, counselors, probation officers, and psychologists. They packaged me up and reported to the court, trying to find me suitable placement. I told and retold my life story, spilling all my transgressions, hopes, and fears to people who looked nothing like me, and who couldn't possibly understand me.

The strange thing was that I was comfortable being honest with them, since they judged me on a different scale than the one in the streets. They didn't care if I was tough or weak; I could just be me. It was like taking a long breath. The adults I met in lockup were expecting me to project weakness, vulnerability, all the hallmarks of adolescence. Christine went out of her way to let me know that it was okay to show myself, that I wouldn't be attacked if I did.

"How do you feel about selling drugs?"

A psychologist was sitting across from me in a closed room at Beach Avenue, yellow walls and open windows. I could hear free kids running around outside, horns honking. On nice days I felt more stuck than others.

"I feel terrible about it," I said. "Like I'm destroying families and that's wrong."

"Well, that's good," he said, writing it down in his leather notebook. "But—" I hesitated.

"Go ahead."

"To be honest, at the same time I feel like if I don't do it, someone else will do it, you know?" I said. "I got friends that sell drugs to their mothers and if I don't do it, someone else is gonna do it anyway."

"So you recognize that it's wrong," he said, more a statement than a question.

"Of course. I'm taking food away from children." "How's that?"

"Because their mother's coming to me to buy drugs."

I was trying to charge through the opening I saw, use my charm to make sure I got access to the resources that were offered. The process was backward—throughout my childhood I needed help, support, and services. But it wasn't until I got arrested that people and services came out of the shadows.

"You've had a hard life," he said, peeking at my files.

"Yes, sir," I said. I recognized that how I spoke was as important as what I said. "I know a lot of people that do. But yes, I did. I do." I didn't say it, but I believed that growing up the way I did, especially in Haiti, forced me to mature quicker. That experience helped me know what I needed from my new environment.

But I was fifteen, so I had a loose understanding of my motivations. Christine said since I was still a teenager I had an "under-informed brain." I allowed negative influences to exert too much control, and I let impulsive behavior govern my actions. The malleable adolescent brain provided fertile ground for the criminal life. The doctors and social workers thought it was a good sign that I attempted to rationalize why I sold poison to society's most vulnerable.

"How do you feel about being placed somewhere?" a social worker asked. She was a mousy woman with small glasses.

"I don't know. I guess I was sad at first but I know that if I stayed in the community I'd be killed," I said. I was getting good at playing my role, though it was also starting to feel more and more like the truth. "Going to a place that gives me medical care, and where I have to be in school every day. I'm excited to learn, to read, better myself. Get opportunities."

"Do you think you can avoid conflict with your peers?" she asked. "Wherever you go, there will be other kids your age. Some like you." It was like she was lobbing underhanded pitches. I knew what she wanted me to say.

"Oh definitely. I don't really have the heart to hurt someone like for real. No doubt. I haven't fought with anyone here."

> The respondent presented a history of markedly poor judgment ... His capacity for sympathy impressed as intact, but sympathy does not appear to play a significant role in the respondent's decision making ... it does appear that if he remains in the community, he will continue to encounter considerable danger.

> The respondent's strong desires to better himself impressed as genuine, not manipulative. He impressed the examiner as a youth who, in spite of his turbulent history and markedly poor judgment, might seize upon opportunities for self-improvement that are presented to him. These strengths will serve him well in the future.

One night at Beach a staff member came to my room and told me to get my things. I did as I was told but he wouldn't answer any of my questions as I packed my few things. I had no idea where I was going and wasn't even allowed to say good-bye to anyone. I was escorted outside into a black car where a Department of Juvenile Justice supervisor sat at the wheel. I felt like a hostage as we drove into the night.

At the stoplight, the supervisor turned to me, seeing the anxiety on my face. "Don't worry," he said. "You're going to like this place."

I didn't even know what neighborhood I was in or where I was going. I took a deep breath and looked out the car window, watching the lights flash by. It was like we were driving into a black hole.

Points

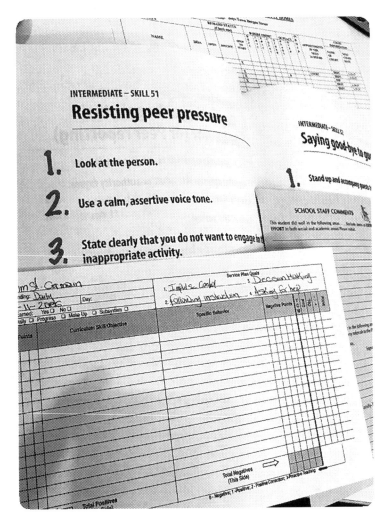

On our life map, he drew a bright circle around twelve through eighteen. This was the abyss here, unguided, black boys were swallowed whole, only to reemerge on corners and prison tiers. Dad was at war with this destiny. He was raising soldiers for all terrain.—Ta-Nehisi Coates, *The Beautiful Struggle*

We pulled up in front of a three-story brownstone in a nice neighborhood not far from downtown Brooklyn. I thought it was a mistake: the building didn't look like a facility at all. I was expecting another high-walled place where I waited out my case. I noticed the quiet, the clean streets, the absence of all the typical late-night elements.

The Boys Town NSD was a sunburnt brick townhouse on Dean Street with gated windows of black metal. It was three train stops from my grandmother's apartment on Crown Street—a five-minute ride—but it felt worlds apart. As the Juvenile Justice supervisor brought me inside, the door opened to hallways, rooms converted into offices. On the first floor was a secretary, security monitors, a computer, and file cabinets. I sat down for intake, a routine I knew well by that point. An older white woman fired questions that I answered automatically:

Jim St. Germain. Tenth grade.

Crown Heights.

Oh, Beach Avenue NSD.

Ricot St. Germain, my mom's not around. I'll eat anything.

A couple of shirts, these sneakers. No.

No, my friends are Crip. Were Crip. They're still Crip but I'm not really friends with them anymore.

No, not me.

I don't know. Next month? My lawyer would know.

Possession with intent to distribute. I don't know.

No.

I went through all this at Beach. And Spofford.

These question-and-answer rounds were never about imparting information. Boys Town already had my file. It was about *me*. They wanted to see whom they were dealing with. What hand they were dealt. What a kid like me was like right there in the flesh—not on paper.

A young staff member in a collared shirt knocked as he opened the door to the office. He put a plate in front of me—fried chicken, mashed potatoes. "Here you go, son," he said. I was starving and cleared the plate, ate like I hadn't in a while. I had been eating at long tables with other kids under tight watch and time frames for a few months. It was now hours past dinnertime but the food was hot; they had saved it for me and kept it warm. It was the first indication that this place saw me as more than a case file or money from the state.

After intake, he came back in and sat across from me on my side of the secretary's desk. He was light-skinned and leanly built, two-day beard and a shaved head. He looked right at me and said, "Hello, my name is Charles," corny and formal. Then he shook my hand and said, "It is nice to meet you."

I mumbled my name.

"Okay," he said. "I'm going to walk you through the Boys Town system. First off, you have to introduce yourself the way that I just introduced myself to you."

"Wait. Really?"

"Really. Look at me. Then shake my hand and say, 'Hello my name is Jim.' Maintain eye contact with me as you say, 'It is nice to meet you.'"

We went through this sequence a few times. He modeled it and I copied. He corrected me and I did it again. Charles and I introduced ourselves to each other five or six times. It was forced and awkward and I resisted it. It just seemed phony.

"The purpose here is to retrain your behavior," Charles said, more direct than before.

"That's the model." He handed me a thick booklet, bound and laminated.

"We start with the first four basic skills: following instruction, accepting consequences, greeting skills, and reporting whereabouts." I knew immediately that this place was nothing like Beach or Spofford. This felt like school. School for the outside world. School for after school.

"First, following instructions," he said. "There's steps in there to follow." He took my manual and opened it to a page, then handed it back to me.

I followed along as he recited: *1. Look at the person. 2. Say okay. 3. Repeat the instruction. 4. Complete the task. 5. Check back.*

"We go over these every day, all day," Charles said, "until it's automatic, unconscious. We're going to instill that in your brain," he said, pointing at my head.

He then handed me a wide index card, with boxes and a divider down the middle. One column read "Positive Points," the other "Negative Points." "Jim St. Germain" was already written at the top.

"What's this?"

"That's your point card," he said. "My what card?"

"Point card. To keep track of your points. You earn positive points for positive behavior, negative points for negative behavior. We're trying to teach you consequences. By the time you leave here, hopefully it'll stick."

"I gotta give this to you anytime I do something bad?"

"No, you keep track. Your life, your card, your points. And it's for positive and negative."

I looked at the card in disbelief. *When in the world was I ever going to use a point card?*

"That card needs to be on you at all times. Think of it as an extension of yourself. Even not having it will get you negative points."

I smiled. "But where you gonna write it down then?"

"That's funny," he said. "You're smart." He flashed a brief smile that quickly got swallowed up by his face. "You always get meals, you always go to school, but a lot else is in your hands. If you accumulate a certain amount of points, you get to play basketball in the back, time to play video games, a later bedtime. Maybe we give you cookies and milk."

"Oh. Okay." I was having trouble processing most of it.

Charles stood up. "Okay, follow me," he said. I grabbed my bag and my new point card, and followed him up the stairs.

On the second floor Charles pointed out the living room, a TV and video game console, a large dining room table, pantries, an almost industrial-size kitchen. The tight hallways had motivational posters framed along the walls. We then went up another flight to where the kids slept—it was after nine so everyone was in bed. The shared bedrooms were college dorm–size with wooden bunk beds and blue-sheeted mattresses. We stopped at one of the rooms with three crumpled figures under blankets, and an empty and made top bunk. Laid out were a clean white T-shirt, boxers, soap, toothbrush, and toothpaste. "This is you," he said. "Now, take a shower. When you're done, store your property for me to lock up." He gestured to a labeled basket. "Wake-up is 6:30."

"Okay," I said.

"Good, that's 750 points." "Huh," I said, confused.

"Write it down," he said. I patted my pockets and Charles took a pencil from behind his ear and handed it to me. I filled in my card, wondering how long I'd be able to do this.

It was a tight space for four people, with small wooden dressers, one thin closet. On a bulletin board I saw family pictures, a magazine photo of Tupac, a test with "Great job!" in red marker. Most kids lived out of bags, as they were only there a couple of weeks, sometimes less. I didn't know how long I'd be there. All I knew was that this was my new home, my fourth in as many months.

Boys Town was built on structure and routine. That's the heart of the system. We woke up at the same time every day, showered, and brushed our teeth. Everyone made their bed, tidied up their area, did their scheduled house chores, and got checked. Chore checker was a responsibility they'd give to a resident, as were manager and book-keeper. It was about creating a "buy in" culture. New residents see the kids taking responsibility so they fall in line.

After our morning routine, we lined up to go down to the dining room table. Two or three staff members would join the twelve kids for toast and cereal, maybe waffles. The teaching continued through the meal. You couldn't escape it. I was in a constant state of being watched and being taught, down to the most basic things. If I grabbed the milk without asking permission, I'd earn negative points. Someone would correct me and have me redo it. I had to give eye contact and ask respectfully, "May I please have some milk?"

At first it felt oppressive, and repressive. The goal was to teach me behavior, unlearn old habits, and train proper ones: everything from greeting someone to following instructions to accepting criticism. There were steps on how to disagree respectfully, select appropriate clothing, even how to contribute to a conversation.

No matter our crimes or situations we all had the same issue. We hadn't been following the rules: at home, at school, in the world, so there was a precision to everything at Boys Town. The lining up, the constant asking of permission, the overly proper way we had to speak, especially toward authority figures. It was like boot camp for my behavior.

One of my first mornings at Dean Street I had to use the bathroom during breakfast, so I got up from the table and did so. I was almost sixteen years old. It didn't occur to me to ask permission to go to take a piss.

"Hey, Jim," one of the staff, a burly dude we called D Dub, said when I returned. He was round, genial, with a beard and glasses. "Just now you got up and you went to the bathroom." The staff always immediately stated what you just did. Rather than "Hey, what are you doing?" or hitting you upside the head, they immediately identified your behavior. It's like the burn from the hot stove, creating a direct connection between behavior and consequence.

"Yeah. So?" I said.

"And you didn't ask permission and you didn't report your whereabouts. For that you're going to earn a negative two thousand points." D Dub spoke calmly, which was the method there. Staff wanted us to focus on our role. This was new: Teachers threw me out of class, cops cuffed me, and my father smacked me. Boys Town staff clearly stated what I did wrong, what the consequence was, and made sure I accepted it.

That last part was the crossroads moment. If you could control your anger, accept the consequences, and write your points down, you would automatically get half of them back. That day, that's not what I did.

"What?! That's fucking stupid," I said. "I'm not asking permission to piss. You want to hold it too?"

Everyone at the table froze.

"I understand you're upset," D Dub said. "You feel like you didn't do anything wrong, but this is part of the system and you have to accept the consequences."

"That's fucking st—"

"Okay, now that you're not accepting the initial consequence I'm going to assign you another five thousand negative points. Plus, because you're cursing—"

"I don't give a fuck about stupid points!" I snapped back.

A calm exhale. "Okay, I'm going to have to give you another …"

I kicked over my chair in protest and started yelling. I was caught in a loop, accumulating more and more negative points, getting further away from my privileges. D Dub stayed locked in on the steps. For all my exploding emotions, he remained even. In order to see if I'd calm down and be willing to accept the consequences, he gave me another instruction—"Please sit down and finish breakfast with us."

That was another chance to end it right there and I took it. Those little opportunities—to earn back points—were hugely valuable. Everyone at that table was paying for a series of bad decisions and consequences going back years. I huffed and sat back down, ten thousand points in the hole for the day. It wasn't even 8:00 a.m.

The Boys Town model makes sure you end on an upswing to show we can always make amends and get redemption, every time. After I accepted and wrote down my points, D Dub role-played it all over again with me. To demonstrate the proper behavior, we tracked back through the incident, which was psychologically powerful. We rewrote the negative incident as a positive one. An erasure. Something about that concept appealed to me.

For the first time in my life I was forced to follow rules, mostly because I had to face accountability on a daily basis. I was also regularly exposed to authority figures invested in my success. Rather than the occasional conversation with Christine or meeting with Dean Walton, this was day in and day out, every little thing I did, from every adult I encountered. But I couldn't always see it for what it was, so I rebelled frequently. It was like I'd been sick for so long that my body rejected the medicine.

After breakfast we lined up for the staff to escort us to the first floor where one by one we'd retrieve our shoes. Every time we entered the brownstone, we'd get searched, and have to take off our shoes and jackets so we'd be less likely to go AWOL, hurt others, or ourselves.

We then lined up again in the front hallway waiting for the blue passenger van to pull up.

Staff transported us one at a time using a grip called manual guidance where they held our arm with one hand, the other on our bicep, and guided us to another staff member at the van door. We were all pre-adjudication, and unlikely to run, but that's how we were transported everywhere. A solid reminder that we were not free. The system's claws were in us.

Behind the wheel of the van was Patrick, Big Pat we called him, one of the morning staff, who treated the van like it was his own. He had a slowly graying beard, glasses, and a gleaming smile. We gave him a hard time because he played only old-school jazz and R&B.

"C'mon, let's hear some hip-hop," I said one time. "You got any Nas in there?"

"That's the problem with you kids—your music is soulless." Big Pat turned back to look at me, then turned the volume up. He pointed at the radio.

"What are you talking about? You been alive like a minute. That's the Commodores. This is the song right here."

She's a brick howwwse. She's mighty mighty, just letting it all hang out.

"Mato mato! What is that?" I said.

"Mighty mighty," he said; then he started singing, dancing in his seat. "She's mighty mighty, just letting it all hang out." The whole van busted up laughing.

"The lady is stacked is what he's saying," Pat explained, drowned out by our laughter. After that anytime that song would come on he'd turn it all the way up and we'd "mato mato" while he waved us off, saying we didn't know anything.

Boys Town had its own school, a small brick building on Willoughby Street downtown, which was part of the larger Passages Academy, the school system's program for kids in detention. It was the twelve of us at Dean Street, another twelve from the other Boys Town NSD on Bergen Street, along with kids serving longer sentences at the two residential homes—about forty kids total. As NSD kids we wanted to help our cause with the judge by getting a good "adjustment report," so we tended to stay in line. It was like an old schoolhouse where we started at homeroom in the lunchroom, and rotated through English, math, history, and science. An assistant teacher would work with individuals on the side, so as not to expose or embarrass them in front of the class.

The points system carried over to the school. Boys Town staff members would stand by the door, handing out discipline and teaching the model. I had barely gone to school and when I did, I had avoided work as much as possible. But I couldn't disappear in this classroom—the size, structure, and staff made that impossible. The spotlight was on me, and it felt like I couldn't get away with anything.

Ms. Oglio, the history teacher, was a small Italian woman with a fiery personality and a strong New York accent. I couldn't shake a feeling that she singled me out, not telling me the answers that she told others.

I remember a time a month into my time there, when we were reading about world religions. The class was filling out a worksheet on rituals and traditions. I kept raising my hand but Ms. Oglio was ignoring me and instead was helping Alan, an Albanian kid who seemed to already know everything.

"Jim, I can't show you exactly where the answer is," she eventually said. "You have to figure it out for yourself. If I give you the answer, you won't remember it or know how to find it again," she said.

"So I'm stupid?"

She opened her mouth like she was going to say something, but didn't. She just leaned over and went back to Alan.

"That's some racist shit, Ms. O. Fuck you!" I shouted, tossing my book and notebook on the floor.

"Jim. Jim! Step out the room, now," Mario called out from the door. A short and stocky staff member with coolie hair, Mario was earnest but had a black belt and an aura that commanded respect. Sometimes he rode a Harley motorcycle to work and we'd gather around to ask him questions about the bike.

"She's fucking racist!" I shouted as Mario walked me out of the room.

"Stop cursing and calm down," Mario said. He walked me out into the small foyer outside the classroom and I sat on the windowsill. Mario didn't speak a word, waiting for me to breathe it down. I stared into the classroom through the glass of the closed door at Ms. Oglio.

"What happened?" Mario asked.

"That bitch, Ms. Ugly-o, called me stupid," I said. "She's racist, man."

"First of all, don't call her a bitch. And her name is Oglio." "I don't care, man. She's racist," I said.

"What are you talking about? You're more racist than she is. She cares about you. And she does *not* think you're stupid."

"She *is* racist! You been here so long you can't see it," I said, still staring through the glass.

"Jim, can you calm down?" he asked. "What does racism have to do with this?"

"That racist bitch—"

"Jim, take a deep breath," he suggested. "Do you remember the skill of expressing your feelings appropriately?"

"Yeah," I mumbled. "Okay, let me hear it."

Once I was revved up, it wasn't easy to bring me down. Reluctantly, I began, "Remain calm and relaxed."

"What else?"

"Look at the person you're talking to, tell them how you feel." "And?"

"Don't curse, and tell the person you appreciate them hearing you," I said. Just saying the steps aloud helped me follow them, which in turn calmed me down.

"So you just proved to me you're intelligent by telling me these skills. You need to practice what you already know. You need to check yourself and give yourself credit. Can I be real with you?"

"Yeah," I said.

"One of the skills was look at the person you're talking to, right?" "Yeah," I said, turning to look at Mario for the first time.

"You forgot to take responsibility for how you feel. You feel you're stupid because that is how we describe our struggles of not knowing something. Raising your hand proved you're not stupid. Ms. Oglio's been doing this a long time. Don't project how you feel about yourself onto her. The only thing that's stupid is giving up, like a punk. You a punk?" he asked.

"Hell no. I'm no punk," I said.

"Then fight for your future. You can win only with proper training. We believe in you, but that means nothing if you don't believe in yourself."

I quietly soaked in what he said, but I was all in the moment. I couldn't see the future, even the immediate future. I couldn't see the very next thing, like returning to the classroom.

"Now, straight, that cost you five thousand points and you owe her an apology. She wants you to use your own brain. People cheat on tests but fail to realize that they don't know what they're supposed to know. Would you want a doctor that cheated on his board exams to operate on you?"

"No."

"I'm going to bring you back in there so you can apologize.

Ms. Oglio is gangster. She might look like a little white lady, but don't get it twisted."

After that incident, I cooled down toward Ms. Oglio and she went out of her way to teach me basic things like how to write a sentence. I'd always had an interest in history and politics so I was drawn naturally to what went on in her class. I had an appetite to know what happened before me. I was always asking why, and when there was an answer, it was history that provided it.

Ms. Oglio wouldn't let me hide or slip by. She was tenacious and had a kind of X-ray vision, seeing me as more than my file. She had a habit of touching my shoulder when she was proud, and warmth flowed out of her. Teaching wasn't just about imparting information for her; it was about connection and relationships and love. Ms. Oglio understood there was a brain, an experience, and a soul on the other side of her instruction.

She was a small woman so I became protective toward her and tried to make her job easier. There were authority figures—in school, at Dean Street, back home—whose job I wanted to make harder. Part of acting out was about creating resistance for those I didn't respect, exerting my power and influence. With Ms. Oglio I wanted to do the opposite.

But the truth is that I was nearly illiterate and mostly overwhelmed in those classes. I had been truant for so long, with such a weak foundation, that things were difficult. English was my second language, I lacked basic knowledge of history, and I had a background in a different math system. I either tried to hide what I didn't know or, if put on the spot, made it hard to teach me. I wore the bully cape sometimes, intimidating other kids and initiating conflict with the Boys Town staff and teachers. Survival instincts are like concrete; it takes a long, sustained force for them to crack. Asking questions meant showing my vulnerability and as a kid you never want to do that—you just nod your head and go along with the teacher. Plus, it was all so overwhelming; I didn't even know where to start.

After school we'd return to Dean Street for our prescribed study hours. Then we'd total up our points for the day. If you made your privileges ("privs"), you'd get television time or a sweet snack— another indication we had our feet in two worlds. We were young enough that cookies and milk was a reward yet we were escorted in and out of a van like state property.

Behind a high white fence in back was an enclosed courtyard with a basketball hoop, and thick leaves drooping down. We'd have barbecues back there in the summertime and play three on three before dinner. Our math teacher let us play chess in class so we got into that for a while. There was also a basketball court on the other side of Dean Street, but we needed permission from the city, state, and Boys Town to go there. Even then we'd get escorted and staff would stand at all exits around the gates.

Lights out was 8:30 unless you were on the highest level, Achievement, and you got to stay up later. That was another psychological and biological wall I hit. I was used to being out on my own, doing what I wanted, staying up late hustling, getting high and drunk, and sleeping in. Now I had to be in bed at 8:30, which was usually before my night even got started. And then I was up with the sun, which I only ever saw on the other side of the night. The point system reset every day, so no one was ever so far in the hole that it was hopeless to climb out. The next day was literally a brand-new day, which spelled something rare: hope.

Boys Town broke me down, forced me to relearn how to behave in the most literal sense. It went against everything I'd ever known. I got tired of early bedtimes, not being able to eat what I wanted, shut off from TV or video games. When I did fall in line, it was often in a superficial way, like I was gaming the system. I got my points, earned my privs, but mostly through tricks.

Once I mastered it, it was easy. Even if I had a horrible day, I knew how to still earn my privs. Before Total Up, I'd ask people if they needed help, every little thing. If someone dropped a pen, I'd rush over and grab it; I'd walk up to a new person and greet him properly. I knew which staff had which sweet spots or weak spots. And I developed keener negotiation skills that allowed me to work myself out of negative consequences. I started to follow the model, but I would not call it buying in at all.

In my heart of hearts, I knew what I was doing. I had turned it into my new hustle.

10

Boredom: A Key Experience of Youth Imprisonment

Tea Torbenfeldt Bengtsson

Introduction

In this chapter, the role of boredom as a significant temporal experience of youth imprisonment is analysed and discussed. The structure of time under confinement is different from that of everyday life on the outside. The institutional routines on the inside are structured to resemble those of normal everyday life, with school-time, rest-time, eating-time and so on. Routines were created with the pedagogical aim of providing the young people with "normalised" everyday rhythms that they often lack in their everyday lives outside. However, there are significant temporal differences between life on the inside and on the outside (Armstrong 2018; Meisenhelder 1985; Scarce 2002; Wahidin 2006). One of the most salient is the lack of control that young people have over their routines and time and consequently the experience of all-encompassing boredom. Boredom "sits in the walls" of institutions designed to confine youth and comes to characterise everyday life (Bengtsson 2012a). Thus, boredom in youth confinement may be linked to individual feelings of restlessness and lethargy, but is conditioned by the wider structures of imprisonment and youth as a formative life phase.

T. T. Bengtsson (✉)
VIVE, Danish National Centre for Social Science Research, Copenhagen, Denmark
e-mail: ttb@vive.dk

To understand the social and cultural meanings of boredom in youth imprisonment, the analysis draws on ethnographic data collected in three Danish secure care facilities in 2009. These facilities hold children and youth between the ages of 10 and 18 and accommodate both youths charged with or sentenced for a crime and youth in protective care, Danish secure facilities operate simultaneously within the criminal justice system and the child protection services. Unlike many other countries, Denmark has no juvenile courts, meaning that youth above the age of legal responsibility (age 15) are tried in the same courts as adults. On 1 January 2019, a specialised youth crime board was established to deal with youth between 10 and 15 suspected of committing crimes and with the option to refer children and youth to secure care facilities. Seeking to meet the demands of both the social and the legal system, these facilities are to care for both "the child in danger" and "the dangerous child" (Donzelot 1979) within the same institutional context providing both treatment and punishment (Bengtsson 2015). Treatment is ideally based on individual pedagogical and educational plans and not, as in other countries, on more formalised institutional requirements or programmes (see Cox 2011; Enell 2017).

As a result, Danish secure facilities are organised around ideas of normalisation and to mimic (family) life on the outside; the youth have private rooms, meals are cooked or prepared in a shared kitchen by staff and youth, there is a common living room with TV, PlayStation and stereo for the youth to use at their own free will, and a gym and other recreational rooms for the youth to use together with the staff. A homely feeling is sought maintained with sofas, curtains, books, plants and paintings on the walls. The staff wear their own private clothing and are not trained as professional guards but as educators or social workers, but not all have professional training. Despite these facilities' resemblance with a "youth club," they also have a number of prison-like characteristics, such as locked doors, barred windows, surveillance cameras, and high walls and fences.

There are eight secure care institutions in Denmark with room for 106 youth at one time (Danish Regions 2018). The average length of stay is two months; however, in the present study the lengths of stay varied from one week to over one year. The institutions consist of three to five units accommodating up to six youth in each unit. The units are gender-integrated and there is no contact between youths in different units. Recently there has been a stronger emphasis on secure care facilities as a place for treatment and learning but there are no fixed treatment programmes. However, the uncertainty of the duration of most youths' stay and the short length of most stays challenges the possibilities of more long-term treatment within these secure care facilities.

Although during the weekdays the youth attend the facility school and workshops (e.g. metalwork), they have an excess of spare time which is often spent sleeping, staying in their private rooms, watching TV and often just "hanging out" in the common rooms and the corridors of the facility (Bengtsson 2012b). This "hanging out" is closely connected to youths' temporal experiences of "doing nothing" (Corrigan, 1975). "Doing nothing" is a way of trying to control temporality by signalling, "I do what I want with my time." However, "doing nothing" in secure care is not an active choice but linked to the burdensome experience of "prison waiting" where time stands still but passes way while the rest of the world moves on (Cox 2017; Armstrong 2018; Wahidin 2006). Thus, to reduce the pains of waiting, "hanging out doing nothing" arguably becomes the youths' response to their lived embodiment of boredom in the secure care facilities (Bengtsson 2012a).

The chapter begins with a presentation of how boredom as a temporal experience of youth imprisonment can be conceptualised on the background of existing literature on time, imprisonment and youth. The next section describes the empirical study focusing on the setting, the method and the data used in the study.

Boredom as a Temporal Experience of Youth Imprisonment

Boredom is, also outside prison and prison-like institutions, a common human experience but often disregarded as an individual emotional state linked to individual emotions and feelings. However, boredom is not merely part of individual experiences but conditioned by wider structures and therefore must be analysed as a collective sociality (Anderson 2004). In their general definition of boredom, Darden and Marks (1999, p. 18) writes, "[boredom] is the socially disvalued emotion we experience in a setting where the drama fails for some reason […] The situation has no apparent future, in the sense of anticipation, although it may have a temporal dimension, because time seems to stretch endlessly ahead without a foreseeable denouement." Despite living a chaotic and at times dramatic life on the outside, most of the time there is little action in secure care facilities. Rather, time often passes exceptionally slow with little action going on, creating an ongoing atmosphere of dullness (Cox 2017).

Being bored is part of a common human experience but may be especially prevailing in the formative phase of young adulthood (Conrad 1997; Anderson

2004; Furlong et al. 2011). Youth generally occupy a social position defined by uncertainty and a state of becoming, with youth itself being a period of experimenting and waiting for adulthood (Miles 2000; Furlong 2009). Youth in vulnerable life situations who often have little stability and support in their everyday lives can especially experience their futures as uncertain.

While boredom can be seen as a common emotional experience, it is found to be present in total institutions, which Goffman (1991, p. 11) defines as, "a place of residence and work where a large number of like-situated individuals, cut off from the wider society for an appreciable period of time, together lead an enclosed, formally administered round of life." The locked doors of prisons become especially defining for the experience of boredom, highlighting the *total* takeover of personal freedom. Boredom in an institutional setting is therefore necessarily conditioned by the temporal structures of imprisonment and not only individual sentiments (Meisenhelder 1985). Boredom in the life of young people placed in secure care facilities thus springs from a collective sociality formed by their imprisonment, rather than their personal dispositions.

Boredom as an experience of imprisonment is linked to the (lack of) action and the structures creating situational meaninglessness. However, the experience of boredom is more than a lack of meaning "in that it does not merely register meaninglessness, but it is also an imperative toward meaning" (Barbalet 1999, p. 633). Boredom constitutes a back door for tackling or avoiding meaninglessness when the person or group of persons experiencing boredom will seek a way of escaping it and will create meaning in the attempt to escape. Boredom-aversion can therefore play a role in the formation of meaning through action or risk-taking, such as engagement in rule-breaking or even crime (Katz 1988). However, deliberate efforts to manage or control various dimensions of time are reduced by the imprisonment and loss of personal freedom (Cohen and Taylor 1972). "Time work," defined by Flaherty (2003, p. 19) as an "effort to promote or suppress a particular temporal experience," is thus limited under the restrictions of the imprisonment, such as not being allowed to go outside for fresh air. At the same time, a central way to cope with imprisonment can be through active "time work" where the experience of time is sped up, such as through laughing and having fun. The room for active "time work" is thus limited while the need for it to better cope with imprisonment is intensified, signifying young people's limited room for agency within total institutions (Wästerfors 2011; Bengtsson 2012a).

Seeking to break with boredom creates a back door for "time work" to manipulate the experience of time as a strategy to tackle and hopefully avoid the niggling meaninglessness of imprisonment. The role of boredom-aversion has been linked with aspects of gambling and risk taking in general, and also intergroup conflict to create meaningfulness (Barbalet 1999; Anderson 2004). Boredom therefore carries within it a dynamic element for creating action through the creation of a situational meaningfulness in an attempt to escape.

The creation of boredom-aversion through risk-taking is well demonstrated both in relation to youths' involvement in crime (Matza and Sykes 1961; Katz 1988; Ferrell 2017) and in other risk-taking activities, such as skydiving, rock climbing, bungee jumping (Lyng 2004b). Lyng (1990, p. 877) uses the term "edgework" to theorise a variety of risk-taking activates as a way of creating "creative, skilful, self-determining action." The engagement in edgework activities can thus provide a refuge from the formal institutional environment of secure care but also resonates with their lifestyles outside secure care. Outside the institutions, many youths are also deeply immersed in a restless search for action where "thrills" and "kicks" and the creation of excitement is a well-known feature in relation to risk-seeking youth cultures (Bengtsson and Ravn 2019). Boredom and boredom-aversion can therefore not merely be ascribed as experiences linked to being on the inside but also carries strong resemblance with the youths' experiences from the outside. While imprisonment in general provokes negative emotions, such as boredom, humiliation and powerlessness, these emotions are not new but often reflect a general position of subordination (Messerschmidt 2000; Soyer 2014).

Setting, Method and Data

The majority of youth (67%) placed under suspicion of crime are in court-ordered remand or serving a sentence (Danish Regions 2018).[1] The facilities are thus primarily used as an alternative to adult jail in order for Denmark to meet the statement of the UN Convention of the Child that the confinement of children should be used only as a measure of last resort and for the shortest appropriate period of time (OHCHR 1989, Article 37b).[2] The average length of stay is two months (Danish Regions 2018). Over the past ten years, there has been an increase in the number of girls going to secure care facilities but often there is only one girl in a unit at the time as the majority of the residents (88% in 2018) are still boys (Danish Regions 2018)

In the study drawn on in the analysis, the aim is to investigate the life of young people placed in secure care and its connection to the young peoples' life outside secure care facilities. In so doing, I seek to develop a perspective on their imprisonment, youth lives and general situation from their own position. For the study, I conducted ethnographic field work in three secure care units during which I met with 40 young people, 21 of which agreed to be interviewed by me. Access to all three secure care units was given by the director of each facility. I adopted the position that informed consent from the youth was not something to be obtained or collected, but rather it became an integrated part of our relationship and thus an integrated part of the research process. Thus, I continually reminded the young people of the role of the research during the period of the field work (Bengtsson 2020). All youth are given pseudonyms and some of their personal details are changed to secure their anonymisation. In Table 10.1, I present some salient details about the youth presented in the following analysis. These five youth are all boys and not representative of all youth populating secure care facilities, but their details give an impression of the background of youth in secure care.

I spent three months and more than 350 hours observing in the facilities, coming and going as I wished. I did not partake in the work of the staff and mostly just "hung out." Unlike the staff, I did not attempt to create special activities. As discussed in the introduction in relation to the youth, "hanging out" has a blurred character because it is not a predefined activity but rather about the importance of "just being." Thus, hanging out as a research method "makes it challenging for a researcher to follow any strictly defined protocol on ethical principles" (Tani 2014, p. 367). When hanging out with the youth, I obtained an approach that positioned me primarily as an observer and an inactive participant, giving me the in-between role of being neither staff nor youth. Most of the time, the youth appeared to accept my presence and, with time, even share intimate information with me.

Writing field notes while at the unit proved difficult so I did them afterwards, taking care to recall most of each day's interactions in detail while they were still fresh in my mind (Emerson et al. 2011). I noted episodes, interaction and speech as well as details about the physical setting such as clothes, the position of furniture and other objects. Furthermore, I noted questions and uncertainties about how to understand episodes. I would always keep pen and paper in my pockets to write down direct dialogue while it was fresh in my mind in the privacy of the lavatory. The field note data included in this article are taken from my field notes but are shortened to focus on the analytical purpose. The more than 200 pages of field notes thus function as a situational record helping to structure episodes, experiences, conversations and feelings conditioned by the context of the secure care facilities. All field notes and interview transcript included in the analysis have been translated from Danish by me.

The significance of boredom in everyday life in these facilities arose as a clear pattern of meaning during the field study, manifesting itself as a shared

10 Boredom: A Key Experience of Youth Imprisonment   211

Table 10.1 Details about the five youth presented in the following analysis. All information shared by the youth

Name[a]	Age	Duration of stay in secure care	Domestic situation outside secure care	Occupation/school outside secure care	Nationality	Accused crime	Parents' occupation
Imran	17	1 month	Living with mother and father and sister and brother in a flat in a suburb	No occupation	Parents from Turkey	• Dealing cannabis • Handling stolen goods	Mother: housewife Father: taxi driver
Rodez	16	Unknown (more than 2 months)	Living with mother and sister in a flat in a suburb	Apprenticeship as a painter	Parents from Algeria/Denmark	• Breaking and entering • Robbery	Mother: unskilled work Father: living in Algeria
Allan	16	2 weeks	Living with mother and father and older sister in a house in the countryside	Secondary school	Parents from Bosnia	• Robbery	Mother: bus driver Father: shop owner
Abham	16	1.5 months	Living in residential home in the countryside	Secondary school	Parents from Palestine	• Fighting • Robbery • Threatening a witness	Mother: housewife Father: small shop owner
Elias	17	Unknown (more than 2 months)	Living on the street/residential home	No occupation	Danish	• Street robbery • Dealing cannabis	Mother: on early retirement Father: Absent

[a]All names are pseudonyms

experience between the youth and me as an observer. Multiple readings of the field notes and the interview transcripts helped me unravel the lived meaning of boredom as highly relevant and directly related not only to the institutional frame of secure care but also in part to the youths' everyday lives outside the secure care facilities (see also Bengtsson 2012a).

Boredom as Part of Waiting

> I sit opposite the kitchen door on a hard chair next to a small table full of old magazines halfway down the dark, empty corridor. The smell of burned toast drifts into the corridor. It blends with the distinct smell of basement and soap always present. I've been sitting on the chair in the corridor for more than an hour and haven't seen anyone enter the kitchen. I try to think; how can it smell of burned toast when the kitchen is locked? One of the five blue doors on the other side of the corridor opens and Imran, 17 years old, comes into the corridor. "Are we having toast?" He looks at me. I shrug my shoulders. "I don't know," I say, "the kitchen is locked." Imran walks over and tries to open the door: "Yes." We stand a little while looking at the locked door. Imran shakes his head a little and then goes back into his room leaving me alone in front of the kitchen door. I sit down again waiting for something to happen. Nothing really happens that afternoon, sometimes one of the five boys residing in the unit comes out of their rooms but quickly returns when they see that I'm the only one there.
>
> (Field notes from secure care facility 1, 2009)

These mundane and trivial observations reveal that although my stay in secure care was professionally revealing and at times exciting, it was primarily characterised by an all-encompassing feeling of boredom. For hours on end, I was sitting in the corridor on the same chair, at the same table, reading the same magazines. As the hours passed, there was a change of consciousness in which my awakening and enthusiasm transformed in to a much slower and "grayer form of awareness" (Meisenhelder 1985, p. 43). There was seemingly very little for me to observe and very little to do. Boredom, I soon discovered, formed the core of my experience, especially at the beginning of my stay, and led me to the embodied insight that it was one of the central aspects of everyday life in the institution. Thus, my boredom was not merely personal but led me to focus on the more general collective experience of boredom in the unit and integral to the experience of imprisonment.

I set out to explore this encompassing experience of boredom and discovered that it was closely linked to my initial expectations of what observing in secure care would be like. I realised that I was waiting for the "wild" life of crime and excitement of these supposedly "dangerous" and "wild youth" to emerge. Because it never really did, I was left with a feeling of disappointment. However, I soon realised that I was not the only one waiting for something to happen. So were the confined youth, and their waiting was in many ways more real than mine. They were waiting to get their lives back and for their chance to get out of the facility and back into freedom. The youth often wondered why I was there and why I did not use my key and leave. Marcus, age 17, commented on my presence by shaking his head, stating, "Only a fool would stay in this place unless they had to." Before I could think of a reply, he went away laughing.

Waiting is known to create experiences of boredom and the youths' waiting time carried some of the amorphousness of waiting. When placed in the secure care facilities under remand awaiting trial, the youth did not know how long they had to wait and when they would be released. Being in remand is an open-ended period that can be prolonged by the judge as long as the police investigation takes place. Therefore, the immediate future of the majority of youth was defined by uncertainties and open waiting time. Not surprisingly, this influenced many of their daily conversations in the facilities. Their concerns were revealed in statements such as, "They have nothing on me, I'll get to be released in court next week" and or "I'm going to call my lawyer [again] to hear if he's got any news." Conversations about the uncertainty of the future were common between the youth and the staff, with the youth desperately waiting for some new information, anything—the indictment, the trial, news from the police, or even a phone call from a mother or girlfriend.

While new information from the "outside" was highly valued, it did not remove or reduce the enduring boredom. Time moves slowly on the "inside" and deliberate efforts to manage or control various dimensions of time, such as waiting, are reduced by the incarceration and loss of personal freedom (Cohen and Taylor 1972; Scarce 2002). The youth daily faced the challenges of dealing with time. Although they seemingly had a lot of "free" time on their hands that was not pre-scheduled, they generally lacked power over the allocation of their time and their daily routines. Despite the simulation of the routines of normal daily life, they become both monotonous and artificial because they are always predetermined by others.

Through active "time work" the youth created strategies for handling waiting time, such as seeing multiple TV series or trying to sleep as much as possible. They often shared such strategies of "time work" dealing with the duration of their stay trying to help each other better cope with their lack of power over the allocation of their time. As Scarce (2002, p. 306) writes from his own experiences of imprisonment, "To some extent, inmates have lost control over time, and thus they have lost some control over themselves." While the "time work" strategies at times could reduce restlessness, they did not signal an end to boredom nor mark the end of their waiting. Thus, boredom in these facilities springs out of the situation of continuous waiting and thus from a lack of control, not only over physical space but also over time.

Breaking with Boredom

> It's almost ten o'clock in the evening. Rodez, Allan and Abham, all 16 years old, are sitting in the corridor together with Bryan, one of the staff, and me. Abham gets up to show how easily he can jump over the football table further down the corridor. Bryan gets up but before he finishes telling Abham not to jump, Abham is flying over the table in a long jump. We all laugh, Rodez and Allan cheering. "Try it," Abham tells them. Bryan gets on his feet: "No, it's off to bed now."
>
> I stand in the corridor next to the kitchen door when Bryan and Shaman from the staff a little later tries to get the five boys to go to bed. "Now stay in your rooms" Bryan shouts in a friendly tone from the corridor. We can hear Abham shouting out of his window to the other boys. Bryan shakes his head and goes into Abham's room to make him stop. I'm alone in the corridor when Rodez pops his head out of his room looking up and down the corridor. He puts his fingers across his lips signalling for me to be quiet as he quickly sneaks into Allan's room. I smile as I hear the two boys giggle. Shaman comes out of Nick's room. "All in bed," he states. I don't reply.
>
> (Field notes from secure care facility 1, 2009)

In a playful way the youth tried to gain control of the situation by challenging the nighttime rules and routines. By running around hiding, the youth constitute a momentary respite or time-out from institutionally expected routines so that the institutional order is momentarily bracketed (Wästerfors 2016). For once, the evening routine was not defined by boredom. No doubt the fun was short lived, but its spontaneity arguably created an atmosphere of excitement. I could easily follow the excitement as the five boys momentarily created an alternative course of events. By shouting out the windows and running to each other rooms, they shortly influenced the daily routines over which they had very little influence.

The small excitement created by the youth often began in the moment when the unexpected happened. Often it began with small signals between the boys: One boy looking at another in a particular way, such as smiling and lifting an eyebrow, signalling so that the other youth knew who would be in on the fun and support an attempt to break the routines. When the youth were all in on the joking, they could quickly create a situation of excitement and momentarily influence daily routines and speed up their experience of time. Through the generation of excitement, the boys could actively influence the experience of duration, sequence and timing of the institutional routines and thus, at times, gain control over the routines and disrupt the institutional rhythms.

In these little attempts at breaking with boredom, the youth skilfully read the situation and thus gained a little control by exploring the limits of the "total institution." It was an opportunity to act like kids and play around. While their rule breaking in the context of the bed-time routine was quite un-harmful, there was often an edge to their actions, as it was never clear how the situation would develop or end. This uncertainty added to the excitement of the actions and also reassured the youth that they were not completely disconnected from controlling their own lives (Wästerfors 2011).

In other situations, the youths' attempts to gain control were more radical, with severe rule breaking, such as stealing keys from a member of staff and harassing a female member of staff by calling her sexually insulting names and trying to remove her skirt with a vacuum cleaner (see Bengtsson 2012a, 2016). Not surprisingly, such attempts to try to break up boredom carried the risk of severe consequences (such as being reported to the police or moved to jail). These attempts of rebellion only rarely led to severe sanctions. Unlike the findings from other countries, these youth did not have to be evaluated or follow a programme to be released and therefore their rule-breaking most of the time did not impact decisions about their futures (see Cox 2011; Abrams and Anderson-Nathe 2013). In a similar way as when taking risks on the outside these youth were willing to face the consequences and possible sanctions to create moments of excitement. While they could not create the "high life" excitement of the streets, the small moments of rule breaking was an institutionalised strategy for boredom-aversion (Conrad 1997; Barbalet 1999).

When the youth were asked about these episodes, they fleetingly explained that they engaged in them "because they could" and that "it was a way of having some fun and killing time" (see Abrams and Anderson-Nathe 2013). Breaking with the rules and routines generated the feeling of being in control, a feeling from which the youth were otherwise excluded. In short moments, they experienced the joy and excitement of "edgework" action and thus momentarily broke out of the boredom of daily life in the facility (Lyng 1990; Bengtsson 2012a). Through the playful use of knowledge of institutional life in the facility the youth in their small rule-breaking demonstrated skills in momentarily challenging the institutions core values of order and obedience. This "institutional edgework" not only formed an escape from boredom but also made them gain a little of their lost power over the present institutionalisation. The escape and fun, however, was always short-lived, as staff always regained control and re-established the institutional routines (Wästerfors 2011; Bengtsson 2012a; Abrams and Anderson-Nathe 2013).

Boredom and the Future Outside

Both in the interviews and when hanging out together in the unit, the youth described their daily lives outside the facility as characterised by an excess of spare time. Especially for the youth who did not attend school or go to work on the outside, "doing nothing" and "hanging out with friends" were familiar "time work." The lack of routines and natural "time work" that school or work can provide often resulted in quite extensive experiences of meaninglessness and the future as out of control. I interview 17 years old Elias in his private room. After having talked about how he experience the unit as "a nice place, with cool people," he reveals how he on the outside tries to navigate difficult circumstance and uphold a sense of control:

Tea:	So have you left school?
Elias:	Yes, yes, it is two years ago. I don't really care for that.
Tea:	What do you do then [with your time] …?
Elias:	I ran away for half a year so I just hung out in Copenhagen …
Tea:	Where did you live then? With some friends or …?
Elias:	It varied …
Tea:	Wasn't it hard not to have a place to live?
Elias:	No, because I prefer being with my friends, instead of being at some kind of residential home. That's killing you. A bit like being here but just worse because there's no getting out. Now I would like to get my own flat.
Tea:	So are the plans [with his social worker] for you to try and get your own flat when you turn 18?
Elias:	No, another institution. I just turned 17.
Tea:	What do you think about that?
Elias:	I'm not going to live there, that's for sure.
Tea:	So what will you do instead?

Elias:	I don't know. Go back to the streets or something. I still have friends, you know.
Tea:	I'm sure they will help you. What about school then?
Elias:	It's not for me. I do things differently.

Just as Elias, several other youth explained that they often did not know what to do with themselves or expect of the future. When I asked about their plans, hopes and dreams, the boys appeared vague and uncertain as if the future was out of their hands. Elias had dreams about getting his own flat, but these dreams appeared unrealistic to fulfil. Instead, he returned to his former lifestyle where living on the street became his solution. Elias and a majority of the other youths experienced a lack of control over their future and a disdain for personal ambition. Thus, the youth often focused on the present and immediate enjoyment, not on long term planning involving stable housing, school or employment.

This focus on the immediate enjoyment also linked to their engagement in criminal activities. Later in the interview Elias, who was charged with street robbery and dealing cannabis, explains how most of the time these criminal activities are just a way of "getting by" and that they are not planned. In general, the youth often talked of their crimes as if they "just happen" to find themselves in situations where crime is a possibility, such as walking along with some friends seeing an attractive victim in the street and deciding to do a robbery. For some youth, especially when "hanging out" together, recollecting and sharing their crimes from the outside could give them a feeling of being creative and skilful (in their past criminal activities) (see also Lyng 2004a). By reliving their crimes and positioning themselves in the stories as "the heroes," this created a feeling of freedom and control that is otherwise nearly absent under imprisonment (Sandberg 2009; Earle 2011).

Just as the institutional edgework, stories of (fun) situations of crimes was relived and shared with excitement. Both institutional edgework and criminal edgework thus became active strategies of gaining momentary feelings of control in situations which otherwise appears to be uncontrollable for the youth (Bengtsson 2012a). While the momentary excitement of the "edgework experience" actively break with experiences of boredom both on the inside and on the outside, the hold no of little promise for the future. The youths' general lack of schooling creates a more constant situation in which the future appears to hold no great promise for the majority of youth. Collison (1996, p. 437), in his study of young disadvantaged men in Britain in search of the "high life," has similar findings: "Schooling is a passport to success yet it is repetitively denied young men like these, as they deny it." Not having the skills, inclination for or chance of being successful in school and education these youth turned to different areas for success, such as leading the "high life" with excitement generated through crime.

Contrary to Elias, some youth did talk about their time under imprisonment as a possible turning point after which a better future could be imagined if they actively focused on improving their schooling. Some took on more responsibility and self-control, but often these attempts to influence their future was often short lived. Being disconnected from the social processes of schooling on the outside, the inside schooling becomes an artificial and detached experience (see also Soyer 2014). While the youth at times envisioned a future without crime (especially in conversations with adults), they also struggled to combine different discourses and expectations into a coherent narrative (Sandberg 2009; Sandberg et al. 2015). Consequently, the youths' attempts of tackling experiences of boredom through different types of "edgework" both on the inside and on the outside were for most of them active attempts at dealing with a profound experience of wide-ranging marginalisation.

Conclusion

Boredom does not spare anyone under imprisonment. Although as an ethnographer, I found ways of handling the boredom during the fieldwork and with time even broke out of it, boredom was also for me the feeling that underlay the entire experience. Together with the imprisoned youth I was waiting for something exciting to happen but it never really did and as Conrad (1997, p. 474) writes, "an unmet expectation, justified or not, is a sure creation of boredom." I gradually learned that boredom was an inseparable part of everyday life in these facilities, not only for me but also, and even more so, for the imprisoned youth.

That youth imprisonment is marked by boredom and the meaninglessness that accompanies it is not surprising. However, the youth did not merely use boredom as an excuse or a way of feeling sorry for themselves; rather, it was an experience that pervaded their everyday lives in these facilities. Their boredom springs out of their situation of continuous waiting and thus from a lack of control, not only over physical space but also over time. Both the youth and I shared the bodily understanding that our internally experienced time did not synchronised with that of clocks and calendars and that in some situations large differences occur (Flaherty 2002). While the youth constantly did active "time work" for handling time, they were only momentarily able to challenge the routines and rhythms of institutional life. Life on the outside filled their conversations and minds, leaving them little motivation for engaging in the artificial routines of the facilities. The intuitional imitation of a "normal everyday life," focusing on regularity and the value of work, was often so far from the lives that most of the youth lead on the outside that this imitation in itself emphasised their experience of alienation.

By creating new situations of "institutional edgework" and reformulating past situations of "criminal edgework," the youths attempted to tie together the separate worlds of outside and inside. A whole host of risk-laden criminal acts such as joyriding, drug use, football hooliganism, fire-setting, street robbery and "binge" drinking may create "illegal forms of excitement," argues Hayward (2007, p. 239) and "represent a break with the banalities of everyday life and mark an entry into a new world of possibilities and pleasures." Looking at the youths breaking with institutional rules and their (most often petty) crime as a form of edgework generating ruptures in daily boredom can make these otherwise meaningless actions meaningful in the concrete situation. These "edgework actions" merely becomes meaningful in their immediate context, as in the long run they are often reduced to isolated situations, which disconnected the youth from daily life and their future. Therefore, these edgework pockets of cheerfulness and excitement, although helping the youth to keep up their spirits when "hanging out doing nothing," did not change their dominant experience of lacking control over both their daily life and their future (Bengtsson 2012a).

"Hanging out" with friends "doing nothing" became especially meaningful for those youth who had abandoned school. From their perspective, schooling is not an option for them and they find other spaces such as the street where they find a kind of freedom from the constraints of educational expectations. While under imprisonment, most youth have no idea to what to expect of their immediate future (such as when they are released). However, this feeling of uncertainty was for many not only linked to their present situation but also well known from their everyday life on the outside. These youth were struggling to handle the pressures of daily life and the (lack of) expectations of the future. While the youths' stories about outside life initially appeared spectacular with excitement and edgework crimes their stories made clear that their reality was more often that of advanced marginalisation with comprehensive experiences of having little or no agency (Bengtsson 2012b; Soyer 2014).

Boredom appeared to be a wide-ranging experience both under imprisonment and in the youths' everyday lives on the outside. Regardless of being on the inside or on the outside, as soon as the excitement ended, the respite or break from the banalities and boredom of everyday life likewise ended. The end of the "edgework action" thus created a situation of "no action." The relationship between action and boredom therefore becomes a vicious circle: Although creating action through edgework activities constituted a rupture with boredom in the here and now, its fleeting nature also generated possible future boredom.

Breaking with or avoiding boredom under youth imprisonment is not easily solved. As demonstrated in this chapter boredom has not merely to do with lack of activities but is embedded in the system as a lack of individual freedom and control. Pedagogies that are directed at creating meaningful activities and treatment plans may be able to temporarily supress boredom in the facilities. However, boredom links to the pains of imprisonment and the negative effects of punishment, which cannot be removed through fun activities, treatment, or by focusing on education (Crewe 2011). For these youth boredom is linked to marginalisation and structural disadvantage in their individual lives and in the lives of their families and communities (Cox 2017). Almost all youth have histories of extensive contact with social agencies and interventions of the wide-ranging Danish welfare state. These social interventions may help and support the majority, but for the individual youth, they have not been able to prevent them from ending up in confinement. Despite the often short duration of the confinement, for the individual youth, it is likely to be experienced as the ultimate exclusion.

Notes

1. The total population aged 15–18 was approximately 345,000. A total of 535 were placed in secure care facilities in 2018 and those not placed under remand were placed for observation or protection.
2. The facilities are regulated by the child protection act and further regulated by a special legislation for the confinement of minors.

References

Abrams, L. S., & Anderson-Nathe, B. (2013). *Compassionate confinement: A year in the life of unit c*. Rutgers: University Press. https://doi.org/10.1177/0094306115588487.

Anderson, B. (2004). Time-stilled space-slowed: How boredom matters. *Geoforum, 35*(6 special issue), 739–754. https://doi.org/10.1016/j.geoforum.2004.02.005.

Armstrong, S. (2018). The cell and the corridor: Imprisonment as waiting, and waiting as mobile. *Time and Society*. SAGE PublicationsSage UK: London, England, 27(2), 133–154. https://doi.org/10.1177/0961463X15587835.

Barbalet, J. M. (1999). Boredom and social meaning. *The British journal of sociology*, 50(4), 631–646. https://doi.org/10.1080/000713199358572.

Bengtsson, T. T. (2012a). Boredom and action-experiences from youth confinement. *Journal of Contemporary Ethnography*, 41(5), 526–553. https://doi.org/10.1177/0891241612449356.

Bengtsson, T. T. (2012b). Learning to become a "gangster"? *Journal of Youth Studies*, 15(6). https://doi.org/10.1080/13676261.2012.671930.

Bengtsson, T. T. (2015). Controlling young people through treatment and punishment. In Bengtsson, T.T., Frederiksen, M., & Larsen J.E. (eds), *The Danish welfare state: A sociological investigation*. doi: https://doi.org/10.1057/9781137527318.

Bengtsson, T. T. (2016). Performing hypermasculinity: Experiences with confined young offenders. *Men and Masculinities*, 19(4). https://doi.org/10.1177/1097184X15595083.

Bengtsson, T. T. (2020). Informed consent as a situated research process in an ethnography of incarcerated youth in Denmark. In P. Billett, M. Hart, & D. Martin (Eds.), *Complexities of researching with young people* (pp. 130–142). Abingdon: Routledge.

Bengtsson, T. T., & Ravn, S. (2019). *Youth, risk, routine: A new perspective on risk-taking in young lives*. London: Routledge. https://doi.org/10.4324/9781315440767.

Cohen, S., & Taylor, L. (1972). *Psychological surival. The experience of long-term imprisonment*. Harmondsworth: Pelican Books.

Collison, M. (1996). In search of the high life: Drugs, crime, masculinities and consumption. *British Journal of Criminology*. Narnia, 36(3), 428–444. https://doi.org/10.1093/oxfordjournals.bjc.a014104.

Conrad, P. (1997). It's boring: Notes on the meanings of boredom in everyday life. *Qualitative sociology as everyday life*, 20(4), 123–133. https://doi.org/10.1023/A:1024747820595.

Corrigan, P. (1975). Doing nothing. In S. Hall & T. Jefferson (Eds.), *Resistance through rituals: Youth subcultures in post-war Britain* (pp. 84–87). Abingdon: Routledge.

Cox, A. (2011). Doing the programme or doing me? The pains of youth imprisonment. *Punishment & Society*. SAGE PublicationsSage UK: London, England, 13(5), 592–610. https://doi.org/10.1177/1462474511422173.

Cox, A. (2017). *Trapped in a vice: The consequences of confinement for young people*. New Brunswick: Rutgers University Press. https://doi.org/10.1093/sf/soz071.

Crewe, B. (2011). Depth, weight, tightness: Revisiting the pains of imprisonment. *Punishment & Society*. SAGE PublicationsSage UK: London, England, 13(5), 509–529. https://doi.org/10.1177/1462474511422172.

Danish Regions. (2018). Den årlige statistik på de sikrede institutioner 2017 (Year statistic for the Danish secure facilities).

Darden, D. K., & Marks, A. H. (1999). Boredom: A socially disvalued emotion. *Sociological Spectrum*. Informa UK Ltd, *19*(1), 13–37. https://doi.org/10.1080/027321799280280.

Donzelot, J. (1979). *The policing of families*. New York: Random House.

Earle, R. (2011). Boys' zone stories: Perspectives from a young men's prison. *Criminology & Criminal Justice*. SAGE PublicationsSage UK: London, England, *11*(2), 129–143. https://doi.org/10.1177/1748895811398458.

Emerson, R. M., Fretz, R. I., & Shaw, L. L. (2011). *Writing ethnographic fieldnotes*. Chicago: University of Chicago Press.

Enell, S. (2017). I got to know myself better, my failings and faults. *Young*. SAGE Publications Sage India: New Delhi, India, *25*(2), 124–140. https://doi.org/10.1177/1103308816638978.

Ferrell, J. (2017). Boredom, crime and criminology. In K. Hayward (Ed.), *Cultural criminology* (pp. 179–194). Routledge. https://doi.org/10.4324/9781315095202-8.

Flaherty, M. G. (2002). Making time: Agency and the construction of temporal experience. *Symbolic Interaction*, *25*(3), 379–388. https://doi.org/10.1525/si.2002.25.3.379.

Flaherty, M. G. (2003). Time work: Customizing temporal experience. *Social Psychology Quarterly*, *66*(1), 17–33. https://doi.org/10.2307/3090138.

Furlong, A. (2009). The emergence of emerging adulthood. In A. Furlong (Ed.), *Handbook of youth and young adulthood: New perspectives and agendas*. London: Routledge Taylor & Francis Group.

Furlong, A., Woodman, D., & Wyn, J. (2011). Changing times, changing perspectives: Reconciling "transition" and "cultural" perspectives on youth and young adulthood. *Journal of Sociology*, *47*(4), 355–370. https://doi.org/10.1177/1440783311420787.

Goffman, E. (1991). *Asylums: Essays on the social situation of mental patients and other inmates*. London: Penguin Books.

Hayward, K. (2007). Situational crime prevention and its discontents: Rational choice theory versus the 'culture of now'. *Social Policy & Administration*. John Wiley & Sons, Ltd (10.1111), *41*(3), 232–250. https://doi.org/10.1111/j.1467-9515.2007.00550.x.

Katz, J. (1988). *Seductions of crime: moral and sensual attractions in doing evil*.

Lyng, S. (1990). Edgework: A social psychological analysis of voluntary risk taking. *American Journal of Sociology*. University of Chicago Press, *95*(4), 851–886. https://doi.org/10.1086/229379.

Lyng, S. (2004a). Crime, edgework and corporeal transaction. *Theoretical Criminology*. Sage PublicationsSage CA: Thousand Oaks, CA, *8*(3), 359–375. https://doi.org/10.1177/1362480604044614.

Lyng, S. (Ed.). (2004b). *Edgework: The sociology of risk-taking.* New York and London: Routledge. https://doi.org/10.1017/CBO9781107415324.004.

Matza, D., & Sykes, G. M. (1961). Juvenile delinquency and subterranean values. *American Sociological Review, 26*(5), 712–719.

Meisenhelder, T. (1985). An essay on time and the phenomenology of imprisonment. *Deviant Behavior.* Taylor & Francis Group, *6*(1), 39–56. https://doi.org/10.1080/01639625.1985.9967658.

Messerschmidt, J. W. (2000). Becoming "real men": Adolescent masculinity challenges and sexual violence. *Men and Masculinities.* Sage Publications, Inc., *2*(3), 286–307. https://doi.org/10.1177/1097184X00002003003.

Miles, S. (2000). *Youth lifestyles in a changing world.* Philadelphia: Open University Press.

OHCHR. (1989). Convention on the rights of the child. Adopted and opened for signature, ratification and accession by General Assembly resolution 44/25 of 20 November 1989.

Sandberg, S. (2009). Gangster, victim or both? The interdiscursive construction of sameness and difference in self-presentations. *The British Journal of Sociology.* John Wiley & Sons, Ltd (10.1111), *60*(3), 523–542. https://doi.org/10.1111/j.1468-4446.2009.01254.x.

Sandberg, S., Tutenges, S., & Copes, H. (2015). Stories of violence: A narrative criminological study of ambiguity. *British Journal of Criminology, 55*(6), 1168–1186. https://doi.org/10.1093/bjc/azv032.

Scarce, R. (2002). Doing time as an act of survival. *Symbolic Interaction.* John Wiley & Sons, Ltd, *25*(3), 303–321. https://doi.org/10.1525/si.2002.25.3.303.

Soyer, M. (2014). The imagination of desistance: A juxtaposition of the construction of incarceration as a turning point and the reality of recidivism'. *British Journal of Criminology.* Narnia, *54*(1), 91–108. https://doi.org/10.1093/bjc/azt059.

Tani, S. (2014). The Right to be Seen, the Right to be Shown: Ethical Issues Regarding the Geographies of Hanging Out. *YOUNG, 22*(4), 361–379. https://doi.org/10.1177/1103308814548102.

Wahidin, A. (2006). Time and the prison experience. *Sociological Research Online.* SAGE PublicationsSage UK: London, England, *11*(1), 127–138. https://doi.org/10.5153/sro.1245.

Wästerfors, D. (2011). Disputes and going concerns in an institution for "Troublesome" boys. *Journal of Contemporary Ethnography, 40*(1), 39–70. https://doi.org/10.1177/0891241610377199.

Wästerfors, D. (2016). Playfights as trouble and respite. *Journal of Contemporary Ethnography.* SAGE PublicationsSage CA: Los Angeles, CA, *45*(2), 168–197. https://doi.org/10.1177/0891241614554087.

11

Friendship in the Juvenile Correctional Institution

Anne M. Nurse

Introduction

> Well, I don't really got no friends here. I mean, I don't got no friends here. I'm just here to do whatever I need to do. I ain't here to make friends or anything.—Nick

When I met Nick, he had just begun serving time at an Ohio Department of Youth Services facility. He, like many young men entering prison for the first time, planned to do his time alone. But that is not the way it turned out—over time, Nick ended up making a small number of close friends. This chapter examines how, why, and when prison friendships like Nick's form. It draws on interview data collected as part of a longitudinal research project with forty incarcerated and paroled young men.

Understanding friendship formation in juvenile prison is important because research suggests that adolescents who have emotionally supportive friendships tend to have better mental health than those who do not (Almquist et al. 2014). These adolescents are also more psychologically resilient (van Harmelen

---

Sections of this chapter are reprinted from *Locked Up, Locked Out: Young Men in the Juvenile Justice System* (Vanderbilt University, 2010).

A. M. Nurse (✉)
The College of Wooster, Wooster, OH, USA
e-mail: anurse@wooster.edu

et al. 2017). Similarly, strong friendships appear to lessen depression in youth who have experienced high levels of stress in childhood (van Harmelen et al. 2016). Offering further support for these conclusions, neurobiologists find that adolescence is a key time of brain development. One of the influences on healthy development is the strength of social network connections (Lamblin et al. 2017).

There is mixed evidence about the impact of friendships on youth behavior. The "peer contagion effect" suggests that youth influence each other into delinquency. In fact, some research has shown that close relationships with nondelinquent peers outside prison inhibits criminal behavior while those engaged in delinquent or illegal behaviors can increase it (Giordano et al. 1986). Researchers have also found some limited peer contagion effects when youth in juvenile correctional centers learn new criminal techniques from others (Halsey 2007) and when peer group membership encourages increased levels of misconduct in the institution (Reid 2017a). At the same time, however, Weaver's research (2012) shows that under some circumstances, friends who engage in delinquency can help support each other's efforts to desist. Similarly, Lee and Thompson (2009) conducted a study of a youth in a group care setting and while they found some limited evidence of peer contagion, they also found evidence that peer relationships can have pro-social benefits.

The clear links between friendship, mental health, and delinquent behavior are compelling reasons to pay attention to relationships youth build—and do not build—in prison. To date, we have limited information about this topic. Below is a summary of the main findings from the existing literature.

Literature Review

Starting in the 1940s with the publication of Donald Clemmer's *The Prison Community*, academics have studied prison friendships and social structure. Clemmer's work, and other early studies in adult prisons, suggested that there was some level of group solidarity and that friendships existed but were somewhat weak and transitory (Clemmer 1940; Goffman 1961; Sykes and Messinger 1960; Zamble and Porporino 1988). Later work, however, found that solidarity had decreased due to the increased presence of gangs, younger people, and racial hostility (Hunt et al. 1993; Jewkes 2002; Owen 1988).

The findings from adult facilities are a good guide to help us think about friendships among incarcerated juveniles, but they are unlikely to apply exactly. As described above, adolescence can be seen as a distinctive developmental stage which may have an impact on the relationships young people form. Scholars have also suggested that the conditions in juvenile prison are less conducive to the formation of friendships than are those in adult prisons. First, young people generally receive shorter sentences, causing the population to be more transitory and limiting the opportunity for friendships to form (Genders et al. 1989). Second, indeterminate sentences—like those being served by most U.S. youth who have been adjudicated as delinquent—function as a disincentive for friendship formation. Under indeterminate sentencing, youth are held until they age out of the system. They can be released earlier, however, if they exhibit good behavior and complete their prescribed program. Indeterminate sentences are similar to programs in adult prisons that reward good behavior with early release. Crewe's study of British adult prisons (2005) concluded that when good behavior programs are available, it is rational to limit emotional ties with other incarcerated people because those ties might require rule breaking, threatening the possibility for early release.

Research suggests that the staff in juvenile facilities often discourage friendships. In their ethnographic work, Abrams and Anderson-Nathe (2013, p. 59) found that the juvenile correctional staff encourage youth to "work their own program" and stay out of each other's business. They also blame and punish the whole group for the behavior of individuals, potentially causing anger and resentment between youth. Similarly, Cox found that staff tell youth that they "come here alone and leave here alone" in an effort to discourage them from seeking the approval of their peers and to encourage personal responsibility (2017, p. 304).

While many factors work to prevent friendships in juvenile prison, research finds that they exist nonetheless. Recently, Reid (2017a) asked young men incarcerated in California about their friendship networks. Just about one-third of the respondents, disproportionately those who were older and less gang involved, reported having no close friends. Reid speculated that these older youth have less need for peer affirmation and may avoid friendship to avoid negative influences. Among the two-third of the sample who reported having friends in the facility, the mean number was 3.8 friends (SD = 2.69). Interestingly, gang affiliation was not associated with increased numbers of friends, but involvement with gang activities was. This may indicate that simply affiliating with a gang is self-protective and does not necessarily reflect actual identification with the gang (Reid 2017b).

Drawing on data from the same California study, Reid and Listwan (2018) identified three patterns of friendship formation in prison. One group of youth heavily involve themselves in prison and gang life and report high numbers of friends. There are also youth who isolate themselves as much as possible and report no or few friends. The third, and largest, group carefully selects friends, recognizing the need for protection from violence. These youth try to select friends who will provide them with a social outlet and will also decrease (or at least not increase) their risk of victimization. It is likely, however, that the structure and security level of institutions affects these patterns. Where Reid and Listwan's work was conducted in a large state institution, Inderbitzin (2005) conducted ethnographic work in a facility that housed youth in cottages (with 15–20 other residents). She found that many residents came to form friendships and even planned to stay in touch after incarceration. Yet, as their release dates neared, these friendships seemed to be less and less important to them (see also Inderbitzin 2009). In terms of security level, Sieverdes and Bartollas (1986) found the highest level of peer group cohesion in maximum security institutions, possibly because the population was less transitory than in the lower security institutions.

Not surprisingly, it appears that another factor that strongly affects friendship formation is race and ethnicity. Researchers asked adult men incarcerated in Pennsylvania about the people they "get along most with." They found that there was "moderate race/ethnic clustering." (Schaefer et al. 2017). It is often difficult to tease out the respective influences of race and region on friendships in juvenile prison, however. Because the carceral state draws disproportionately from impoverished communities of color, many of the youth either know each other or know of each other. These pre-existing ties often determine friendships in the institutions (Lopez-Aguado 2018). Racial segregation outside the institution ends up translating to racial segregation within it.

The influence of race on friendship is further complicated by institutional policy. In California, for example, the prison system categorizes youth by both race and geography and assumes gang identity based on those factors. Patrick Lopez-Aguado finds that groups that are commonly labeled gangs are really "racialized, place-based collective identities that are established in how individuals are categorized and separated in the punitive facility" (2018, p. 60). These groups not only provide protection; they racialize the youth as they come to accept the classifications given to them by the institution. In his ethnographic work on jails, Walker (2016) concludes that both staff and incarcerated people use race as an organizing principle. Because the two processes come to legitimate and reinforce each other, it becomes very difficult for incarcerated people to make friends across racial lines. The institution, for example, cites gangs as a reason to racially segregate housing and the inmates go on to police each other to ensure that the groups created by the institution are maintained (Walker 2016).

In sum, the literature indicates that friendships do exist in juvenile prisons but that they are shaped and limited by institutional factors as well as by social groupings like race and gang membership. The project from which this chapter draws extends and deepens our knowledge of friendship in juvenile prisons through its unique ethnographic and longitudinal design. The project's goal was to ascertain whether newly incarcerated youth seek out friendship, whether and how their plans change over the course of their incarceration, and the criteria they use to select friends.

Methods

This study included young men who were starting their first sentence with the Ohio Department of Youth Services (DYS) system in 2002. The DYS is responsible for supervising youth convicted of serious or repeat offenses. At the time of the study, the agency housed about 2000 youth in eleven institutions. I only selected youth from two of these facilities: Oak Hill which was a maximum-security prison housing about 200 young men, and Perry Point, a medium-security prison with about 500 male residents (the institution names are pseudonyms). Both were large institutional-looking buildings walled off with barbed wire. In Oak Hill, residents slept two to a locked room while in Perry Point, fifty residents slept in one large room filled with bunk beds.

The sample's distribution reflected the different sizes of the two institutions: twenty-seven youth were housed at the larger Perry Point facility, and thirteen were at Oak Hill. These institutions were ideal for this study because young men were assigned there based not on what type of crime they had committed, but rather on perceived security risk and available beds. Thus, a diverse group of young men from across the state resided in each facility. Both institutions also housed the full range of ages found in the DYS—from twelve to twenty-one years. I chose to limit the sample to first-time admissions in order to follow youth from their first impressions of the system through their release. Excluding youth who had spent time in the system before, however, meant that there were likely differences between my sample and the whole DYS population.

A challenge associated with interviewing incarcerated Ohio youth is the requirement that researchers obtain parental permission for youth under the age of eighteen. This proved to be difficult and I ultimately only received permission from 20 percent of the parents I tried to contact. This low response rate raises concerns about sample bias because it is likely that the most marginalized parents were less likely to respond and allow their sons to participate. Fortunately, 100 percent of the youth whose parents signed forms agreed to participate. In addition to these youth, fifty percent of the final sample included youth who were able to consent for their own participation because they had committed their crimes as seventeen-year-olds and had subsequently turned eighteen. As with the younger age group, all of the eighteen-year-olds I spoke with agreed to participate in the study, decreasing the chance of bias. The sample slightly overrepresented white teenagers (58 percent, compared to their institutional population of 50 percent). Black teenagers made up 40 percent of the sample but 47 percent of the population and one youth (2 percent) identified as Latino (Ohio Department of Youth Services 2002).

I met with the youth three times over approximately three years. I used a semi-structured interview schedule. The initial interview focused on the young men's early experiences at the institution. The second round of interviews took place between nine and fifteen months after the first. Because the youth in this study were first-time admissions to the DYS, their sentences were relatively short, and the majority (twenty-nine of the forty) had been released to parole by the time of the second interview. The meetings with the paroled youth took place in a variety of locations in their communities but generally occurred in a restaurant of their choice. During this round, thirty-five of the youth were re-interviewed (a response rate of 88 percent). About two years after the original interviews, I returned once more to ask each youth about his life, family, friends, and future plans. I was able to interview thirty-four of the original forty (a response rate of 85 percent over the period of the study).

This chapter focuses on the friendships that incarcerated young men make in correctional institutions. "Friendship" is a difficult concept to operationalize and different researchers define it in different ways. For example, Schaefer et al. (2017) asked adult prisoners about the people they got along with most. The researchers made that decision based on other work had that found that incarcerated men are unwilling to claim friends in the institution (Crewe 2005). Although aware of this potential problem, I chose to use the word "friend" and I asked the young men to describe what the term meant to them. They said that a friend is someone they have known for a long time, who has proven his or her loyalty ("someone I can trust to be there for me"), and who will listen to them talk about their problems. It became clear that the youth reserve the term "friend" for relationships with a high level of trust and proven loyalty. Even though they used this somewhat specific definition, it did not appear to inhibit them from claiming friends in the institution.

In the time since this research was conducted, there have been a number of structural changes at the DYS which may impact friendship formation. Like many states, Ohio has decreased the population in its state-level correctional facilities and has reduced the number of facilities as well, from eleven to three.

While both Oak Hill and Perry Point are still open, the average young man living there has a much more extensive mental health and criminal (often violent) history than average youth in 2002 (Harrell et al. 2015). Additionally, to comply with PREA (the Prison Rape Elimination Act), Oak Hill moved from housing two youth in a room to all single rooms. Because of these changes, I returned to Oak Hill in 2019 and conducted a short survey with eight youth. The survey included open-ended questions about their friendships both inside and outside the institution. Because it was a small and non-random sample, I simply use the responses to verify the earlier findings. Only one significant difference emerged, which I discuss at length below.

Findings

In the initial round of interviews, the young men indicated that friendships between youth at the facilities are rare. They were quite adamant that they planned to avoid others as much as possible and do their time alone. When I asked why, the most common response was that the other youth in the institution were not suitable friends, primarily because they could not be trusted. Doug told me,

> You can't really have friends in here 'cause the people you think you're friends with, they will go stealing your stuff, so I don't really have any friends. I've got certain people that I talk to and certain people that I don't. I got like one friend, but I know him from the outs and I know he wouldn't do anything like that.

Marcus made a similar comment about the other youth in the institution: "I see a couple that's headed for the good but most of 'em they still gotta a long way to go. A long way to go." Other youth described their fellow residents as being "liars," "stupid," and "violent." These sentiments echo those expressed by incarcerated people in other studies. For example, respondents in one study of a maximum-security prison said that other prisoners were "superficial" and "unhelpful" (Toch 1992, p. 79). Similarly, the adults in another study repeatedly insisted that they were "not like those other guys" (Zamble and Porporino 1988).

While distrust of others was the primary reason given for avoiding friendship, the youth also felt that there was little point in investing time in a friendship that would not last past their stay in prison. Richard, for example, said, "The way I look at it, if you're not gonna see this person again why try to make friends with them? Just while you're there at your stay? But there is no point of making friends while you're there because you won't see them when you get out." Nick, who was quoted at the beginning of the chapter, also thought that it was not worth his time to make friends.

Youth were also aware that friendships might pull them into trouble. They told me that friends might cause them to enter into fights or other illegal activities, resulting in extra time being added to their sentences. For example, Jason commented, "If you were to fight someone, your friend might join you in an act of violence which will cause seclusion or extended time in the institution and security threat group punishment." The young men also talked about how the prison staff reinforce the idea that friends lead to trouble. They said that from the time they walked through the door at orientation, guards and counselors stressed that the best way to get out of the prison is get involved with as few people as possible. This reinforced the link between friendships and trouble.

It is clear from the first round of interview data that most youth do not enter prison with the intention of making friends. Getting to know this study's participants over time, however, gave me the opportunity to see whether they followed through on their plans. Early in the second round of interviewing, indications began to emerge that doing time alone was not easy. Alex, for example, spoke at length about how he tried and failed to refrain from friendships:

> It's just hard, because, I mean, when I went in there I tried to keep to myself, but you just get so lonely that, oh my God, I just want someone to talk to. You just, you get so lonely, that's why I had just one friend in there and that was that kid, Mick. I talked to him every day. Every day at lunch, I talked to him every day. That's the only person I really communicated with besides staff. I don't know. It just, it got me through my time faster.

As it turned out, Alex was not alone—the majority of the youth in this study ended up making friends with at least one or two carefully selected prison residents. The sections below detail the criteria they used in choosing friends.

Area Codes and Gangs

In Ohio juvenile prisons in the early 2000s, one of the most important forms of social organization involved telephone area codes. When a young man arrived at the DYS intake center, other youth immediately asked what code he was from, and once this was ascertained, someone from his area usually approached him to find out more about his neighborhood. In the prisons I visited, the largest area code groupings were Cleveland, Columbus, Akron, and Dayton. Youth from smaller cities sometimes managed to establish and maintain their own groups, but because of low numbers they were usually forced to combine with the larger urban groups. Virtually every young man in this study emphasized the importance of the area code system in the prison culture. For example, Freddie said,

> This is how it is in here though—all Cleveland people hang out with each other. I mean they all clique up, like if you're cool with a certain person or something, then you're going to be cool with 'em. Like if this man's cool with that kid and he's from Toledo, then all his Toledo boys is cool with him. He's from Cleveland and I'm from Cleveland, then I'm going to be cool with him and I'm going to be cool with his boys over there. If they got problems with those boys over there from Akron and … I don't know anybody from Akron and he don't know anyone from Akron …, we're going to be messing around with them. We are going to have problems with them. That's how it is.

The area code groupings Freddie describes were fairly rigid, and a newly admitted youth was not usually able to lie about his home code. He was questioned intensely about his school and friendship history, and if he refused to divulge any personal information, other young men would ask a guard or steal his prison identification papers. I asked Charles what happened when a new young man from his area arrived. He said, "[We] just sit down and talk about stuff. I just start talking about people in my neighborhood and the other person will know the person in my neighborhood and then we start being cool." On a rare occasion, it was possible for a youth to switch code affiliations if he knew a lot of people from another area code or if he had cousins or other family members in the same prison who claimed another affiliation.

Area codes served as a useful group marker because they were obvious and could be quickly assessed. They also gave new arrivals a temporary identity while they figured out the more personal identity they would like to project. Coretta Phillips (2008) points out that regional affiliation is particularly meaningful to youth in prison because it gives them an outside identity (rather than an institutional identity) with which to define themselves. Area codes are also a rich form of group solidarity because they are based on shared spatial knowledge as well as common connections. Regional affiliation is not a peculiarity of the Ohio prison system—these types of alliances have been found in adult facilities other U.S. states as well as in a British juvenile facility (Irwin 2004; Phillips 2008).

Area code groups shared some features with gangs and were sometimes identified as such by Ohio prison staff. The 2002–2005 interview data indicated that gangs and area codes were linked. The young men said that gangs outside prison were often regional, and consequently, area codes and gang territory overlapped considerably. At the same time, the youth in the original study saw the two as distinct entities. They reported that what they regarded as true gangs were present but not prominent in the Ohio system. Freddie and I talked about gangs during an interview shortly after his release. He confirmed the presence of gang members but said that it was safer to claim an area code instead:

> Anne: Are there gangs in there?
> Freddie: There's not gangs there. It's not gangs. It just people cling Cleveland to Cleveland, Columbus to Columbus.
> Anne: So there are no Bloods and Crips?
> Freddie: Oh, you can find those. There is people that are in there that are Bloods and Crips but they don't say it 'cause you never know who is and who is not. So you might as well run with your city. And just keep it clean, you know?

Freddie and other young men's assessment of the weak presence of gangs in Ohio juvenile prisons surprised me because it strongly contrasted with what was being reported at the same time in other states (Curry et al. 2000). It appears, however, that at some point after 2005, gangs began to establish a stronger presence in Ohio juvenile correctional facilities. In the 2019 follow-up survey, respondents mentioned area codes as important in determining friendships, but gangs were a much more prominent theme. In response to a question about whether there are informal rules about who can be friends with whom, all eight respondents said that gang affiliation is one of the primary factors that drives friendship patterns.

Race

Racial identity plays a powerful role in social relationships in juvenile correctional centers both independently and through area code and gang affiliations. The interviews made it clear that a shared racial identity can lead to some level of solidarity—at least among Black people—but that it did not automatically lead to friendships. The Black respondents told me that they rarely united on the basis of race unless a white person did something that was perceived to be racist. When that happened, the Black youth came together,

11 Friendship in the Juvenile Correctional Institution 235

using words or physical violence to punish the white youth. In less conflictual situations, Black youth generally hung out together but did not feel a strong loyalty to the group. Chad even told me that he thought much of what passed for solidarity was simply talk:

> Niggas always talking about we stick together and this and this, but they be the first ones trying to knock you. You know what I'm saying? Or bring you down when they on another level to get you on their level. You know what I'm saying? 'Cause it's all about the mind thing. They want to bring you down to their level 'cause they feel bad about theirself.

Chad's views reflect the general level of distrust of others in the institution—a distrust that tends to override potential friendships that might be based on racial allegiances. At the same time, the somewhat higher level of solidarity among Black than white youth mirrors findings from earlier research in juvenile facilities (Sieverdes and Bartollas 1986).

Unlike the Black teenagers, whites said that they rarely came together on the basis of race. In fact, a small group of white teenagers actively avoided other white youth as they tried to curry favor with Black people. They would also, in the words of multiple interviewees, "act Black" as a method of gaining status. They believed that having Black friends would elevate their social standing. This finding is consistent with work conducted outside prison in which white adolescent males were found to perceive select racial groups (particularly Black and Puerto Rican) as cooler and more masculine than whites (Way 2011).

As described, conclusions about friendships and racial identity should be drawn carefully because racial identity overlaps with other characteristics. For example, while gangs and area code groupings are theoretically interracial, in practice they tend to be fairly homogeneous due to residential segregation outside the prison. In fact, Ethan, who is white, told me that when he arrived in prison and told people where he was from, everyone laughed because every single other young man from that area code was Black. Normally, youth are constrained from making friends across race lines due to these area code or gang groupings—not by race per se. However, unlike the situation in 2002, some of today's gangs are specifically organized around race. For example, the Aryan Brotherhood and other white supremacist gangs have gained ground in Ohio prisons and have added a much stronger racial overtone to the social organization of prison life. It should be noted, of course, that adolescents outside prison also tend to associate with people from within their own races (see, e.g., Wimmer and Lewis 2010 for a study of Facebook friends). The presence of racially based gangs in prison, however, creates strong and explicit rules that enforce homogamy whereas the forces driving racial segregation outside prison are far less obvious.

Safe Spaces

As described above, the young men in this study felt that friendships had the potential to pull them into trouble, but some found ways to make friends whom they considered to pose less risk. First, many told me that they intentionally cultivated friendships with acquaintances from outside prison. These prior associations allowed youth to assess whether potential friends were acting out their "true selves." Because everyone in prison understands the rigorous impression management requirements imposed by the informal culture, it becomes hard to trust that anyone's act is real. In other words, if a youth knows that he is being forced to put on an act himself, he has good reason to believe that everyone else is too. Having known someone prior to prison provides some protection from duplicity as it enables a comparison of the potential friend's prison self to his outside-world self.

A somewhat surprising second space where youth met friends was in the DYS intake center (named Scioto). Jeremy said,

> When I was in Scioto, I met these kids, Trevor and Adam. We were real good. We got to be real good friends and always hung around in Scioto. I came here and they both in my unit. So yeah, I was happy about that. And there is this other kid I know, kinda know, from the outside. I've only seen him like once or twice. So now I talk to him too. Besides that, I kinda stay to myself.

Like Jeremy, Gabe also made friends with someone he knew from the intake center. He said, "I talk to some kids, but I don't make friends here ... But I have one friend that I was in Scioto with. He was in my unit ... He left though." The intake center differs from a permanent placement institution because its population is extremely transitory. This transience may result in fewer pre-set social groupings and somewhat less pressure to put on an act. The youth seem to trust others who entered intake with them more than they trust youth they meet in their permanent placements. If nothing else, a youth from intake is an appealing friend because he represents a familiar face in a new and frightening environment. Rarely, however, did these—or any—friendships made in custody survive once the youth went home.

While friendships are most common among youth who know each other from outside their current institution, there are certain circumstances that appear to foster friendship among those who were not connected prior to serving their sentence. Several young men told me that Bible study was a safe space because it brought together others who shared their interests and values. When I asked Kevin whether he had made friends in the institution he said, "There was one youth there that … actually there were a couple of them … one of them I talked to almost every day while I was there. And the other one I met at Bible study one time and me and him was walking around one day talking about the Bible and religious stuff. He said he needed some spiritual support." Other young people told me that Bible study was one of the few places where they felt free to "really talk" and that friendships formed there had the potential to be genuine.

In addition to Bible study, housing provided a possible avenue for friendship. As described, the two prisons in this study had different sleeping arrangements with Oak Hill having rooms with double occupancy and Perry Point having large rooms with bunk beds. There were clear differences in the two groups' propensity to make friends. Specifically, youth in the facility with semi-private rooms were more likely than those in the communal bunkroom to report making friends. Being together in a separate room provided the opportunity for a youth to come to know his roommate well enough to consider him a friend. For example, Nick talked about his roommate with great enthusiasm. I asked him what they talked about and he said, "As far as just talking we, you know what I'm saying, down in our rooms, sharing conversations. Talking about what he gonna do when he go home. I talk about what I'm gonna do when I go home. Mutual." The tendency to make friends with a roommate obviously has something to do with proximity (see Slosar 1978, on effects of proximity on friendships in prison), but it also has to do with the relative privacy a shared room affords. As described above, today Oak Hill no longer double bunks youth. Research suggests that this reduces violence (Krisberg 2003; McCain et al. 1980), but it also takes away opportunities for youth to make supportive friendships.

Conclusion

I began this chapter with a quote from Nick about how he planned to avoid friendships while incarcerated. By our second interview, however, he had made several friends, including his roommate. Nick is representative of most of the youth in the study. The prison is a lonely place and time goes by slowly.

Friends can provide support and companionship in this bleak environment. At the same time, friendships are difficult to forge when youth do not trust each other and so it generally takes place around the edges—between roommates, in Bible study class, or between youth with outside connections. Friendship choices are severely constrained by where the young men are from or by their gang affiliation. They are also constrained by race, although that is partly a byproduct of segregated housing outside the prison leading to equally segregated area codes and gangs.

Staff members at many juvenile correctional facilities actively discourage friendship formation, fearing that it will make youth more likely to participate in illegal activities or gang violence and thus be harder to control. Cox's (2017) work suggests, however, that this assumption may be incorrect. During her fieldwork New York juvenile correctional facilities, she found that the most relaxed and controlled moments happened when staff allowed themselves and the youth time to play and hang out together. Conversely, it was at moments the youth were not allowed to speak and were highly regulated that the greatest tension and potential for trouble occurred. Restricting the opportunity to make friends can also have unforeseen negative consequences. As described above, considerable research suggests that friendships are important for mental health, resilience, and even healthy brain development (Almquist et al. 2014; Lamblin et al. 2017; van Harmelen et al. 2016, 2017). There is also evidence to suggest that friendships can aid in desistence from delinquency (Lee and Thompson 2009; Weaver 2012).

The potential benefits of friendships between incarcerated youth make it important to consider ways to change structural elements of juvenile prisons to encourage their healthy development. For example, it appears that the small cottage model may make it easier to make friends (Inderbitzin 2005). The project from which this chapter draws suggests that creating more groups formed around common interests (like sports, Bible study, music, video games, or writing) might give youth a safe space to interact with others who they perceive as like themselves. Cox (2017) finds that allowing down time, when staff and youth are able to just hang out, can build relationships. These kinds of programs, however, will require modification in staff training. Rather than reinforcing the mantra about doing time alone, staff need to learn that friendship can have positive effects for youth and for the institutional environment. Given that many young people are locked up for the majority of their adolescence, prison friendships can play a key role in their emerging adulthood.

References

Abrams, L. S., & Anderson-Nathe, B. (2013). *Compassionate confinement: A year in the life of Unit C*. New Brunswick, NJ: Rutgers University Press.

Almquist, Y. B., Östberg, V., Rostila, M., Edling, C., & Rydgren, J. (2014). Friendship network characteristics and psychological well-being in late adolescence: Exploring differences by gender and gender composition. *Scandinavian Journal of Public Health, 42*(2), 146–154.

Clemmer, D. (1940). *The Prison community*. New Braunfels, TX: Christopher Publishing House.

Cox, A. (2017). Fetishizing the will in juvenile justice policy and practice. In J. Jacobs & J. Jackson (Eds.), *The Routledge handbook of criminal justice ethics* (pp. 301–314). London: Routledge.

Crewe, B. (2005). Codes and conventions: The terms and conditions of contemporary inmate values. In A. Liebling & S. Maruna (Eds.), *The effects of imprisonment* (pp. 177–208). Cullompton, UK: Willan Publishers.

Curry, D. G., Howell, J. C., & Roush, D. W. (2000). *Youth gangs in juvenile detention and corrections facilities: A national survey of juvenile detention centers*. Washington, DC: U.S. Department of Justice, Office of Juvenile Justice and Delinquency Prevention.

Genders, E., Player, E., & Johnston, V. J. (1989). *Race relations in prisons*. Oxford: Clarendon Press.

Giordano, P. C., Cernkovich, S. A., & Pugh, M. D. (1986). Friendships and delinquency. *American Journal of Sociology, 91*(5), 1170–1202.

Goffman, E. (1961). *Asylums: Essays on the social situation of mental patients and other inmates*. New York: Anchor Books.

Halsey, M. (2007). On confinement: Resident and inmate perspectives of secure care and imprisonment. *Probation Journal, 54*(4), 338–367.

van Harmelen, A. L., Gibson, J. L., St Clair, M. C., Owens, M., Brodbeck, J., Dunn, V., et al. (2016). Friendships and family support reduce subsequent depressive symptoms in at-risk adolescents. *PLOS ONE, 11*(5), e0153715.

van Harmelen, A. L., Kievit, R. A., Ioannidis, K., Neufeld, S., Jones, P. B., Bullmore, E., et al. (2017). Adolescent friendships predict later resilient functioning across psychosocial domains in a healthy community cohort. *Psychological Medicine, 47*(13), 2312–2322.

Harrell, W., Dedel, K., & Schuster, T. (2015). *A report on the transformational reform of the Ohio Department of Youth Services, 2007–2015*. (Online). Washington, DC: Federal Court Monitoring Report, p. 39. Retrieved July 12, 2019, from https://www.scstatehouse.gov › 083116 ohio_report_on_transformation.

Hunt, G., Riegel, S., Morales, T., & Waldorf, D. (1993). Changes in prison culture: Prison gangs and the case of the "Pepsi Generation". *Social Problems, 40*(3), 398–409.

Inderbitzin, M. (2005). Growing up behind bars: An ethnographic study of adolescent inmates in a cottage for violent offenders. *Journal of Offender Rehabilitation, 43*(3), 1–22.

Inderbitzin, M. (2009). Reentry of emerging adults: Adolescent inmates' transition back into the community. *Journal of Adolescent Research, 24*(4), 453–476.

Irwin, J. (2004). *The warehouse prison: Disposal of the new dangerous class.* New York: Oxford University Press.

Jewkes, Y. (2002). *Captive audience: Media, masculinity, and power in prisons.* Portland, OR: Willan Publishers.

Krisberg, B. (2003). *General corrections review of the California youth authority.* Sacramento, CA: California Youth Authority.

Lamblin, M., Murawski, C., Whittle, S., & Fornito, A. (2017). Social connectedness, mental health and the adolescent brain. *Neuroscience & Biobehavioral Reviews, 80*, 57–68.

Lee, B. R., & Thompson, R. (2009). Examining externalizing behavior trajectories of youth in group homes: Is there evidence for peer contagion? *Journal of Abnormal Child Psychology, 37*(1), 31–44.

Lopez-Aguado, P. (2018). *Stick together and come back home: Racial sorting and the spillover of carceral identity.* Oakland, CA: University of California Press.

McCain, G., Cox, V. C., & Paulus, P. B. (1980). *The effect of Prison crowding on inmate behavior.* Berkeley, CA: University of California Libraries.

Ohio Department of Youth Services. (2002). *Annual report 2002.* Columbus, OH: State of Ohio.

Owen, B. A. (1988). *The reproduction of social control: A study of Prison workers at San Quentin.* New York: Praeger.

Phillips, C. (2008). Negotiating identities: Ethnicity and social relations in a young offenders' institution. *Theoretical Criminology, 12*(3), 313–331.

Reid, S. E. (2017a). Friendship group composition and juvenile institutional misconduct. *International Journal of Offender Therapy and Comparative Criminology, 61*(2), 191–209.

Reid, S. E. (2017b). The curious case of loners: Social isolation and juvenile incarceration. *Legal and Criminological Psychology, 22*(1), 180–195.

Reid, S. E., & Listwan, S. J. (2018). Managing the threat of violence: Coping strategies among juvenile inmates. *Journal of Interpersonal Violence, 33*(8), 1306–1326.

Schaefer, D. R., Bouchard, M., Young, J. T. N., & Kreager, D. A. (2017). Friends in locked places: An investigation of prison inmate network structure. *Social Networks, 51*, 88–103.

Sieverdes, C. M., & Bartollas, C. (1986). Security level and adjustment patterns in juvenile institutions. *Journal of Criminal Justice, 14*(2), 135–145.

Slosar, J. A. (1978). *Prisonization, friendship, and leadership.* Lanham, MD: Lexington Books.

Sykes, G. M., & Messinger, S. L. (1960). The inmate social system. In R. Cloward (Ed.), *Theoretical studies in social organization of the Prison* (pp. 5–19). Brooklyn, NY: Social Science Research Council.

Toch, H. (1992). *Living in prison: The ecology of survival.* (Rev. ed.). Washington, DC; Hyattsville, MD: American Psychological Association.

Walker, M. L. (2016). Race making in a penal institution. *American Journal of Sociology, 121*(4), 1051–1078.

Way, N. (2011). *Deep secrets: Boys' friendships and the crisis of connection.* Cambridge: Harvard University Press.

Weaver, B. (2012). The relational context of desistance: Some implications and opportunities for social policy. *Social Policy & Administration, 46*(4), 395–412.

Wimmer, A., & Lewis, K. (2010). Beyond and below racial homophily: ERG models of a friendship Network documented on Facebook. *American Journal of Sociology, 116*(2), 583–642.

Zamble, E., & Porporino, F. J. (1988). *Coping, behavior, and adaptation in prison inmates.* New York: Springer-Verlag.

12

Juvenile Facility Staff: Research, Policy, and Practice

Alexandra Cox

Juvenile Facility Staff: Research, Policy, and Practice

Workers arguably lie at the heart of our understandings of youth imprisonment. When a young person is removed from their homes and their families and detained in custody, the state assumes responsibility for their care and safety. In most youth imprisonment contexts, the state assumes the role of *in loco parentis*, or the 'place of a parent', while a young person is incarcerated. Thus, the adults working in facilities for youth in trouble with the law, which includes juvenile detention, corrections, and residential facilities, serve as not only custodians of a population that has been incarcerated beyond their will, but also carers who must ensure the well-being of a population of young people who are considered to be legally and socially vulnerable. The core tension between 'care' and 'control', then, is one which arguably animates the relationship between young people and staff in juvenile facilities (see also Inderbitzin 2006).

Juvenile facility work is also important to understand in the broader context of labor and labor rights, and the transformation of juvenile

---

A. Cox (✉)
Department of Sociology, University of Essex, Essex, UK
e-mail: alexandra.cox@essex.ac.uk

imprisonment around the globe, particularly in the context of the implementation of the United Nations Convention on the Rights of the Child and global reforms which have sought to keep the detention of children to the minimum and transform the treatment of young people. Workers lie not only at the heart of organizational change initiatives, as they are the key individuals who implement those reforms, but also at the center of discussions about the future of care work (Armstrong et al. 2013; Himmelweit 2018). They are also the individuals who are most likely to lose their work in the face of substantial reforms.

This chapter provides an overview of the dynamics of work in juvenile facilities, focusing on the critical role that workers place in shaping juvenile facility life, as well as a focus on the microculture of juvenile facility work, drawing on data from a US-based study of juvenile facility staff.

The microdynamics of work in facility life, and particularly the relationships between young people and the staff who manage them, have been studied by a number of scholars and researchers, and these dynamics have revealed some key and core issues: the tensions between care and control, the experience of trauma, both that which is imported into facility life by staff and young people and that which occurs in facility life, and the dynamics of staff training. The macro studies of work in juvenile imprisonment have pointed to the history of juvenile incarceration and their impact on local communities and the nature of work, the effect of decarceration on staff resistance to reform, and broader theoretical discussions about the abolition of juvenile imprisonment and whether treatment can ever really be effective in juvenile justice landscapes (Schlossman 1977; Miller 1991; Bernstein 2014; Cox 2015).

Staff in Juvenile Facilities

Not all staff members working in juvenile facilities across the globe are focused on custodial matters, nor are all staff members in juvenile facilities that are primarily focused on custody and control involved in the work of control. In general, juvenile facility frontline staff (sometimes referred to as 'juvenile care workers') involved in custodial matters are often not referred to as 'guards', despite engaging in roles similar to those as prison guards or corrections officers. They often do what is termed 'direct care' work in the field of social work and social care, which involves direct interactions with young people as clients, as opposed to administrative or managerial work or supervisory social care. These frontline staff workers are generally tasked with order maintenance, surveillance and control, the management of movements within the facility, and the uses of restraints when an incident triggers them. They are also tasked with enforcing rules and behavioral expectations, as well as implementing behavioral change strategies, often either solely or in conjunction with treatment or counselling staff members, as well as mentoring and support of young people (Kupchik 2007). Staff members can play a critical role in assisting young people to adjust to institutional life, particularly through the support they offer (Cesaroni and Peterson-Badali 2010). Yet these staff members also often transcend their traditional 'control' role, building close relationships with young people on their units, sometimes even as surrogate parents or guardians, often because they are the staff members in the facilities with the most frequent forms of contact with young people (Inderbitzin 2006). It is thus often noted that frontline staff in juvenile facilities struggle with a role conflict as they manage the often-competing goals of punishment and rehabilitation (Abrams and Anderson-Nathe 2013).

In her study of the role of staff working in a small cottage setting in a rural juvenile training school in the United States, Michelle Inderbitzin (2006, p. 433) found that frontline staff members engaged in more than simply the 'control' of the young people under their care; they serve simultaneously as "correctional officers, parents, counselors, coaches, friends, and guardians" in a living unit context which demanded close cooperation and interaction between staff and young people. Inderbitzin's work helpfully contributes to our understanding of the tensions at play in a facility environment where staff are charged with transforming the lives of young people charged with crimes.

In addition to frontline staff, there are a number of other workers in juvenile facilities that play a critical role in the life of the facilities. In North American and British contexts, counselors, social workers and therapists are increasingly common in facilities, whereas in Scandinavian facilities which are more child welfare and 'pedagogically' oriented (van der Laan and Eichelsheim 2013), staff members play a blended role between security and treatment. In the Netherlands, for example, 'group workers' are employed in juvenile correctional institutions, and they are tasked with "stimulating behavioral change" through in-depth, intensive interactions with young people (Geenen 2017). Institutions in Sweden, for example, include a combination of young people placed for reasons of child welfare ('problematic home conditions') or behavior, and the placements can range from being voluntary or done through a court order (Franzén 2014). Staff members in these institutions are generally considered to be parent-like, providing physical and emotional affection to young people while also expected to deliver treatment (Franzén 2014).

Juvenile facilities are also overwhelmingly full-time educational institutions, and thus employ teachers and other full-time educational staff. Teaching staff in juvenile facilities often have to enforce the broader sets of norms and rules in the facilities themselves. Although there have been some informal accounts of the lives of teachers and other educational staff in juvenile facilities (Zeman 2014), there are few empirical studies of the role that teachers play in the context of confinement (Benner et al. 2016; Flores 2012, 2015; McCray et al. 2018). Despite the fact that juvenile facilities are intended to be largely therapeutic institutions, some researchers have found that the delivery of services and care, as well as education provision, is often limited (Domenici and O'Leary 2015; Ashkar and Kenny 2008), even in comparison to adult prisons (Kupchik 2007), even though it is federally mandated in U.S. contexts which receive federal funding for education.

Developmental Role of Staff

Juvenile facility staff arguably play a critical role in enforcing norms and expectations of behavior amongst young people during their time in confinement. They are also often working with young people during a core moment in their development, and thus arguably play an important role in either facilitating or interrupting that development, particularly through their joint roles as mentors and enforcers, as well as their ability to engage young people successfully in treatment and promote readiness to change (Mulvey et al. 2010; Kupchik and Snyder 2009; Schubert et al. 2011). Positive relationships between young people and staff are said to be at the core of healthy institutional functioning (Mulvey et al. 2010).

The extant research on juvenile facility staff, primarily from Western contexts, indicates that poor relationships between young people and staff are correlated with young people's sense of safety and their well-being, and in particular their experiences of anxiety, depression and hopelessness (Biggam and Power 1997; van der Laan and Eichelsheim 2013; Harvey 2007). Marsh and Evans (2009) argue that the traditional literature on helping or mentoring relationships may not sufficiently address the unique relationships that are established in juvenile correctional settings, because juvenile justice staff spend a significant amount of time with the young people under their care. There has been a substantial amount of research which has looked at mentoring relationships, however, which demonstrates that young people benefit from strong and consistent relationships with adults in these mentoring contexts (Marsh and Evans 2009, pp. 47–8). In a study conducted in juvenile facilities in four Western states, researchers evaluated youth perspectives on the quality of relationships with staff, with an emphasis on how those relationships would impact on young people's self-efficacy with respect to their release plans. They found that the types of relationships that young people developed with staff impacted on their levels of stress, sense of self-worth, their forecasts about their future, and their general orientations, all of which may impact on their sense of self-efficacy about their release (Marsh and Evans 2009). In a study comparing young people's experiences with staff in prisons as compared to juvenile facilities, young people in juvenile facilities rated staff members more highly for their abilities in being supportive mentors (Fagan et al. 2007).

Young people have also identified key concerns with the procedural fairness and legitimacy of institutions. Young people incarcerated in correctional institutions place a high value on fairness; they point to authoritarian rule-making and cultures of institutions, the limited privacy rights, and an obsessive focus on rule-making as key concerns related to the legitimacy of the institutions (Ashkar and Kenny 2008; Harvey 2007; Miller and Ohlin 1985; Geenen 2017). Gover et al. (2000) their study of 48 U.S. juvenile facilities, found that young people who perceived their institution to have less 'justice' were more likely to report higher levels of anxiety. Dutch researchers similarly found a relationship between "experienced perceptions of justice of the rules and fairness of treatment in the institution" and feelings of safety by young people in juvenile institutions (van der Laan and Eichelsheim 2013). A British study revealed that young people's experiences of unfairness at the hands of staff related to their levels of stress (Harvey 2007).

Gender Dynamics Between Staff and Young People

Since juvenile facilities are often gender segregated, the gender dynamics at play in the facilities, both between staff members and young people, and between young people themselves, can be an important dimension of life inside of those facilities. Some researchers have examined the gendered dynamics of staff-youth relationships, and have found that staff members can play a vital role in young people's self-understandings, their gender identity, and in enforcing normative gender role expectations (Galardi and Settersten 2018). Researchers have found that girls are often described by staff members as more emotionally labile, and more manipulative and difficult to work with (Bond-Maupin et al. 2002; Baines and Alder 1996; Lanctôt et al. 2012). This, some have argued, may play a role not only in how staff treat young people, but also how they communicate normative gender role expectations to them, and how and what they expect of young people after they leave facilities (Galardi and Settersten 2018). Researchers have found that staff members tend to draw on gendered stereotypes and expectations of young people's behavior, and thus when a young person does not conform to those gender role expectations or stereotypes, they may often be perceived to be more difficult or are judged negatively (Galardi and Settersten 2018; Cox 2018). Although some facilities in the United States and the United Kingdom, for example, have started developing what they call 'gender-responsive' programming, it is unclear to what extent this programming engages with the views of frontline staff (Galardi and Settersten 2018). However, there is less research on the gendered performances of staff members in juvenile facilities, and how these performances may play a role in the dynamics of care and control (although see Abrams and Anderson-Nathe 2013).

Staff Abuse and Violence

Allegations of abuse and violence by staff members in juvenile facilities against young people are common (see also the chapter by Liz Ryan in this volume). Young people have died at the hands of staff members involved in aggressive restraints, they have suffered serious physical and sexual abuse, and they have sustained life threatening injuries. Novelist Colson Whitehead's book *The Nickel Boys* (2019), which was a fictional account of the horrific abuse and violence, and sometimes homicides, that were revealed to have occurred at a reform school in Florida called the Arthur Dozier School for Boys, illustrates the full scope and scale of this violence.

Sexual violence and victimization by staff members against young people remains a problem in juvenile facilities. In the United States, the most recently available data reveals that the number of allegations of sexual victimization has increased between 2005 and 2012, and 45% of the reported incidents involved staff-on-youth sexual victimization (Beck and Rantala 2016).

In a large scale study of the role of officers in violence in juvenile facility life which took place in Canada, researchers found that staff "allowed, and induced" young people to use force on other young people in the facilities (Peterson-Badali and Koegl 2002, p. 41; Cesaroni and Peterson-Badali 2010). Negative relationships between young people and staff have also been found to be related to violence between young people and in the facilities, as identified in a study of German juvenile facilities (Klatt et al. 2016), Young Offender Institutions in England and Wales (Bottoms 1999), and in the United States (Poole and Regoli 1983). On the flip side, positive relationships between staff and young people have been found to be correlated to lower levels of violence (Lai 2018).

Occupational Stress

Researchers have found that occupational stress amongst individuals working in juvenile facilities is common. Staff turnover rates in juvenile correctional facilities are relatively high (Mitchell et al. 2000; Armstrong et al. 2013). Occupational stress in correctional environments has not only been linked to negative health outcomes, including lowered life expectancy, but also to negative personal behaviors, such as alcoholism and family problems, but also to chronic absenteeism, problems at work, low morale, and problems with co-workers (Mitchell et al. 2000).

High sources of stress for individuals working in juvenile facilities include negative relationships between administrators and line staff and work in institutions with a strong treatment orientation, potentially because staff members experience higher levels of role ambiguity (Mitchell et al. 2000).

In recent years, practitioners and policymakers have recognized that staff members in juvenile facilities can experience two kinds of trauma related to their work in juvenile facilities: vicarious trauma, associated with their work with young people who have entered the facilities having experienced high levels of neglect and abuse, as well as the trauma associated with exposure to abuse and violence within the facilities (McNamara 2010).

A New York Case Study

There is a dearth of qualitative research on the experiences and lives of juvenile facility staff. The research below documents staff perspectives on care and control in the context of reforms that were taking place in a US state-level juvenile justice system. This state, New York, is used as a case study here to reveal staff perspectives in the context of a state which was under federal and state scrutiny for its staff practices—not only had sexual and physical violence and abuse been identified in custody, but the state's treatment and behavioral change practices were also being assessed.

In order to develop an account of staff perspectives on confinement, I undertook a period of qualitative research between 2011 and 2012 inside of New York's residential juvenile facilities. The research involved observations and interviews with over 75 frontline staff members, including teachers and recreational staff, and 40 site visits to facilities, where I conducted observations in various areas of the facility, from the units, to the security booths, to the recreational areas. The research took place during a period of substantial reform in New York's system aimed at addressing allegations of abuse and violence by staff against young people, the overuse of physical restraints, as well as the state's overreliance on incarceration. The state had been under federal oversight and monitoring for a period after allegations were made that staff were engaged in sexual violence against girls in some facilities, and that they engaged in an overuse of force (King 2009, 2010). In order to address these issues, the state introduced a new model of care that was designed to be 'trauma informed', implemented a restraint monitoring system, and began to implement changes in the daily life of facilities in order to make the facilities more home-like, like allowing young people to decorate the walls of their rooms, or receive more rewards, such as video games on their units. The research study itself was focused on understanding the staff dynamics of resistance to organizational change, staff-youth relationships, and the role of behavioral change programming in the lives of staff members.

This chapter is based on interviews with 50 frontline staff members across three facilities, union members, staff at the central administration, and court-based staff and observational research which took place in five juvenile residential facilities across New York State. Where available, the length of time that the staff member worked in the system is indicated. Staff members from several positions in the facilities were interviewed. YDAs, or Youth Development Aides, spent the most time during the day with young people, and were responsible for security, movement, and monitoring of progress. Youth Counselors, or YCs, met on a regular basis with young people to monitor their treatment and behavioral change program progress and to provide some support for their release. Mental health workers were relatively sparse in the facilities, but represented a range of professions, from social workers to psychiatrists, who worked closely with young people diagnosed with a serious and persistent mental health disorder. I also interviewed teachers, recreational staff, and facility management.

Methods

The study involved semi-structured interviews and observational research with staff members serving in a range of roles in the facilities, and who represented a mix of ages, race and ethnicity, and genders (Table 12.1). The research also included a group of young people incarcerated in the facility who were trained in interview research and who conducted several research interviews, as well as a university-based research assistant who had previously been incarcerated at one of the facilities, and who participated in interviews and observations. The young people were incarcerated in the same facility where the staff were interviewed, and they conducted several of the interviews themselves. A purposive sample was generated based on the goal of interviewing participants occupying a range of positions, who had worked in the system for varying lengths of time, and who were identified by other staff members as representing a perspective that was pertinent to the research focus. The interviews followed an Appreciative Inquiry approach (Cooperrider and Whitney 2007), in which staff members were asked to describe what they saw working well in the organization and in their relationships with young people.

At the time of the research, New York State managed juvenile facilities across the state, which ranged in size from just a handful of young people to a facility with a capacity for 200 young people. The facilities range in security from being staff secure to being locked and heavily secure, with hurricane wire fencing around the perimeter. All facilities in New York are centrally managed and overseen by the state's Office of Children and Family Services, but have their own facility directors who make day-to-day decisions about young people's movements, care and treatment. Every facility has a school, which young people attend daily. They also generally participate in some recreational activities and had staff counselors assigned to them to monitor their progress in a behavioral change program. The behavioral change program was a token economy system, whereby young people would earn privileges based on their compliance with particular behavioral norms and rules (Kazdin 1982;

Table 12.1 Interview sample demographics

Total sample	N = 50
Gender	
Male	86%
Female	14%
Race/ethnicity	
Black	28%
White	66%
Latino/a	6%

Tompkins-Rosenblatt and VanderVen 2005; Doll et al. 2013). This kind of system is also used in residential treatment facility contexts.

The disciplinary system in New York's facilities included tickets or write-ups for young people who violated rules, which would prevent them from advancing in the behavioral change system. But informally speaking, discipline also involved the use of 'room confinement', which sometimes involved young people being locked in their rooms (which were locked from a central unit in the facility). Although physical restraints were only triggered if a young person was considered to be a threat to themselves or others, some young people experienced the use of physical restraints as a form of punishment for misbehavior.

Young people lived on small units in the facilities, and had their own rooms. They traveled throughout the facility by unit; in the larger facilities, they would rarely interact with other units, and the 'movements' between units were orchestrated carefully by senior security staff, ensuring that no two units met each other in hallways. At least two staff members would generally accompany units of young people at all times. Young people attended school daily, for most of the day.

At the time of the research, frontline staff members in New York's juvenile facilities wore uniforms and, by all accounts, looked like prison guards (although they did not carry weapons or have pepper spray). The youth counselors in the facility wore their own clothes. But it was the frontline staff—referred to as Youth Division Aides (YDAs)—who spent the most time with young people. They sat with them on the facility units, accompanied them around the facilities, ate with them, and even sat in classrooms with them. YDAs would often work eight-hour shifts, but the regular use of overtime, involving 16-hour shifts, was not uncommon during the study period, as a number of staff had called out sick.

Emotion Management and Labor

Engaging in work with young people in custody involves a great deal of emotional labor. The sociologist Arlie Hochschild has defined emotional labor as "the management of feeling to create a publicly observable facial and bodily display" (1983, p. 7). Juvenile facility work arguably creates particular demands to manage feelings, as staff members are expected to manage a group of young people who are held in custody against their will, and thus uphold a performance of 'control', but residential juvenile facilities also often demand strong attention and care to relationships, or 'care', and thus staff members sometimes struggle to perform work within these competing demands. Elaine Crawley (2004) has studied the management of emotions required by corrections officers working in adult facilities, and argues that prison work demands a performative attitude in order for staff members to manage their life at work. Crawley (2004, p. 414) describes prison as an 'emotional arena' in which, because people are held against their will, where the experience of prison can be painful for people who are incarcerated, and where the "degree of intimacy" between staff and people who are incarcerated is great.

Performances of Control

The physical presence and performances of the YDAs, or frontline staff, was a critical part of their emotion and identity management. The YDAs wore uniforms that resembled the uniforms of prison guards; they had military-style cargo trousers and a collared shirt with the insignia of the agency on it, and carried radios (see also Abrams and Anderson-Nathe 2013). Although the staff were relatively diverse by gender and age, the frontline staff were predominantly male, and a number of these male staff members were physically large, and participated in heavy weightlifting. Some would come to work carrying protein milkshakes for bulking up their muscles, and some would speak to the young people in the facility about their muscle-building and weightlifting strategies. For some of those staff, their physical bulk was deemed essential for their performance as staff members who were capable of exercising physical control over the young people they had custody over. YDA French, a white man who was in his 20s and had just started working at a small facility for boys in a rural part of the state, was himself physically strong and large. When I asked him what made a good staff member, he said that he said that if a staff can "be aggressive without being aggressive," or looks like the kind of guy who "would rip your head off," this would be important. Referring to another physically strong and large staff member, he said that he "probably has more respect than anyone else." French had recently joined the facility after being told by a friend, who was also a staff member, that he could come to the facility to work "and you can beat the shit out of them." However, French said that he quickly realized that this approach was wrong, and that "talking" to young people, coupled with a strong physical appearance, was the preferable route to maintaining control.

French's description of "be[ing] aggressive without being aggressive" refers to the potential *threat* of physical violence that physically strong and large staff members represented to the young people, at least in the minds of staff members. Other staff members spoke about their need to instill a kind of fear in young people about the consequences of their actions, which may result in the ultimate enactment of physical violence. Brooks, a Black staff member and a former American football player who stood at over six feet tall, and who often dominated the room as he barked commands at young people to follow rules, said that he felt that staff needed to "grandstand" a little in front of the young people to demonstrate to them that they were in authority.

The threat of physical violence was a tenuous one for staff members at the time of the research. Prone physical restraints were a 'tool' that staff members could use against young people, but only if they posed a threat to themselves or others, not as a kind of discipline. But this standard had recently been changed, and a number of staff members who had worked in the system for a long time felt somewhat resentful that they couldn't use the tool of restraints as often as they once had. In an interview with a staff member working in a unit in the large boys' facility where young people were sent for disciplinary violations, the staff member said that he felt that the number of fights between kids had gone up since the restraint policy had changed. He felt that the kids knew that the staff probably wouldn't intervene, so they felt they could "get away with more."

Exerting control over the young people in the facility environment contributed to a number of staff feeling that this would facilitate the smooth and efficient management of what was a very complex facility environment, often with large numbers of staff and young people, frequent movement throughout the facility of staff and young people, and high levels of turnaround and transition, of both staff (on daily shift changes) and young people (who cycled through the facilities for their sentences). Movements were highly orchestrated, observed and controlled. Each facility had a central unit where staff watched over extensive surveillance cameras, logged notes, and were at the ready to send out an emergency response if a staff member 'pulled the pin', which meant that they initiated a call for a response from multiple staff in the case of an emergency. There were elaborate handbooks detailing rules for young people's comportment and their behavioral regulation and control, their personal grooming, and their need to have their trousers above their waist. Staff members spoke frequently about the importance of these elaborate sets of rules and regulations, and at the time of the research, one of those rules, which many staff deemed to be important for the exercise of control, had been removed. This involved a requirement that young people hold their hands behind their backs when they moved throughout the facility, in theory to prevent any fist fighting or physical action as they moved throughout the facility. Graves, a Black male YDA who had been working in the system for 30 years, spoke about the perceptions of the decline in control, and why he felt that this had changed:

> Just the whole morale has totally changed, especially with the staff. Before, all moves were done before. The residents, they had their hands checked behind their backs. The wardens didn't want the control we had. They knew they went through a lot of stupid things then at that time. They were told to keep their pants pulled up, which they were. They were dressed in order. Their uniform was basically the same.

Graves' sense was that the facility morale had declined as the ability to control young people's physical movements declined. His perception, was, like a number of others, that the facilities had declined into chaos and disorder, and that the staff ability to control young people's movements physically contributed to their overall sense of control over their environment. Sally, a white staff member for the union that represented workers, said that she had heard from staff aggrieved members that "there are no consequences for low level behaviors, so it ends up escalating into bigger behaviors." Yet, some of the staff members who had been brought into the facility under the reforms, including the mental health staff, struggled within this system to manage their roles. According to Mandel, a white woman who was a new social worker in the facility charged with working with young people with mental health issues, since she saw the priority of the facility to be "security first," she found that it was hard to do things with the young people which were "therapeutically useful." This tension between management and development was a struggle for all of the staff, but from the different positions that they operated from in the facility.

Managing the Loss of 'Control'

A number of staff members also expressed anxiety and frustration about what they perceived to be a loss of 'structure' and control in the face of reforms to the system which were aimed at making the system ostensibly more rehabilitative, but which, they argued, resulted in a confused array of practices. Some wished for greater access to restraints; others felt that they had always been engaged in rehabilitation, but that the constant churning of reforms required them to focus increasingly on controlling what was a chaotic facility. YDA Tompkins, a Black woman who had worked in the system since 1979, said that she had observed staff rely *more* frequently on the use of physical restraints in the face of increasing role confusion, and that staff had used fewer restraints when she had first started, and that there was less fighting amongst the teenaged residents. She said that she felt like when she first started in the system, "we tried to rehabilitate" the kids, and "show them a different life." Now, she said, "we're warehousing" them.

Staff members often expressed a sense of frustration and difficulty in managing what they felt was a loss of control imposed on them from above by the central management. Thus, at the level of the facility unit, where they had more discretion, they would try to manage that sense of frustration by doing what they could to exert control, often through their tone of voice or their demeanor. A number of staff members invoked the word "structure" to describe the kind of work that they did in their day to day work of the unit; this kind of "structure" was a form of boundary maintenance for them—it contributed to their sense that if they provided consistent management, rules, and a firm set of demands for the young people, they would respond well. YDA Marshall, a white staff member who worked in the large boys' facility said, "if there's no structure, there's no use" meaning for the staff (or for their jobs), saying that "if we don't provide structure, we're just like another set of bad parents." Residential childcare workers and administrators have similarly expressed a desire for 'structure' (Pazaratz 2003; Rose 2000).

Yet, even without explicit training in boundary management, the staff members often sought to strike a balance with the young people which required them to draw a delicate line between being too tough and too warm. Pagano, a white YDA, expressed this sentiment when he described his approach:

> the kids know where my line is. They know we can have a fun time, we can fool around ... but there are lines we do not cross. There's a lot of respect. They pick on me because I am a big guy and I do not care about that. We don't talk about our families ... They all know I want to have a daughter, and they would respect the fact. They would never ever cross that line. It is a firm affair, they know when I am on duty this is going to happen. They know they should be respectful and have a good time. They do get out of line sometimes. I just haul them back in.

Pagano describes the withholding of personal information, but also his ability to let his guard down and "fool around" with young people, but make it clear to them that they cannot take advantage of him.

12 Juvenile Facility Staff: Research, Policy, and Practice

Staff members frequently invoked their own parenting experiences—or experiences of being parented—to describe their approach to working with the young people under their care. This partially reflected the disconnect in training and practice for the staff, especially the frontline staff; training programs for staff largely relied on teaching them the tools of de-escalation, control, and administration. Very rarely, if ever, did the trainings focus on relationship building, boundary setting, and issues of projection, introjection, and care, issues which may typically be presented in trainings with direct care workers in other settings. Thus, in managing their relationships with young people, staff members often reached for the tools that were most readily available to them—their perceptions and experiences of 'good' parenting. Some even spoke about the complex interplay between their lives at home and those in the facility. According to a white frontline staff member at the small boys' facility, Masterson, for example, "you try not to be frustrated and angry with their behavior, you try to understand their behavior, and we have, and that's what we're trying to do, behavior modification, and I'm a single parent-bingo!- I take all this stuff home and practice it on my kids." Bryce, a white former YDA who had moved to the central office, saw the role of the YDA as "de facto counselor" and role model, and that their job is to set limits and rules. He described the staff as "house parents."

Expressions of Care

It was this role as "house parents" that most often revealed the staff members' expressions of care and investment in the young people they worked with. And yet there were tensions in their expression of care, most often around their support of the young people after they were released. Brooks referred to the unit that he worked on as "almost like family," and said, of the residents, "they are all our sons." YDA Bryce described his role as a "de facto counselor," "role model," and "house parent." Another YDA said that "I'm the psychologist, bartender, and cab driver" for the young people. Montano, a white teacher in the large boys' facility, commented on the staff-youth relationships in this way:

> A YDA who looks like one of the boys, talks like one of the boys, I will hear saying to the boy, hey, that's not right, talk right, do right or they're talking about stuff and the YDA is counseling him. It's so nice. It's just lovely. I think it's the hidden beauty of this place. That the YDAs, each in his own way, forms a relationship with a boy and that's why you see them hugging each other so

much, even shadow boxing or fake boxing. It's a way of interacting that is playful and shows a relationship.

This teacher's observations of staff-youth relationships reveal the part of the relationships which are often obscured for reformers—the banal, everyday interactions which form the glue of facility life.

Staff members would often express tenderness and care towards young people, sometimes in contravention of the rules of the agency. Although hugging and physical contact wasn't allowed, I often observed staff members put their arms around young people and sometimes hug them. They would engage in often complex conversations with the young people, and some saw those conversations as essential to doing their work well. According to YDA French, "If you're not talking with them, then you are having a hard day." Bonta, a white staff member who worked as a Youth Counselor at the small boys' facility said, "'if there's no relationship, we can't do anything." After a Latino YDA, Ramirez was out of work for some time after receiving an injury during a restraint, I observed young people express joy at seeing him upon his return, hugging him and giving him a pat on the shoulder. In the context of facilities which were dominated by boredom, downtime and restlessness, staff and youth relationships were often collegial, filled with humor, and built on camaraderie and fun. One weekend day at a small boys' facility, I went with a unit of boys and a young staff member in his twenties to a game room in the facility, and I observed the staff member playing pool with one of the boys, joking around with him and talking about playing pool with his friends in a local bar. The boys and the staff members shared cultural references with each other, laughed together, and teased each other. A white YDA, Taylor spoke about how much he enjoyed taking young people on outings like hiking, which he said was done a bit more in the facility, before the reforms:

> Yeah, when you do stuff like that, you can more or less kind of, it's a break for, it's kind of a break for the staff, and a break for the kids, and you have more of a chance to bond and build better relationships with them. And if you have good relationships with the kids for the most part you don't have a lot of problems, and they're more apt to trust you and listen to what you have to say, and that spills over into like your groups, your behavioral groups, and all the other groups that you teach. They're more apt to listen to you.

Taylor's argument—that trusting relationships are the cornerstone of well-managed facilities—has also been found in research conducted in adult prison contexts (Liebling and Arnold 2004).

It was the explicit policy of the agency that frontline staff—YDAs in particular—were not to engage in planning a young person's reentry into the community. In fact, not only were the YDAs given no training in boundary management or relationship building, they were also not provided with any information about reentry resources. Yet, a number of staff members expressed despair about the rate of return of young people to the facility, and their perception that the young people weren't receiving the appropriate support or resources while they were on the inside to prevent them returning from the outside. Echoing Tompkins' comment about 'warehousing', according to YDA Close, for example, "what we are doing is we house them so they can come right back and so we can keep our jobs."

Despite that, a number of staff members built close relationships with young people and became invested in their lives and motivations. Many of the staff did not identify as guards, but instead saw themselves as youth workers; this reflects the blended role of 'care' and 'control' that other researchers have identified. Some staff members would suggest ideas for jobs to young people, and get job applications for them to start before their release. Others would obtain university applications and help young people apply. Another particular area of concern for staff members was for the housing and foster care of young people. As has been demonstrated elsewhere, access to housing for teenagers involved in the justice system, particularly for so-called dual-system youth, who have both juvenile justice system involvement and involvement in the child welfare system, is very limited. Yet, the staff members were not only prohibited from obtaining information about housing opportunities or attempting to link young people to those opportunities, they were also prohibited from contacting the young people after they left the facilities, as there was an explicit 'no contact' policy between staff and young people imposed for the purposes of preventing sexual 'grooming'.

Staff members would often express frustration at the seeming futility of their work and investments, and they would seek to manage the complex emotions connected to working with young people who they saw cycling through the system. YDA Pagano said: "Mostly I try to keep an even mind about it. Unfortunately, with statistics and figures, most of these kids are not gonna make it. You have to have to have the wherewithal to keep coming back. Maybe you will reach one."

Implications

The research with staff in New York revealed the tensions inherent in the work of frontline juvenile facility staff, particularly in the context of reforms which aim to close large scale facilities and shift to smaller 'care home'-style facilities. There is thus a tension at the heart of efforts to close large institutions in favor of smaller facilities; staff will still play a major role in the lives of young people incarcerated in these facilities, and their role may still raise questions about the relationship between care and control. Juvenile justice systems in the United States have arguably experienced a near-constant 'cycle' of reforms over the last 150 years (Bernard and Kurlychek 2010). There are not only significant implications for recent reforms for the structure of treatment and aftercare programming (Sankofa et al. 2017), but also for the ways that frontline staff themselves manage the difficult terrain of exercising structure and discipline while also facilitating development and growth, particularly for the young people they develop close bonds and attachments to. In a clinical trial of technology transfer in a juvenile justice office, Taxman et al. write about the critical role that frontline staff members play in the implementation of reforms:

> Building support for innovations involves more than the initial commitment by management or staff. In fact, organizational scholars recommend… penetrating the social structures and networks to address the concerns of the staff as well as the practicalities of how the content would be implemented in each specific organization. The staff reaps both the benefits and losses associated with using the innovation, and ultimately are the ones responsible for determining whether the new practice(s) will be integrated into their work repertoires. (2014, p. 12)

Taxman et al. recognize how essential staff members are for the functioning of a healthy organization, in part because, as demonstrated above, they develop a close relationship with young people that has implications for the well-being of both staff and young people. Yet, as some have recognized, the anxieties and emotions of workers may create instability and uncertainty in an organization (Hirschorn 1988). In the research documented above, staff members conveyed the daily strategies of emotion management and performance that they engaged in as they sought to balance care and control in the juvenile facility environment. Yet, as new reforms were introduced, those abilities were challenged.

The research above demonstrated not only the intimate and complex role that staff play in everyday life in the facilities, but also the limitations of organizational models that neglect to treat frontline staff members as critical participants in young people's development. In fact, staff members have been widely criticized by juvenile justice reformers for their role in obstructing reforms. Some work is being done, for example, by the Annie E. Casey foundation to more fully attend to juvenile facility staff resistance to reform by equipping frontline staff members with more ongoing support in enacting reforms (Annie E. Casey Foundation 2019). Other jurisdictions have engaged in a coaching model, where staff receiving ongoing support in boundary management and relationship building. This could more closely resemble the clinical supervision model employed in social work contexts, which more arguably attends to both the internal and external dynamics of relationships that exist in juvenile justice contexts (McNamara 2010).

Juvenile prisons and detention facilities are complex environments where relationships matter. From the explicit role that violence and abuse play in harming young people, to the more subtle dynamics at play in facilities where staff seek to support young people while also attempting to manage them, frontline staff should not be neglected in the study of juvenile imprisonment. Indeed, they are essential to understanding it.

References

Abrams, L., & Anderson-Nathe, B. (2013). *Compassionate confinement: A year in the life of Unit C*. New Brunswick, NJ: Rutgers University Press.

Annie E. Casey Foundation. (2019). Casey selects 15 sites to train juvenile justice frontline staff. *Annie E. Casey Foundation Blog*. April 9, 2019 Ed.

Armstrong, M. M., Hartje, J. A., & Evans, W. P. (2013). Factors affecting juvenile care workers' intent to continue working in juvenile corrections. *Criminal Justice Review, 39*, 5–18.

Ashkar, P., & Kenny, D. (2008). Views from the inside: Young offenders' subjective experiences of incarceration. *International Journal of Offender Therapy and Comparative Criminology, 52*, 584–597.

Baines, M., & Alder, C. (1996). Are girls more difficult to work with? Youth workers' perspectives in juvenile justice and related areas. *Crime & Delinquency, 42*, 467–485.

Beck, A. J., & Rantala, R. R. (2016). *Sexual victimization reported by juvenile correctional authorities, 2007–12*. Washington, DC: United States Department Of Justice.

Benner, G., Zeng, S., Armstrong, A. L., & Carpenter, E. (2016). *Strengthening education in short-term juvenile detention centers: Final technical report*. Tacoma: University of Washington.

Bernard, T., & Kurlychek, M. (2010). *The cycle of juvenile justice*. New York: Oxford University Press.

Bernstein, N. (2014). *Burning down the house: The end of juvenile prison.* New York: New Press.

Biggam, F., & Power, K. (1997). Social support and psychological distress in a group of incarcerated young offenders. *International Journal of Offender Therapy and Comparative Criminology, 41*, 213–230.

Bond-Maupin, L., Maupin, J. R., & Leisenring, A. (2002). Girls' delinquency and the justice implications of intake workers' perspectives. *Women & Criminal Justice, 13*, 51–77.

Bottoms, A. E. (1999). Interpersonal violence and social order in prisons. *Crime and Justice, 26*, 205–281.

Cesaroni, C., & Peterson-Badali, M. (2010). Understanding the adjustment of incarcerated young offenders: A Canadian example. *Youth Justice, 10*, 107–125.

Cooperrider, D. L., & Whitney, D. (2007). Appreciative inquiry: A positive revolution in change. In P. Holman & T. Devane (Eds.), *The change handbook.* Berrett-Koehler Publishers.

Cox, A. (2015). Fresh air funds and functional families: The enduring politics of race, family and place in juvenile justice reform. *Theoretical Criminology, 19*(4), 554–570.

Cox, A. (2018). *Trapped in a vice: The consequences of confinement for young people.* New Brunswick, NJ: Rutgers University Press.

Crawley, E. (2004). Emotion and performance: Prison officers and the presentation of self in prisons. *Punishment and Society, 6*, 411–427.

Doll, C., Mclaughlin, T. F., & Barretto, A. (2013). The token economy: A recent review and evaluation. *International Journal of Basic and Applied Science, 2*, 131–149.

Domenici, D., & O'leary, R. (2015). No more closed doors: Ending the educational exclusion of formerly incarcerated youth. In N. Dowd (Ed.), *A new juvenile justice system: Total reform for a broken system.* New York: NYU Press.

Fagan, J., Kupchik, A., & Liberman, A. (2007). Be careful what you wish for: Legal sanctions and public safety among adolescent felony offenders in juvenile and criminal court.?

Flores, J. (2012). Jail pedagogy: Liberatory education inside a california juvenile detention facility. *Journal of Education for Students Placed at Risk (Jespar), 17*, 286–300.

Flores, J. (2015). A race conscious pedagogy: Correctional educators and creative resistance inside California juvenile detention facilities. *Association of Medical American Educators, 9*, 18–30.

Franzén, A. G. (2014). Responsibilization and discipline: Subject positioning at a youth detention home. *Journal of Contemporary Ethnography, 44*, 1–29.

Galardi, T. R., & Settersten, R. A. (2018). "They're Just Made Up Different": Juvenile correctional staff perceptions of incarcerated boys and girls. *Children And Youth Services Review, 95*, 200–208.

Geenen, M.-J. (2017). A tailored approach for incarcerated boys: Q study into the needs of incarcerated boys in the interaction with group workers in a juvenile correctional institution. *Residential Treatment for Children & Youth, 34*, 227–243.

Gover, A. R., Mackenzie, D. L., & Armstrong, G. S. (2000). Importation and deprivation explanations of juveniles' adjustment to correctional facilities. *International Journal of Offender Therapy and Comparative Criminology, 44*, 450–467.

Harvey, J. (2007). *Young men in prison*. Cullompton: Willan.

Himmelweit, S. (2018). Transforming care. In L. Macfarlane (Ed.), *New thinking for the British economy*. London: Opendemocracy.

Hirschorn, L. (1988). *The workplace within: Psychodynamics of organizational life*. Cambridge, MA: The MIT Press.

Hochschild, A. (1983). *The managed heart: Commercialization of human feeling*. Berkeley: University Of California Press.

Inderbitzin, M. (2006). Guardians of the state's problem children. *The Prison Journal, 86*, 431–451.

Kazdin, A. (1982). The token economy: A decade later. *Journal of Applied Behavior Analysis, 15*, 431–445.

King, L. (2009). *Investigation of the Lansing Residential Center, Louis Gossett, Jr. Residential Center, Tryon Residential Center, and Tryon Girls Center*. Washington, DC: U.S. Department Of Justice.

King, D. (2010). 'Culture of Violence' Plagues New York's juvenile prisons. *Gotham Gazette*.

Klatt, T., Hagl, S., Bergmann, M. C., & Baier, D. (2016). Violence in youth custody: Risk factors of violent misconduct among inmates of German young offender institutions. *European Journal of Criminology, 13*, 727–743.

Kupchik, A. (2007). The correctional experiences of youth in adult and juvenile prisons. *Justice Quarterly, 24*, 247–270.

Kupchik, A., & Snyder, R. B. (2009). The impact of juvenile inmates' perceptions and facility characteristics on victimization in juvenile correctional facilities. *The Prison Journal, 89*, 265–285.

Lai, Y.-L. (2018). Determinants of importation and deprivation models on committed juvenile offenders' violent misconduct: A Taiwanese perspective. *International Journal of Offender Therapy and Comparative Criminology, 63*, 1242–1264.

Lanctôt, N., Ayotte, M.-H., Turcotte, M., & Besnard, T. (2012). Youth care workers' views on the challenges of working with girls: An analysis of the mediating influence of practitioner gender and prior experience with girls. *Children and Youth Services Review, 34*, 2240–2246.

Liebling, A., & Arnold, H. (2004). *Prisons and their moral performance: A study of values, quality, and prison life*. Oxford: Oxford University Press.

Marsh, S., & Evans, W. (2009). Youth Perspectives on Their Relationships With Staff in Juvenile Correction Settings and Perceived Likelihood of Success on Release. *Youth Violence and Juvenile Justice, 7*, 46–67.

Mccray, E. D., Ribuffo, C., Lane, H., Murphy, K. M., Gagnon, J. C., Houchins, D. E., & Lambert, R. G. (2018). "As Real As It Gets": A grounded theory study of a reading intervention in a juvenile correctional school. *Child & Youth Care Forum, 47*, 259–281.

Mcnamara, P. M. (2010). Staff support and supervision in residential youth justice: An Australian model. *Residential Treatment for Children & Youth, 27*, 214–240.

Miller, J. (1991). *Last one over the wall*. Columbus: Ohio State University Press.

Miller, A. D., & Ohlin, L. E. (1985). *Delinquency and community: Creating opportunities and control*. Beverly Hills, CA: Sage.

Mitchell, O., Mackenzie, D. L., Styve, G. J., & Gover, A. R. (2000). The impact of individual, organizational, and environmental attributes on voluntary turnover among juvenile correctional staff members. *Justice Quarterly, 17*, 333–357.

Mulvey, E. P., Schubert, C. A., & Odgers, C. (2010). A method for measuring organizational functioning in juvenile justice facilities using resident ratings. *Criminal Justice and Behavior, 37*, 1255–1277.

Pazaratz, D. (2003). The application of a reinforcement/level system in the residential treatment of adolescents. *Residential Treatment for Children & Youth, 21*, 17–32.

Peterson-Badali, M., & Koegl, C. J. (2002). Juveniles' experiences of incarceration: The role of correctional staff in peer violence. *Journal of Criminal Justice, 30*, 41–49.

Poole, E. D., & Regoli, R. M. (1983). Violence in juvenile institutions. *Criminology, 21*, 213–232.

Rose, M. (2000). The management of boundaries and an organisation's therapeutic task. *Residential Treatment for Children & Youth, 18*, 15–33.

Sankofa, J., Cox, A., Fader, J. J., Inderbitzin, M., Abrams, L. S., & Nurse, A. M. (2017). Juvenile corrections in the era of reform: a meta-synthesis of qualitative studies. *International Journal of Offender Therapy and Comparative Criminology, 62*, 1763–1786.

Schlossman, S. (1977). *Love and the American Delinquent: The theory and practice of "Progressive" juvenile justice, 1825–1920*. Chicago: The University Of Chicago Press.

Schubert, C. A., Mulvey, E. P., Loughran, T. A., & Losoya, S. H. (2011). Perceptions of institutional experience and community outcomes for serious adolescent offenders. *Criminal Justice and Behavior, 39*, 71–93.

Taxman, F. S., Henderson, C., Young, D., & Farrell, J. (2014). The impact of training interventions on organizational readiness to support innovations in juvenile justice offices. *Administration and Policy in Mental Health, 41*, 177–188.

Tompkins-Rosenblatt, P., & Vanderven, K. (2005). Perspectives on point and level systems in residential care: A responsive dialogue. *Residential Treatment For Children & Youth, 22*, 1–18.

Van Der Laan, A., & Eichelsheim, V. (2013). Juvenile adaptation to imprisonment: Feelings of safety, autonomy and well-being, and behaviour in prison. *European Journal of Criminology, 10*, 424–443.

Whitehead, C. (2019). *The Nickel boys*. New York: Doubleday.

Zeman, M. (2014). *Tales of a jailhouse librarian: Challenging the juvenile justice system one book at a time*. Brooklyn: Vinegar Hill Press.

Part IV

Gendering Justice

Epigraph to Section IV

When I Look in the Mirror ...

I'm surrounded by hate people that are out for me.
I see a girl who suffered through months with depression and pain.
I see myself isolating over tears and over my mom and little sister that I miss so much.
I see my mom by my side and always being there for me saying stay strong. I love you.
I see a beautiful confident girl that has been through a lot of pain and hurt.
I see a girl who is really respectful, mellow and nice in a place she shouldn't be in over a mistake.
I see a girl that always keeps a smile on her face no matter what.
I see a girl whose dad had a drinking problem because he was so stressed but stopped because he cares about his kids.
I see a girl who now is trying to stay strong and not cry even though its hard.
I see a girl who had a brother and a sister that she was so rude to but at the end of the day, they are still there for her.

March 7, 2020
Central Juvenile Hall, Los Angeles, CA, USA

13

Straight and Narrow: Girls, Sexualities, and the Youth Justice System

Lisa Pasko

Before the 1970s, most research on juvenile arrests, court involvement, and corrections in the United States did not include an explicit focus on girls. Today, however, girls have become one of the fastest-growing segments of the juvenile justice system and account for nearly a third of juvenile arrests, one-fourth of all court referrals, and one out of every six youth adjudicated and placed in secure confinement in the United States (Federal Bureau of Investigation 2015; Office of Juvenile Justice and Delinquency Prevention 2016; Puzzanchera et al. 2011). These data have led scholars to examine girls' court involvement, current custodial conditions, the institutional policies that affect their future criminal trajectories, and the rationale behind the decisions made about and for them (e.g., Bloom et al. 2002; Chesney-Lind and Shelden 2014; Mallicoat 2007; Pasko 2011, 2017).

Despite this growing academic interest in girls who come into conflict with the law, studies on girls, sexualities, and juvenile court and corrections remain fairly unusual in criminology. In particular, the literature fails to consider how system-involved girls react to the ways the contemporary youth justice system manages their sexual and reproductive choices and sexual identities. This chapter addresses this dearth of knowledge in the extant literature and explores girls' perceptions of the court and correctional sexual regulatory policies and techniques.

L. Pasko (✉)
University of Denver, Denver, CO, USA
e-mail: Lisa.Pasko@du.edu

Girls, Sexuality, and the Justice System

The U.S. juvenile system has a long history of adjudicating and punishing girls for sexual immorality, incorrigibility, and resistance to gendered expectations for behavior (Chesney-Lind and Pasko 2013; Chesney-Lind and Shelden 2014; Pasko 2010; Platt 1977). In the early years of the U.S. juvenile justice system, the movement to create separate institutions for children who offended was part of the larger Progressive movement that, among other things, was fervidly concerned with "social evils," such as prostitution (Chesney-Lind and Pasko 2013; Rafter 1990; Schlossman and Wallach 1978). Spearheaded by privileged women, the child savers' movement and the establishment of family courts provided an opportunity for these women to patrol the normative boundaries of the social order and enforce gender roles of chastity, obedience, and marriageability (Chesney-Lind and Pasko 2013). Particularly concerned with sexual morality, "fallen women," rescue homes, homes for unwed mothers, and girls' reformatories served the multiple functions of reforming girls, providing prenatal and natal care, and controlling girls' sexuality and venereal disease (Knupfer 2001). Whereas the first U.S. juvenile court in Chicago, Illinois, originally defined "delinquent" as those under 16 who had violated a city ordinance or law, when the definition was applied to girls, the court included "up to the age of eighteen when activities included incorrigibility, associations with immoral persons, vagrancy, frequent attendance at pool halls or saloons, immoral conduct, and use of indecent language" (Knupfer 2001). Indeed, social reformers at the time viewed sexual enticements as an ever-present danger and believed that a morally functioning society required sexual restraint (Abrams 2001).

Despite policy and legal changes in juvenile justice, the treatment of girls who were considered "delinquent" changed very little, with girls seldom charged with serious law violations and commonly judged in terms of their moral welfare. Examinations of early juvenile courts found that "wayward" girls were sentenced to reform schools for exercising freedoms, such as going on unsupervised dates or spending their paychecks and refusing to relinquish funds to their fathers (Alexander 1995; Pasko 2010). Other girls were institutionalized for their own good: to punish petty larceny; to supply a home; to provide protection from physical abuse; to prevent further lewd acts; and to effect moral salvation (Brenzel 1983, p. 130).

Odem (1995), in her study of juvenile justice during late-nineteenth-century Los Angeles and Oakland, also found that working-class young women who sought opportunities for social and sexual independence ended up in police holding cells, juvenile courts, and training schools for their morally offensive behaviors. Receiving penalties for their willfulness and self-defense against sexually aggressive men, not only the girls remained sexually vulnerable, but their victimization was openly questioned by justice professionals as well as intimates. Knupfer found similar themes in her analysis of the early juvenile court in Chicago; between 1904 and 1927, 60 to 70% of delinquent girls placed on probation or in institutions were first-time offenders, virtually all of them brought in on charges of incorrigibility (2001). Indeed, judges more frequently institutionalized girls than boys for sexual delinquency or immorality, considering it a "more dangerous" sex offense. Embedded in these courtroom discussions was a juxtaposition—one image of the girl offender as victim, essentially good but wayward, contrasted by the other image of a promiscuous "sexualized demon" who was a danger not just to herself but to the larger community (Knupfer 2001, p. 94). An examination of judicial sentiments and sentencing practices of girls throughout the mid-twentieth century reveals few changes (Andrews and Cohn 1974; Odem and Schlossman 1991). Overall, girls, in comparison to their male counterparts, were sentenced more harshly for status offenses and, despite the absence of serious law violations, were as likely as boys to be institutionalized.

What is clear from the contemporary research on girls and sexuality is that the pattern of sanctioning and institutionalizing girls for minor offenses, status offenses, and sexual misconduct continues in present-day conservative moral movements as well as juvenile justice processing. For example, in her work on girls' sexuality and the control of unplanned reproduction, Nathanson (1991) examines the historical redefining of nonmarital pregnancy from a moral to a medical problem—one that could be treated through medically overseen contraception rather than religiously imposed moral redemption. She also illustrates the countermovement that aimed to restore traditional values of sexual morality and to define teen pregnancy as a moral issue to be handled by parents instead of intrusive public health professionals. In conclusion, Nathanson shows that the problem of teenage pregnancy was constructed as a problem with impish girls' flawed choices, rather than in the structural conditions that shaped their lives or the men who participated in such activities.

Under a paternalistic ideology, current juvenile justice institutions—police, courts, and corrections—continue to "protect" these "delinquent daughters," usually from sexual experimentation and other dangers on the streets (Chesney-Lind and Shelden 2014; Pasko 2017). With a focus on their physical appearance and sexuality, research has demonstrated that the characterization of girls in court, at probation, in their official court and correctional records, and in their case files regularly obscures girls' agency and deems them to be deceitful, manipulative, hysterical, wildly sexual, and verbally abusive (Bond-Maupin et al. 2002; Gaarder et al. 2004; Mallicoat 2007; Pasko 2010; Pasko and Lopez 2018; Schaffner 2006). At the same time, the court frequently labels girls as sexually promiscuous, untrustworthy, and unruly, without meaningful connection of such behaviors to their life histories and social contexts (Pasko 2010).

Despite the growth of gender-responsive reforms in juvenile court and corrections (see Cooney et al. 2008; Cusworth Walker et al. 2015; Sherman 2012) and research evaluating such initiatives (e.g., Davidson et al. 2010), scholarly examinations of how system-involved girls respond to policies and procedures used to control their sexualities remain few. This chapter examines such system responses from the girls' perspectives. It explores how girls encounter, negotiate, and resist these justice institutional reactions to sexualities.

Methodology

The data are derived from a larger project that focused on the lives and correctional involvement of girls who offended; it was performed across eight different jurisdictions in a Western state of United States from 2008 to 2012. This chapter centers on the narratives of 18 girls who were involved in the juvenile court (nine Latina girls, five African-American girls, and four white, non-Latina girls) who discussed their pathways toward correctional involvement. Overall, the sample was gathered through referrals from justice professionals with whom the author made throughout the project. These professionals and program staff were essential in referring girls to be interviewed, helping to secure a safe and private place where the girls felt comfortable completing such interviews, and serving as an additional contact for the girls, in order to facilitate their return for future conversations.

To gather participants' interpretations of their experiences and life narratives and attenuate preconceived notions about the lives of girls who offended, repeat intensive interviewing with a broad, open-ended instrument was used. Repeat, intensive interviewing also allowed multiple opportunities for discussion about topics that respondents may guard and conceal. Ten participants were interviewed twice; eight were interviewed three times. Each interview took place five to seven months apart. The first conversation was used chiefly to develop rapport with the interviewee, to ameliorate concerns about judgment that they feared might arise in the interviews, to alleviate trepidation, and to create trust and comfort in thinking and talking about their life experiences. Each initial interview took place in a private setting and lasted from 60 to 90 minutes.

Employing an interview guide of loosely structured topics, the second (and sometimes third) interviews of the participants were performed to gather more detail, elicit more depth to their thoughts and feelings about their narratives, return to themes that had emerged earlier, chart new experiences and progress in their lives, and offer each participant a well-developed sense of appreciation, understanding, and affirmation, consistent with feminist methodology. Approaching interviewees with this regard allows room for acknowledgment of the research-subject relationship, while it also opens space for more authenticity in representation and narrative sharing (see Reinharz 1992). Girls were asked open-ended questions about their significant childhood to contemporary experiences, and were prompted intermittently to discuss family structures and relationships, neighborhood and community dynamics, school participation, significant relationships, sexual behavior and identity, drug use, criminal behavior including violence, mental and physical health, and social/justice system involvement. In the overall research project, such information was also used to examine how well the programming girls received matched their needs. This multiple interviewing technique allowed for opportunities to study the data and return to the participant with additional queries that would add to their narratives and analysis. It also gave interviewees time to be reflexive in their recollections and interpretations. The second and third interviews lasted between two and three hours each.

Altogether, nearly 80 hours of interview data were analyzed. Institutional Review Board approval was given for all interviews. Extensive notes were taken during the interview and all but five interviews were audiotaped. After recording and transcribing notes, the author and her research assistant worked independently in their coding to ensure incisive thematic analysis. Although not purposeful, we interviewed the young women at various stages of the correctional process: probation ($n = 7$); and probation/parole with experience in a secure facility ($n = 11$). The young women ranged in age from 15 to 22 years old, with those over 18 reflecting on their experiences with juvenile court and corrections (though not currently under supervision); see Table 13.1. This chapter summarizes the girls' and young women's experiences with court and correctional responses to their sexual behavior, sexual identities, and reproductive choices. It includes girls' personal histories of sexual exploitation and trauma before justice involvement and the techniques and mechanisms used by the justice system to address such abuse, to "protect" them from further victimization, and to control sexualized behaviors while in custody.

Table 13.1 Summary background of girls

Race	Age	Age of first arrest	Number of detentions, confinements
African-American	22	12	5
African-American	19	14	2
Latina	18	15	0
White	18	14	1
Latina	18	12	1
White	19	13	1
White	15	14	0
Latina	17	14	1
African-American	19	13	1
Latina	16	14	0
African-American	15	13	0
Latina	18	13	1
Latina	18	12	1
White	16	14	0
Latina	18	14	0
Latina	18	13	1
African-American	17	12	0
Latina	18	13	2

At Court and on Probation

When reflecting on institutional reactions to their sexual behaviors and identities, interviewees often first spoke of victimization and the institutional responses—by both child welfare and juvenile justice systems—to reports of sexual abuse. Indeed, nearly half of the girls ($n = 8$) had histories of sexual abuse and/or exploitation and two-thirds ($n = 12$) had some intervention by police or child protective services during their childhoods. Interviewees reported, however, that this intervention did not help them deal with feelings of anger, depression, abandonment, and isolation. Instead, contact with this system further propelled them into delinquent and criminal behavior, as girls in this study saw their system involvement as a turning point and the beginning of "placing all my behavior, and yeah, like sex especially, under a microscope" (Interviewee, age 19). The following comments also illustrate such sentiment:

> "It seemed like everyone was worried I get hurt again so I got watched all the time. (*asked if that meant getting caught too*) Yeah, meant I got caught doing stuff too!" (Interviewee, age 15)

> "I was watched a lot after [the sexual assault]. You know, my mom worried about me and felt bad for me, but then she'd call the cops after I'd be like late or something, and it's like, well, yeah, maybe you're worried, but you keep calling

the cops and we keep fighting and then more cops, and just keep on getting me into trouble, I guess, she wants to help me, but it ain't like anyone is helping me ... just making me sit in [detention]." (Interviewee, age 17)

"It does feel like I got into trouble [after reports of sexual abuse]. I started drinking and partying and not listening to my mother and getting arrested, and I guess it all started then. I didn't really get help." (Interviewee, age 18)

Interviewees with such histories reported intervention by child welfare services without "good" results, often feeling responsible when they (or the perpetrator) were removed from the home, being exposed to assessments without meaningful follow-up treatment, or engaging in therapy they felt did not help. No interviewees could relate specifics about the counseling sessions they received, and none had records of receiving trauma-informed therapy. As one interviewee explained (age 18), "When my dad first left, and part of going back to live with my mom was that I had to go to therapy with this woman who I felt didn't really care. She didn't speak Spanish, so my mom couldn't talk to her and it just seemed stupid. Like now, it seemed pointless."

Girls' reflections on their justice involvement rang similarly, especially in terms of the system's confusing and contradictory messaging between offender and victim. On the surface, girls were reluctant to plead responsible (juvenile court language synonymous to a guilty plea) because they wanted to avoid consequences, punishment, and added surveillance to their lives. However, during court hearings and in meetings with their probation officers, as girls were told they must "take responsibility for their choices" for offending behaviors; they were also told they were not responsible for their sexual victimization. When their victimization and exploitation connected to their offending (e.g., status offenses, drug use) or were part of their charges (e.g., prostitution), interviewees expressed this awareness and consequent dissonance with their court involvement as a result of these charges. They were resistant to accepting responsibility for their choices—especially for involvement in sex trafficking, as such choices were circumscribed by restriction, a sense of inferiority, criticism, inflexibility, and lack of understanding. Referring to conversations with her probation officer as well as with staff in her previous court-ordered program, one interviewee (age 19) explained, "Do you know how many times I have been told that no matter what I did, I do not deserve to be [sexually assaulted]? Or how many times I am not at fault for what someone else did to me? And yet, I am in court being told found responsible, found responsible, found responsible. Ridiculous."

Once adjudicated by juvenile court and placed on probation, all interviewees reported experiencing the use of a valid court order (VCO) (even if they did not use such terminology) as a means of surveilling their romantic and sexual relationships. Previous publications by the author have shown that the use of a valid court order is a key way the court can sanction girls for maintaining associations considered as risky, dangerous, and/or facilitating criminal behaviors (Pasko 2017). While VCOs were used to discipline probationers and restrict movements (e.g., go to school, follow curfew, maintain employment, etc.), they also were used to prevent contact with specific individuals (i.e., boy/girlfriends) and/or general "undesirables"—terminology used by the justice professionals to describe other probationers, gang members, drug users, and so on. If girls pursued such relationships, the court had a means of revoking probation and placing her in custody. Interviewees presented in this chapter were aware of this tactic to control their movements and relationships and framed it as a way to control their sexual behavior, occasionally linking it to their families' and court's fear that they may be (re)victimized or become pregnant:

> "I was put into [detention] for not following what I had to do on probation. But I thought it was unfair that I couldn't see my boyfriend because I, you know, he's not the problem. My mom is more the problem." (Interviewee, age 16)

> "I am always told not to hang around undesirables …. My PO [probation officer] don't get that everybody I know is undesirable!" (Interviewee, age 19)

> "I don't like being on the pill, so I think they're just worried I'll get pregnant." (Interviewee, age 17)

For sexual minority young women in this study ($n = 5$), they often described it as indicative of homophobia:

> "I know he [judge] hates gay people. He said something like my girlfriend was the problem and relationships like this are always a problem so then I couldn't see her. It was part of my probation. You know, being gay, having a girlfriend. That's why I get into trouble. But if anyone asked me about how being gay or my girlfriend caused me to get into trouble, I'd tell them it's because I'm fucking homeless after I came out to my parents." (Interviewee, age 19)

> "I think they (judge and probation officers) just hate gay people and that's why they are hard." (Interviewee, age 22)

Speaking directly about probation, some girls reported a complicated relationship with their probation officers, often questioning trust but appreciating care and connection:

> "My PO (probation officer) is great. She is one of my closest friends and took me to my ultrasound. But then when I tell her certain stuff, she's like, I could send you back to [detention] or maybe I should do a UA (urinalysis) on you and then I'm like, wait, I thought you cared about me, not just looking to screw me up in some way." (Interviewee, age 19)

> "I like my PO but sometimes I feel like she's just waiting to get me on something … [with laughter] like a friend who can jack you up whenever they want and there ain't nothing you can do about it." (Interviewee, age 18)

> "My PO is out to get me. He can be nice, but he doesn't like me. But I have had one who was OK, seemed to care." (Interviewee, age 22)

Overall, girls expressed frustration with the social welfare and justice system involvement they experienced, ranging from feelings of ineffective intervention and constant judgment, especially over sexual relationships and identities. Additionally, when probation officers were the ones responsible for doing group therapy—oftentimes without trauma-informed training that fosters safety, connections, and emotional management skills--interviewees felt suspicious about and defiant toward such services. As one interviewee (age 19) described, "I think [PO] thought she was doing a good job with the group, but we would all sit there and be like, oh hell no, we ain't telling her."

During Secure Confinement

Detention and correctional facilities in this study varied in terms of policies and programming, although all of them employed methods of regulating girls' bodies and sexualities. Such methods were arguably designed to reduce conflict among residents and between staff and residents, to create physical sameness among residents, to desexualize the body and the custodial environment, to minimize time when the body is exposed (showering) or susceptible to sexual contact (alone with staff or other residents), to modulate physical intimacy, and to instill cognitive and physical discipline. Although policies and programming differed among the different facilities, the most common methods included 30-day probationary periods of not talking to other residents (in three of the facilities); loose gender-neutral gym outfits; upon admission, immediate standardized "bowl" haircuts; no touching (although in group therapy girls were allowed "one-arm" hugs if permission was asked and granted); no make-up or other accessories to the body; separate rooms, locked at night; regular lock-down hours; in room/cells, no sexualized or provocative artwork; 90-second showers; no team recreation or sports—physical exercise that focused on aloneness (running, elliptical bike, weights); and maintained distance between residents when riding in van/bus or occupying desks, chairs, or sofa. For those interviewees who had been committed to one of these facilities, they noticed such "sexual sanitation" of the environment immediately:

> "You get the message right away. No one ain't going to believe shit you say because you're all like just manipulating us." (Interviewee, age 18)
>
> "I know they want to make sure we get along and not have drama and stuff ... it did seem like a lot." (Interviewee, age 18)
>
> "It's like I said before, they hate gay people. The staff and the other girls, all ... you know, like sex is the worst thing." (Interviewee, age 19)

As girls showed they could follow rules for appropriate behavior, they slowly gained rewards and privileges, ranging from better (single room) accommodations, choice of daily vocational and educational activities, freedom to move around the campus, and, in some facilities, off-campus recreational activities. If such regulations were violated, girls could be subjected to loss of privileges, longer detention/commitment, solitary confinement, physical restraints, stays in "soft rooms" (furniture-less padded rooms), stays in administrative segregation, or, in the case of sexual contact between residents, criminal charges. Indeed, facilities followed the rules and guidelines put forth by the United States Prison Rape Elimination Act (PREA)—a "zero tolerance" policy on prison rape that works to identify, prevent, and punish sexual violence in all custodial settings, including juvenile justice settings, regardless of whether the facility is federal, state, or local, privately or publicly run.

In 2003, the United States Congress unanimously passed PREA, a "zero tolerance" policy for prison rape. The act seeks to identify, prevent, and sanction sexual violence in all custodial settings—including juvenile—regardless of whether the facility is federal, state, or local, private or publicly run. Spearheaded by human rights, faith-based, and prison rape advocacy groups, PREA's genesis can largely be attributed to growing conservative concerns about homosexuality and the spread of AIDS in male prisons as well as

13 Straight and Narrow: Girls, Sexualities, and the Youth Justice...

concern about the growing number of white men (who are more frequently victimized) placed in custody (Smith 2008). PREA does address sexual misconduct of staff against inmates, although this is of minor focus. After the final passing of PREA, U.S. states and agencies were required to comply with all federal standards and reporting or risk losing 5% of criminal justice assistance.

PREA has had the unintended consequence of criminalizing institutionalized girls' sexual activity with each other and has contributed to the emergence and growth of the female juvenile sex offender population. In the year after its passing, the number of committed girls with registered sex offenses increased by 120% since 1997 (Sickmund 2004). It has made the loss of sexual autonomy an apparent corollary to imprisonment (Smith 2008). For girls, this has meant the disappearance of any continuum of permissible sexual behaviors in institutional settings.

When girls entered the correctional institution, their sexualized behaviors and histories were often understood in terms of disordered personalities and other psychological pathologies, while the social and economic situations structuring their actions and development remained documented in their case files, but largely unaddressed, except for occasional economic literacy courses and limited vocational training. As many facilities hired (as staff or through contracts) clinical social workers, individual therapy sessions and group therapy were also available. However, in four of the facilities noted in this study, such therapy was guided by line staff or a case manager, with such sessions becoming part of the residents' correctional record. In addition, programming also focused on cognitive discipline, which included identifying and staying away from undesirables, making more responsible choices, mastering mood regulation, raising moral reasoning (understanding and prioritizing others' feelings and needs), and reversing thinking errors that brought them to commitment. Part of cognitive discipline also included aggression management training, which was achieved, in part, through frequent rituals of reproach for challenging staff, being manipulative with staff or other residents, acting in a sexualized manner, or using sex as power over others. Several girls interpreted these techniques of cognitive discipline as punitive and oppressive, occasionally relaying careful acts of resistance to such policies:

> "You get into trouble if you talk back so you can't complain about anything. Like they can just do whatever they want because if you say something, you're the liar." (Interviewee, age 19)

"Some girls will try to run away or have their parents complain or like, break something, or like mess something up, and try not to get caught. It always just gets you more trouble." (Interviewee, age 18)

"They cut your hair when you first get there and then they will cut it if you break the rules. So like you might grow out your hair for a year and then they chop it if you break a rule." (Interviewee, age 18)

Focusing on sexual minority girls in custody, current research demonstrates how girls regularly experience heteronormative policies and overall homophobia, from both staff and other inmates (Curtin 2002; Majd et al. 2009; Pasko 2011). In particular, lesbian and bisexual identities are often ignored in juvenile court and corrections, with staff assuming youth are always "straight." In addition, girls in lock-up are often encouraged to develop a heterosexual understanding of themselves and their sexuality and engage in hetero-feminine forms of gender conformity. Such forms of conformity include pressuring them to wear makeup, prohibiting them from shaving their heads, and offering them only heterosexual life skills and safe sex education. Additionally, "sexually acting out" while in secure confinement was often viewed by correctional staff as part of the girls' pathology, attempts at gaining power or popularity, and always deviant and abnormal. The sexual minority young women in this study often felt such pressure:

"If you're gay, you're gross." (Interviewee, age 17)

"There was a counselor who was gay and would speak openly about it to us (sexual minority residents), but that was not … something that happened a lot." (Interviewee, age 19)

"There's a lot of sex that happens and it can cause drama, so I get it, but that doesn't mean all gay people are screwed up or like, there's something wrong with me." (Interviewee, age 18)

"We had one group, a family group thing, and we talked about it (being gay). And I think that was it." (Interviewee, age 18)

"I like to shave my head. Keep it real close …. I was never allowed to do that. Felt like I had to grow it out." (Interviewee, age 22)

Additionally, while interviewees spoke of sexual activity during confinement as experimental or for popularity, they also noted—especially for those who identified as lesbian—as ways to maintain a "true" self, to express what feels normal, and to create a connection. As one interviewee noted, "It's like they just want me to stop being gay. But I didn't. I actually did meet [partner] in there." However, others noted that they didn't discuss their sexual identities while confined, for fear of repercussions from both staff and residents:

"I learned not to talk about it because you could get jacked up." (Interviewee, age 18)

"I only talked about it with other girls I knew were gay, like gay on the outside, too." (Interviewee, age 19)

"I didn't want [staff] treating me differently. I heard that if you're gay, they will put you in administrative segregation." (Interviewee, age 17)

Similar to juvenile justice efforts in earlier eras, the facilities the young women in this study experienced placed tremendous focus on risky sexual behavior and pregnancy. Unlike the first eras of juvenile courts and reformatories, where efforts were primarily rooted in the moral reformation of the wayward girl into a marriageable woman (Odem 1995), in the current era of juvenile justice in the United States, the use of medical advances and pharmaceuticals made it possible to exert control more effectively through the body. Pregnancy was often the biggest concern cited by justice professionals, especially when considering placement and as girls began to exit a facility, to leave on family furloughs for a weekend, or to finish/age out of probation. Indeed, some private facilities in this study did not take girls who were pregnant, or insisted that girls take oral contraception as part of acceptance into the program (Pasko 2010). Other programs regulated girls' sexual activity by administering birth control, completing vaginal examinations for evidence of sexual activity, and mandating pregnancy tests, when returning to the facility after furlough, even if the girls identified as lesbian. If girls did not agree with such requirements, they may not be placed in the private facilities that had such policies (and these facilities may be closer to their homes and/or provide better services or dormitory/campus-like environments) or they may not be allowed furloughs and opportunities to spend time with their families. Despite such focus on sexual behavior, several interviewees ($n = 8$) demonstrated little knowledge about sexual and reproductive health and had no access to services upon release (unless they became pregnant). Indeed, six of them were pregnant or parenting while system-involved (probation, detention, or correctional facility). For example, one interviewee (age 16) commented, "I don't remember giving birth. I don't really recall how it all happened … or making any decisions. I was just told what to do. I'm not sure how you get pregnant. I mean, you just have sex?"

Despite these forms of regulations and control, some facilities sought to develop girls' sexual agency and integrated education and training on sexual health, sexually transmitted diseases, self-care, reproductive options, healthy romantic relationships, and parenting classes into their programming. However, in most facilities, such programming followed a heteronormative script and/or promoted abstinence. Undeniably, other facilities offered nothing, leaving education and access to services up to the young women's self-advocacy and responsibility once in the community:

> "I actually had [staff] ask me if I wanted to talk to [the pastor] when we asked about birth control." (Interviewee, age 18)

> "They gave us exams if we need one or they want us to have one, but nothing else." (Interviewee, age 18)

> "I had [son] while I was [in facility], and he died 'cause he was really sick. I don't think anyone said anything to me …. I'm not sure what happened. My foster mom had to look into it for me. But no, no help or anything." (Interviewee, age 22)

Conclusion: Sexualities and Girls' Imprisonment

The juvenile court and correctional system in the United States has consistently sanctioned and criminalized aspects of girls' sexualities. Despite a juvenile justice system that has deinstitutionalized status offenses and noncriminal behavioral problems, the capture and custodial confinement of girls for sexual impishness or indecency continues, even if some of the processes and definitions have changed (Pasko 2010). For example, refusing to accept responsibility for actions, refusing to follow terms of probation, making poor choices (especially in terms of romantic attachments and sexual behavior), and engaging in risky lifestyles continue to be reasons why girls need secure confinement—for their own good and protection (Pasko and Lopez 2018; Pasko 2017).

This chapter's findings show that sexual stereotypes and heteronormative policies leave young women in conflict with the law, especially sexual minority girls, few options for treatment and services that are more open to and understanding of their experiences and environments. It also denies them girl-sensitive treatment (see Bloom et al. 2002; Davidson et al. 2010, for examples) that comes without judgment or micro-management of their choices and orientations and underscores relationships and healthy connections, across the sexual and gender identity spectrums. Indeed, the heteronormative construction of sexuality and the enforcement of conservative heterosexual choices and identity can have profound impacts on girls in the youth correctional system, and these damaging effects often go unnoticed.

What is important to note is that the girls profiled in this chapter represent only a portion of all young women who find themselves in the justice system. The small number of cases shared here is a limitation of this research. Further research on larger samples of sexual minority and/or pregnant/parenting girls and young women would add to this analysis. Additionally, although girls of color in this study did not report much variation in the treatment of sexualities as compared to their white counterparts, future research should explore such intersectionality. For example, findings that emerged from this project's interviews with justice professionals found that the majority of them considered girls of color to be less trustworthy, more prone to violence, and more sexually promiscuous, especially when speaking of Latina girls on probation (Pasko and Lopez 2018).

This study also raises significant policy implications. Schools and other welfare and health service systems are in need of reform and repair in order to adequately address system-involved girls' lives and needs, especially in terms of recognizing risks, understanding the complexities of sexualities, and offering trauma-informed care for those who have histories of sexual abuse and assault. This, however, might be a somewhat geographic-specific recommendation. In the United States, many districts remain focused on identifying and punishing delinquent girls, and policymakers often refuse to address these multiple failing systems. The content of gender-specific (or girl-sensitive) programs formed within the juvenile justice system requires special attention, since the family court has a long history of policing of girls' behavior without sensitive, nuanced, girl-centered approaches (Pasko and Chesney-lind 2016; Pasko 2010). Programming for this population often fails to offer girls spaces, experiences, and relationships that will depart from traditional, heteronormative practices and policies. As many of the interviewees demonstrated throughout their comments, many girls are in need of specific life skills training and honest sexual education, in addition to treatment of past trauma and exploitation.

The young women presented in this chapter demonstrate how, from their perspective, the court and correctional system seems hyper-sensitive to sexual deviations in behavior and alternative identities, utilizing approaches often perceived as overly unfair and uncompromising. Indeed, programming needs to be culturally sensitive as well and incorporate diverse and inclusive staff who can dismantle stereotypical assumptions. Programming elements that utilize intersectional perspectives include the use of art, poetry, dance, and both fictional and biographical story-telling to relate their experiences with racial, sexual, and gendered micro-aggressions and inequalities. Such discussions and presentations also require staff to confront their own biases in their approaches and decision-making relating to system-involved girls, especially in their personal understanding of and belief systems regarding sexual behavior and reproductive choices, and their thoughts and treatment of sexual minority girls.

References

Abrams, L. (2001). Guardians of virtue: The social reformers and the "girl problem," 1890–1920. *Social Service Review, 74*, 436–452.

Alexander, R. (1995). *The girl problem: Female sexual delinquency in New York, 1900–1930*. Ithaca, NY: Cornell University Press.

Andrews, R., & Cohn, A. (1974). Ungovernability: The Unjustifiable Jurisdiction. *Yale Law Journal, 83*, 1383–1409.

Bloom, B., Owen, B., Deschenes, E. P., & Rosenbaum, J. (2002). Improving juvenile justice for females: A statewide assessment for California. *Crime and Delinquency, 48*, 526–552.

Bond-Maupin, L., Maupin, J., & Leisenring, A. (2002). Girls' delinquency and the justice implications of intake workers' perspectives. *Women and Criminal Justice, 13*, 51–77.

Brenzel, B. (1983). *Daughters of the state*. Cambridge, MA: MIT Press.

Chesney-Lind, M., & Pasko, L. (2013). *The female offender: Girls, women, and crime* (3rd ed.). Thousand Oaks, CA: Sage Publications.

Chesney-Lind, M., & Shelden, R. (2014). *Girls, delinquency, and juvenile justice* (3rd ed.). Belmont, CA: Wadsworth.

Cooney, S. M., Small, S. A., & O'Connor, C. (2008). *Girls in the juvenile justice system: Toward effective gender-responsive programming*. What works, Wisconsin—Research to Practice Series, No. 7. Madison: University of Wisconsin–Madison and University of Wisconsin-Extension.

Curtin, M. (2002). Lesbian and Bisexual Girls in the Juvenile Justice System. *Child and Adolescent Social Work Journal, 19*, 285–301.

Cusworth Walker, S., Muno, A., & Sullivan-Colglazier, C. (2015). Principles in practice: A multistate study of gender-responsive reforms in the juvenile justice system. *Crime & Delinquency, 61*(5), 742–766.

Davidson, J. T., Pasko, L., & Chesney-Lind, M. (2010). She's way too good to lose:' An evaluation of Honolulu's girls court. *Women and Criminal Justice, 21*(4), 308–327.

Federal Bureau of Investigation. (2015). *Uniform crime reports, 2014*. Washington, DC: Department of Justice.

Gaarder, E., Rodriguez, N., & Zatz, M. (2004). Criers, liars, and manipulators: Probation officers' views of girls. *Justice Quarterly, 21*, 547–578.

Knupfer, A. (2001). *Reform and resistance: Gender, delinquency, and America's first juvenile court*. New York: Routledge.

Majd, K., Marksamer, J., & Reyes, C. (2009). *Hidden injustice: Lesbian, gay, bisexual, and transgender youth in juvenile courts*. San Francisco, CA: Autumn Press.

Mallicoat, S. (2007). Gendered justice: Attributional differences between males and females in the juvenile courts. *Feminist Criminology, 2*(1), 4–30.

Nathanson, C. (1991). *Dangerous passage: The social control of sexuality in women's adolescence*. Philadelphia, PA: Temple University Press.

Odem, M. (1995). *Delinquent daughters: Protecting and policing adolescent female sexuality in the U.S., 1885–1920*. Chapel Hill, NC: University of North Carolina Press.

Odem, M., & Schlossman, S. (1991). Guardians of virtue: The juvenile court and female delinquency cases in early 20th century Los Angeles. *Crime and Delinquency, 37*, 186–203.

Office of Juvenile Justice and Delinquency Prevention. (2016). *Survey of youth in residential placement*. Washington, DC: Office of Juvenile Justice and Delinquency Prevention. Retrieved from https://syrp.org/default.asp.

Pasko, L. (2010). Damaged daughters: The history of girls' sexuality and the juvenile justice system. *Journal of Criminal Law and Criminology, 100*(3), 1099–1130.

Pasko, L. (2011). Setting the record 'straight:' Girls, sexuality, and the juvenile correctional system. *Social Justice, 37*(1), 7–26.

Pasko, L. (2017). Beyond confinement: The regulation of girl offenders' bodies, sexual choices and behavior. *Women and Criminal Justice, 27*(1), 4–20.

Pasko, L., & Chesney-Lind, M. (2016). Running the gauntlet: Understanding commercial sexual exploitation and the pathways perspective to female offending. *Journal of Developmental and Life-Course Criminology, 2*(3), 275–295.

Pasko, L., & Lopez, V. (2018). The Latina penalty: Juvenile court and correctional attitudes toward the latina juvenile offender. *Journal of Ethnicity in Criminal Justice* (published online). https://doi.org/10.1080/15377938.2015.1015196.

Platt, A. (1977). *The child savers*. Chicago, IL: The University of Chicago Press.

Puzzanchera, C., Adams, B., & Sickmund, M. (2011). *Juvenile court statistics 2008*. Pittsburgh, PA: National Center for Juvenile Justice.

Rafter, N. (1990). *Partial justice: Women, prisons, and social control*. Piscataway, NJ: Transaction Publishers.

Reinharz, S. (1992). *Feminist methods in social research*. Oxford: Oxford University Press.

Schaffner, L. (2006). *Girls in trouble with the law*. Piscataway, NJ: Rutgers University Press.

Schlossman, S., & Wallach, S. (1978). The crime of precocious sexuality: Female juvenile delinquency in the progressive era. *Harvard Educational Review, 48*(1), 65–94.

Sherman, F. T. (2012). Justice for girls: Are we making progress? *UCLA Law Review*, 1585–1628.

Sickmund, M. (2004). *Juveniles in corrections*. Washington, DC: Office of Juvenile Justice and Delinquency Prevention.

Smith, B. (2008). The Prison Rape Elimination Act: Implementation and unresolved issues. *Criminal Law Brief, 3*, 10–18.

14

"This Place Saved My Life": The Limits of Christian Redemption Narratives at a Juvenile Detention Facility for Girls

Mary E. Thomas

Introduction

"This is an opportunity." These words were spoken by an adult Christian volunteer to incarcerated teenage girls at Juvenile Correctional Facility (JCF). I attended the Christian evangelical program one evening when I visited the facility conducting research on girls' experiences of incarceration. For two years (2012–2014), I typically went weekly to JCF, located in the Midwestern United States on the banks of a tributary of the Ohio River. That evening, I planned to hang out on the housing unit as usual, but all of the girls participating in my research were on their way to religious programs. Four girls went to a Catholic program led by a priest, and seven attended the programming provided by the evangelical group, Epiphany Ministry. Epiphany's volunteers visited the facility monthly to hold a Christian fellowship meeting with youth who had attended what Epiphany calls a "three-day short course in Christianity." The three-day event focuses on guiding youth to a decision to make a spiritual and personal commitment to Christ. According to Epiphany Ministry's website, the structure of the three-day event is as follows: "Day one is you are loved and you are not alone. Day two is you are forgiven. Day three

M. E. Thomas (✉)
Ohio State University, Columbus, OH, USA
e-mail: thomas.1672@osu.edu

is God is counting on you."[1] The monthly program's purpose is to "follow up" with youth who had previously completed the course or who were planning to participate at the next offering.

I tagged along with the girls to the cafeteria building at their insistent invitation and with the welcoming permission of both Epiphany's volunteers and JCF facility staff. Volunteers outnumbered girls by about three to one at the meeting. I hung back that evening, chatted with the middle age and elderly volunteers, mostly staying out of the way of the attention that the girls were receiving. The cookies and fruit laid out on the tables in the facility's cafeteria looked promising, and after several songs, some prayers, and lots of hugging, we sat down to eat the snacks. Soon, an African-American woman, 58 years old, stood to witness to the teenage girls in attendance. To witness is to provide a personal testimony about the power of God's and Jesus' love over one's life at a moment of change, to offer this evidence as an example for others to consider their own conversion, and to provide guidance and prayer while others grow their faith. Epiphany Ministry's mission statement is "To show Christ's transforming love to at risk and incarcerated youth."[2]

The woman surprised the girls by beginning her story with the memory of her own imprisonment when she was an adolescent at the same location where we now sat. She recounted the intense frustration and anger she had felt as an incarcerated teenager, musing that she had concocted schemes for escape by swimming across the facility's adjacent river to freedom. This part of her story was evidence provided to the girls that she was once just like them and that they should relate to her, despite the age difference. However, it was her language about swimming the river to freedom that immediately sharpened my attention. Prominent scholar-activists including Angela Davis and Michelle Alexander refer to the US prison system as "the rebirth of caste" (as Alexander (2010) puts it) and draw a direct connection between enslavement and the contemporary mass incarceration of people of color. Racism, Alexander writes, is "highly adaptable" (Alexander 2010, p. 21). The volunteer's language of swimming the river to freedom also invoked the regional importance of the Ohio River as a border between northern and southern/slave-holding states. The National Underground Freedom Center in Cincinnati stands on the northern shoreline of the river and memorializes the estimated 100,000 who escaped slavery (30,000 of them through Ohio) through the activities and safe havens of the Underground Railroad.

However, the volunteer did not overtly make that connection, nor did the girls who listened to her story. They instead laughed at the idea of escape—and in fact, a couple of the girls had previously described to me their own fantasies of escape over the razor wire fencing and beyond the river's border.

None of them, either that evening or later when we talked about the woman's story, made the connection that many scholars have between race, imprisonment, and freedom struggles. Rather, the volunteer urged the girls to turn *away* from the river and instead focus on themselves and the opportunities that imprisonment could provide for them. While as an incarcerated youth she had failed to reflect on her life and future prospects, she told the girls that hindsight had showed her the error of that lost moment at the facility. For you, she said, "This is an opportunity."

While the volunteer insisted that the opportunity was part of God's plan for the youth, youth justice scholars, including Cox (2018), Morris (2016), and Rios (2011), insist that the punitive social control of Black and Brown youth starts very early in their lives. Rather than an absent, retreated state made familiar by themes of neoliberalism, the over-policing of Black and Brown neighborhoods and urban schools has inaugurated a path, especially for boys and girls of color, to criminalization. Girls who offend also face the scrutiny of their sexuality and so-called mis-performances of proper femininity. Girls have always been punished more severely than boys for status offenses, are more likely to be picked up than boys for being outside the home, and experience the connections between victimization and offending more acutely than boys (Pasko 2008). I learned early in my research from the girls and the staff at the facility that a shocking, near universal percentage of incarcerated youth there experienced sexual and gender abuse prior to their adjudications. In the United States, lesbian, queer, and gender non-conforming girls are charged and sentenced more harshly than feminine girls and are thus overrepresented in prison populations, especially when they are not white (Morris 2016). The so-called opportunity, as the Christian volunteer put it, of youth incarceration exists squarely within a pronounced racist and sexist punitive shift in the US carceral state.

On the other hand, juvenile detention in the United States emphasizes rehabilitation efforts as centrally as it does punishment—though the lines between the two are almost always blurred. Increasingly, juvenile justice advocates and policy makers emphasize, as Abrams and Anderson-Nathe (2013, p. 3) point out, the "immense capacity for change" of young people. Yet, the failure to achieve change is often placed squarely on the backs of youth despite the overwhelming evidence that individual youth cannot merely overcome the obstacles they face through "better decision-making" (Cox 2018). Thus, while most facilities housing incarcerated youth highlight their work to rehabilitate, educate, and support the specific needs of adolescents, teens, and young adults, core to this work is an overwhelming discourse of personal responsibility and changed behavior. Whether based in therapeutic practices in cognitive behavioral approaches, merit systems of reward and punishment, or youth-staff relations emphasizing youth accountability, these routes of engagement with youth place the onus of change onto the individual child herself (also see Sankofa et al. 2017).

In my research I found that youth quickly learn when incarcerated to conform their life stories and experiences to the expectations of staff and program requirements for changed attitudes and behaviors. Thus, while girls' stories to me over the course of my research overwhelmingly illustrated the effects of what Rios (2011) calls the "youth control complex" on their lives, they predominantly articulated their pathways to incarceration by blaming their own bad decision-making (Thomas 2019). Despite recounting the tragic contexts of their upbringing in communities and families wracked by economic precarity, over-policing and incarceration, sexual violence, gang involvement, and substance abuse, they summarized their hopes for post-prison futures around their individual capacity for change. This focus on personal responsibility and the capacity to make better choices about their lives also aligned with the Epiphany volunteer's witnessing. The work and effort of Christian volunteers sit neatly beside the state's mission to reroute girls' experiences through personal responsibility, and the girls also told me that the majority of facility staff regularly integrated their own Christian faith and belief into mandatory, daily group sessions meant to teach girls routes to more successful futures. Thus, the everyday Christian religious expression of facility staff buttress volunteer activities and messaging just as much as the reverse.

Cox (2018, p. 6) defines the juvenile justice system as "a palimpsest: the system we have today bears many traces of its predecessors." The classist, racist, and heterosexist foundations of the earliest "child-saving" movements are clear and evidenced in justice scholarship, but it is important to remember that the people who inaugurated the juvenile justice system were also grounded by their Christian faith and practice (as was the birth of the US penitentiary). The very idea that the child and adolescent could be reformed came from a modern belief in the inherent malleability of young people and the increasing command of the state to provide replacement institutions for moral education of youth when upstanding adults and parents failed to do so (Bernard and Kurlycheck 2010). While the belief in child-saving was not applied to all youth equally, since, as Cox writes, "not every child was worth saving" (such as those who are racialized, have disabilities, are sexually active, or live in poverty: see for example, Cox 2018, p. 6; Agyepong 2018; Simmons 2015; Pasko 2008), the moral education and training of youth through Christian belief and practice was firmly in place in the palimpsest.

A developmental approach to age and childhood remains the primary framing device for justifying reform to the juvenile justice system (nowadays this is most evident through the use of neurological discourses about brain maturation), but the Christian notion of the eternal soul retains its guiding role in everyday facility investments in youth reform and change. The role of staff fueling this retention in the facility where I did my research include staff praying with girls, sharing witnessing and religious beliefs, everyday chatting about church activities, and forging direct connections between staff's church communities and adult volunteers (e.g., often staff recruited friends from their own church communities to volunteer with "their" kids). Overwhelmingly, staff and adult volunteers both situated predominant lessons about individual responsibility and reform as a service to a higher power and as enabled by that higher power, whether couched in the present time for immediate gain, or for their future prospects and eternal salvation.

Scholars who explore religious programming in US adult prisons mostly consider the Constitutional implications of state-religion interactions, the rights withheld for freedom of religious expression for incarcerated people, and the extensive and increasing reach of Christian ministries' influence on incarcerated people and prison spaces. However, in this chapter, I am most aided by the work of Erzen (2008, 2017), whose book *God in Captivity* examines faith-based prison ministries. She astutely shows that the transformation process of evangelical conversion allows incarcerated adults to distance themselves from their confinement and the everyday depersonalization and shame that is an effect of incarceration. In her extensive research at faith-based adult prisons, Erzen (2008, pp. 663-664) found that religious transformation

> removed prisoners from the authority of the state and placed them under the dominion of a supreme being. The Christian narrative of born-again transformation especially, in which one has ceased to be the sinner and now exists in an irrevocable state of grace, functions to alleviate guilt and shame.

Faith-based Christian programs, she continues, "are successful because recipients feel comfortable with a theology that stresses grace and forgiveness instead of questioning their moral worth or defining them solely by their crimes" (Erzen 2008).

Many tens of thousands of nondenominational Christians make up the bulk of adult volunteers visiting prison populations in US states, referring to themselves and their organizations as "faith-based," Erzen writes, in order "to avoid violating the establishment clause of the First Amendment, which prohibits government from favoring one religion over another" (2017, p. 5).

These groups provide a range of programming from worship and Bible study to addiction self-help groups, yet the underlying goal for activities is to transform "the hearts of prisoners" through faith in God. "Heart change," Erzen argues, "exemplifies the faith-based idea that religious belief will alter someone from the inside out" (p. 4). Faith programs in adult facilities often provide the only semblance of reform efforts in otherwise harshly punitive contexts. Maruna (2009) importantly points out, however, that redemption requires an observer, either as an adjudicator of change or as a recipient of the benefits of one's change. This fact is vital to consider in the context of youth incarceration, because the state's assessment of youth focuses intently on their capacities for changed behavior.

In youth facilities, mandated to incorporate the care and rehabilitation of young people adjudicated of offenses, the alignment of faith-based and carceral programming is perhaps more uniform than in adult facilities, but very little scholarship exists on the use of religion in contemporary youth facility programming. Further, the question of how adult volunteer/incarcerated youth relations add an intergenerational dimension to the dynamics of conversion also remains to be examined (on intergenerationality, see Kallio and Thomas 2019). This chapter offers an initial contribution on these issues by considering the effects of Christian faith-based programming on girls' experiences of incarceration. It addresses the ways that the young women at JCF articulated their everyday struggles of confinement with commitments to take responsibility for changed lives through religious belief and faith framed by the guidance of adult volunteers. After next describing my study's research methodology, I turn to a repeated theme in girls' stories that prison saved them and provided them an opportunity for profound change. I relate these narratives to the ways that girls detail their changed behaviors at the facility, especially subsequent to religious programming and involvement with church volunteers. In the penultimate section I ask what limits girls relate about their abilities to carry out change, both in the facility and when they imagine leaving it, and finally I offer brief conclusions.

Methodology

At the time of my research (2012–2014), JCF was one of four state-operated juvenile correctional facilities overseen by the Ohio Department of Youth Services (DYS), and the only one of the four that housed girls. In 2014, the state shuttered JCF in response to the decreasing numbers of girls adjudicated of felonies and sentenced to detention; for more than a decade, widespread and persistent claims, legal suits, and media reporting of sexual misconduct at the facility also plagued DYS. Girls have since been routed to community based alternatives and residential mental health facilities. In 2012, when my research began, the average monthly facility population count for girls was already low, at 39, compared to highs near 200 in previous decades, and that number fell further until the facility closed in May 2014 (the annual state-wide profiles for adjudications and commitments for all of these years are publicly accessible online at dys.ohio.gov). Across all four DYS facilities, the average age of both male and female youth was 17.7 years in 2012 (most were 16 and 17 year olds). Youth adjudicated and committed as minors before age 18 age out of DYS facilities no later than the eve of their 21st birthday.

Between 2012 and 2014, I recorded interviews with 15 girls (10 identified as African-American and 5 as white, roughly representative of the facility's racially disproportionate demographics), most multiple times and a few only once. I saw eight girls with long tenures of one-and-a-half to three years almost weekly over most of the timespan of the research. All youth who participated in an interview with me had to give consent (if 18 or over) or assent with parental or guardian consent (if under 18). I also knew about 45 other girls who went through the unit and whom I did not interview. I also frequently provided extracurricular programming which was classified as "volunteer" activity by facility staff. Examples of these activities include craft projects like card-making and tie-dying, or hosting secular holiday parties. My university's Institutional Review Board recommended that my general knowledge of the facility formed through activities as a "volunteer" also be considered as research data, given the impossibility of discerning impressions made through research and volunteer time at the facility. Only interviews with girls who provided consent or assent/parental consent are directly quoted in research publications. I did not interview any facility staff or adult volunteers as part of the project, nor have I tracked youth after their release, per the restrictions placed on the research by the Department of Youth Services.

In the span of the research, I attended numerous religious programs as an observer. I also met and talked informally with at least a dozen Christian volunteers at the facility, during required volunteer training (I went through training three times, once per year), the annual volunteer appreciation event, and at the front gate on frequent occasion while we were all waiting to be escorted on site by staff. I did not meet any religious volunteers who were not Christian. Thus, I was able to meet religious volunteers frequently and to garner a strong sense of their programming at the facility over the years that helps me to contextualize girls' stories and experiences.

"This Place Saved My Life": From Crisis to Heart Change

An experience of incarceration, for girls in the facility for the first time or even on a second or third stint, obviously presented a radical change in everyday life for the youth. In my interviews with girls and during activities at the facility, they all shared longings for what they missed during their confinement, yet *all* the girls who participated in my research repeated similar phrasing to this section's title. They marveled at their sheer luck in being incarcerated, because without the separation from the contexts that led to their arrests, they claimed that their paths would surely have led to a premature death. While not all girls' narratives about gratitude for prison involved a religious conversion or were accompanied by proclamations of Christian faith, most did. In this section I particularly highlight girls' narratives of redemption about the savior prison, or in other words, this place that saved them through an opportunity for heart change and Christian testimony.

For Marie, a white 20 year old who was released from the facility just days after I talked to her, change at JCF came through a religious transformation. She explained to me that she was suffering from being away from home upon her arrival because a friend had just died. She described feeling alone, often isolating herself in her room and skipping meals. But within days, through what she thought was a message from God through the repeated references to 1 Corinthians 13 (especially, "And now abide faith, hope, love, these three; but the greatest of these is love."), she felt she was saved:

> That Sunday the pastor read off Corinthians 13. The next week I went to Bible study and chose reading a book, and the first story in the book, I had the passage Corinthians 13. My grandma sent me a cute little thing with Corinthians 13 on it. I had prayer guides. Three times other people kept talking about Corinthians 13. And I just started crying. That was the first thing. Then I just prayed to God to help me. I started reading my bible. It really helped me get through. I started being myself again.

Marie noted the importance of the volunteers in bringing her to her "salvation." The pastor and the leader of Bible study both served to guide her while at JCF, as well as her grandmother's mail which bridged her experiences in the facility to her life at home. Since she was saved, she told me, "Things have changed a lot for me. I had to do it myself, but I had [a church volunteer] to lean on."

Marie explained to me that prison was the break she needed from her life at home, in order to accomplish lasting change for a new future. She said, "I'm glad I came here. I really am. I didn't care [before]. 'That is the best way to live. What I was doing was okay. Violence is good.' I just had that mindset. I don't anymore. I never thought that I would change. I never thought I would change. I thought I would end up dying in the streets." Marie also placed her religious conversion and changed self as a path to return to the past, when she said, "I started being myself again." Faith therefore brought change but also a renewed sense of self. The connection to much older others—her grandma, the pastor, church volunteers—was the impetus to both religion and adjustment to the facility. Emphatically, she said, it was not the other girls. No girl described to me that another girl helped her be saved—it was only through relations to adult volunteers that girls expressed their pathways to faith and renewal.

When Marie said that she "started being myself again," that self was formed by the spatial and emotional context of the facility, both in terms of what it offered and in terms of what it prohibited. The self with an inherent capacity for change, reformed behavior, and good intentions saturated the therapy materials that girls received, and in daily group meetings on the unit, girls had to provide regular narratives about how they were performing against these expectations for reform (see also Thomas 2019). On the other hand, a range of other personal identities and senses of self were prohibited or treated as a basis from which to change. For example, a desiring or sexual self was displaced onto future contexts since even expressions of desire or lust were considered evidence of failed reform. However, as Goodkind (2009, p. 401) notes, "the self is not some innate essence … [Therefore,] an examination of residential programs for girls must necessarily consider the types of selves that such programs seek to create." Because self-help is paramount to juvenile justice settings, especially for girls, emotional encouragement and support from adults are techniques of self-help promotion (Goodkind 2009). Therefore, while Marie saw the repetition of 1 Corinthian 13 as a message from God, that message was ubiquitously cited by the adults (both at the facility and her grandmother) seeking to offer love as a technique of reform. "Faith, hope, love" is specifically resonant for a context of incarceration where hope for a "successful" future undergirds all programming, though the bleak routine of prison life displaces hope always to the future for its accomplishment. In other words, hope is articulated in terms of what life holds in the future; while sometimes girls hoped for "a good day tomorrow," the magnitude of hope from Biblical references places emphasis on the long term, indeed, adult futures that awaited youth on their release.

"Love," on the other hand, was offered by the adult volunteers at the facility, a sharp contrast to daily unit life where love was outright discouraged. I saw volunteers, for example, express their love verbatim to girls in programming, and they were allowed to hug girls and hold hands during song and prayer. Any likewise expressions of "love" between incarcerated youth is prohibited, either as intimate expressions of friendship or fellowship, or as romantic love. Any touching, doing each other's hair, and even joking too loudly can lead to punishment, depending on the day and the mood of staff. Further, staff also sometimes expressed love and care to youth, including through hugs and by saying, "I love you." The expressed care and so-called love that staff offer is conditional on an incarcerated youth's behavioral performances and success, however, with often painful results for youth—many of whom come from families with embedded traumatic histories and abusive relations (see Thomas 2019). Thus, when "love" from the older volunteers comes to youth like Marie, with the warmth of contact and the genuine sentimentality of prayer and care, this is a unique form of adult comfort than they usually experience. In turn, that experience of comfort and "love" led to youth engagement and commitment to the Christian programming.

Marie went home the week after I talked to her, and tragically, within a year she was dead. Most of the girls insist that their heart change will not change again upon release, that they are forever changed. Despite Marie's acknowledgment that her change in "mindset" followed a change in context (that forced segregation from "the streets"), she was not able to ensure a permanence to the change once she returned home and back to the same challenges and struggle with drug addiction that laid the groundwork for her incarceration. The volunteers who were present during her stay at JCF do not provide that same support upon release; the "place that saves" is contingent on its restricted geographies. A more appropriate phrasing would be, "this place saves my life as long as I remain confined here."

Goodkind offers a perspective on the contradictory messages involved with juvenile justice when she questions, "[I]s it reasonable to ask girls to value themselves when they have been so utterly devalued by those around them and society more broadly?" (Goodkind 2009, p. 417). Marie began using drugs very early in her life, and her parents had both struggled with addiction and prison stays. She told me, "When I go home, it is the first time in 12 years that I'm clean. I wasn't just addicted to drugs. I was addicted to a whole lifestyle. The guns, the violence, the money and the people ... That's no way to live." Christian volunteers seek to foster girls' faith in Jesus Christ and God so that they can cement an inner strength for their return home, yet, in the case of Marie, survival demanded more than prayer and behavioral reform. She left

JCF at the height of the opioid "epidemic" in Ohio, and the painful irony of Marie's death at home is obvious—for girls experiencing struggles with drug addiction, the place often did save their life, if only temporarily in her case.

The fear of an early death arose repeatedly in girls' change narratives, and all of the girls had lost young friends, siblings, and/or cousins prior to their incarceration. Nia, an African-American 18 year old, was the girl who stated, "This place saved my life." Nia described to me situations where she thought death was imminent to her before her adjudication and incarceration (e.g., she lost very close family members to gun violence, and she was involved in the drug trade). God, she explained, removed her from that harmful and violent life in order to save her:

> I was baptized before I came here, but I actually wasn't as sincere as I am now. But I really sincerely believe in God, and I trust in him. And I believe that everything that he does is for a reason. So that's another reason why I'm just so humble. Sometimes when I get angry, I just—instead of just running my mouth or something, I could just cry, like I'm just being humble. Like I'm holding it in, but he's letting me let it out by just crying. So he is working with me, and he has changed my life tremendously.

Nia took part in the volunteer church services at the facility, and she planned to join one group's church when she got out: "I feel like they have a lot to teach me, and I look up to them. You know, they are just so sweet, and I feel like surrounding myself by people, it's like triggers. Like, people, places and things that can trigger me. I just feel like I surround myself with people, I will start learning better places to be—that is their church. They said it's a very good church." In her story, the church-place serves as a desire to be "better" and represents a location to her of personal advancement. "Good" in her quote signals a Godly place, and her wording that "I will starting learning better places to be"—rather than "I will learn to be better"—illustrates the displacement between the desire for change on the one hand, and the capability for change, on the other. Like Marie, Nia also associates where she is with her potential to be better, whether the "streets" to Marie which signifies danger, or the "very good church" for Nia which signifies adult support and personal advancement. The racialized connotations of "good" in this example are also central to how advancement and care are articulated by Nia, in addition to the intergenerational support from the much older and mostly white Christian adults.

Unlike Nia, Jessica (a white 16 year old) had not gone to church before JCF. She expected the inundation of faith-based messages while incarcerated, but she did not expect to find their messages compelling. The excerpt from our conversation about the scene of her "saving" at Epiphany illustrates the power of the caring attention from the adult volunteers on her religious experience (ellipses indicate where I removed some text for clarity and brevity):

Jessica: I've never really been religious but you know this is going to sound really, really crazy—I guess it's really not, because I guess it's typical for people in jail—but we went to this [Epiphany] program, and I was like, "Holy crap, I need God." The last song they sung, it was talking about not wanting to go back [to previous behaviors and beliefs] and how you're ready to change, you know? "You don't want to have to go through this kind of stuff anymore." [...] I broke down and I started crying, and at the end they're like, "Who is ready to change?" And I was like, "I'm ready to do this."

Mary: So what makes that group able to reach you? What is it about them, do you think?

Jessica: They're just all so kind. [... It] seems easier to talk to them, like they're kind and they're like—some of them have had really bad lives, like there was this lady who sat at my table with me, and her son killed his wife on accident. They were drunk, and they got in a fight, she broke her neck, and then she died like a year later because she was paralyzed. And he just wants to get out of prison, he's been there for like eight years, and he's about to get out of prison, and her other daughter refuses to talk to him. They're kind, because they believe that God's going to handle it.

Jessica has family members who were incarcerated as adults, and family members who went through 12-step programs that emphasize a "higher power." She expected to remain skeptical about this discourse but expressed surprise that she was swayed by a religious program; I think she was slightly disappointed in being "typical" for her conversion experience. Yet, her narrative shows the seduction of the Christian programming for a young person dealing with the sadness of being removed from home. The kindness of the older volunteers, despite the grief and violence they have experienced in their own lives, is a salve to Jessica, and that staging of witnessing, music, and singing, engages the emotional vulnerability in her. The findings of scholars focusing on adult incarcerated people who "find God" emphasize the ways that religious conversion provides people with a route to communicate new self-identities, to express remorse, and to reconcile past with present life narratives (e.g., Maruna et al. 2006). However, Jessica's narrative here also points importantly to the difference age makes; she emphasizes the kindness of volunteers and their painful histories, as opposed to her own need to reconcile "what she did" with "who she is now." Some days Jessica has the opportunity to channel her newfound faith by attending two Bible studies, on in the afternoon and one in the evening.

Perhaps the most telling aspect of her story, however, is the message conveyed to her that conversion and faith will help prevent her from "going through this kind of stuff anymore." Incarceration is meant to "save her" through reform, rehabilitation, and removal from home, but the journey through "this stuff" in the future requires faith in God to steer her clear. The interior life of belief and prayer allows Jessica to hand over her problems to God, as the mother did after her son's incarceration: "God's going to handle it." In the next section, I consider how girls confront challenges in the prison on the path to reform through faith.

The Savior Prison and the Path to Reform Through Prayer

Faith in God allows girls to fantasize possible lives beyond the contexts of their communities and families, and they often articulate hopes for their futures that jump from the present to the dream, without clear paths on how to get there. A key mechanism of the witnessing of adult volunteers is to show that the path to success comes through faith in God and Jesus Christ. If change through faith and prayer can be witnessed through the dozens of religious volunteers that some girls encounter over a year or two (or more) of confinement, then why not for them? Not to mention the fact that the detention facility does not invite visitors to share their experiences without a happy ending. Every adult volunteer who witnessed the girls had evidence that their faith led to positive outcomes. Armstrong (2014) emphasizes that volunteer messages to incarcerated people mediates their response to altruism. She writes, "The nature of voluntary input as an unearned gift both extended and invited trust" (Armstrong 2014, p. 307).

Nia told me about one Christian program she attended where several adult women shared their stories of overcoming hardship and achieving success. This example resonates with Armstrong's argument that the "love and care offered" by volunteers "was sensed as authentic, not arising out of superiority, piety, or pity, and it offered a sense of commonality" (Armstrong 2014, p. 307):

> A lady came in and shared her testimony and told us about how when she was young, she got molested by her daddy and her brother for a long time. It was so much. It was just sad. It was sad. She had a good story. She's a school teacher. She teaches kindergarten. Actually, there was [another woman] who was here six years out of her life. She was here for six years out of her life, and she shared a story with us about how she used to be, and how now she's changed. She just signed a contract to be making fifty thousand a year.

In Nia's recounting of the evening's testimonies, she is most affected by the jobs the women are able to have now, despite the years of suffering and hardship that they had had to endure. The "change" that the previously incarcerated youth and now successful woman was able to achieve came with her faith—which allowed her to flourish after spending a very long number of years in a juvenile prison. Nia's sentence of several years was one of the longest sentences of any of the youth I met during my research, so the similarity between her and the adult volunteer allowed her to relate and slot herself into a hopeful trajectory for the future. The path to that future requires change "now" through a religious commitment to Christ. The adult volunteer's "authentic" experience was proof to Nia that other futures were open to her, and the volunteer's testimony differed from staff efforts to provide that same message through mandated therapeutic approaches.

Having the ability to change at the moment of testimony is, obviously, severely restricted for youth who are incarcerated. They have little control over their lives, as every moment is determined for them through daily scheduling, including meals and bedtime, every relationship they are allowed to have with people on the outside must be approved by their social workers, and even their emotional responses to hardship and grief are tightly choreographed by staff expectation and comportment requirements (e.g., expressions of anger, frustration, or self-harm are prohibited and are considered rule infractions). Thus, because girls must relinquish autonomy constantly to "succeed" in their rehabilitation, the logic of God's plan for them is a way to contend with a context of control that does not completely define their selves. In other words, they would rather believe that God's plan for them allows them some capacity for change and self-control in spaces of hyper-surveillance and punishment.

Thus, many girls explained to me that their religious practice in prison included handing over control to God. The Serenity Prayer was commonly referenced by the girls and in their religious programming, as well as familiar

14 "This Place Saved My Life": The Limits of Christian Redemption... 299

to them through its use in 12-step addiction programs. The prayer goes like this: "God grant me the serenity to accept the things I cannot change, courage to change the things I can, and wisdom to know the difference." Having faith in an idea of God's plan means that girls can defer everyday challenges to him to resolve for them. They can pray and hope that he sends success to them, rather than confront the overwhelming contexts of devaluation that shape their everyday lives. Because they cannot change those contexts, they seek comfort in Christian belief and the faith that someone is looking out for them (God is that someone).

For example, De (17 years old and African-American) told me that she was able to smoke marijuana in a bathroom at the facility with Nia, and this "temptation" became a test of her faith (I do not know where or how they obtained the drugs):

> I'm blessed to be in a place like this because I have had the opportunity to change what I can, you know. But only, one thing that's been happening bad, well, it ain't happened again, but I think it was a test from God: I had smoked some weed with Nia. [...] But, I felt bad [about it]. 'Cause I'm like, "You [God] brung me here to change." I said, "You brung me here to get closer to you. Why make me go through all this stuff, disrespecting my auntie, running away, had to go through a unhealthy relationship, being beat, stripping, doing all those things for me to have to come to this?"

In this narrative, the Serenity Prayer is evident with the phrase "change what I can." In her explanation to me of what's "been happening," De explains that when Nia offered the drugs to her, it is a test from God rather than a practical, ethical, or perhaps even moral decision for her to refuse or accept the smoke. Because using drugs while in prison is a very serious infraction, De places this "test" in comparison to the "stuff" she went through over the course of her whole adolescence. She reminds me of the violence, abuse, and economic and familial precarity that she experienced prior to her incarceration (she was only 17 at the time she told me this story), as a way to say that her fear of getting caught could instantly erase all the good work of reform she had been doing—the change she had welcomed in her life through her faith in God. She was very anxious about getting caught, and I asked if they are ever drug-tested. She replied that there had been no random drug tests recently, and that she thought it was out of her system. She continued:

> I just been drinking water all the time, and I have some cranberry juice. [She giggles.] I thank God, because how did I get all that? We had some volunteers

that came in that same night. They brung me cranberry juice. And, you know, I cracked a fortune [cookie]. And you know what it said on the fortune? It said: "Trouble will bypass you." Oh, I'm like, Jesus, I hope this is really true. Cause I can't get in trouble. But I was crying because I'm like, this is ridiculous. This is crazy. I'm like, "God, why would you tempt me here?"

De thought that God graced her by letting trouble bypass her. She thanks God for bringing the volunteers to the facility that very night with cranberry juice (which the youth thought would undo the ability to detect THC in any drug test; the myth that cranberry juice's properties would mask THC is common among young people).

The route through which De's story explains "temptation" mimics the Christian ministries' language, which encourages youth to place control into God's hands. In turn, youth like De explain lucky breaks through God's divine grace. When their luck runs out, however, God doesn't shoulder the blame. The girls do. De is worried about getting in trouble because she had already been given a "primary" for writing a boy in another facility (see Thomas 2019). A primary means your judge is notified of a serious rule violation, and youth may even receive extra time on their sentences, or be refused early release with even one primary. The juvenile justice system also threatens youth with loss of privileges and wages with rules violations, too. Thus, detention and the justice system overall blend with redemption narratives and the personal struggle of living a life through Christ. Successes are celebrated with prayers of gratitude, and failures with punishment and enticements for more prayer. On the other hand, no one is required to take accountability for drug availability in the prison except for the girls who must decide to refuse it. The youth cannot control the context of surveillance and punishment, but they can pray to God to give them a pass when they mess up.

On another day, pondering her incarceration, De she said to me, "I'm really not a bad kid. I just made a bad decision." I replied, "Do you believe in bad kids?" Expecting her to say no, since most girls in the facility had faced similar challenges and caught similar charges, she surprised me by replying, "I do believe in bad kids. I can't even lie and say I don't. I do. Because I see a lot of them on the unit. [... But] I know *deep down in my heart* I'm not one of those types of kids." She explained, "It is a good thing that God brought me here because I am not the same person that I used to be." Implying that it was her faith in God which made her more able to make different—and better—decisions, De believes that faith allowed for her to change. This example resonates with Erzen's argument (2008) about heart change in prison settings. De is questioning her own moral worth and looking for change so that she can imagine a future that is not the same as her past. As I noted earlier, Erzen argues that the promise of redemption in prison through religious conversion means that the incarcerated person can absolve herself. With the guiding language of Christian ministry, De examined her own worth "deep down in her heart," and there she can find a good kid who has just made bad decisions. As opposed to a "bad kid," Christian discourse allows her to understand herself as having interior worth—that is, a kid whose actions were bad and whose self is good. Maruna et al. (2006) teach us that narratives about self-worth—here reflected in De's juxtaposition between good and bad—often follow experiences of "hitting rock bottom." Christianity (especially evangelical) offers clear mechanisms for shame management by, as they put it, imbuing prison stays with "purpose and meaning" and providing incarcerated people "with a language and framework for forgiveness" (Maruna et al. 2006, p. 174).

Conclusion

When I initially went to a mandatory volunteer training at the facility before I began my research, I found myself in a room of Christian volunteers, predominantly over age 65, retired, and white (I am also white). I asked the man running the training what percentage of volunteers are from religious groups. The chaplain—who was in charge of training volunteers at the facility at the time, no surprise—said 98%. "It's who shows up," the chaplain told me. The saturation of Christian religious programming for the youth at the facility is therefore not surprising. The ways that programming affects girls' everyday understandings of their confinement, themselves, and their relations to others, however, is less straightforward to understand. In this chapter, I have provided an initial exploration of the power of faith-based messages to youth, especially since they derive from adult volunteers and not just the regular staff that that girls must encounter involuntarily on a daily basis on the unit and in their required programming and education. The fact that adult volunteers come from "outside" and can bring with them hugs, food and juice, songs, love, and prayers has a dramatic effect on the girls who participate. These programs are unlike anything else the youth experience while incarcerated, and the adult attention is unique in the girls' lives during their incarceration, too.

I have cautioned, however, that faith-based volunteer activities ask youth to turn away from broader understandings of how the carceral system operates and to place faith in a personal, spiritual relationship to Christ. The volunteers especially encourage youth to place their faith in God and Christ because they will then lead the youth along better, righteous pathways and toward eventual success as adults. Volunteers, such as those from the evangelical group Epiphany, do know and have acknowledged to me in conversation that the girls shared their stories of family abuse and addiction, dire poverty, and struggles with the over-policing of Black communities. But despite their knowledge of the girls' difficult and trauma-filled lives, their approach highlights the ways that they emphasize Christian conversion rather than social change or continued mentoring after girls' release. Faith-based approaches, as Erzen also shows, insists that success follows from heart change and love of God.

The idea of change itself begins even earlier in girls' experiences with the justice system, with their adjudications and placement at the facility, where they are greeted with the challenge—and the requirement—to make the most of their stay through reform and rehabilitation. The idea that the place would be required to save their lives often began through their judges and carried through to social workers and therapeutic approaches at the facility (Thomas 2019). The repeated message that the prison was a savior space was impossible to ignore, as it recurred in *all* rehabilitation efforts at the facility, including girls' meetings with social workers and counselors, their educational activities, group sessions on the unit, and in fun and spiritual activities with adult volunteers. Once girls are institutionalized and undergo this regime of redemption and reform from both staff and the volunteers, the "religious belief that someone [can change] from the inside out" (to requote Erzen 2017, p. 4) means that when girls falter or face challenges, they often feel that they have failed God as well as themselves. Challenges include experiences of trauma from histories of abuse and neglect, drug addiction, family incarceration, poverty, the over-policing of girls of color, among many other experiences beyond any one young person's capacity for change and control.

The shame and punishment of failing to live up to the reform narrative or to God's expectations, tragically, is borne by the girls alone. Both the adult volunteers and the prison staff redirect girls' attention constantly to their selves, their moral worth, and the merits of their eternal souls. Indeed, the insularity of prison disallows girls' own understanding of what lies ahead. Just as they do not usually have an analytical framework for understanding their treatment by an often sexist and racist juvenile justice system, or the underlying reasons for their pathways to felony offenses, without a more comprehensive understanding of challenges they must face beyond their own capacities of "better decision-making," they are easily seduced by the ideal that they can change their pathways through personal choice and faith in God. The river, they learned from the volunteers, must be crossed through personal redemption, not with the support of safe havens on the road to freedom.

Notes

1. http://www.epiphanyministryinc.org/program.html, last accessed 08 September 2019.
2. Also http://www.epiphanyministryinc.org/home.html, accessed 08 September 2019.

References

Abrams, L. S., & Anderson-Nathe, B. (2013). *Compassionate confinement: A year in the life of Unit C*. New Brunswick, NJ: Rutgers University Press.

Agyepong, T. (2018). *The criminalization of Black children: Race, gender, and delinquency in Chicago's juvenile justice system, 1899-1945*. Chapel Hill: University of North Carolina Press.

Alexander, M. (2010). *The new Jim Crow: Mass incarceration in the age of colorblindness*. New York: The New Press.

Armstrong, R. (2014). Trusting the untrustworthy: the theology, practice, and implications of faith-based volunteers' work with ex-prisoners. *Studies in Christian Ethics, 27*(3), 299–317.

Bernard, T., & Kurlycheck, M. (2010). *The cycle of juvenile justice*. Oxford: Oxford University Press.

Cox, A. (2018). *Trapped in a vice: The consequences of confinement for young people*. New Brunswick, NJ: Rutgers University Press.

Erzen, T. (2008). Religious literacy in the faith-based prison. *PMLA, 123*(3), 659–664.

Erzen, Y. (2017). *God in Captivity: The Rise of Faith-Based Prison Ministries in the Age of Mass Incarceration*. Boston: Beacon Press.

Goodkind, S. (2009). "You can be anything you want, but you have to believe it": Commercialized feminism in gender-specific programs for girls. *Signs: Journal of Women in Culture and Society, 34*(2), 397–422.

Kallio, K., & Thomas, M. (2019). Intergenerational encounters, intersubjective age relations. *Emotion, Space and Society, 32*, 100575.

Maruna, S. (2009). 'Virtue's door unsealed is never sealed again': Redeeming Redemption and the Seven-Year Itch. (pp. 52–60). In Natasha A. Frost, Joshua D. Freilich, and Todd R. Clear (Eds.), *Contemporary Issues in Criminal Justice Policy: Policy Proposals From the American Society of Criminology Conference*. Belmont, CA: Cengage/Wadsworth.

Maruna, S., Wilson, L., & Curran, K. (2006). Why God is so often found behind bars: Prison conversions and the crisis of self-narrative. *Research in Human Development, 3*(2&3), 161–184.

Morris, M. (2016). *Pushout: The criminalization of Black girls in schools*. New York: The New Press.

Pasko, L. (2008). The wayward girl revisited: Understanding the gendered nature of juvenile justice and delinquency. *Sociology Compass, 2*(3), 821–836.

Rios, V. (2011). *Punished: Policing the lives of black and latino boys*. New York: New York University Press.

Sankofa, J., Cox, A., Fader, J., Inderbitzen, M., Abrams, L., & Nurse, A. (2017). Juvenile corrections in the era of reform: A meta-synthesis of qualitative studies. *International Journal of Offender Therapy and Comparative Criminology, 62*(7), 1763–1786.

Simmons, L. (2015). *Crescent city girls: The lives of young black women in segregated New Orleans*. Chapel Hill: University of North Carolina Press.

Thomas, M. (2019). "Y'all trying to make a mockery out of me": The confined sexualities of girls in a US juvenile detention facility. *Emotion, Space and Society, 32*, 100533.

15

Horizontal Surveillance and Therapeutic Governance of Institutionalized Girls

Carla P. Davis

Introduction

At any given time, the more powerful side will create an ideology suitable to help maintain its position and to make this position acceptable to the weaker one. In this ideology the differentness of the weaker one will be interpreted as inferiority, and it will be proven that these differences are unchangeable, basic or God's will. It is the function of such an ideology to deny or conceal the existence of a struggle. (Horney 1967, p. 116)

Institutions serve as the locale at which the molding of citizens occurs. Previous research on how power is enacted through institutional practices provides insights about the significance of these sites in shaping citizen-subjects. Social institutions reproduce citizens and citizenship status through processes of attempting to impose dominant societal meanings/discourses (Cruikshank 1999; Garland 1997; Glenn 2002; Foucault 1965, 1977, 1978, 1983, 1988; Rose 1988). These meanings are represented in an institution's logic, as reflected in documents, programs, policies, and daily practices.

This chapter examines the processes by which a juvenile justice institution reproduced a model of gendered and racialized citizenship through therapeutic discourses and techniques regulating women's sexual morality and perceived

---

C. P. Davis (✉)
Beloit College, Beloit, WI, USA
e-mail: daviscp@beloit.edu

emotionality. Discourses regulating sexual morality and emotionality are part of broader discourses of meritocracy emphasizing notions of the ideal worker-citizen as rational; thus, free of "bodied" processes, such as emotions or sexuality. Under pressure to demonstrate acceptance of institutional ideals, the girls actively participated in using these dominant ideals to police each other (horizontal surveillance) in competing for status in the institution's meritocratic social order. These processes illustrate how surveillance by colleagues not in positions of power contributes to reinforcing the power of governing authority, as well as reinforcing hierarchies of gender, race/ethnicity, and class.

Institutional Power and the Reproduction of Worker-Citizens

Research on women and therapeutic governance largely draws upon Foucault and/or Acker's Theory of Gendered Organizations (1990). Foucault's theories outline how institutional power is enacted, and citizens reproduced, through processes reinforcing dominant ideologies. Acker draws upon Foucault's theories of power to elaborate on how processes that reproduce citizens through reinforcing dominant ideologies simultaneously reproduce gender hierarchies or "gendered" citizens. She particularly focuses on the workplace. United States (U.S.) citizenship status has always been intricately connected to labor status in that establishing oneself as an independent laborer has always been a critical element of demonstrating eligibility for U.S. citizenship. In theorizing about gendered processes in workplace institutions, Acker (1990) asserts that although current institutions have seemingly gender-neutral policies and programs, institutional practices reveal gendered institutional logic that reproduces gender hierarchies. According to Acker, although seemingly gender-neutral, the logic by which workplace organizations operate is inherently gendered in that it reflects understandings based on differences between sexes, with greater value being accorded to those qualities associated with being male.

Embedded in this hidden assumption of the ideal worker-citizen as male is the assumption of the ideal, gender neutral, worker and workplace as being rational and free of "bodied" processes, such as sexuality or emotions. In the abstract construction of job, "the abstract, bodiless worker, who occupies the abstract, gender-neutral job has no sexuality, no emotions" (Acker 1990, p. 151). Thus, in molding this ideal worker-citizen, one way that organizations reproduce gender hierarchies is through the control and suppression of sexuality or other bodied processes such as emotions since these are seen as disrupting the ideal functioning of the organization. This is achieved through organizational logic or arguments about women's sexual morality, or emotionality, or reproduction and managing institutional members through penalizing or rewarding their sexuality or emotionality management.

Race and the Construction of Worker-Citizen

Acker (1990), as well as previous literature on gendered institutions (including therapeutic governance), posits gender as the primary organizing factor in institutional citizenship processes. These studies view the historical construction of the ideal worker-citizen as rational and free of "bodied" processes such as emotions or sexuality as solely a gendered construction evolving from the historical context of industrialization and the separation of spheres (private vs. public). However, the reproduction of labor and citizenship in the U.S. arose out of a slave-based economy. A slave-based economy provided the foundation for reproducing racialized and gendered notions of worker-citizen ideals. The economic development of the U.S. relied on a racially based stratified labor system comprised of labor from Africa, Latin America, and Asia. "Racialization in the labor market has been buttressed by a system of citizenship designed to reinforce control of employers and to constrain mobility of workers" (Glenn 2002, p. 5).

In historical processes of the construction of labor and citizenship, a language of meritocracy (rationality, self-sufficiency, bootstrap, individual responsibility) evolved as a system of beliefs justifying the underlying racial/ethnic hierarchy of the distribution of resources, status, and power. "Notions of which groups had the intellectual capacities to do conceptual work were similar to notions of which groups had the rational, self-governing capacity required for citizenship" (Glenn 2002, p. 2). Thus, discourses of rationality/emotionality have underpinnings in this context. With the rise of industrialization, ideas of cultural inferiority began replacing biological explanations for Blacks' social location at the bottom of the economic, political, and social hierarchy. U.S. expansion westward and the need for cheap labor resulted in similar ideologies for Mexican immigrants. Thus, hierarchies of race and ethnicity are embedded in the language of meritocracy embodying worker-citizen ideals. These justifications or rationalizations are currently manifested in explanations attributing the marginalized social location of racial and ethnic groups to lacking appropriate cultural values.

These cultural explanations are part of the overarching ideology accompanying a competitive economic system.

Discourses of sexual morality have their roots in the production of dominant ideals of womanhood, produced during slavery. The hierarchical structures of slavery in which Black women were subjects of rape and sexual entanglements with white slave masters shaped a dual construction of dominant ideals of womanhood. Black women were not accorded the same values of femininity and chastity as white women. White women were accorded the ideal of "chaste virgin," and sexually pure while notions of Black women and promiscuity/whore became synonymous (Collins 2008; Hurtado 1996). Black women have occupied the position in the popular imagination of "promiscuous whore," and disrespected accordingly (Davis 1983; Hurtado 1996). This dichotomous construction remains as a dominant idea that permeates the web of institutional structures. This construction of sexual (im)morality evolved to include many women of color, as well as white women at the bottom of the socio-economic hierarchy. Thus, contrary to assertions of the literature on gendered organizations, regulating sexuality and emotionality are not merely gendered phenomena.

Theoretical Frameworks

This institution's reinforcement of worker-citizen ideals through group therapeutic sessions reflects Foucault's (1983) conception of how power is constituted through the processes of disciplining thoughts. Power operates through imposing a definition of the nature of the self and circumstances that is consistent with the definitions and interests of governing authority. Foucault hypothesizes that a critical element of processes of social control and discipline is placing individuals' everyday lives under surveillance through the imposition of language that reflects and emphasizes dominant ideologies. This imposition of dominant meanings works to enact institutional power by encouraging particular self-conceptions of ideal citizens that are in line with institutional expectations; thereby instituting a form of self-policing. This process negates the need for more coercive forms of power. These dominant ideals are embedded in institutional structures; thus, power is enacted through an institution's processes, including programs, evaluations, policies, and routine practices. Foucault's (1977) "web of discipline" proposes that discursive power operates through an institution's various actors. The findings in this chapter expand upon Foucault by providing an example of the ways and extent to which institutional subjects are *themselves* actively involved in perpetuating the process of molding subject-citizens.

These findings also expand upon Foucault's (1965) notion of modern therapeutic practices as moralizing therapy, where subjects are condemned as violators of social norms whose morals should be reformed. However, Foucault's conception of moralizing therapy does not emphasize the significance of moralizing therapy in a group-based forum. To the extent that the group-based forum is of significance in these processes, Durkheim's emphasis on the significance of social occasions or public forums serving as a means of re-enforcing moral codes/community beliefs also provides a useful lens in analyzing interaction patterns that emerged in the group therapy sessions of this institution. Durkheim believed that public forums of punishment served the necessary function of preserving a society's social order by clarifying a society's norms and boundaries of acceptable behavior. This process affirms collective identity and beliefs, and inhibits future deviations from these norms and boundaries of acceptable behavior. This institution uses group therapy sessions as a public forum in which to clarify and reinforce dominant meanings reflecting the greater societal moral/social order.

In a meritocratic system or society, navigating place in the social order entails employing discourses or symbols of meritocracy to construct an ethical self. This encompasses a form of self-policing. In a meritocratic structure in which progress and worth are always relative, self-policing is a form of competition for place in the social order. Self-policing inevitably incorporates policing others (O'Grady 2005) in the constant incentive to rank one's own behavior in the hierarchical structure. Thus, self-policing is mirrored in individuals' relationships with others through practices of using dominant ideas to police others. The group therapy sessions served as social occasions or public forums that provided the girls opportunities for demonstrating acceptance of institutional ideals in competing for place in the meritocratic social order. The institution used various techniques for enlisting the girls to use these discourses to monitor each other. I refer to these practices of policing others with dominant ideas as horizontal surveillance.

Research Setting

This study is based on ethnographic research I conducted at a co-ed county juvenile justice institution in a large North American city. Although this institution was a lock-down facility comprised of sixty residents, it attempted to encompass group home living by dividing the residents into bungalows comprised of groups of ten. This is one of a handful of institutions to which youth may be sentenced after spending time in juvenile hall and being charged with a minor offense. However, this was the only lock-down institution that included therapeutic practices as part of the rehabilitation program. Although the institution is co-ed, the girls and boys are kept separate from each other with the exception of time spent in the classroom and time spent during recreational activities. The only gender-integrated sphere within this institution was the school.

Sample Population/Methodology

The data on which this chapter is based consist of field notes from two years of participant-observations of fifty girls, periodic taped interviews with thirty of those girls during incarceration, and fieldnotes and interviews with seven of the thirty after they were released from incarceration. The ethnic composition of the girls was predominately African-American and Latina (Salvadoran and Mexican), and they were from predominately underprivileged to lower-/working-class neighborhoods. Of the thirty girls periodically interviewed, fifteen were Latina, fifteen were African-American, and one was Anglo. At the time I began the research, all of the girls were incarcerated in a co-ed public detention facility for minor offenders between the ages of thirteen and eighteen.

Of the thirty girls interviewed, the following charges were represented (the total number of charges is greater than thirty because each girl had multiple charges): twenty-one girls had violation of probation charges (including violating curfew, dirty drug tests, and missing court dates); seventeen girls had assault charges (including assault and battery, and assault with a deadly weapon); seven girls had prostitution charges; seven girls had grand theft auto charges; five girls had shoplifting charges; four girls had possession of drug charges (two of these had possession and sales charges); four girls had terrorist threat charges; two had vandalism/destruction of property charges; and two girls had charges of receiving stolen property. Many of these girls had been in and out of the system, and spent time in other institutions. Cycling in and out of institutions is a common phenomenon in the juvenile justice system.

Data Analysis

I used grounded theory methods to conduct an inductive analysis of the interview and fieldnote data to discover the patterns that provide the basis for the book's primary argument. Grounded theory consists of a set of inductive strategies for discovering patterns and meanings in large masses of disorganized information. Grounded theory methods involve analyzing processes in data by looking at words and actions in relation to meaning; thus, avoiding static analyses that merely provide a literal accounting of words and actions. Rather than viewing data through preconceived categories, new ways of representing and understanding reality are revealed through the analytical process of integrating and assimilating data inductively.

Moralizing Discourses: Regulating Women's Sexual Morality

Discourses of individual responsibility provided the groundwork for discourses regulating women's sexual morality and emotionality. One way that the institution shaped a gendered, racialized model of citizenship regulating sexual morality was through discourses of prostitution. This was most evidently reflected in discourses indicating that prostitution was considered the most heinous crime and was the criteria that sparked the strongest responses in evaluating and regulating the girls:

STAFF: "You really have to watch them though. I mean some of these kids have done some really serious stuff." I said "really?" (thinking that he was about to speak of rape, murder, etc.) He nodded and said "yeah, I mean we have some prostitutes in here."

Discourses of prostitution reflect the institution's techniques of reinforcing women's sexual morality through the ranking of crimes. That prostitution is considered the most heinous offense speaks to not only the moral basis, but also the gendered and racialized nature of the institutional logic governing regulation. However, ideologies in and of themselves do not convey power. Rather, power lies in the enactment of these ideologies. Power lies in instilling in subject-citizens a definition of self that is consistent with the state's definition (Foucault 1977, 1978, 1983). The perception that prostitution was the most heinous of crimes was mirrored in the girls' self-conceptions:

[CARLA]: Do you feel—that in some kind of way, that what you're in here for is worse than what other people are in here for?

RENEE: Yes. I do—I really do ... after like my eyes have been opened, you now, like—I knew it was wrong ... I know it wasn't like ladylike to do .... I'd rather—assaulted somebody, than be on the streets and have people run up in me ... people are so used to like "oh yeah, I'm here for assault and battery or attempted murder," whatever, or GTA, you know, and that's nothing. Because you know, it's just a—a crime. Like a—I don't know how to explain it, but it's not like the same ... it's not the same as like prostitution.

The girls adapted perceptions of self that mirrored the institution's perception through the practice of adapting the institution's ranking of crimes. Renee is, in effect, saying that being a woman who violates sexual codes is a greater offense than any crime (e.g., assault and battery, attempted murder, Grand theft auto, etc.) and violates acceptable moral standards of what it means to be a woman ("ladylike"). Self-policing resulted in policing each other (horizontal surveillance), as well:

TERESA: I don't think it's gonna help me, because—the majority of these kids—they're here for prostitution or—drugs—and I have nothing to do with that—I'm just here because _ I committed a crime out there of assault and battery ... everybody else is in here for prostitution or drugs. And it's like—dang—I'm in here with just drug addicts and some prostitutes ... I seem like every day, we get a prostitute ... I mean I'm surrounded by prostitutes.

In the reproduction of the social order, institutional power lies in the extent that governing authority can get the girls to form a perception of self (and others) that is consistent with governing authority's perception. Alice reinforces the moral order through the defining/ranking of self in comparison to others ("I mean I'm surrounded by prostitutes.") In this moral order, her offense of assault and battery accord her higher status than drug addicts and prostitutes, and in her comment she draws this contrast. Objects of disciplinary control internalize norms and become monitors of their own behavior (Foucault 1977).

However, this is not solely a gendered phenomenon. It is not just the low status of women that makes prostitution so stigmatized in the social/moral order. It is also about race. In the historical construction of womanhood, there was a dual construction based on race—"white goddess/black she-devil, chaste virgin/nigger whore, the blond blue-eyed doll/the exotic 'mulatto' object of sexual craving" (Rich 1979, p. 291). In this construction, Black women and promiscuity/whore became synonymous (Hurtado 1996). Because poor Black women occupy the lowest status along hierarchies of race, class, gender, they are the most stigmatized and thus any category associated with this social location is perceived as posing the greatest threat to the moral order.

Moralizing Discourses: Regulating Girls' Emotionality

As Acker (1990) notes, the disembodied, ideal citizen is not only free of sexuality, but also free of emotions as well. The institution's techniques also used discourses of emotionality to reproduce a gendered and racialized citizen. One of the ways that ideas of women's emotionality were manifested in these discourses was the constant use of the word "drama" to refer to the girls. The perception of the innate nature of girls as being characterized by excessive displays of emotion was reflected in recurring staff characterizations of the girls as "drama queens":

STAFF MEMBER: She was a drama queen. She was a major drama queen … she would go to her room and she would have these little episodes … she needed attention—all the time.

These elements have a broader societal context in that the label "drama" is often used in the broader society as a derogatory characterization reflecting images of excessive or inappropriate displays of emotion. The essence of drama (theatric, cinematic, etc.) has two defining dimensions: fictional or unreal, perhaps exaggerated depictions of reality; containing some quotient of emotional content beyond what is acceptable in the daily navigation of "real" life.

These dominant understandings are reflected in staff perceptions of the girls as displaying emotions beyond what is acceptable. The implication is that the girls' concerns were something they created—not real concerns of substance—but fiction—somehow trivial. For example, the common concern of expressing emotions over romantic relationships was often held up by the staff as evidence of the girls' being governed by their emotions:

> The new staff person added that the girls would always be crying over some boy, while she had never seen a boy cry over a girl. She frowned and repeated, "they just *cry* over some *boy*." Ms. F. nodded, enthusiastically agreeing. She said that when she came there, she had thought that she would be working with boys.

The staff person expresses her disdain for the display of emotions by emphasizing the word *cry*, while simultaneously indicating girls' irrationality by suggesting girls' inability to distinguish matters significant enough to warrant such emotion ("over some *boy*"). That girls are seen as ruled by emotions and their relative position in the hierarchy is reflected by the staff person comparing; thus, suggesting that boys are in control of their emotions (she had never seen a boy cry over a girl). The policing of emotions by staff in this institution mirrors the processes of regulation of emotions in the workplace in the construction of accepted ways of being of the model worker-citizen. The staff person's last sentiment in the above narrative reflects a recurring theme in staff narratives of a preference for working with boys. A preference for working with boys is one way that staff reinforced notions that girls are emotional:

STAFF: In the Halls, I loved workin' with the boys—that's where I was for sixteen months and then they stuck me with the girls—when I found out—I cried. That night that they gave me my letter and told me that you're gonna be workin' with the girls startin' such and such date—my whole attitude for the rest of the night was really sour and then—when I got ready to leave, I just cried … because I *knew* how it was gonna be … the girls *always* have problems—you always see staff runnin' over to the girls' cottages—*all the time*—or you hear about it—"them girls is off the hook—we had to *spray* somebody- … they'll be callin' the staff … " we need your third to go over to such and such cottage … a girl is outa control, " and I'm like—"Jesus no …."

This narrative reflects recurring themes of underlying elements comprising discourses of girls' emotionality. One gets the sense that working with girls is an environment of continuous heightened state of alert (the girls *always* have problems … *all the time* … always see staff runnin' to girls' cottages). The implication is that the girls lack control ("them girls is off the hook …" … "a girl is outa control …") and thus need to be controlled. This perception of lack of control is further exemplified in her account of the need for additional forces brought in from the outside ("we need your third to go over to such and such cottage …") to subdue the girls in an attempt to regain control ("we had to *spray* somebody"). Indeed, the impression is that conditions are so bad working with the girls that circumstances call for appeals to a higher authority ("*Jesus* no …") than mere human backup forces to subdue the girls. These accounts of working with girls evoked images tantamount to battle scenes, in which physical battles are the foundation. The expression that the girls were somehow "out of control" suggested perhaps physical violence was at play here. However, upon further inquiry, the narratives revealed that verbal expressiveness was at the heart of these exchanges.

A recurring theme was that girls = drama, and this drama was somehow related to verbal expressiveness. In attempting to tease out and to get a better sense of the connections between discourses of girls' emotionality and verbal expressiveness, I asked the school principal whether he noticed any difference between girls and boys in the frequency in which they were cited for misbehaving in class. He thought about it and responded:

School principal: "[W]ell, the girls seem to be more temperamental …." He said this slowly—thinking—as if he either wanted to qualify this or make sure that it was placed in the appropriate context, then added—"the girls seem to be more temperamental, but I don't know if that's because they're just more verbal in expressing themselves,"

In these discourses of girls' emotionality, expressing oneself verbally gets categorized with notions of excessive display of emotions. The underlying theme evolves into a sentiment of—"are they emotional or is it just that they talk a lot—emotional—talks a lot—it all runs together … what's the difference?" These sentiments echo those of authority in the rest of the institution with respect to attributing an underlying propelling force of girls' institutional navigation to their emotionality ("temperamental"). In essence, the dominant perception was that the innate inability of girls to control their emotions manifested itself through excessive (uncontrollable) verbal expressiveness. Regulating emotions through regulating verbal expressiveness is embedded in intersecting hierarchies of gender, as well as race/ethnicity. In her study of Black Women navigating academia, Fordham (1993) explored the significance of talk in navigating status in institutions. Fordham found that in navigating the academy, successful Black girls achieved academic status through intentional silence. Fordham explains that this is because in order to be successful, they must pass at being the ideal student-citizen, that is, white male, embodied by the utmost sign of rationality—lack of emotions. Expounding upon Fordham, verbal expression inevitably carries the potential for revealing emotions. This is particularly the case for those at the bottom of hierarchies of race/ethnicity. For them, navigating daily life requires suppressing accumulated layers of pain emanating from their degraded status. Verbal expression increases the possibility that this pain will surface in the form of emotions. These processes result in successful members of a stigmatized racial/ethnic group being simultaneously silent and *silenced* by the institutions they navigate. Of course, it is not the case that white men are necessarily void of emotions; however, it is the case that their display of emotions is far less likely to call into question their capacity for reasoning and rational judgment.

While verbal expressiveness was a target for regulation in all of the girls, the African-American girls were particularly targeted on this front. This was manifested in the staff and girls' using "loudness" as a criterion for exclusion and policing African-American girls:

> Ms. B. asked who wanted to work and Diedre (African-American) said that she did. Diedre said she had a question for Teresa (African-American) …. Diedre said that she was trying to be Teresa's friend, and she asked Teresa why she didn't talk to her anymore. Teresa responded by telling Diedre that she (Teresa) didn't know what Diedre was about yet and that she wanted to wait and see what Diedre was about first. Teresa said "you know you came in here talking about you changed your ways, and I'm just waitin' to see whether you really changed your ways or not … and from what I've seen, you still loud … So I'm just waitin' to see whether or not you changed your ways—what you all about first …." … Diedre said that she was tired of people saying she was loud. Diedre said that she was sorry if she didn't come from a nice neighborhood like the other girls. She said she was from the ghetto and people were loud in the ghetto …. "You not staff—if the staff think I shouldn't be doing something, then let them tell me—if the staff think I'm too loud, then let the staff tell me—you not staff."

Just as drama is a symbol of excessive display of emotions, loud also symbolizes excessive display of emotion through modulated voice tones. Thus, attempts to regulate voice may be seen, in part, as attempts to regulate emotion. Teresa is evaluating Diedre regarding whether she (Diedre) has demonstrated that she has accepted and is working to modify this perceived deficiency. "Loud" embodies dominant ideas (stereotypes) about those at the bottom of the hierarchical structure: loud is equated with ghetto; "ghetto" is a term used to describe those associated (or actions associated with) being at intersections of the bottom of race and class hierarchies. Diedre's reminding the girls that they are not staff reflects the extent to which power operates horizontally in that the girls assume the surveillance of governing authority. Staff does not have to assume sole responsibility for discipline because the girls reinforce dominant ideals in policing each other.

Placed in a broader societal context of how these dominant discourses function as criteria for policing, the following exchange illustrates how "loud" is intertwined with dominant meanings of race, both within this institution and in the broader society:

> [O]ne of the staff entered with an African-American girl who was to be a new girl in the cottage … Roxanna (Latina) who was sitting to my left said "Oh man—*another* Black girl. We have too many Black girls." … Jackie (African-

American) and Brenda (African-American) began talking about how every time there were Blacks around, Mexicans would always think that they (the Blacks) were going to be loud … Jackie said "In the Halls, the staff be like "No talking" and they be looking at all the Black girls and the Mexican girls be steady talking and they don't say anything to them. But they always be looking at the Black girls because they think the Black girls gon' be loud." Sonya said "They always think—whenever they see Black people—they always think they gonna be loud." Brenda (African-American) said "I *know* I'm loud—and I ain't gon' change." … Brenda (African-American) and Jackie (African-American) continued talking about how whenever Blacks came around people would either be afraid of them or think they were loud.

The girls share their experiences in the broader society to legitimize their use of dominant racialized ideals to draw exclusionary boundaries, policing each other. The conversation was a complex combination of jest and complaint about being feared … being too prominent … always being watched. These processes of policing each other mirror historical, as well as current, processes in the broader society that rationalize the location of racial minorities at the bottom of the socio-economic hierarchy by attributing this status to cultural deficiencies. "Loud" is advanced as an inherent (seemingly natural), culturally deficient trait of being Black (compounded by simultaneous structures of class and gender). The intersection of race and gender is reflected in that similarly to how the institution and girls sanction each other for violating ideals of womanhood with respect to chastity, the same sanctioning occurs with respect to dominant ideals dictating that respectable women should be seen and not heard. Thus through utilizing these dominant discourses of emotionality, the girls simultaneously reinforce hierarchies of race, class, and gender even though these are stereotypes associated with their own social positions in the broader society. In her study of Puerto Rican gang girls, Campbell (1987) revealed how girls used denigrated aspects of their identities to insult each other. However, Campbell focused on these insults as a mechanism for identity construction, rather than as a mechanism for negotiating power. The criteria used for policing are about much more than constructions of identity. Through these interactions, the girls are negotiating power and status in an institution that both reflects and reinforces competition for resources/status in the broader society. The girls' dominant discourses of loudness mirror the previous narratives of staff's dominant discourses associating the girls with excessive verbal expressiveness and being out of control.

Regulation of emotions is reflected and reinforced through the institution's formal practices of evaluating the girls' attitudes, as reflected in a daily form filled out by staff, with each girl's name and a place where the staff person for each shift ranks the behavior of that girls for the shift: options are "fair," "good," and so on. For example, one day, on a form that was completed by the morning shift person who left at 2:00 pm, it said something to the effect of "so & so ran a fair program this morning" and then gave a three line description of the minor's behavior. I noticed that next to one name Ms. T. had written "minor displayed negative attitude when leaving the shower." It is noteworthy that her sanctions are not for any overt wrongdoing or misbehavior but instead based on her attitude in navigating her morning routine. In the daily evaluation of the girls' merits, failure to demonstrate the appropriate attitude results in failure to accumulate merit points. These interactions also reflect previous literature's assertions regarding how displays of deference may be more significant than actual wrongdoings in determining sanctions by social control agents (Becker 1963).

Just as dominant perceptions of girls being "naturally" inclined to instigate conflict due to their innate emotionality was manifested in the staff's narratives making sense of the conflict, these ideologies were similarly manifested in the girls' narratives:

ANDREA: It's gonna be drama … it's just like—we're all girls—so, we're gonna take our anger out on each other.

Similar to expressions in previous staff narratives, in Andrea's understanding, the conflict evolves from girls' inherent emotionality and the consequent expression in sanctioning other girls. In using these dominant meanings to sanction and draw hierarchies, girls reinforce these ideas, thus reinforcing the system of existing power imbalances.

Just as staff perceptions of girls' emotionality leads to their privileging working with boys over girls, so do girls' perceptions of girls' unreliable emotions and untrustworthiness lead to the girls privileging the company of boys, thus further distancing themselves from the degraded status of being a girl:

Monica and another girl said that they would rather hang around kicking it with the guys, rather than girls. Monica said if she saw a lot full of girls & then a lot full of boys, she would pick the guys any day. A lot of the other girls, particularly Miranda agreed. Monica continued by saying that when you talk to girls about things, they just go on forever. A few of the girls laughed and nodded their heads. Monica continued by saying that when you say something to a girl, she takes it to heart and holds a grudge—she emphasized *forever*. Monica said she didn't hold a grudge. If you told her something she would be over it and that was that. She said "but girls just take things to heart and hold a grudge forever."

The message is that girls are untrustworthy as comrades because of their emotionality (holding a grudge) and she simultaneously defines and distances herself from the degraded status of the category (i.e., by contrast, she does not hold a grudge). The implication is that boys are able to control their emotions, thus do not hold grudges and she is more like a boy in that she is able to control her emotions. Once again, the emotional realm of not being able to control their emotions incorporates verbal expressiveness perceived as uncontrollable talking ("when you talk to girls about things, they just go on forever").

This disparaging of emotions can be illustrated with the way that Miranda views love. Miranda views love as a loss of control and portrays love as being ruled by emotions. This is exemplified in the following exchange in which she elaborates upon the perceptions of women's weakness evolving from emotionality by suggesting how women's inferiority as a result of emotionality is manifested in their relations with men:

MIRANDA: They are *so* stupid … they hoish—they can't control their little emotions … fall in love with every nigga they go with … then there's the females who like—who let niggas—I aint even gone lie—that's what really annoys me about Sabrina—how she let her nigga whoop her ass after she tried to commit suicide over that nigga … girls wanna be all cuddled up and everything.

The use of dominant ideologies to demean girls is a way of separating themselves from other girls and a symbolic way to "move up" hierarchically to the position of boys. In talking about other's girls' perceived weaknesses, the girls are punishing themselves while simultaneously moving away from the stigmatized status. If they can criticize it, it is assumed they are not it. As reflected in the previous staff narrative in which girls were demeaned for crying over boys, Miranda similarly demeans girls for displaying emotions over a man. Miranda expresses an annoyance with the perceived weakness of what it means to be a woman: not to be in control of one's emotions—to be under the control of men, as exemplified by "falling in love." This perceived lack of control is further emphasized by suggesting an indiscriminate pattern of girls' object of affection: it is not just that they fall in love, they fall in love with *every* man, suggesting that they do not possess the rational faculties to choose. Further, Miranda's comments suggest that she even views the abuse as the byproduct of Sabrina's lack of control of emotions/falling in love.

Techniques Reinforcing a Gendered, Racialized Model Through Horizontal Surveillance

While the institution's organizational logic provided a foundation for power, institutional power is enacted or negotiated daily through micro level interactions and practices. One technique that the institution used to enlist horizontal surveillance in the reproduction of institutional ideals was using each girl's initial group therapy session as a mechanism for teaching the significance of judging and ranking each other through the ranking of offenses. This technique entailed the practice of requiring, upon arrival, each girl's initial group therapy session as involving revealing her name, age, and formal charge, as well as learning and memorizing all of the other girls' names, ages and formal criminal (misdemeanor) charges. The institution's requirement of the girls to publicly establish and recognize their own, as well as each other's, diminished status provided the groundwork for enlisting the girls to engage in the process of "working" to remanufacture immoral selves into citizens through judging themselves and each other. Through these introductions in group sessions, the institution enlists the girls in a form of "setting-up"/ identifying the problem (flawed, immoral selves), before beginning the "work" of individual transformation making one worthy of citizenship:

> In order to get their Level Ones, two of the new girls had to go around the group and state all of their cottage sisters names, ages, and charges. The first one to go was Cathy. When she got to Renee, instead of saying "Prostitution," she said "two forty seven." Renee turned to her and said, "*Thank you*." During the second girl's turn, when she got to Renee, she said "two fifty seven" and kept going. Ms. Y. said, "Wait a minute—two *forty* seven." The girl said "two forty seven." Ms. Y. said, "Do you know what that is?" The girl nodded and said "prostitution" and kept going.

Institutions shape citizens' understanding of themselves by imposing particular definitions of the nature of self (Foucault 1988). The institution must first establish the girls as having a morally devalued status, one unworthy of "citizenship." As Garfinkel (1956) noted in summarizing characteristics of successful denunciations or ceremonies of degradation, both perpetrator(s) and circumstances defining perpetrator(s) must be defined/redefined as a uniformity or "type" that is not the norm or "out of the ordinary" (422). Learning to identify themselves and their colleagues by their official conviction is one of the first lessons in thinking of their circumstances in individualistic terms. A girl's charges provided the first piece of information forming the basis for assessing worthiness of self and thus worthiness for citizenship. This technique reinforces the notion that their charges are as important as their names and ages in defining them, thus reinforcing the message that the problem primarily lies within them; that it is merely an individual attribute. Through these initial sessions, the girls learned that using background information for the purposes of judging was a normal part of the processes of working to obtain the institution's citizenship. The fact that stating their own, as well as other community members' misdemeanor charges is a requirement for attaining level one of the institution's merit system conveys the message to the girls that hierarchical ranking is a fundamental element of social mobility.

While each girl's initial therapy session provided the mechanism for enlisting horizontal surveillance through teaching to judge self and others according to offenses, subsequent sessions provided mechanisms for reinforcement. This was generally accomplished through the staff using one or more girls' resistance to institutional definitions as an opportunity to incite hierarchical competition (girls' judging). Inmate resistance reflects the inmate's perception of irrationality of particular rhetoric (Fox 1999). In essence, these exchanges became a competition of defining oneself—defining one's worthiness for citizenship—in the social order in accordance with ideals of women's sexual morality and using each other as targets of comparison in this process of defining. One technique of using resistance to enlist competition was for the therapists to frame a girl's resistance in a manner that suggested she was placing herself above the other girls in the social order. This is exemplified in the following exchange in which Cathy and Renee's use of ideals of sexual morality to distinguish their own, as well as each other's place in the social order, was sparked by the therapist's framing Cathy's resistance in a manner that suggests that Cathy sees herself as not belonging there—out of place with the other girls:

> Cathy said she was having a hard time adjusting to being here. Ms. Y. (therapist/p.o.) said, "Could you be more specific?" … Cathy said … "this is just really affecting me." Ms. Y. said, "*how* is it affecting you?" Cathy was crying. She said I feel like I'm in a mental hospital—I just can't take it." Ms. Y. said "Cathy, could you say how it's affecting you without insulting your cottage sisters?" Cathy continued … "And I talk to my mom about it. And she tells me to just stay to myself and not to have anything to do what the other girls." … Ms. Y. told Cathy that while she was there, she had to learn to get along with her peers and in order to do that she had to not put everything off on her peers, but had to recognize the part she played in it. Ms. Y. said, "Because you're presenting it as if you really don't belong here and everyone else is a criminal or a mental case.

And that's insulting to your cottage sisters. You did something to get here. And you need to look at your role and what you can do to ease your stay here." ... Renee loudly told Cathy ... "you're in denial Cathy and you better just start smellin' the funk—cause you're no better than the rest of us—some of the things you told me you did and the people you were hanging around with—about doing drugs and having sex-" Cathy said "I never said I had sex." Renee said "Oh right—you're a virgin." Cathy said that she hadn't said she was a virgin, but it's not like she was a prostitute.

The power of these group-based forums in the molding of sexually moral girls is illustrated by the fact that whereas in Cathy's initial group therapy session (illustrated above), she avoided stating Renee's charge as a show of courtesy or respect, as if to diffuse the stigma of prostitution, by this later date, Cathy has learned and accepted the practice and is willing to wield Renee's charge of prostitution to rank herself and Cathy in the social order. As a response to the therapist's suggestion that Cathy is placing herself above the other girls in the social order, Renee uses ideals of women's sexual morality in an attempt to establish Cathy's immorality, thereby suggesting that she does belong there. Renee does so by revealing and using Cathy's background activities as evidence. The significance of sexual morality is reflected in that Renee includes "having sex" as one of the pieces of evidence. The implication is that having sex ranks on par with doing drugs or engaging in illegal activities. The significance of women's sexual morality is further reflected in that of all the activities Renee listed, it was the charge of "having sex" to which Cathy responded. Renee further attempts to define Cathy's sexual (im)morality ("oh right—you're a virgin."). Cathy counters Renee's definition of her (and thus her place in the social order), by using Renee's formal charge of prostitution as evidence defining Renee's ranking at the bottom of the social order. The implication is that while having sex may be immoral, the unofficial activity of "having sex" at least accords her higher status than having an official charge of prostitution. It is noteworthy that Cathy does not address the charge of doing drugs; rather, it is the charge of having sex that she addresses. Both Renee's and Cathy's comments reflect how, for girls, having sex is on par with, and perhaps worse than official categories of illegal activity (i.e., "doing drugs and having sex").

The primary practice of group sessions consisted of therapists in some way initiating the judging, then retreating to let it unfold. However, sometimes the therapists utilized intervention techniques even after the policing by the girls had begun. One such technique was to join the girls in the chorus of judging. Therapeutic techniques of joining the girls in the judging once the competition was underway were likely to happen when there was overt

15 Horizontal Surveillance and Therapeutic Governance... 323

challenging of the institution's ideals, such as discrediting the institution's view of prostitution, particularly when it was perceived that the girls' sanctioning was ineffective. This was particularly salient when a girl suggested that prostitution was a viable avenue for achieving meritocratic ideals equated with citizenship:

> Mr. F. (therapist/p.o) came in for group. Sabrina said she wanted to work. She said she was nervous about going before her judge and worried about to whom her judge would release her ... Mara said "you're eighteen—why don't you just live on your own—get a job ... Sabrina said "but I'm scared, what if my money gets low?" Mara said, "It's called a Job." Sabrina said "but—what is minimum wage—three something—? ... Sabrina began talking about how she didn't want to get a 9–5 job and work her way up. She began talking about how she had been on the top. She said "I was on the *top*—..." Jackie said, "that was just an illusion." Dr. A. (clinical director) had already begun to lean forward on his knees to say (loudly whisper) "Sweetheart, no you weren't—and there's a flip side to that feeling that you were on top—because you know that on the other side of that little voice in your head telling you that you were on the top was a little voice saying "you ain't nothing but a ho"—(Sabrina had a surprised/startled look on her face & she said "Dr. A. stop") She sat back in her chair. Dr. A. continued by saying that she knew that was true, that that was the flip side of the voice telling her that she was on top. When he finished, Sabrina said "Dr. A. how did you know that?" Ms. S. said, "because he's Dr. A." Everyone, including Dr. A., laughed ... Ms. S. said, "you needed to hear that." Then added "and coming from a man—you especially needed to hear it from a man—you needed to get a man's point of view." Jackie added *especially* coming from a *man*." The session ended shortly thereafter.

Sabrina's resistance to institutional ideals is reflected in her assertion that she does not want to work her way up in a minimum wage job when she had already achieved a high degree of social mobility working as a prostitute. In questioning whether she could support herself on a minimum wage job, she challenges the meritocratic notion that minimum wage jobs can be a viable avenue for social mobility while simultaneously suggesting that prostitution can be a viable avenue for social mobility. This prompts the direct intervention of the therapist. Both the message ("you ain't nothing but a ho") and the manner of delivery (dramatic effect of leaning toward her) reflect how value commitments are often reinforced through manipulation of emotion, consistent with Garfinkel's (1956) conceptions of public ceremonies of degradation. In essence, these group therapy sessions operate as shaming sessions. Dr. A.'s whispered voice represents the voice of authority, which is, in essence, the voice of society reflecting back to Sabrina how society views her and the judgment of her shame. In her study of therapeutic group sessions of teen mothers (Fujimoto 2001) also notes the significance of emotions in the therapeutic process and calls for further research on "how institutional representatives employ emotions in the construction of 'compliant' and 'resistant' types of clients" (20).

Because the sessions were preoccupied with reinforcing morality, Sabrina's practical concerns of how to raise a child on minimum wage were not addressed. Sabrina's fears (said she was nervous ... "I'm scared") about navigating structural complexities ("what if my money gets low?") are ignored in favor of institutional rhetoric of self-sufficiency and bootstrapping. In effect, Dr. A.'s focus on Sabrina's individual responsibility de-contextualizes her circumstances. His message conveys that material circumstances are not the important issue; rather, what is important is that she upholds standards of morality. The implication in Dr. A.'s message is that somehow adapting the appropriate values will address the material concerns.

Dr. A. is reinforcing values reflecting prostitution as a grave (moral) crime, serving as a lesson reminding the girls of appropriate codes of sexuality and appropriate standards of womanhood. However, because race and sexuality have a particular social-historical context in which they are intricately intertwined, Dr. A.'s whispered sentiments carry a more nuanced meaning. As discussed previously, hierarchical structures of slavery in which Black women were the victims of rape and objects of non-emotional sexual entanglements of white slave-masters, shaped dichotomous conceptions of "woman." The material location of working alongside men, as well as the sexual entanglement with white slave masters, was critical in shaping a dual construction of dominant ideals of womanhood such that Black women were not accorded the same values of femininity and chastity as white women. As previously mentioned, white women have historically been accorded the ideal of "chaste virgin," while Black women have occupied the position in the popular imagination of "promiscuous whore" (Davis 1983; Hooks 1981; Hurtado 1996). This historical context illuminates the significance of race and gender hierarchies in shaping the power embedded in the delivery of the message "you ain't nothing but a ho" from a white man in a position of authority to a powerless African-American girl.

Just as with discourses of women's sexual morality, therapists used techniques to regulate and reinforce ideals of women's emotionality. Governing authority creates and reinforces narratives of girls' emotionality, and girls, in turn, reinforce these dominant ideologies through utilizing them to sanction each other. Similar to the way that therapists reinforced sexual morals, therapists reinforced discourses of women's emotionality. They did so by encouraging horizontal surveillance through group therapeutic techniques that introduced the girls' judgments of each other as a basis for work in the session. This included encouraging the girls' snide or sarcastic comments made on the side to be introduced as part of the assessment or evaluation process of group therapy sessions. The following exchange illustrates how governing authority through the processes of group therapy reinforces girls' policing each other's emotionality:

> Renee wanted to know from Dr. A. why he had called for Roxanna to say her sidebar (mumbled/whispered something under her breath to the person sitting next to her) comment "drama" to the whole group … Dr. A. said … he thought this particular comment was useful … Renee wanted to know how that was useful & said that if someone made a comment that was negative, it should not be asked to be repeated to the group … Roxanna said that she did not mean it to be negative. Renee … told her that it was mean … Dr. A. said that maybe she [Renee] should pay attention to the comment "Drama" because it applies to her and that she does tend to be on the dramatic side.

Renee is referring to events of the previous evening's (mandated) family therapy session in which one of the girls whispered the comment "drama" under her breath, not to the group, but as an aside, to which Dr. A. responded by asking her to repeat her "sidebar" comment aloud to the group. "Drama" serves to discredit Renee's perceived excessive display of emotions; thereby, instructing Renee, as well as the group, on the acceptable expression (or lack thereof) of emotions. Renee challenges the therapist by asking the reason for his encouragement of Roxanna's comments of "Drama." Dr. A. responds by simply validating the assessment of "drama" as "useful." Renee persists by wanting to know the logic behind his action and counters his perception of "useful" with her own definition, "negative." Dr. A. counter's her resistance and reinforces his definition by simply stating that the term "drama" "applies." These exchanges illustrate how these sessions are primarily negotiations of competing definitions of the girls' circumstances. Through these expressions, both the woman staff person and the girls validate Dr. A.'s definition of the circumstances as a male expert, thus illustrating how those at the bottom of the hierarchical structure internalize and actively participate in reinforcing dominant ideologies.

In these negotiations, the power imbalance prohibits recognition of interpretations other than those embedded in institutional ideals. The power of the institution in these negotiations is reflected by the fact that although

Renee initially challenges Dr. A., in the end, his definition of the circumstances (Renee's emotionality) prevails:

> Renee became even more upset and told Dr. A. that she hated him & said "You always try to make me look stupid." ... Renee rattled off a list of other unsettling events and ended by saying "and I'm on my period now in case you didn't know."

Power is demonstrated as an entity's ability to influence interpretations of self and circumstances. In the end, the institution's definition of Renee prevails, and she publicly concedes and defines herself accordingly. In claiming, "I'm on my period," Renee publicly discredits her interpretations/judgment/rationality/self, attributing her logical inquiry to biological circumstances beyond her control; thus, substantiating the institution's claims. Resistance is subsumed into dominant discourses such that what is taken as self-knowledge is in actuality knowledge of the self and circumstances that are the institution's definition of the self (Fox 1999). "Discourses of Truth" (Foucault 1977) prevail: if governing authority says she is emotional, then it must be true. In her frustration, her emotions surface, thus validating the institution's perception. Thus, the allegations of emotionality become a self-fulfilling prophecy.

Discussion and Conclusion

This institution created a gendered and racialized citizen through discourses regulating sexual morality and emotionality during group therapy sessions. These models of citizenship were reflected in discourses of prostitution, as well as discourses characterizing the girls and their needs as "drama." Discourses of sexuality and emotionality were part of the broader worker-citizen discourses of meritocracy and individual responsibility. Group therapy sessions served as vehicles for therapists to utilize techniques enlisting the girls to use these ideals to rank and judge self and others, as well as a vehicle for the girls to engage in this process. Although not in positions of authority, the girls actively participated in bringing resisters into line with institutional ideals. Similar to Acker's conception of a job evaluation, in the rehabilitation processes of this institution, group therapy sessions may be seen as an evaluation mechanism tantamount to job evaluations. In essence, each group therapy session served as a forum for evaluating the girls' progress in accepting the institution's dominant discourses and thus for assessing their ranking in the social order. The findings of this chapter reflect Foucault's (1965, 1977, 1983, 1988) conception of how institutional power is enacted through the imposition of dominant ideologies.

These forums provided the therapists opportunities to clarify ideals, as well as opportunities to enlist the girls to reinforce these ideals with each other, often by using one or more girls as examples of deviation or resistance to these ideals. Girls who in some way seemed to resist the dominant ideals were used by therapists to clarify and reinforce the ideals through enlisting the girls to use this example as a reference to rank self and others. To this extent, these group sessions functioned as public forums of punishment, similar to what Durkheim viewed as necessary for preserving a society's social order by clarifying a society's norms and boundaries of acceptable behavior, affirming collective identity and beliefs, and inhibiting future deviations from these norms and boundaries of acceptable behavior.

Previous studies have primarily focused on reinforcement efforts by governing authority. Yet although not in positions of authority, the girls in this study actively participated in bringing resisters into line with institutional ideals. More research is needed to illuminate the ways that dominant meanings are enacted, not only by governing authorities, but by institutional colleagues not in positions of authority. These findings also expand upon previous literature on institutional gendering processes by linking the micro dynamics to broader societal historical citizenship processes to suggest how seemingly gendered processes are simultaneously reproductions of race/ethnic hierarchies.

Research examining court practices reveals a history of preoccupation with girls' sexuality. This institution's reproduction of gendered and racialized citizenship through therapeutic techniques regulating girls' sexual morality is a continuation of that historical process. Controlling girls' sexual morality through punishment has its historical context in the development of the juvenile justice system's attempt to separate supposedly "wayward" children from "criminal" children. For girls, waywardness included sexual promiscuity and the remedy was instilling values of sexual morality. The activities of white middle-class women moral reformers revolved around using ideals of female sexual propriety to monitor the moral and sexual behaviors of working class, particularly immigrant girls (Chesney-Lind and Shelden 2014). Girls who did not conform to these ideals were deemed to be wayward and in need of control through state institutions such as reformatories or training schools.

This institution reinforced colleague surveillance by setting up a highly competitive structure in which the girls demonstrated their institutional competency for citizenship by publicly reinforcing institutional ideals in the monitoring of colleagues. Horizontal surveillance is a way for those under surveillance to gain a sense of control/power—a way to affirm their worth in a meritocratic structure in which worth is relative. Through reinforcing the institution's rules, the girls demonstrate to governing authority their own acceptance of these rules; thereby, providing the opportunity to make a favorable impression and elevate their own status in the hierarchical structure. These dynamics suggest how a peer governance system that encourages the demonstration of the attainment of institutional ideals through the public evaluation of colleagues fosters disciplinary mechanisms of surveillance. This also lessens the appearance of coerciveness from those in positions of authority. As a result, participants in the process become performers in order to demonstrate their acceptance of institutional ideals.

The exchanges in these sessions illustrate the particular coerciveness of evaluation processes within structures in which public and private spheres are within close proximity of each other, or in which there is no separation between public and private. Privileged or private setting information is wielded as weapons to invalidate rational, as well as moral competency, thus rendering the girls powerless to construct alternative meanings of their selves and circumstances. This ability to introduce as evidence activities that would otherwise be privileged information reinforces the institution's power (Fujimoto 2001). It is likely that processes of horizontal surveillance are particularly heightened in circumstances where public/private spheres are merged since private sphere actions become a base for evaluation.

While these findings raise questions about the impact of meritocratic structures (or types of) on therapeutic governance, these dynamics also raise the larger question of how merit based rehabilitation programs may foster processes of horizontal surveillance. Further exploration is needed on the viability of "rehabilitation" programs solely based on a merit structure in which the primary grounds for evaluation is one's attitude since these processes are more likely to premise morality as the basis of rehabilitation. In rehabilitation programs in which merit is the basis, at the very least there should be content of evaluation other than the transformation of attitude. This would be a step in moving evaluation away from morality as the primary basis of evaluation. To the extent that these findings invite the re-thinking of merit-based rehabilitation programs, it moves beyond current literature on gender equity in the criminal justice system, which has focused the debate on comparisons between women and men's programs.

The findings in this chapter also expand upon previous studies of therapeutic governance by studying gendering processes among adolescent girls, rather than adult women, and by studying these dynamics in a co-ed institution. This is significant because previous studies of therapeutic governance have suggested that therapeutic governance reproduces gender hierarchies through a therapeutic division of a more likely presence in women's institutions. This gendered division of therapy is explained as being a factor of gendered organizational logic attributing women's circumstances to psychologically disordered selves. The logic is that women's crimes are a factor of something wrong on the inside while men's crimes are a factor of their responses to structural/economic conditions (McCorkel 2003). However, in this institution, the therapeutic regime's gendered organizational logic of this coed institution is that the girls (as well as the boys) have immoral selves resulting from a lack of appropriate values, rather than "psychologically disordered" selves. Neither the boys' nor the girls' circumstances were attributed to structural circumstances. This lack of distinction was perhaps shaped by the co-ed structure of the institution. It is possible that gender-segregation shaped gendering processes in this co-ed institution such that they resembled that of single-gender institutions. Had group therapy sessions been integrated, perhaps discourses would have been more "gender-neutral" and perhaps discourses of girls' sexuality and emotionality would not have dominated group therapy sessions—at least not to the same degree.

Reinforcing worker-citizen ideals as rationalizations for the girls' circumstances distracts attention from the underlying structures of state/governing power and unto the "cultural" habits/deficiencies of the powerless. Historical and social reproduction processes (Feld 1999; Glenn 2002; MacLeod 1995) shaping the girls' location at the bottom of socio-economic structures make it unlikely that they will accrue significant substantive rewards of citizenship once they leave the institution. Upon leaving the institution, the girls' lives are structured such that they are overwhelmed with reacting to the daily circumstances emerging from their marginalized social locations shaped by hierarchies of race/ethnicity, class, and gender. A program that recognizes these structural conditions and helps the girls navigate these structural circumstances would be a more logical and effective approach.

Finally, these findings have broader societal implications for thinking about the reproduction of gender, race/ethnic, and class hierarchies on a broader societal level. They show the significance of group-based horizontal surveillance processes in the reproduction of hierarchies in merit-based systems. Further research is needed on how, and the extent to which, horizontal surveillance processes may reproduce gender, race, and class hierarchies in other institutional settings, such as workplace merit-based evaluation processes.

References

Acker, J. (1990). Hierarchies, jobs, bodies: A theory of gendered organizations. *Gender & Society, 4*(2), 139–158.

Becker, H. (1963). *Outsiders*. New York: Free Press.

Campbell, A. (1987). Self definition by rejection: The case of gang girls. *Social Problems, 34*(5), 451–466.

Chesney-Lind, M., & Shelden, R. (2014). *Girls, delinquency, and juvenile justice*. Wadsworth.

Collins, P. H. (2008). *Black feminist thought: Knowledge, consciousness, and the politics of empowerment*. Routledge.

Cruikshank, B. (1999). *The will to empower: Democratic citizens and other subjects*. Ithaca, NY: Cornell University Press.

Davis, A. (1983). *Women, race & class*. Vintage Books.

Feld, B. (1999). *Bad kids: Race and the transformation of the juvenile court*. Oxford University Press.

Fordham, S. (1993). "Those loud black girls": (Black) women, silence, and gender "passing" in the academy. *Anthropology & Education Quarterly, 24*(1), 3–32.

Foucault, M. (1965). *Madness and civilization*. New York: Vintage Books.

Foucault, M. (1977). *Discipline and punish: The birth of the prison*. New York: Vintage Books.

Foucault, M. (1978). *The history of sexuality: An introduction* (Vol. I). New York: Vintage Books.

Foucault, M. (1983). The subject and power. In H. L. Dreyfus & R. Rabinow (Eds.), *Michel Foucault: Beyond structuralism and hermeneutics* (2nd ed., pp. 208–226). University of Chicago Press.

Foucault, M. (1988). Technologies of the self. In L. H. Martin, H. Gutman, & P. H. Hutton (Eds.), *Technologies of the self* (pp. 16–49). Amherst: University of Massachusetts Press.

Fox, K. (1999). Changing violent minds: Discursive correction and resistance in the cognitive treatment of violent offenders in prison. *Social Problems, 46*(1), 88–103.

Fujimoto, N. (2001). What was that secret? Framing forced disclosures from teen mothers. *Symbolic Interaction, 24*(1), 1–24.

Garfinkel, H. (1956). Conditions of successful degradation ceremonies. *The American Journal of Sociology, 61*, 420–424.

Garland, D. (1997). 'Governmentality' and the problem of crime: Foucault, criminology, sociology. *Theoretical Criminology, 1*(2), 173–214.

Glenn, E. N. (2002). *Unequal freedom: How race and gender shaped American citizenship and labor*. Harvard University Press.

Horney, K. (1967). *Feminine psychology*. W. W. Norton & Company.

Hurtado, A. (1996). *The color of privilege*. Ann Arbor: University of Michigan Press.

MacLeod, J. (1995). *Ain't no makin' it: Aspirations & attainment in a low-income neighborhood*. Westview Press.

McCorkel, J. A. (2003). Embodied surveillance and the gendering of punishment. *Journal of Contemporary Ethnography, 32*(1), 41–76.

O'Grady, H. (2005). *Woman's relationship with herself: Gender, Foucault and therapy*. New York: Routledge.

Rich, A. (1979). *On lies, secrets, and silence: Selected prose, 1966–1973*. New York: W. W. Norton.

Rose, N. (1988). Calculable minds and manageable individuals. *History of the Human Sciences, 1*, 179–200.

16

'Hypermasculinity' in Interaction: Affective Practices, Resistance and Vulnerability in a Swedish Youth Prison

Anna G. Franzén

Introduction

In this chapter, I aim to demonstrate what a discursive perspective on emotion and masculinity can contribute with to the field of youth imprisonment. Prisons are highly emotional spaces, often described as filled with, for instance, aggression, pain and fear (Crewe et al. 2014; Sykes 1958). Incarcerated men, and young men in particular, are often deemed as having emotional trouble in terms of uncontrollable and explosive anger, which can be seen, for instance, in that rehabilitation strategies often are aimed at helping young men control their anger (Andersson 2008a; Franzén 2015; Laursen and Henriksen 2019). Studies on prison masculinities have often highlighted emotions such as anger as intentionally and strategically enacted as a response to the violent prison environment (De Viggiani 2012; Jewkes 2005; Ricciardelli et al. 2015). This study departs from a different viewpoint: rather than understanding emotion and identity as something that individuals carry, hidden deep inside, a *discursive* perspective highlights emotions as intrinsically tied to social discourses, for instance, the discourse of masculinity. Through a detailed analysis of the complexities of emotions in a research interview with young incarcerated

A. G. Franzén (✉)
Department of Child and Youth Studies, Stockholm University, Stockholm, Sweden
e-mail: anna.franzen@buv.su.se

© The Author(s), under exclusive license to Springer Nature Switzerland AG 2021
A. Cox, L. S. Abrams (eds.), *The Palgrave International Handbook of Youth Imprisonment*,
Palgrave Studies in Prisons and Penology, https://doi.org/10.1007/978-3-030-68759-5_16

men, the study demonstrates how emotions and identities emerge from intricate interactional processes where both participants contribute to meaning-making. This illuminates less intentional or strategic performances of masculinities, and also showcases the less familiar prison masculinity of being vulnerable.

Hegemonic Prison Masculinities

Prisons have been argued to be key sites for the reproduction of hegemonic masculinity (Sabo et al. 2001) and numerous studies have investigated the construction of masculinities among incarcerated men. The notion of hegemonic masculinity has been both disputed and reworked since it was first introduced by Connell (1995; see, for instance, Connell and Messerschmidt 2005; Jefferson 2002). It assumes masculinities in the plural, and presupposes one dominant and desired ideal of masculinity in a specific context, and an ideal that always is constructed in relation to other subordinated masculinities and femininities (Connell and Messerschmidt 2005). However, among the criticisms of the concept is that it often, paradoxically, is used for masculinities that simultaneously are depicted as desirable and dominant, and as being in a crisis (Jefferson 2002). Furthermore, studies drawing on the concept of hegemonic masculinities often have failed to illuminate the relational complexities of doing masculinity, rendering hegemonic masculinity as a set of static traits (Connell and Messerschmidt 2005; Jefferson 2002). In prison studies, hegemonic masculinity is often described as *hyper*masculinity, and understood as involving an exaggerated and especially narrow combination of qualities and values found in hegemonic masculinities in other contexts (Bengtsson 2016; Sabo et al. 2001). This hypermasculinity is often described as drawing heavily on characteristics such as courage, physical strength and control, heterosexuality, stoicism and independence (cf., Abrams et al. 2008; Bengtsson 2016; De Viggiani 2012; Jewkes 2005; Phillips 2001). To date, scholarship on prison masculinities has mainly explored adult masculinities and have tended to focus solely on the '*hyper-*' aspects of masculinities, leading to a depiction of prison masculinity as too unitary, and highlighting mainly aggression, violence and emotional detachment. However, a few recent studies have demonstrated more complex and varied constructions of masculinity in prison (Crewe 2014; Crewe et al. 2014; Maycock 2018; Ricciardelli et al. 2015); for instance, how softer masculinities can be found in certain spaces in prison, such as visits rooms (Crewe et al. 2014).

In this chapter, I aim to contribute to this emerging research field of complex and multiple prison masculinities. Specifically, by engaging deeper with the subtle emotional aspects of *young* prison masculinities in the context of a prison unit for young men in Sweden. I will zone in on how emotional issues are played out in action, by taking a closer look at emotion work in a research interview, and drawing on a perspective on affect as productive of subjectivities (Ahmed 2014; Wetherell 2012, 2013). Following Wetherell (2012, 2013), affect will be understood neither as an individual property hidden deep inside, nor as an intentional strategy, but rather as something that is both non-conscious and co-constructed, both constituted and constitutive. Through emphasizing the social in affective processes, this perspective avoids separating between individual/embodied affects and cultural emotions, but rather understands the social/discursive and emotional as intrinsically intertwined. Thus, I will use terms such as 'emotion' and 'affect' interchangeably.

In the research interviews which centered on childhood relationships and emotions, I will argue that the interviewer empathetically positions the young men as vulnerable when they talk about difficult or traumatic circumstances. The analysis will illuminate affective practices related to hypermasculinities in detail, and in particular, both resistance to and the affective expression of vulnerability.

Emotion and Young Prison Masculinities

While there has been a recent (re-)turn to emotions in criminology (for instance, Karstedt 2002; Jacobsen and Walklate 2019; Spencer and Ricciardelli 2017), the topic of emotions and criminology is an evolving and emerging research field (Jacobsen and Walklate 2019). Accordingly, despite the bulk of studies of prison masculinities highlighting the use of emotional control by incarcerated people, including extreme forms of aggression and concealing of vulnerabilities, there are few that specifically (and theoretically) zone in on the emotional work involved in enacting masculinity (but see Crewe 2014; Crewe et al. 2014; Laws and Crewe 2016). In studies of incarcerated youth, the lack of studies of emotions is especially clear. This might be understood as surprising, considering that rehabilitation methods aimed at youth often focus on a combination of cognitive and emotional issues—that is, aggression problems (Andersson 2008a; Franzén 2015; Laursen and Henriksen 2019). Furthermore, studies of young masculinities, to a larger extent than studies of adults, highlight how hypermasculine ideals are constructed and enforced within rehabilitation programs (see, for instance, Andersson 2008a; Cox 2011; Laursen and

Henriksen 2019), and by staff (Abrams et al. 2008). Abrams and colleagues found that boys in a secure correctional facility were paradoxically both encouraged to express their feelings, and at times punished or mocked for expressing vulnerable emotions which were not in line with the hegemonic masculine ideals at the facility (2008). Studies of young men in secure youth institutions have also highlighted how institutional ideals of hegemonic masculinity intersect in significant ways with both ethnicity (Bengtsson 2012) and class, by disciplining young men into a working class masculinity emphasizing manual labor and physical strength (Henriksen 2018).

While the majority of studies on masculinity in prison have been focused on adult men, the institutional reinforcement of hegemonic masculinities appear to be similar among incarcerated young men as well (Abrams et al. 2008; Bengtsson 2016). Gooch (2019) illuminates the importance of both age and masculinity in prison violence, where violence is connected to both performance of 'boyhood' and 'manhood'. Cesaroni and Alvi (2010) have also pointed out that many of the masculine ideals relevant to adult men are unavailable to youth (such as autonomy and domination). However, since the studies on young prison masculinities and emotion are so few, I will draw on studies on both young and adult men in the following brief review of hypermasculinities and emotion in prison.

Strategic Emotions? Masking, Fronting and 'the Prison Code'

Studies on hypermasculinities in prison often focus on the intentional and strategic aspects of emotion work (Goffman 1959, 1961; also see Laws and Crewe 2016; Spencer and Ricciardelli 2017). Hypermasculinity is typically described as involving both a display of certain emotions (i.e., related to hardness, toughness and aggression) and suppressing others (i.e., related to vulnerability, love, fear; cf., Abrams et al. 2008; Crewe et al. 2014; Evans and Wallace 2008; Jewkes 2005; Sabo et al. 2001).

Controlling of emotions and emotional displays (along with hypermasculine behavior) among men in prison is often conceptualized as a survival strategy, a response to risk of assault, and to the pains of imprisonment (Buston 2018; De Viggiani 2012; Jewkes 2005; Ricciardelli et al. 2015; Sabo et al. 2001), or as an effect of being deprived of a vital sense of masculine self, as part of the mortification processes of the prison as a total institution (Cesaroni and Alvi 2010; Goffman 1961). Emotion work such as wearing a 'mask' (De

Viggiani 2012), or putting up a front (Cesaroni and Alvi 2010; De Viggiani 2012; Jewkes 2005: 48), is often described as part of living up to a 'prison code' (Sabo et al. 2001). De Viggiani's study, for instance, emphasizes prison masculinities as a kind of strategic performance, separating the men's 'public and private façade' in order to reach social acceptance in prison (2012: 287). Strategically used tactics involve, for instance, acting and talking aggressively and hiding vulnerability. In a study of the 'emotional geography' of prisons, however, Crewe et al. (2014) give a more complex view of the emotional universe of the total institution by highlighting the variety of emotional strategies of the different 'emotion zones' in prison, pointing to 'leakages' where inmates may display vulnerabilities, for instance.

There are many virtues of these studies of strategic employment of hypermasculine expressions, among them, as pointed out by Crewe et al. (2014), highlighting the immensely painful conditions of prison life and the agency expressed by people in prison to tackle their situation. However, as these studies tend to primarily focus on emotion processes as intentional and strategic, they leave out the less agentic aspects of emotional processes relating to masculinity. Therefore, in this chapter, in order to investigate and illuminate the fluidity and variation of masculinities among young men in prison, I will adopt a broad discursive perspective on affect and subjectivity that understands affect as performative and productive, and attempts to find a middle ground where the individual is neither completely free to pick and choose his subjectivity or affects, nor completely agentless.

Affect, Affective Practices and Subjectivity

A discursive perspective on subjectivity involves understanding identity as dynamic and exterior (rather than interior), and as constituted (rather than reflected) in discourse (see, for instance, Benwell and Stokoe 2006; Foucault 1978; Wetherell 1998). Discourse can be understood a system of representations that provides a language for speaking about a particular topic at a specific moment in time (Foucault 1978). This means that discourse is productive in that it produces meaning and subjectivity, which can be conceptualized through the notion of subject positions (Wetherell 1998). Discourse also always produces opportunities for resistance (Foucault 1978). In a detention home setting, this can, for instance, be done by incarcerated young men refusing to draw on the official problem formulation of the institution: for example, by refusing to talk about themselves as needing rehabilitation they are resisting the subject position that is imposed on them by the institutional discourses (Franzén 2015, see also Fox 1999). In this chapter, I will zone in specifically on how subjectivity is constituted, and resisted, through affect.

Sara Ahmed (2014) has illuminated how emotions contribute to the production of subjectivities and boundaries between groups of people, and how affects circulate and stick to certain bodies, constructing meaning. For instance, drawing on Ahmed's theory, Spencer and Ricciardelli (2017) have demonstrated how disgust produces the boundaries between men who are incarcerated for sex offenses and prison staff. Men imprisoned for sex offenses are constituted as objects of disgust, and the staff members' maintenance of the feeling of disgust is an important aspect of separating themselves from the incarcerated men. Thus, disgust constructs meaning for sex offending and consequently both about the individuals who are imprisoned for sex offences and the staff who are not charged with sex offences. Disgust, then is productive of their subjectivities. Ahmed highlights how this production of subjectivities happen *in between* people, rather than being isolated *within* separate individuals: 'It is not simply that the subject feels hate, or feels fear, and nor is it the case that the object is simply hateful or is fearsome: the emotions of hate and fear are shaped by the 'contact zone' in which others impress upon us, as well as leave their impressions' (Ahmed 2014: 194). So, while we feel emotions in our bodies, they are also relational and cultural. We are angry *at* someone, or we are happy *for* someone, and we are affected by other's feelings. Interaction is one 'contact zone' where feelings are transmitted (Kiesling 2018), and Margaret Wetherell (2012, 2013) has detailed a perspective on emotions as affective-discursive practice (I will call these *affective practices*), which is useful for investigating emotions and subjectivity in interaction.

Understanding emotions as affective practice, this perspective sees affect as inseparable from the discursive context in which it is produced and made meaningful (Wetherell 2012). Affect and discourse are understood as 'coupled, feeding back to one another' (Kiesling 2018). Thus, affect is both embodied and intertwined with social interaction and discursive practice—always situated in specific contexts. The affective processes which are productive of subjectivity can therefore be studied in people's interaction, for instance, by investigating recurring ways of talking about, and enacting, affect and how these produce subject positions, which can be drawn upon, negotiated or resisted in interaction (Wetherell 1998, 2012). This is not to say that affective displays or subject positionings are intentional or planned but rather that discourse is 'construct[ing] physical arousal, turning it into recognizable and communicable emotion' (Kiesling 2018, Wetherell 2012: 52).

Scott Kiesling (2011) highlights the connection between affect and identity though the individual's desire to have a specific (masculine) identity, something that requires a constant re-enactment of, and investment in, acts and affects discursively associated with the masculine self. In a study on masculinity in an American college fraternity, Kiesling has illuminated, for instance, how 'ease' appears to be an important affective practice that constructs masculinity among young American men, and that similar types of 'emotionlessness' are typically perceived as masculine (2018, see also 2011).

In line with this perspective, the aim of this study is to investigate emotions as affective practices, rather than as inner entities which are either held back or expressed. Specifically, the focus is on how affective practices are involved in the production of subjectivity, alongside other discursive practices. This involves analyzing (i) the recurring ways of talking about and enacting affect, (ii) how they produce affective subject positions and, lastly, (iii) how these affective subject positions are negotiated in interaction.

Data and Method

This study is part of a project[1] on young incarcerated men, narrative identities and affective practices, and it draws on data from a larger, previous research project[2] on incarcerated young men and the use of treatment programs in Swedish prisons. Scandinavia has at times been considered exceptional in terms of imprisonment, primarily regarding low imprisonment rates and humane prison conditions, as well as a heavy emphasis on rehabilitation and re-socialization (Lappi-Seppälä 2015; Pratt 2008a, b). Lappi-Seppälä (2015) argues that the Scandinavian exceptionalism is particularly visible in the realm of youth justice, were major parts of youth justice lies outside of criminal justice. The age of criminal responsibility in Sweden is 15, and all under the age of 15 are dealt with by the child welfare authorities. Youth between the ages 15 and 17 are dealt with by either child welfare authorities or the criminal justice system, but it is very rare that youth under the age of 18 are sentenced to prison; rather, they are sentenced to closed youth care (Lappi-Seppälä 2015). Youth between 18 and 21 who are sentenced to prison may get a reduced sentence because of their young age, and are typically placed in wards dedicated for youth aged 18–21.

This study was carried out in a closed medium-security prison, comprising several wards, two of which were designated for incarcerated young men aged 18–21. A total of 42 young men were included in the study and all had a sentence of at least three months; the average sentence was 19 months. They were convicted of various crimes: the most common were robbery, drug offence and assault and battery. The average age of the participants was 20.1 years.

The project involved ethnographic fieldwork (conducted by myself) at the youth wards, and interviews with both staff and incarcerated youth. This chapter zones in on a specific type of psychological interview conducted for the research project by a researcher in the team who also is an experienced psychologist.[3] The so-called adult attachment interview (AAI) is a standardized interview focused on relationships, thoughts and feelings primarily during childhood. The interview is structured in that it uses an interview schedule with a battery of structured questions, but also allows the interviewer to ask follow-up questions. The AAI is mainly focused on childhood experiences and relationships, personal loss and feelings and thoughts about these experiences. In the prison setting, the interview questions brought about stories of childhood trauma, loss and difficult circumstances. Many of the young men produced long and rich narratives, and several also appeared to enjoy talking; some invited the interviewer to talk more after the interview. The data consists of 42 video-recorded and transcribed interviews,[4] most of which were about one to two hours long.

While the AAI typically is used in psychological research or clinical practice in order to study attachment or mentalization (a psychological concept about individuals' ability to reason about their own and other's mental states, cf., Möller et al. 2014), the present study involved a different take on the interviews—a discursive take. In order to analyze emotion as affective practice, rather than inner entities, and as situated and negotiated in interaction, the analyses draw on methods from primarily discursive psychology (Benwell and Stokoe 2006; Potter 1996) and discourse analysis (Foucault 1978; Wetherell 1998). These discursive methods entail analysis that goes beyond the topic of the interviews, and rather treats interviews as discursive practice, where discourses, affective practices and subject positions are being reproduced and negotiated in interaction. This means that instead of perceiving the research interview as a means to reveal emotions or identities that the young men carry around hidden in their inner selves, the analysis aims to study these phenomena as produced and co-constructed in the interview (cf., Benwell and Stokoe 2006; Potter 1996; Wetherell 2012). Thus, this type of discourse analysis involves analyzing the interview as social action and as a collaborative meaning-making process, where both interviewer and the interviewee co-construct meaning. Therefore, both participants' contributions in the interview must be included in the analysis.

Affective Repertoires in Youth Prison

At immediate sight, the youth ward could be recognized as a type of hypermasculine environment. The prison consists mainly of long, empty corridors, aligned with rows of locked, heavy doors, dividing the space into smaller, locked partitions, including the gym, where many of the young men would lift weights, displaying muscular bodies and tattoos. During my ethnographic fieldwork I became accustomed to the many distinctive prison sounds that speaks to the general atmosphere—the echo of boots in the corridors, the clinking of keys and bleeping of walkie talkies, the sound of machines in the work shop, and all the deep voices: arguments, loud laughter and excited yells, and the authoritative voices of the staff. This is not an environment that appears to invite emotional talk. At large, the prison can be understood as designed to deal with dangerous and aggressive young men, including the rehabilitative program offered which was primarily focused on anger problems (a version of Aggression Replacement Training, cf., Andersson 2008a). From a discursive perspective (Foucault 1978; Wetherell 1998, 2012), this means that the prison may be understood as discursively constructing specific, primarily aggressive, subjectivities (cf., Andersson 2008a; Fox 1999; Franzén 2015).

However, in the analysis of the AAIs, a different affective repertoire (Wetherell 2012) emerged, one of the young men as relational and emotional beings. The interviewer addressed the young men, not primarily as 'inmates' or as young men with 'aggression problems', but asked them questions about their childhood experiences and their thoughts and feelings connected to these. Many of the young men responded with narratives about personal loss and childhood trauma. The interview can thus be understood as discursively constructing the young men as having other emotions than merely aggression. This involved an affective process that produces quite different subjectivities (Ahmed 2014; Wetherell 2012) than in the everyday life and rehabilitation at the prison.

There were a variety of affective practices (Wetherell 2012) drawn upon in the interviews. In the following, I will argue for two main points: firstly, that the interviewer positions the young men affectively, as having some kind of emotional pain. Secondly, that many of the young men respond to this affective subject positioning with resistance in the form of affective practice: indifference and irritation. However, I will begin by analyzing one of the few cases where the young men talked more openly about difficulties in their childhood and painful experiences affected them negatively.

Empathy and Vulnerability as Affective Practice

While many of the young men talked about difficulties or trauma during their childhood, a few positioned themselves as sad or in pain in relation to these events. Below I will analyze one such case, and illuminate the affective practices of empathy (enacted by the interviewer) and vulnerability (enacted by the young, incarcerated man, Martin). In the interview, Martin is talking about his relationship with his mother, giving detailed narratives of feelings and memories, including being beaten by her. When answering the question 'can you name three words to describe the relationship to your mother', he chose the words 'sad', 'miserable' and 'uninterested'. Below, the interviewer asks him to give some examples of memories connected to the word 'sad'. Martin produces a long answer, looking and sounding sad throughout, and speaking with a soft voice.

Ex. 1

```
7    Mar    I have horrible memories, I don't even want to say it
8           in front of the camera (int: oka:y, oka:y) but I was
9           simply sad, every time she came- I didn't get happy, I
10          got sad (int: mm) I don't know, it's like that for me
11          still ((looks sad)) sure I love my mom but I actually
12          feel better without her (int: mhm) in some strange way,
13          I don't know why ((little smile, sad look)) (int: mm)
14          but I don't miss her in here, so to speak, I miss no
15          one ((looks sad)) (int: no)
            [...]
17   Mar    I don't know, it's her behavior I don't like, she was
18          always drunk you know? (Int: mhm) and eh, yea, there's
19          something about her I don't like, I don't know if these
20          kinds of things occur in this world, like, that
21          children don't like their mother, but yea, is that
22          abnormal? ((shakes head with sad look and looks at the
23          interviewer for an answer))
24   Int    It can be like that, sure
25   Mar    It can be like that, huh? (int: absolutely) yea
```

Something that stands out in the case is that not only is Martin telling stories of painful memories from childhood and of being vulnerable and in a victim position as a child, but he also connects these childhood events to who he is now and emotions and feelings he has now, for instance, that he still feels sad when he sees his mom (lines 9–11). In this excerpt, the negative effects of his childhood experiences and relationships are also described as a lack of positive feelings, where they would be expected: not feeling happy when he

16 'Hypermasculinity' in Interaction: Affective Practices, Resistance... 343

sees his mom, not missing her, and not liking her. But furthermore, he is clearly displaying sadness and pain in the moment, both sounding and looking sad, and the interviewer responds with empathy.

One might argue that empathetic communion is foundational to social relationships and moral order (Durkheim 1915). When someone reports of a personal experience involving intense emotion such as joy, pain or sorrow, it socially, and therefore morally, demands of the recipient to respond by affirming the experience and affiliating with the persons' stance towards it (Heritage 2011). An empathetic response is here understood as 'an affective response that stems from the apprehension or comprehension of another's emotional state or condition, and that is similar to what the other person is feeling or would be expected to feel' (Heritage 2011: 161). Discursive psychologists have demonstrated how empathy and sympathy (for the purposes of this analysis it is not necessary to differentiate between the two, but see Hepburn and Potter 2012) can be seen in alignments and prosody, for instance, in stretched turns, softened volume and a creaky or 'breathy' delivery (Hepburn and Potter 2012). Furthermore, response cries such as 'oh!' or 'ah' work as vehicles for empathic alignments (Heritage 2011). In prosody, these empathetic turns can mirror elements of crying, in interaction they are heard as sympathizing or soothing (Hepburn and Potter 2012).

In extract one, the interviewer can be seen to enacting empathy, using a soft and breathy voice in her responses to Martin's sad story. The interviewer and Martin can be seen to be aligning affectively (Heritage 2011) here. A painful story of 'horrible memories' and of being 'sad' rather than 'happy' with his mother as a child, is met with soothing empathy, and Martin develops his narrative, with a sad look upon his face and a sad tone in his voice. This narrative also stands out in the data because of Martin's reasoning about there being something abnormal about him, and here, in his question about this, directed to the interviewer/psychologist, he is further aligning with her as an authority on emotions, and seemingly accepting her reassurance that this is not abnormal. In a subtle way, Martin and the interviewer are positioning him as a victim of a difficult circumstance—leading to some kind of subtle emotional pain, in particular through the affective practices of empathy and sadness. In most AAIs, however, the young men tell similar stories, but resist the position of being in some kind of pain. In the following, two types of affective resistance will be analyzed.

Indifference: Affective Practice as Resistance

The following case exemplifies 'indifference' as an affective practice. In his interview, Johannes narrates how he and his two older brothers were brought up with their grandparents, because both parents were in prison. He was one year old when they moved in with the grandparents and he describes having a very close relationship with both of them, but at the age of seven he was transferred to a foster home, and since then he has moved between multiple foster homes and youth institutions. So far, the interview has revolved around the adults Johannes had close relationships with during his childhood, and now the interview has moved into more detailed questions about the different relationships, significant childhood events and emotions associated with these.

Ex. 2.

```
1   Int  What did you use to do when you were emotionally upset as
2        a child? (3)
3   Joh  ((Breathes in)) E::h I dunno, I got- eh like instead of
4        getting sad I usually got aggressive, angry, you know,
5        like (3) yea, I got angry a lot, fought a lot when I was
6        little, fought a lot […] black- blacked out and stuff,
7        got angry and stuff (int: right) so that's kind of it.
8   Int  Right, were your grandparents around then or, do you
9        remember what they used to do [when you got like that?]
10  Joh                                [No this was] more later
11       on, like after- when I had moved from my grandma and
12       grandad ((opens up his arms wide, strokes his head,
13       massages neck)) like, more then (.) (int: yea:) that I
14       got angry and stuff a lot, and like eh, yea, like (int:
15       mm)) ((folds his hand on his lap)), before that I don't
16       remember that much (2) ((smacks his lips)), there
17       weren't so many of those feelings like sad […] it was
18       more the last- when- after- like at seven, eight like
19       (int: yea) that you e:h started to fight a lot and stuff
```

In the excerpt above, both Johannes and the interviewer are speaking calmly and softly. The interviewer asks a question that zones in on difficult emotions, but without specifying what specific emotions she's looking for (lines 1–2). Johannes answers (lines 3–7) by drawing on what can be understood as an affective interpretative repertoire, that is, a recurring way of talking about affect (Wetherell et al. 2015). In this case it involves constructing 'what the problem is'. In this research context, the young men recurrently describe that they were angry rather than, for instance, sad or anxious, and that loss of control due to anger, such as blacking out, is their main problem. In this repertoire, anger is understood as an individual problem, generally talked about as

16 'Hypermasculinity' in Interaction: Affective Practices, Resistance... 345

simply being there, something they are born with. This way of understanding the young men's 'problem' can also be found among prison staff and in the different treatment methods commonly used for treatment of young men in locked institutions (for instance, Cox 2011). These methods have been connected with hypermasculine ideals (Andersson 2008a), and, notably, they can be understood to construct the young men as emotional beings with emotional problems, but exclusively anger and aggression (cf., Fox 1999). In the interviews, the affective repertoire is drawn upon both in the young men's childhood narratives and in narratives of the crimes they have been convicted for. Often, the young men describe aggression or anger as an innate problem stemming from a personality disorder or some type of diagnosis, and many describe that they have had these problems since they were children, as Johannes does here.

However, in lines 8–9, as the interviewer asks about what the grandparents used to do when he got 'like that' (a question that presupposes the proximity of the grandparents) this repertoire of innate anger problems is challenged, as it turns out that the problems only began after he was removed from his grandparents (lines 10–19). As Johannes describes that prior to the move he had not experienced a lot of sadness or anger, a different narrative begins to take shape, one where the difficult emotions might have been connected to his removal from the grandparents at age seven. It is also at this moment in the interview that Johannes begins to display a body language of being very relaxed or tired—of not really being faced by what is talked about: stretching and massaging himself, with an indifferent look upon his face. A few lines later, the interviewer returns to questions about the move from the grandparents. The interviewer asks how he reacted and how they reacted when the move happened.

Ex. 3

```
1   Int  Mm do you remember why it turned out that way, that you
2        were to move [to a new family?]
3   Joh                [yea::] there was all this mess
4        with the social services eh just as my mom was let out
5        of prison ((stretches for several seconds)) [...] it
6        turned out that I had- eh eh that I had to move since I
7        was the youngest, you know
8   Int  So your brothers stayed? ((empathetic voice))
9   Joh  Yea my older brothers stayed ((scratches face, pokes at
10       chin for a few seconds)) (int: oka::y) and so I got to
11       move- move to a foster home (int: yea) so- yea
         [...]
12  Int  Okay mm, eh did you ever feel rejected as a child?
```

```
13 Joh   No, not that I can remember ((faint smile)) (int: no?)
14        not that I can remember anyways (1) I don't think so, it
15        was more that ((scratches face)) yea, I thought it was
16        strange, like ((shrugs shoulders, smiles)), it was more
17        that, like.
```

This excerpt exemplifies the negotiation and co-construction of affect (cf., Wetherell 2012). When the new information arises that Johannes was the only one of the brothers that had to move, the interviewer can be seen to upgrade her empathetic responses (lines 8, 10 and 12). She is picking out this specific information from a longer narrative, and using a soft and breathy voice, emphasizing words in a manner that constructs the story as sad. By displaying empathy, the interviewer makes visible the interpretations of the story of a seven year old being removed from his family—that it likely would be an emotional event, and, consequently, positioning Johannes as having gone through something difficult—a subject position that also includes affect, since difficulties are (culturally) expected to lead to some emotional pain.

However, while Johannes confirms that this fact is correct, he displays no signs for emotional pain or sadness, but rather engages in the relaxed body language again (lines 5, 9–10). Scott Kiesling (2018) has shown how interactions like this can be part of performing a type of 'masculine ease', of not caring or being bothered, and in this case, Johannes is displaying that he is not faced with what culturally could be understood as traumatic. Johannes could thus be seen to resist this affective subject position of (subtle) painful emotions. To clarify, however, this does not mean that he is intentionally or strategically denying some emotion (Kiesling 2018; Wetherell 2013). There is no way of knowing what feelings Johannes is 'actually' experiencing in his body in this moment. As highlighted by discursive psychology, the only way we can think about and make meaning of our inner life is though discourse (Potter 1996), and this further means that affects cannot be separated from the unfolding sequence of the interaction it is embedded in (Wetherell 2013). Furthermore, as Kiesling points out, even when we abide by cultural norms or discourses, such as on how to be a man, we rarely do it consciously or intentionally (2018).

The interview continues for a few more minutes, revolving around the move and the grandparent's reactions. Then the interviewer moves on to a standard question about experiencing rejection during childhood (line 12). In light of Johannes's narrative so far, there appears to be an expected answer to this question: Johannes had to move and the brothers got to stay with the grandparents—a feeling of rejection would have been warranted. But Johannes answers 'no' to the question. He does, however, relate the question to the move from the grandparents, in a sense confirming that it would be expected to feel rejected under the circumstances. As he explains that he rather thought that it was strange, the body language returns again. Thus, as the interviewer turns to questions of negative emotions, Johannes can be seen to upgrade his affective resistance to these, through body language (shrugging and smiling, lines 13, 15–16) and restating that he cannot remember. Discursive psychology, highlights how statements such as 'I don't know' or 'I don't remember', should not be understood to simply reflect the speaker's level of knowledge, but rather as a social action that is used to handle delicate subjects in interaction (Potter 1996). This is sometimes called 'stake inoculation' (Potter 1996), a way of avoiding being blamed for attempting to present oneself in a positive manner. By pointing out that one does not remember or does not really know, the risk for being blamed for fabricating or embellishing a story is handled, since it signals that whatever issue is discussed, it cannot be so important, since the speaker cannot remember. The way the question is constructed arguably demands that he answers from the position of a vulnerable child. By giving the account that he does not remember, coupled with his displayed indifference, he manages to escape the vulnerable position altogether (see Jonsson 2014 for similar examples of 'dispreferred responses' among boys in school).

Anger: Affective Practice as Resistance

In this second example of affective resistance, one of the young men, Peter, responds with irritation at a point during the interview when the focus of the interview approaches the subject of personal loss, and the interviewer asks questions about feelings and experiences surrounding the loss. Peter has told her that he lost one of his closest friends a few years ago.

Ex. 4

```
1   Pet  He was murdered.
2   Int  He was murdered ((soft, breathy voice)) (4) How did you
3        find out?
4   Pet  He was in the hospital. (5)
5   Int  So you found out he was in the hospital?
6   Pet  Yea he was in a coma first.
7   Int  Mhm (5) did you visit him there, or?
8   Pet  Yea of course. ((irritated voice))
9   Int  mm mm (3) how was that?
10  Pet  Bad ((irritated voice)) (2)
11  Int  mm mm (2) do you remember what it felt like? (1) (Pet:
12       what?) Do you remember how that felt for you?
```

```
13  Pet  What do you think? ((dismissing hand gesture)) of course
14       it felt bad! ((irritated voice))
         [...]
15  Int  Yea, yea (3) how is it for you when I ask?
16  Pet  You get irritated, you know ((shakes head slightly)) it's
17       stupid questions.
```

The excerpt begins about 15 minutes into the 45-minute-long interview. As the interview zones in on personal losses, and questions about the loss of Peter's friend, Peter sounds increasingly irritated. It is important to note that no other inmates expressed irritation as clearly during the interview, although subtler versions of this did occur. What is particular with the affective practice here, is that Peter's irritation emerges as the interviewer asks him about the death of his friend, and increases as she is asking follow-up questions and displaying empathy.

Through empathetic intonation and breathiness, the interviewer's response to the information that the friend was murdered constructs it as a sad story. However, as opposed to the case of Martin above, there is an affective disalignment (cf., Kiesling 2018) here—the interviewer is treating the story of the murdered friend as a sad story, using a soft, empathetic voice, but Peter is responding with upgraded resistance, partly in the form of irritation. The interviewer continues asking questions with a soft voice, leaving time for Peter to pick up his turn, but Peter resists. The point here is that the interactional struggle that is going on is not only about urging Peter to talk more, or whether the questions are relevant or not, but also involves affective practices and affective subject positioning (Wetherell et al. 2015). When the interviewer empathetically handles Peter's story as a sad story, she is simultaneously positioning him as feeling sad or being vulnerable, albeit in a subtle way. These are not emotions that typically are associated with performing prison masculinities. Resistance here, is therefore not referring to resistance to the interview, per se (although for a moment, there is definitely that type of resistance as well), but rather, resistance toward a subject position that is produced through affect and in discourse (see, for instance, Franzén 2015; Franzén and Aronsson 2013) in particular this resistance is aimed toward the affective subject positioning.

Eventually, the interviewer departs from the interview questionnaire, and asks a meta question about the interview, to which Peter confirms that he is getting irritated (by the stupid questions). After this they move on to other subjects and Peter sounds less irritated. It appears then, that Peter's resistance is concentrated to talking about, and being positioned as, having vulnerable emotions such as sadness or pain.

16 'Hypermasculinity' in Interaction: Affective Practices, Resistance... 349

At the end of the interview, Peter is encouraged to talk about whatever he finds important for the researchers to know, and he then engages in long and rich narratives of when he has been mistreated by the police and prison staff.

Ex 5.

```
5    Pet   [...] when they finally get to the scene they point the gun
6          at me, 'get on the ground, get on the ground' [...] then in
7          the ambulance their boss comes up to me and asks if I can
8          help them and say where the perpetrator went and stuff,
9          'the perpetrator is in your mama's cunt you fucking pig'
10         I say (int: mm) 'first you want me to lay on the ground
11         and then you do this (int: mm) when you want help, huh'
12         ((looks down and picks at a soda bottle throughout))
13   Int   Right, and hadn't given you any help, right
14   Pet   They're really some cowardly bastards
            [...]
15   Int   Eh how- like- now this might be one of those stupid
16         questions again, but what did that feel like for you, I
17         can't really imagine what that is like? (3)
18   Pet   Well it's really not easy (int: no) I've always grown up
19         hating them (int: yea, okay) And it was the same thing
20         then ((shakes his head while talking, looking down))
```

This is part of a longer narrative of an incident when Peter felt that the police wanted to let him die after he had been shot, and he can be seen to draw on several of the characteristics typically described as valued in prison hypermasculinities: aggression, violent and sexist language, and hatred towards the police. In this instance, Peter is fully up-taking a hypermasculine, affective subject position of an angry young man. This is also a type of underdog position of being a victim of structural injustice of the criminal justice system (cf., Presser 2008), although it is a victim position that does not involve emotional vulnerability or weakness. Quite the opposite, despite Peter's physically vulnerable state of being shot and believing that he might be left to die, he manages to strike back verbally at the police who have mistreated him badly. It is thus a subject position that manages to combine a victim-hero position which can be understood as a way of performing masculinity (see also Andersson 2008b; Presser 2008) and that has the affective practice of anger at its core.

However, it is also noticeable that it is an affective subject position that is relational and co-constructed (Wetherell 2012) by the interviewer and Peter. The narrative is developed though follow-up questions and encouragements to talk more. We can also see the affective practice of empathy in this instance. In line 13, the interviewer is aligning with Peter, when she is supporting and confirming his narrative, along with his account for hating the police: that the police had not helped him when he was shot. Furthermore, as opposed to the previous excerpt that revolved around vulnerability, Peter shows no resistance to the interviewer's follow up questions about feelings—when the feeling in question is anger. However, this is not to imply that Peter is deliberately planning his display of anger here, or withholding a felt sadness in the previous excerpt, but rather that 'the flow of activity is both constrained by past practice and the immediate situation and context' (Wetherell 2013: 360).

Discussion and Conclusion

In this chapter, I strived to illuminate how prison masculinities come about through affective-discursive practices in a psychological research interview, adopting a perspective on affects as productive of subjectivities (Ahmed 2014) and co-constructed in interaction (Wetherell 2012, 2013). While previous studies primarily have highlighted aggressive and dangerous masculine prison subjectivities, mainly as strategic responses to the painful and dangerous environment (i.e., Sabo et al. 2001; Ricciardelli et al. 2015), this study reveals subjectivities and affects as emergent from an intricate interactional process, and as intrinsically intertwined with discourse (Kiesling 2018; Wetherell 2012). As the young men are encouraged to talk about their childhoods and emotions, and through the interviewer's empathetic affective practices, both the interviewer and the inmates are constructed as subjects. In the process, a less familiar prison masculinity emerges—one of being vulnerable, of experiencing (subtle) pain or sadness stemming from trauma and loss.

The affective practices highlighted in the analysis might be seen to challenge the discursive and affective order (Wetherell 2012) of the prison, and therefore also the young person's subject positions. The young men resist the subject positioning though nuanced and varied affective practices, indifference and anger/irritation, both recognizable as characteristics of 'hypermasculinity'. Furthermore, while the analyses show that most young men enacted resistance to vulnerability, it was also found that some did not, as exemplified with the case of Martin, who enacted vulnerability and sadness clearly in the interview. Even if the examples of enacted vulnerability are few, these cases are highly significant as they showcase the variety and complexity of affective masculinities in youth prison.

The study contributes to the field of affect and masculinities in prison by demonstrating how affective practices related to hypermasculinities can be investigated in action, even in interviews. This means, for instance, that by zoning in on how affective practices are accomplished it is possible to analyze 'hypermasculine' emotion work in action, without strictly focusing on intentional and strategic emotion work. In all three cases of affective practice, the affect in question (vulnerability, indifference, irritation) emerged in relation to topics of trauma or loss, and when the psychologist responded with empathy to a 'sad story'. The analyses suggest that affective practices related to hypermasculinity here are performed in instances that appear to have little to do with survival or immediate response to risk. Thus, affective practices that at other times may be drawn upon intentionally as a strategy for survival, here appears more automatic in response to being empathetically positioned as vulnerable, as suffering from loss of loved ones. To conclude, I have strived to illustrate that a discursive perspective on subjectivities and affect is a useful perspective that grants possibilities for a fine-grained analysis that may contribute to further investigations of the fluidity and range of, as well as discursive constraints for, young prison masculinities.

Notes

1. This study was supported by a grant from Forte: The Swedish Research Council for Health, Working Life and Welfare (Forte: 2016-01038) and has been approved by the regional ethics committee in Linköping (ref. no. 54-08).
2. The larger project involved multiple researcher and a range of research questions, both qualitative and quantitative, and focused on interplay between staff and youth, rehabilitation programs and mentalization. The present project aims to draw on a wide range of data, including the interviews conducted for quantitative purposes, in order to analyze narrative identities, including affective practices.
3. Clara Möller.
4. Transcription notations:

:	Prolonged syllable
[…]	Omitted lines
[word]	Overlapping talk
(.)	Micropause
(2)	Pauses in seconds
((word))	Comments from the transcriber
<u>Word</u>	Emphasized utterance
word-	Abrupt cut-off

References

Abrams, L. S., Anderson-Nathe, B., & Aguilar, J. (2008). Constructing masculinities in juvenile corrections. *Men and Masculinities, 11*(1), 22–41.

Ahmed, S. (2014). *Cultural politics of emotion* (2nd ed.). New York: Routledge.

Andersson, K. (2008a). *Talking violence, constructing identity: Young men in institutional care.* PhD, Tema Institute, Linköping University.

Andersson, K. (2008b). Constructing young masculinity: A case study of heroic discourse on violence. *Discourse & Society, 19*(29), 139–161.

Bengtsson, T. T. (2012). Learning to become a 'gangster'? *Journal of Youth Studies, 15*(6), 677–692.

Bengtsson, T. T. (2016). Performing hypermasculinity: Experiences with confined young offenders. *Men and Masculinities, 19*(4), 410–428.

Benwell, B., & Stokoe, E. (2006). *Discourse and identity.* Edinburgh: Edinburgh University Press.

Buston, K. (2018). Inside the prison parenting classroom: Caring, sharing and the softer side of masculinity. In M. Maycock & K. Hunt (Eds.), *New perspectives on prison masculinities* (pp. 277–306). Cham: Palgrave Macmillan.

Cesaroni, C., & Alvi, S. (2010). Masculinity and resistance in adolescent carceral settings. *Canadian Journal of Criminology and Criminal Justice, 52*(3), 303–320.

Connell, R. W. (1995). *Masculinities.* Berkeley, CA: University of California Press.

Connell, R. W., & Messerschmidt, J. W. (2005). Hegemonic masculinity: Rethinking the concept. *Gender & Society, 19*(6), 829–859.

Cox, A. (2011). Doing the programme or doing me? The pains of youth imprisonment. *Punishment & Society, 13*(5), 592–610.

Crewe, B. (2014). Not looking hard enough: Masculinity, emotion, and prison research. *Qualitative Inquiry, 20*(4), 392–403.

Crewe, B., Warr, J., Bennett, P., & Smith, A. (2014). The emotional geography of prison life. *Theoretical Criminology, 18*(1), 56–74.

De Viggiani, N. (2012). Trying to be something you are not: Masculine performances within a prison setting. *Men and Masculinities, 15*(3), 271–291.

Durkheim, E. (1915). *The elementary forms of the religious life.* New York: Free Press.

Evans, T., & Wallace, P. (2008). A prison within a prison? The masculinity narratives of male prisoners. *Men and Masculinities, 10*(4), 484–507.

Foucault, M. (1978). *The history of sexuality, vol. 1: An introduction.* New York: Pantheon.

Fox, K. J. (1999). Reproducing criminal types: Cognitive treatment for violent offenders in prison. *The Sociological Quarterly, 40*(3), 435–453.

Franzén, A. G. (2015). Responsibilization and discipline: Subject positioning at a youth detention home. *Journal of Contemporary Ethnography, 44*(3), 251–279.

Franzén, A. G., & Aronsson, K. (2013). Teasing, laughing and disciplinary humor: Staff–youth interaction in detention home treatment. *Discourse Studies, 15*(2), 167–183.

Goffman, E. (1959). *The presentation of self in everyday life.* New York: Anchor Books.

Goffman, E. (1961). *Asylums: Essays on the social situation of mental patients and other inmates*. Harmondsworth: Penguin.

Gooch, K. (2019). 'Kidulthood': Ethnography, juvenile prison violence and the transition from 'boys' to 'men'. *Criminology & Criminal Justice, 19*(1), 80–97.

Henriksen, A. K. (2018). Vulnerable girls and dangerous boys: Gendered practices of discipline in secure care. *Young, 26*(5), 427–443.

Hepburn, A., & Potter, J. (2012). Crying and crying responses. In A. Peräkylä & M.-L. Sorjonen (Eds.), *Emotion in interaction* (pp. 194–210). Oxford: Oxford University Press.

Heritage, J. (2011). Territories of knowledge, territories of experience: Empathic moments in interaction. In T. Stivers, L. Mondada, & J. Steensig (Eds.), *The morality of knowledge in conversation* (pp. 159–183). Cambridge, UK: Cambridge University Press.

Jacobsen, M. H., & Walklate, S. (Eds.). (2019). *Emotions and crime: Towards a criminology of emotions*. Routledge.

Jefferson, T. (2002). Subordinating hegemonic masculinity. *Theoretical Criminology, 6*(1), 63–88.

Jewkes, Y. (2005). Men behind bars: 'Doing' masculinity as an adaptation to imprisonment. *Men and Masculinities, 8*(1), 44–63.

Jonsson, R. (2014). Boys' anti-school culture? Narratives and school practices. *Journal of Anthropology and Education Quarterly, 45*(3), 276–292.

Karstedt, S. (2002). Emotions and criminal justice. *Theoretical Criminology, 6*(3), 299–317.

Kiesling, S. F. (2011). The interactional construction of desire as gender. *Gender and Language, 5*(2), 213–239.

Kiesling, S. F. (2018). Masculine stances and the linguistics of affect: On masculine ease. *NORMA, 13*(3–4), 191–212.

Lappi-Seppälä, T. (2015). Juvenile justice without a juvenile court: A note on Scandinavian exceptionalism. In F. E. Zimring, M. Langer, & D. S. Tanenhaus (Eds.), *Juvenile justice in global perspective* (pp. 63–118). New York: NYU Press.

Laursen, J., & Henriksen, A. K. (2019). Altering violent repertoires: Perspectives on violence in the prison-based cognitive-behavioral program anger management. *Journal of Contemporary Ethnography, 48*(2), 261–286.

Laws, B., & Crewe, B. (2016). Emotion regulation among male prisoners. *Theoretical Criminology, 20*(4), 529–547.

Maycock, M. (2018). Introduction: New perspectives on prison masculinities. In M. Maycock & K. Hunt (Eds.), *New perspectives on prison masculinities* (1st ed., pp. 1–16). Cham: Palgrave Macmillan.

Möller, C., Falkenström, F., Holmqvist Larsson, M., & Holmqvist, R. (2014). Mentalizing in young offenders. *Psychoanalytic Psychology, 31*(1), 84–99.

Phillips, J. (2001). Cultural construction of manhood in prison. *Psychology of Men & Masculinity, 2*(1), 13–23.

Potter, J. (1996). *Representing reality: Discourse, rhetoric and social construction.* London: Sage.

Pratt, J. (2008a). Scandinavian exceptionalism in an era of penal excess: Part I: The nature and roots of Scandinavian exceptionalism. *British Journal of Criminology, 48*(2), 119–137.

Pratt, J. (2008b). Scandinavian exceptionalism in an era of penal excess: Part II: Does Scandinavian exceptionalism have a future? *British Journal of Criminology, 48*(3), 275–292.

Presser, L. (2008). *Been a heavy life: Stories of violent men.* Urbana, IL and Chicago, IL: University of Illinois Press.

Ricciardelli, R., Maier, K., & Hannah-Moffat, K. (2015). Strategic masculinities: Vulnerabilities, risk and the production of prison masculinities. *Theoretical Criminology, 19*(4), 491–513.

Sabo, D., Kupers, T., & London, W. (Eds.). (2001). *Prison masculinities.* Philadelphia, PA: Temple University Press.

Spencer, D., & Ricciardelli, R. (2017). 'They're a very sick group of individuals': Correctional officers, emotions, and sex offenders. *Theoretical Criminology, 21*(3), 380–394.

Sykes, G. (1958). *The society of captives: A study of a maximum-security prison.* Princeton, NJ: Princeton University Press.

Wetherell, M. (1998). Positioning and interpretative repertoires: Conversation analysis and post-structuralism in dialogue. *Discourse & Society, 9*(3), 387–412.

Wetherell, M. (2012). *Affect and emotion: A new social science understanding.* London: Sage.

Wetherell, M. (2013). Affect and discourse—What's the problem? From affect as excess to affective/discursive practice. *Subjectivity, 6*(4), 349–368.

Wetherell, M., McCreanor, T., McConville, A., Barnes, H. M., & le Grice, J. (2015). Settling space and covering the nation: Some conceptual considerations in analysing affect and discourse. *Emotion, Space and Society, 16,* 56–64.

17

Incarcerated Young Men and Boys: Trauma, Masculinity and the Need for Trauma-Informed, Gender-Sensitive Correctional Care

Nina Vaswani, Carla Cesaroni, and Matthew Maycock

Introduction

Custodial establishments across the world are dominated by cisgender men, with males comprising 95% of prisoners in the United Kingdom (Ministry of Justice 2019; Scottish Prison Service 2018) and 93% of prisoners in the United States (Bronson and Carson 2019). These ostensibly homo-social spaces have particular implications for performances of masculinity within and after prison (Maycock 2018b; Sabo et al. 2001). We frame this chapter in a theoretical context within which we consider the multiple and changing masculinities (Connell 1995) in the countries within which this research is located (Anderson 2009; McCormack 2012).

N. Vaswani
Centre for Youth & Criminal Justice, University of Strathclyde,
Glasgow, UK
e-mail: nina.vaswani@strath.ac.uk

C. Cesaroni (✉)
Faculty of Social Science and Humanities, Ontario Tech University,
Oshawa, ON, Canada
e-mail: carla.cesaroni@uoit.ca

M. Maycock
University of Dundee, Dundee, UK
e-mail: mmaycock001@dundee.ac.uk

The prison as a place of significant trauma is also becoming increasingly recognised, from the extensive trauma histories of prisoners (Welfare and Hollin 2015; Akyüz et al. 2007), the potential for re-traumatisation within the prison system (Burrell 2013) as well as incarceration being the source of new trauma (Honorato et al. 2016). Yet, little is known about the trauma of incarcerated men, and even less attention has been paid to the trauma of incarcerated young men and boys (both before incarceration and as a consequence of incarceration). While we agree that women are missing from data relating to many areas of public life (Criado-Perez 2019), the particular context we consider in this chapter illuminates the ways in which research on trauma has tended to be gendered through a focus on women and girls, with young men relatively overlooked. The literature on trauma among incarcerated women and girls is arguably much more robust (Sloan 2018). The lack of academic, policy and practice attention on the trauma of incarcerated males may reflect the widely held perception that prison has been designed for men, compounded by society's acknowledgement of the often-great harms caused by male violence, dominance and oppression and the fact that men are often the source of women's trauma (Sloan 2018).

These challenges to compassion and consideration towards imprisoned males do not diminish the need to focus on the implications for human rights, prison management, rehabilitation and trauma recovery that arise from unaddressed trauma in incarcerated males, within a context that more fully considers the gendered experiences of male prisoners. As Sloan (2018, p. 127) observes "men's gendered experiences of prison may need just as much sympathetic attention as women's if they are to become less violent or harmful upon release from prison." Furthermore, there are important interactions between trauma, prison masculinities and incarcerated males that warrant further attention in the literature if we are to better understand the manifestation of trauma in males (especially in relation to offending and violence) and advance both recovery and rehabilitation practice.

This chapter emerges from a desire to bring together and reflect on the work of the authors (and others) that occurred individually in three spheres (trauma and prison, trauma and masculinity, prison masculinities), but had rarely been considered together as a whole. One of Nina Vaswani's key areas of research is the impact of trauma, bereavement and loss in young people in prison and the vulnerability of young men. For the past two decades, Carla Cesaroni has studied the adjustment and experiences of incarcerated adolescent and young adult males. She has recently completed a comparative study of incarcerated young adult males (18–24 years old) in Scotland and Canada. Matthew Maycock is the recent co-editor of *New Perspectives on Masculinities*, the first book to use theories of masculinity to analyse contemporary slavery. Matthew has consistently worked on gender issues, with masculinity being a particular focus across a number of studies.

By drawing together the literature and exploring the intersections of trauma, prisons and masculinities, and with an emphasis on adolescent boys (12–17 years old) and young adult males (18–24 years old), this chapter highlights a much overlooked area of study and make the case for dedicated scholarship and gender-sensitive practice in relation to trauma and incarcerated males. Our argument is that prison masculinities and the prison experience itself compound the trauma (and masculine "performance" associated with it) that incarcerated males experience, making help-seeking difficult, and potentially re-traumatising and causing new traumas.

Trauma and Prison

Incarcerated adolescent boys and young men have experienced high levels of trauma, at a rate not dissimilar to their female counterparts. Between 62% and 98% of incarcerated young men in Australia, the United Kingdom and the United States report at least one lifetime experience of trauma prior to incarceration (Abram et al. 2013; McMackin et al. 2002; Moore et al. 2013; Pettus-Davis 2014). This includes experiencing childhood physical and/or sexual abuse, experiencing serious life threats and/or injuries, witnessing severe injury or death of another and being involved in gang violence (Abram et al. 2013; McMackin et al. 2002). Approximately three-quarters of young men in custodial settings, or who have histories of gang involvement, have experienced traumatic losses, separations or bereavements (such as murders, suicides and distressing accidents) (Dierkhising et al. 2019; Vaswani 2014). It is important to recognise that imprisoned young men and boys tend to come from violent and traumatic environments such that male trauma is far more likely to be experienced in public, compared to incarcerated women and girls, who are more likely to experience violence and trauma in private settings (Chesney-Lind and Paramore 2001; Greenfeld 1999; Schwartz 2013). However, it is difficult to establish reliable estimates of male victims of intimate partner abuse as men tend to be reluctant to report (Leonard 2003; Barber 2008).

Arriving in custody with pre-existing vulnerabilities from trauma means that prisoners are also at risk of re-traumatisation (Burrell 2013) and may have difficulties in adaptation and coping within the prison environment (Cesaroni and Peterson-Badali 2005, 2010, 2016). The environment and regime inherent in carceral spaces, including bright lights, overcrowding, noise, isolation, strip-searching, fear and the actual or perceived threat of violence, can trigger trauma symptoms. Awareness of these conditions has resulted in more attention towards 'trauma-informed' prison design (Jewkes 2018; Miller and Najavits 2012). In addition, incarceration is often a traumatic event in itself, and once in custody, the risk of experiencing and witnessing violence, victimisation, suffering, self-harm and death rises (Daquin et al. 2016; Hales et al. 2003). Young people in their teenage years are especially vulnerable to the distress and trauma of prison, as not only are they in a crucial developmental phase between childhood and adulthood, but also the youth custodial estate often contains the highest levels of bullying, victimisation, self-harm and suicide (Gooch 2016, 2019; Shepherd et al. 2018).

Trauma symptomology is unsurprisingly prevalent among prison populations. Post-traumatic Stress Disorder (PTSD) is a diagnostic category characterised by a collection of symptoms including intrusive thoughts; flashbacks; sleep disturbance; avoidance of stimuli associated with the trauma; psychological and physiological reactions to triggers; negative alterations in cognitions or mood such as dissociation, emotional numbing, fear and detachment; and alterations in arousal and activity, such as hypervigilance, anger and risky behaviour (American Psychiatric Association 2013). There are added complications for individuals who experience severe and/or chronic abuse, neglect or other trauma during childhood who are at greater risk of suffering long-lasting effects of trauma compared to those who first encounter trauma in adulthood or children who experience a one-off traumatic event in the context of an otherwise secure childhood. The inability to escape trauma by virtue of the child's powerlessness and dependency, as well as the disruption that trauma has on the child's developing brain, their subsequent world view and template for life, love, attachment and relationships (Herman 1992; Perry and Szalavitz 2017), arguably leaves a lasting legacy. The additional complexities and symptomology of developmental trauma have been termed Complex PTSD by clinicians in the field (Cloitre et al. 2009), which was included as a new and distinct diagnosis in the 11th edition of the *International Statistical Classification of Diseases and Related Health Problems*, although has yet to be formally acknowledged in the *Diagnostic and Statistical Manual of Mental Disorders* (DSM) (Rosenfield et al. 2018).

Research from the United States and Canada suggests that PTSD occurs in approximately 4% of the general public but reaches up to 48% in prison populations (Briere et al. 2016). Importantly Briere et al. (2016) found that although women had slightly higher rates of PTSD in both the community and prison, the differences were not statistically significant. There is also some evidence that while women tend to become 'safer' in custody, due to their community experiences of violence and victimisation, men are at increased risk of victimisation once incarcerated (Miller and Najavits 2012). Despite this, trauma is far more likely to be addressed among incarcerated women than men (Miller and Najavits 2012). A study of 34 adolescent males aged 15–17 convicted of murder or serious violence in the United Kingdom (Welfare and Hollin 2015) found that all of the boys had experienced trauma, 44% presented with symptoms that warranted a full PTSD assessment, yet none of the boys had received any assessment or treatment for their trauma either in custody or in the community. There are important implications for both trauma and justice policy and practice arising from the prevalence of this unrecognised and untreated trauma among young men in prison, as well as specific factors related to the interplay between trauma and masculinity that this chapter will now turn to.

Trauma and Masculinity

Perhaps surprisingly, throughout most of the twentieth century much of the scholarly and clinical attention on trauma was focused on very male-dominated experiences. The recognition of trauma-related nervous disorders emerged from the horrors and fall-out from two global conflicts, with around 80,000 men believed to be suffering from 'shell shock' in WWI and the re-emergence of the disorder as 'combat fatigue' in WWII (Chan 2014). These conditions were associated with shame and stigma for failing to live up to the masculine ideal of the strong and fearless soldier (Shields 2016), and sufferers were even deemed 'malingerers' and 'cowards' (Chan 2014).

With each major conflict, understanding of the disorder evolved, indeed, the hard-fought inclusion of PTSD in the DSM-III in 1980 stemmed from the distressing experiences and intense lobbying from Vietnam veterans (Herman 1992). This also meant that conceptualisation and understanding of the disorder originated in male experiences of combat. While Herman (1992) rightly argues that women's more 'ordinary' experiences of violence, victimisation and trauma in homes, streets and communities were largely overlooked until the 1970s, today trauma scholarship is firmly weighted towards women. The literature on trauma and masculinity remains largely confined to work on men in the military, but this narrow focus does not capture either the trauma experiences of the majority of people (men or women) or the complexities of childhood developmental trauma and Complex PTSD.

Yet with gender remaining the biggest predictor of violent behaviour (Perry and Szalavitz 2017), and an association between trauma and the risk that men can pose to both themselves and others (Walsh 2020; Mejia 2005), there is a pressing need to focus on male trauma. While females tend to report greater exposure to trauma over the life-course, males frequently present with more PTSD symptoms, have lower usage of therapeutic interventions and respond less well to treatment than females (Shields 2016; Wade et al. 2016; Morrison 2012). While trauma therapies may be tailored towards women, aspects of the experience and performance of masculinity are also implicated in this discrepancy. Trauma shapes masculinity, as the very nature of trauma calls into question traditional notions about what being a man entails in that "at the core of most traumatic experiences are overwhelming states of fear, helplessness and vulnerability. These states are extremely difficult for anyone to deal with, but they carry an added message and burden for male trauma victims" (Mejia 2005, p. 38). Elder et al. (2017) note that male survivors of military sexual trauma report disrupted assumptions about masculinity such as strength, control, self-worth and the ability to protect oneself and others from harm.

Trauma can also affect the performance of masculinities. Experiencing trauma, along with the entirely human responses to such an experience, often leaves men feeling stigmatised, humiliated and ashamed, resulting in exaggerated displays of heteronormative and traditional displays of masculinity in an attempt to reassert power and control (Ellis et al. 2017; Elder et al. 2017). These behaviours can include excessive exercise, overtly enacted heterosexuality, aggression, risk-taking and violence (Elder et al. 2017; Ellis et al. 2017).

The performance of a traditional, hegemonic masculinity can also shape the experience of, and recovery from, trauma as there are many barriers to help-seeking, assessment and treatment. In a study of 197 male veterans, emotional restriction was significantly related to PTSD symptom severity (Morrison 2012). Many people, both male and female, who have experienced trauma find it difficult to articulate their emotional and psychological symptoms, a phenomenon known as alexithymia (Van Der Kolk 2014). Research has found that alexithymia is more prevalent among males, especially for young men involved in the justice system, and is also associated with poor mental health in this population (Snow et al. 2016). Being able to identify and describe problematic emotions is an essential first step in the help-seeking process and trauma recovery (Van Der Kolk 2014), and trouble in doing so puts males at a disadvantage. Attachment to traditional masculine norms, such as strength, control, restrictive emotionality, stoicism and gender-role socialisation can also be a barrier to help-seeking (Addis and Mahalik 2003), a barrier that is intensified further by the shame and stigma of having experienced trauma. Even once help has been sought, these features of masculinity also affect assessment for PTSD and related disorders, as assessment methods typically rely on the verbal expression of emotional and psychological symptoms (Elder et al. 2017). Treatment interventions often require some form of emotional processing, and confronting these emotions may cause men to feel additional loss of agency and control and result in added distress (Elder et al. 2017; Morrison 2012). For these reasons, men have higher drop-out rates from treatment and a lack of success with trauma interventions.

Prison Masculinities

Masculinities are often constructed, maintained and restructured according to particular social networks and social institutions (Connell 2002). Arguably, the behaviour that men engage in or exhibit may depend upon the types of masculinities that are available—and safe to adopt—in a given environment or social setting (Lutze and Murphy 1999; de Viggiani 2018). Masculinity is a cultural resource that can be drawn upon in a presentation of self, something to be negotiated over a wide range of situations (Carrabine and Longhurst 1998). Masculinities are multiple, contested, dynamic and socially located in both time and place (O'Brien et al. 2005).

Earlier we discussed the intersection of masculinities, trauma and the military, and perhaps there is no other institutional site that compares to the military (in terms of masculinities and the masculine performance) as prisons. Indeed Goffman (1961) asserts that both prisons and the military constitute total institutions that transform outsiders to insiders, breaking down the very nature of a person's identity through a type of status degradation ceremony. According to Sabo et al. (2001) prisons constitute a key institutional site for the expression and reproduction of hegemonic masculinities. In the social context of prison, power is partially exercised through the expression of identity, specifically through signifiers of gender (de Viggiani 2018). Close social proximity in prison means traditional discourses of masculinity regarding what it means to be a man become acute and magnified, oriented around narrow values associated with heterosexist masculine ideology, compelling individuals to present a tough front even if this means concealing their emotions (de Viggiani 2018; Curtis 2014). The performance of hyper-masculinity offers men the possibility of navigating prison life and long-term survival in the prison milieu (Brown and Grant 2018; Toch 1998). Even amongst incarcerated men who do not believe in hyper-masculine values, the social policing of masculine codes is sufficiently strong that they must keep their viewpoint secret (Evans and Wallace 2008). Kimmel (1994, p. 122) argues that "masculinity must be proved, and no sooner proved that is again questioned and must be proved again." Nowhere is this probably more so than in the prison.

There is an abundance of prison research that has detailed the gendered nature of prison including its aggressive, hierarchal, emotionally detached and violent aspects (Maycock 2018a). According to Sim (1994) institutions for young men are the site of a dominant and uncontrolled culture of masculinity. Despite this prevailing narrative about prison masculinities, a more complex picture emerges within which alternative masculinities have been analysed within prison spaces (Cox 2018; Laws and Lieber 2020; Maycock 2018a; Morse and Wright 2019). More recent masculinity research has uncovered the existence of more subtle, nurturing and engaged performances of masculinity in prison (Maycock 2018b). For example, this includes the possibility of caring and, in some senses, softer performances of masculinity by young people in prison (Buston 2018). This is within a wider context in which the study of masculinities is exploring the possibilities for more emotionally available inclusive performances of masculinity, where homophobia and the hyper-masculinity described above are less formative (Anderson 2009; McCormack 2012). Critically, much of the research analysing inclusive masculinity has been undertaken in University and Fraternity settings, within the Global North. While some theoretical work has explored the possibilities of inclusive masculinity in prison settings (Maycock 2018a), little empirical work has been undertaken that explicitly analyses inclusive masculinity in prisons.

Caution must therefore be exercised in failing to recognise the pluralities of masculinities that are exercised and contested in the prison setting (Carrabine and Longhurst 1998). Indeed our own research points towards this complexity and diversity of the performance of masculinity by young people in custody (Cesaroni and Alvi 2010; Maycock et al. 2018a; Vaswani 2014). Displays of toughness, bravado and masculinity, however, may be particularly important to adolescent boys and young adult males who are attempting to establish a masculine identity, feeling pressure to engage in what they perceive as "adolescent appropriate" ways (Steinberg 1999) and secure a sense of self-identity (McNess 2008).

Trauma, Prison Masculinities and Incarcerated Young Men

Experiencing trauma does not inevitably lead to offending or violence, and survivors of trauma are far more likely to grow up to be further victimised rather than become the perpetrators of harm to others (Herman 1992). However, unaddressed trauma in boys and young men can lead to maladaptive coping strategies that help to relieve the symptoms of unresolved trauma, such as anger, aggression, substance misuse, risk-taking and violence (Van Der Kolk 2014). A history of being marginalised or victimised coupled with gender socialisation that stresses stoicism, toughness and physicality can lead to aggressive over-compensation and violence (Ellis et al. 2017; Abrams et al. 2008). Trauma symptoms can increase the potential for violence, in that hyperarousal and hypervigilance may result in misinterpretation of social cues and provoke inappropriate hostile reactions (Walsh 2020; Martin et al. 2015). These behaviours often cause young males to be rejected and excluded from prosocial activities and support mechanisms (Honorato et al. 2016), thereby increasing the likelihood that trauma will go unresolved. Involvement in violent offending can also lead to an additional layer of offence-related trauma (Welfare and Hollin 2015), and contact with the justice system and incarceration only adds to trauma experiences.

Once incarcerated, the interplay between youth, trauma, masculinity and prison becomes ever more complicated. We have documented that prison is the site of a multitude of traumas and re-traumatisation, that trauma histories can affect how people present to authority, engage with services and treatment agencies, and that hypervigilance and mistrust can lead to even relatively benign interactions being misinterpreted and responded to inappropriately (Martin et al. 2015). These factors often cause people to come into contact with the justice system or cause people to rub up against the regime while in custody, creating additional hardships (Miller and Najavits 2012; Martin et al. 2015).

We have also noted that masculinity can exacerbate trauma symptoms and reduce help-seeking and responsiveness to available treatments (Chan 2014; Wade et al. 2016). Prison too is conventionally seen as a hyper-masculine environment (Toch 1998), in which traditional masculine norms, those associated with power and aggression, are amplified in order to obtain and maintain status (Iwamoto et al. 2012), although a more complex picture of prison masculinities is now acknowledged (Maycock 2018a). Ricciardelli et al. (2015), Gooch (2019) and Sim (1994) have all observed that males in prison are on constant guard and permanently vigilant to potential risk and threats to their masculinity, causing anxiety even among the strongest characters, but it is important to note that the hypervigilance of trauma causes people to do the same. Prison masculinities can therefore create an added trauma burden for those who are already vulnerable through trauma. We also know that trauma can result in an exaggerated masculinity, often helping to perpetuate the distress caused by trauma and creating the potential for new trauma related to offending, violence and incarceration (Ellis et al. 2017; Elder et al. 2017; Honorato et al. 2016).

Power, agency and autonomy are reduced for all prisoners, but are even less available to young people due to their age and status (Cesaroni and Alvi 2010). But with youth at a crucial stage of transition to adulthood, the need to assert independence and establish identity and status can lead to an extra emphasis on the performance of aspects of certain masculinities such as physical strength, aggressiveness and bullying (Cesaroni and Alvi 2010; Gooch 2019; Maycock 2018b), helping to intensify the level of fear (Ricciardelli et al. 2015), victimisation and re-traumatisation in youth institutions. At least one study of adolescent custody facilities suggest that young offender facilities not only modelled and encouraged hegemonic masculinities but supressed young men's experimentation with alternative masculinities (Abrams et al. 2008), highlighting both the importance of context and the influence of role modelling in the development of a masculine identity.

In short, it is clear that trauma can exaggerate hegemonic masculinity, prison can exaggerate hegemonic masculinity and youth can exaggerate hegemonic masculinity, and aspects of masculinity can increase the likelihood of trauma, exacerbate trauma symptoms and reduce opportunities for receiving help as well as to reduce the effectiveness of any trauma treatment. Thus when trauma, masculinity, youth and prison coincide there are very real ramifications for prison management, care, rehabilitation and trauma recovery (see Fig. 17.1).

Trauma-Informed Care and Masculinity

Based on these factors, we argue that prison needs to be not only trauma informed but gender sensitive in a way that resonates with the needs of diverse gender identities and performances, evident in the wider communities within which prisons are located. Miller and Najavits (2012) and Griffin et al. (2012) offer approaches to trauma-informed practice that, in theory at least, should be feasible even within the complex prison environment. As a minimum, trauma-informed approaches within correctional settings should ensure that institutions do no further harm to already traumatised individuals (Miller and Najavits 2012). Overarching principles include a focus on trauma-specific screening, assessment and clinical provision, but also emphasise a whole establishment approach, with the role of frontline prison staff and the wider prison environment (structure, safety, predictability etc.) an essential component of treatment (Griffin et al. 2012). The requirements underpinning a

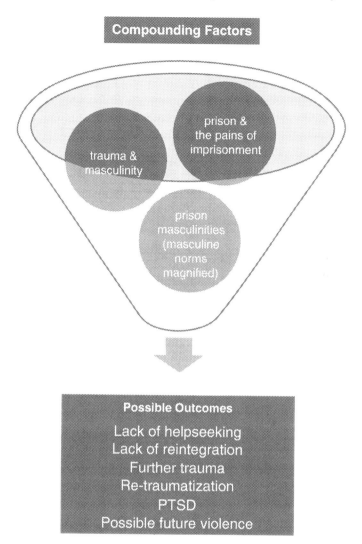

Fig. 17.1 Complicating factors and outcomes arising from the interaction of trauma, masculinity, youth and prison

trauma-informed approach include staff training (including stress management and self-care), valuing relationships and evidence-based interventions (Griffin et al. 2012; Miller and Najavits 2012). Additionally, it is important to consider the extent to which working in prison can result in trauma for prison staff (Cassidy and Bruce 2019; Ruck et al. 2013).

That said, there remain few trauma-informed, or gender-sensitive interventions for men in custody (Pettus-Davis 2014), and even fewer for young men with complex developmental trauma (Welfare and Hollin 2015) or that consider trauma-informed practice across the whole institution (Vaswani and Paul 2019). More recently, practitioners have made attempts to adopt a whole-prison approach to trauma, loss and bereavement with emerging evidence of effectiveness and impact, but also an acknowledgement that the confines of custody impinge upon successful implementation and delivery (Pitt and Thomson 2018). It appears that even the most well-intentioned policies and approaches encounter considerable challenges in the translation to practice, with the realities of implementing trauma-informed care in prison particularly complex on the frontline (Vaswani and Paul 2019).

Vaswani and Paul (2019) argue that genuinely trauma-informed care in prison is unattainable because custodial settings are fundamentally at odds with trauma-informed practice in terms of their purpose, values, environment and organisational culture. A recurring theme throughout this chapter is the powerlessness, fear, loss of agency, disconnection and hopelessness that is at the heart of trauma experiences (Herman 1992), but these are also key features of young men's experience of prison regardless of their trauma histories, with young men in prison describing the loss of hope for the future, loss of safety and stability, loss of relationships, and loss of power and agency (Vaswani 2015). This has major implications for trauma recovery as almost all models emphasise the establishment of safety, regaining control and agency, identifying and processing the emotions associated with trauma in some way (directly or indirectly) and reconnecting with trusting and healing relationships as essential elements of the recovery process (Perry and Szalavitz 2017; Van Der Kolk 2014; Herman 1992), and all of which are compromised in prison.

For example, Judith Herman's book *Trauma and Recovery* (1992) outlines the main phases of recovery as establishing safety and stabilisation (essentially restoring power, control and healing relationships), remembrance and mourning (processing and reconstructing the traumatic memory so that it can be assimilated into the survivor's ongoing life narrative) and lastly reconnection and integration (with an emphasis on reintegrating back into ordinary life), although the stages do not necessarily progress in a true linear fashion. But on reflecting upon the challenges posed by the interactions between prison and masculinity, trauma and masculinity, and trauma and prison, it becomes apparent that this is a process that cannot unfold for incarcerated young men without overcoming significant barriers.

Safety and Stabilisation

While Miller and Najavits (2012) argue that the prison regime can provide the structure, stability and predictability needed to provide a safe space for trauma recovery, they also acknowledge that males often become less 'safe' upon incarceration. Furthermore, the pains of imprisonment have long been documented (Sykes 1958), and more recent research on the experiences of young men and boys in prison describe a climate of fear, mistrust, bullying and disempowerment that persists today (Cesaroni and Alvi 2010; Cox 2011; Gooch 2016; Vaswani 2015).

The aggression many youth display in custody and prison may actually be a reflection of impaired coping (Coid et al. 2003; Kolivoski and Shook 2016; Leigey and Hodge 2013; MacKenzie 1987). Young people differ in important ways from older adults that render them more vulnerable. Younger people are less able to cope with the stress of imprisonment and experience much higher levels of anxiety as a result of having been deprived of their families and social networks (Bala and Anand 2012; Schulman and Cauffman 2011). MacKenzie (1987) provides a number of theories regarding youth and prison adjustment. She argues that a young person's violence in prison is an impulsive reaction to stress and may be a sign of immature coping ability. This may also manifest not only in striking out at others but in self-harm; for example, unlike older prisoners—whose risk of self-harm or suicide risk is often related to psychiatric illnesses—young people's self-harm or suicide vulnerability can also be connected to their inability to cope with the custody environment itself (Liebling 1999).

Thus loss of power, control and safety are key features of prison life, yet Herman (1992, p. 159) advises that "the guiding principle of recovery is to restore power and control to the survivor." Herman also acknowledges that, as trauma destroys relationships, "recovery can take place only in the context of relationships; it cannot occur in isolation" (p. 133), and that the capacity for developing (or redeveloping) a sense of safety, trust, intimacy and autonomy is within these healing relationships. This is why social support is often found to be the critical success factor in recovery (Van Der Kolk 2014; Perry and Szalavitz 2017; Pettus-Davis 2014). However, males with trauma histories are less likely to have access to quality social support (Pettus-Davis 2014), and prison disconnects people from the social support networks they do have and places them in an environment where even positive relationships with staff and others are tinged with mistrust.

Remembrance and Mourning

This stage involves processing the trauma in one way or another, but has frequently been achieved through attaching words and meanings to emotions and reconstructing a story of trauma, as well as mourning the losses associated with trauma (Herman 1992). This is a challenging process for any traumatised individual, but is further complicated by certain displays and characteristics of traditional masculinity (i.e., stoicism, emotional restriction, alexithymia) which are intensified within the prison environment due to the need to put on a front, and to obtain and/or maintain status (Walsh 2020; Vaswani 2014; Cesaroni and Alvi 2010). In addition, the constraints of the prison environment limit the ability to provide safe and private therapeutic spaces for treatment interventions (Pitt and Thomson 2018; Vaswani and Paul 2019).

Reconnection and Reintegration

In the final phase of recovery, the focus is on the creation of a new sense of self and moving forward and reconnecting with ordinary life and activities. In much the same way as healing relationships are crucial for the two earlier stages of recovery, much of this development and growth needs to take place within the context of new and/or re-established relationships, a challenge for incarcerated individuals. This new self is also drawn from the aspects of the self that the individual valued from before the trauma, as well as from the experience of trauma itself, and from the recovery period. As Herman (1992) writes, "integrating all of these elements, [s]he creates a new self, both ideally and in actuality" (p. 202). Yet the loss of a 'future possible self' (Markus and Nurius 1986) is a real and pervasive loss for young men in prison, caused by a sense of overwhelming hopelessness as well as perceived and actual barriers to development and growth (Jewkes 2011; Vaswani 2015) imposed by the justice system. Thus the potential for rehabilitation, reintegration and trauma recovery are sharply inhibited.

Although a truly trauma-informed practice or milieu may not be possible within the custodial context, it remains that more can and should be done to alleviate the trauma symptoms of men in prison (Vaswani and Paul 2019), not least with prison care and management, human rights and public protection goals in mind. There are also implications for gender-sensitive trauma treatment and trauma-informed practice with males both within and outside of the prison. Understanding the obstacles that postures and attitudes associated with masculinity place on the presentation and assessment of trauma (Elder et al. 2017), and on an individual's ability to respond to trauma (Fox and Pease 2012; Wade et al. 2016), is essential. Exploring masculinity, and the legacy of gender-role socialisation, is likely to be beneficial as part of trauma treatment for men (Mejia 2005; Iwamoto et al. 2012; Fox and Pease 2012), as well as in the juvenile justice system more broadly (Abrams et al. 2008; Abrams and Anderson-Nathe 2013). Custodial institutions can make greater progress towards trauma-informed practice by focusing more strongly on organisational culture change, and support mechanisms for staff (such as training, supervision and self-care) as well as the wider physical environment and provision of appropriate therapeutic spaces (Vaswani and Paul 2019).

Discussion

Sloan (2018) argues that there are many reasons we fail to explicitly consider men's trauma in prison research, including their avoidance of vulnerabilities. Most of the work which has been done on incarcerated males, trauma and masculinity have been small-scale, qualitative studies. Though this exploratory research is important, more research needs to be conducted which speaks directly to men about their trauma, the prison setting and how they see masculinities in prison as potential conflicts with help-seeking. Moving forward it will be imperative that clinicians be sensitised to their own personal concept of masculinity, which may shape their approach to treatment and intervention (Chan 2014).

The importance of hope should not be neglected. While trauma, and prison, are so typically characterised by hopelessness, the potential for post-traumatic growth following recovery from trauma, or release from prison, should not be discounted. Just as trauma, or a period of incarceration, can disrupt a person's world view in a negative way, so too can it lead to new perspectives, insights or wisdom (Dierkhising et al. 2019; Fox and Pease 2012). Recovery from trauma, particularly that which explores masculinity as part of treatment, may also involve a redefining of traditional ideas about what it means to be a man. For young men in particular, there is still the opportunity for masculine biographies to be rewritten, and young men provided new mechanisms for expressions of vulnerability and masculinity (Abrams et al. 2008).

There is hope too in the fact that alternative masculinities, co-operation and compassion already exist among incarcerated men (Buston 2018; Laws and Lieber 2020), and can likely be emphasised and celebrated in order to open the window to recovery. As part of this a new understanding of masculinity in terms of a subtler strength that incorporates the agency behind emotional expression, therapeutic endurance, acceptance and help-seeking can be developed (Fox and Pease 2012). This can only have positive outcomes for recovery, rehabilitation, reintegration and desistance.

References

Abrams, L. S., & Anderson-Nathe, B. (2013). *Compassionate confinement. A year in the life of unit C*. London: Rutgers University Press.

Abrams, L. S., Anderson-Nathe, B., & Aguilar, J. (2008). Constructing masculinities in juvenile corrections. *Men and Masculinities, 11*, 22–41.

Abram, K. M., Teplin, L. A., King, D. C., Longworth, S. L, Emanuel, K. M., Romero, E. G., McClelland, G. M., Dulcan, M. K., Washburn, J. J., Welty, L. J., & Olson, N. D. (2013). PTSD, Trauma, and Comorbid Psychiatric Disorders in Detained Youth. *Juvenile Justice Bulletin*. OJJDP. https://ojjdp.ojp.gov/sites/g/files/xyckuh176/files/pubs/239603.pdf.

Addis, M. E., & Mahalik, J. R. (2003). Men, masculinity, and the contexts of help seeking. *American Psychologist, 58*, 5–14.

Akyüz, G., Kuğu, N., Şar, V., & Doğan, O. (2007). Trauma and dissociation among prisoners. *Nordic Journal of Psychiatry, 61*, 167–172.

American Psychiatric Association. (2013). *Diagnostic and statistical manual of mental disorders: DSM-5*. Arlington, VA: APA.

Anderson, E. (2009). *Inclusive masculinity: The changing nature of masculinities* (Paperback ed.). New York: Routledge. ISBN 9780415804622.

Bala, N., & Anand, S. (2012). *Youth criminal justice law*. Toronto: Irwin Law.

Barber, C. F. (2008). Domestic violence against men. *Nursing Standard, 22*, 35–40.

Briere, J., Agee, E., & Dietrich, A. (2016). Cumulative trauma and current posttraumatic stress disorder status in general population and inmate samples. *Psychological Trauma: Theory, Research, Practice, and Policy, 8*, 439–446.

Bronson, J., & Carson, E. A. (2019). Prisoners in 2017 (U.S. Department of Justice, Ed.). Washington, DC: Bureau of Justice Statistics.

Brown, G., & Grant, P. (2018). Hear our voices: We're more than the hyper-masculine label—Reasonings of black men participating in faith-based prison programme. In M. Maycock & K. Hunt (Eds.), *New perspectives on prison masculinities* (pp. 91–121). Cham: Palgrave Macmillan.

Burrell, S. (2013). *Trauma and the environment of care in juvenile institutions*. Los Angeles, CA and Durham, NC: National Center for Child Traumatic Stress.

Buston, K. (2018). Inside the prison parenting classroom: Caring, sharing and the softer side of masculinity. In M. Maycock & K. Hunt (Eds.), *New perspectives on prison masculinities* (Palgrave Studies in Prisons and Penology). Palgrave Macmillan.

Carrabine, E., & Longhurst, B. (1998). Gender and prison organisation: Some comments on masculinities and prison management. *The Howard Journal of Criminal Justice, 37*, 161–176.

Cassidy, T., & Bruce, S. (2019). Dealing with death in custody: Psychosocial consequences for correctional staff. *Journal of Correctional Health Care, 25*(4), 304–312.

Cesaroni, C., & Alvi, S. (2010). Masculinity and resistance in adolescent carceral settings. *Canadian Journal of Criminology and Criminal Justice, 52*, 303–320.

Cesaroni, C., & Peterson-Badali, M. (2005). Young offenders in custody: Risk and adjustment. *Criminal Justice and Behavior, 32*, 251–277.

Cesaroni, C., & Peterson-Badali, M. (2010). Understanding the adjustment of incarcerated young offenders: A Canadian example. *Youth Justice, 10*, 107–125.

Cesaroni, C., & Peterson-Badali, M. (2016). The role of fairness in the adjustment of adolescent boys to pretrial detention. *The Prison Journal, 96*, 534–553.

Chan, S. T. (2014). The lens of masculinity: Trauma in men and the landscapes of sexual abuse survivors. *Journal of Ethnic and Cultural Diversity in Social Work, 23*, 239–255.

Chesney-Lind, M., & Paramore, V. V. (2001). Are girls getting more violent? Exploring juvenile robbery trends. *Journal of Contemporary Criminal Justice, 17*, 142–166.

Cloitre, M., Stolbach, B. C., Herman, J. L., Kolk, B. V. D., Pynoos, R., Wang, J., & Petkova, E. (2009). A developmental approach to complex PTSD: Childhood and adult cumulative trauma as predictors of symptom complexity. *Journal of Traumatic Stress, 22*, 399–408.

Coid, J., Petruckevitch, A., Bebbington, B., Jenkins, R., Brugha, T., Lewis, G., Farrell, M., & Singleton, N. (2003). Psychiatric morbidity in prisoners and solitary confinement: Disciplinary segregation. *The Journal of Forensic Psychiatric and Psychology, 14*, 298–319.

Connell, R. W. (1995). *Masculinities*. Cambridge, UK: Polity Press.

Connell, R. W. (2002). On hegemonic masculinity and violence. *Theoretical Criminology, 61*, 89–99.

Cox, A. (2011). Doing the programme or doing me? The pains of youth imprisonment. *Punishment and Society, 13*(5), 592–610.

Cox, A. (2018). *Trapped in a vice: The consequences of confinement for young people*. Rutgers University.

Criado-Perez, C. (2019). *Invisible women: Exposing data bias in a world designed for men*. London: Chatto & Windus.

Curtis, A. (2014). 'You have to cut it off at the knee': Dangerous masculinity and security inside a men's prison. *Men and Masculinities, 17*, 120–146.

Daquin, J. C., Daigle, L. E., & Listwan, S. J. (2016). Vicarious victimization in prison: Examining the effects of witnessing victimization while incarcerated on offender reentry. *Criminal Justice and Behavior, 43*, 1018–1033.

De Viggiani, N. (2018). 'Don't mess with me!' Enacting masculinities under a compulsory prison regime. In M. Maycock & K. Hunt (Eds.), *New perspectives on prison masculinities* (pp. 91–121). Cham: Palgrave Macmillan.

Dierkhising, C. B., Sanchez, J. A., & Gutierrez, L. (2019). "It changed my life": Traumatic loss, behavioral health, and turning points among gang-involved and justice-involved youth. *Journal of Interpersonal Violence*. Advance online publication.

Elder, W. B., Domino, J. L., Mata-Galán, E. L., & Kilmartin, C. (2017). Masculinity as an avoidance symptom of posttraumatic stress. *Psychology of Men & Masculinity, 18*, 198–207.

Ellis, A., Winlow, S., & Hall, S. (2017). 'Throughout my life I've had people walk all over me': Trauma in the lives of violent men. *The Sociological Review, 65*, 699–713.

Evans, T., & Wallace, P. (2008). A Prison within a Prison?: The Masculinity Narratives of Male Prisoners. *Men and Masculinities, 10*(4), 484–507.

Fox, J., & Pease, B. (2012). Military deployment, masculinity and trauma: Reviewing the connections. *The Journal of Men's Studies, 20*, 16–31.

Goffman, E. (1961). *Asylums: Essays on the social situation of mental patients and other inmates*. New York: Anchor Books.

Gooch, K. (2016). A childhood cut short: Child deaths in penal custody and the pains of child imprisonment. *The Howard Journal of Crime and Justice, 55*, 278–294.

Gooch, K. (2019). 'Kidulthood': Ethnography, juvenile prison violence and the transition from 'boys' to 'men'. *Criminology & Criminal Justice, 19*, 80–97.

Greenfeld, l. A., & Snell, T. L. (1999). Women Offenders. *Bureau of Justice Statistics Special Report*. https://www.bjs.gov/content/pub/pdf/wo.pdf.

Griffin, G., Germain, E. J., & Wilkerson, R. G. (2012). Using a trauma-informed approach in juvenile justice institutions. *Journal of Child & Adolescent Trauma, 5*, 271–283.

Hales, H., Davison, S., Misch, P., & Taylor, P. J. (2003). Young male prisoners in a Young Offenders' Institution: Their contact with suicidal behaviour by others. *Journal of Adolescence, 26*, 667–685.

Herman, J. L. (1992). *Trauma and recovery*. New York: Basic Books.

Honorato, B., Caltabiano, N., & Clough, A. R. (2016). From trauma to incarceration: Exploring the trajectory in a qualitative study in male prison inmates from north Queensland, Australia. *Health & Justice, 4*, 1–10.

Iwamoto, D. K., Gordon, D. M., Oliveros, A., Perez-Cabello, M. A., Brabham, T., Lanza, A. S., & Dyson, W. (2012). The role of masculine norms and informal support on mental health in incarcerated men. *Psychology of Men & Masculinity, 13*, 283–293.

Jewkes, Y. (2011). Loss, liminality and the life sentence: Managing identity through a disrupted lifecourse. In A. Liebling & S. Maruna (Eds.), *The effects of imprisonment*. Oxon: Routledge.

Jewkes, Y. (2018). Just design: Healthy prisons and the architecture of hope. *Australian & New Zealand Journal of Criminology, 51*, 319–338.

Kimmel, M. (1994). Masculinity as homophobia. In H. Brod & M. Cauffman (Eds.), *Theorising masculinity* (pp. 119–141). Thousand Oaks, CA: Sage.

Kolivoski, K. M., & Shook, J. J. (2016). Incarcerating juveniles in adult prisons. *Criminal Justice and Behaviour, 43*, 1242–1259.

Laws, B., & Lieber, E. (2020). 'King, Warrior, Magician, Lover': Understanding expressions of care among male prisoners. *European Journal of Criminology*. https://journals.sagepub.com/doi/abs/10.1177/1477370819896207

Leigey, M. E., & Hodge, J. P. (2013). And then they behaved: Examining the institutional misconduct of adult inmates who were incarcerated as Juveniles. *The Prison Journal, 93*, 272–290.

Leonard, J. (2003). The hidden victims of domestic violence. *Victimology, 7*, 1–22.

Liebling, A. (1999). Prison suicide and prison coping. In M. Tonry & J. Petersilia (Eds.), *Prisons* (pp. 283–360). Chicago: University of Chicago Press.

Lutze, F. E., & Murphy, D. W. (1999). Ultramasculine prison environments and inmates' adjustment: It's time to move beyond the "boys will be boys" paradigm. *Justice Quarterly, 16*(4), 709–733.

MacKenzie, D. L. (1987). Age and adjustment in prison: Interactions with attitudes and anxiety. *Criminal Justice and Behaviour, 14*, 427–447.

Markus, H., & Nurius, P. (1986). Possible selves. *American Psychologist, 41*, 954–969.

Martin, M. S., Eljdupovic, G., Mckenzie, K., & Colman, I. (2015). Risk of violence by inmates with childhood trauma and mental health needs. *Law and Human Behavior, 39*, 614–623.

Maycock, M. (2018a). Introduction. In M. Maycock & K. Hunt (Eds.), *New perspectives on prison masculinities* (Palgrave Studies in Prisons and Penology). Palgrave Macmillan.

Maycock, M. (2018b). "They're all up in the gym and all that, tops off, fake tan". Embodied masculinities, bodywork and resistance within two British prisons. In M. Maycock & K. Hunt (Eds.), *New perspectives on prison masculinities* (Palgrave Studies in Prisons and Penology). Palgrave Macmillan.

McCormack, M. (2012). *The declining significance of homophobia how teenage boys are redefining masculinity and heterosexuality*. Oxford: Oxford University Press.

McNess, A. (2008). Happy to Talk…To a Point: Bereaved Young Men and Emotional Disclosure. *Youth Studies Australia, 27*(4), 25–34.

McMackin, R. A., Leisen, M. B., Sattler, L., Krinsley, K., & Riggs, D. S. (2002). Preliminary development of trauma-focused treatment groups for incarcerated juvenile offenders. In R. Greenwald (Ed.), *Trauma and juvenile delinquency: Theory, research, and interventions* (pp. 175–199). Binghamton, NY: Haworth Maltreatment and Trauma Press.

Mejia, X. E. (2005). Gender matters: Working with adult male survivors of trauma. *Journal of Counseling & Development, 83*, 29–40.

Miller, N. A., & Najavits, L. M. (2012). Creating trauma-informed correctional care: A balance of goals and environment. *European Journal of Psychotraumatology, 3*.

Ministry of Justice. (2019). *Population bulletin: Weekly 6 September 2019*. London: Ministry of Justice.

Moore, E., Gaskin, C., & Indig, D. (2013). Childhood maltreatment and post-traumatic stress disorder among incarcerated young offenders. *Child Abuse & Neglect, 37*, 861–870.

Morrison, J. A. (2012). Masculinity moderates the relationship between symptoms of PTSD and cardiac-related health behaviors in male veterans. *Psychology of Men & Masculinity, 13*, 158–165.

Morse, S. J., & Wright, K. A. (2019). Imprisoned men: Masculinity variability and implications for correctional programming. *Corrections*, 1–23. https://www.tandfonline.com/doi/full/10.1080/23774657.2019.1694854

O'Brien, R., Hart, K., & Hunt, G. (2005). 'It's caveman stuff, but that is to a certain extent how some guys operate': Men's accounts of masculinity and help seeking. *Social Science and Medicine, 61*, 503–516.

Perry, B. D., & Szalavitz, M. (2017). *The boy who was raised as a dog: And other stories from a child psychiatrist's notebook. What traumatized children can teach us about loss, love, and healing*. New York: Basic Books.

Pettus-Davis, C. (2014). Social support among releasing men prisoners with lifetime trauma experiences. *International Journal of Law and Psychiatry, 37*, 512–523.

Pitt, D., & Thomson, L. (2018). The evolution of change. Factors involved in the design and delivery of a therapeutic service within the confines of a custodial setting. In S. Read, S. Santatzoglou, & A. Wrigley (Eds.), *Loss, dying and bereavement in the criminal justice system*. Abingdon: Routledge.

Ricciardelli, R., Maier, K., & Hannah-Moffat, K. (2015). Strategic masculinities: Vulnerabilities, risk and the production of prison masculinities. *Theoretical Criminology, 19*, 491–513.

Rosenfield, P. J., Stratyner, A., Tufekcioglu, S., Karabell, S., Mckelvey, J., & Litt, L. (2018). Complex PTSD in ICD-11: A case report on a new diagnosis. *Journal of Psychiatric Practice®, 24*, 364–370.

Ruck, S., Bowes, N., & Tehrani, N. (2013). Evaluating trauma debriefing within the UK prison service. *Journal of Forensic Practice, 15*(4), 281–290.

Sabo, D. F., Kupers, T. A., & London, W. J. (2001). *Prison masculinities*. Temple University Press.

Schulman, E. P., & Cauffman, E. (2011). Coping while incarcerated: A study of male juvenile offenders. *Journal of Research on Adolescence, 21*, 818–826.

Schwartz, J. (2013). A "new" female offender or increasing social control of women's behaviour? Cross-national evidence. *Feminist Studies, 39*, 790–821.

Scottish Prison Service. (2018). *Annual report and accounts 2017–2018*. Edinburgh: SPS.

Shepherd, S., Spivak, B., Borschmann, R., Kinner, S. A., & Hachtel, H. (2018). Correlates of self-harm and suicide attempts in justice-involved young people. *PLoS ONE, 13*, e0193172.

Shields, D. M. (2016). Military masculinity, movies, and the DSM: Narratives of institutionally (en) gendered trauma. *Psychology of Men & Masculinity, 17*, 64–73.

Sim, J. (1994). Tougher than the rest? Men in prison. In T. Newburn & E. Stanko (Eds.), *Just boys doing business? Men, masculinities and crime*. London: Routledge.

Sloan, J. (2018). Saying the unsayable: Foregrounding men in the prison system. In M. Maycock & K. Hunt (Eds.), *New perspectives on prison masculinities*. London: Palgrave Macmillan.

Snow, P. C., Woodward, M., Mathis, M., & Powell, M. B. (2016). Language functioning, mental health and alexithymia in incarcerated young offenders. *International Journal of Speech-Language Pathology, 18*, 20–31.

Steinberg, L. D. (1999). *Adolescence*. Michigan: McGraw-Hill College.

Sykes, G. M. (1958). *The society of captives: A study of a maximum security prison*. Princeton, NJ: Princeton University Press.

Toch, H. (1998). Hypermasculinity and prison violence. In L. H. Bowker (Ed.), *Masculinities and violence* (pp. 168–178). Sage Publications, Inc.

Van Der Kolk, B. (2014). *The body keeps the score: Mind, brain and body in the transformation of trauma*. Penguin UK.

Vaswani, N. (2014). The ripples of death: Exploring the bereavement experiences and mental health of young men in custody. *The Howard Journal of Criminal Justice, 53*, 341–359.

Vaswani, N. (2015). A catalogue of losses: Implications for the care and reintegration of young men in custody. *Prison Service Journal, 220*, 26–35.

Vaswani, N., & Paul, S. (2019). 'It's knowing the right things to say and do': Challenges and opportunities for trauma-informed practice in the prison context. *The Howard Journal of Crime and Justice*. Advance online publication.

Wade, D., Varker, T., Kartal, D., Hetrick, S., O'donnell, M., & Forbes, D. (2016). Gender difference in outcomes following trauma-focused interventions for post-traumatic stress disorder: Systematic review and meta-analysis. *Psychological Trauma, 8*, 356–364.

Walsh, C. (2020). The utility of a psycho-social approach for understanding and addressing male youth violence: The interface between traumatic experiences and masculinity. *Journal of Aggression, Maltreatment & Trauma, 29*(2), 186–205.

Welfare, H. R., & Hollin, C. R. (2015). Childhood and offense-related trauma in young people imprisoned in England and Wales for murder and other acts of serious violence: A descriptive study. *Journal of Aggression, Maltreatment & Trauma, 24*, 955–969.

Part V

Coming Home: Life After Youth Imprisonment

Walking Dark Streets …

Walking in the dark streets with my two brothers wondering if any of my brothers' enemies will pass by and blast us. Who knows. I was just a 12-year-old girl walking her brothers. As one year pass by, I turn 13 then I'm the one on the street with my homies. Now, it's me walking looking out for enemies.

Now that I think of it, I should have never followed my brothers, sister, aunt, uncle, and dad's footsteps. I ask myself "why?" Is it because I was always around that when I was a baby? Is it because I saw my brother get shot 15 times when I was 5 years old? I don't know. I still ask myself that question the more I try to get out of it and stay away from it. I can't. I'm always surrounded by it. Now I'm here in Juvenile Hall. Where is my family? And siblings?

I wonder when I get out, will I keep talking the dark streets or will I keep doing what I always do. I don't know. I'm trying to do good. I don't want my baby brother to follow my steps.

February 22, 2020
Central Juvenile Hall, Los Angeles, CA, USA

18

The Expectations and Challenges of Youth Reentry

Elizabeth Panuccio

Introduction

The number of youth confined in correctional facilities in the US has declined by over 60 percent since the year 2000, but there are still over 43,500 youth in residential placement each day (Puzzanchera and Hockenberry 2019). Two-thirds of them are held in the most restrictive facilities, two-thirds are held for over a month, and nearly one in ten are held in adult jails or prisons (Sawyer 2019). Furthermore, despite the overall decline in juvenile incarceration, youth of color continue to be overrepresented in correctional facilities. While 14 percent of youth under the age of 18 in the US are Black, 39 percent of committed youth and 45 percent of detained youth in juvenile facilities are Black (Puzzanchera and Hockenberry 2019).

While estimates vary, nearly 200,000 of individuals released each year from juvenile and adult correctional facilities are under the age of 24 (Mears and Travis 2004). Young people returning to the community from custody during young adulthood face a unique set of challenges as they transition not only

---

Sections of this chapter were drawn from the previously published article: Panuccio, E., & Christian, J. (2019). Work, family, and masculine identity: An intersectional approach to understanding young, Black men's experiences of reentry. *Race and Justice*, 9(4), 407–433.

E. Panuccio (✉)
Department of Criminology & Criminal Justice, Fairleigh Dickinson University, Teaneck, NJ, USA
e-mail: elizpanu@fdu.edu

from custody to the community, but from adolescence to adulthood. Evidence suggests that young people have a difficult time desisting from crime after release from residential correctional programs. Studies tracking youth released from juvenile correctional facilities have consistently reported high recidivism rates (Mendel 2011). State estimates indicate that rearrest rates for youth within one year of release average 55 percent and reincarceration rates average 24 percent (Snyder and Sickmund 2006). Within two to three years 70–80 percent of youth are rearrested, and 26–62 percent are reincarcerated on new charges within three years (Mendel 2011).

Young people who have been incarcerated are at an increased risk of both adult criminality and incarceration (Gatti et al. 2009), which may result in part from the numerous obstacles young people face after spending time in a secure confinement facility. The majority have few options but to return to the homes they resided in prior to their incarceration (Altschuler and Brash 2004; Todis et al. 2001), but they often come from families of limited economic resources and a multitude of other problems, including mental health problems, substance abuse, histories of physical or sexual abuse, parental incarceration, and the involvement of child protective services (Snyder 2004; Teplin et al. 2013; Uggen and Wakefield 2005), all of which may limit the availability of support to returning youth. Through a qualitative study of the experiences of African American males between the ages of 19 and 25, this chapter will explore some of the challenges of reentry during young adulthood.

Literature Review

Challenges of Youth Reentry

Between the ages of 18 and 25, young people are in a unique developmental phase as they are no longer adolescents but not quite adults—they are living in the context of an "emerging adulthood" (Arnett 2000). Young people reentering their families and communities after a period of secure confinement undergo a dual transition from prison to community and adolescence to adulthood (Altschuler and Brash 2004; Fader 2013). Even for youth who have not been incarcerated, the transition to adulthood is arguably more complex. In the twenty-first century, young people take longer to reach the traditional markers of adulthood such as finishing school, moving out of their parents' home, starting a career, and getting married (Furstenberg, Rumbaut, and Settersten 2005). Emerging adults are relying increasingly on their families for continued financial support, and socially, economically, and racially disadvantaged youth are not afforded the same safety nets as their more affluent peers (Roy and Jones 2014). They may be additionally subjected to police surveillance and other forms of criminal justice control such as probation or parole (Rios 2011). Young people in disadvantaged communities, and those in foster care and the juvenile justice system, may lose most of their support at the age of 18, especially since transitional services from the youth custodial context to the community are limited (Furstenberg et al. 2005; Osgood et al. 2005).

There are many other obstacles during the reentry process that complicate the transition to adulthood. Many youth return to their communities with drug and alcohol problems that were untreated during incarceration (Altschuler and Brash 2004; Snyder 2004; Uggen and Wakefield 2005), many suffer from mental illnesses (Mears 2001; Snyder 2004; Steinberg et al. 2004; Uggen and Wakefield 2005), and many have learning disabilities and low educational attainment (Altschuler and Brash 2004; Sedlak and McPherson 2010; Snyder 2004). In Bosick and Gover's (2010) study of at-risk males at the age of 25 who had previously been incarcerated, the majority of their participants were fathers and spent significant time behind bars away from their children, less than a quarter graduated from high school, none went on to college, and few had achieved stable employment by the age of 25. Their study demonstrates the cumulative disadvantage experienced by young incarcerated males. In Abrams and Terry's (2017) study of desistance during emerging adulthood, many participants experienced marginalization and instability due to limited work and educational histories and ongoing discrimination after release from incarceration. Some even retreated from the work force due to self-perceptions that they would not fit in.

Formerly incarcerated individuals rank securing employment as one of their primary objectives (Fader 2013; Travis et al. 2014; Western 2002, 2006), yet they face substantial barriers in doing so (Abrams and Terry 2017; Arditti and Parkman 2011; Crutchfield 2014). Even employers who express a willingness to hire people with criminal records do not necessarily hire them (Pager and Quillian 2005), and studies demonstrate that Black and Latinx people are particularly disadvantaged when seeking jobs, irrespective of prior involvement with the justice system (Pager 2008). Hence, formerly incarcerated young Black men pursue jobs in the face of constricted opportunities, while they may be distinctly compelled to find work because of their family's precarious economic circumstances (Burton 2007; Roy et al. 2014). Following a conviction, the poor prospects for stable employment and the decline in earnings perhaps create even more pressure, as young men achieve legal adulthood and a greater expectation to support their families (Abrams and Terry 2017; Arditti and Parkman 2011). In the absence of well-paid employment opportunities, hustling may become a viable option, leading some to increasingly criminal activities over time (Fader 2013; Rios 2011). In their study of emerging adults, Salvatore and Taniguchi (2012) reported a correlation between economic instability and levels of offending, and Abrams and Tam (2018) similarly found that some emerging adults remained engaged in crime after release from incarceration due to economic constraints.

Social Bonds and Family Support

Faced with decreased support from the government and blocked opportunities in the labor market, social support may be especially important during reentry to motivate success in the absence of a wide array of services (Simon 1993). Studies of adult prisoners indicate that support from family members post-release is vital to their successful reintegration (Bahr et al. 2010; Herman-Stahl et al. 2008; La Vigne et al. 2004; Martinez and Christian 2009; Nelson et al. 1999; Naser and Visher 2006; Sullivan et al. 2002). In the *Returning Home Study* (Naser and Visher 2006); 80 percent of respondents interviewed after release from prison identified family as an important factor in staying out of prison. Most families provide some type of instrumental support, which includes tangible resources such as a place to live, transportation, and financial assistance (Cullen 1994; Naser and Visher 2006; Nelson et al. 1999). Expressive support, involving acceptance and encouragement, has also been linked with positive post-release outcomes (Nelson et al. 1999; Sullivan et al. 2002).

Research on young people who have spent time in custody and who are reentering the community is not as abundant, but affirms that family support is equally important. A study examining desistance among formerly incarcerated youth found that active family involvement and communication was a factor leading to the discontinuation of illegal activity (Todis et al. 2001). Many juvenile delinquency studies have illuminated the significance of social bonds to the desistance process (see Eggleston 2006; Gilmore et al. 2005). Born et al. (1997) found that stable relationships and a decrease in family and personal problems are associated with resiliency and subsequent desistance from crime among young people. These studies highlight the importance of post-release support in the desistance process.

Sampson and Laub's (1993) life-course theory considers the role of social bonds in crime prevention across the life course, and they argue that the formation of strong social attachments, such as getting married or becoming a parent, fosters desistance from crime. Unlike other life-course theories, Sampson and Laub (1993) emphasize the *quality* and *strength* of social attachments more than their occurrence or their timing. Berg and Huebner's (2011) examination of the link between social ties and recidivism supports this notion. The authors found that the quality of social ties was important in the post-release process. Giordano et al. (2002) argue that social ties can be a "hook" for change that helps offenders to desist from crime. Although they believe that individuals must first develop an openness to change, social support can motivate them towards desistance. Similarly, Panuccio et al. (2012) argue that motivation is essential to the desistance process, but that informal support can both trigger and sustain motivation in youth who return from incarceration.

A study of young people who engaged in offending found that a shift in attitude along with life-changing events, such as parenthood, marriage, and employment, led to a termination of offending (Council on Crime and Justice 2006). Abrams and Tam's (2018) research on desistance among formerly incarcerated emerging adults suggests that romantic bonds in particular encourage a shift in attitude and promote desistance. For all of the young men in their study who were in committed romantic partnerships, their partners motivated and encouraged them to avoid crime and remain positive. Interestingly, the same did not hold true for the young women in their study, who experienced instability in their romantic partnerships.

In addition to romantic bonds, parenthood might also encourage desistance. Todis et al. (2001) found that becoming a parent had a positive impact on formerly incarcerated young men. Fatherhood motivated some of the males to remain drug-free, employed, and out of trouble. Curtis and Schulman (1984) found that men who lived with their wives and children after release from prison experienced more success than those who lived alone or with parents. Hairston's (1988, 1991) research similarly demonstrated that men who took on husband and parenting roles after release from incarceration had higher rates of success than those who did not step into these roles. In Nurse's (2002, 2004) study of newly paroled young fathers in California, incarceration heightened the participants' desire to be involved in their children's lives after release. Although many of them faced obstacles in reclaiming the "father role" for the children they left behind, their thoughts about their children while they were incarcerated reveal a significant source of motivation for change. Edin et al.'s (2004) research on fathers revealed that for some men, incarceration presented an opportunity to rebuild ties with children, providing a powerful motivation to transform their lives. In addition, they found that fear of incarceration, combined with becoming a father, can deter criminal activity. The extent to which this is true for younger men, however, remains unclear. Some researchers have found that even though some young men are initially motivated by their children, some relapse into crime and reincarceration as a result of blocked job opportunities and disadvantage (Berger and Langton 2011; Smeeding et al. 2011; Tach and Edin 2011).

While many life-course studies emphasize the importance of marriage and parenthood to the desistance process, the role that their own parents play in desistance is often overlooked as youth transition to adulthood. Schroeder, Giordano, and Cernkovich (2010) argue that individuals' relationships with their parents continue to evolve as they enter adulthood, and an examination of how these relationships promote or inhibit criminal behavior is warranted. Using data from the Ohio Life Course Study, they found that strong relationships with parents are a significant predictor of adult desistance and an even stronger predictor of desistance for those with poor romantic bonds. Similarly, a study of formerly incarcerated men and women found that men and women with quality parental relationships had a delayed time to recidivism (Cobbina et al. 2012). In an analysis of data from the Toledo Adolescent Relationships Study, researchers examined the influence of early and late parenting factors such as support, monitoring, and conflict on the offending patterns of participants who were interviewed first as adolescents and later as young adults (Johnson et al. 2011). They found that monitoring during adolescence and continued parental support are associated with lower rates of offending during young adulthood. Clearly, strong relationships with parents have the potential to influence post-release outcomes.

The Study

A qualitative study was conducted to explore the challenges of reentry from incarceration during emerging adulthood. The study was guided by a grounded theory approach with the intent of generating theory based on the experiences and views of participants who have all been through a similar process (Creswell 2007; Strauss and Corbin 1998). Many recidivism studies utilize quantitative data, which does not fully capture the social processes involved in reentry. Qualitative methods are arguably best suited for the purpose of gaining a deeper understanding about the way things are and why (Gay and Airasian 2000).

Sample Recruitment

The sample was generated in several ways. At the outset of the study, a social worker I had worked with previously suggested that I speak with a former client, Antoine, who had recently been released from a five-year prison term. Antoine agreed to participate in a pilot interview to help refine research questions. After the interview, Antoine was hired as a research assistant to help recruit participants. Antoine provided access to the study population, enabled me to establish trust with participants, and gain a deeper understanding of the population being examined, all of which have been cited as advantages to establishing a relationship with members of the community (Fader 2013). We began by contacting some of the people Antoine knew from the neighborhood where he was raised. We also reached out to individuals that Antoine knew from prison and people he knew from his place of employment. Finally, a snowball sampling method was utilized to identify potential participants by asking subjects to recommend friends and acquaintances.

The sample of 31 participants, included 17 formerly incarcerated young adults released between the ages of 19 and 25 and 14 of their family members. The sample included ten family dyads and an additional five young adults for whom family member interviews could not be completed. The sample also included an extended case study with six additional family members beyond the primary dyad—two of whom were also formerly incarcerated young adults. Participants were recruited throughout Middlesex County, New Jersey, with the majority residing in New Brunswick. The inclusion of family members in the sample allowed for an analysis of how individuals' circumstances are intertwined with those of their family members, but also strengthened the validity of the participants' reflections on their life histories. While the sample size is small, it is sufficient for a grounded theory approach which involves sampling toward theory construction, not population representativeness (Charmaz 2006).

The inclusion criteria for participants in this study were that they had been incarcerated and were released between the ages of 18 and 25 (although the youngest participant was 19 at the time of release) and they had been back in the community for a minimum of one month. Incarceration was defined as a period of confinement in a juvenile or adult secure correctional facility. All participants were African American males from high-poverty communities in an urban area.

While the results of this study are not generalizable to the population of young adults released from incarceration, they do have important implications for young, urban African American males who reside in communities that experience high rates of poverty, crime, and incarceration. The participants ranged in age from 19 to 25 years when they were released from incarceration. Length of the most recent incarceration ranged from one month to four-and-a-half years. Participants had been in the community from a range of one month to five years. Half of the sample members were gang affiliated. Eleven of them had prior convictions, but all of them had previous involvement in crime prior to the most recent committing offense. Eight of them had prior incarcerations. Four participants had charges pending at the time of their interviews. Of the family members interviewed, six are significant partners, five are cousins, one is a brother, one is a mother, and one is a father. See Table 18.1 for detailed information about the participants.

Limitations of the sample include wide variation in both length of time incarcerated and time at risk. Another limitation is the variation in type of confinement facility participants were released from, which included juvenile detention centers, county jails, and adult prisons. Facility type undoubtedly has implications for the conditions of confinement as well as the availability of services and programs, all of which have the potential to influence the post-release transition. These types of variations, however, provide access to a broad range of experiences and allow for a closer examination of the impact of incarceration length, time at risk, and facility type on post-release experiences. An in-depth analysis of these factors is not included in the current chapter, where the focus is on challenges of reentry for emerging adults.

Data Collection

Data collection occurred from January 2012 through March 2013. In-depth interviews were conducted with participants, primarily in their homes, lasting approximately an hour to an hour-and-a-half. Interviews occurred at least one month after participants were released from incarceration. Research on post-incarceration experiences has shown that the first month out is a difficult time but also a time of opportunity, as returning prisoners try to reestablish family ties, find employment, and remain drug and crime free (Nelson et al. 1999). The first month out was a sufficient length of time for participants to discuss the challenges and opportunities they faced early on in their post-release transitions. Participants were asked to discuss the immediate challenges they faced upon returning to the community and the challenges they continued to face as time went on. They were also asked about the nature of their family relationships and sources of support. The questions allowed for an exploration

18 The Expectations and Challenges of Youth Reentry

Table 18.1 Descriptive characteristics of participants

Family	Young adult name	Age	Incarceration length	Committing offense	Prior convictions	Total No. of lockups	Gang member	Time at risk	Family member name	Relation to young adult	Criminal history
1	Antoine	24	4.5 years	Drug distribution	Y	2	Y	1 mo	Keisha	Girlfriend	N
	Andrew	23	4 months	VOP; Theft	Y	1	N	7 mos	Divine	Mother	Y
									Sam	Cousin	Y
	Dustin	20	3 months	Possession of CDS	Y	1	N	1 yr	Divine	Mother	Y
									Divine	Mother	Y
2	Clyde	24	18 months	Conspiracy to attempted murder; weapon possession	Y	Numerous—exact number not known	Y	1 mo	Miles	Father	Y
									Chantal	Girlfriend	Y
									Moesha	Girlfriend	Y
3	Mitchell	21	3 years	Robbery	Y	3	Y	19 mos	Ailee	Girlfriend	N
4	Ty	22	10 months	Robbery	Y	2	Y	3 yrs	Shemar	Cousin	Y
5	Terrance	23	1 year	Weapon possession	N	1	N	1 yr	Lateisha	Fiancé	N
6	Lamont	24	2 years	Home invasion	Y	3	Y	1 mo			
7	Darnell	23	5 months	Drug distribution	N	1	N	3 mos			
8	Davay	25	6 months	Possession of CDS	N	1	N	7 mos			
9	Kevin	25	3 years	Robbery	Y	1	Y	2 yrs	Marcus	Cousin	Y
10	Trey	19	7 mos	Robbery	Y	2	N	1 mo			

(continued)

Table 18.1 (continued)

Family	Young adult name	Age	Incarceration length	Committing offense	Prior convictions	Total No. of lockups	Gang member	Time at risk	Family member name	Relation to young adult	Criminal history
11	Seth	23	3 months	Possession of CDS	N	1	N	9 mos			
12	Allaquan	25	1 year	Possession of CDS	N	1	N	1 yr	Chester	Cousin	Y
13	Randall	25	1 month	Drug distribution	N	1	Y	4 mos	Darius	Brother	Y
14	Ernest	24	2 years	Robbery; possession of CDS	Y	5	Y	5 yrs	Latoya	Girlfriend	N
15	Eddie	22	7.5 months	VOP	Y	6	Y	2 mos	Alwan	Cousin	Y

Y = yes; N = no
VOP = violation of parole/probation

into the nature of relationships and support systems, employment, and desistance.

Data Analysis

Data analysis occurred simultaneously with data collection. Early data analysis involved reading through transcribed interviews and writing theoretical notes about preliminary findings. Many emerging themes were identified through this type of preliminary analysis, allowing us to examine them more closely in subsequent interviews. Interviews were transcribed verbatim and uploaded into the software program NVivo, which can be a useful tool for storing, organizing, and analyzing qualitative data. Interviews were initially coded using an open coding approach, which involves identifying and labeling phenomena found in the text (Corbin and Strauss 2014). In relation to their reentry challenges, for example, initial coding included an identification of social factors such as *family expectations* and *family support*. Further coding exercises, using an axial and selective approach, involved an identification of more specific codes in relation to the broader concepts (Glaser and Strauss 1967; Strauss and Corbin 1990). For example, within the core category of *family expectations*, the impact of *parenthood* was a theme underlying the challenges associated with adult roles.

Through this process, I was able to draw connections between the broad categories that emerged early on, such as *family expectations*, and the specific ways that the young men's lives were impacted by these as they navigated the reentry process. It became clear, for example, that as they near adulthood, young men experience heightened expectations to fulfill family obligations at the same time that they are experiencing blocked opportunities, making it difficult for them to achieve their conceptions of manhood. The narratives presented in the sections that follow provide an in-depth look at the challenges of reentry for young men as they transition to adulthood.

Findings

Employment

The biggest obstacle faced by the study participants when they returned home was finding and maintaining a steady job with decent wages. Even though some participants ultimately found steady work, all of them experienced frustration at some point over their ability to secure employment. Lamont described the difficulties he faced in securing employment and the devastating impact this had on his outlook:

> To me, I'm getting older. When I was 19, I felt like I still had a chance. I never had to deal with anything like this. I was able to get a job anywhere. When I caught that adult charge, everything is real serious. I got a job out on Route 1. I was supposed to start on a Monday, but I got a background check showing the drug charge that I came home on. I was so happy that I got that job. Do you know how bad that really crushed me? When you catch an adult charge that changes everything.

Like Lamont, when Terrance was unable to find a job, his fiancé Lateisha could see a change in his mood. She described how frustrating the process was for him:

> I think in the beginning it was so hard for him because he was having a hard time finding a job. I think that would stress him out because everybody wants to carry their own weight and I guess he felt like he wasn't carrying his own weight at that time, so he was really stressed out. And you know, taking care of his self, having his own money, he don't have to ask nobody else for money… I can pick up on stuff like that because I lived in a house with guys, like, with my dad and my brother, so I know. Plus, I can see when he goes to an interview and then he didn't get good feedback from it, I could tell his mood will change. Filling applications day after day, like three applications a day, and not getting no phone call, I can see that he was getting really frustrated. Like, he was just trying his hardest to find a job and it was like it was not going good for him at that time. So, it really affected his mood where it was obvious. Like, it was obvious that was hurting him.

Part of Terrance's frustration stemmed from his inability to contribute in a way that he perceives a man is supposed to contribute, suggesting that having a job is a major step toward becoming an adult.

Interviews illuminated how truly important employment is to the desistance process for young adults (see Sampson and Laub 1993; Tripodi et al. 2010). Kevin, Davay, and Eddie all discussed their ongoing criminal activity after their release when they were unable to earn a legitimate salary. After he was released from his most recent sentence, Kevin was hopeful about his future when he earned a degree in medical coding and billing and completed an internship. When he was unable to find a job, however, he fell into despair and gravitated toward the streets.

> Right there I got off my positive side. I didn't feel like there was any hope, like, you know what I mean, it was hard. I started going actually more back to the streets and then I caught two charges and then after them two charges though, I was like, "No, that negative side has to go right now. I got to get back on my positive one."

Ultimately, Kevin found a job at a warehouse and has been staying away from crime. He discussed the importance of his employment in keeping him on a straight path:

> This job keeps me out of trouble because, like I said, if I ain't got that type of money, I'm easily influenced by negative things. If I don't have like a steady income, it's like, I know one thing I know how to do for sure to get some.

When money is not available through legitimate means, there may be an insurmountable temptation to return to crime, particularly when returning youth are faced with the expectation that they will make significant financial contributions to their families or even to become fully independent. Davay admitted that he did return to crime initially after his release because he could not find a job:

> When I came home, I had to do something to get money, but I was looking for a job at the same time, but nobody would hire me because of my record. I'm a black man out here, you know what I mean? So it was hard for me to get a job and have money and my mom was pressuring me for money, you know, "You need to get a job, you need money, how do you have all this money if you don't have a job?" I had to keep lying to her.

Davay's passage highlights the discrimination faced by young Black men in the labor market (see Pager 2003; Pager et al. 2009). Many participants also believe that due to their criminal records, their access to legitimate means of success is blocked by the perception that they are "bad" and untrustworthy. In discussing why he could not find a job when he first came home, Davay expressed that employers are quick to judge:

> Getting a job at first was hard cuz of my record. They see your record and automatically think, "He's no good." That doesn't mean I'm not good. That just means I messed up… They see a record, "No, we don't want to hire him, he has a record," but that don't mean anything. That just means I slipped. That don't mean I won't come to work every day for the rest of my life. That don't mean none of that, but they don't see that. They see a Black man with a record.

In Davay's opinion, his potential as an employee was never even assessed. Employers did not look beyond the fact that he is a young Black man with a criminal record. Like Davay, Eddie discussed how the desistance process has been complicated by his inability to find a job, which he believes is largely the result of his drug charges:

> I was trying to slow down, but it's hard out here. It's hard. People don't want to hire anybody. They've got convictions. They don't want to hire you. They look at your background, anything that you're going to continue to commit crimes or you might steal from them or do something to them or something, but it's not like that.
>
> It's like when you come home, you want to do better. You want to get a job, but if no one is hiring you, then what are you supposed to do? How are you supposed to eat and feed yourself? You can't because you can't get any job. You can't pay your bills.
>
> And then when you come home, the court system, they want you to pay them $50 every month. How are you supposed to do that if you don't have a job? You're looking for a job and you're trying, but no one is hiring you. What are you supposed to do?

Although Eddie reported that he is currently refraining from crime, the temptation to return to it is strong. He describes this feeling below:

> If you got a drug charge, they're really not going to hire you, and that's what I've got. So, some days I just wake up thinking like, "What am I going to do? I've got to get some money somehow, some way." I don't want to go back to my old ways because I really need money. Everybody needs money. You need money to survive. Without money, I'll be like one of the bums out there walking around begging for dollars, sleeping outside.

Eddie said he is determined to avoid crime because he does not want to go back to prison, but if he continues to face barriers to employment, he may find it difficult to fight the temptation to resume a criminal lifestyle. He stated, "I have to pay bills now. I can't live anywhere for free, so I got to do what I got to do."

While some participants spoke about being discriminated against in the hiring process, others indicated they experienced stigmatization at work. Ty, who works in a warehouse, explains the negative treatment he receives in his place of employment:

18 The Expectations and Challenges of Youth Reentry

Once you come on my shift—second shift—you ain't got nothing but convicts—3:30pm–12am—nothing but convicts. Everybody's, like, Black and everybody got a record. First shift is different ethnicities and it's like a whole different ballgame. Once you come home and they give you a chance to work, like my job, they give second chances, but while they doing that we get blamed for everything. If something is missing or something happens, our shift is like the worst shift. That be the second shift all the time and it sucks… I don't like it. I'm tired of it cuz of all the, excuse me, bullshit! At the end of the day, it's a good job but it needs to change or something. I could tell, someone like you working in the office, you might feel comfortable during the first shift but once the second shift comes, like, they don't say nothing. They just walk right past you and it's like totally different… It's just like that cuz once you see second shift and once you see people with dreads, you automatically think they bad. Man, it sucks. You trying to turn your life around and people won't give you that chance. They just look down upon you. It's like, why is he doing that when he don't know nothing about me?

You think the world is gonna change but people criticize us and look down. Lynching is still here but people aren't getting hung. We're getting hung because we can't get no jobs. What's the point? If y'all want us to better ourselves when we locked up and do this and do that, but when we come out here it's a whole totally different world. You feel me? They don't want to give you that chance. They don't want to see you succeed.

Even though he is supposedly being given a chance to better himself, it is made known to him as well as to the other "convicts" who work the second shift alongside him that they are not trusted. They are judged based on both their appearance and their background. Ty believes that this discrimination extends beyond his place of employment. He described how structural forces keep convicted Black men trapped in the system by making them unemployable and untrustworthy. The lynching metaphor is a reference to a period in American history when Blacks were hung from trees by angry White mobs as a punishment, an act of terror meant to instill fear. Ty's reference illustrates his view that following the abolition of slavery, the legal system has been used as a tool for oppression through the mass incarceration of African Americans and, consequently, their exclusion from the labor market (see Alexander 2010, for further reading on the oppression of African Americans through mass incarceration).

The discrimination the young men face in the labor market further complicates their ability to meet their families' expectations of them. As emerging adults, there is an expectation that they will provide for their families, and as their narratives will reveal, there is also an expectation that they will serve as positive role models, but they need to be able earn an income through legitimate means to fulfill these obligations (Arditti and Parkman 2011). For several participants, the desistance process has been a long, bumpy road, as evidenced by their multiple convictions. Even some of the participants who had only one conviction at the time of their interviews reported having to resume criminal activities after their release until they secured jobs. Now that they are adults, the pressure they feel to support themselves or to contribute to their families may set them back if they are unable to achieve success in the labor market.

Family Support

As they attempted to meet the demands of adulthood in the face of blocked opportunity, the majority of the participants were able to access some type of family support when it was needed. Some of them described feeling frustrated by having to ask for help when they recognize they should be stepping into adult roles. Darnell, who was convicted for selling drugs, discussed how a felony conviction diminished his ability to get a job, so he has consequently become dependent on his parents.

> Well, you can't get a job. You got to be more dependent, like, I'm not used to it. You got to be more dependent, like, on your parents and just like loved ones and stuff like that to make sure they're holding down the little bit of things that you need and stuff like that.

Having to depend on his parents for financial support is especially difficult for Darnell, who was used to earning fast money in the illicit market. Others expressed a similar frustration in having to ask for assistance. Mitchell gets by on some money he has saved in the bank, along with income from intermittent employment, but he acknowledged that he frequently has to rely on family.

> Sometimes I ask my mom to help me. Sometimes I ask my friends. I work on the side. Last year I worked the whole time until I went to the halfway house. I went to school at night and I worked in the morning. I had a car last year too, so I was able to get around. Now, it's mad hard for me. When I got sent back in the summertime, it messed me up with school and with work. It messed me up a lot. It's just mad hard. I gotta keep asking my mom, or my dad, or my brother. I gotta keep asking people to help me out. Every little bit of money that I do get I put towards this music that I'm working on so every time I do that, I'm back

18 The Expectations and Challenges of Youth Reentry

to square one. So, it's like, who's gonna help me this time? It's just hard. I want to work but I don't want to settle. I don't want to do no warehouse or nothing. I still got some money in the bank from financial aid so I'm using that to get around for now.

While having to ask for help may be frustrating, many participants stressed that both instrumental and expressive support were critical to their survival as well as their emotional well-being. Instrumental support involves assistance with tangible items such as money, shelter, food, clothing, transportation, and connections to jobs. Expressive support involves checking in on loved ones, offering words of encouragement and advice, and providing a shoulder to lean on. In the following passage, Antoine describes the importance of having a strong support system:

Without my mother I wouldn't be nothin.' I wouldn't be able to get no job because I need her for transportation. If I couldn't live here, I don't know what my mind frame would be. I'd be involved in too much stuff. Maybe I would turn back to being negative again, maybe not, but the support system plays a major part. Having somebody that's there for you and makes you be better—that's just it basically. A lot of people don't have people to be supportive. I'm just blessed. I got my mother. My family just want to help me out and stuff like that. Cuz nobody give you nothin.' Anything somebody do for me, I appreciate it cuz they don't owe me nothin,' they don't, at the end of the day.

Antoine's statement reveals that without a home to reside in and a source of transportation, his physical survival would be difficult. Equally important, however, is knowing that someone is there for him. Without that type of support, he acknowledges that his mental state would suffer and potentially lead him to make bad decisions.

Eddie, who had a conflicted relationship with his mother and her boyfriend prior to his incarceration, now relies on them heavily for both instrumental and expressive support. He described the ways in which his family supported him upon his return:

They gave me a place to live. The only person that does help me is my mom and her boyfriend. They gave me a place to live and I could go to my aunt's house anytime. That's my mom's twin. If I need money, I could just call her or something like, "Can I have this? And she'd give it to me and I'll pay her back. But most of the time, she doesn't want to get paid back because she knows how it is.

My mom, she'd say, "I know it's hard out here. We're going to support you all the way." If I need a ride for a job interview or something, she would take me. She'd help me out a lot like, "Yeah, just keep trying, keep trying. You're going to get it one day. Just don't go back to the streets."

Like Antoine, Eddie makes clear that tangible forms of support such as financial assistance and transportation, and expressive forms of support offered through verbal affirmations, are both critical in being able to survive without resorting to crime as well as in keeping a positive outlook.

Some may require assistance with basic life skills as they transition to adulthood. Scholars have argued that some people who offend lack the psychosocial maturity necessary to succeed after they return from prison and that young adults who exhibit deficits in psychosocial maturity struggle with desistance (Monahan et al. 2009; Steinberg and Cauffman 1996). Randall, who lived with his mother until he was 24 years old and did not move into his own place until his release from incarceration at the age of 25, routinely looks to his mother for guidance when it comes to basic decisions like which milk to purchase or how to change a lightbulb. Randall transitioned from his mother's house to prison, and when he was released and living on his own, it was the first time he had to make decisions about daily life. Decisions that seem basic to most people, like which type of milk to purchase, may be confusing for those who have never purchased groceries. Fortunately for Randall, his mother is willing to provide the level of support that he requires.

While most of the participants did have access to much-needed support, some family members acknowledged the strain that it placed on their time and resources. In the following passage, Antoine's mother Divine highlights the burdensome nature of reentry for family members:

Well, let me say this to you. Indirectly the families are involved because, okay, Antoine had to do all these things, going down to this program twice a week, go to parole twice a week, do this, but in actuality how is he going to get there from where we are? Now, most places there's a bus or a train. If I did not have a car and I was not—I mean, how would he really? [...] even a train station is not in walking distance. Your family has to be involved. Whoever is supporting you has to be involved because if not, then you're breaking the law. How are you going to get there if you're going to drive with no license? So, to me, it's almost like they set you up for failure. I don't think they set you up to prosper yourself. Once you get into this system if you don't have anybody that cares about you enough, you're f*cked. You're doomed probably just to go back to where you started. I got his back 100% no matter what. But say if I was like, maybe, "You ain't using my car, you ain't doing shit, I gave you somewhere to live," how are

18 The Expectations and Challenges of Youth Reentry

> you going to get back and forth? And, if he don't go back and forth, they're going to violate him, you know? Where we live, there's no public transportation—no train and no buses. He got to go all the way to [...]to get on a train, but again, how are you going to get there? And if you're thinking of yourself, "Man, if I don't get to this program, they're going to violate me," you're going to break another law to get there. I mean I'm just being real. If you don't have anybody that's supporting you and behind you most of the time, nine out of ten the way they have this set up you're going to do something wrong to end up back in jail and that's the way I look at it, the way that they have it. And the way they have the jail set up now, you can't call, you can't even eat if you don't have somebody that's supporting you in some kind of way.

Divine's narrative highlights how critically important social support is in navigating the reentry process and points out that not all returning youth have the level of support needed to fulfill their obligations. For those who do not have access to the types of tangible support she described, Divine perceives that the rigid nature of the criminal justice system dooms them to failure.

Some families may have the means to offer assistance but are skeptical when their loved ones return home, particularly if they have extensive histories of criminal involvement or incarceration. For Ernest, although his sister lends a tremendous amount of support by caring for his son while he recovers from serious injuries sustained in a car accident, she keeps Ernest at arm's length by letting him know she does not trust him. Ernest explained:

> I guess they're happy to see me feeling good, but they still have that side that I can see like, "Oh," like they waiting to see me mess up. Like they know it's going to happen, like they have that, "Oh, I know he's going to do something. I know he's going to go out there and do something crazy." I mean because they—you hear everybody when they talk, "Oh, I'm just happy to see you doing good, and I hope you won't be back out there again." I feel as though if you're confident in me or believe in me, you won't even mention that part. So that's how I see it like they played a role of "Oh, we're here for you, but—"

Ernest clearly expressed frustration over his sister's continued mistrust of him, even though he has been in the community for a few years. Ernest went on to explain that since so much time has passed, he feels that his family should not be skeptical anymore, but he knows that time will not ease their concerns.

Some of the participants discussed the potential impact of not having family encouragement. In the following passage, Antoine explains how family members, mothers in particular, can become fed up with their children when their behavior leads to incarceration, and that this frustration may lead parents to withhold support:

> I know for a fact, when you come home if you ain't got the support around you, basically positive people, just knowing somebody cares and loves you, some people have nobody. If you have nobody, especially the men, if you have nobody to talk to or nothing, it's like, "What do I care for? Nobody loves me." Mom's probably dead, Dad's gone, so it's like, "F*ck everything," basically. Some people just don't care. You gotta have support around you, positive friends and stuff like that. Some people go to jail and got nothing. Some people talk to Mom and Dad on the phone, some people go like three or four years without any conversation with them cuz Mom said, "That's it, I'm done," and she washed her hands with them. If you burn your bridges on the streets, when you go to jail nobody gonna be there for you. You only get one mom, you can get a thousand friends. At the end of the day, your mom is all you got, your mom and your dad. Your mom is always there anyway. Your dad's probably not in your life. You better bond with your mom or she'll push you out. If you cross your mom, you think she's gonna be loyal to you? It be like that though.

Antoine commented on how a negative mindset can develop for those who are released from incarceration without a strong support system in place. When asked what happens to people who are released and have no support, Seth remarked, "They go right back in." Ty commented, "I seen people go home on Friday and come back in on a Sunday. I be looking like, 'Yo, you just went home, how you back so quick'?"

Family Expectations

While they may be receiving support from their families, returning youth face mounting pressure to meet heightened responsibilities. In talking about their families' expectations for them and their expectations for themselves, most participants described themselves as being "men," suggesting that age is meaningful to the post-release transition. As they approach adulthood, young adults are expected to contribute to their households by pitching in financially, doing chores, serving as positive role models, and even working toward independence. For some, being a man means they should be self-sufficient and living on their own. Terrance explained how his parents expressed this expectation for him now that he's an adult:

18 The Expectations and Challenges of Youth Reentry

You're grown, you've already been grown so just, I mean, handle your business how you have to handle it. So, basically get a job or find some type of income and basically, you got to move out or whatever. Like, you're getting older, you can't stay here forever.

In Terrance's case, becoming an adult clearly means to become financially independent, but participants described a variety of expectations that their families would find meaningful beyond financial support. In discussing the family's expectations for Antoine after his release, his fiancée Keisha, with whom he shares a child, commented:

I know the family would expect more for him now than before because he's a man. You have to look at a lot of things differently, like, life differently, period. Basically, to take care of what he's supposed to and be a man in the family. Like, you know your situation. You don't have your father so you have to be that strong person for everyone. That's something that you *should* do as a man because this is *your* sentence, this is where you gotta pick up—do your bid, do your time. So, they would expect him to do more, to go that extra mile.

In Keisha's opinion, being a responsible adult involves being a positive role model and being there to support the family the way his family supported him when he went through a difficult time. A participant named Ty described how being a man could involve taking on household responsibilities:

You can't be the man if you ain't doing shit, know what I mean? That's part of being a damn man. You could be a man in the house but ain't doing shit and he's lazy, don't want to do this, don't want to do that, don't want to take out the garbage. Do something, like, take out the garbage, clean up, do something. Don't just be a man and say you're a man when you really not. Do what you gotta do.

Ty's statement clearly expresses the opinion that you cannot be a man without doing your part in the home. It is evident in their discussions of what it means to take on adult male responsibilities that some of the young men, as well as some of their family members, had internalized notions of hegemonic masculinity as the standard for success.

For returning young adults who have or are expecting children while they are transitioning to community life, the expectations for them may be even greater. Seth has three children—two were born before he was incarcerated, and one was born about a month after he came home. In a conversation Seth had with his mother after he returned home, she expressed to him that he was growing up and that he has to do better for his children. Seth describes this conversation below:

> When I came home my mom was just, like, done with all that. We sat down and talked and my mom was like, "You need to get your stuff together for your kids and for you. You're getting older now and you need to be on your own." So, that's what I'm doing—getting everything in order.

Seth's mother communicated to him that as an adult, he should work toward becoming independent and being able to provide for his children. Dustin's mother similarly described how she spoke to her son about the importance of taking care of his responsibilities as a father and being a positive role model for his child:

> I said, "You've got to be a man. You're going to be a better man than your father was." I said, "You know what it was like sitting, waiting at the window. That means you've got to straighten up and that's the only piece of advice I could offer you." It's the same thing that my grandmother said to me, that when you have this baby, this is your baby not until you're 18, but for the rest of your life.

Several of the participants talked about their children as a source of motivation to do better. Seth described how the need to provide for his kids keeps him motivated to stay on the right path:

> I'm doing better. I got three kids so I gotta do what I gotta do. They do keep me focused. If I don't got it, they don't got it. So, I gotta get it so they can have it. Kids are expensive. They need clothes, food, daycare, school, all that. I contribute every week. I get paid, "Here, pay that, pay this." I don't spend nothin' until they done.

Terrance's fiancée Lateisha indicated that Terrance also derives motivation from wanting to be a good father. She described how, since his release, the desire to be a good stepfather to her daughter as well as a good father to their newborn son has kept him focused on being a family man:

> From the beginning to now, I see a lot of changes. I see that he's focusing more on like, just, on being a family man. He wants to be a good role model in a family, like, he wants to be a good husband, good stepfather, good father. That's where he's trying to set his mind at right now—being a family man, not being young or whatever.

18 The Expectations and Challenges of Youth Reentry

Terrance agreed that having a child is motivational. He commented on how a child is a positive force because he wants to remain in the community to play an active role in his child's life:

> Having a child is positive. Knowing that you ain't really trying to be out of that child's life because if you're not in that child's life somebody else is going to be supporting your child, and why would you want somebody else supporting your own child? You made that decision to have that child so why would you put that on somebody else?

Many discussed the failings of their own fathers in talking about what it means to be a man and the responsibilities they want to fulfill as they mature into adulthood. For many, a desire to do better than their parents was a powerful motivator in turning their lives around.[1] As they reflected on the absence of their fathers in their lives, participants reported a desire to be present and to be positive role models for their own children now that they have reached adulthood. Below, Seth discusses how he sees his children as often as he can, nearly every day, because he does not want to be absent from their lives the way his father was absent from his life:

> I see my two, the oldest and the youngest, almost every day. I see the other one like twice a week. I ain't trying to say I'm gonna be the best. I'm gonna do what I can. I came up with no father so I don't want to do that to my kids.

Like Seth, other participants talked about the impact of their fathers' absence, and they do not wish their children to have the same feelings of loneliness or abandonment. Allaquan described how being a presence in his kid's life is the most important thing he can do because he knows what it feels like not to have a father:

> Most all of us grew up without a father. I think it plays a big part really because I know what it's like. Some days you think about it, like, you ain't thinking about your father but there's going to be days and it hits you and now you want to think about certain situations. You could go through anything and it's like somebody to talk to, you know. You would rather talk to them. So, you don't go to your mother about everything, you know. Like certain things I couldn't even talk to my mom about. I knew if my father was there then I would have been able to talk to him, you know. So, it's like I went through a lot of stuff on my own and if he was there, he probably would have helped me get through it a little easier. I think it plays a big part. I think about it now, I got to stay in my kid's life, that's the main important thing.

He desires to be involved in his child's life not only to provide for her but also to provide moral support. While the participants with children acknowledged the importance of being there for financial as well as moral support, those who experience difficulty in achieving adult responsibilities may find it challenging to remain a constant in their children's lives or to make significant monetary contributions. Becoming independent and being able to provide for family requires a steady income. For nearly all participants, finding a job after their release proved to be a challenge and some were tempted to return to crime. Eddie's cousin, Alwan, who had just turned 26 and was released from incarceration as a young adult himself supports five children. He pays child support for his oldest child who resides with her mother and the remaining four children reside with him and his girlfriend, the oldest two being hers from a previous relationship. Based on his past experience with employment, Alwan admits to being fully involved in drug dealing to support his family, and he is not seeking legitimate employment at this time. Aside from his frustration over low wages, Alwan has experienced problems with the child support system which does not allow for adjustments when earnings are reduced, making it difficult to meet legal obligations.[2] Providing for his family is his top priority, and he believes that drug dealing is the most gainful approach.

Discussion and Conclusions

The current study sheds light on numerous challenges associated with reentry for emerging adults, including meeting the demands of adulthood and family expectations, securing employment, experiencing stigmatization, and accessing family support. It was evident that social bonds, such as parenthood, romantic partnerships, and relationships with parents, help young adults aspire to set legitimate goals, but their ability to achieve them is difficult given the financial difficulties they face along with declines in optimism. Family support plays a large role, especially for young adults who do not have jobs and need to rely to a greater extent on their support systems than youth who do not have criminal records. In an examination of social ties, employment and recidivism, Berg and Huebner (2011) reported that good quality social ties are particularly important for men with histories of frequent unemployment.

The interviews in this study highlighted the importance of family support to the post-release transition. All participants relied on family members for instrumental support upon their return, such as a place to live, transportation, and other economic assistance. While some families had few resources to share beyond providing a place to live, other types of support were equally important. Expressive support was crucial in keeping the young men motivated to succeed, which is consistent with Panuccio et al.'s (2012) finding that family support can motivate offenders toward desistance. Participants in this study derived a great deal of motivation from the acceptance and encouragement they received from family.

Complicating matters is that even though families were generally supportive, most of their family members expected them to take on greater responsibilities over time, especially given the burdensome nature of reentry on the family's time and resources. The young men themselves desired to make significant contributions to the family and felt it was their responsibility as men to do so, suggesting they feel compelled by hegemonic masculinity. The extent to which they could make meaningful contributions, however, was limited by the exclusion they faced in the labor market. Overwhelmingly, the participants identified employment as their biggest post-release obstacle. They drew close connections between their inability to maintain a steady job with decent wages and their inability to contribute to family and meet their own expectations about what it means to be a man. Arditti and Parkman (2011) describe a developmental paradox, in which young men in reentry are chronologically mature enough to hold jobs and earn money, yet repeatedly encounter obstacles to securing employment, in part because of their criminal records. Inability to find jobs leads to a cycle of dependency on family members, who are themselves in economically precarious situations (Arditti and Parkman 2011). For some, the barriers they face in achieving their goals may tempt them to revert to a life of crime. Participants in the current study who experienced frustration finding or maintaining a job thought about returning to crime at various points, supporting Abrams and Terry's (2017) description of young adults who are "running in circles," meaning they are trying to make positive steps toward desistance but unable to fully disengage in crime due to economic struggles. In the current study, and in Abrams and Terry's study, those who were able to secure jobs and provide financial support to their families had a more positive outlook for the future.

A strength of this study was the inclusion of family voices, which are typically neglected in research about reentry, even though research has highlighted the prominent role that families play in the reentry process. Dependence on family was a source of concern for the young men in this study, as it contradicted socially constructed norms of masculinity. In addition, family members played a dual role of both pressuring the men to find jobs because their financial contributions were necessary for family well-being, but also empathizing with the barriers they faced, and attempting to offer encouragement and support. Both the men and their family members were caught in binds imposed by their location within the social structure and criminal justice system.

An understanding of the problems that these individuals experience and gaps in the types of assistance they receive can inform policies for addressing the needs of emerging adults reentering from incarceration. Reentry programs for emerging adults should include a component that links individuals to structural opportunities such as employment and education. For those who are released to parole or have been on probation, they are required to work, but participants said there is very little support in finding jobs. Vocational training immediately following release might be a good starting point for those without jobs, particularly for those who have not received vocational training previously. Research that has examined participation in vocational programs while incarcerated has shown that participants report a more positive outlook and are more likely to experience identity transformation when doing work that they perceive to be rewarding and will help them develop valuable skills to be used in securing legitimate work post-release (Edwards 2014). Studies of post-release vocational programs have shown a reduced likelihood of recidivism in program participants compared to those who do not participate (Aos et al. 2006).

At the policy level, parole expectations need to be adjusted for individuals with low educational attainment and/or disruptions in schooling and for those with limited work histories. There should also be leniency in paying fines. When people on parole are unable to pay their legal fees because either they are unable to find work or their families' needs are more pressing, many find themselves violated and reincarcerated, which only worsens their problems. Interventions that account for the challenges experienced by the specific population being supervised or treated have the potential to reduce negative outcomes and increase the likelihood of long-term success.

Given the importance of family support, programs aimed at strengthening families may lead to improved outcomes for individuals transitioning to the community. Boeck et al. (2008) point out that, "for young people with key choices to make, widespread network relationships contribute to processes of self-assurance, personal development and, in turn, resilience and desistance" (p. 16). Ideally, programs should begin prior to release. The criminal justice system does little to help incarcerated individuals maintain or strengthen their social bonds, and social capital is diminished by the emotional and geographical distance created by imprisonment (Wolff and Draine 2004). Participants in the current study agreed that maintaining contact with family members while incarcerated is difficult for various reasons ranging from embarrassment to the cost associated with staying in touch. Correction agencies can remove barriers to the maintenance of family ties and encourage contact between incarcerated individuals and their loved ones (Christian et al. 2006; La Vigne et al. 2005; Bobbitt and Nelson 2004; Hairston 2003; Petersilia 2003; Hirsch et al. 2002; Couturier 1995). In addition to encouraging ongoing relationships during incarceration, pre-release programs could help families prepare for the challenges they will face during the reentry process. Such programs, for example, could offer parenting and relationship classes, provide pre-release family counseling, and allow families to be involved in the discharge planning process (Christian et al. 2006). A continuum of services should continue to be provided post-release to continue to engage families in the rehabilitation process.

Notes

1. Unfortunately, there is considerable evidence that their commitments to their children do not work out over time for many young fathers. Tach and Edin (2011) argued that when casual romantic relationships result in pregnancy, the majority of unmarried fathers are supportive throughout the pregnancy, are optimistic about their romantic relationships, and are committed to being involved with their children. The cumulative disadvantage they experience, however, makes it difficult for them to meet their commitments. The employment and earnings prospects of young fathers, particularly those who have been incarcerated, combined with the likelihood that they will have children with multiple partners and receive little income support from the government, place them in desperate economic situations and lead to instability in their families (Smeeding et al. 2011). Relationship instability over time between unwed couples lessens the involvement that fathers have with their children (Berger and Langton 2011). Although the participants in this study are initially motivated by their children and feel hopeful about their futures, existing research suggests that the barriers they face in achieving economic success and stability in their romantic relationships could limit the involvement they have with their children, in terms of their financial support as well as their engagement.
2. Smeeding et al. (2011) discuss the complexities of child support policy at length. While access to income support has decreased for young males, child support policy has demanded more from them. Their child support obligations continue to mount as they experience blocked opportunities and decreased earnings.

References

Abrams, L.S., & Tam, C. (2018). Gender differences in desistance from crime: How do social bonds operate among formerly incarcerated emerging adults? *Journal of Adolescent Research, 33*(1), 34–57.

Abrams, L.S., & Terry, D. (2017). *Everyday desistance: The transition to adulthood among formerly incarcerated youth.* New Brunswick, NJ: Rutgers University Press.

Alexander, M. (2010). *The new Jim Crow: Mass incarceration in the age of colorblindness.* New York: The New Press.

Altschuler, D. M., & Brash, R. (2004). Adolescent and teenage offenders confronting the challenges and opportunities of reentry. *Youth Violence and Juvenile Justice, 2*(1), 72–87.

Aos, S., Miller, M., & Drake, E. (2006). *Evidence-based public policy options to reduce future prison construction, criminal justice costs, and crime rates.* Olympia, WA: Washington State Institute for Public Policy.

Arditti, J. A., & Parkman, T. (2011). Young men's reentry after incarceration: A developmental paradox. *Family Relations, 60,* 205–220.

Arnett, J. (2000). Emerging adulthood: A theory of development from the late teens through the twenties. *American Psychologist, 55,* 469–480.

Bahr, S. J., Harris, L., Fisher, J. K., & Armstrong, A. H. (2010). Successful reentry: What differentiates successful and unsuccessful parolees? *International Journal of Offender Therapy and Comparative Criminology, 54*(5), 667–692.

Berg, M. T., & Huebner, B. M. (2011). Reentry and the ties that bind: An examination of social ties, employment and recidivism. *Justice Quarterly, 28*(2), 331–361.

Berger, L. M., & Langton, C. E. (2011). Young disadvantaged men as fathers. *The Annals of the American Academy of Political and Social Science, 635,* 56–75.

Bobbitt, M., & Nelson, M. (2004). *The front line: Building programs that recognize families' role in reentry.* New York: Vera Institute of Justice.

Boeck, T., Fleming, J., & Kemshall, H. (2008). Social capital, resilience and desistance: The ability to be a risk navigator. *British Journal of Community Justice, 6*(3), 5–20.

Born, M., Chevalier, V., & Humblet, I. (1997). Resilience, desistance and delinquent career of adolescent offenders. *Journal of Adolescence, 20*(6), 679–694.

Bosick, S. J., & Gover, A. R. (2010). Incarceration during the transition to adulthood. *American Journal of Criminal Justice, 35*(3), 93–104.

Burton, L. (2007). Childhood adultification in economically disadvantaged families: A conceptual model. *Family Relations, 56,* 329–345.

Charmaz, K. (2006). *Constructing grounded theory: A practical guide through qualitative analysis.* London: Sage.

Christian, J., Fishman, N., Cammett, A., & Scott-Pickens, L. (2006). *Bringing families in: Recommendations of the incarceration, reentry and the family roundtables.* A

Joint Project of the Rutgers University School of Criminal Justice and the New Jersey Institute for Social Justice.

Cobbina, J., Huebner, B., & Berg, M. (2012). Men, women and post-release offending: An examination of the nature of the link between relational ties and recidivism. *Crime and Delinquency, 58*(3), 331–361.

Corbin, J., & Strauss, A. (2014). *Basics of qualitative research: Techniques and procedures for developing grounded theory.* Thousand Oaks, CA: Sage.

Council on Crime and Justice. (2006). *The juvenile offender study: A retrospective examination of youth offenders.* Minneapolis, MN: Council on Crime and Justice.

Couturier, L. C. (1995). Inmates benefit from family service programs. *Corrections Today, 57*(7), 100–105.

Creswell, J. W. (2007). *Qualitative inquiry and research design: Choosing among five approaches* (2nd ed.). Thousand Oaks, CA: Sage.

Crutchfield, R. D. (2014). *Get a job: Labor markets, economic opportunity, and crime.* New York: New York University Press.

Cullen, F. (1994). Social support as an organizing concept for criminology: Presidential address to the Academy of Criminal Justice Sciences. *Justice Quarterly, 11*(4), 527–559.

Curtis, R. & Schulman, S. (1984). Ex-offenders' family relations and economic supports: The significant women study of the TARP project. *Crime & Delinquency, 30*(4), 507–528.

Edin, K., Nelson, T. J., & Paranal, R. (2004). Fatherhood and incarceration as potential turning points in the criminal careers of unskilled men. In M. Patillo, D. Weiman, & B. Western (Eds.), *Imprisoning America: The social effects of mass incarceration* (pp. 46–75). New York, NY: Russell Sage Foundation.

Edwards, K. (2014). Prison work: Transforming identity and reducing recidivism. In M. S. Crow & J. O. Smykla (Eds.), *Offender reentry: Rethinking criminology and criminal justice* (pp. 51–74). Burlington, MA: Jones & Bartlett.

Eggleston, D. E. (2006). Self-control, social bonds, and desistance: A test of lifecourse interdependence. *Criminology, 44*(4), 807–833.

Fader, J. (2013). *Falling back: Incarceration and transitions to adulthood.* New Brunswick, NJ: Rutgers University Press.

Furstenberg, F. F., Jr., Rumbaut, R. C., & Settersten, R. A., Jr. (2005). On the frontier of adulthood: Emerging themes and new directions. In R. A. Settersten, Jr., F. F. Furstenberg, Jr., & R. G. Rumbaut (Eds.), *On the frontier of adulthood: Theory, research, & public policy* (pp. 3–25). Chicago, IL: The University of Chicago Press.

Gatti, U., Tremblay, R. E., & Vitaro, F. (2009). Iatrogenic effect of juvenile justice. *Journal of Child Psychology and Psychiatry, 50*(8), 991–998.

Gay, L. R., & Airasian, P. (2000). *Educational research: Competencies for analysis and application* (6th ed.). Upper Saddle River, NJ: Prentice Hall.

Gilmore, A. S., Rodriguez, N., & Webb, V. J. (2005). Substance abuse and drug courts: The role of social bonds in juvenile drug courts. *Youth Violence and Juvenile Justice, 3*(4), 287–315.

Giordano, P., Cernkovich, S., & Rudolph, J. (2002). Gender, crime and desistance: Toward a theory of cognitive transformation. *American Journal of Sociology, 107*, 990–1064.

Glaser, B. G., & Strauss, A. L. (1967). *The discovery of grounded theory: Strategies for qualitative research*. Chicago, IL: Aldine Publishing Company.

Hairston, C. F. (1988). Family ties during imprisonment: Do they influence future criminal activity? *Federal Probation, 52*(1), 48–52.

Hairston, C. F. (1991). Family ties during imprisonment: Important to whom and for what? *Journal of Sociology and Social Welfare, 18*, 87–104.

Hairston, C. F. (2003). Prisoners and their families: Parenting issues during incarceration. In J. Travis & M. Waul (Eds.), *Prisoners once removed: The impact of incarceration and reentry on children, families, and communities* (pp. 259–282). Washington, DC: The Urban Institute Press.

Herman-Stahl, M., Kan, M. L., & McKay, T. (2008). *Incarceration and the family: A review of research and promising approaches for serving fathers and families*. Washington, DC: U.S. Department of Health and Human Services.

Hirsch, A., Dietrich, S., Landau, R., Schneider, P., Ackelsberg, I., Bernstein-Baker, J., & Hohenstein, J. (2002). *Every door closed: Barriers facing parents with criminal records*. Washington, DC: Center for Law and Social Policy and Community Legal Services, Inc.

Johnson, W. L., Giordano, P. C., Manning, W. D., & Longmore, M. A. (2011). Parent-child relations and offending during young adulthood. *Journal of Youth and Adolescence, 40*(7), 786–799.

La Vigne, N. G., Naser, R. L., Brooks, L. E., & Castro, J. L. (2005). Examining the effect of incarceration and in-prison family contact on prisoners' family relationships. *Journal of Contemporary Criminal Justice, 21*(4), 314–335.

La Vigne, N. G., Visher, C., & Castro, J. (2004). *Chicago prisoners' experiences returning home*. Washington, DC: Urban Institute.

Martinez, D. J., & Christian, J. (2009). The familial relationships of former prisoners: Examining the link between residence and informal support mechanisms. *Journal of Contemporary Ethnography, 38*, 201–224.

Mears, D. P. (2001). Critical challenges in addressing the mental health needs of juvenile offenders. *Justice Policy Journal, 1*, 41–61.

Mears, D. P., & Travis, J. (2004). *The dimensions, pathways, and consequences of youth reentry*. Washington, DC: Urban Institute.

Mendel, R. A. (2011). *No place for kids: The case for reducing juvenile incarceration*. Baltimore, MD: The Annie E. Casey Foundation.

Monahan, K. C., Steinberg, L., Cauffman, E., & Mulvey, E. P. (2009). Trajectories of antisocial behavior and psychosocial maturity from adolescence to young adulthood. *Developmental Psychology, 45*(6), 1654–1668.

Naser, R. L., & Visher, C. A. (2006). Family members' experiences with incarceration and reentry. *Western Criminology Review, 7*(2), 20–31.

Nelson, M., Deess, P., & Allen, C. (1999). *The first month out: Post-incarceration experiences in New York City*. New York: Vera Institute of Justice.

Nurse, A. (2002). *Fatherhood arrested: Parenting from within the juvenile justice system*. Nashville, TN: Vanderbilt University Press.

Nurse, A. (2004). Returning to strangers: Newly paroled young fathers and their children. In M. Pattillo, D. Weiman, & B. Western (Eds.), *Imprisoning America: The social effects of mass incarceration* (pp. 76–96). New York, NY: Sage.

Osgood, D. W., Foster, E. M., Flanagan, C., & Ruth, G. R. (2005). *On your own without a net: The transition to adulthood for vulnerable populations*. Chicago, IL: University of Chicago Press.

Pager, D. (2003). The mark of a criminal record. *American Journal of Sociology, 108*(5), 937–975.

Pager, D. (2008). *Marked: Race, crime, and finding work in an era of mass incarceration*. Chicago, IL: University of Chicago Press.

Pager, D., & Quillian, L. (2005). Walking the talk? What employers say versus what they do. *American Sociological Review, 70*, 355–380.

Pager, D., Western, B., & Sugie, N. (2009). Sequencing disadvantage: Barriers to employment facing young black and white men with criminal records. *Annals of the American Academy of Political & Social Science, 623*, 195–213.

Panuccio, E., Christian, J., Martinez, D. J., & Sullivan, M. L. (2012). Social support, motivation, and the process of juvenile reentry: An exploratory analysis. *Journal of Offender Rehabilitation, 51*(3), 135–160.

Petersilia, J. (2003). *When prisoners come home: Parole and prisoner reentry*. Oxford: Oxford University Press.

Puzzanchera, C., & Hockenberry, S. (2019). *Trends and characteristics of youth in residential placement, 2017*. Washington, DC: Office of Juvenile Justice and Delinquency Prevention. Retrieved March 4, 2020, from https://www.ojjdp.gov/ojstatbb/snapshots/DataSnapshot_CJRP2017.pdf.

Rios, V. M. (2011). *Punished: Policing the lives of Black and Latino boys*. New York: New York University Press.

Roy, K., & Jones, N. (2014). Theorizing alternative pathways through adulthood: Unequal social arrangements in the lives of young disadvantaged men. *New Directions for Child and Adolescent Development, 2014*, 1–9.

Roy, K., Messina, L., Smith, J., & Waters, D. (2014). Growing up as "man of the house": Adultification and transition into adulthood for young men in economically disadvantaged families. *New Directions for Child and Adolescent Development, 2014*, 55–72.

Salvatore, C., & Taniguchi, T. A. (2012). Do social bonds matter for emerging adults? *Deviant Behavior, 33*(9), 738–756.

Sampson, R. J., & Laub, J. H. (1993). *Crime in the making: Pathways and turning points through life*. Cambridge, MA: Harvard University Press.

Sawyer, W. (2019). Youth confinement: The whole pie 2019. Northampton, MA: Prison Policy Initiative. Retrieved March 4, 2020, from https://www.prisonpolicy.org/reports/youth2019.html

Schroeder, R. D., Giordano, P. C., & Cernkovich, S. A. (2010). Adult child-parent bonds and life course criminality. *Journal of Criminal Justice, 38*(4), 562–571.

Sedlak, A. J., & McPherson, K. S. (2010). *Youth's needs and services: Findings from the survey of youth in residential placements*. Washington, DC: U.S. Department of Justice.

Simon, J. (1993). *Poor discipline: Parole and the social control of the underclass, 1890–1990*. Chicago, IL: The University of Chicago Press.

Smeeding, T. M., Garfinkel, I., & Mincy, R. B. (2011). Young disadvantaged men: Fathers, family, poverty, and policy. *The Annals of the American Academy of Political and Social Science, 635*, 6–21.

Snyder, H. N. (2004). An empirical portrait of the youth reentry population. *Youth Violence and Juvenile Justice, 2*(1), 39–55.

Snyder, H. N., & Sickmund, M. (2006). *Juvenile offenders and victims: 2006 national report*. Washington, DC: U.S. Department of Justice, Office of Justice Programs, Office of Juvenile Justice and Delinquency Prevention.

Steinberg, L., & Cauffman, E. (1996). Maturity of judgment in adolescence: Psychosocial factors in adolescent decision making. *Law and Human Behavior, 20*(3), 249–272.

Steinberg, L., Chung, H. L., & Little, M. (2004). Reentry of young offenders from the justice system: A developmental perspective. *Youth Violence and Juvenile Justice, 2*(1), 21–38.

Strauss, A., & Corbin, J. (1990). *Basics of qualitative research: Grounded theory procedures and techniques*. Newbury Park, CA: Sage.

Strauss, A., & Corbin, J. (1998). *Basics of qualitative research: Grounded theory procedures and techniques* (2nd ed.). London: Sage.

Sullivan, E., Mino, M., Nelson, K., & Pope, J. (2002). *Families as a resource in recovery from drug abuse: An evaluation of La Bodega de la Familia*. New York: Vera Institute of Justice.

Tach, L., & Edin, K. (2011). The relationship contexts of young disadvantaged men. *The Annals of the American Academy of Political and Social Science, 635*, 76–94.

Teplin, L. A., et al. (2013). *The Northwestern Juvenile project: Overview*. Washington, DC: Office of Juvenile Justice and Delinquency Prevention.

Todis, B., Bullis, M., Waintrup, M., Schultz, R., & D'Ambrosio, R. (2001). Overcoming the odds: Qualitative examination of resilience among formerly incarcerated adolescents. *Exceptional Children, 68*(1), 119–139.

Travis, J., Western, B., & Redburn, F. S. (2014). *The growth of incarceration in the United States: Exploring causes and consequences*. Washington, DC: National Academies Press.

Tripodi, S. J., Kim, J. S., & Bender, K. (2010). Is employment associated with reduced recidivism? *International Journal of Offender Therapy & Comparative Criminology, 54*(5), 706–720.

Uggen, C., & Wakefield, S. (2005). Young adults reentering the community from the criminal justice system: The challenges of becoming an adult. In D. W. Osgood, E. M. Foster, C. Flanagan, & G. R. Ruth (Eds.), *On your own without a net: The transition to adulthood for vulnerable populations* (pp. 114–144). Chicago: University of Chicago Press.

Western, B. (2002). The impact of incarceration on wage mobility and inequality. *American Sociological Review, 67*(4), 526–546.

Western, B. (2006). *Punishment and inequality in America*. New York, NY: Russell Sage Foundation.

Wolff, N., & Draine, J. (2004). Dynamics of social capital of prisoners and community reentry: The ties that bind? *Journal of Correctional Health Care, 10*(3), 457–490.

19

Nothing's Changed but Me: Reintegration Plans Meet the Inner City

Jamie J. Fader

Preface

The following is excerpted from *Falling Back: Incarceration and Transitions to Adulthood Among Urban Youth* (2013). When I began preliminary research for the project a decade earlier than its publication, very little had been written about the unique experiences of youth returning home from confinement settings. Having visited many campuses of "residential placements," as they are called (in an effort to sanitize the fact that they are in fact prisons with therapeutic designs), I could only imagine what it must feel like for them to be removed from urban communities, dropped into the middle of wooded rural areas to receive treatment, and then returned back to the same social and economic contexts that led them to drug selling. As I reviewed the scant literature on the subject, I realized how rare it was to ask youth to articulate their own experiences and became determined to invite them to narrate the process of incarceration and reentry. Although securing access to the inner workings of these facilities is difficult because of the opaque nature of juvenile corrections, my former role as a program evaluator provided me entree.

Reprinted from *Falling Back: Incarceration and Transitions to Adulthood Among Urban Youth* (Rutgers University Press, 2013) Edited for length

---

J. J. Fader (✉)
Department of Criminal Justice, Temple University, Philadelphia, PA, USA
e-mail: jfader@temple.edu

Philadelphia is an important site to study juvenile incarceration and reentry because its landscape of residential placements is largely comprised of private facilities employing a wide variety of treatment modalities and contracted by the city's Department of Human Services. This distinguishes it from many other jurisdictions that rely heavily or exclusively on state-run facilities that are more visibly jail-like and less therapeutic in nature. "Mountain Ridge Academy"[1] was an ideal study setting because it was considered by decision makers such as Family Court judges and juvenile probation officers (POs) as one of the highest-quality placements available to Philadelphia's adjudicated youth. It was often reserved for young people who were old enough to be on their "last stop" before their next arrest made them eligible for the adult criminal court. Court commitments to placements were indeterminate, lasting an average of nine to ten months, but adjusted up- or downward based on each youth's progress through treatment benchmarks and consistent compliance with rules. As the young men I studied were returning home, they were encountering a newly reformed system of supportive aftercare services, which were evidence based, but—due to budget constraints—half as long (90 days) as the prior regime had offered.

This study draws upon three years of intensive participant observation with 15 young Black and Latino men aged 17–19 who were incarcerated at a private juvenile facility called "Mountain Ridge Academy." The administration and staff generously opened their doors to me, allowing me to shadow residents throughout their daily routine inside the facility and to participate in staff training. I observed classes, dorm life, and mealtimes. After selecting 15 residents on the basis of their race, age, Philadelphia resident status, and length of stay at the program, I conducted in-depth pre-release interviews focused on their perceptions of treatment at Mountain Ridge Academy and their plans for return to the community.

The young men were released between November 2004 and July 2005, and their first eight weeks at home involved weekly audio reentry journals, documenting their daily activities, goals, and challenges. During this time, and for the next three years, I conducted participant observation in a number of settings and situations: searching for work, providing care for their children, meeting with their probation officers, going to court, or passing leisure time on front stoops, corner stores, or basketball courts. I also got to know the people in their social circle, including parents, extended family members, girlfriends and baby's mothers, kids, and friends.

To triangulate their accounts of further involvement in the system, I conducted record checks of the juvenile and adult systems and spoke with their probation officers and reintegration workers. I conducted formal interviews at regular intervals, but spent the bulk of my research time during 2004–2007 spending focused time with the young men. Some of them dropped out of the study immediately, never having built the required level of trust to participate. Others were incarcerated fairly quickly after returning to the community. When this happened, I exchanged letters and visited when I could. The young man featured in this chapter—Tony—remained active for the duration of the study and I am still in contact with him 14 years later.

I conducted analysis using an inductive framework consistent with grounded theory (Glaser and Strauss 2017). I coded field notes the old-fashioned way, without any software, assigning open (broader) thematic codes in the first round, followed by focused codes in the subsequent rounds. I tested hypotheses by generating thematic memos whereby I collated all the evidence pertaining to a claim and paid special attention to negative cases. I then developed case studies designed to exemplify key themes, particularly how they played out sequentially and where they allowed me to highlight the confluence subjective perceptions of life events.

Falling Back (Fader 2013) examines the approach used by staff at Mountain Ridge Academy to promote change among youth in conflict with the law and contrasts the good intentions of the adults behind the program with the deeply stigmatic and disempowering experience of receiving this treatment, as narrated by my participants. The program's "hidden curriculum" identified urban life and Black culture as criminal in nature, and the staff made negative predictions about the young men's futures. Although the men contested these labels, they ultimately internalized them and bought into the premise that self-control and decision-making skills would be sufficient to overcome the structural barriers associated with poverty and racism. The chapter I have selected for this volume highlights this disjuncture between their expectations that were framed by therapeutic discourse and the demands of urban street contexts, which they experienced most acutely immediately upon their return to Philadelphia.

Introduction

Tony, 19, was light-skinned, thin, and quiet. We met in the cafeteria at Mountain Ridge, where he approached me about being part of my study. Although I realized that a clerical error had prevented him from being on my list, I soon learned that Tony often felt overlooked and left out, and for good reason. His mother had smoked crack for the past 12 years and was still an addict. He and his sister had different fathers, neither of whom was present in their lives. During his childhood, they teetered on the brink of homelessness, moving from one house to the next. His relatives took him in for a week at a time, only to return him. "They dropped me off, literally on the street" at the drug house where his mother was at the time. He felt a fierce loyalty to family, even those who didn't care for him in return. His sister Gniesha, also a former drug seller, got her life together and became a nurse. Tony planned to go to nursing school when he came home, viewing it as a way to pay society back for the harm he had caused while selling drugs. Shortly before he was released from Mountain Ridge, he told me,

> I feel, for me just to think how I was so dumb, that school really is power, right? The more education you got, the more power you have. I wish I was still young, like I wish I could do it all again. Drugs made me forget about school but if I woulda just stopped using drugs, man, I woulda been better off. School is so much, so good. That's all I think about right now, go to school, stay in school, I wanna stay in school for … the next six years of my life … And if [only] I can just start it now, 'cause I get the tendency to get lazy and not do it.

Tony appeared very anxious to continue the cognitive momentum he started at the facility, revealing a fear of "forgetting" to pursue his goals when he got home.

Tony was released after 15 months at Mountain Ridge with plans to join Job Corps, a no-cost education and training program sponsored by the U.S. Department of Education. Part of the appeal of Job Corps was that it had a residential component; it would provide him a stable, rent-free place to stay and require him to move to Virginia, away from his criminal networks.

Two weeks after his release, I visited him at Gniesha's place. "I saw my PO yesterday," he said. "She wants to keep me on probation, but I'm not hearin' that." He had called the number for Job Corps listed by his counselor on his continuing care plan several times, but got no response. Tony's reintegration worker, Karen, and probation officer, Lisa, had worked together to recommend a shorter term of probation so he could be enrolled at Job Corps, but the special arrangement depended on his enrollment. A month after his release from Mountain Ridge, he had instead enrolled himself at a Manpower employment agency and spent two abysmal shifts doing day labor, first at a meat packing plant and then at a cotton factory.

Eventually, Tony learned that Job Corps had done a criminal background check and found an outstanding summary (noncriminal) charge for disturbing the peace generated five years before. Unfortunately, the civil court in charge of summary offenses did not share a computer system with the juvenile

19 Nothing's Changed but Me: Reintegration Plans Meet the Inner City

court, so the matter had to be cleared up by scheduling a hearing at the civil court. Until that hearing, scheduled for five months after his release from Mountain Ridge, Tony was in limbo. "That's on Lisa! How did she not know that I had a bench warrant from that long ago when I been locked up all this time?" he said angrily.

Now that his probation would be extended, Lisa required Tony to attend the Empowerment, Education, and Employment (E3) Center, a community-based program for "disconnected" or out-of-school youth. His experience there only added to his frustration and sense that the system was screwing him over. E3 Centers had been recently added to the repertoire of services for returning youth as part of the city's attempt to "reinvent reintegration" using best practices that are supported by research. Unfortunately for Tony and several of the other men I followed, the centers were just getting off the ground during their reentry period and weren't fully staffed or offering a full range of programming.

Tony admitted that he had walked out of the center of his first day. "I told them they were wasting my time. They had me working math problems and I haven't been in school for eleven months!" He explained that they had put him in a remedial math class because their systems weren't up yet. "The program just started. They don't even have teachers for most of their classes yet. But they expect us to be there four and a half hours a day, five days a week." Reintegration services often assume that any required activity is better than leaving young people with unstructured time. Tony realized that this program was ritualistic and put his probationary status on the line by rejecting it.

He decided to enroll in Thompson Institute to study nursing. On the drive to campus, he expressed anxiety about going back to school, where he had never experienced much success, and worried aloud about whether training to become a nurse threatened his masculinity. He also wondered how he was going to pay $75 per month for tuition and find a job on the second or third shift to work around his school schedule.

One of the key problems the men I studied encountered as they tried to pursue advanced education and training was that it required an intricate balancing act among work, school, and, for many (though not Tony), fatherhood. Tony was not an attractive job applicant and was very sensitive to rejection. He and many of the other young men looked for work only sporadically because repeated rebuffs by employers were too great an assault on their sense of self-worth. Tony was also so embedded in street life that he felt like he was missing something when he had to work indoors. As he sold bags of weed outside a major train stop in West Philly, he could hang out with his friends and get girls' phone numbers. His knowledge of goings-on in his neighborhood was a form of social currency and an important source of status that he didn't see as worth giving up for traditional employment.

Six weeks after starting school, Tony's best friend was found slumped over in his car, riddled with gunshots. When he stopped by the makeshift grave, the police picked him up for questioning and found a bag of weed in his pocket. They let him go without charging him but had been following him since. The next month (five months after his release from Mountain Ridge), Tony was arrested and charged with possession of marijuana with intent to deliver. "I was in the Chinese store when the cops rolled in and popped another guy for carrying a gun. I had just shook his hand. We knew each other, but wasn't friends."[2] That had been enough to charge him with conspiracy for the gun charge, which they used as a pretext to search him. When they did, they found a small bag of weed for personal use. He admitted to me later that he was selling drugs that day, but not to the guy they said he was. They also missed a couple hundred dollars' worth of coke that was hidden in his jacket pocket.

Tony had stopped attending Thompson Institute. His attendance before the arrest was sporadic, but he didn't return at all after he was locked up. Each month, he received a bill for $75, even though he was not attending. All his momentum and enthusiasm about the importance of education that he had felt while locked up was now washed out by the realities of his life. It had been easy to see the value of education in a bubble.

Meanwhile, he owed hundreds in fines and in court fees for the old disorderly conduct offense. By the time we sat down for a formal interview a year after his discharge from probation (September 2006), he had moved from small-time drug dealing to having his own block with a partner. They were selling "weed, powder, and rocks" for a guy who fronted them the money. They paid themselves $200 every three days, provided they had sold that much. Meanwhile, he had spent more time locked up after he arrived late for his court date and the judge found him in contempt. In December he was arrested for robbery and simple assault; in July 2007 he was charged with statutory sexual assault. In September, two years after being discharged from juvenile probation, he began serving a one- to two-year sentence for the sexual assault charge. The following January, he began serving five to ten years in adult prison for the robbery charge.

There is no way to know what would have happened to Tony if he hadn't encountered the problem with the old bench warrant and had been able to move to Virginia with Job Corps to pursue a nursing degree. Perhaps he would have viewed the experience as outside his comfort zone and would have found trouble no matter where he moved. Maybe, with a nursing degree in hand, he would have turned out more like his sister, who had left that old life behind. In the language of desistance scholars, Job Corps might have served as a "turning point," moving him out of a criminal pathway and into a more conforming one. It does seem regrettably certain that this was a lost opportunity for someone who had few opportunities growing up. Moreover, Tony, who had already been profoundly disappointed by the people in his life, felt that "the system" that was supposed to help him succeed upon his return from Mountain Ridge had failed him.

Tony's story is emblematic of so many of the reentry trajectories of the young men I followed home to Philadelphia. Most encountered a stunning disjuncture between plans and reality. As Tony left Mountain Ridge, he felt simultaneously hopeful that his life would be different when he returned to the city and fearful that he would lose the momentum and social support he had built up at Mountain Ridge. Like many of the other young men I followed, he strove to pull himself away from the streets by pursuing an education, but discovered that his precarious position in relation to the labor market and the criminal justice system prevented him from maintaining his investment. His reintegration worker and probation officer had good intentions, but ultimately forced him to participate in services for their own sake, rather than offering meaningful and appropriate programming or assistance. Their ignorance of his outstanding bench warrants was a function of the size and decentralized nature of the justice system in Philadelphia. How quickly his reintegration plans crumbled is a testament to their shaky foundation, as they were built to compensate for a lifetime of structural disadvantage.

Juvenile Reentry

Despite the mass of research on the challenges confronting former adult prisoners as they reenter their communities, relatively little attention has been paid to juvenile reentry from residential facilities. Those who have examined the problem point out that the process is different because young people make a "dual transition" from facility to community and from adolescence into early adulthood (Altschuler and Brash 2004). We know that young men are particularly vulnerable as they struggle to disentangle themselves from the sticky web of supervision by the justice system. Failure is all too common. As many as two-thirds of returning youth are rearrested and up to one-third are re-incarcerated within a few years after release (Mears and Travis 2004). Fewer than a third are either in school or employed a year after release (Bullis et al. 2002). Because young people sent to residential placements present greater needs than their counterparts who remain in the community, they face even greater problems afterward. They encounter significant challenges in terms of family stability, educational attainment, mental health, and substance abuse. They are also particularly likely to already have children of their own (Snyder 2004).

The remainder of this chapter explores the reentry period for the young men I studied. Beginning with the ground-level, day-to-day experience of returning home from confinement, it documents their activities and concerns during the first eight weeks after release from Mountain Ridge Academy. Weekly audio journals and field research provide a window into their attempts to fall back by navigating the conditions of probation, avoiding further contact with the police, and reestablishing relationships with family members. The young men detail their struggles to view themselves in new ways. Finally, they convey the simple pleasures of freedom, including long showers, sex with women, and the personal autonomy to act, speak, and dress as they wish.

The second lens through which I examine youth reentry involves mapping the disjuncture between the young men's plans at the point of release and what actually happened when they returned to their families and communities. I move back and forth between the intentions they articulated shortly before their release from Mountain Ridge and the realities they faced upon their return to Philadelphia. Few of these young men were able to follow through with the concrete reintegration plans developed in conjunction with their counselors at Mountain Ridge. Time and time again, I witnessed their hopes and expectations for employment, schooling and technical training, relationships with family members and romantic partners, and falling back dashed shortly after their release.

I analyze the reasons why things fell apart so quickly and in so many ways for these young men and why they expected their circumstances to be changed upon their return. I conclude that the problem stems from the tenuous relationships that these men have with social institutions such as the labor market, families, and criminal justice system, including police. Neither good planning on the part of professionals nor a simple willingness to accept accountability for past behavior and a desire to "do good" is enough to overcome the structural barriers to healthy adulthood among vulnerable youth.

We begin with excerpts from in-depth interviews with the young men shortly before they were released. Despite their skepticism toward many aspects of Mountain Ridge's program of change, these young men bought into the deterrence language used inside the facility and believed that falling back after their return was simply a matter of thinking more rationally than in the past. They expressed a new appreciation for weighing the risks and rewards of their actions and viewed the costs of offending as no longer worth the meager benefits.

Findings

Regrets and Plans for Change

The framework of criminal thinking errors used at Mountain Ridge Academy (and many other facilities around the U.S.) offers little hope for change because it assumes that the criminal personality is largely fixed in early childhood. At Mountain Ridge, it was translated in practice into deterrence theory, the idea that readjusting the ratio of risks to rewards prevents offending. Once residents were taught to identify criminal thinking errors, it presumed, they would make better decisions when opportunities to offend arose. While the young men were skeptical about this form of therapy, they did understand their process of change in terms of rational choice.

During his pre-release interview, Keandre explained that his view on falling back changed during his time at Mountain Ridge:

> [Falling back] ain't somein that I wanna do when I first came up here but, I done took seven months out my life to sit back and just think clearly, and this is not where I wanna end up at or live my life as a drug dealer, so it's all up to me to make that choice. If I find myself getting back into the same thing I just gotta think twice about it and just stop thinking my first thing. You know how people say your first instinct is your best instinct? Well my first instinct always seems to be kinda shaky, so when I think twice the answer's better so the results is better.

Being locked up gave these young men a "time out" to reflect upon their past actions and imagine a different future (Edin et al. 2004). Eddie told me, "You actually got the time to sit and get your head straight, get your head screwed on straight. Rather than in Philly it's a lot of distractions." Sharif reported,

> Once I came here I started looking at that stuff, analyzing it and finding a solution for all that stuff. And it's like now I look at things differently … It's like everything just changed my view from negative to goin' positive. And it's like everybody ask me, do you really think you could stay positive when you get home? And I'll say, yeah, if I'm determined to do that and I'm confident in myself that's what I'm gonna do.

Many talked about regretting the past and wishing they had taken another path. Shortly before his release, I asked Gabe if he agreed with the program's assertion that he was locked up because he made bad choices. He replied,

> I agree. Selling drugs was bad because I let my instant gratification get the best of me, you know. Like, 'cause I wanted to provide for myself, but I ain't wanna get no job, you know what I mean? That was a bad choice right there, just goin' out there and sellin' drugs to get money when I could have just got it the legal way and I'd a been still home right now, you know. But I ain't gonna say 'what if' 'cause if what if was a fifth we'd all be drunk.

All of these young men had more or less specific plans for schooling and/or work and housing. All (with the exception of Akeem, who quite honestly said he wasn't sure if he could stay away from the game) appeared sincere when they talked about feeling changed as a result of the program and their plans for falling back on the outside. Some, like Raymond, were probably skilled liars, trained over months at Mountain Ridge to "fake it to make it" and tell adults what they want to hear. I am inclined, however, to interpret their desire to make good as genuine, whether it stemmed from aspirations to better themselves or simply to avoid being locked up and deprived of their liberty again. So we must take seriously the harsh reality associated with returning home to the most disadvantaged and violence-ridden neighborhoods, which has the power to rapidly eliminate all hopes and plans for a crime-free future. In the next section, these realities are described in detail.

Coming Home: The First Eight Weeks

The First One to Two Days Home

Being released from Mountain Ridge Academy and returning to Philadelphia prompted a conflicting array of emotions for the young men in my study. All were excited to reunite with family members and other loved ones and to regain their freedom. After taking a bus across the state, most spent their first night at home celebrating. Eddie's mom cooked his favorite meal, short ribs and cabbage. Isaiah's girlfriend, Tamika, prepared him a full breakfast after they had stayed up all night playing with their son. Several of the young men mentioned that they had taken a long, hot shower to compensate for months or years of three-minute showers at the facility. Like Isaiah, many also reported spending sleepless nights with old girlfriends.

19 Nothing's Changed but Me: Reintegration Plans Meet the Inner City

Their first few days at home were an opportunity to recover their former selves by reestablishing their urban identity kit: heading to the barber for a "shape-up," buying a cell phone so that they could reconnect with their friends, and wearing the street clothes that had been prohibited inside Mountain Ridge. It also was important to announce their renewed presence in the community by visiting the corner store and hanging out on their stoop, two key neighborhood staging areas. Sitting on his grandmother Ida's front stoop with Leo, I observed the way that neighborhood residents in inner-city communities adapt to the constant in-and-out flow of their neighbors from juvenile facilities, jails, and prisons.

While we were sitting there, several people stopped to greet him and ask if he was home for good. A young woman named Candy approached us, wearing her arms inside her jacket. "I'm going to be a mom," she said. "No way. Who?" he asked. She smiled. "No one from around here," she said. "Who's this, your PO?" she asked. "Yeah," he said. She looked at me warily. He laughed. "She's writing my life story," he said. She looked doubtful. "He goin' to be locked up again by December." While we sat there, we observed open-air drug dealing and observed a man storm by with what looked like a handgun in his pocket.

Leo and the other men returning from reform schools soon realized that the opportunities for trouble were the same as they were before they were incarcerated. These unchanged circumstances are the reason why cognitive behavioral therapy (CBT) in which youth in the juvenile justice system learn and practice prosocial behaviors inside facilities does not easily translate to their urban neighborhoods. Eddie summed it up when he said, "Mountain Ridge is so far away from reality, it's so different from the street, it's so structured. Here in the streets, there's structure, but we make it ourselves."

When Candy predicted that Leo would be locked up again by December, she was doing what some describe as "hating." In neighborhoods of concentrated disadvantage, signs of personal success may be scrutinized by other community members. If Leo goes to college, then Candy's failure to succeed could be viewed as the result of personal shortcomings. Misery loves company. I observed hating in James's Southwest Philly neighborhood, where the young people who hung out near the corner store attempted to sabotage his efforts to fall back by falsely accusing him of selling drugs. Correctly identifying his uncle Clifton as the cornerstone of his plan to make good, they reported to Clifton that James was back to the grind, which had the intended effect of eroding the trust that the two were building.

These young men's concerns about returning home were a sobering counterpoint to their excitement. A couple of them mentioned that they needed to watch their backs carefully because they had ongoing beefs with other young men. Warren had an SOS waiting for him, which he explained meant that a gangster in the city had warned him he would be shot on sight.[3] Eddie, who lived in Southwest Philly with his mom, wasn't safe in South Philly because he had angered some guy named Estaban by dating his baby's mom.

Young men like Isaiah and Sincere had another reason to be wary about their return. Sincere's mother, Teresa, spent much of his childhood battling an addiction that resulted in her becoming HIV positive. He continued to worry that she would relapse or get sick, leaving the family without a parent. (His father had died of AIDS-related complications while he was at Mountain Ridge.) Isaiah was released to live with his aunt, whom he alternately called "my guardian" and "mom" and whom he blamed for getting him locked up. He believed that she called the police and turned him in so that she could get rid of him and be free to operate an unlicensed day care in her home. When he returned home, he was dubious about her motives. "We'll see. Only time will tell."

Their most common concerns were about returning to their old ways and the consequences that could bring, especially now that they had left the "last stop" in the juvenile system. They worried that their counselors were right all those times they had predicted that they would end up back in the system or dead. Those who worried most about slipping back into old habits, such as James and Eddie, often spent their first days at home looking for work. Others engaged in desistance talk, a kind of self-talk designed to support a narrative of prosocial change.

Desistance Talk

One of the windows through which I was able to view these young men's struggle to fall back was through their audio reentry journals. Many used "desistance talk" as a cognitive and linguistic tool to help reinforce their determination not to return to their old ways. Luis, the only young man I followed who regularly used drugs other than marijuana and who saw his reentry process largely in terms of sobriety, underscored this point:

> Trying to start off another session of some good talking and hopefully see something better than what I was seeing out here. Start off a better relationship with my family and other the people that I know that I love, deep down inside. I gotta do it, do it soon. Trust is something you keep when you gain it. I came between death a lot of time but I guess God gave me a chance and to this day,

19 Nothing's Changed but Me: Reintegration Plans Meet the Inner City

I'm trying to understand the chance that I got and why I got it. I guess I needed that chance and now I'm doing what I need to do. I thank you, Jamie, for letting me speak into this. I want to do some more speaking about the streets, about my life. It puts me in the space to know that I can talk about my past. I have it on tape, where people can listen to it and understand what I'm going through right now. I think it's good for me.

Akeem reported during his first week home,

The smell of weed it takes me back to the old days. When I smelled that, I wanted to say forget probation and wanted to smoke, but y'know, I wasn't trying to deal with the consequences all over again just for a blunt. I feel like the drug game is calling me. I see everybody out here, makin' all this money. Stuntin' on people and shit. That's what I feel like. Goin' back to hustlin' and shit. But I also know that I don't want to deal with the consequences of that action, so I gotta think real hard about what I want to do. If a job comes in line, then that's a good thing. If not, that's a bad thing. This is my story. And it's to be continued.

I got chills listening to Warren's first journal entry; he had brought it along as he and his buddies were driving around in an SUV at night and were talking into the recorder at the moment when another young man they knew was shot and killed. His account, clearly influenced by what he had just seen, echoed these concerns about the future. "Deuce Deuce gang [from 22nd Street] is everywhere. Everybody Deuce Deuce. It's going down. Everybody got pistols. Y'know what I'm saying? How it's happening. And me? I'm going either way, right or wrong. But you know I love my freedom too much." About the shooting, he said, "On the real tip, man, I felt kinda scared, man, because these guys don't give a fuck."

These messages were more tenuous and reveal more uncertainty than the claims the young men made while they were locked up. As they came home and slipped back into old patterns, I was reminded of addicts who are able to clean up inside rehab, but find that returning to people, places, and things associated with their old lives is simply too much to counter.

Young people do not make this transition alone. Although services are not available to all young people returning from reform schools nationwide, all Philadelphia youth receive these services as mandated by the Pennsylvania Juvenile Court Judges' Commission. Juvenile reintegration consists of supervision and support designed to smooth the transition from facility to community. Before release, reintegration workers and/or juvenile probation officers help youth reenroll in school, work with the young person's family to ensure that there is a stable home environment, connect youths to employment opportunities, and locate other community-based services that fit their clients' individual needs. Young people are required to meet specific conditions of their release, such as paying restitution, doing community service, and passing regular drug screens. In Philadelphia, the supervisory role is played by the juvenile probation officer housed at Family Court, and support services are offered by a reintegration worker employed by a private agency.

Conditions of Probation and Interactions with Reintegration Professionals

Returning youth meet with the various professionals to whom they will be held accountable during their probationary period at their discharge hearing, the morning after they take the bus home from their facilities. Often, the reintegration worker will have met with clients in person during their monthly facility visits. He or she is supposed to visit the client's home several times to determine whether the household and the parent or guardian living there are conducive to a smooth transition and develop an individual service plan designed to address the client's needs upon return. In addition to working with their reintegration workers to develop plans for employment or schooling, youth often meet with their probation officers on discharge day to discuss the conditions of probation. When I took Eddie and his mother to his discharge hearing, I sensed how overwhelmed he was about meeting all the obligations his PO, Lisa, laid out for him. They held a brief conference outside the courtroom while he expressed his displeasure at having to attend Narcotics Anonymous (NA) meetings four times per week. "Listen, NA isn't for everyone. If you don't feel comfortable there, don't just stop going. Talk to me and I can get you in somewhere else that is a little more in line with the therapy you've been getting," she added. She told Eddie that she expected to see him the following week for a urine screen. Karen, his reintegration worker, added that she would be seeing him three days per week. His mom suggested that he get a calendar to help organize his daily and weekly itinerary. "You're going to be a busy man," she said.

Eddie's was a high-risk case for Karen and Lisa. He had been enrolled in a four-year university while he was at Mountain Ridge and had to make it only through the summer without any new trouble before he planned to move to central Pennsylvania, where it was assumed it would be harder for him to find trouble. No one wanted to allow a kid with real potential to slip through the cracks. Eddie's conditions of probation hint at a mismatch of services surrounding substance abuse needs and resources. Eddie was eventually tempted to smoke marijuana with his friends, despite the possible consequences that hot urines (positive drug tests) would have for his case and his ability to leave the jurisdiction to attend college. However, Eddie, like the other young men in the study (except Luis), never reported—nor did their drug tests indicate—using drugs other than marijuana.

Home and Family Life

The young men released from Mountain Ridge trickled back into their communities with varied levels of stability and support at home. Seven (Malik, Hassan, Keandre, Luis, Raymond, Sincere, and Warren) moved in with their mothers; Sharif moved in with his father and stepmother; Leo went back to living with his grandmother; James moved into his uncle Clifton's spare room; Tony stayed with his sister, Akeem with his brother, and Isaiah with his aunt. Gabe was the only one to return to a home with parents who had been married and living together his whole life. Three young men—Sincere, Gabe, and Isaiah—quickly moved in with their girlfriends, retaining their original addresses for the purposes of probation.

Most of the young men had betrayed their family members' trust during their days in the drug game. They stored drugs, money, and weapons in their homes and brought over friends who stole anything of value that wasn't tacked down. They lied about their whereabouts and activities and engaged in behavior that resulted in police raids and other unwanted attention from the authorities. Their involvement in the system had been costly, both financially and emotionally, for many of their family members. Their return was greeted with a mixture of relief at having them home and a nagging concern that they had not changed their ways. This ambivalence was evidenced by the common practice of withholding a house key until a period of trouble-free time had passed. Without a house key, the young men's status was diminished to that of a guest; if they returned home when others weren't there, they had to bide their time elsewhere. I watched as they phoned upstairs to see if anyone was available to drop keys down from an open window.

Many chafed at the new house rules, particularly with regard to visitors. Some felt the rules challenged their autonomy and manhood by infantilizing them in similar ways that Mountain Ridge had. All but two (Eddie and Malik) had turned 18 while incarcerated, fueling their expectations that they would be treated as adults when they returned home. This disappointment often resulted in conflict, leading to instability in their housing. Akeem, for instance, battled with his older brother over house rules and his brother's demands that he find work. "His rules are really simple, really easy. I don't know why I don't follow them. I do know why, I just got my own tendency to do what I want."

Within four months of returning home, Akeem had been kicked out of his brother's house for failing to pay his portion of the bills and refusing to meet with his caseworker during scheduled visits. He then moved in with his mother in a neighborhood adjacent to Temple University. I lost touch with Akeem during this period, although I was able to keep tabs on him through his probation officer's notes. Five months after his release from Mountain Ridge, he was refusing to meet with the family counselor the court had assigned. According to his PO, he was suffering from suicidal ideations and it was "doubtful" that he was still in school.

Scrutiny by and accountability to parents and guardians paralleled another unpleasant aspect of Mountain Ridge: being treated like a criminal. Criminologist Shadd Maruna et al. (2004, p. 272) note that "a hundred nondeviant acts may not be enough to earn someone the recognition of nondeviance." This "negativity bias" caused the greatest problems for those like James, who viewed himself as transformed after his period of incarceration. He wondered how, if people who were supposed to be in his corner, such as his uncle Clifton, didn't believe in him, he could continue to believe in himself. James repeatedly moved out of Clifton's home when Clifton accused him of stealing things from the house or returning to the drug game. When he moved in with his mother, who claimed to believe his story of personal transformation, she pressured him to "pick up a packet" here and there to help her make the rent.

Reentry Plans Versus Reality

Table 19.1 provides a snapshot of rearrest and offending activity during the three years following release from Mountain Ridge.

The youths' concerns about falling back into old routines were certainly justified. Within six weeks, at least four had returned to drug selling, and a fifth, Sharif, was dead. Akeem never admitted directly to selling drugs, but within three weeks of coming home he told me that he needed $300 for an "illegal transaction gone bad." Gabe sold drugs only during his first few weeks at home, as he was waiting for his first paycheck, and ended up as one of two whom I identify as having gone straight during the three-year period of follow-up. Keandre and Luis were both arrested for drug selling, at 20 days and 5 weeks post-release, respectively. After a stint inside a state-run juvenile facility, Luis established the longest record, with four more arrests for receiving

19 Nothing's Changed but Me: Reintegration Plans Meet the Inner City

Table 19.1 Reoffending, reincarceration, and other criminal justice outcomes, three years after release

	< 6 wks	6 wks–6 mos	6–12 mos	12–24 mos	24–36 mos	Total arrests 3 years	Reincarceration 3 years
Akeem	Self-report					0	
Eddie			Arrest	Arrest	Arrest	4	6–23 mos, 1–2 yrs, 6–12 mos
Gabe	Self-report					0	
Hassan		Bench warrant	Arrest	Arrest	Arrest	5	3–6 days
Isaiah		Report by domestic partner	Self-report	Arrest		2	
James				Arrest		1	
Keandre	Arrest			Arrest	Arrest	4	
Leo		Self-report	Self-report	Arrest	Arrest	3	1–2 yrs
Luis	Arrest		Arrest	Arrest	Arrest	5	5 mos juv; 1–2 yrs adult
Malik		Arrest		Arrest	Arrest	4	8–14 mos juv; 2–5 yrs adult
Sharif	Deceased						
Sincere		Self-report		Arrest	Self-report	1	
Tony		Arrest		Arrest	Arrest	3	2 mos/1–2 yrs/ 5–10 yrs
Warren		Arrest		Arrest	Arrest	4	Jail max 23 mos

stolen property (twice), carrying a firearm, and robbery. Sharif was brutally gunned down and killed five weeks after his return to North Philadelphia. Although the *Philadelphia Inquirer* reported that he was found clutching 38 bundles of crack, his family and friends believed his death was payback for signing a subpoena to testify in a murder trial less than 24 hours prior to his murder. At the six-month mark, six more had resumed offending and a seventh, Hassan, was on the run from the police. By the time 3 years had passed, 7 had spent time in jail or prison, and they had generated a combined total of 36 arrests.[4]

These young men were vulnerable to pressures to return to drug using and selling and to violent victimization. Two months and four days after returning home from Mountain Ridge, Hassan was shot after he and some young men from his block were leaving a game of pickup basketball against men from a neighboring block. Soon after, his PO, Anthony, received a phone call from a city detective saying that he had been trying to get him to cooperate with the investigation of the shooting, but that Hassan refused. The detective claimed that several witnesses had seen Hassan with a gun and threatened to file charges against him if he did not give up the name of the person who shot him. Anthony told me he believed the police were trumping up charges and using Hassan's tenuous status as a probationer to coerce him to comply. Later, when the prosecution dropped the charges, it looked like he was right. Faced with a new arrest and probation violation or the strong likelihood that he would be killed for snitching, Hassan chose to become a fugitive. He remained on the run for most of the next three years.

Being embedded in street culture involves young men in a repertoire of activities that are counterproductive to successful transitions to adulthood. When a crisis occurs, usually when money is needed quickly, their reaction is to use the tools that have worked in the past to resolve it. Recognizing criminal thinking errors and employing correctives become inadequate and irrelevant to meet the demands of the situation. This reliance on drug selling to solve short-term financial problems is clearly seen in the case of Malik.

Malik was one of two 17-year-olds I followed. His reentry plan involved moving back in with his mother, getting a job doing carpentry with his father, and going to community college. He had already filled out the financial aid forms while he was at Mountain Ridge. Although he did start working with his father, I never heard him mention college again. His first month at home seemed promising; he was working so many hours that he barely had time to spend with his old friends who were still selling drugs. He said, "Carpentry is hard, man! But you should see my check. $5,000 at the end!" All his efforts came screeching to a halt five weeks after returning home when the money he'd been saving for his son Tyrik's first birthday party was stolen from his house. I ran into him at Family Court, and he told me the story. He looked terrible, his eyes puffy and small, like he'd been crying or up all night. "It's one thing to steal from me, but they stole from *my son*," he said in disbelief. When I asked what he planned to do, his next comment was telling: "Whatever it takes. I'm in debt now." Later he asked to be dropped off at his old drug block, and it was clear he had returned to the game.

The next month, Malik was arrested for carrying a gun. After he was committed to one of the state-run juvenile facilities, I lost touch with him. Just over a year after he was committed there, Malik, then 19, was arrested for selling drugs in central Pennsylvania. While he awaited his hearing, he was arrested twice more, once for possession of marijuana and once on a firearms charge. In November 2007, he was sentenced to prison for 22 months to 5 years on the drug charge. Just over three years after his release from Mountain Ridge, he was sentenced to three to six years in state prison on the gun charge.

Warren, the young man who witnessed the shooting during his first week home and Malik's cousin, was similarly embedded in street culture. He also struggled to manage bipolar disorder, which was diagnosed when he was in detention. A month after he came home, his mother who told me he had visited a local outpatient mental health clinic. They had given him a number of medications, but he didn't like to take them because they made him sleepy. After several discouraging months, he had returned to drug selling, but this time he was working behind the scenes, connecting buyers and sellers in a manner that reduced his risk of arrest. He also drew a new line about what he would sell, saying that crack was just too risky.

Five months after his release, Warren was arrested for drug dealing. Ironically, according to his story (which I believe, since he had already admitted to me that he was selling drugs), he was not actually doing anything wrong at the time of his arrest. He explained that he had been getting Chinese food down on Washington Avenue and had seen some guys inside from his neighborhood that he usually avoided. He had just walked up to the window to pick up his food when a couple of police officers came in and told all the young men in the store to get up against the wall. Warren had been indignant. "I ain't doing anything wrong. I'm not getting up against the wall," he told them defiantly. Of course, this made them angry and they proceeded to search him. When they didn't find anything but money, they searched the store and found a nickel bag of weed in a wastepaper basket. The store owner tried to explain to the police that Warren had just walked in, but they put him in the car, allowing the other two guys to go free.

Warren kept talking smack to them from the back seat of the cruiser. When he heard a 187 (code for homicide) called in over the radio, he derided them for wasting time on a nickel bag of weed when there were murders going on in the city. At his arraignment, he was advised that he would likely get only community service if he pled guilty. Refusing to plead, he went to trial and received a jail sentence for a maximum of two years. After spending a short time in jail, he was arrested again for aggravated assault, for which he received two more years of probation.

Isaiah avoided drug selling for a comparatively long period. His first signs of trouble involved domestic violence against his baby's mom, Tamika. After dropping out of college and working sporadically, he, like Warren, set up a "silent partnership" in which he fronted money for a drug operation. He was never apprehended for this business, but was arrested almost exactly one year after his release from Mountain Ridge for simple assault against Tamika and again the following year for harassment and violation of a protective order.

Similarly, Sincere returned briefly to the drug game but was never detected by police. His one arrest during my study involved buying a $5 "blunt" (marijuana cigarette) for personal use; the charge was later dropped. Sincere's involvement in the drug game since I've known him has been characterized by what criminologists call "intermittency," moving back and forth between periods of selling drugs or paraphernalia and of non-offending.

Finally, Eddie, the college-bound Mountain Ridge graduate, illustrates how criminal behavior can become a familiar routine that young people fall back upon in moments of uncertainty. When he went away to attend the university, he quickly established himself as a small-time dealer in the college town where he had moved. By Thanksgiving of his freshman year, he had been arrested for a check-kiting scheme and had been suspended from school. He spent approximately a year in state prison as a result.

The young men I followed were released from Mountain Ridge with solid reentry plans, a desire to make a better life for themselves and their families, a set of decision-making skills provided by the facility, in most cases a diploma or GED, the deterrent effect of knowing their next arrest would likely land them in the adult system, and a network of professionals who were there to support and control them during their first months at home. While these ingredients may seem necessary conditions for them to succeed on the outside, they certainly did not prove to be sufficient. Although many felt changed as a result of their time at Mountain Ridge, their material conditions remained the same. They returned to neighborhoods plagued by violence, households prone to financial crises, a legal labor market offering low-paying, degrading jobs, and an illicit economy that beckoned them with the promise of fast cash and masculine pride.

These material conditions, and the cultural and developmental adaptations to these conditions, are the real reason why young men began offending in the first place and why so many continued to offend. Because the juvenile justice system is ill equipped to restructure the labor market to create better jobs, allow young people the financial freedom to invest in higher education, dismantle racial discrimination or residential segregation, or fix families struggling with poverty or addiction, it must recast the problem in terms of poor decision making, as a matter of individual deficits on the part of the young men who are part of the system.

Postscript

Since I began the research reported here, knowledge about youth reentry has greatly expanded. In 2004, the journal, *Youth Violence and Juvenile Justice*, published a special issue dedicated to the subject, providing a statistical portrait of the youth reentry population (Snyder 2004) and making a case for developmentally tailored reintegration services (Altschuler and Brash 2004). A number of other ethnographic portraits of juvenile incarceration and reentry were conducted in a variety of jurisdictions. This body of scholarship has identified numerous structural barriers to desistance from offending, including finding stable employment, educational attainment, parenthood, managing conditions of probation supervision, and navigating peer networks (Abrams and Terry 2017; Inderbitzin 2009; Panuccio and Christian 2019; Sullivan 2004). This research has also unpacked the internal contradictions of therapeutic-carceral logics, which attempt to produce compliant citizens and encourage the framing of future success in individualistic terms as they simultaneously reinforce stigmatic identities as men who pose a risk to society (Abrams and Lea 2016; Cox 2018; Inderbitzin 2007; Sankofa et al. 2018; Soyer 2016).

As the *Falling Back* men have moved into their 30s, I have continued to follow their progress. By 2016, eight had been incarcerated in the adult system within the five years prior to the follow-up, eight had been rearrested during the prior two years (with two others incarcerated), and three were serving long-term probation sentences. Only 3 of the 13 men still living in Pennsylvania had avoided contact with the justice system as adults. Tony, featured prominently in this chapter, spent a decade in adult prison and returned to Philadelphia under a restrictive set of probation conditions (Fader and Henson 2020). At the time of this writing (age 34), he is in jail for a violation of his probation related to a new arrest for possession of marijuana.

Moreover, the men's lives in other respects were chaotic, characterized by housing and food insecurity, permanent labor market discouragement, untreated mental health problems, frequent losses of friends and family members to violence or chronic illness, and continued "drama" (as they referred to it) in their relationships with baby's mothers and families of origin. Tragically, soon after I conducted this follow-up, "Warren" (age 30) was the victim of a home invasion and fatal shooting.

Although we cannot conclude that these trajectories were caused by their period of incarceration as teenagers, it seems certain that therapeutic treatment in the context of confinement did not improve their life chances. Indeed, as the influence of adolescent development science has grown over the last 15 years (Cauffman and Steinberg 2012), many policy makers and practitioners have had to acknowledge the widespread failure of juvenile incarceration as a tool for positive change. The U.S. reliance on residential placements for youth has declined dramatically and the use of smaller, cottage-like facilities sited closer to home, as well as other community-based alternatives, have expanded (Juvenile Residential Facility Census Databook 2018). This shift in juvenile justice philosophy, supported by continued low youth crime rates, has resulted in a reversal of many of the "get-tough" era policies, including a movement to raise the age of criminal responsibility in many jurisdictions (Justice Policy Institute 2017) and a new focus on emerging adult (18–25) justice (Perker and Chester 2017). Future research will be needed to document the effects of these changes, particularly when juvenile crime rates eventually begin to regress to the mean and the policy context is no longer so favorable to treatment over punishment.

Notes

1. "Mountain Ridge Academy" is a pseudonym employed throughout to protect the confidentiality of the young men who agreed to be part of the study.
2. The "Chinese store" is a term used to describe both Chinese food stores, which are plentiful in poor urban neighborhoods, and corner bodegas run by Asians of all nationalities.
3. Sadly, his concern foreshadowed his death many years later. In 2017, he was killed during a home invasion at age 30.
4. Raymond is missing from this count because I did not have access to his criminal records after he moved to South Carolina.

References

Abrams, L. S., & Lea, C. (2016). Becoming employable: An ethnographic examination of life skills classes in a men's jail. *The Prison Journal, 95*(6), 667–687.

Abrams, L. S., & Terry, D. (2017). *Everyday desistance: The transition to adulthood among formerly incarcerated youth.* Rutgers University Press.

Altschuler, D. M., & Brash, R. (2004). Adolescent and teenage offenders confronting the challenges and opportunities of reentry. *Youth Violence and Juvenile Justice, 2*(1), 72–87.

Bullis, M., Yovanoff, P., Mueller, G., & Havel, E. (2002). Life on the 'outs'—Examination of the facility-to-community transition of incarcerated youth. *Exceptional Children, 69*(1), 7–22.

Cauffman, E., & Steinberg, L. (2012). Emerging findings from research on adolescent development and juvenile justice. *Victims & Offenders, 7*(4), 428–449.

Cox, A. (2018). *Trapped in a vice: The consequences of confinement for young people*. Rutgers University Press.

Edin, K., Nelson, T. J., Paranal, R., Patillo, M., Weiman, D., & Western, B. (2004). Imprisoning America: The social effects of mass incarceration.

Fader, J. (2013). *Falling back: Incarceration and transitions to adulthood among urban youth*. Rutgers University Press.

Fader, J., & Henson, R. (2020). This individual may or may not be on the Megan's Law registry: The sex offender label's impact on reentry. Pp. 235–256 in A. Leverentz, E. Chen, & J. Christian (Eds.), *Moving beyond recidivism: Expanding approaches to research on prisoner reentry and reintegration*. New York University Press.

Glaser, B. G., & Strauss, A. L. (2017). *Discovery of grounded theory: Strategies for qualitative research*. Routledge.

Inderbitzin, M. (2007). Inside a maximum-security juvenile training school: Institutional attempts to redefine the American Dream and 'normalize' incarcerated youth. *Punishment & Society, 9*(3), 235–251.

Inderbitzin, M. (2009). Reentry of emerging adults: Adolescent inmates' transition back into the community. *Journal of Adolescent Research, 24*(4), 453–476.

Justice Policy Institute. (2017). Raise the age. Retrieved from http://www.justicepolicy.org/research/11239.

Juvenile Residential Facility Census Databook: 2000–2016. (2018). Retrieved from https://www.ojjdp.gov/ojstatbb/jrfcdb/asp/aboutJRFC.asp.

Maruna, S., Lebel, T. P., Mitchell, N., & Naples, M. (2004). Pygmalion in the reintegration process: Desistance from crime through the looking glass. *Psychology, Crime & Law, 10*(3), 271–281.

Mears, D. P., & Travis, J. (2004). Youth development and reentry. *Youth Violence and Juvenile Justice, 2*(1), 3–20.

Panuccio, E., & Christian, J. (2019). Work, family, and masculine identity: an intersectional approach to understanding young, black men's experiences of reentry. *Race and Justice, 9*(4), 407–433.

Perker, S. S., & Chester, L. (2017). *Emerging adult justice in Massachusetts*. Harvard University Kennedy School of Government.

Sankofa, J., Cox, A., Fader, J. J., Inderbitzin, M., Abrams, L. S., & Nurse, A. M. (2018). Juvenile corrections in the era of reform: A meta-synthesis of qualitative studies. *International Journal of Offender Therapy and Comparative Criminology, 62*(7), 1763–1786.

Snyder, H. N. (2004). An empirical portrait of the youth reentry population. *Youth Violence and Juvenile Justice, 2*(1), 39–55.

Soyer, M. (2016). *A dream denied: Incarceration, recidivism, and young minority men in America*. University of California Press.

Sullivan, M. L. (2004). Youth perspectives on the experience of reentry. *Youth Violence and Juvenile Justice, 2*(1), 56–71.

20

Young Women and Desistance: Finding a Net to Fall Back On

Laura S. Abrams and Diane J. Terry

Introduction

I already knew it was going to be hard for me, so I already had prepared myself. I wasn't scared, I was just more preoccupied with how to get home; the way. I don't even remember where the streets are at, how to get home. I hope I'm going the right way. (Irene)

These were Irene's thoughts upon exiting the California Youth Authority (CYA), the harshest form of imprisonment for youth in the state, after five years of incarceration, a twenty-year-old young woman with five dollars in her pocket and a small bag of belongings from when she was fifteen. Nearly all of her former friends were by then incarcerated, had moved, or were no longer reachable. She had no close family members to help with her transition, and

---

Reprinted from:
Everyday Desistance: The Transition to Adulthood Among Formerly Incarcerated Youth (2017) Rutgers University Press.

L. S. Abrams (✉)
Luskin School of Public Affairs, University of California Los Angeles, Los Angeles, CA, USA
e-mail: abrams@luskin.ucla.edu

D. J. Terry
Loyola Marymount University, Los Angeles, CA, USA

© The Author(s), under exclusive license to Springer Nature Switzerland AG 2021
A. Cox, L. S. Abrams (eds.), *The Palgrave International Handbook of Youth Imprisonment*, Palgrave Studies in Prisons and Penology, https://doi.org/10.1007/978-3-030-68759-5_20

no cell phone to connect her with people that could possibly provide some support. How does a young woman survive these conditions?

In this chapter, we showcase young women's experiences with desistance on their pathway toward adulthood. Prior research has found that young women are more likely to achieve desistance in young adulthood than their male counterparts in part due to the bonds they are able to forge with friends, family, and significant others. Whereas women's movement away from crime is often facilitated by social relationships, men appear to be more instrumentally or individually oriented toward their own successes (Benda 2005; Salvatore and Taniguchi 2012). In this chapter, we investigate how these relationships operated for the young women.

While the young women in our study struggled to becoming economically self-sufficient, they did not grapple with temptations to continue in criminal activity. However, stemming from a dearth of family stability and poverty, all of these young women were still teetering on the edge of solid ground, putting them at risk for criminal activity either for survival or through their associations with romantic partners and friends. For the young women, their sense of stability post-incarceration appeared to be dependent on their own resourcefulness as well as the generosity of the people around them. Many of their struggles revolved around finding a stable base when the very sense of home had been quite elusive to them throughout their lives. All of the women's stories are hence interconnected through the themes of finding home, breaking the cycle, caregiving, social bonds, gendered violence, and survival and resilience.

Method

A qualitative, narrative methodology guided this study. This methodology provided a framework to understand and interpret the participants' lived experiences through repeated in-depth interviewing (Sandelowski 1991). The research method is fitting with our exploratory questions as we seek to build knowledge in an understudied area. The University of California at Los Angeles Institutional Review Board approved all aspects of the research.

Sampling and Recruitment

The researchers recruited participants purposively from community-based agencies in Los Angeles, California. The young women were recruited through information sessions held at two community agencies providing services to formerly incarcerated youth. All of the reentry organizations involved as recruitment sites were voluntary. In accordance with the methodology, the sampling procedure was purposive and was not intended to be generalizable.

Data Collection

Following informed consent, two in-depth interviews were conducted with each participant within a four-to-six-week timeframe. Of the seven young women, four also participated in third, fourth, and/or fifth interviews over the course of two years. Two researchers were present at each interview. The interviews lasted from 60 to 90 minutes and were conducted in private settings. Participants were compensated $25 for the first and $30 for the second interview and subsequent interviews. Each interview was digitally recorded and transcribed verbatim.

The first interview covered life history information, and the second interview focused on narrating the process of desistance from crime during emerging adulthood. During the second interview, the respondents also participated in a social support exercise in which they were asked to identify their primary, secondary, and tertiary supports, and describe how they utilized these supports. The authors adapted this exercise from Kahn and Antonucci's (1980) convoy model of social relations to include questions that were specific to the participants' experiences as formerly incarcerated young people (e.g., "who can you count on to help you stay out of trouble?"). The adapted convoy exercise was used as a visual tool to elicit more in-depth information about understandings and uses of social bonds and supports. Subsequent interviews consisted of updates and conversations about career, relationships, parenting, and other issues. These were loosely structured and largely directed by the participants.

The Young Women

Twenty-five formerly incarcerated emerging adults participated in the study as a whole. For this chapter, the authors focus exclusively on the seven female-identified participants from the larger sample of 25. Table 20.1 contains information about each of the seven participants according to pseudonyms. All seven were cisgender women between the ages of eighteen and twenty at first interview, were Black and/or Latinx, and nearly all had been in foster care as at some point in their childhood. Two of the young women were parents of one or more children, and three were in romantic partnerships.

Table 20.1 Sample characteristics

Name	Age at first interview	Age at first incarceration	Race	Relationship status[a]	Number of children[a]	Foster care history
Carina	20	12	Latina	Single	0	Yes
Irene	20	14	Latina	Partnered	0	Yes
Lupe	19	13	Latina	Partnered	0	Yes
Sara	19	13	Latina	Single	0	Yes
Desiree	20	14	African American	In flux	1	Yes
Amber	18	12	African American	Single	0	No
Keira	18	16	African American	Partnered	1[a]	No

[a]Had a second child during the study period

Analysis

Data analysis consisted of an open and focused coding, data reduction, and comparison across gender groups. Once all of the transcripts were coded, the codes and preliminary concepts were discussed and synthesized to conduct more focused coding. Once focused coding was completed, data reduction activities included generating conceptual maps and matrices of main themes in regard to desistance. Final themes were crosschecked between the authors and with the raw data. Multiple data reduction strategies were used including conceptual maps and matrices, and the authors worked together on interpreting the overall findings.

Findings

Irene: Finding a Family

When Irene was released from the state youth prison, she had no family members to return to, no job, and limited concrete plans for her future. As may be all too customary, her parole officers had done little to prepare her logistically for her release. Irene was unable to return to her mother, as their relationship had not recovered from its contentious history, and her mother had not visited her even one time during her lengthy incarceration. By the time Irene was set for release, she had heard from a relative that her mother had moved out of state and was serving her own prison term. This news sent Irene into a bit of shock but also gave her motivation to change course, to steer clear of her

20 Young Women and Desistance: Finding a Net to Fall Back On

mother's destructive path. She explained: "So, in reality now I see it as a big step that I don't want to see myself. When I look at the mirror I don't want to see my mom, right, I want to see me. Something else—break the chain at least."

Irene's sincere motivation to "break the chain" was compromised by her tenuous circumstances, particularly in finding a place to call home. When we first met Irene, we were impressed with her mature sense of understanding how her history of abuse and trauma had led her to criminal activity. Although she had largely committed crimes of economic survival, she sorely regretted the cost of these actions to her victims, which is one major component of desistance (Maruna 2001). After five years of contemplation, she was mentally and emotionally committed to a new way of life. Notwithstanding Irene's emotional maturity and will to change, her circumstances were still very much in flux; she had been out of prison for seven months and was already on her fourth living situation. Irene described some of the difficulties that she had experienced in finding a stable home:

> I had a 'so-called' friend that I called my aunt and I went to her house but after I stayed there for a whole week … She was a big girl. She had her boyfriend come over and stuff and I guess her boyfriend made a comment saying that 'oh, I saw her naked when she came out of the bathroom. She did it on purpose'—when I *never* do that. So she started tripping, I started to leave and she called my mentor, and told her 'she can't be here.' So they found a halfway home for me and I didn't like it because they are racist. It was all Black girls and there were elder people, too, so they were kind of jealous, too—this halfway home had girls and guys. So the guys would talk and they thought 'oh, she's trying to take my man da da da,' so that made me go 'like, ok, I need to get outta here. I need to find a job as soon as possible.' So I found me a job and then I moved.

Fleeing the halfway house due to the suspicions and threats surrounding her from other young women, Irene landed a part-time stocking position at a drugstore and rented a room in an apartment for about $200 a month, which was still a stretch on a limited income. Yet soon she had to exit that situation because of a potential danger from the landlord. Once again, she felt threatened by her position as a woman in a world that she knew very well from her history—one with the potential for sexual exploitation: "males think that if I'm a young lady by myself they want something else." Fearing another problematic situation and with her survival instinct in high gear, she quickly moved on.

Seven months after her release, Irene appeared to have found a sense of stability. Now in her fourth home, she was renting a room in a house from an unrelated adult woman in a modest neighborhood and had obtained some part-time work. The apartment was fairly void of furniture and decoration yet she had her own bedroom and seemed comfortable there. She mentioned that she was still a bit lonely living with a stranger.

Just four weeks later when we arranged to meet for her second interview, we were surprised that Irene had moved again—this time with her boyfriend Javier in his family home. Irene had met Javier at a bus stop just a few weeks after she was released. While she had not had many intimate relationships due to her history of abuse and a significant amount of time behind bars, she felt she had found someone with whom she could finally feel "at home." She articulated how the relationship with Javier moved her from a space of being isolated in the apartment with a stranger to feeling loved and protected. She said: "We've gone through our ups and downs but it's just like, we, he … similar background. We understand each other and he helps me out and he gave me his family because he knows I don't have no family." So several months into the relationship, she moved into his family home in a working-class neighborhood in South Los Angeles. There she and Javier shared a small room with one of his other brothers.

Irene's immersion into Javier's large family fulfilled a deeply seated longing: a safe sense of place and home. Initially, Javier's family appeared to be an ideal setting to find this peace. During her lonely times of incarceration, Irene had "a vision that I was being on my own for all the time... alone." The loneliness of confinement had caused her to accept that she was always going to be alone, so she was very pleasantly surprised by her good fortune. Javier had a large family with seven siblings and many nieces and nephews. Moving into a family had broken her longstanding sense of isolation. She also finally found a mother figure that she felt she could trust and confide in—someone with whom she could cook meals and have intimate talks.

However, living with Javier was not without its own risks. Irene knew that Javier was on parole and that some of his siblings, cousins, and friends were actively involved in a local gang and on probation or parole. Some also had a gang target on their backs with the police. With Javier, she frequently went to parties where trouble could emerge at any moment; yet she willingly took the risk because she enjoyed feeling finally free after so many years behind bars. She explained: "So, me and him, we're just alike. We work 'cause, like, we drink together, we hang out, we have lots of fun, you know, like, life of the party." These activities obviously placed Irene in situations where she could get into trouble with the police simply by being at the wrong place at the wrong time. For Irene, the benefits of being part of this family clearly outweighed the risks.

Four months later, Irene's life took another sharp turn when Javier was arrested for attempted murder. Although she believed in his innocence and viewed the evidence against him as circumstantial, she worried that his past convictions might be enough for his lawyers talk him into a plea deal that might carry a very long sentence. While awaiting trial, Javier had also proposed to her, and she accepted his offer of marriage. Irene was emotionally torn about staying loyal to a man who was facing a long sentence. She was not sure he would get out of prison in the foreseeable future, yet she desperately wanted to maintain the sense of security she had found with him and his family. So while he was awaiting trial, Irene continued to operate as a member of the family who took her in as Javier's fiancée, as she explained in the way that "a traditional Mexican family does."

Javier was a person who could pull Irene into trouble yet also protect her from criminal influences and past associations. Yet one of the ways that he protected her was through his extreme jealousy. Although Irene was involved in positive activities, such as job training and attending community programs for formerly incarcerated youth, Javier had asked her to cut down on these activities due to his fear of her meeting other men. On the one hand this deeply annoyed her, as it reminded her of years of being told what to do while she was confined; yet still, lying low and minimizing going out protected her from getting into trouble. When Javier was locked up, she found herself with a degree of freedom that she did not feel she was ready to handle. Being only minimally employed, she also had time on her hands. So during his trial, Irene began to contact old boyfriends and others through social media but still tried to keep her relationship with Javier in the forefront of her everyday decisions.

A few months later, Irene had moved on, ending her engagement to Javier (even though he was acquitted and returned home), leaving the family home, and landing a new job, one that she saw as having more potential for her future. This decision was not without significant turmoil as she had survived some abuse within the relationship. This relationship mistreatment was understandably very emotionally triggering due to her history of abuse and difficulty with intimacy. Yet Irene managed to find the emotional resources that she needed to feel whole—in herself and through her outside support system. Many of the friends and networks she had developed, including the mentor she worked with while in prison, came "to her rescue" to help her find an apartment and move. She felt blessed with the outpouring of support from her community. During our final interview, she explained:

> So, I'm just trying right now to little by little to control myself and have back what I've built up before because I've lost myself. Because he <Javier> made me something ... I really wanted to just turn around and ask him, you know that I've gone through so much and you didn't even make it easier for me ... I feel bad because basically, I waited for a jerk that is just going to come back to me and abuse me. Use me and abuse me. But I'm doing better. I'm going to school and going to work. I'm about to get my license to get a car. Other than that, I have a nice spot.

Despite having to contend with violence and to sever ties with her post-prison family, Irene managed to find her way back to herself and was working to move forward. She relied on her social supports—mostly those who were new in her life, to get her to a better place and to interrupt the cycle of abuse.

Irene's story is distinctly her own—one of strength, survival, and emotional resilience. Yet it also touches on many of the young women's struggles post-incarceration: seeking to find a place to call home, contending with the threat of abuse or sexual victimization by men, depending at times on others for economic protection, and enduring several moves, twists, and turns before finally landing on her own two feet. Among the eight women in the study, five moved at least once just during the course of our interviews with them, three moved more than once, and two moved out of state and became unreachable. And while Irene with these uncertainties and criminal associations managed to move forward with her life, others were unable to gain the momentum needed to propel them toward a more positive and stable future. Lupe's story represents the latter of these possibilities.

Lupe: The Cost of Good Fortune

At age eighteen, Lupe was in the process of transitioning out of both the juvenile justice and the foster care systems. Wearing a backward ball cap and baggy jeans, she appeared tougher than her actual personality, which was open and soft-spoken. As described in Chap. 2, Lupe had a turbulent childhood that included an absent mother, paternal abuse, familial rejection based on her gender non-conformity and sexual orientation, and drug addiction. Her crimes of survival were quite common among the young women in this study, including theft, drug use, and running away from foster care.

We first met Lupe when she had been out of her juvenile camp placement for about seven months and was living in a transitional home for young women who had been in foster care. Lupe's few years prior to emancipation had been extremely unstable, both logistically and emotionally. She met the self-described "love of her life" while in a group home at age sixteen. With Lydia, Lupe felt that she could better control her compulsion to abuse drugs. So when Lydia was released from their shared group home placement, Lupe felt lost and started using drugs more heavily again. Although she was court-mandated to live in her group home placement, she ran away to be with Lydia. Soon after she went AWOL she got caught and was sent back to a different group home—one of over fifteen placements she had lived in since age nine.

Three months later, Lydia was on her own and pressuring Lupe to move in with her. Technically still on the run from the law, Lupe moved into Lydia's apartment in a low-income neighborhood in East Los Angeles, where they fit into the densely populated Mexican American community. They lived together in a relatively stable situation for about a month. However, the police soon picked up Lupe again, this time as a result of her brother's gang associations. This was her closest brush with the law as a newly minted legal adult. She recounted:

> I was there for a month until one day we decided to go to the movies.... I guess we got stopped because my brother was bald headed—he was banged out. It was like a White cop—a White old cop. What the fuck, why'd he have to fuck with us… They stopped us because of my brother. I had a warrant, so they ran it. They run my brother's name and they run my name, they run my girlfriend's name and they're like 'you, you have a warrant for your arrest.' I'm like 'oh, fuck.' And my girlfriend's just like 'you should have given them a fake name.' I'm like 'you know what, I'm going to just get over it. Do my time and get out.' So they took me in, back to juvie for 3 days. I had court the third day and I guess my girlfriend and my brother showed up. So they showed up to my court date and I guess they told him 'she has a place to stay at,' that my girlfriend would help me look for a job and you know go back to school. And I guess my judge was tired so he agreed to release me off of probation. I was like 'what!?'

Much to her surprise, Lupe finally had some unexpected good fortune—at age eighteen, she was dismissed from her probation, evaded a potential adult jail sentence, and was released from court supervision.

Set free from dependency and delinquency courts, Lupe moved in with Lydia. Without structure from the state for the first time in over nine years, she did not know quite what to do with her time. She had not completed high school due to her transience, and she did not have a job. Quickly, she fell into a static place and began to smoke weed "around the clock." She explained:

> We had a neighbor, he smokes a lot and he would like smoke us out. I didn't go back to school; I didn't attempt to find a job—I just was smoking weed every day, and my girlfriend didn't like that. She would hate to see me smoke. She hated it; she hated me at the time. And at that time we were all living off of GR <General Relief> ... so like, I would spend it on her but the rest I would go buy some weed. She hated it. Then I started drinking—like drinking a lot, a lot.

The situation quickly deteriorated as the apartment was crowded (her brother and his children also stayed there), and they had very little money. Lupe spiraled into heavier drugs and alcohol use. By her own admission, she wasn't at all prepared for the freedom of adulthood or absence of state supervision. The relationship with Lydia had also descended into a negative cycle to the point where Lupe was worried that she would replicate her own violent victimization patterns. She remarked: "I thought to myself 'you know, I don't want to turn into my dad. 'Cus when my mom and my dad used to be together my dad used to beat the fuck out of her, you know? Like, I'm not going to do that no more, you know?" Similar in many ways to Irene's desire to "break the chain," Lupe wanted to make sure that she did not fall into the trap of becoming like her own abuser. Both Irene and Lupe had enjoyed few positive adult role models in their lives, particularly as children, and they were determined to forge their paths differently.

Although the relationship with Lydia stabilized to a more peaceful place, they eventually came to the realization that they needed the financial support of transitional housing. They applied to housing programs for former foster youth and were accepted at separate residences. When we first met with Lupe, she was living in a transitional program where she had access to GED classes, case management services, rent, and food. She lived with eleven other young women in what she described as a "gang banging" and violent neighborhood that she despised. Despite the support of the transitional housing staff, she was feeling stuck about moving forward in her life. As Lupe stated, her major downfalls were always "drugs and girls." During our first interview, she was trying to refrain from using any substances without the support of AA or any other program, remarking that she was proud to be three weeks sober.

Three weeks later, Lupe appeared a bit more disoriented, and we suspected that she might have been high during our interview. She was still living at the transitional home but had stopped attending her GED prep class. When asked why she had quit, she replied: "I don't know. I started getting high so I got lazy and stopped going." To fill her time, she often helped out her brother with his kids, but since he was "slinging" (meaning selling weed), she would visit him and basically spend the day getting high. Also, since he was selling drugs, hanging around her brother put her at risk of police contact—a risk she was willing to take for the free pot. At the same time that Lupe was slipping into having no structure, Lydia had found a full-time job and was bringing in a steady paycheck. Lupe felt a bit hopeless about her own future because she had no GED and feared "dirty drug tests." In comparison to Lydia, she felt worthless.

By her own admission, Lupe was unable to stop using drugs, was lying to Lydia about the extent of her use, and was trapped in a cycle that she knew was a slippery slope toward self-destruction. When asked about these patterns, she explained:

Lupe: Yeah, so I just stopped. This past week and a half I haven't smoked. I've had money on me but I haven't gone and bought some.
Laura: But it seems pretty up and down for you?
Lupe: Yeah, it's like up and down, you can say. I can stay clean for a certain amount of time, but then I'll relapse.
Laura: So what draws you back, do you think? Is there a trigger?
Lupe: The feeling, I don't know.
Laura: Like, when you're upset.
Lupe: Bored, I guess … and when I'm mad, too, sometimes … Yeah. It makes me forget about … 'Cus usually when I'm upset it's because of my girlfriend. It makes me forget about her for a minute and then it just comes back to me … the problems and shit.

In the absence of a clear direction, Lupe had returned to the comfort that she knew from an early age: to numb herself from emotional pain by getting high. This cycle of use and numbness may have protected her emotionally but also prevented her from accomplishing any of her goals.

At the same time that she felt unable to move forward, Lupe also had made some important changes in her life. This was particularly the case around desistance. Similar to the "On the Road to Desistance" young men, Lupe had spent a great deal of time thinking about changes in her appearance and mannerisms that would create a more pro-social outward identity. All of this was part of her growth and transformation toward a law-abiding self. She explained:

The way I changed … The way I dress, the way I talk. A lot of my appearance, the way I treated people, 'cus like, I go back and I read the letters I used to write to her and I think to myself like 'what? I used to talk like this? I used to write like this?.' And just the things like I used to dress like banged out and I used to treat people like shit, you know. But now I have more respect for others, you know? I treat them just like everybody else, you know?

In addition to the outward appearance, Lupe felt that a large part of her change was the way she treated other people. She saw herself moving from a disrespectful teenager to a kinder and more thoughtful adult. She explained:

I didn't care. I didn't care about nobody's feelings. I used to break cars and I didn't think about 'oh, it's going to come back to me one of these days.' Like, I didn't care. I'd tell you 'I love you' just to get in your pants. I was disrespectful to staff when I was in placement. I don't know, I just didn't care. I didn't care about nothing, nobody. But now I do.

Hence despite her lack of progress around drug use and obtaining a career path, these two elements, appearance and respect for others, were a large part of her growth over the past year since her emancipation from the system.

One of the lessons that we learned from Lupe was the role of good fortune in helping to pave the road for a more positive future. Just as in many ways Irene had stumbled upon the protective, although temporary confines of Javier's family, Lupe also happened to come into a degree of financial security. As a child, Lupe was in a serious car accident that left her with a pocket of money to receive upon emancipation from foster care. Using her resourcefulness, Lupe enlisted the help of an advocacy organization to retrieve the trust fund (she estimated at over $200,000), which she received around her nineteenth birthday. Thus when we next spoke to Lupe four months later, she was renting a one-bedroom apartment with Lydia. These resources allowed her to finally make a clean break from public benefits, which also made her feel more confident about her future.

A lot had changed materially for Lupe as a result of retrieving this substantial sum of money. She could afford an apartment and furniture, and she was not pressured to get a job. She moved out of the group home right away. Christina, one of the project interviewers, remarked in her field notes:

The place was very clean, and I was half expecting the apartment to be less than furnished, considering they had moved not long ago. Her disposition was much more cheerful this time around. She led us into her bedroom where we could get some privacy—I noticed that the furniture in this room was matching and particularly new-ish.

20 Young Women and Desistance: Finding a Net to Fall Back On

As Christina remarked, the new furniture and belongings represented a huge change from our last meeting, when she was on General Relief and struggling to make ends meet at the group home. Lupe agreed: "I didn't have nothing, we didn't have nothing, you know—all we had was our clothes and a couple of things. Everything in here, we bought it."

Lupe explained her radically changed circumstances very openly. When she finally got a hold of the trust fund, she quickly moved out of the transitional shelter and into an apartment. At the same time, Lydia moved out of her group home and quit her job. She was not entirely pleased with her new neighborhood, but she was relieved to finally have her own space and security. She explained: "I'm happy about it because I don't have to worry about being homeless. Because I used to worry about that a lot, you know? Like, when I was in transitional, worrying about getting kicked out for smoking, you know? Right now I got no worries." Like Irene experienced when she moved in with Javier, Lupe finally felt a sense of relief in finding a place to call home, creating her own comfort and family without being told what to do or how to spend her time. She also welcomed in her brother and his children to her apartment with open arms; she wanted to sustain a connection with his brother and her nieces and nephews as a whole family.

Lupe was also in the process of trying to get custody of one of her teenage brothers, who was still in foster care at the time. She had applied for custody and was taking steps to seal her juvenile record. But to follow through on this reality, she knew that she needed to show that she had some stable income, and to do this she had to stop getting high. While she was admittedly still using drugs on a regular basis, she also wanted to become a good role model for her little brother. In the past four months, however, she had not been able to make a great deal of progress toward those goals partially because of the freedom that the trust fund was providing.

While clearly the money made a world of difference for Lupe, she knew that she had spent too much too quickly. Not only had she furnished the apartment and bought expensive electronics and gadgets, she also had taken her family members on trips to amusement parks and other places that she never got to enjoy in foster care. This produced both a sense of liberation and anxiety. She described:

> Yeah, I get bored, I wish I had more stuff to do. I have to wait for this class <educational program>. That's all I have to wait for to get out. I don't really like to go out because every time we go out we spend. I'm trying to like … they're kind of used to eating out a lot. We used to not have the chance to go out to all these places and now that I do we just go.

While Lupe relished in her ability to finally provide for herself and her family, she was also very concerned about spending the money too fast. She was still battling some of the same demons of drug use, boredom, and a sense of malaise. She, along with Lydia and her older brother, had applied to participate in a job training program and were on a wait list for enrollment. Meanwhile, they were spending most of their time smoking weed and playing video games—a life that Lupe described as less than fulfilling. She said:

> Next week I'm going to start going to job training stuff. I don't know—some class me and my girlfriend and my brother are all going to go to, to like get more help to find a job and to go to school. Because I'm tired of living like—not this life—but always buying stuff. It gets kind of boring.

After this interview, we left feeling hopeful about Lupe's future. She finally had found a home, she had resolved some of the issues with Lydia, and she seemed happy and more motivated. We were thus surprised when, two months later, we found out that she had suddenly moved out of state and was living with a distant relative; we were unable to find out exactly why she left California and were unable to establish any further contact with her. The sudden moved seemed out of place and abrupt.

Lupe's story illustrates a few themes regarding the desistance process for young women. The desistance journey is clearly not entirely gendered. Lupe was battling some of the same demons as Tyrone, whose drug use habits were also holding him back from making concrete progress in his life. She also had a similar script as some of the young men, such as Oscar and Gabriel, who felt that desistance started with the outward projection of identity to coincide with the newer person inside.

There was, however, a sense that we got from Lupe that she felt very compelled to care for everyone else—particularly her girlfriend, brothers, nieces, and nephews. It seemed easier for Lupe to focus on the well-being of others rather than herself, and within that paradigm of caring for those around her, she did not attend much to her own problems. Coupled with her drug use, this lack of attention to her own goals made her indeed vulnerable to staying stuck in a cycle of depression and addiction that was detrimental to her overall well-being. Although she was the only young woman in this study to struggle so extensively with substance dependence, she was certainly not isolated in having others depend on her both financially and emotionally. Whether it was parents who depended on them, such as were the cases for Carina and Theresa, or small children, such as in the cases of Amber and Desiree, the women had to balance caregiving with their own desistance journeys.

Mothering and Desistance

For Amber and Desiree, the challenges of desistance were overshadowed by their more immediate needs to provide a safe environment for their own children—one that would be very different from the turmoil of their own childhoods. While Desiree was essentially on her own, relying on public benefits and occasional work to make ends meet (as profiled in Chap. 4), Amber had family support from her mother and aunt as well as a romantic partner, her children's father. Both of their stories provide insight into how a balance of caregiving and perseverance factors into young women's journeys toward desistance.

Amber. At age seventeen, Amber gave birth to a baby girl, April, with her boyfriend of then about two years. She was nervous about having to provide for a child without any work experience or a high school diploma, but she decided to raise April with the support of her family (her mother, aunt, and sisters) and her boyfriend Devon. To make ends meet, she and April moved in with her mother, while Devon lived about fifty miles away with his parents. She described to us her strained financial situation:

> To tell you the truth, the County helps me but when I run out of County money I try to do chores around the house to earn money from my mama but she don't be giving me money like that. She's like 'you got a baby-daddy, so he's got to help you' so I don't even ask her for anything anymore. I don't tell her about needing no bras or panties or nothing—I just get it on my own.

Amber was not happy living under her mother's roof due to their ongoing conflicts and also the location of the home, which she considered to be an extremely dangerous neighborhood. Like the young men described in Chap. 6, Amber struggled with living in a neighborhood where "anything can happen," including gunfire, violence, and crime. She described this sense of continuous fear:

> It's just my neighborhood is bad, horrible. So I'm nervous. I'm stressing. When we're there <at Devon's home>, I'm at peace. I love it. But once we come back to LA I start stressing. I don't know when he's coming, I don't know anything, you know? So it's like—'oh my G-d.'

While Amber would have much preferred to live with Devon on their own, neither had enough money to rent their apartment. She was in the midst of trying to finish high school, and Devon was unemployed and receiving disability benefits. She was very unhappy with her living situation, but it was the only option that made financial sense at the time.

Although having a baby at a young age posed financial strains, April provided her with a strong motivation to move her life in a more positive direction. That said, Amber had not been in juvenile hall or a camp since her initial stay around age fifteen, mostly because she described it as a terrible experience: "When I tell people like—when people are like 'oh, have you been to camp before?' I tell them 'yeah' and they look at me like 'for real?' 'Yes, I've been to that horrible place before—it's horrible, horrible, horrible.'" So while Amber's original source of motivation toward desistance was a fear of being incarcerated, having a child had helped to solidify her desistance goals and to "get my act together." Despite her intense motivation, Amber dropped out of school shortly after the first motivation, and like so many of the other young women, her life had changed dramatically in a very short period of time.

Four months after our initial meeting, we were surprised to find out that Amber had a three-week-old infant in tow. She had not mentioned that she was pregnant at the time of the first interview, but now she had another baby girl whom she named September. Both April and September were present during the interview, this time at her mother's home where she still resided.

Amber explained that just after we met, her boyfriend's disability had worsened and landed him in the hospital, so she had dropped out of school in order to provide more care for him. She recounted: "He got sick and put in a hospital. He was in there for a month. And then his mom was always working, so I had always had to go to where he lives at and help him because his whole right arm had stopped working." Around this time, she also discovered that she was pregnant with their second child, which was quite a surprise to both of them. With a year-old daughter and another baby on the way, Amber was not able to juggle her care for Devon and April while also attending school during the day.

Once she gave birth to September, she started to realize how difficult it was to live on a public assistance income and take care of two children. She was still in the house with her mother, and they were still fighting frequently. All of this financial strain was weighing on Amber, who was desperately trying to figure out how to care for two small children, get a job, and finish her GED or high school credits. Eventually, she wanted to become a nurse.

Nevertheless, the seemingly long and arduous upward climb to reach her goal of becoming a nurse made her propensity for fighting or getting into trouble an invention of the past: "I was horrible. I was bad, fighting and all that. I just didn't care." Now as a mother, she has so much more to focus on. She explained:

20 Young Women and Desistance: Finding a Net to Fall Back On

> Yea everything has changed a lot. <as a mother>. Because I don't really be out like that unless, they somewhere I know that they safe. If they are at my auntie house, like my auntie is obsessed with April. If I go out to party with my best friend, if we go out and people see us. I don't want to say they are hating on us but they will look at us up and down. They'll say stuff. I'll be like 'you don't even know me and you're talking like that. They be like 'what?' And then they be like 'we can fight and all that.' And I'm like 'I don't have time for all that.' It has changed. I haven't been fighting at all.

Amber was just eighteen at that time, still trying to hang out with her friends on occasion and have a young adult life. However, with two children under two years of age and a lot of responsibility on her shoulders, she could not afford to make silly mistakes or to run away from her problems as she had done in the past.

Similar to the situation that Irene faced with Javier, Amber's relationship with Devon was a complicating factor in her journey toward desistance. Devon also had a history of crime and gang involvement, but he, too, was trying to get his act together with the two children. She described the transition to fatherhood as sobering for him:

> He's calmed down. He felt that when he was young, that was his time. Now he's older, he felt he has done his stuff and he don't need to do nothing else. So it's time to take care of my kids. He's got kids to live for so I don't got time to be, you know going after this person … going to jail.

Despite her recognition that Devon was trying to do well, Amber was still concerned that he would not fulfill his promises and was not certain they would end up together in the long run. Thus she was hopeful that they would eventually get married and live together but did not count on this as a sure reality. In the meanwhile, she was very focused on her immediate tasks: raising two young daughters, finding a more stable income, and trying to get along with her mother. Overall, with the support of her friends, family, and boyfriend, Amber was hopeful and energized about her future.

Desiree. Desiree was similar to Amber in regard to criminal desistance in that she found her motivation to stay out of trouble for the sake of her daughter. In many ways, her pregnancy was the impetus for ending the revolving door of running away, juvenile hall, and group homes. However, because she was a single mother and still in foster care when she gave birth to Kianna, having a young child also put her at risk of police and child protection surveillance in a way that Amber did not experience. This type of over-policing caused major mistrust of state systems, fear, and high stakes for small mistakes.

At age seventeen, Desiree found herself pregnant and very much alone, having been thrown out of both her mother's and grandmother's homes and waiting for a new placement. Like Lupe, she found out by chance she was actually terminated from the juvenile justice system. Yet unlike Lupe, who was overjoyed about her sudden turn of events, this abrupt termination left Desiree in a bind. She explained:

> I'm telling the lady 'oh yeah, I'll be out of your house Tuesday—don't worry.' Tuesday come—no. Wednesday come—she's like 'ok, why are you not out?' So, Thursday—I called, I just happened to call the court and I was like 'do I have court scheduled, you know, for Tuesday?'... And they were like 'oh, you don't have court and your probation was terminated two weeks ago' and I was just like 'what?'... So I found out I was off probation and was just crying, crying, crying. I had a PO <probation officer> that actually I used to give a hard time when I was at camp and I ran into him. He seen me; I told him I was pregnant ... He was like 'ok, keep in touch with me if you need any advice or whatever' so I called him and I was like 'I don't have anywhere to go, I don't have any money. I don't have my birth certificate, my social security—nothing.' And he was like 'this is what you do, go to the county building and tell them everything you just said to me and they should help you.' I was like 'I don't have money to get on a bus, like, I don't have anything.'

As she explained, Desiree used the last of her remaining resources to go to the county office to get back into the child welfare system. It was her only option at this point besides a homeless shelter. She was one of the crossover youth in this study who had been essentially booted out of foster care and handed fully over to probation; but once her probation ended, foster care had to take her back because she was technically a pregnant minor without a home.

Desiree was placed at a group home for pregnant and parenting foster youth. Even with such horrible childhood experiences in foster care, she had high hopes for this placement, wanting to learn independent living and parenting skills. Yet when she got there, she was very disappointed with the placement and particularly the group home staff, whom she felt were trying to control her every move. For example, the group home told her that she had to give birth at a designated hospital, but she had heard from the other women that this specific hospital had substandard care. So Desiree communicated with her attorney and social worker to make sure that she could have the baby at the hospital of her choice and one that her insurance would cover. The group home did not relent in their decision, so she had to violate the rules just to find the best care in her labor and delivery. She stated, "I had to AWOL when I was having contractions." Subsequently, every time she left the group home she was at risk of getting picked up by the police. Desiree explained:

> The placement supposed to take me to get my birth certificate. They told the social worker 'we're going to take them, we go on trips every weekend, or every week' to get my social security, my birth certificate and my ID. I was like … 'you guys are going to take me this week or next week, something. You gotta fit it into the schedule because it's supposed to be there.' I had to sneak out … And my baby was two days old and as bad as it may seem I was out there with her. I had like a pouch and I covered her with blankets and stuff. I took her everywhere. I had to AWOL to go to the doctor but I would tell—my judge knew everything I was doing. My lawyer knew everything I was doing. I was calling her constantly and my social worker knew everything.

Although Desiree was doing everything that she could to advocate for Kianna's care, she was well aware that she was also skirting the system and defying the staff's rules. In her view, because she had refused to follow the rules, the group home staff members were out to get her by calling child protective services and reporting her for maternal unfitness.

After giving birth, by state licensing rules for foster care she had to switch to her own room where she and the baby could have their own beds. Prior to that date, she had a roommate and a room with two twin beds. When she brought Kianna back to the group home, her new "mother and baby" room had been freshly painted, but the fumes were so strong that she refused to sleep in her newly designated quarters. She had to fight vociferously for her right to sleep in a room that wasn't toxic, and she moved back into her old room, sleeping with Kianna in her bed. This choice led to a call to the Department of Children and Family Services (DCFS) for suspected child abuse:

> So they call the hotline because, what did they say? I was refusing to go into the other room and I was sleeping with my baby in the bed. But what I did was, everybody—the girls—had felt sorry for me—'oh, they're trying to take your baby.' And I was like 'I'm not scared of what they're trying to call…' So they called the hotline on me. I got into it with the hotline lady because she was like 'you're being defiant and blah blah blah' and I was like 'you know what? I'm not going into that room until the 24 hours is up and if it still smells like fumes in the room I'm not going in there, period. Because if my baby catches pneumonia or something like that you guys are going to be at fault for it and I'm going to

deal with that' and she was like 'um, well you're going to go in the room and if not we're going to come out and you're going to have to deal with that later.' And I was like 'as a matter of fact, since you have a lot to say—you're going to come down here, you're going to go into the room, walk in the room, smell the room and then tell me that I have to go in there. That way if something happens you're going to be at fault for still not going in the room.' And she was like 'I'm not going to do that so you and the staff are going to have to handle that on your own' and I was like 'ok, I thought so.'

Subsequent to that call, DCFS left her situation alone. However, a few days later, the group home called the hotline on her again for sleeping with her baby in the bed when Desiree was worried about her baby's fever. She explained:

They had to call the Hotline on me again because I was sleeping in the bed with my baby but I had woke up in the middle of the night and my baby had threw up all over her face and I was scared because I didn't see, I didn't hear it or anything. I just woke up - and she was in the swing—and she just threw up everywhere. And I was scared—if she had been in the crib she would have drowned in her own throw up. So, she slept in the bed with me, on my chest. And they were all 'oh, people have rolled over the baby and give the baby SIDS' and I'm like 'I really don't care about any of that, I just experienced something that I don't ever want to experience again.'

Maintaining her most remarkable spirit of survival, self-determination, and care for her daughter, Desiree fought to get out of that group home, and she wound up in an independent living program. This program allowed her to get into her own apartment, which was subsidized for former foster youth, and to receive welfare benefits for Kianna and food stamps. For the first two years, she devoted her time to being the best possible mother that she could be.

Yet still, her position of being an African American young single mother with a juvenile record left her open to further monitoring and investigation. The second time we met with Desiree she had just moved to a different supported independent living apartment and was in the process of getting settled into her new environment. She had a stable place to live, and despite not having a job, she had the support of public benefits and a boyfriend, Chris, who helped with Kianna's care.

Although Chris had provided her support in the past, Desiree did not like his overall attitude, particularly his jealousy, so decided to break up with him. When she tried to get him to leave her apartment, he became physically abusive in front of Kianna, so she called the police. She recounted that the situation hit rock bottom such that he punched her in the gut and broke her phone, and she had to knock on several doors in the building to get help. To her shock and horror, when the police came they called DCFS to file a report for emotional abuse because Kianna had seen her mother being punched and beaten by her boyfriend. This was a no-win situation, in that the very authorities whom she called to help her in a time of danger were now threatening the one thing she had fought so hard to protect: her daughter. To prevent a DCFS investigation, she had to file a restraining order against Chris, which she did the next day. Still, her own experiences in foster care left her even more untrusting of the system that had essentially raised her, her mother, and her siblings. She explained:

> They came on the emotional abuse that one time and they're looking for it I got food in my house, or if she has somewhere to sleep—just stuff like that and I'm just like 'you guys are dramatic and I don't want you here.' No, seriously, I don't like DCFS because they're not looking for the traits in bad parents. There's a lot of kids I've seen that *should* have been taken away from their parents and they didn't. But the one's that shouldn't have—they take them and then they end up all screwed up. ... So, they traumatize these kids and then they just give them back to their parents all messed up. ... Like, they say they're trying to help—Department of Children and Family Services—it's not a department of children and family nothing. And I'm not just upset because of what's going on with my daughter, it's just never been right.

Desiree experienced being marked in her own way: being a poor single woman of color on public assistance. She was doing everything that she could to raise her child the best way she knew how, far surpassing the care she was ever provided in her own life. Yet still, she ended up with DCFS involved in her life. At that point, she just hoped that they would close the case and she could move on.

Four months later, Desiree reported that DCFS dropped the case, but a short while later she let Chris back into her life. She needed the childcare help to look for a job, and also Chris was the one person that Kianna had ever called "dad." Desiree felt guilty about taking him away from Kianna. Soon after she let him back in, though, his violent behavior and jealousy escalated, so she had to kick him out again. This time, she relied on the support of her friends and her faith to get her through hard times.

> One of my other friends told me that certain people being in your life might block your blessings. I feel like every time he leaves everything works out smoothly. I didn't have childcare last time. I just happened to call this lady, said

yes I'll watch her and I'll watch her for free. God has been taking care of me ... I know that I had appointments in the past couple of days that I had to go to and I was just making up excuses to keep him around and then every day God was sending me signs. Little signs, signs by signs and even after the fight he was begging—he called me like 40 times in the middle of the night. He came to the house and I was praying. She <Kianna> stayed up. She was scared. I was praying that she didn't hear him. She has little fits. But for the most part, I just don't want him to come because I don't want her to be bothered—I don't want to be bothered.

In the few months in between interviews, Desiree had undergone significant changes largely due to the community she was developing with other formerly incarcerated young people. Together, they had encouraged her to leave Chris for good and assured her that she would be okay on her own. They also helped to care for Kianna. Desiree had many new people in her life and a strong network of formerly incarcerated youth that she called her family. She described her new way of love and support by her chosen family:

I'm just excited to actually have a family behind me to help kind of support that and knowing in foster care, it's not like that. You don't have people who really stand by you and a lot of support. People move in and out ... We are a family—no one should be struggling by themselves. Everybody should be looking out for each other. I don't have much, but if someone needs help—I'm going to help them. We volunteer... So, that's another thing—I want to go and volunteer. At least give a little bit of my time to the schools.

With the help of her community and relatives, she also had secured a part-time job, enrolled in school, and was planning to move in with her grandmother's sister, who also ran a daycare out of her home. This was fortunate as her eligibility for transitional housing benefits was soon coming to an end. Remarkably, after fighting the system for so many years, she seemed more than ready to be free of many of her past burdens: abuse at home and in foster care, mental health wards, juvenile justice, and then domestic violence. Desiree knew instinctively that she was repeating a cycle of trauma that she refused to extend to Kianna. Exuding self-confidence, she exclaimed: "I'm changing my life ... I have wings, and I'm moving on."

Discussion

The young women's stories were replete with diverse experiences, setbacks, and triumphs. However, through these narratives, as well as those not fully examined in this chapter from the three other women, we identified the themes of finding home, breaking the cycle, caregiving, social bonds, gendered violence, and survival and resilience as being critical to the young women's desistance journeys.

Finding home was not just a practical need for these young women but also an emotional pursuit. Many of the young women had not actually had a stable space to call home for nearly their whole childhoods. Thus the search for this place of "home" had multiple layers of meaning, including a way to start over and break the cycle of the abuse or negative experiences they had witnessed in their own childhoods. This desire to break the cycle was related to not only desistance, but also just being a better person, parent, sister, or friend than their own caregivers had been to them.

Caregiving and social bonds are intimately connected themes through close relationships with others, and both are associated with desistance (Salvatore and Taniguchi 2012). Having strong social bonds and/or adopting a caregiving role is protective with regard to recidivism, particularly for women (Benda 2005). These young women created meaning in their lives through both providing care to others (boyfriends, children, friends), clearly in the case of the young mothers, but also in the other stories, particularly Lupe and her care for her family and her girlfriend. Caregiving was important to them and something that motivated them to stay out of trouble for the sake of those who depended on them.

A bit more reluctantly than with caregiving relationships, they also relied on social bonds to support their own movement forward or at times to bail them out of difficulty. We use the term reluctantly here as these young women were used to relying on themselves, their own street smarts, and their ingenuity to create their own path forward. Yet still, we were struck that many formed bonds with groups, mentors, or friends that really came through for them in times of need. The young women spoke about these relationships as though they happened just in the nick of time to avoid a crisis, but they were also forged through their own deliberate involvement in positive social groups. From the stories of Irene and Desiree, it was quite clear that social support played a huge role in keeping them connected, committed to their goals, and feeling safe.

One of the major threats to that sense of safety was gendered violence. In some ways similar to the young men explored in the book as a whole, the young women had to navigate risky neighborhoods, watch where they went at night, and steer clear of danger. Yet on top of these everyday risks associated with disadvantaged neighborhoods, the young women had to contend with fears or actualities of gendered forms of violence such as intimate partner violence, rape, and sexual assault. As many had already suffered trauma from these forms of violence in their own childhoods, this violence had the potential for emotionally and practically destabilizing their progress toward their goals. Even when trying to protect oneself from violence as in Desiree's situation, any contact with the police led to further complications with DCFS. This was clearly a no-win situation in which being the target with gender-based violence led to her being double targeted by the authorities.

Last, through all of the ups and downs in the search for a safe place to call home, the young women exhibited what we would have to call extraordinary resourcefulness and resilience. Reflecting back to Irene's narrative that opened this chapter, we must reflect back on the survival skills that weave a thread throughout these stories. Life changed quickly and dramatically in between each interview and many challenges remained, yet still, these women managed to find places to live, ways to support themselves, and mechanisms for growth and self-improvement.

References

Benda, B. B. (2005). Gender differences in life-course theory of recidivism: A survival analysis. *International Journal of Offender Therapy and Comparative Criminology, 49*(3), 325–342. https://doi.org/10.1177/0306624X04271194.

Maruna, S. (2001). *Making good: How ex-convicts reform and rebuild their lives*. Washington, DC: American Psychological Association.

Salvatore, C., & Taniguchi, T. A. (2012). Do social bonds matter for emerging adults? *Deviant Behavior, 33*(9), 738–756. https://doi.org/10.1080/01639625.2012.679888.

Sandelowski, M. (1991). Telling stories: Narrative approaches in qualitative research. *Journal of Nursing Scholarship, 23*(3), 161–166. https://doi.org/10.1111/j.1547-5069.1991.tb00662.x.

Part VI

Young Adulthood and Long-Term Confinement

"Untitled": Epigraph to Section VI

Central Juvenile Hall is where I'm at.
I miss my family.
I made some mistakes and hope they are not mad at me.
I live my life in a fantasy world.
Everything I saw didn't happen to be.
All my problems are like hide 'n go seek
life in the streets is like demons to me.
Whatcha thinks is scary is funny to me.
Life is so cold.
Everything I saw is getting old.
I'm tired of getting judged by the way the story was told
Fighting this case the Judge expects me to fold.
Mom is working hard making sure we have some clothes.
I try not to tell my mom what I was doing
So i kept it on the low
I tried to show my mom I was on the right flow.

March 11, 2020
Central Juvenile Hall, Los Angeles, CA, USA

21

My Shame

Christian Branscombe

The Intention

The truth is, I justified my actions, wrong or right, I believed in what I was doing or I wouldn't have done it. This chapter is about how I became capable of believing that murder was a solution, and the way to redemption. We often look at the secondary aspects of trauma: anger, resentment, aggression and fail to see the true cause of these interactions, the very nucleus that we don't want to see, that we are blind to. The ethics of shame dictate that we are not weak when we become the experience that made us feel weak. In truth, my road to redemption would bring me to face my greatest fears, that feeling I feared the most complete powerlessness and the idea that I was truly unacceptable.

When I committed first-degree murder 25 years ago, my intention was to rise up out of the pit of shame that I had spent most of my life in, only to find that I would be cast into a justice system that intended to shame me to within an inch of my life under the hammer of punitive segregation. Where justice embraces the same shame ethics that I had perpetuated in my crime. If you are more oppressive than your oppressor then you are no longer oppressed, right? It all made sense to me at the time. It's the language of shame ethics, in a seemingly never-ending cycle of trauma. We pass our masks from one to the

---

C. Branscombe (✉)
Healing Dialogue and Action, Los Angeles, CA, USA

other, where everything is polarized (winner and loser; weak and strong) and you learn what strength is from your weakest moments. For a justice system focused on penance, it proves to be much less redemptive than the language would suggest. Becoming a bigger, more organized version of your opposition does not represent justice or promote what is best for our society as the law should, it only perpetuates the cycle of shame as a social disease. This traumatizes our society as a whole. Living in this land of the lost for 25 years, and condemned to Death By Incarceration (Life Without the Possibility of Parole, also known as LWOP—the other death penalty) at 19 years old, I can say without a doubt that redemption comes from facing your greatest fears, not instilling them in others.

I would like to share my journey to redemption because the need for this journey has never changed, but how I approached it would radically change my life and others. Many do not know what healing looks like or that it is possible. It always seemed like a fairytale that called people to a leap of faith, which I did not believe in. Where were these people on the other side of this healing bridge, smiling and full of well-being?

In November of 2018, I was commuted from serving a sentence of Life Without the Possibility of Parole and resentenced to 25 years to life in prison. This gave me the opportunity to be reviewed by the Board of Parole Hearings for potential release. I was released in August 2019 having been found suitable for parole in my initial hearing. I was given great mercy by Jerry Brown, the Governor of California, and I have been deeply impacted by the magnitude of that action, fortifying my fervent desire to continue in my life of service and greatly humbled by the power that we all have in an act of mercy. That can only be understood and appreciated fully after seeing the heart of the trauma cycle.

The Beginning

Where does it come from, the idea or intention to kill as a form of redemption? It lies so far outside the normal realms of rational thought that it confounds those who try to gain their bearings in that mental space. In truth, it is a rabbit hole that brings about the surreal and deeply disturbing mindsets that become realities and plague our communities today. I see these social dynamics as countless shadows cast from a nucleus of shame. It is a trauma cycle that needs to be understood in order to heal these wounds within ourselves, within others, and within our justice system. As the psychiatrist James

Gilligan (1997) so aptly described it in *Violence: Reflections on a National Epidemic*, shame is a social pathogen; each person infected with it passes it on to many others before they are healed or die. If we do not focus on this social virus, we will fall short of the cure, getting lost in the symptoms.

It took a long time to face the powerful impact of shame in my life and to develop the courage to do what it took to overcome the notion that *if you really knew me, you wouldn't accept/respect/love me*. This is the core and voice of this social disease: shame, that which does not want to be named.

When I was conceived, it was not my parents' intention to have me. They were running from the ugliness in their lives with intense sexuality and were trying to get away from all the things that complicated it. My father's failed marriage with three children and my mother's fight to get away from her domineering mother didn't include the responsibility and economic strain of having a child. I would have been aborted had not my mother been forced to have an illegal abortion when she was just 15 years old. She could not face reliving another abortion. I was cast into the arms of an absent father and a mother who resented having me.

I was severely neglected for the first two and a half years of my life and, as a result, I could not find a connection with others. When I cried, felt pain, sat in my waste, or even laughed, I shared that with no one. I had long periods of hysterical crying and sensory deprivation, and I developed abnormally. As my mother coped with severe depression and having all the baby duties dumped on her by my father, she would become overwhelmed and shake me when I wouldn't stop crying. Later in life, as my mother healed in group therapy, she would confess these things to me in hopes of clearing her conscience. Though I had experienced this trauma, I had not experienced it consciously, or had the ability to understand the profound effects it would have in my development in that moment. Faced with my mother's tears, I didn't want to see her in pain so I gave her what she wanted: acceptance. This was a dynamic that would play out between us for as long as she was alive. Her love always took more than it gave and was all about her well-being. Her shame and insecurities could not allow for anything else ... some of which centered around how she had treated me. The evidence of her actions was present every day that she saw the dysfunctional child in front of her. This compelled her to pawn me off on others and abandon me further. When others smiled, I did not return it. When others shared space, I walked alone. When I felt pain, I did not look for solace from others. When someone said, "I love you," I wondered what they wanted that I didn't want to give. This was my personal development and something I couldn't know was lost, because I never had it—a connection to others.

These forms of neglect would create deep feelings of worthlessness, and they conditioned me to be a target for what would become my turning point to violence. When I was eight years old I was groomed and molested by a 17-year-old boy in my neighborhood, who molested me as well as my crush, a girl my own age. Wanting acceptance and a connection with someone else would lead to an easy grooming process for my molester. Acceptance came through sexuality. As an eight year old, I did not understand what sex was, but the need to be relevant was compelling. This would be some of my first symbiotic experiences, and they were based in deception and manipulation. I could not endure the pain as he tried to sodomize me and I was assaulted, belittled, and threatened with death if I ever shared what we had done. These were my first experiences with violence and intimidation, which were terrifying and confusing. Suddenly alone again in life, I felt regret and a sense of great failure. When the girl I was molested with abandoned our friendship at the behest of our molester, the very bond that had been manipulated for our grooming, I was left feeling utterly worthless.

I would try to give my parents the same kind of attention that my molester wanted, reflexively feeling that this might make them love me, by crawling into their bed one night and touching them inappropriately while they slept. The following morning they would coax the truth out of me. I was terrified to share where I had learned these things from and was convinced that I would be safe if I shared what had happened. I was promised safety by my mother, father, and the authorities. So I shared what had happened, and my molester was arrested. I was left feeling very confused and ashamed. I didn't want to betray the people that had accepted me or for him to go to Juvenile Hall. I wanted their acceptance back and I realized that others would look down on me for that, for what we had done and that I was complicit in these things.

Inside of all of this was something that would linger within me. My mother was a devout Christian and had uncompromising views about what was condemned by God. One was homosexuality. The venom and hatred she spewed toward my molester landed on my conscience. My first experiences of acceptance were through the trauma of molestation. I was deeply ashamed for the first time. If my mother really understood everything, she would hate me the same way. I belonged in Hell, too, I told myself. The only moments I had felt love or appreciation was in this secret society the three of us shared, and yet this was my greatest regret. I had betrayed them and created chaos by sharing it with my family. This is where the voice of shame was born within me: "If they really knew me, they wouldn't accept me." Everyone—my molester, my friends, my family—was untrustworthy so this is when I started to choose isolation: I felt unacceptable.

When my molester got out of Juvenile Hall two months later, I was terrorized for my betrayal. He would beat me up in front of his friends as they laughed. He humiliated me publicly and swore that he would come to kill me in the middle of the night. I didn't want to ask my family for help. They'd left me to the wolves and everything had gotten worse when I trusted them and the cops. Both my parents worked and I was on my own most of the time, with the exception of spending time with my sister, who was two and a half years younger than me, who I felt I had to protect.

It didn't take long to start developing my persona of aggression. I would fantasize about being the victor instead of the victim and what I would do to my molester and his friends for messing with me. Then came my inspiration for this struggle, the heroes I related to: Michael Myers, Jason, Charles Bronson, and Dirty Harry. Like me, they had all been betrayed, hurt, and looked down on. They didn't trust the law and took matters into their own hands. These men were who I wanted to be and I did everything I could to live up to their narratives. I carried knives, imitated the warriors I saw on TV, made homemade weapons, thought of escape plans, built traps, learned how to survive, and fantasized about causing fear versus feeling it.

Despite my fantasies of harm, I still felt a deep-seated shame. I fantasized about the closeness that I experienced with my secret club. This was the most shameful thing: wanting the acceptance. I hated myself for it. I knew I was evil for wanting to please my companions. I didn't want to feel this shame, so I shut down all of my emotions in the process.

By the time I was ten, I was completely shut down and conditioned to cope with life in the most negative ways. I was weak, insecure, and feeling worthless, isolated, accepted only through sexuality, numb, and inspired by violence. Soon, the insecurities would start to spill out into harming others (shame cycle/addiction to violence). These were all baby steps toward the belief that redemption could be found through extreme violence or murder.

Twenty-One and in Prison: Serving Life Without Parole

When they offered me a 30-to-life deal at the age of 19, I couldn't imagine taking it. It was 11 years longer than I was alive at that time, and it was longer than a lifetime away. I chose to face the death penalty or death by incarceration (LWOP) instead. I was found guilty of first degree murder in the commission of a robbery and sentenced to die in prison.

During the sentencing phase of the hearing, I was remorseless. *I* felt like the victim. Everyone was playing in a charade from my perspective. The State was attempting to kill me for being a killer; the survivor of my crime had broken our outlaw code and used the State as a form of revenge; the surviving families knew the rules of our lifestyle and had betrayed every bit of it because they had lost their son. I felt like I was the loser because I upheld our code unconditionally and this was their parade. I couldn't have had more hatred than what I felt for the system and the survivors of my crime. They were scum, and I was the stand-up one, having not caved in under the pressure of the court and did what officers would have been honored for. The judge called a halt to the phase where the families could share their loss and the impact of my crime on their lives, due to the open disdain and disregard I had for their emotions.

Some of these sentiments stemmed from something that transpired just before sentencing. The officers took me and my co-defendant into a secluded part of the jail and had us wait. By the looks of it, we were going to get beaten up. The opposite happened; a long procession of deputies came down the hall single file to shake our hands. Each intimated some form of encouragement: "If you had been wearing a badge you would have gotten a medal," "You *will* make it home some day," "I can't believe they convicted you for this." I felt like a political prisoner. I did what society needed done but no one wanted to take responsibility for. This positive feedback mixed with my criminal thinking resulted in me feeling I wasn't wrong for having killed someone or attempting to kill another.

I was sent to prison on my 21st birthday. It was surreal to contemplate the dichotomy of what this moment was and what it should have been compared to most men's coming of age stories. I was condemned to die in prison and it seemed like I had been born again, a spawn from some beast born into hell for eternity. I was a man now, the man I had always wanted to be, a killer. I had the ethos of a vigilante, justifying my perceptions of redemption and the eternal condemnation of society.

Chipping Away

Coming to prison did not change me. If anything, it made me more resolute in my persona, the badge of honor I hung my self-respect upon. I didn't want to feel the pain of my life, the loss of my freedom, the indignities of incarceration. Any time it would come close to the surface, I would do something more horrifying to pull myself back into the darkness. The numbness that can only take joy in other people's pain, knowing that someone else feels like me, is the closest thing to friendship I could experience. Being confined in a system that invests solely on punitive segregation only compounded the issues that contributed to my murderous commitment offense. Shame and humiliation were at the core of my inadequacies, systematically inflicting these things on me as a form of penance would only result in further damage within and without.

Some part of me wanted to be free of these masks and the shame, even though at that time I could not name it. I started challenging my beliefs, studying (which I had never done before, having been borderline illiterate when I was arrested), and experiencing new things.

I would start this journey by getting my GED (high school equivalent) degree. This felt like the biggest accomplishment ever. I had gotten it on my own, and learned that I could *learn*. I no longer had to rely on others for secondhand information I could find my own way. That created a much different approach to socializing and making personal decisions. There were many reasons that I felt like I was a failure and my lack of confidence in learning was a major hindrance in my life up to that point. I had deep interests in learning and began to explore my thinking intently. That ultimately would challenge many negative traits I had developed growing up, though only intellectually at this point.

I found my way into a philosophy that became a spiritual path for me: Buddhism. I spent several years in a meditation practice where I explored abstract thoughts and questioned my core beliefs. The answers to which would later become deep convictions and guiding principles in the direction I chose in life.

Buddhist concepts of not clinging to expectations and temporality are helpful in an environment like prison, where life is fluid; it is clear that you have no control of what is allowed in or out of your life. My run with active Buddhism would end when our sponsor was denied access to the prison. I maintained my practice in the cell and started to explore other philosophies and traditions that employed metaphysical ideologies. I explored spirituality in a way that did not remind me of the madness my mother had imposed on us with religious manipulation and condemnation. While I had not given up my negative coping skills that would lead to justifying my antisocial behavior, something deeper in me was calling for growth.

When I was 27, my mother died. Suddenly struck with her death and an end to our unresolved relationship, I had a downward spiral that led to a drug binge, resulting in a mental breakdown. This made me vulnerable to the prison population. In this fall from grace, I lost my privileged standing as an active member of the prison population and became the target of their misgivings.

This isolation and ostracization was crippling as someone who defined himself by aggression and courage. Though it was one of the hardest things socially I have had to face, it would be one of the greatest blessings over time. I was banished from everything that was holding me back from finding my true center and well-being. I even questioned my compulsions at that time, as if my unconscious self was placing me in a position to die or progress. In a true death ground strategy (a place in Sun Tsu's *Art of War* that depicts a moment when an army becomes an army—when they are at the point of no return). Whether it was an unconscious push toward enlightenment or the mere product of defunct thinking and coping skills, it would amount to the same end: I had to find a new way to function in life. What I'd been doing would not work anymore.

In Time All Things Change…

Seeking different social circles, I became dedicated to an art community in prison where I had some friends that hadn't given up on me. Many of those friends had been a part of my Buddhist Sangha. A volunteer staff that ran a program called Arts in Corrections took a liking to me and pushed my talents to a new level. They got me to consider different styles of art outside of realism and compelled me to see art as expression versus a skillset. This approach to art would become a powerful tool of introspection for me and a lifeline as I tried to connect to myself and others. In this progressive environment, it stood out that I had no coping skills outside of aggression. It had been my cure-all, and even my most basic coping skills were stilted due to the blunt force trauma that was my existence up to that point. I had to start growing in order to be a part of things.

In the art program, we gave back to the community. We made toys for kids during Christmas, and donated paintings to auctions for the Battered Women's Shelter annually. It felt good to be giving back to others in a tangible way. In prison, there are very few opportunities to reach out into the real world and make a contribution. These philanthropic efforts would become a source of well-being and compel us to consider our impact on others' lives as a whole, a taste of what it is like to find contentment from giving.

For close to a decade I would slowly mature in this environment. In my late thirties, something very unexpected would happen: a close friend of mine that I had known for years in prison and worked with in the art room had his LWOP sentence reduced due to some new legislation for juvenile offenders. I was attentive to each step of this process, and impressed that he would have a second chance to live again. Then something unexpected would strike me to the core of my being. As I read his board hearing transcripts, the hostility and anger of his survivors stood out to me. Their calculated effort to exact revenge upon him and to not let go of the pain shocked me. I had the epiphany that they had not healed like we had. Their wounds were ones that we had inflicted upon them. It was surreal to read my friend's enemies' words and to feel compassion for their pain. I knew what it was like to have to face the pain that others had pushed into your life without cause, and felt great sorrow for them. I immediately thought of the survivors of my crime. I wanted to help them heal in some way and share that I was no longer the angry kid that had no remorse for what I had done to their son, Patrick, who I had not acknowledged before. I wanted them to know that I felt deep regret for what I had done and how it affected so many lives since then. More so, that I live a life of service in hopes of preventing others from having to experience this pain and to honor the potential that Patrick should have had in this world.

When I looked for ways to reach out to the survivors of my crime, all I would find were roadblocks. The hardest part was finding the words. I would sit down in front of a piece of blank paper and attempt to process what needed to be expressed, only to become overwhelmed with the magnitude of the subject and abandon my efforts. Not wanting to give up, I started taking self-help classes, hoping to find a way to get what I needed to make amends. It would be an incredibly slow process. I still have the first draft of my letter of amends. It was two paragraphs long and seemed like it could never be reproduced. I guarded it like something sacred. Which it was, but I would have to do some major soul searching and face my greatest fears to make it sacred enough to acknowledge the pain I had caused in order to make it a healing gesture.

About two years after I had started this quest to better understand my remorse, I came across the first group in prison that addressed the issue head on: Healing Dialogue and Action. The class they led was appropriately titled Victim Sensitivity and we started digging. In the middle of this course, Javier Stauring—a 35-year restorative justice veteran who works extensively with survivors of violent crime as well as offenders in an attempt to resolve trauma within communities—showed up with a survivor of violent crime named Noel. All of the personal work I had done up to that point could not compare to what happened as I listened to this woman's experience and received her compassion. For the first time in my life, I felt everything, all at once. I was reconnected to myself and others in one grand, overwhelming moment. That would leave me an emotional mess anytime I attempted to recount it. I was confronted by something I had never fully experienced and was unable to process: my full spectrum of emotions.

The effects of that moment told me loud and clear that we, as offenders and survivors, can impact each other deeply and that interaction is symbiotic. Noel intimated how coming in to meet with us was part of her healing process and the experience had been deeply impactful for her as well. In these moments, we are confronted with our innate and reflexive responses. These can prove cathartic, revealing, and often transcend our cerebral justifications or rationalizations about what we *should* experience. In other words, these moments center us and bring us back into the moment we are in and help us to become more self-aware in the healing process. Sometimes it is a slow process and in others, it is lightning fast. We can become detached from our empirical knowledge when we don't take the time to update our personal awareness. The depth of our emotional awareness is often revealed on the playing field. We cannot conjure up deep emotions without intense experiences or process them properly without experiencing a sense of safety. This stage of healing is not the first stage by any stretch of the imagination, but a much needed one on our quest for wholeness and well-being.

I started asking myself what led up to this moment. What process had I used to heal that gave me the strength to be vulnerable in that interaction and be open to Noel's experience? What was I bringing to the table for her, and was this something that others could or should experience? What I found was that every time I found a root cause of my healing experiences, it had to do with confronting my shame. I didn't see some part of myself or my experiences as acceptable. Suppressing that deep pain shut me down, and I became dysfunctional and disconnected from my feelings and others in the process.

The most important part of this understanding came to me after I explained these things to Javier and he found some literature on shame he had lying around the house. In it, a psychiatrist named James Gilligan described the cycle of shame as a social disease that spreads through trauma reenactment within our societies. Demonstrating how someone harmed in this cycle is most likely to become a person that reenacts their experience of weakness from the place of their traumatizer in an attempt to seek the sensation of strength. This makes the cycle of trauma very personal. We pass it on like a pathogen, often times exactly as we received it. It suggests that if we can heal from it, we have a deep insight into what those we have harmed are going through and will need to find their way out of this similar process. James Gilligan made the connection I needed to build my approach to making amends for my crime, and it was based on the idea that I cannot make amends until I am connected to myself and have healed considerably. This was enough to connect to others again and truly relate to the impact of my traumas and the symbiotic nature of my decisions/actions upon others following those experiences. Facing my greatest fears and taking responsibility for the ethos of my trauma reenactment was the only real offering of amends I could extend. That was the first step to any real attempt at amends. Like in poker, this was the ante.

As I designed a group in prison called the Bare Bones Society for healing from shame, my intention was to make direct amends to our survivors.

Though that was not common or legal for us to accomplish on our own, it was the purpose of this group. This would allow us to confront our shame cycles, take responsibility for our decisions and actions, and give what we could in the way of information for our survivors to find the understanding they may need to find their way to well-being.

Shame is something that is born out of our perceptions of how others perceive us. (Which is an interesting dynamic when you consider that more often than not these perceptions are not true to others' thinking and would appear as more of a projection from our shadow, those hidden parts of us that can be dark, reflexive, and are often not factually driven.) The courage in healing is having to face the shame in a public/group setting where you could be judged, and finding connections with others despite or because of the omission. This involves accepting yourself, as is, and knowing the person you are today is the product of all your history, not just the fun stuff.

During this group, we discussed the idea that taking responsibility for our actions in this case is different than saying, "I did it." It has to do with acknowledging where it came from as a demonstration that we have taken the time to deal with its origins and own that what we did was an intentional act. No matter how circumstantial it might seem, it was a deeply personal act within the offender, and for the recipient of our actions. This was the context of ownership as I created the curriculum for the Bare Bones Society. Revealing one's healing process intimates what is often needed for the survivor to answer many questions they have in order to understand and let go of the confusion and seeming senselessness of it all. Even when the thinking is irrational, knowing where it came from gives some context to the situation, and shows the survivor that in no way were they responsible for the actions we committed. Owning the history of these decisions throughout our lives and how they led to such incredible loss shows that they are our burden to bear, not the survivors.

Once the curriculum for the Bare Bones Society was written out and prepared through what we called "sitting in the fire" due to the intense nature of the work, we described our "turning point" which is a euphemism for the moment our shame ethics completely failed us and we hit rock bottom, often years *after* our commitment offense. The final stage before the direct amends is our path to change, which is when we completely let go of our old thinking and invested wholeheartedly in changing ourselves, becoming dedicated to a life of living amends. We also work with survivors of violent crime to tap into the impact of our actions and connect to ourselves emotionally. This enriches their healing process as well. This is a truly symbiotic, and all too often avoided, healing experience.

Collectively, the intention is to give our survivors and others the opportunity to have greater insight into the factors causing their trauma and to have what they need to choose a healing path through this understanding. The hardest thing for an offender or survivor to learn is that we are responsible for how we receive our trauma. It is the only thing we actually have control of in this healing process. It is very hard for an offender to find a sense of responsibility until they heal and don't feel like the victim of their experiences and take responsibility for their reactionary/defensive mindset; because they feel weak, it does not justify them harming others. Survivors don't want to accept that their well-being is their choice and they are also responsible for every action after a traumatic experience. An extreme debt that was not asked for can be difficult to come to terms with and develop ownership for; that can and does often lead to trauma reenactment. This is a nasty cycle that cannot be avoided to some degree. We see in the intention of amends that healing cannot be extended until it has been achieved on either side of this issue. We cannot relate to another's pain when we normalize our own.

As I pushed through a year-long process working on these issues with no hope of direct amends in sight, I was extremely fortunate to have had a survivor of my crime reach out to my family. It had been years before I started the Bare Bones Society, but I was never informed of his expressed forgiveness due to my lack of contact with the family member it was extended to. When I shared the project and my heartfelt intentions with my family member, they told me that my survivor had reached out some time ago and was available to talk if I wanted to. It was almost too much to believe.

The process that would follow would be documented in a CNN special with Van Jones and Javier Stauring call the *Redemption Project*, Episode 7, titled: *Left for Dead*. This would be an experience that would be deeply impactful to Joshua "Gunner" Johnson, the survivor of my crime, as well as for myself. We had a Healing Dialogue, also known as a Victim Offender Dialogue (VOD). The bond we share post-healing dialogue is surprising to say the least. Not only did he advocate for my release more fervently than I at my board hearing, he also shared his sentiments publicly at an event that same evening. They showed our on-camera VOD at the event and Gunner advocated for more amends projects to high ranking State of California officials. This ultimately led to Governor Jerry Brown allocating $2,000,000 to fund VOD work for the first time in California's history. Thanks to his advocacy and the mercy of Governor Brown's commutation of my LWOP sentence, Gunner and I now share the stage with our experience of healing and display the power of these interactions with other survivors and offenders of violent crime. This is the very example of the work we advocate for: a path to healing within ourselves and in our communities.

At the start of this chapter, I mentioned two paths to redemption. In the beginning of my life, I sought to redeem myself through the violence and terror that I had received at a young age. I was stuck in the trauma cycle like an addiction, guided by my insecurities and feelings of deep inadequacy. I was convinced that I was defending myself as I terrorized others for making me feel weak and ashamed, whether that was their intention or not. This was a cycle that could not be broken, no matter how much violence I pushed into it. This left me with my life and others in the balance as my shame ethics spiraled beyond my capacity, where the only redemption was death. I was disconnected from myself and others in every way. I was numb to every emotion, blocked by the need to avoid the shame that I feared more than death itself. In this psychotic state, the only redemption was murder. I was driven by the coping skills of an abandoned ten year old, deeply damaged, crippled by shame and fear. I was trapped in a self-induced isolation where safety took precedence over all other human needs that I desired like a deep aching within my soul. I wouldn't let anyone in.

To observe the outer effects of shame as a social disease, we often draw a blank on what we are experiencing and question what humanity is. When we see no shred of it in another human being, we don't believe in extending those beliefs to something (or someone) that cannot relate to those forces within us. Our humanity is symbiotic, or we are in breach of contract, where both sides believe that we can do the most awful things to redeem ourselves. Such is the hypocrisy that so many call "justice" and the broken call redemption. This is the ethos of the trauma cycle: it should be banished, punished, tortured, or it should die, because I cannot relate to it. In fact, that is the only time we can act in that accord is when we do not see someone as a human being. The question we should be asking is, "Why don't I see this person as a human being?"

Essentially this is what someone has to do to heal: they have to ask themselves that question. To redeem themselves, they have to face the truth of the answer to that question and be willing to confront what they often fear the most. This is not just for people who offend, it is a question we all have to face when we believe that violence will cure our societal ills.

What I have found in this journey from adolescence to adulthood, from damaged to healed, from offender to amender, from disconnected to whole, is that if we see these things as outside of us, we are mistaken. That redemption resides in being connected to ourselves and others unconditionally, because there is no condition when we are not affecting and affected by each other. Even when I must take action because of someone else's disconnection, it will come from a place of connectedness within me and be focused upon the best intention possible for the person I am affecting. It is a false notion to think that we are separate, more so, that I am defined by my opposition to them.

In Brian Stevenson's book, *Just Mercy*, he writes:

> The power of just mercy is that it belongs to the undeserving. It's when mercy is least expected that it is most potent, strong enough to break the cycle of victimization and victimhood, retribution and suffering. It has the power to heal the psychic harm and injuries that lead to aggression and violence, abuse of power, and mass incarceration. (Stevenson 2014, p. 294)

As someone that has been deeply humbled by the connection I have developed with my survivor, I can speak to the power of mercy, and I have not experienced a more powerful exchange with another human being.

This quote demonstrates the essence of my point on redemption. The voice of shame always says we must be redeemed. That connotation implies we are still within the grips of shame's ethics: we are the only ones that can redeem ourselves and are the only ones that can redeem others in our own eyes. When we understand this, we are free from the trauma cycle and can become a guide to others through unconditional acceptance and connection. Life itself is an amends when we come to terms with this understanding.

References

Gilligan, J. (1997). *Violence: Reflections on a national epidemic*. New York: Random House.

Stevenson, B. (2014). *Just mercy: A story of justice and redemption*. New York: Spiegel and Grau.

22

The Pains of Life Imprisonment During Late Adolescence and Emerging Adulthood

Serena Wright, Susie Hulley, and Ben Crewe

Introduction

The vast body of literature on "juvenile" offending has historically focused on those whose age profile fits the state definition of a "minor": that is, those above the age of criminal responsibility (in England and Wales, 10 years old) but below the age of 18—the traditional and legal threshold of "adulthood" (Prior et al. 2011). Yet Prior et al. (2011) highlight recent developments within the fields of developmental psychology and neurobiology which "point emphatically to the inappropriateness" of processing those in their late teens and early 20s through criminal justice systems in accordance with expectations and punishments designed for "adults" (p. 35). This emerging body of work challenges long-held normative assumptions about "maturity" and offers a more "complex" model of maturational development among young adults as a means of demonstrating how individual experience and context dictate "maturity" with far greater accuracy than chronological age (see e.g. Cauffman and Steinberg 2000). This growing recognition of the contextual nature of "maturity" as a prerequisite for a more legitimate criminal justice system has

S. Wright (✉)
Royal Holloway, University of London, Egham, UK
e-mail: Serena.Wright@rhul.ac.uk

S. Hulley • B. Crewe
Institute of Criminology, University of Cambridge, Cambridge, UK

occurred in tandem with developments in global health research which acknowledge a "shift in popular perceptions of when adulthood begins" (Sawyer et al. 2018). While there is no unified approach to such matters, recent developments point to the need to reconceptualise and refine our understanding of the demarcation between childhood, adolescence, and adulthood.

Such developments are of direct relevance to our study on long-term imprisonment from young adulthood (reported in full in Crewe et al. 2020), which explored the experiences of men and women who had been convicted of murder and sentenced to imprisonment for life[1] or the youth justice system equivalent[2] for a minimum of 15 years when they were aged 25 years or younger. For clarification, while this study involved interviewing a broad cross-section of individuals of varying ages and stages of the life course, this chapter focuses only on the experiences of men and women aged between 18 and 25 years *at the time of the study*. Drawing on the literature on maturational development above, we do so with the explicit aim of offering a contemporaneous account of the experience of serving a life sentence for murder during the period of "late adolescence" (defined as 18–19 years) or "emerging adulthood" (defined as 20–25 years).

The chapter begins by documenting the increase in life sentences in England and Wales and setting this against the literature on the pains of long-term incarceration, before going on to outline the methodological landscape of our study. We then consider how it feels to be convicted of murder when young and to be facing a minimum period in prison equal to, or longer than, the number of years you have lived. We ask how individuals aged between 18 and 25 years at the time of the study—some of whom were convicted prior to their 18th birthday[3]—experienced the daily deprivations of the carceral environment, and how they negotiated the challenges of their sentence. Combining quantitative survey findings relating to the top-ranking "problems" of long-term imprisonment and qualitative interview data from young life-sentenced prisoners, three core analytical streams can be identified for discussion. Firstly, we reflect on the *relational/social* pains conveyed by young people; these chiefly centred on missing and worrying about loved ones outside of the prison. Secondly, we explore the *temporal/existential* pains they described, particularly as they pertained to the length of the sentence and implications of this in terms of "wasted" years. Lastly, we turn to the pains induced by the *deprivation* of various forms of stimuli—most notably discussed in terms of boredom and the absence of "little luxuries", social life and sex.

Within this context, we conclude by reflecting on the long-term implications of the growing trend towards longer life sentences being handed to increasing numbers of individuals and pose critical questions about the necessity of exposing those in late adolescence and emerging adulthood to the pains of imprisonment for life.

The Rise of Longer Life Sentences in England and Wales

Following the abolition of capital punishment in the 1960s, sentences of imprisonment for life (and their equivalent for children and adolescents) have represented the ultimate sanction available to the courts in England and Wales. Since that time, the use of life sentences has risen inexorably—for instance, the annual number of individuals sentenced to mandatory[4] life imprisonment increased by 75% between 1998 and 2008, representing the most significant proportionate increase across the penal estate during that period (Ministry of Justice 2009, p. 2). The rapidity of growth can also be demonstrated through numbers of life-sentenced prisoners in the current prison population, which rose from just under 2000 individuals in the late 1980s (Blom-Cooper 1987) to 8309 in 2010 (Freedom of Information request 68520).

While the most recent figures indicate a life-sentenced population of just over 7000 in England and Wales (Ministry of Justice 2019), a greater proportion are serving longer terms than ever before, being sentenced—even in late adolescence—to minimum custodial periods which would have hitherto been considered barely survivable. For instance, between 2000 and 2003, less than 100 life sentences carried 'tariffs'[5] of 15 years or more; however, by 2008 this figure had more than doubled (Freedom of Information request 68152). By 2010, 2309 prisoners—more than a quarter of all life-sentenced prisoners in England and Wales at that time—were serving sentences of imprisonment for life with a tariff of 15 years or more. Of these, 319 had been convicted and sentenced between the ages of 18 and 20 years (Freedom of Information request 68152).

Taken together, these trends point to an increasing number of individuals being sentenced to life imprisonment, some barely at the cusp of "emerging adulthood", and being subjected to the complex and multifarious pains of long-term imprisonment within a system that was never designed to cater for those spending decades in confinement (see Flanagan 1995).

The Pains of Long-Term and Life Imprisonment

The concept and terminology of the "pains of imprisonment" stems from Gresham Sykes' (1958) seminal work, *Society of Captives: A Study of a Maximum Security Prison*. Based on a small number of informal interviews in the US with prisoners and staff, observations, and questionnaires at New Jersey State Maximum Security, Sykes critiqued claims from contemporaries that prisons of the era were a comparatively "humane alternative" to previous carceral regimes, drawing attention to the specific pains of the deprivations of *liberty*, *goods and services*, *heterosexual relationships*, *autonomy*, and *security*. Building on this seminal study, more contemporary studies—within the specific context of England and Wales—have highlighted a diverse range of additional "pains", including the deprivation of "certitude, legitimacy and hope" (Warr 2016), and the pains of "uncertainty and indeterminacy, psychological assessment and self-government" (Crewe 2011). Bearing in mind these broad range of "pains", indicators suggest that prisons in England and Wales are now experienced as more painful and "less safe than they have been at any point since records began" (Prison Reform Trust 2019, p. 4), signalled by significant increases in self-harm, prisoner-on-prisoner violence, and serious assaults against staff.

In addition to the pains of imprisonment noted above, individuals serving very long sentences face exposure to a host of "special problems and stresses" and may experience these to a greater "degree" than their short-sentenced counterparts (Flanagan 1982, p. 115). Specifically, the uncertainty of indeterminate sentences bears down heavily and cumulatively on long-term and life-sentenced prisoners, forcing individuals to try and manage these concerns alongside a prolonged exposure to the ubiquitous violence, despair, and disempowerment of prison life.

Despite the increases in global long-term imprisonment described above and the recognition that long-term sentences generate particular pains, there has been little sociological or criminological interest in recent years in the phenomenon of long-term imprisonment. The bulk of studies in this area are squarely grounded in the latter half of the twentieth century (e.g. Cohen and Taylor 1972; Gunn et al. 1973; Richards 1978; Flanagan 1980, 1982, 1995; MacKenzie and Goodstein 1985; Porporino 1990; Zamble 1992; Sapsford 1983) and as such unlikely to be able to account accurately for the experience of the twenty-first-century "lifer". While recent studies have strived to correct this balance (e.g. Schinkel 2014; Toch 2010; Johnson and McGunigall-Smith 2008), this body of work has tended to focus on adult males, with women (whom we have considered in depth elsewhere) (see Crewe et al. 2017, 2020) and young people featuring as largely peripheral concerns. The failure to consider the ways in which the particular pains of long-term imprisonment might intersect with the challenges of late adolescence and emerging adulthood is a significant gap in the literature, and one which we aim to stimulate discussion about using the empirical data generated by our study.

Research Design: Generating and Analysing the Data

The aim of the overall study was to understand the experience of receiving, making sense of, and managing long custodial sentences (of 15 years or more) received at a young age (aged 25 or younger). Given the exploratory nature of the study and the desire to account for the twenty-first-century experience of these phenomena, the research sought to address three broad sets of research questions:

- Firstly, what are the main problems that this group of prisoners encounter and in what ways do they respond to them? How do they make sense of their predicament, find meaning, manage time, and think about the future?
- Secondly, how do they adapt socially to the demands of the environment?
- Thirdly, how do such extreme sentences shape their perceptions of the prison's legitimacy?

Fieldwork for the study took place between February 2013 and December 2014. Participants were drawn from 25 prisons across England, 16 of which held men and nine of which held women. The women were accommodated in both open and closed prisons and the men in all types of establishments, from high-security to open conditions, as well as Young Offender Institutions. The National Offender Management Service (now "Her Majesty's Prison and Probation Service") provided data on all current prisoners who met the eligibility criteria for the original study (who were serving a life sentence with a tariff of 15 years or more, which they received when they were 25 years old or younger). At the outset of the study, 808 people were identified as meeting these criteria (789 men and 27 women). All prisoners were serving life sentences for murder and sentenced to imprisonment for life or equivalent.

Generating the Data: Interviews and Survey Instrument

The study employed a mixed-methods approach, involving surveys and semi-structured interviews. In-depth qualitative data were generated through a series of two-part interviews. Part I was a detailed life history interview, which drew heavily on the literature on narrative inquiry and life stories (e.g. Holloway and Jefferson 2000). Part II focused on participants' post-conviction lives (the "life inside" interview), particularly in relation to the experience of serving a very lengthy life sentence from a young age. Interviews were primarily conducted in recreation rooms or offices on prison wings, almost always on a one-to-one basis, and lasted on average between one and four hours. The sampling strategy for the interviews was broadly purposive. During the first phase of the study, undertaken exclusively in male prisons, individuals within the overall population were targeted by *sentence stage*[6] and type of prison. While we conducted interviews with prisoners at the early, mid-, and late stages of their sentence, we deliberately oversampled men in the "early" stage (within the first four years), because they represented a fast-growing group about whom little was known.[7]

In addition to these in-depth interviews, a survey instrument was developed, which drew on and adapted (based on our early experiences in the field) the "problems of long-term imprisonment" tool utilised by Richards (1978), Flanagan (1980) and Leigey and Ryder (2015). Surveys were completed in 25 prisons (16 men's prisons and 9 women's prisons, accounting overall for 21% of the 117 prisons in England and Wales) with individuals who met our overall research criteria. Survey participants were presented with 39 statements reflecting key "problems" of long-term imprisonment (based on previous studies noted above and our observations and discussions during the initial month of fieldwork). Respondents were asked to report on 2 five-point Likert scales the *frequency* and *intensity* with which "problems" were being experienced at that point in time—where frequency represented how often the problem happened and intensity measured how hard it was to deal with (when it did happen). Problems included "Wishing that time would go faster", "Feeling that my life is being wasted", and "Thinking about the time you might have to serve" (see Hulley et al. 2016 for a complete list of all survey "problem" statements).

The Research Sample

In total, 309 men and 21 women participated in the broader study ($N = 330$), either through completing a survey, an interview, or both; this sample represented 39% of men within the target population and 72% of women. Of these, 126 men and 21 women participated in interviews ($N = 147$; respectively 16% of the male population and 72% of the female population fitting our criteria), while 294 men and 19 women completed a survey ($N = 313$; respectively 37.26% of men and 70.37% of the women within the population).

The specific sub-sample upon which this chapter is based (participants who were aged 18–25 years at the time of the research) represented almost 41% ($N = 128$) of our total survey participants and 43% ($N = 64$) of our total interviewees. The first two tables (Tables 22.1 and 22.2) detail the key characteristics of survey participants and interviewees within this younger sub-stratum of the total sample (for more on the full sample, see Crewe et al. 2020).

Taken together, the data from Tables 22.1 and 22.2 draw our attention to four important observations. Firstly, that this was a carcerally inexperienced group, with just over two-thirds of survey participants being first-time entrants to the prison system with no prior custodial record. Secondly, that many fell within the "early" stage of their sentence—a period we have already identified elsewhere as being significantly and disproportionately painful compared to later stages of long sentences (see Wright et al. 2017; Crewe et al. 2020). Thirdly, that both survey participants and interviewees aged 18–25 years were convicted of murder and sentenced to life imprisonment at an average age of 19 years (i.e. during late adolescence). Lastly, young men and women in both the survey and interview sample were facing an average minimum period of confinement just longer than the average number of years they had lived.

It is also relevant to our analysis here that more than half of the *survey* respondents in the "late adolescence and emerging adulthood" sub-stratum had served an average of just over four years ($M = 4.02$, $SD = 1.81$), with 57% falling in the "early" stage of their sentence (within the first four years). Due to the sampling strategy adopted for the qualitative part of the study, the majority (roughly 95%) of *interviewees* aged between 18 and 25 years at the time of the study fell also within this "early" stage. However, it is important to note that the analysis that follows did not control for "sentence stage", and that owing to the high percentage of survey participants and—particularly—interviewees who were in the "early" stage of their life sentence, age, and stage are unavoidably conflated to some degree in the findings. The aim of the

Table 22.1 Frequencies and means for key demographic variables: Survey participants and interviewees aged 18–25 years at the time of the study

		Survey participants aged 18–25 years at time of study N (%)	Interviewees aged 18–25 years at time of study N (%)
N (total survey sample N = 313; total interview sample size N = 147)		128 (40.89%)	64 (43.54%)
Gender[a]	Male	121 (94.53%)	56 (87.5%)
	Female	7 (5.47%)	8 (12.5%)
Sentence stage	Early	73 (57.03%)	61 (95.31%)
	Mid	0	3 (4.69%)
	Late	0	0
	Post-tariff	0	0
	None	55 (42.97%)	0
Ethnicity	White British, Irish, or Other (incl. Gypsy or Traveller)	63 (49.22%)	33 (51.56%)
	Black/Black British (incl. African, Caribbean, or other)	38 (29.69%)	20 (31.25%)
	Dual heritage (Black African or Black Caribbean and White)	13 (10.16%)	7 (10.94%)
	Asian/Asian British (incl. Chinese, Indian, and Pakistani)	6 (4.69%)	4 (6.25%)
	Dual heritage (Asian and White)	2 (1.56%)	0
	Other ethnic group	4 (3.13%)	0
First custodial sentence[b]	Yes	86 (67.19%)	–
	No	42 (32.81%)	–

Note: Valid data only—percentages therefore do not necessarily add up to 100
[a]While we acknowledge that gender is not a binary concept, none of the study participants identified outside of these two categories when asked to self-identify their gender
[b]This data was only collected during surveys, and not during interviews; therefore no comparative data for interviewees exists

Table 22.2 Mean averages, standard deviation, and range for key demographic variables: Survey participants and interviewees aged 18–25 years at the time of the study

		Survey participants aged 18–25 years at the time of study	Interviewees aged 18–25 years at the time of study
Age at time of study: years	Average (std dev)	23 (1.93)	21.94 (2.14)
	Range	18–25	18–25
Age at sentencing: years	Average (std dev)	19.37 (1.98)	19.14 (2.19)
	Range	13–24	13–24
Tariff length: years	Average (std dev)	21.15 (4.43)	20.92 (4.38)
	Range	15–36	15–33
This sentence—time served: years	Average (std dev)	4.02 (1.81)	3 (1.53)
	Range	1.25–9.08	0–9

conceptual discussion that follows then is not to separate out the causal mechanics of the experiences reported, but rather to emphasise the *particular burdens* that *young prisoners at the start of a lengthy life sentence* experience.

Analysing the Data

Interviews were digitally voice-recorded (with informed consent), then transcribed verbatim. Each interview was coded using NVivo software by at least one member of the research team. The analysis process proceeded based on an "iterative" approach, a method grounded in constant interpretation and revision, based on reading, discussion, reflection, revision, and re-reading, with the goal of "deepening understanding" of the data (see Berkowitz 1997, cit. in Srivastava and Hopwood 2009, p. 77). Though this, we sought to establish thematic connections and points of conceptual convergence (as well as divergence), both according to specific characteristics (i.e. gender, age, and sentence stage) and across the broad spectrum of the data.

Analysis of the survey data focused on quantifying the "severity" of the "problems" of long-term imprisonment—measured on a scale from 0 to 25 (where 0 denotes lowest severity/least painful and 25 indicates greatest severity/most painful), severity scores were calculated by multiplying the Likert scores for item *frequency* and *intensity* ratings (each measured on a five-point scale). A Principal Components Analysis was then conducted on these data to group the variables into nine meaningful subsets of "problems" or "dimensions" (for a more detailed discussion of this process and the findings from the survey, see Hulley et al. 2016, and Crewe et al. 2020).

The Pains of Life Imprisonment in Late Adolescence and Emerging Adulthood

This final substantive section draws on both the quantitative and qualitative data to identify and describe the ten "most severe" problems identified by life-sentenced prisoners (abbreviated throughout the findings to "LSPs") who were aged 18–25 years at the time of the study (see Table 22.3). In order to determine the *particular* problems of experiencing a life sentence at this age, a series of t-tests were conducted to test for significant differences between the mean severity scores for this group and their older counterparts (aged 26 years and older) within the overall sample.

Of the 39 "problem" statements presented in the survey, those accruing the ten highest mean scores among participants aged 18–25 years are presented in Table 22.3 in rank-order (from 1 to 10, in descending order of "severity").

Table 22.3 Ranked (top 10 of 39 "problems") mean severity scores comparing survey respondents aged 18–25 years and ≥26 years at the time of study

"Problem of long-term imprisonment" survey item (n = 39 items total)	Respondents aged 18–25 years Rank score	Respondents aged 18–25 years Mean severity score for survey item	Respondents aged ≥26 years Rank score	Respondents aged ≥26 years Mean severity score for survey item	p values for t-tests
Missing somebody	1	17.90	1	16.67	0.152
Feeling that you are losing the best years of your life	2	**16.07**	4	**13.85**	**<0.001**
Worrying about people outside	3	15.74	2	15.00	0.418
Feeling that the length of your sentence is unfair	4	**14.95**	11	**11.42**	**0.001**
Feeling that your life is being wasted	5	14.88	5	13.77	0.221
Missing social life	6	**14.02**	9	**11.80**	**0.012**
Thinking about the amount of time you might have to serve	7	13.09	8	12.28	0.409
Being bored	8	**12.75**	25	**8.78**	**<0.001**
Missing little "luxuries"	9	**12.66**	15	**10.62**	**0.012**
Feeling sexually frustrated	10	12.50	16	10.59	0.45

Note: Mean severity scores represent total group means. The lowest possible score is 0 (least severity) and the highest is 25 (greatest severity). These scores are presented in descending order and assigned a rank position to denote relative importance to each group

Data in bold highlights those 'problems' for which the difference in severity scores between the two age groupings was statistically significant

Alongside, the severity scores and ranks for adults aged ≥26 years old in the overall sample are presented for the same items. While this comparative data is useful in highlighting which problems were experienced with particular severity by younger participants, these data should also not be interpreted as implying that age is the causal variable (for those reasons noted in the section above).

Briefly, the data in the table below indicate that young LSPs experienced six of these top-ten "problems" with *significantly greater severity* than their older counterparts, specifically: "feeling that you are losing the best years of your life"; "feeling that the length of your sentence is unfair"; "missing social life"; "being bored"; "missing little 'luxuries'"; and "feeling sexually frustrated". The salience of these statistical observations is explored in greater detail below.

The sections that follow draw together conceptually similar items within the ten highest-ranking "problem" to explore three different areas of concern identified as particularly challenging among young LSPs. Firstly, we discuss *relational* pains ("missing somebody" and "worrying about people outside"), followed by *temporal* pains ("feeling that your life is being wasted"; "feeling that you are losing the best years of your life"; "feeling that the length of your sentence is unfair"; and "thinking about the amount of time you might have to serve"), and concluding with the pains of *deprivation* ("missing social life"; "being bored"; "missing little 'luxuries'"; and "feeling sexually frustrated").

These reflections are then drawn together in the final section, which concludes the chapter.

Relational Pains: Missing and Worrying About Others

Consistent with earlier survey-based studies on the problems of long-term imprisonment (Richards 1978; Flanagan 1980; Leigey and Ryder 2015) and the findings of our broader study (see Hulley et al. 2016), the relational pains of imprisonment were among the highest-scoring problems reported by young LSPs—specifically "Missing somebody" (ranked 1st of 39 survey items) and "Worrying about people outside" (ranked 3rd of 39 survey items). That relational pains were among the highest severity scores for both age groups (and that no statistically significant differences existed between the two) brings into sharp relief the omnipresent pains of relational dislocation induced by long-term imprisonment, irrespective of years lived or years served (see Crewe et al. 2020 for more detail).

Young men and women consistently talked in loving and nostalgic terms about their family, expressing deep pain at the separation induced by their imprisonment; "I miss my family more than anything" (Oscar, 21, 18-year tariff)[8]; "The thing I miss the most? It's *always* going to be my family, and being with them" (Jeremiah, 20, 16-year tariff). Interview data demonstrated the value that these individuals placed upon the love and support received from members of their natal family, particularly their parents. As Connie explained:

> [The most important people to me are] my mum and dad—I speak to them on the phone every day. [...] They're like my support. If I've got any problems, I'll get on the phone and just let it all out to them. (Connie, 20s, <20-year tariff)[9]

Interestingly, despite the challenges typically faced by families forced to live in the "shadow of the prison" following the incarceration of a relative (see Codd 2008, p. 1), young life-sentenced prisoners (particularly male) consistently reported that their familial relationships had improved rather than diminished following conviction (albeit often from a low baseline). For instance, Thomas (21, 16-year tariff) explained how he had come to re-evaluate the value of parental love and support since being imprisoned:

> When you're a life sentenced prisoner your whole world comes crashing down. So you realise just how important family is and you learn to appreciate them, and you just feel so lucky to have a mum and dad who [...] love you the same. And that feels amazing, absolutely amazing.

Similarly, Carl reflected that even though his mother was "not happy" with what he had done, she and other family members had "really stepped up and shown that they care", adding:

> Before I might not have really considered [my family] as quite close to me, but [...] my mum, my family [...] they've always just supported me and said that they loved me, and they're here for me. (Carl, 20, 24-year tariff)

While the separation from family was painful, it was made bearable in some ways by the support provided by these relationships. What was less bearable, however, was the loss of peer support, as within a relatively short period of time—sometimes just months into the sentence—friends had either actively "stepped back" (Dan, 23, 15-year tariff) or simply "faded away" (Carl). Young men in particular spoke about the pain associated with the feeling of being deserted by lifelong friends; those who had "lived on the same estate, gone through the same shit, the same struggle" (James, 21, 22-year tariff), and whose abandonment consequently "hurt a lot more" (Carl) than the loss of briefer or more transitory friendships.

Contrary to these (predominantly male) experiences, it was less common for young women to reflect extensively on missing parents, partners, or peers, often because such relationships had either broken down prior to imprisonment or because women had actively severed ties to such individuals (who were regularly implicated in the women's extensive histories of pre-prison trauma and abuse). Instead, when asked about "missing" and "worrying" about people outside the prison, those young women with children (11 of the 21 interviewed) focused on the extreme pains of separation from their children, as Kathryn and Connie explained:

> I only get to see [my daughter] three times a year, so in a sense I've lost the main part of her. But she's still alive, and then that makes it really difficult because every time I see her it brings up all my feelings for her again, and then I spend the next four months grieving. And that's really difficult because you're constantly going through it—you're breaking your heart a little bit more every time. (Kathryn, 20s, >20 years tariff)

> I came in when my son was two and he'll be 21 [when I'm released], and that's *if* I get my first parole. So I've missed a lot of his life […] Like his first days at school and stuff like that. (Connie)

These relationships were consistently at the epicentre of fears and frustration related to the length of the sentence being served and represented a lens through which the pains of life imprisonment for young women were often brought into the sharpest relief. Such concerns are discussed in more detail at the end of the following section.

Temporal Pains: Time Left to Serve and Losing the Best Years of Your Life

The notion of "temporal vertigo" conveys the disorienting and distressing feelings arising from becoming overwhelmed by the length of the custodial sentence received (see Wright et al. 2017). Ranked the 7th most severe of problems of long-term imprisonment among young LSPs, "thinking about the amount of time you might have to serve" was felt to be largely incomprehensible and best avoided, as Curtis (25, 19-year tariff) explained:

> I was 19 when I got sentenced. Basically, all them years I've just done, growing up, I've got to do them again in prison, and it's, like, whoa. […] I just didn't want to think about it, cause I knew [did] it would just mess up my head.

In the main, young men and women acknowledged that ruminating on the dizzying existential implications of time to be served was particularly detrimental to psychological well-being, and that living exclusively in the present acted to defend against this:

> [The sentence] is a bit daunting at times. […] But you try not to think about it—you just try to take it day-by-day and crack on, really. (Oscar)

The "overwhelming and overpowering" realisation of having "longer to serve than I've been alive" (Maria, 20s, >20-year tariff) created a sense among some that life was being "wasted" and would be "almost pointless" (Carl) at the expiration of the tariff; this was reflected in the severity with which young people identified with "feeling that your life is being wasted" (ranked 5th of 39 problems). Interviewees expressed their sense that being incarcerated during late adolescence and early adulthood was uniquely painful because it "robbed" them of an inimitable opportunity to experience "that vital period between 18 and 21, 22 […] when you really sort of find out who you are as a person" (Carl). Being forced to confront the fact that this stage of life had been irrevocably lost was reflected in the significantly higher severity scores among young LSPs when compared to their older counterparts for the item "feeling that you are losing the best years of your life" (ranked 2nd of 39 problems; $p < 0.001$). Contact from friends in the outside world compounded this acute sense that these "formative years" (Dan) were being lost in real time, "constantly" reinforcing their inability to follow their peers in "setting up a career" or "settling down with a family and getting married" (Dan). For many, these conventional life goals were little more than an elusive fantasy, fostering a deep sense of resentment and despair; sentiments that were often enhanced by the perceived illegitimacy of the conviction and tariff length, reflected in the significantly higher severity score among young LSPs than older prisoners for the item "feeling that the length of your sentence is unfair" (ranked 4th of 39 problems; $p = 0.001$).

Such temporal anxieties and despair were often brought into the sharpest relief when considered through a relational lens: that is, when young LSPs reflected on the aspects of family life they would be missing while serving their sentence. For example, Kathryn explained her tariff length only "really hit" her when considered in the context of her daughter's age ("I'm thinking 'what the *fuck* am I going to do; my little girl's going to be like 30 before the time I get out'"), while Blake (20, 22-year tariff) recognised that the length of his tariff meant that he might never spend time in the community again with ageing family members ("My nan's seventy. My mum's fifty. I don't know if I'll be out there with them again").

In this sense the support of family members described in the previous section was a somewhat bittersweet experience, forcing young LSPs to constantly reflect on the ways in which familial others were "doing time" with them. As Maria acknowledged, as a life-sentenced prisoner "you're not the only one that's being punished. Your whole family is being punished too".

Deprivation Pains: Being Bored, Missing "Little Luxuries", Social Life, and Sex

The mean severity scores for "being bored" were significantly higher ($p < 0.001$) for young LSPs, for whom this was the 8th most severe problem of long-term imprisonment (compared to being ranked 25th among participants aged 26 years or older at the time of the study). Given that "repetition" and "minimal variation" is at the very core of "boredom" (Conrad 1997, p. 473), it might be relatively unsurprising to find prison life—a routinised and monotonous experience for most—described as "boring", particularly among an age group known for being "boredom-prone" (cf. Weybright et al. 2020). However, a broad range of existential challenges were communicated by young LSPs when they dismissed something as "boring". In some instances, it was little more than an "all-purpose term of disapproval" (Conrad 1997, p. 468), with young people describing as "boring" any aspects of prison life which they found particularly annoying or disagreeable (e.g. prison rules, staff behaviour), or which was tedious because it was "too easy" (Blake, discussing his prison's low-level/basic educational offer) or not "intellectually stimulating" (Dan, reflecting on conversation with "criminals"). In this sense, "being bored" reflected the absence of activities that specifically "aroused interest" (Conrad 1997, p. 470); moreover, even activities that once provided a degree of relief could become "boring" when repeated ad nauseum. For example, Hugo (21, 18-year tariff) explained that he was so "bored" of "playing pool and table tennis [every evening] for the last five years" that he was somewhat grateful that the recent curtailment of evening association[10] had relieved him of this obligation.

However, discussions or tasks which were conversely far too challenging, either intellectually or emotionally, were *also* described as "boring". Such sentiments reminiscent of Conrad's (1997, p. 471) notion of "boredom as alienation", which seemingly underpinned Maria's interpretation of letter-writing as "boring". She explained that she struggled to connect with the task, which required reading "meaningless" descriptions of an outside life which remained inaccessible and largely irrelevant, and the tedium of her prison life, which made her feel that she had nothing of interest or importance to offer up in return.

The disproportionate sense of "being bored" among young LSPs might also be explained by the sense of "boredom as a function of social expectations" (Conrad 1997, p. 468). Growing up in an intensely "boredom-avoidant" society, where most young people exist in a "constant state of activity, connection and stimulation" (Madden 2019, p. 67), no doubt meant that the monotonous and technologically deprived nature of prison was especially painful for this group (particularly when compared to older peers, some of whom had never used the internet or seen a smartphone). To some degree, this perhaps also shaped the significantly greater severity with which young LSPs experienced "missing little luxuries" (ranked 9th of 39 problems in terms of severity; $p = 0.012$) compared to older prisoners. The ways in which young men and women reflected on this issue not only reflected the pains induced by the deprivation (absolute and relative) of "luxury" items (i.e. non-essential but desirable goods such as quality chocolate, 18-rated video games, and take-away pizza), but also the sharp contrast between their current circumstances and their memories of a recent past in which they had been free to obtain and consume such items at will. In this sense, the absence of luxuries was all the more painful for young people—most of whom were only a matter of months or years into their sentence, and had scant carceral experience—as it represented an attack on their autonomy; an assault to which they had not yet adjusted, as Carl explained:

> I went from being able to go to the shops and order whatever you wanted, to having to order [my] items once a week [...] [I miss] being able to go wherever you want and do whatever you want—that *freedom*, in a sense? For someone who is *just coming into prison and who has never been in it before* [...] to have that completely taken away from you? It's a wake-up call. It's a shock.

This painful disjuncture between pre-prison life and current carceral reality was also reflected in the significantly greater severity with which young men and women missed their "social life" (ranked 6th of 39 problems) compared to their older counterparts ($p = 0.012$). Many described how they had "loved living a bit wild" (Liz, 24, 15-year tariff) prior to their conviction, and so the stark comparison between recent lives—characterised by "drinking, going out, partying [...] and doing what lads do" (Seb, 23, 21-year tariff)—and the routine monotony of prison life was a particularly painful burden to bear. The inability for heterosexual males (who made up the bulk of the sample) to "do what lads do" was also expressed in the significantly greater severity with which young LSPs reported "being sexually frustrated" (ranked 10th of 39 problems; $p = 0.045$). Young men—and to a lesser extent, young women—expressed anguish at the disconnect between their current circumstances and the construction of their pre-prison sexual self, and raised concerns about the long-term impact of the absence of sex:

Obviously, *of course* I miss sex! I'm a man like, so-I'm a young boy like, I'm active like, you get me? So I miss it, you know. *Obviously*! When you used to do something a lot, like, you miss it. (Zaid, aged 20, 22-year tariff)

[My vagina] will be shrivelled up by the time I get out! (Eloise, 20s, <20-year tariff)

It was not simply the absence of the physical act of intercourse which was painful, however, with young men and women also mourning the loss of everyday affection. For example, Kathryn "miss[ed] having someone to stroke your hair" while Harris described how much he missed "cuddling and kissing" women. Such experiences and feelings impacted on attitudes towards coping strategies for this, as well as shaping fears about the possibilities of a "normal" sexual relationship following release, citing the damaging and "dehumanising" effects of the deprivation of "intimacy" more broadly (Dan).

Discussion and Concluding Thoughts

While long-term imprisonment has long been acknowledged as an experience that is "unsettling [...] disruptive and disorganizing" for most, Gibbs (1982, p. 100) has argued that it is a uniquely "cataclysmic" phenomenon for young people. Little work, however, has sought to explore this claim within the context of the pains of long-term imprisonment among young people, and even less in a contemporaneous (rather than retrospective) manner.

In response to this perceived lacuna, this chapter has drawn on data from our broader study of long-term imprisonment from a young age to explore the lived experience of serving a long life sentence in England and Wales during the specific life-course period of late adolescence and early adulthood (aged 18 to 25 years inclusive). In doing so, we identified the most dominant pains of life imprisonment for young people—many of whom were in the initial years of a sentence that was similar to, or exceeded, the years they had lived—as existing within three core conceptual areas: *relational* pains; *temporal* pains; and *deprivation* pains.

Notwithstanding the methodological caveats noted above, the comparative aspect of the analysis between these young prisoners and their older peers (aged between 26 and 66 years at interview) drew attention to a series of observations about the nature and challenges of long-term imprisonment during late adolescence and emerging adulthood. Firstly, the analysis supported broader findings that the most painful aspects of long-term imprisonment are often *relational*, and the absence of statistically significant differences between the groups indicates that this observation holds irrespective of age or years served. Fears that parents and grandparents would become ill or die during the course of the sentence were common, as was a general sense of despair among young parents that they would miss the entirety of their child's developmental years, and all that this entailed (missing first steps, words, and day at school, for instance). Of specific concern to young women without children (and indeed, those across our broader sample) was that the length of their sentence would exceed their reproductive capacities, meaning that the sentence also crushed hopes of a family. This was less of a concern for young men, who did not anticipate release in their 40s or 50s to impede their opportunities to have children, adding to our earlier work on the ways in which the pains of long-term imprisonment are gendered (see Crewe et al. 2017).

Secondly, the analysis identified that the *temporal* pains of long-term imprisonment and deprivational pains were *particularly* painful among those aged 18–25 years when compared to those aged 26 or above. In terms of the temporal pains, the sense of being "robbed" of one's late teens and 20s resulted in a sense of deep despair and irrevocable loss. Long-term imprisonment during late adolescence and emerging adulthood crushes what Shaw et al. (1995, cit. in Caldwell et al. 1999, p. 105) identify as the "normative developmental impetus towards autonomy" associated with this specific stage of the life course. And while Sykes (1958) identified "autonomy" as a separate pain from the deprivation of goods and services or of sexual intimacies, the accounts of these young LSPs revealed these concerns to be inextricably intertwined. Indeed, feeling bored and being *deprived of* "little luxuries", social life and sex shattered existential expectations of late adolescence and emerging adulthood. These brief years of hedonistic excess and freedom from responsibility were recognised as a rite of passage among the young, and many interviewees had severed contact with friends from the outside who represented a painful reminder of what life could, or should, have been. It is likely that these temporal pains and deprivations were felt more keenly by young LSPs because they had spent significantly less years in prison than their older peers. As O'Donnell (2014, p. 207) notes of the initial phase of imprisonment more broadly, the deprivation of liberty is felt most harshest when the outside world is still part of the "immediate past", and that the "dependence on external points of reference" for what life is, or should be, act to smother adaptive potential in carceral settings. For young life-sentenced prisoners only a matter of months or years into a 15, 20, or 30-year tariff, the outside world was still painfully tangible and far more familiar than the prison world; a new reality to which many had yet to adjust.

In a broader sense, these findings raise important questions and challenges about the nature, utility, and legitimacy of the trend in England and Wales towards a greater number of people serving increasingly lengthy minimum tariffs, particularly young people. It is likely that young people are cognitively and socially more vulnerable and therefore struggle more with the specific pains of long-term confinement (as demonstrated in the comparative analysis with adults) and that the system may not recognise the specific needs of young men and women in a system set up primarily for adult males. It is clear that targeted support is required for this group, particularly in the initial months and years of a long sentence.

These findings should also force us to consider more carefully the presumed heterogeneity of the experience of long-term imprisonment; specifically, how age and generation might shape the challenges experienced (particularly in terms of mental health and well-being) and hinder the ability to adapt to or cope with a lengthy period of confinement.

It is particularly important to address such concerns given that we know so little of the nature of long-term change and post-release outcomes for individuals whose maturational processes in late adolescence and emerging adulthood are played out within a carceral context. Research on adults released from lengthy custodial sentences points to poor outcomes, with mental health issues akin to post-traumatic stress disorder (see Liem and Kunst 2013, p. 335), relationship problems (due to the complexity of managing complicated relationships over extended periods) (Jamieson and Grounds 2005), and a general lack of preparedness for life on release (Munn and Bruckert 2013). With this in mind, it is essential that we understand the impact of (increasingly long) life sentences on young men and women, who will be catapulted back into the community at middle age, with a significant portion of their lives still ahead of them.

Notes

1. In England and Wales, "imprisonment for life" is technically a term of 99 years but with the expectation that this term will be served partially in custody (guided by a minimum period known as the "tariff"; see footnote 5) and—following a successful parole hearing—partially in the community. Upon release, such individuals must adhere to a set of strict conditions known as "life licence" for the rest of their natural life.
2. Only "adults" (aged 21 years or older) can be sentenced to "imprisonment for life". However, equivalent sentences—also for an indeterminate period and for which a minimum tariff will be set—exist for young people: "Custody for Life" (most typically for those convicted of murder) for those aged 18–20 years and "Detention during Her Majesty's Pleasure" (also known as an "HMP" sentence) for children aged 10–17 years.
3. Of those interviewees aged 18–25 years at the time of the study (n = 64) who represent the focus of this chapter, 17% (n = 11) were convicted prior to their 18th birthday (range = 13–17 years inclusive). For context, 8.3% (n = 26) of all survey and interview participants within the broader study, who ranged from 18 to 66 years in age, were convicted as a "minor" (aged under 18 years).
4. In England and Wales, life imprisonment is the *mandatory* sentence for murder convictions, in that no judicial discretion exists in terms of the nature of the sanction handed down. Individuals may also be sentenced to imprisonment for life for other set offences; these are known as *discretionary* life sentences.
5. The "tariff" is the *minimum* custodial period to be served before being considered eligible for parole; unless the defendant is aged 16 years or younger at conviction, the full tariff *must* be served, with no possibility of reduction or early release. Trial judges set the tariff length, guided by the minimum "appropriate starting points" legislated for in the Criminal Justice Act 2003 (Schedule 21)—these are then scaled up or down depending on aggravating and mitigating factors. Importantly, these are differentiated according to age—for example, 30 years is the minimum tariff starting point for an adult (aged 18 years or older) convicted of murder involving a firearm, or for gain, compared to 12 years for individuals aged 17 years or younger convicted of the same offence. Further, "whole life" orders—where the minimum term is for the remainder of an individual's natural life—are only available for specific offences and for individuals aged 21 years or older.
6. The concept of "sentencing stage" was primarily a tool for sampling interviewees, whereas surveys sought to draw data from a broader spread of the population; therefore, while all interviewees fit within this framework, most survey participants fell outside of it.

7. "Mid" stage was calculated as half of the overall sentence tariff, plus or minus two years, and the "late" stage as two years prior to their tariff point, or beyond their tariff point. The second phase of the study, which focused exclusively on women, had a far smaller overall population, meaning that it was possible (and indeed desirable) to instead adopt a "total population" sampling strategy, regardless of sentence stage.
8. Names, age at time of interview, and tariff length are given only for the initial reference to an individual; subsequently only the pseudonym will be given, to reduce repetition.
9. Given that the women are a potentially identifiable group within the sample, information which could jeopardise their anonymity has been written in a manner that is deliberately vague and obfuscatory rather than giving specific age and tariff length.
10. Assigned opportunities within the prison regime, often in the evening, set aside for socialising with other prisoners and calling friends and family.

References

Blom-Cooper, L. (1987). The penalty of imprisonment. *The tanner lectures on human values*. Lecture delivered at Clare Hall, University of Cambridge, UK, 30th November to 2nd December 1987. Retrieved from https://tannerlectures.utah.edu/_documents/a-to-z/b/Blom-Cooper88.pdf

Caldwell, L., Darling, L., Payne, L., & Dowdy, B. (1999). Why are you bored? An examination of psychological and social control causes of boredom among adolescents. *Journal of Leisure Research, 31*(2), 103–121.

Cauffman, E., & Steinberg, L. (2000). (Im)maturity of judgment in adolescence: Why adolescents may be less culpable than adults. *Behavioral Sciences & The Law, 18*(6), 741–760.

Codd, H. (2008). *In the shadow of prison: Families, imprisonment & criminal justice*. Cullompton: Willan.

Cohen, S., & Taylor, L. (1972). *Psychological survival: The experience of long-term imprisonment*. Middlesex: Penguin.

Conrad, P. (1997). It's boring: Notes on the meanings of boredom in everyday life. *Qualitative Sociology, 20*(4), 465–475.

Crewe, B. (2011). Depth, weight, tightness: Revisiting the pains of imprisonment. *Punishment & Society, 13*(5), 509–529.

Crewe, B., Hulley, S., & Wright, S. (2017). The gendered pains of life imprisonment. *British Journal of Criminology, 57*(6), 1359–1378.

Crewe, B., Hulley, S., & Wright, S. (2020). *Life imprisonment from young adulthood: Adaptation, identity and time*. Houndmills: Palgrave Macmillan.

Flanagan, T. J. (1980). The pains of long-term imprisonment: A comparison of British and American perspectives. *British Journal of Criminology, 20*(2), 148–156.

Flanagan, T. J. (1982). Lifers and long-termers: Doing big time. In R. Johnson & H. Toch (Eds.), *The pains of imprisonment* (pp. 115–129). Prospect Heights, IL: Waveland Press Inc.

Flanagan, T. J. (1995). Preface. In T. J. Flanagan (Ed.), *Long-term imprisonment: Policy, science and correctional practice* (pp. xi–xiv). Thousand Oaks: Sage.

Gibbs, J. (1982). The first cut is the deepest: Psychological breakdown and survival in the detention setting. In R. Johnson & H. Toch (Eds.), *The pains of imprisonment* (pp. 97–114). Thousand Oaks: Sage.

Gunn, J., Nicol, R., Gristwood, J., & Foggitt, R. (1973). Long-term prisoners. *British Journal of Criminology, 13*(4), 331–340.

Holloway, W., & Jefferson, T. (2000). *Doing qualitative research differently*. Thousand Oaks: Sage.

Hulley, S., Crewe, B., & Wright, S. (2016). Re-examining the problems of long-term imprisonment. *British Journal of Criminology, 56*(4), 769–792.

Jamieson, R., & Grounds, A. (2005). Release and adjustment: Perspectives from studies of wrongly convicted and politically motivated prisoners. In A. Liebling & S. Maruna (Eds.), *The effects of imprisonment* (pp. 33–65). Cullompton: Willan.

Johnson, R., & McGunigall-Smith, S. (2008). Life without parole, America's other death penalty: Notes on life under sentence of death by incarceration. *The Prison Journal, 88*(2), 328–346.

Leigey, M. E., & Ryder, M. (2015). The pains of permanent imprisonment: Examining perceptions of confinement among older life without parole inmates. *International Journal of Offender Therapy and Comparative Criminology, 59*(7), 726–742.

Liem, M., & Kunst, M. (2013). Is there a recognizable post-incarceration syndrome among released "lifers"? *International Journal of Law and Psychiatry, 36*(3–4), 333–337.

MacKenzie, D. L., & Goodstein, L. (1985). Long-term incarceration impacts and characteristics of long-term offenders: An empirical analysis. *Criminal Justice and Behavior, 12*(4), 395–414.

Madden, C. (2019). *Hello gen Z: Engaging the generation of post-millennials*. Sydney: Hello Clarity.

Ministry of Justice. (2009). *Population in custody monthly tables—February 2009: England and Wales*.Ministry of Justice Statistics Bulletin. Retrieved from https://assets.publishing.service.gov.uk/government/uploads/system/uploads/attachment_data/file/218181/population-in-custody-february-091.pdf

Ministry of Justice. (2019). *Offender management statistics quarterly: April to June 2019*. Retrieved from https://assets.publishing.service.gov.uk/government/uploads/system/uploads/attachment_data/file/842590/OMSQ_2019_Q2.pdf

Munn, M., & Bruckert, C. (2013). *On the outside: From lengthy imprisonment to lasting freedom*. Vancouver: University of British Columbia Press.

O'Donnell, I. (2014). *Prisoners, solitude, and time.* Oxford: Oxford University Press.

Porporino, F. J. (1990). Difference in response to long-term imprisonment: Implications for the management of long-term offenders. *The Prison Journal, 70,* 35–45.

Prior, D., et al. (2011). *Maturity, young adults and criminal justice: A literature review.* Birmingham, UK: University of Birmingham. Retrieved from https://www.t2a.org.uk/wp-content/uploads/2011/09/Birmingham-University-Maturity-final-literature-review-report.pdf.

Prison Reform Trust. (2019). *Prison: The facts—Summer 2019 Bromley briefings.* Retrieved from http://www.prisonreformtrust.org.uk/Portals/0/Documents/Bromley%20Briefings/Winter%202019%20Factfile%20web.pdf

Richards, B. (1978). The experience of long-term imprisonment: An exploratory investigation. *British Journal of Criminology, 18*(2), 162–169.

Sapsford, R. (1983). *Life sentence prisoners: Reaction, response and change.* London: Open University Press.

Sawyer, S. M., Azzopardi, P. S., Wickremarathne, D., & Patton, G. C. (2018). The age of adolescence. *The Lancet Child & Adolescent Health, 2*(3), 223–228.

Schinkel, M. (2014). Punishment as moral communication: The experiences of long-term prisoners. *Punishment & Society, 16*(5), 578–597.

Srivastava, P., & Hopwood, N. (2009). A practical iterative framework for qualitative data analysis. *International Journal of Qualitative Methods, 8*(1), 76–84.

Sykes, G. (1958). *The society of captives.* Princeton, NJ: Princeton University Press.

Toch, H. (2010). "I am not now who I used to be then": Risk assessment and the maturation of long-term prison inmates. *The Prison Journal, 90*(1), 4–11.

Warr, J. (2016). The deprivation of certitude, legitimacy and hope: Foreign national prisoners and the pains of imprisonment. *Criminology & Criminal Justice, 16*(3), 301–318.

Weybright, E. H., Schulenberg, J. and Caldwell, L. L. (2020). More bored today than yesterday? National trends in adolescent boredom from 2008 to 2017. *Journal of Adolescent Health, 66*(3), 360–365.

Wright, S., Crewe, B., & Hulley, S. (2017). Suppression, denial, sublimation: Defending against the initial pains of very long life sentences. *Theoretical Criminology, 21*(2), 225–246.

Zamble, E. (1992). Behavior and adaptation in long-term prison inmates. *Criminal Justice and Behavior, 19*(4), 409–425.

23

Surviving Life: How Youth Adapt to Life Sentences in Adult Prisons

Kaylyn C. Canlione and Laura S. Abrams

Surviving Life: How Youth Adapt to Life Sentences in Adult Prisons

The United States is a global outlier in its harsh treatment of young people who come into conflict with the law. Compared to other nations, the United States imprisons youth (in this chapter, referring to persons under age 18) for longer periods of time and transfers youth into the adult criminal justice system at greater rates (Bochenek 2016). In the early 1900s, social reformers developed the institution of the juvenile courts because they viewed children and adolescents as different from adults in their maturity and capacity for rehabilitation, and hence deserving of a more flexible and informal response to alleged misconduct (Feld 2017; Whitehead and Lab 2018). By the 1990s—nearly a century after the initial juvenile court was founded—the trial and sentencing of youth in conflict with the law had become more harsh and formal, including laws that made it easier to transfer youth to the adult criminal court (Feld 1997, 2017). The possibility of extreme sentences for youth—including life without the possibility parole and the death penalty—made the United States distinct in its harshness and reliance on such extreme sanctions (Bochenek 2016).

K. C. Canlione (✉) • L. S. Abrams
Luskin School of Public Affairs, University of California Los Angeles, Los Angeles, CA, USA
e-mail: kcanlione1@g.ucla.edu

Many scholars have documented and studied the transformation and paradigm shifts of the U.S. juvenile court and correctional institutions over the course of the twentieth century (c.f., Feld 2017; Tanenhaus 2004; Whitehead and Lab 2018). All concur that in the 1980s and 1990s, a surge of violent crime among adults and youth, along with racialized, distorted media representations of "violent youth," coincided with legislative changes that ushered in harsher and more extreme sentences for youth (Feld 2017). State transfer policies—those that allow youth to be legally adjudicated as adults in criminal court—dramatically increased the number of youths sentenced in criminal court and sent to adult jails and prisons (Feld 2017). For example, from 1990 to 1999, the number of youths housed in adult jails rose by 311% (Troilo 2018). In 2000, the first year that the numbers of youth in adult prisons were measured, there were 3892 youth under the age of 18 in adult prisons (Bureau of Justice Statistics 2000). Although crime rates fell dramatically after their peak in 1994, harsh penalties for youth convicted of crimes—including life sentences and life without parole—remained state law (Blumstein 2002).

Due to the steep rise of harsh punishments doled out for youth in the 1990s, in 2017, there were 11,745 adults serving *life sentences* in state prisons for crimes they were charged with when they were under age 18 (Nellis 2017). The vast majority of these cases involve a homicide, often as the primary perpetrator, but sometimes as an accomplice. Additionally, juvenile life sentencing in the United States is extremely racially disparate, with roughly 80% of individuals serving life without parole or "de-facto" life sentences (i.e., the length of the sentence exceeds the offender's natural life) for crimes convicted as minors are persons of color, meaning non-White (Leiber and Peck 2013; Nellis 2017). All told, 9% of all "lifers" in the United States were convicted for crimes committed when they were under age 18 (Nellis 2017).

Current Conditions: Policy Changes and Advocacy

Over the last 15 years, several U.S. Supreme Court decisions have dramatically altered the legal understanding of culpability as it pertains to youth. Beginning with *Roper v. Simmons* (2005), the majority decision established that youth differ from adults in key ways, namely in their lack of maturity and sense of responsibility, unformed character, and their relative lack of control over their own environments. These mitigating factors resulted in the determination that death sentences for juveniles violate the Eighth Amendment's prohibition on cruel and unusual punishment. Building upon the *Roper* decision, *Graham v. Florida* (2010) equated life without parole sentences for juveniles convicted of non-homicide offenses to the death penalty, establishing these sentences as unconstitutional under the Eighth Amendment. Further, *Graham* set precedent that the characteristics of youth must be taken into account when considering the appropriateness of extreme sentences.

Following *Graham*, *Miller v. Alabama* (2012) held that mandatory life without parole sentences for juveniles convicted of homicide also violate the Eighth Amendment and that youth sentenced under these conditions must be given "some meaningful opportunity to obtain release based on demonstrated maturity and rehabilitation" (*Miller v. Alabama* 2012). This decision eliminated *mandatory* juvenile life without parole (JLWOP) sentences, but did not categorically ban the use of JLWOP.

Moreover, *Montgomery v. Louisiana* (2016) held that the decision in *Miller* should apply retroactively so that those already serving a mandatory JLWOP sentence would be entitled to case review. That said, how these resentencing and parole determinations are made is left to the 50 states to determine. This discretion proves problematic, as some states function with fully discretionary parole systems, meaning they have no stated standards and are not subject to examination under the Due Process Clause (Bell 2019). States with presumptive parole systems, in which statute directs parole boards to vote in favor of release unless certain factors are found, still provide little assurance despite the Due Process Clause, as the factors are often so ambiguous that they provide little restraint on discretion. As a result, parole decisions for those seeking relief under these statutes are dramatically inconsistent (Bell 2019).

Extreme Sentencing

The series of Supreme Court decisions referenced in the preceding section created an opportunity for release of roughly 2100 people serving JLWOP sentences in the United States (Nellis 2017). Of these 2100 imprisoned individuals, 1000 are estimated to have been resentenced and nearly 400 released, largely due to changes in state policy prompted by *Miller* (Nellis 2017; The Campaign for the Fair Sentencing of Youth 2018). For those who have been resentenced or released, the average sentence length served was 25 years (The Campaign for the Fair Sentencing of Youth 2018), meaning that vast majority of their lives have been spent in prison.

Despite this significant paradigm shift, there are two other groups of "juvenile lifers" who are not directly impacted by this series of supreme court decisions: those sentenced to an *indeterminate* life sentence, also called juvenile life *with* parole (JLWP), such as 25 to life, 50 to life, and so on, and those sentenced to de-facto life sentences, in which the sentence exceeds the offender's natural life. As of 2018, there were 7346 people serving JLWP in the United States, and an additional 2089 serving de-facto life sentences for crimes committed as minors (Nellis 2017). While the *Miller* decision does not directly impact these two groups, several states, including California, have enacted policies on behalf of these groups that align with *Miller's* reasoning.

In the state of California, where this study took place, several key policies resulted from the mandate in *Miller v. Alabama*. California has pushed *Miller's* intent beyond just mandatory JLWOP cases, also instituting reforms for other types of juvenile life sentences, such as JLWP and de-facto juvenile life. Here is a brief summary of these laws and their reach.

- *SB9:* Allows for a person who was sentenced to JLWOP to seek review of his/her sentence after serving 15 years. Those eligible still must serve at least 25 years before they are eligible for parole. (S.B. 9, 2011–2012 Leg., Reg. Sess. (Cal. 2012) 2012).
- *SB 260:* Established Youth Offender Parole Hearings (YOPH), requiring the board to give "great weight" to the diminished culpability of youth in making their parole decisions for those whose offense occurred when they were under 18. This applies to youth offenders who have received either an indeterminate life sentence or a lengthy determinate sentence. (S.B. 260, 2014–2015 Leg., Reg. Sess. (Cal. 2014) 2014)
- *SB 261:* Extends SB 260 to those whose offense occurred when they were under 23, recognizing that the hallmark features of youth extend beyond the age of majority (S.B. 261, 2015–2016 Leg., Reg. Sess. (Cal. 2015) 2015)
- *SB 394*: Makes individuals sentenced to life without the possibility of parole as juveniles eligible for parole on their 25th year of incarceration through a Youth Offender Parole Hearing (S.B. 394, 2017–2018 Leg., Reg. Sess. (Cal. 2017) 2017)

All of the men who participated in this study were released based on one of these policies. While this group of "released" youth lifers shares a unique experience, there is little research about how their lives have been impacted by the policies that both permitted their sentencing and allowed for their eventual release. In a separate paper, we have discussed how these men located motivation for desistance behind bars despite the odds (Abrams et al. 2020). Here we focus on another key facet of this experience: how youth adjust to serving a life sentence. Our key questions are: how do young people adapt to serving a life sentence in an adult prison? How are they socialized to adult prison life? What strategies do they use to cope, find community, and make a life for themselves? While we in no way endorse the continued use of extreme sentences for youth or adults, our intention is to shed light on how young people coped with their sentence in the midst of deplorable and adverse conditions.

Related Literature and Theory

Prior scholarship has examined issues related to our study questions such as prison adaptation, trauma, and the process of adjusting to life sentences. Adjustment to prison for most people is a difficult and significant transition. Loss of freedom, the noise and the routine of prison, and the environment itself causes an immediate need for psychological adjustment. This adjustment is profoundly disruptive, forcing those facing the condition of imprisonment to reckon with their expectations of how the world ought to function (Crewe et al. 2020). Some people have been in jail or prison many times and may be more immune to these conditions; but for most, being imprisoned causes extreme transition stress, anxiety, and fear (Haney 2001).

Adult prisons often differ from youth prisons in that they are less staffed, more crowded, and more violent; they also have less access to educational, recreational, or counseling services. Adult prisons are, for the most part, violent and harsh environments (Lopez-Aguado 2018; Wood 2012). As such, most people who enter a prison sentence experience a sense of hypervigilance around personal safety while adjusting to the local norms set by the "elders" of prison life. These are the people, often those with more experience, who control access to resources and other social and economic facets of prison life (McCorke 1992).

Added to this typical stress, lengthy sentences, and especially life without the possibility of parole, is arguably more than devastating to the individual psyche than any other type of sentence. The longer people are incarcerated, the more their well-being and positive self-perception can deteriorate. Psychologist Craig Haney (2001) conceptualizes prisonization—also known as institutionalization—as experiencing one or more of the following symptoms: dependence on the institution for structure, distrust and suspicion of others, controlling emotions, social withdrawal and isolation, normalizing prison culture, loss of dignity and self-worth, and post-traumatic stress. Moreover, he argues that people with longer terms of imprisonment are especially vulnerable to the effects of prisonization (Haney 2001).

In examining long-term imprisonment for young adults in the United Kingdom, Crewe et al. (2020) compare the experience and subsequent trauma of entering an institutional setting for a long sentence to being diagnosed with a chronic or terminal illness, referencing the way in which it is often inconsistent with the individual's sense of self and serves as "sudden interruption of lifecourse" (Crewe et al. 2020). Jewkes (2005) contends that this interruption to the lifecourse, and subsequent feelings of loss and grief, "may be regarded as the ultimate sanction of life imprisonment" creating a sense of "bereavement for oneself; the loss involving lost worlds, lost futures and lost identities" (p. 370).

In addition to these pains and emotional losses, incarceration is also traumatizing due to physical and sexual violence, which is even more prevalent among those incarcerated at younger ages (Troilo 2018). California state prisons are notoriously violent, overcrowded, and prone to the use of solitary confinement for months and years on end (ProPublica and the Sacramento Bee 2019). Beyond routine prison adjustment, these contexts lend themselves to heightened risks of trauma, PTSD, depression, suicidality, and other mental health conditions (Haney 2001).

Despite the trauma inherent in incarceration—and especially in long-term incarceration—research finds that many people with lengthy sentences will eventually come to a point in which they move past the sense of shock and bereavement that often accompanies long-term imprisonment (Crewe et al. 2020). Cohen and Taylor (1972) describe this "coming to terms" as the point in which individuals "reflexively negotiate […] an 'extreme and immutable environment, imposed upon them as a punishment'" (p. 58). Crewe et al. (2020), using Margaret Archer's theory of reflexivity, describe this process as individuals using their own power to internally deliberate on how to navigate situations that are "not of their choosing" (Crewe et al. 2020; see pp. 18–19).

These theories offer a guiding framework from which to understand how and why young people with long sentences find meaning and create lives in the harsh environment of the prison. However, this related literature is largely based on research conducted in the United Kingdom, where youth, even up to age 21, cannot be sentenced to life without the possibility of parole, and most life sentences in England/Wales does not mean a "whole life sentence" (Criminal Justice Act 2003). In this study, we seek to build from this literature, and examine how people sentenced to life in prison as youth adapt to this sentence in the contexts and conditions of California state prisons.

Method

This study is grounded in the epistemological approach of constructivism, which understands individuals' reflections of their lived experience to be the primary way in which they make meaning of the world (Berger and Luckmann 1967; Lock and Strong 2010; Schutz and Luckmann 1973). The authors conducted this study using a phenomenological methodology (Sokolowski 2000), which attempts to uncover "core" facets or process of shared experiences through in-depth interviewing.

Recruitment and Sampling

Participants were recruited purposively through presentations about the study at several halfway houses in Los Angeles, California, and through the assistance of advocacy organizations. To be eligible for the study, participants met the following criteria: (a) sentenced to life without parole, de-facto life, or life with the possibility of parole for a homicide offense committed as a young person (age 20 or under); (b) obtained release through one of California's youth offender resentencing polices; and (c) released from prison within at least one month. In total, 22 men expressed interest in the study. Of those, we prioritized recruitment of those who were sentenced for crimes they committed when they were legally classified minors. Although we did not purposively seek an all-male sample, we were not able to recruit any female participants through these outreach strategies. Of the 10 who participated in the study, in this chapter, we focus on the narratives of 8 men who were under age 18 and transferred from the juvenile court to an adult prison sentence. This small sample with in-depth interviewing follows the phenomenological methodological approach and is not intended to be generalizable (Sokolowski 2000).

Table 23.1 provides demographic information for each member of the study. The 8 participants were Black ($n = 3$), Hispanic ($n = 3$), and White ($n = 2$). The age of the participants ranged from 39 to 50, with a mean of 44.9. The length of time since release from state prison ranged from 2 to 37 months with a mean of 9.6 (and a median of 3.4). The number of years that participants spent incarcerated ranged from 21 to 32 years, with a mean of 26.4.

Table 23.1 Participant characteristics

Name	Race	Age at time of crime	Current age[a]	Length of time served	Sentence type	Months since release[a]
Allen	White	17	42	25	LWOP	2
Christopher	Black	17	41	21	LWOP	20
Darryl	Black	17	50	32	LWP	3
Hector	Latino	16	39	23	LWP	12
Julian	Black	17	46	28	LWP	4
Kent	White	17	48	30	LWP	
Miguel	Latino	17	44	21	LWOP	37
Roberto	Latino	17	49	32	LWP	3

[a]At time of first interview

Data Collection

We (the authors of this chapter and one additional graduate student) conducted two in-depth narrative life-history interviews with each of the eight study participants. The total number of interviews for this analysis was 16. The interviews were comprised of open-ended questions on various segments of the participants' lives, loosely split by pre and post the homicide charge that resulted in a life sentence. Given that the interviews were retrospective, we were interested in the participants' views of their own life course, recognizing that stories get "rewritten" based on years of insight and introspection.

The first interview explored questions about participants' childhood, family life, education, entrée into crime, the eventual crime leading to the life sentence (i.e., life-crime), sentencing, transition to prison life, and survival in prison. The second interview consisted of questions about finding meaning in prison, resentencing, reflections on victim impact, release, and transition to society. Each interview lasted between 90 and 160 min, was digitally recorded, and was conducted with one or two interviewers present. The interviews were conducted in private meeting spaces. We also collected basic demographic information for each participant and compiled public court documents and media pertaining to individual cases.

Prior to the interview, each participant signed an informed consent document. Each received a $35 gift card for the first interview and a $40 gift card for the second, although some declined these incentives. All procedures were approved by the Office of Research Protection for Human Subjects at the University of California, Los Angeles.

Results

The core process that emerged from the phenomenological analysis was the will to *live* rather than merely *survive* in the context of a life sentence in adult prison. Study participants progressed along similar trajectories, moving through a phase of survival into investing in one's life, community, and future, even if that future was confined to prison. This process began with "learning the rules," "participating in prison culture," and for some, "creating their own rules" from the beginning of their sentence. These themes and their subcomponents are described here.

Learning the Rules

For these men, the need to navigate survival as a young person in an adult prison arose quickly upon their entry. Almost immediately, they were faced with the racial dynamics of gang culture within the prison. While many of these men had been involved in gangs outside of prison, they found themselves facing different rules and expectations in adult prison. In prison it was no longer about neighborhood allegiances or even gang, but almost exclusively about race. Allegiances linked to racial identity are necessary for survival, especially for youth in adult institutions, who are uniquely vulnerable. In this sense, outside identities were quickly shed and institutional identities established. Christopher, an African American man who received a JLWOP sentence at age 17, expressed: "You go into prison and you don't know nothin'. So, if you have no allegiance who's going to teach you. Who's going to teach you what not to do in order to not get stabbed?" As Christopher and others explained, if they did not abide by these new race-based allegiances (rather than gang, region, or other forms of alliances), they were often put in danger of victimization. Christopher recalled arriving in prison and learning these race-related rules and allegiances, some of which were not what he had expected. He said:

> So, I see a guy that I was in juvenile hall with. He's been in prison, maybe three years or so before I got there, maybe four. So, I see him, he's over there with all the Mexicans you know. So, I'm walking towards him, like "hey what's up!" He's somebody that's familiar. I'm way up north, I've never been to prison, never been out of L.A. in my life. I'm walking towards him, I'm happy to see him. It feels good, because when I drove to the prison gates it was the scariest stuff of my life. And I knew him, we hung in juvenile hall. But when I went over there,

> I was immediately surrounded. So, I don't know <what's going on>, and he's acting different. So, then all the Blacks come. *And I didn't even know that it's a border there. And if you cross the border, you can be stabbed, and nobody helps you, because you crossed the border. I walked right passed it. So, who's going to tell you those things if you have no allegiance.* (Emphasis ours)

As this story relays, Christopher assumed that the connections he had forged across race in juvenile hall would carry over to adult prison, and yet instead, they put his very survival at risk.

Many of the men described the importance of learning the rules and distinctly remember moments in which those who were imprisoned alongside them took the time to teach them the unwritten rules. Julian recalled: "Gettin' to state prison, like I said, I get around them other guys, and they pretty much took me under they wings." Often times the "teachers" in these moments were members within the participants' former gangs, racial group, older lifers, or cell mates.

These lessons played a large role in their ability to navigate the formal and informal rules of the prison, and, in many cases, the guidance of the older men served as the catalyst for the youths' ability to successfully avoid being targets of violence. Several of the men identified an older lifer or cellmate as the source of advice that kept them out of danger, ultimately allowing them to pursue a life that they found meaningful. An older prisoner, for example, told Allen how to become a clerk (i.e., a job in the front office) in order to avoid trouble. He was told that if he could become useful—to both the prison staff and to other prisoners—he would have a better chance at successfully navigating the impending violence of prison. Allen is a white man who had received a JLWOP sentence at age 17, and by the time he arrived in prison he had decided that he was not going to partake in any prison gang culture—a dangerous decision which leaves one without physical protection. The advice he received from an older lifer provided him the route necessary to make himself useful enough that it would no longer be advantageous for others to harm him.

> I learned early on that I needed to put myself in a situation where I could stay away from the high volatile areas. And I asked him [an older prisoner] one day, how do you become a clerk? And he said, just tell him you're a clerk. Because I knew that being a clerk took me out of this dynamic of prison and put me into this dynamic of prison. Of being around officers and cops and away from all the guys that are causing all the trouble. [...] I didn't know anything about being a clerk, but I learned very quickly. [...] With that came the ability to do bed-moves. And with that, came the ability to help be a liaison between the inmates and the

staff. I can go, "Hey, I can get these bed moves done." I became valuable in that sense, to where I didn't need to be a soldier. I didn't need to be, you know, one of their person-in-their-ranks. In that capacity, I could be the desk-job-guy. Right?

Through his job as a clerk, Allen found two important ways to keep himself safe, both through proximity and utility. His proximity to violence grew further as he was removed from much of the general population during working hours, which placed him at arm's length from danger. Additionally, this job made him useful to staff and inmates alike. Allen was more useful brokering deals such as bed moves than he was on the yard, which allowed him to solidify his safety behind the desk.

Miguel, a Latino man, was also adamant in separating himself from prison politics from the time he entered the adult facility as a young person. Miguel and Allen appeared to be outliers in their approach to prison survival, carving out unique paths to avoid the dangers of their decisions. Sentenced to JLWOP at 17, Miguel experienced a religious awakening while still in county jail awaiting trial, leading to his decision not to participate in prison culture and to fully purge his former gang identity. He describes this experience as related to his youth, as it came out of the realization of being 17 and reckoning with the loss of his future. Similar to Allen, Miguel found a way to become useful in prison, though for Miguel this was through his Christianity. Miguel describes himself as bold in his Christianity, to the point that it became dangerous or even potentially fatal for him to refuse racial or gang allegiances. He said, "I'm ready to go be this light. And I don't care. I'm just ready to do good now. And if I'm going to die, I'm going to die being a good person. And I was bold. I was bold to the point that it became dangerous for me." In order to navigate the danger that followed, Miguel found a way to fulfill a need within the prison—that of providing hope. He made himself known as "Miguel the Christian," establishing his institutional identity as that of a religious confidante for the other men.

> I remember I used to get these guys coming out from the hole. They would send me letters. They would send me little kites <notes>. [...] I remember they would come and be like, hey homie, I've got a kite for you. I would ask who it was coming from, and they'd say it was coming from back there <the hole>. [...] So, I would get these kites, and I'm reading them, and it's like, hey bro, can you call my family and pray for me? [...] They wanted my help. You know, pray for Snoopy bro, he's getting stabbed right here and I don't know what to do. It hurts me, I can't do it, but you're close to God.

In this sense, Miguel made himself uniquely useful to the broader prison population, across racial groups. There was a need among the other men for hope and spiritual connection, and Miguel was able to fulfill this space. Miguel's youth at the time of his incarceration appears to have contributed to his ability to navigate these dangerous decisions, as in some ways, his boldness in his religious identity arose from his naivety and the recklessness that are hallmark feature of youth. Miguel's boldness led to a lack of fear and a stubbornness around his Christian identity, allowing him to assert himself as such unabashedly. Once it was clear to the other men that Miguel was "the Christian" they began to seek him out for their spiritual needs.

Prison Culture: Wearing the Mask

Most of the men were not as fortunate as Allen and Miguel in finding a path in prison that allowed them to avoid violence, nor where they initially as adamant about remaining outside of prison politics. For these men, survival and adaptation often involved participating in gangs, prison violence, and the drug trade. This was especially salient due to their age upon entry, as it was necessary that they solidify their racial allegiances for protection. Julian described it as such:

> You couldn't be a lone wolf with it. Part of my survival was—even with the first staff assault, I was taught you don't disrespect this race, that race, this way. Everything is race, even from the administration on down. They put you in some kind of category no matter what. You're black, white, other, period. Then they promote it as a—no matter what, they treat differently. [...] The race also becomes just part of your mindset, and the concept and the politics of it.

Many of the young men were angry at their situation and their sentence as well, contributing to a dangerous combination of nihilistic youth and the pressures of prison-yard participation. Kent, sentenced to life at 17, described himself as filled with hate upon entry to prison, contributing in his willingness to initially participate in prison violence. The violence he witnessed early in his time in adult county jail fueled his anger as well. On his first day in prison, Kent was given a knife by other whites, and it was made clear that there was an expectation of him as a young person with a life sentence. With nowhere to process his trauma, this provided an outlet for his anger, and his participation in prison violence lasted almost a decade. He recalls his time as such:

I was so brainwashed. I was so warped and twisted. I was already hurting. I was hurt. I was bad hurt whenever I got busted. I was hurt and I was hurting people because of it. Whenever I ended up in the county jail, it added to the fuel. It put gasoline directly on a flame. I just like, "Give it to me more, more, more." I just embraced it. I was caught up in that lifestyle of hatred and anger.

Further, due to their young age at the time of their offense, our participants had not yet had the chance to mature or "age-out" of tendencies toward criminal or reactive thinking until several years into their sentence. The timeline of this inevitable maturation meant that participants were well established in their institutional identities by the time they began to feel a pull toward a non-criminal path, creating complications for the youth as they eventually attempted to distance themselves from these identities. Some participants described this experience as "wearing the mask," in which they were growing up and changing internally but felt obligated to continue their participation in prison politics for safety. These masks allowed them to play both sides, working on internal change but presenting a hard or unchanged exterior to others. Darryl, for example, who had received a life sentence as a youth, described how he protected his reputation while working toward internal change:

Well, I was scared to do it [change] because, again, I had already built up that image to where I didn't have to act any kind of way, but just really walk. You just assume that I was a badass. Then word of mouth, "This is what he used to do when he was a kid." Reputation, like I said, precedes you. I won't say it was an epiphany, but I was tired of doin' the damage. I still cared the way as if I was. I didn't change. It wasn't a change, really. It was a shift in knowing that the sheet off, and I didn't have to do no damage in order to reestablish my reputation. [...] <I still had the> mask forever. I was afraid to let you see what I was.

Interestingly, several of the men who talked about "wearing mask" were familiar with this process; as they had endured many forms of abuse in the past, including sexual abuse, that required other layers of protection of their true feelings and identities. Seemingly, this experience of past trauma translated into a heightened desire to maintain allegiance with their gang, both for protection and for the outlet to perform masculinity. As a young person in an adult facility, the participants were especially vulnerable, making it conceivable that performing masculinity in this way would fulfill the need to reclaim some level of agency and power.

Choosing Life

The shift from focusing on survival to forging one's own life occurred for most of our participants after being incarcerated for a decade or even longer. While the men took different approaches to surviving their youth in an adult prison, they all eventually reached a point in which they began to build community, invest in themselves, and build meaningful lives. We posit that this shift toward investment, for many of our participants, was related to the unlikeliness of their release and their experience growing up inside the prison. With this experience came the realization that the prison was their home and that if they wanted to have any semblance of a fulfilling life, they would need to invest in it as such. To be clear, we by no means intend to insinuate that this "home" was an opportune place for our participants or that it was an easy place to thrive in after their shift from survival toward *living*. Instead, we aim to highlight the mechanisms that the juvenile lifers employed to make their seemingly unending incarceration more manageable, more fulfilling, and more human.

Creating One's Own Community

The role of various forms of community building in finding meaning was particularly salient for the men serving JLWOP sentences, thus having little to no hope for release. Allen and Miguel were among this group and both became active in creating and serving their community within the context of the prison. This contributed to their ability to maintain a sense of purpose and locate meaning in the absence of any possibility for release. They both understood the prison environment as their home and made a conscious decision to invest in that environment, making it as fulfilling as possible. This sense of community building was then bolstered by legislative advocacy to resentence people serving JLWOP, which brought new hope and connection to the community. California resentencing laws (referenced earlier in the chapter) were in the legislative process at this time, and lawyers and social workers kept them abreast of legal developments and possibilities. Allen recalled:

> I can remember as the other juvenile LWOPs were a part of this community that we had built, would go to different lawyer meetings, or whatever. People would be waiting for them to come back. To absorb some of that hope that their lives maybe had meaning. And had worth.

23 Surviving Life: How Youth Adapt to Life Sentences in Adult Prisons

Seemingly, their LWOP status informed their decisions to invest emotional labor and time in their prison communities as they understood their roles within these communities as enduring. Further, the men's status of *juvenile* life-without connected them in a unique way, especially as laws began to change regarding resentencing. They began to invest in their community in a way similar to that of a family, adopting responsibility for one another's well-being. Allen recalled it as such:

> From that moment on <when we found out about SB 9> there was like a, there was an added drive and determination to try to reduce the lack of hope, the pain and the suffering of the community that we had built.[…] The juveniles were really the only life-withouts at that time that had any type of sliver of hope. So, they became bonded by that.

The experience of navigating prison as a youth with a JLWOP sentence, and then suddenly facing the possibility of release, connected the men with a common thread of hope.

Investing in the Self

Another way in which the men transcended survival was through finding meaning from programmatic activities or educational opportunities that allowed them to invest in themselves and recognize their own value. For Hector, a Latino man who received an indeterminate life sentence at age 16, this meaning came in the form of education. Entering an adult prison as a youth, Hector functioned in survival mode for roughly a decade—he was gang-involved and experienced pushback from fellow inmates when he tried to move on from this lifestyle. Eventually, he became more comfortable in the classroom than on the yard. He began investing in himself through education, finding meaning and joy in challenging himself intellectually and developing positive social ties with his professors and peers. Interestingly, the seeds to Hector's educational investment were planted by his first cell mate, an older lifer. Hector recalled:

> He was actually older. He had already been there for 25 years in '97. […] He was the individual that was always reading. […] When I went to a lower level, level three, he actually gave me some books. I had one book there, a psychology book. He told me, 'Look, no matter what you do right now, always learn. Always educate yourself no matter what.'

Even though as a young person, Hector reflected that he was focused on survival rather than investing in himself, this piece of advice stuck with him and eventually propelled him into what he described as his life's most meaningful pursuit—education. Hector described the impact education had on him as follows: "Education, I think 100 percent education is what opened my mind. [...] To me, that's how I feed myself, through my mind. [...] I'm big with education. I can't stop about education. I love education."

Similarly, Julian found deep fulfillment through participating in prison programming and educational degrees. Julian was sentenced to indeterminate life in prison at age 17. His process of investment began after several years of participating in prison politics and violence, sparked by encouragement he received from an instructor. He recalled: "Her <the instructor's> encouragement, that set me off right there. That right there was a major turning point in my life right there." This is important, as most of our participants did not receive positive feedback from educators, caregivers, or their communities as youth. Julian stated, "Growing up I didn't have a lot of people that believed in me except my grandmother. For them to believe in me, it feels good. It feels good." This encouragement seemingly made their in-prison programmatic and educational achievements more important to them, as it was often the first time that they received positive feedback, allowing them to experience themselves as valuable, intelligent, and worthy of investment. This was the case for Julian, who took great pride in this investment, bringing a large binder of his programmatic and educational certificates to our second interview. In the previous interview, he described it as such:

> It's a whole lot of stuff to learn. I should've brought that to you too and let you check that out. [...] A lot of people would be impressed by it, but I don't know. [...] <I'll> let you read for yourself some of the things that the staff has said about me. It's just unbelievable. There's no way that I can—how I feel, the things that they say about me, that I didn't wanna let 'em down.

For Julian, understanding his value in this way helped him make the shift from survival to living, investing in a meaningful life.

Our participants all eventually found an outlet to make meaning of a life behind bars. As they grew up in the context of the prison—all eventually passing more years in than out—they began to understand the prison as their home, despite how unsuitable it may be to serve as such. The men sought out fulfillment, through community, education, and programming, allowing them some semblance of autonomy in the way they chose to make meaning of a situation in which they had little to no control. This translated into the

23 Surviving Life: How Youth Adapt to Life Sentences in Adult Prisons

understanding of imprisonment as a condition of their lives, rather than as the defining factor, leading them to invest in themselves and the shift from survival to *living*.

Discussion

Policies that permitted youth to be sentenced to life in prison have resulted in thousands of "lifers" who have not experienced freedom since before they turned 18. The U.S. context is unique in its commitment of so many young people to die behind bars; life sentences in other countries are indeed time limited and youth are not subject to such extreme punishments (The Sentencing Project 2018). While the literature is clear that any life sentence is devastating and traumatic (Haney 2001), we know little about how young people experience and navigate the transition to a life in prison.

Our phenomenological approach uncovered a core process for study participants, demonstrating how they shifted from survival to choosing to create their own lives in the face of severe adversity, harsh conditions, and lack of control over their environments. Survival consisted of uncovering the racialized code of prison allegiances, which emerged as the first set of rules necessary to protect one's physical safety. Most of the men engaged in prison violence in order to prove themselves, resulting in physical and emotional harm as well as additional layers of self-protection. These survival techniques are part of a well-documented violent prison culture (Lopez-Aguado 2018). Yet prior studies do not necessarily account for the stress and negotiation that occurred with each decision and each stage of development for these young people facing life in prison. They also don't show how much compassion received from cellmates and prison elders that allowed these young men to navigate these conditions and the rules that facilitated their very survival. Indeed, each interviewee had a remarkable memory—from 20 years or more—about each step, each person, and each interaction that contributed to their survival. Even with the retrospective accounts, the participants were still able to reconstruct a vivid timeline and picture of these events and the people that all played a key role in their prison experiences.

The phenomenological methodology identified a core process of moving from survival to forging a life in prison, yet this did not happen consistently or at the same time for each person. Many had to move from what they called their "stubborn" or "reckless" mindset to a more future-thinking and adult perspective. Contrary to what one might expect when facing a full course of life in prison (at that time, perhaps 60 or more years of life), these men all decided that they would indeed forge a life that they could be proud of—one that involved service to others, education, or other ways that they could create meaning.

To contextualize the timeline in which these men participated in programming and educational opportunities (often later in their carceral stays), it is important to acknowledge that many of our participants did not initially have access to any programs at all. Programmatic and educational opportunities that the men found so meaningful were often not available to them during their earlier years in the prisons due to their lifer status. In California prisons, it is common for restrictions to be placed on lifer's participation in any rehabilitative programming (Pro Publica and Sacramento Bee 2019). Some of these restrictions have since been lifted, allowing the men to gain more access as they grew up. And yet, we wonder what may have been different for the men in their youth had they been able to engage with supportive programing and educational programs even sooner.

This is an exploratory, phenomenological study that can be seen as a particular experience in California state prisons—ones that are notoriously violent and subject to racialized prison gangs. We also sampled those who did eventually earn their release, through state law and parole hearings: they were a group of men who likely had fewer write-ups or violations than those in similar circumstances who have not yet earned their parole. That said, we hope that our analysis can contribute to the larger conversation about extreme sentencing for youth (Crewe et al. 2020) and ways that people survive in prison more generally.

Implications and Conclusion

First, our findings strongly echo the works of Craig Haney and other first-person accounts (Lopez-Aguado 2018) that emphasize how dehumanizing prison conditions entrap those who are imprisoned in cycles of violence and repeated trauma. This is very apparent from the narratives of these men, who in detail recall their initiation to adult prison life and how they navigated this transition, sometimes resulting in lasting harm to themselves and others. It is clear from these accounts that institutions so arbitrary in punishment (i.e., length of punishment does not directly correlate with one's capacity for rehabilitation), and inherently violent and dehumanizing, cannot be relied on as our primary response to crime, and therefore to the social issues that often precede crime. This speaks to, first and foremost, the need to radically rethink the context of prisons and life sentences in the United States, not just for youth, but for adults as well. For example, what is the purpose of a life sentence? Does this mean that those who are condemned can never change? Why do we, as a society, continue to believe in life sentences as a remedy for violence and crime?

In regard to the unique experience of youth receiving a life sentence, the 1990s policies that resulted largely from public panic also shaped the life course of many individuals who were banished to prison for life while they weren't even yet adults. These men have lived these policies firsthand, as "tough on crime" policies shaped the life course of young people to grow up in prison, from their teens to middle adulthood. To be transferred at age 18 from "juvie" to a life in prison was experienced as terrifying, unfamiliar, and required quick adaptation and learning the ropes. These men had to shield themselves, both emotionally and physically, by aligning with a racialized prison gang or establishing oneself as outside of prison politics and adopting a different role. These layers built into a core theme of "survival" that for some lasted many years until they found themselves in a place to choose to "live" rather than survive.

The *Miller* case, although applied inconsistently across states, has allowed many with a JLWOP sentence to earn release. We see this as a step in the right direction, although certainly it does not go far enough in preventing extreme sentencing of youth, particularly indeterminant sentencing, from occurring in the future. It is important that the voices of those with lived experience continue to inform state and federal policy to keep children out of the adult system and to further restrict extreme sentences for youth. We hope that this chapter can contribute to one part of this story.

References

Abrams, L. S., Canlione, K. C., & Applegarth, D. M. (2020). Growing up behind bars: Pathways to desistance for juvenile lifers. *Marquette Law Review, 103*(3), 745–773.

Bell, K. (2019). A stone of hope: Legal and empirical analysis of California juvenile lifer parole decisions. *Harvard Civil Rights-Civil Liberties Law Review, 54*, 455–548.

Berger, P. L., & Luckmann, T. (1967). *The social construction of reality: A treatise in the sociology of knowledge*. New York: Anchor.

Blumstein, A. (2002). Youth, guns, and violent crime. *The Future of Children, 12*(2), 38. https://doi.org/10.2307/1602737.

Bochenek, M. (2016). *World report 2016—Children behind bars: The global overuse of detention of children*. Human Rights Watch. Retrieved from https://www.hrw.org/world-report/2016/children-behind-bars

Bureau of Justice Statistics. (2000). *Corrections statistical analysis tool—Prisoners: Inmates age 17 or younger in custody*. Office of Justice Programs. Retrieved from https://www.bjs.gov/index.cfm?ty=nps

Campaign for the Fair Sentencing of Youth. (2018). *Tipping point: A majority of states abandon life-without-parole sentences for children*. Retrieved from https://www.fairsentencingofyouth.org/wp-content/uploads/Tipping-Point.pdf

Cohen, L., & Taylor, L. (1972). *Psychological survival: The experience of long-term imprisonment*. Penguin Books.

Crewe, B., Jewkes, Y, Ugelvik, T. (2020). Life imprisonment from young adulthood: Adaptation, identity, and time. Palgrave Studies in Prisons and Penology.

Criminal Justice Sentencing Act. (2003). Retrieved from https://www.legislation.gov.uk/ukpga/2003/44/schedule/21

Feld, B. (1997). Abolish the Juvenile Court: Youthfulness, Criminal Responsibility, and Sentencing Policy. *The Journal of Criminal Law and Criminology (1973-)*, 88(1), 68–136. https://doi.org/10.2307/1144075.

Feld, B. C. (2017). *The evolution of the juvenile court: Race, politics, and the criminalizing of juvenile justice*. NYU Press.

Graham v. Florida, 560 U.S. 48, 82. (2010).

Haney, C. (2001). *From prison to home: The effect of incarceration and reentry on children, families, and communities—The Psychological impact of incarceration: Implications for post-prison adjustment*. U.S. Department of Health and Human Services, Office of the Assistant Secretary for Planning and Evaluation. Retrieved from https://aspe.hhs.gov/basic-report/psychological-impact-incarceration-implications-post-prison-adjustment#N_9_

Jewkes, Y. (2005). Loss, liminality and the life sentence: Managing identity through a disrupted lifecourse. In A. Liebling & S. Maruna (Eds.), *The effects of imprisonment* (pp. 366–388). Cullompton: Willan Publishing.

Leiber, M., & Peck, J. (2013). Race in juvenile justice and sentencing policy: An overview of research and policy recommendations. *University of Minnesota Journal of Law & Inequality, 31*(331), 331.

Lock, A., & Strong, T. (2010). *Social constructionism: Sources and stirrings in theory and practice*. Cambridge University Press.

Lopez-Aguado, P. (2018). *Stick together and come back home: Racial sorting and the spillover of carceral identity*. University of California Press.

McCorke, R. (1992). Personal precautions to violence in prison. *Criminal Justice and Behavior, 19*, 160–173.

Miller v. Alabama, 132 S. Ct. 2455, 2457-58. (2012).

Montgomery v. Louisiana—136 S. Ct. 718. (2016).

Nellis, A. (2017). *Still life: America's increasing use of life and long-term sentences*. The Sentencing Project. Retrieved from https://www.sentencingproject.org/publications/still-life-americas-increasing-use-life-long-term-sentences/

Pro Publica and the Sacramento Bee. (2019, May 28). Cruel and unusual: A guide to California's broken prisons and the fight to fix them.

Roper v. Simmons, 543 U.S. 551, 575. (2005).
S.B. 394, 2017-2018 Leg., Reg. Sess. (Cal. 2017). (2017).
Schutz, A., & Luckmann, T. (1973). *The structures of the life-world*. Northwestern University Press.
Senate Bill 260, 2014-2015 Leg., Reg. Sess. (Cal. 2014). (2014).
Senate Bill 261, 2015-2016 Leg., Reg. Sess. (Cal. 2015). (2015).
Senate Bill 9, 2011-2012 Leg., Reg. Sess. (Cal. 2012). (2012).
Sokolowski, R. (2000). *Introduction to phenomenology*. Cambridge University Press.
Tanenhaus, D. S. (2004). *Juvenile justice in the making*. Oxford University Press.
The Sentencing Project. (2018). *The facts of life: 1 in 7 people in prison is serving a life sentence*. Retrieved from https://www.sentencingproject.org/wp-content/uploads/2018/12/Facts-of-Life.pdf
Troilo, M. (2018, February 27). Locking up youth with adults: An update. *Prison Policy Initiative*. Retrieved from https://www.prisonpolicy.org/blog/2018/02/27/youth/
Whitehead, J. T., & Lab, S. P. (2018). *Juvenile justice: An introduction* (9th ed.). Routledge.
Wood, A. (2012). Cruel and unusual punishment: Confining juveniles with adults after Miller v. Graham. *Emory Law Journal, 61*(6), 1445.

24

Experiencing the Death Penalty as a Child in Malawi: The Story of Henry Dickson

Linda Kitenge and
Alexious Emmanuel Silombela Kamangila

Introduction

Located in south-eastern Africa, Malawi is a small nation with a population of 18 million people (BBC 2020). Like many developing countries, Malawi's postcolonial penal code is inherited from the colonial state—which called for the mandatory death sentence in cases of murder and treason (Babcock and McLaughlin 2015). Even after decolonisation, every person convicted of homicide, rape, robbery with violence and burglary faced a mandatory death sentence, though these were reserved in practice for a more limited range of cases, primarily homicide (Death Penalty Worldwide 2020). As one of the poorest countries in the world, Malawi's criminal justice system is severely underfunded and characterised by inefficacy, lack of expertise and extreme overcrowding in prisons. This context further exacerbates the suffering of the majority indigent prison population (Reprieve 2019).[1]

L. Kitenge (✉)
Reprieve, London, UK
e-mail: linda.kitenge@reprieve.org

A. E. S. Kamangila
Reprieve, Blantyre, Malawi

© The Author(s), under exclusive license to Springer Nature Switzerland AG 2021
A. Cox, L. S. Abrams (eds.), *The Palgrave International Handbook of Youth Imprisonment*,
Palgrave Studies in Prisons and Penology, https://doi.org/10.1007/978-3-030-68759-5_24

Malawi's criminal justice system was overhauled in 2007 when the High Court struck down the mandatory death sentence in the landmark decision of *Kafantayeni v Attorney General* (2007). This ruling meant that every person who had been sentenced to death was entitled to a new hearing where they could present mitigating evidence (*Kafantayeni v. Attorney General* 2007). In 2014, a coalition of national and international stakeholders came together to form the Malawi Resentencing Project. Lawyers and judges were trained on mitigation, including in the areas of mental health, trauma and foetal alcohol syndrome (Reprieve 2019). As a result of the Resentencing Project, the courts heard 158 resentencing hearings (Reprieve 2019). After hearing the life history of the convicted person and circumstances surrounding the offence, the courts were persuaded to reduce the sentences of every single applicant—no one was resentenced to death and 145 people formerly sentenced to death have since been released back to their communities and have successfully reintegrated (Reprieve 2019). Henry Dickson was one of the beneficiaries of the project and it is in this context that he was saved from the death sentence imposed on him when he was just a child (Reprieve 2019). There are currently 27 people on death row in Malawi and they are all adults (Death Penalty Worldwide 2020), including 26 males and 1 female (Reprieve, March 2021). Reliable statistics on the number of juveniles serving life sentences are not readily available. This is because of low rates of birth registration across the country, which makes it difficult to ascertain a person's age as well as lost or damage prison files (Plan International n.d.). Above all, both government and prison authorities do not document such information regularly. According to the 2019 Prison Inspectorate report, there are 31 prison stations across the country, holding a total of 14,500 inmates. However, this statistic does not specify how many inmates are children (Malawi Inspectorate of Prisons 2019).

Henry Dickson Background

Henry Dickson was born in 1978 and his month and day of birth remains unknown and untraceable, as birth registration rates in Malawi were and continue to be low. He was his parents' fourth child, but his three older brothers died. He grew up in Blantyre, a commercial city in the southern part of the country. His father worked for the civil aviation department and his mother was a housewife.

Before his arrest, Henry aspired to become a pilot or a civil servant. His motivation emanated from his visits to his father at his workplace, which inspired him to pursue the same career as his dad.

24 Experiencing the Death Penalty as a Child in Malawi: The Story...

Henry was arrested in 1992, at the age of 14, by the Blantyre police together with two other men, Joe Kamoto and Richard Matabwa. He was initially arrested for theft. However, the investigation discovered that his co-accused were previously involved in the robbery and murder of an unknown man in Blantyre. The police then charged all of them with the offence of murder. Henry admitted to having been involved in the second theft but denied and continues to deny any involvement in the robbery that led to the death of the man, worse still participating in killing the deceased.

The theft was Henry's first offence. After he was arrested, he was harassed and tortured by the police, who beat Henry and his co-accused severely until they provided coerced caution statements. Mr. Dickson's co-convict Richard Matabwa details the brutal mistreatment inflicted upon the three men:

> [T]he police officers kept accusing me of lying and then started badly beating me to get me to admit to everything, and also did the same to Dickson and Kamoto. [T]hey were beating us one by one with iron rods and batons and slapping us with the side of a panga knife. [T]hey beat us on a daily basis over a month urging us to confess to the murder and other robbery charges around Blantyre. [D]espite being badly beaten we refused to sign the caution statements written by the police, which did not contain the truth. […]
>
> [T]he police forged Dickson and Kamoto's signatures on their caution statements because neither of them could hold the pen after their hands were so badly beaten.[2]

The physical consequences of this mistreatment were witnessed by Mr. Dickson's mother when she visited him in police custody. In her witness statement, she recalls:

> When I saw him I was so shocked. He was covered in open wounds and large bruises. They were all over his back and also some on his arms. He looked terrible.
>
> Henry said that they had been given to him by the police, who wanted him to confess to everything. They had hit him using an iron rod and also their police batons. They beat him so hard because he did not want to confess to something he had not done.
>
> He was in such a bad condition that one of the good police officers there told me to go to the shop to buy medicine for him because he needed treatment. I bought him painkillers and medicines to treat his open cuts and stop them being infected.[3]

Henry was arrested during Malawi's one-party rule period, with a strong and authoritarian state led by Kamuzu Banda, widely regarded as a dictator.

During this period, the police were widely engaged in abuse, corruption and torture. Unfortunately, these practices continue as demonstrated by the recent death of a man accused of killing a person with albinism (Malawi Human Rights Commission 2019).

After he was charged, Henry was taken to Chichiri Prison, an adult prison, notorious for overcrowding and poor conditions. He spent four years on remand awaiting trial. Henry was placed with the rest of the population despite being a child. Henry found life in the prison very tough; he struggled to find food and even space to sleep. Prisoners sleep side-by-side, packed together in cramped communal cells, 'coupled with recurrent general problems of overcrowding, poor sanitation, poor diet, poor ventilation' (Malawi Inspectorate of Prisons 2019, p. 2). Older men would demand sexual favours in exchange for food and sleeping space.

Henry's Trial and Sentence

Henry's trial took five years to be completed. He was found guilty by a jury of the offence of murder and sentenced to death. He was tried together with the others with whom he had been accused to have committed the offence. Henry describes this period as one of the most difficult times of his life. He and his co-defendants were taken to court in highly guarded vehicles with leg irons on their legs and their hands bound in chains. He would only be released from the irons and chains when he briefly entered the witness box.

Henry's trial was long. The jury could not reach a unanimous verdict at first and were split; when they tried to vote again, they decided to convict Henry and his co-accused in a vote of eight to four (non-unanimous verdicts were allowed in Malawi, but juries are no longer in use).[4]

When Henry was sentenced to death, life became unbearable for him. He and his co-defendants initially spent three days at Chichiri Prison in Blantyre before being transferred to Zomba Central Prison, a maximum-security prison, where they were to be executed. According to Henry:

> Life was meaningless. It lost all the sense when I got sentenced to death. At Chichiri prison we were locked in isolation and tiny cells. We couldn't talk to each other or any other person. It was as if we were dead already. It was basically a coffin. When we were transferred to Zomba Central Prison, we were sent straight to the condemned section. We were in total isolation. I was put in cell seven. My room had some fats and other prisoners said these were human fats.[5] At 19 years then, my every vein and bone was traumatized. They said someone

24 Experiencing the Death Penalty as a Child in Malawi: The Story... 529

was refusing to go to the gallows and they just killed him with a hammer. He died right there. This increased my fears. This was a time when we were still in transition from one party rule to multiparty democracy. Although we had a new system, there were still some elements of one-party system lingering. Our group was the first group that followed a group that was executed. We faced death. We couldn't rule out execution. It was such a torturous time.[6]

The people who were sentenced to death were not allowed to walk around the main prison yard as other incarcerated persons at Zomba prison, where the prisoners often play games and socialise; instead, Henry and the others sentenced to death were confined to the condemned section—a small strip of concrete bordered on one side by an open drain and on the other by the cells. They were always forced to wear leg irons and handcuffs, even while confined in the condemned section yard, the most secure, excluded and protected area of the prison.

Sometimes, prison guards came into the condemned section to grease the gallows. Oftentimes, the people on the death row were sent in to help the guards grease and clean the gallows. The prison wardens would proudly tease the imprisoned persons that this was the place where they will die, it was their destiny. Naturally, this terrorising by the guards increased Henry's fears. The whole sense of life had left him. Henry recollects his experience:

> I thought I am a cursed person. I still think I am cursed. It is not ordinary that a young person like me would just be sentenced to death. The fact that I wasn't in any way involved in the murder pained me the most. Unfortunately, there was no way I would have convinced the police to believe me. I couldn't sleep well. I used to have nightmares. I believe the spirits of those who were executed before were still there.

The condemned section is not just an ordinary part of the prison in terms of the rights and opportunities available to the people incarcerated there. Those on the death row were not allowed to go to school or interact with others. Many people died. Henry was fearful for his life, as there was a rumour circulating that a popular security staff member had been charged with murdering another imprisoned person at Zomba. The experience of death row led many people in the prison to develop mental illnesses. In Henry's case, 'the mental torment of his incarceration was for one year and seven months exacerbated by the constant terror that he could at any moment be executed for an offence he insists he did not commit, and which took place whilst he was a juvenile.'[7] Further, nearly half of the prisoners were diagnosed with a mental illness, majority of which is said to have developed or been exacerbated by the terrible living conditions. It is hence conclusive that Henry's experiences in prison were extremely painful.

In the early 1990s, Malawi transitioned from one-party rule to multiparty democracy. This political shift led to the election in 1994 of Bakili Muluzi, who commuted the life imprisonment the sentences of all imprisoned persons on death row (Amnesty International 1994). This was repeated frequently until 2005, when commutations ceased following an election. Henry's sentence was commuted to life imprisonment in 1999, through a routine commutation process.[8]

Following the commutation of his sentence, Henry felt as if he was undergoing a resurrection from the dead as he was transferred to the general population of the prison and he became certain that he would not be hanged in the gallows. He knew that at least he would die of a sickness or something natural, but not through execution (Yadidi et al. 1998; Banerjee et al. 2000). However, as young as he was, he knew he might live for a long time. That meant more years of suffering in prison and a life of incarceration.

Resentencing and Release

In 2010, Henry was interviewed by lawyers and law students from an international human rights clinic at Northwestern University, who informed him that as a result of the *Kafantenyi* (2007) decision, individuals on death row were entitled to a sentence rehearing. The fact that he had someone to talk to about his case was in itself very encouraging because, following his conviction, Henry had tried several times to appeal his sentence, to no avail. When the Malawi Resentencing project started, following the *Kafantayeni* judgment, and people who were eligible started to see lawyers and investigators visiting them frequently and scheduling new hearings for them, Henry's hope was raised. He knew this was a great opportunity. It was a chance to resurrect his life and himself. A chance to live again. On 26 November 2015, after Henry's lawyer had the opportunity to present Henry's case on sentence to the court, including a number of mitigating factors such as Henry's age, lack of criminal history and the lack of evidence that he was involved in a capital crime, Justice Bvundula ordered Henry's immediate release. Henry said, 'I couldn't believe this. I cried. It was like a dream. I only believed it was real when I left for my home ... When I met my family they wouldn't believe either.'

Law on Juveniles and Children in Malawi

International, regional and local legislation and case-law provide an appropriate legal framework for a human rights-based approach to the handling of children who are in conflict with criminal law. The underlying approach in the law is that in all actions concerning children the courts of law should give the 'best interest of the child' primary consideration.[9] In regard to trial procedure, the law emphasises on the need to take into account the vulnerability of child defendants due to their immature age and the desirability of promoting social rehabilitation.[10]

According to international law standards as well as the Malawian Constitution, any child who has been arrested for committing an offence ought to be subjected to child friendly procedures and the mode of conducting the trial ought to be in camera, that is, a closed court to the exclusion of the general public and which respects his or her privacy.[11] None of these safeguards were applied in the trial of Henry Dickson. The first task of the Court in a case like this or any other is to ascertain the particulars of the accused person, which includes the age of the defendant who is before the court. Rep v Mwenda [1999] MLR 356 (HC) alludes to the importance of this step, stating that it is not uncommon that the age as shown on a charge sheet is incorrect. In Henry's case, there was strong evidence that he was a child because when he was arrested he was still in school. Furthermore, a pre-trial mental health assessment document found at Zomba Mental Hospital listed his age as 17 years.[12]

Legislation was in force at the time of Henry's conviction that prohibited trying juveniles as adults.[13] Where a child suspect is found responsible for committing the offences of murder, the Court is not supposed to sentence him/her, but rather order him/her to be detained at a reformatory centre for such a period as may be specified in the order.[14] The Courts in Malawi have also been clear that children cannot be committed to prison at all,[15] so children can only be detained at a safety home or reformatory centre.

Imposition of the death penalty on children is prohibited.[16] Specifically, the Malawian penal code prohibits the imposition of the death penalty on children and requires that such children be detained at the President's pleasure.[17] At the time of Henry's trial, the imposition of the death sentence was also prohibited by the Children and Young Persons Act (CYPA) which stipulated that:

Sentence of death penalty shall not be pronounced on or recorded against a person under the age of eighteen years, but in lieu thereof the court shall sentence him to be detailed during the pleasure of the President, and, if do sentenced he shall, notwithstanding anything in the other provisions of this Act, be liable to be detained in such place and under such conditions as the President may direct.[18]

Finally, the Constitution provides that a child should not be sentenced to life imprisonment without the possibility of release.[19]

It is therefore clear that the entire course of Henry Dickson's trial procedure, from arrest, through to conviction and sentence to death, and even including his later commutation to life imprisonment, represented grave injustices against a vulnerable child.[20]

Life After Prison

Upon release, Henry had nowhere to go and was stranded without support from family or relatives. His direct family, who supported him during his teenager years, were no longer around and were deceased. Whereas the family members who were present had no real bond with Henry while others were also struggling to make ends meet, making it difficult for them to support another person, a full adult. It seemed all was lost. His opportunity to go to school was lost. There were no schools for him in prison during the whole period; he was mostly either on remand or on death row.

After some time, he started working in some shops. With time, an opportunity arose to do driving lessons through the Malawi Resentencing Project, he received driving lessons and qualified as a driver, but struggled to find a job due to stigmatisation against ex-prisoners.

Even after his release, Henry still suffered from nightmares. Sometimes he thought he was still in prison. It was difficult to adapt to life outside. It took some months for Henry to start living a normal life. Some religious groups also played a great role in supporting him. With time, things changed. His hallucinations and horrible dreams ceased.

Henry is currently based in Balaka, where he sells second-hand clothes, bags and shoes. He is married to Noria Dickson Moyo and they have two children.

Henry's Opinion on the Death Penalty

According to Henry, 'the death penalty is not good at all. Even biblically this is not allowed. With the death of Jesus on the cross, there is nothing like an eye for an eye.' The worst situation is where a juvenile is sentenced to death. Children are said to be the future of the nation. It is difficult for children to resist the influence of adults. In my case, for example, I was coerced by older people to go and still. I didn't think of the consequences. In fact, at first, I thought we were taking things that belonged to Richard Matabwa. It was during the day. Until when I heard people shouting then I realised these were not his things. The worst is when I was charged of murder that happened previously by associating with these guys. I couldn't explain convincingly to the police. I lost my future. I lost all I had dreamt of.'

> Henry says:
> I feel sad that I went to prison and through all the hardships when I was very young. Most painful is that I wasn't part of those who committed the offence.
> Prison is a very bad place. I feel prison sentence is enough. I say no to death sentence. I wish the death penalty should end.
> Big thanks to those who initiated the project. It's a good project. Look at me now. I am living again. I wish I had a better forum that I can express my feelings to everyone in the project.
> Children should never be sentenced to death. Not even life imprisonment. Give them chance to reform. The death penalty can never be reparable once the execution is done. In cases where one is not executed like in my case, the effects of it lives in the person forever. Look at me, I live feeling that I am cursed. In fact, I am cursed. How can an eldest son be this poor while my younger ones are doing better? NO WAY.

Conclusion

Despite the existence of international norms, laws and clear domestic legislation, the sentencing of children to death remains a hidden crisis within the Malawi criminal justice system. This is exacerbated by the fact that individuals often spend several years on remand (in some incidences 14 years before a trial-citation Awali Matemba v Republic, High Court, Miscellaneous Application No. 1 of 2021). This means that even though an alleged offence was committed when one is a minor, it results in one being an adult by the time the case is heard. In such circumstances, original files and documents are lost which then make it difficult to present mitigating evidence that one was a juvenile at the time of offence. The sentence of death is nevertheless despite the crime and designated punishment, not permissible (not imposed) where the person is below the age of 18.[21] When the purpose of this limitation is understood, the age limit is and should be considered as against the time of commission of offence and not only as at the point of imposition of the sentence. Unfortunately, there are many imprisoned persons on death row with such stories. Although Henry is now free, and he has had the opportunity to rebuild his life due to the Kafantenyi Project, the death penalty nevertheless robbed him of 22 years that he will never get back. Despite the success of the Malawi Resentencing Project, there remains much work to be done to ensure that all juveniles still trapped in harsh prison conditions get swift access to justice.

Notes

1. *Francis Kafantenyi and others v the Attorney General Constitutional Case No 12 of 2005 [2007] High Court of Malawi.* This ruling declared the mandatory death penalty unconstitutional because it violated the right to access to justice.
2. Affidavit of Richard Matabwa, paras. 53 to 56; para. 59.
3. Supplementary Witness Statement of Esnat Dickson, paras. 5–7.
4. It is established that 'in the event of any of the jurors, after reasonable consultation, dissenting from the remainder, the verdict of a majority consisting of not fewer than eight jurors or, in any case to which section 308 applies, the verdict of the eight remaining jurors, shall be taken to be the verdict of the jury' Section 321C, Criminal Procedure and Evidence Code, Laws of Malawi, Chapter 8:01.
5. Henry believed the 'fats' were human remains of person who had been killed in his cell.
6. Interview with Henry Dickson on 24 February 2020, Balaka, Malawi.
7. Henry Dickson's submissions on sentencing rehearing, page 34.
8. Notably, these routine commutations for those sentenced to death ceased in 2005 and have not been resumed since.
9. Article 3(1) of the Convention on the Rights of the Child (CRC); Article 4(1) of the African Charter on the Rights and Welfare of the Child (ACRWC) and section 23 (1) of the Constitution of Malawi.
10. Section 42 (2) (g) (vi) of the Constitution; Article 14 (4) of the International Covenant on Civil and Political Rights (ICCPR) which Malawi ratified in 1993; Article 40(4) of CRC and Article 17 (3) of the ACRWC.

11. Article 17 (2) (d) of the ACRWC; Article 14(1) of the ICCPR and Article 42 (2) (g) (vii) of the Constitution
12. Henry Dickson's submissions on sentencing rehearing, page 2.
13. Sections 2, 4 and 6 of the Children and Young Persons Act (CYPA).
14. Such requirement is now legislation as per section 141(1) of the Child Care, Protection and Justice Act. Section 140 of the Act specifically provides that 'No child shall be imprisoned for any offence.'
15. Evance Moyo v AG and Rep v Children at Bvumbwe and Kachere Prisons.
16. Article 6 of the ICCPR; Article 37 (a) of the CRC and Article 5 of the ACRWC
17. Section 26 (2) of the Penal Code. It remains unclear what it means to be detained at the President's pleasure.
18. Section 11.
19. Section 42 (2) (g) (i) of the Constitution. A similar provision is contained in article 37 (a) of the CRC.
20. NB: This section has benefited a lot from case of The Republic v MC, Sentence Rehearing Case No. 18 of 2016, Zomba (HC) [Criminal case No. 164 of 2002, High Court of Malawi, Principal Registry].
21. UN General Assembly on 14 December 1984 in its Resolution 39/118.

References

Amnesty International. (1994). The death penalty in Malawi: Recent developments. Retrieved from https://www.amnesty.org/download/Documents/184000/afr360061994en.pdf.

Babcock, S., & McLaughlin, E. (2015). Reconciling human rights and the application of the death penalty in Malawi: The unfulfilled promise of Kanfantenyi v Attorney General. In P. Hodgkinson (Ed.), *Capital punishment: New perspectives*. London: Taylor and Francis.

Banerjee, A., et al. (2000). Prevalence of HIV, sexually transmitted disease and tuberculosis amongst new prisoners in a district prison, Malawi. *Tropical Doctor 2000, 30*, 49–50.

BBC. (2020). Malawi country profile. Retrieved July 28, 2020, from https://www.bbc.co.uk/news/world-africa-13864367.

Death Penalty Worldwide, Death Penalty Database Malawi. (2020). Retrieved July 28, 2020, from https://dpw.pointjupiter.co/country-search-post.cfm?country=Malawi.

Kafantenyi v Attorney General. (2007). *Francis Kafantenyi and others v the Attorney General Constitutional Case No 12 of 2005 [2007] High Court of Malawi*.

Malawi Human Rights Commission. (2019). A report of the investigation into the death of Mr Buleya Lule in police custody.

Malawi Inspectorate of Prisons. (2019). The report of the inspection of prisons and police service cells conducted by the Malawi Inspectorate of Prisons.

Plan International. (n.d.). Digital birth registration in Malawi: Technical Analysis: Strengthening CRVS in Malawi through the appropriate use of digital technologies. Retrieved September 28, 2020, from https://plan-international.org/publications/digital-birth-registration-malawi#download-options.

Reprieve. (2019). Malawi resentencing project: A triumph of collaboration and community decision-making. Retrieved July 28, 2020, from https://reprieve.org.uk/wp-content/uploads/2019/03/2019_03_20_INT_Malawi-Resentencing-Project-overview.pdf.

Yadidi, E., et al. (1998). Pattern of disease in a prison population in Malawi. *Annals of Tropical Medicine & Parasitology, 92*(3), 343–345.

Part VII

Abolition and the Future of Youth Justice

It's Okay by Anonymous

It's okay they say.
It's okay they say.
It's okay.

But it's not society has clearly put their foot on my throat I'm grasping for air.
I'm stuck one man one cell and one decision away from losing myself my life my freedom.

Covered in feces and blood I can't help but wonder why this Covid-19 should have at least been a reason to clean away the stains away another man's scared life.
I call to ease my fear no case yet filed my dear.

One decision away from going back to living in fear.
The struggles that bind my community I'm grateful I had a little money in the bag.
It's not easy for someone like me a gay man.

My breath was almost taken I almost gave
up body in shock they didn't even feed me
breakfast or lunch.

My hairline went back more an inch or two.
My mom came all the way to help out this
Cool.

I'm tired of one choice defining my life.
I want to be rich and keep living my life.
Get a lawyer naw I can't no more money left
bail took everything I had.

Same mistake naw this one was different
same pain yeah I sill live with it.
See scars don't heal they slowly fade away.
So remember that when I continue to make
mistakes.

Just one choice they can take it all away.
I have to keep going trying to live for today.
It's okay it's okay it's okay.

Fuck that no it's not okay it's time to make
a decision to stop playing a system was
created to fill the white man's pocket.

If we realized we had a choice we'd realize
we can go up we have the same rockets.

One choice won't define me they won't put
me away I'll fight and manifest until my
court date.

25

The Pitfalls of Separating Youth in Prison: A Critique of Age-Segregated Incarceration

Hedi Viterbo

Introduction

Debates about youth justice focus on themes all too familiar to those in the field, such as rehabilitation, retribution, welfarism, justice, and the enforcement of international legal standards (e.g., Muncie and Goldson 2012). Very rarely, if ever, is age-segregated incarceration—the separation of youth and adults in criminal custody—called into question.

This taken-for-granted practice, however, is underpinned by two problematic conceptions: essentialism and carcerality. Crudely defined, essentialism is the belief that a type of person or thing, in this case a person within a certain age group, possesses an intrinsic, invariant, and constitutive nature. It is age essentialism that makes the separation of the young in certain sites appear natural and beneficial. Though ageism is often wrongly associated exclusively with older people (Hagestad and Uhlenberg 2005), age essentialism is ageist toward youth (as well as adults, albeit differently, as I argue in this chapter). As for carcerality, it encompasses the ideologies, social forces, and institutions positing imprisonment as a necessary response to transgressions. Combined,

---

For their helpful comments, deep thanks are due to Laura Abrams, Tamar Birckhead, Alexandra Cox, Barry Feld, Maayan Geva, Nicola Lacey, Daniel Monk, Leslie Moran, and Christine Piper.

H. Viterbo (✉)
Queen Mary University of London, London, UK
e-mail: hedi.viterbo@qmul.ac.uk

© The Author(s), under exclusive license to Springer Nature Switzerland AG 2021
A. Cox, L. S. Abrams (eds.), *The Palgrave International Handbook of Youth Imprisonment*, Palgrave Studies in Prisons and Penology, https://doi.org/10.1007/978-3-030-68759-5_25

these conceptions render age-segregated incarceration seemingly self-evident and desirable, or at least the lesser of all possible evils.

Within these prevailing parameters, the only conceivable alternatives are non-segregated incarceration or youth-specific reforms. Illustrating this is the view—voiced by some proponents of a so-called toughness on youth crime—that young people in conflict with the law should be imprisoned in adult facilities. While potentially eroding age segregation, this position remains well within carceral logic. Also problematic, albeit differently, is the ostensibly progressive claim that young people must never be held behind bars, regardless of whether they are separated from their adult counterparts. Here, the opposition to incarceration is reserved exclusively for the young, the implication being that for others—namely, adults—prison may not be out of the question.

My aim in this chapter is to radically challenge both the practice of age-segregated incarceration itself and contemporary debates about it. The next section outlines the enshrining of this practice as a legal and human rights norm, at the international, regional, and domestic levels. In each of the sections that follow, I lay bare a hitherto overlooked pitfall of this norm. First, I argue that age-segregated incarceration reinforces the ageist, essentialist, and historically recent belief that "youth" (a term subject to varying definitions) are inherently different and, hence, must follow constrictive age norms. Second, age-segregated incarceration portrays the separated adults as less vulnerable and less corrigible, and thus sanctions harshness and apathy toward them. Third, this practice legitimizes imprisonment, by entrenching its false image as humane and effective as well as its punitive preoccupation with blame. Fourth, in conflating protection with separation from imprisoned adults, age-segregated incarceration harms youth. It does so in several ways: downplaying the risk youth face from their peers and the prison staff, overlooking the support some incarcerated adults can offer, and leading prison staff to use harmful measures such as solitary confinement in order to maintain age segregation. Lastly, age-segregated incarceration, as well as comparable practices beyond prison, has a long and ongoing history of oppressing communities by breaking their intergenerational ties.

Familiar alternatives, such as non-segregated incarceration, age-specific reforms, or more refined segregation, fail to adequately address these pitfalls and in some respects actually aggravate them. What is needed, instead, is to move past essentialism and carcerality. This chapter provides an outline of the issues in question, with the aim of stimulating further conversations and offering a more exhaustive analysis in the near future.

The Law of Separation: Age-Segregated Incarceration as a Legal and Human Rights Norm

Over the course of the nineteenth century, discrete youth justice systems started to emerge in Western countries (May 1973; Magarey 1978; Platt 1977; Shore 2003). Since then, with very few exceptions, age-segregated incarceration has become the norm across the Global North, including jurisdictions where such separation is not legally mandatory (Siegel and Welsh 2017, p. 652). There remain instances of non-separation (Goldson and Kilkely 2013, pp. 358–360; Goldson and Muncie 2012, pp. 52–54), but these are limited exceptions, rather than the rule. The United States, for instance, generally prohibits "sight or sound contact" between incarcerated youth and adults, defined as "any physical, clear visual, or verbal contact that is not brief and inadvertent" (Juvenile Justice and Delinquency Prevention Act, 1974, §§ 103, 223). Non-separation, though permitted in some US states in certain circumstances, has sharply decreased following recent reforms and is expected to shrink further as a result of a 2018 amendment to federal law (Pilnik and Mistrett 2019, pp. 6–8, 10). In England and Wales, pursuant to statute, youth are held separately in so-called Young Offender Institutions (currently about 73% of incarcerated youth), Secure Training Centers (18%), and Secure Children's Homes (8%) (Her Majesty's Prison and Probation Service 2019).

International law, too, now overwhelmingly enshrines age-segregated incarceration as the norm. Article 37(c) of the 1989 UN Convention on the Rights of the Child (hereinafter CRC), the world's most extensively ratified international treaty, formulates the separation principle in the following terms: "Every child deprived of liberty shall be … separated from adults unless it is considered in the child's best interest not to do so."[1]

Thus, though non-separation is permitted in exceptional and unspecified circumstances, as a default, age-segregated incarceration is presumed to be in young people's best interest. This perceived sanctity of the separation norm is further reinforced by the dominant human rights discourse. Instituted by the CRC, the UN Committee on the Rights of the Child (2007, ¶ 104) has emphasized: "The permitted exception to the separation of children from adults stated in article 37(c) of CRC, 'unless it is considered in the child's best interests not to do so', should be interpreted narrowly." This was later reconfirmed by the UN Special Rapporteur on Torture (2015, ¶ 76):

> Children should be appropriately separated in detention, including … those in conflict with the law, children awaiting trial and convicted children … Children

detained under criminal legislation should never be detained together with adult detainees. ... [T]he permitted exception ... provided for in article 37 (c) of the Convention on the Rights of the Child should be interpreted *sensu stricto* [i.e., narrowly].

So powerful is the separation norm that human rights organizations frequently quote Article 37(c) while entirely omitting its "best interests" exception. Such erasure of the non-separation exception is found in countless and varied human rights publications, including those of Amnesty International (2005, p. 6; 1997, p. 5), Human Rights Watch (2012), Save the Children (2005, p. 16), UNICEF and Terre des hommes (Albanian Ministry of Labor et al. 2010, pp. 34, 100), the US-based Campaign for Youth Justice (2016), the Swiss Institut international des droits de l'enfant (2010), SOS Children's Villages—Canada (2009), Thai Lawyers for Human Rights (2017), and the Scottish Institute for Residential Child Care (2005, p. 4).

Other international legal documents enshrine age-segregated incarceration even more categorically, with no exceptions whatsoever. Thus, Articles 10(2)(b) and 10(3) of the widely ratified International Covenant on Civil and Political Rights (1966) stipulate: "Accused juvenile persons shall be separated from adults ... Juvenile offenders shall be segregated from adults and be accorded treatment appropriate to their age and legal status." Equally unequivocal are two UN General Assembly resolutions: the Standard Minimum Rules for the Treatment of Prisoners (adopted in 1955, revised in 2015, and since the revision called the "Nelson Mandela Rules") and the Standard Minimum Rules for the Administration of Juvenile Justice (1985, also known as the "Beijing Rules"). The former instructs, in Article 11(d): "Young prisoners shall be kept separate from adults" (this provision was not revised in 2015). The latter expands on this unreserved commitment to age segregation (¶¶ 13.4, 26.3): "Juveniles under detention pending trial shall be kept separate from adults and shall be detained in a separate institution or in a separate part of an institution also holding adults. ... Juveniles in institutions shall be kept separate from adults and shall be detained in a separate institution or in a separate part of an institution also holding adults."

In some documents, exceptions to the separation norm are allowed, but they are very specific and narrow. Under Article 77(4) of Additional Protocol I to the 1949 Geneva Conventions (1977), young people "arrested, detained or interned" in times of armed conflict "shall be held in quarters separate from the quarters of adults, except where families are accommodated as family units." Aside from members of the same family, no incarceration of young people with adults is allowed. Beyond armed conflict, the Rules for the

Protection of Juveniles Deprived of Their Liberty (1990, ¶ 29), a UN General Assembly resolution known as the "Havana Rules," permit a similar exception while adding to it: "In all detention facilities juveniles should be separated from adults, unless they are members of the same family. Under controlled conditions, juveniles may be brought together with carefully selected adults as part of a special programme that has been shown to be beneficial for the juveniles concerned."

Age-segregated incarceration has been legally codified at the regional level as well. Thus, Article 17(2)(b) of the African Charter on the Rights and Welfare of the Child (1990) requires party states to "ensure that children are separated from adults in their place of detention or imprisonment." Slightly more flexible are the European Prison Rules (adopted by the Council of Europe in 1973 and last revised in 2006): "Children under the age of 18 years should not be detained in a prison for adults … If children are nevertheless exceptionally held in such a prison there shall be special regulations that take account of their status and needs." Relatedly, the American Convention on Human Rights (1969, Article 5(5)), which has been ratified by most Central and South American countries and is also known as the "Pact of San José," stipulates: "Minors while subject to criminal proceedings shall be separated from adults."

The separation of youth and adults in criminal custody, then, is a potent norm at the international, regional, and (with very few exceptions) domestic levels. Exceptions to age-segregated incarceration tend to be either narrowly carved, outright denied, or simply ignored. That instances of non-separation are relatively limited and roundly criticized helps further cement this as an otherwise uncontested norm.

Pitfall 1: Reinforcing Age Essentialism

The essentialist dichotomy between adults and the young reigns over contemporary social and legal thinking. Notwithstanding contradictions and ambiguities in this dichotomy, society envisages the archetypal adult offender as competent, as fully formed, and, accordingly, as more culpable and less susceptible to reform (relative to youth). In contrast, young people in conflict with the law are perceived as still developing and dependent, easily influenced, relatively vulnerable and impulsive, lacking in knowledge, and, for these and other reasons, in greater need of protection and guidance (e.g., Ainsworth 1995, pp. 944–946). Age-segregated incarceration both manifests and contributes to this age essentialism.

An extensive body of scholarship has challenged this conventional knowledge. Neither natural nor universal, the youth and the adulthood envisioned by practices such as age-segregated incarceration have been shown to be historically and culturally specific social creations. For instance, nearly a century ago, anthropologist Margaret Mead (1928) famously reported that adolescent rebellion—seen from Western eyes as a universal stage in human development—was largely absent in the Samoan Islands due to different local attitudes toward youth. Later anthropological studies have brought to light further intercultural disparity not only in the nature of childhood and youth but also, importantly, in their distinctiveness from adulthood (e.g., Montgomery 2008).

Similarly, from the seminal if imperfect work of Philippe Ariès (1962) to more recent historical literature (e.g., Cunningham 2005), scholars have argued that childhood and youth, as distinct stages separate from adulthood, are in many respects a modern invention. Pre-modern societies saw children working from an early age, mixing freely with adults, and consuming the same information. Age-specific legislation was rare and mostly unenforced at the time, and a person's social status changed not through legal age thresholds but gradually or through rites of passage. There were no universal compulsory education laws, and schools, where they existed, consisted of mixed-age classrooms (e.g., Chudacoff 1989, pp. 10, 16–17, 19; Lesko 2001, pp. 120–122). Neither courts nor prisons segregated youth and adults, and in nineteenth-century England, separation was initially based on the perceived character of the incarcerated individuals, the severity of their offense, and their criminal record (May 1973).

Age essentialism operates to box people into rigid age categories and channel their life along constrictive age norms (Hagestad and Uhlenberg 2005; Lesko 2001; Chudacoff 1989). Having now established itself as received wisdom, it is rarely accounted for. When justifications are provided, they often focus on traits associated with very young children. However, younger children are exempt from criminal responsibility in most countries (Nowak et al. 2019, pp. 278–281), and they are rarely incarcerated even where no statutory age of criminal responsibility exists. Therefore, not only are assumptions about the distinctness of very young children open for debate, they also bear little relevance to incarceration. Those typically separated from adults do not include all young people, in other words.

Regarding youth, age essentialism—not unlike racism, patriarchy, and classism in past times—now finds support in mainstream science, with neuroscience increasingly at the forefront. However, the assumptions neurodevelopmental studies make about brain activity are contested and ever-changing, as is the testing equipment they use. Further, testing in a lab setting is limited, and countless variables that may influence the brain are ignored. Brain maps are also oversimplified to make them accessible to the public, in addition to being normalized for statistical "significance," resulting in misrepresentation of the messy and complex data (Bessant 2008; Kelly 2012; Cox 2014). More fundamentally, neurological development is affected by exposure to social experiences and information (Bennett and Baird 2006), which in the contemporary era have become highly age specific. Therefore, in a mixed-age society, cognitive development may well occur differently. In this respect, rather than bringing to light natural and universal age differences, neuroscience reflects and reinforces the age-stratified order of contemporary society.

Equally open to debate is the close association of young age with inexperience, incompetence, or vulnerability. Only in heavily age-stratified societies such as ours are these traits bound to be so closely intertwined. Insofar as youth lack certain social knowledge and skills, this is largely the consequence of their exclusion from ostensibly adult-only activities and spheres (such as work and politics) and their relegation to age-homogeneous spaces (such as school). "Shielding" youth from the adult world, sometimes with the best of intentions, can end up denying them valuable capacities and thus prolonging their vulnerability, dependence, and ignorance. As for the assumption (to the extent that it exists) that incarcerated youth are physically weaker than their adult counterparts, there is no reason to believe that all 17-year-olds, for example, are weaker than all 46-year-olds (quite the contrary, perhaps). Thus, it is not simply that differences dictate the division into youth and adults, but, to a large extent, the other way around. As youth came to be thought of as distinct from adults, so did their experiences, minds, and even bodies come to be shaped and regarded as different. It is society that attaches importance to, enhances, and sometimes even creates certain differences while deeming others meaningless (cf. James et al. 1998, pp. 147, 150–151). Scholars now widely accept anti-essentialist insights analogous to these when it comes to other identity categories, such as gender, sexuality, race, and disability.

Pitfall 2: Sanctioning Harshness and Apathy Toward Adults

Debates over youth imprisonment tend to consider only its impact on youth (an issue indeed examined later in this chapter). However, it is adults, no less than youth, whom age-segregated incarceration targets. By associating incarcerated youth with vulnerability, plasticity, and the need for special protection, age segregation signals that those at the other side of the divide are more dangerous, culpable, and incorrigible. Consequently, through essentialism, age segregation makes harshness and apathy toward imprisoned adults appear natural, obvious, and hence requiring little if any justification. Once separated, adults in prison can be denied protections reserved exclusively for youth. Notwithstanding differences across time and place in the scope and content of these protections, the overall message tends to be similar: incarcerated adults are less deserving of society's compassion and leniency.

Across the world, in addition to their adult status, adults in criminal custody tend to be predominantly men, from disempowered and marginalized socioeconomic, ethnic, racial, and national groups (e.g., Coyle et al. 2016). As such, they are commonly the targets not only of age essentialism but also of sexism,[2] classism, and racism, all of which potentially exacerbate prejudice toward them. Admittedly, most of these demographic features apply to incarcerated youth as well (e.g., Burns Institute for Youth Justice Fairness and Equity 2016; Goldson and Muncie 2012, pp. 54–55). Nevertheless, their supposedly distinguishing characteristic—their young age—commonly associated with relative innocence, is considered a mitigating factor (see Viterbo 2012a, pp. 142–144, 146, 154 for exceptions), and hence invites relative leniency, at least rhetorically. In actuality, not all youth in conflict with the law are treated leniently: in the United States, for example, the recent decline in youth incarceration rates has been accompanied by a continued and even growing overrepresentation of racial and ethnic minority youth (Rovner 2017; Burns Institute for Youth Justice Fairness and Equity 2016).

Had adults not been locked up separately, their prison conditions would have directly impacted youth as well and, for this reason, may have garnered greater social concern. Conversely, introducing age segregation in prisons might make it easier for state authorities to worsen the conditions of imprisoned adults with relatively little public outcry. This is no mere hypothetical eventuality. There is evidence of youth-specific prison reforms, including age segregation, facilitating a steady erosion in the rights of previously non-separated adults along with the introduction of new adult-focused restrictions (Viterbo 2018, pp. 771, 777–779, 783).

Far from being exclusive to age-segregated incarceration, the legitimation of harshness toward adults is intrinsic to modern child law and policy.[3] To mention but a few examples, in international humanitarian legal discourse, "women and children" are often a shorthand for civilians, while adult male civilians are overlooked. This framing disregards men's unique vulnerabilities in armed conflict and, at times, has even paved the way for their indiscriminate targeting by the belligerent parties (Carpenter 2006). The privileging of young people in humanitarian aid campaigns likewise disenfranchises adults by deeming them less deserving of empathy and assistance (Burman 1994). Similarly, the rhetoric of an endangered childhood innocence has, in some contexts, repeatedly served to expand the policing and incarceration of purportedly dangerous adults (Meiners 2016). Some attempts at redesigning family law courts in a "child-sensitive" fashion, too, have drawn an antithesis between innocent children, who are assumed to need protection, and adults in conflict with the law (parents or others), who are portrayed as culpable criminals deserving imprisonment (Ananth 2014). It is probably no coincidence that across these contexts, as in age-segregated incarceration, the adults bearing the brunt are often from "othered" and disempowered groups.

Time and again, supposedly progressive critiques of the youth justice system play into society's abandonment of incarcerated adults (Cox 2015). Some of them do so while decrying insufficient age segregation, as exemplified by an op-ed titled "Children, even teenagers, don't belong in adult jails" (Washington Post editorial board 2013). The piece rehashes essentialist claims about the reduced capacity of youth for moral reasoning, impulse control, and mastery over their environment, and then adds: "There is also more hope of rehabilitating young offenders. … When minors are thrown into adult jails and prisons, … they don't get the structure and educational opportunities necessary for growth or rehabilitation. They are also extremely vulnerable to harm." The implication is that adults, unlike their younger counterparts, do belong behind bars, that they are relatively irredeemable, and that they deserve less support and protection.

Other youth justice reforms leave intact the mistreatment of incarcerated adults by, for instance, banning solitary confinement only for youth (Equal Justice Initiative 2016) or ensuring that no person under 18 in prison is legally considered an adult (Kelly 2018). Calls to abolish youth imprisonment exhibit similar sentiments. A *Guardian* op-ed titled "Child prisons are beyond reform—it's time to stop jailing young people" thus maintains: "Desperate levels of child suffering combined with terrible outcomes [of youth incarceration] should lead us all to reject imprisonment" (Willow 2018). Far from rejecting imprisonment, however, the piece reserves its compassion exclusively for youth. In so doing, it effectively condones the damaging incarceration of those making up the overwhelming majority of the prison population: adults.

Rather than trickling into adult incarceration, the reforms that self-identified progressives advocate for thus cement age differentiation. A case in point is the steady decarceration of youth in Canada in recent decades: it has not reduced the adult incarceration rate and, in addition, has arguably enabled the government to focus its punitive rhetoric on adult crime (Webster et al. 2019, pp. 1094, 1121–1124). This ubiquitous approach—reinforcing harshness and apathy toward adults by reserving decarceration or reforms for youth—figures centrally in academic studies (e.g., Bowman 2018), journalistic books (e.g., Bernstein 2014), and NGO publications (e.g., Equal Justice Initiative 2017). This leads me directly to the next pitfall of age-segregated incarceration: its legitimation of incarceration.

Pitfall 3: Legitimizing Incarceration

Incarceration is irredeemably problematic. As some critics argue, the endemic violence in prisons stems first and foremost from the punitiveness and violence inherent to incarceration itself (often compounded by staff violence), not from the imprisoned population—most of whom tend to be there for physically nonviolent crime, primarily property and drug offenses. Further, imprisonment has repeatedly proven to be effective neither in discouraging harmful behavior nor in preventing reoffending. Incarceration and policing are also damaging to the public, socially and economically, among other reasons because their high costs come at the expense of funding for welfare, healthcare, education, housing, and other imperative areas. For these and other reasons, prison abolitionists and other critical prison scholars have pressed for non-punitive responses to harm, which focus on healing and, by addressing root causes, prevention. Such alternatives, it has been argued, must be flexible and context specific, with possible examples including various forms of restorative justice, anti-poverty policies, community-based restitution initiatives, affordable housing, free and high-quality healthcare and education, recreational projects, decriminalizing drug use, and empowering marginalized communities (Goldman 1910; Hulsman 1991; Davis 2003; Lamble 2011).

In order to understand the role age-segregated incarceration plays in this regard, one must recognize the ties it encapsulates between imprisonment and reform. The genesis of prison was in attempts to reform punishment: to place lawbreakers behind bars as a more humane substitute for castigating and torturing them in public (Foucault 1995, pp. 3–31; Davis 2003, pp. 40–42). As criminal punishment became less publicly visible, so did its violence become more deniable (Kahn 2008, pp. 2–3). Against this backdrop, age-segregated incarceration emerged. As noted earlier, youth were initially tried and imprisoned with adults, but the transformation of childhood into a separate social realm entailed age segregation within the criminal legal system. Age segregation thus served as a reform enabling prison to maintain its false image as a humane, effective, and hence acceptable solution to transgressions.

Rather than undermining carceral thinking, then, separate incarceration entrenches it, making prison more immune to criticism. This problem is by no means unique to age segregation. Comparable issues arise from separating imprisoned people based on their gender or sexual identity, as well as from attempts at making prisons "responsive" to their needs. Such measures, some critics have argued, occasion new—and sometimes more far-reaching—forms of punishment, while also jeopardizing incarcerated people who do not fit into the binaries imposed on them (Spade 2011; Shaylor 2008; Carlton and Russell 2018; Davis 2003, pp. 60–83).

There is yet another sense in which age segregation lends legitimacy to incarceration. By dividing imprisoned people on grounds including their perceived culpability, it feeds into the punitive fixation with blame—a fixation with identifying and distinguishing between the blameworthy and those deemed less blameworthy (cf. Ananth 2014; Meiners 2016). Indeed, age has come to dictate both culpability and the spatial arrangement of prison. On its one side, age-segregated incarceration places adults, whose purported maturity and competence are said to render them fully culpable, and on its other side youth, who are supposedly unknowing, undeveloped, impressionable, and hence less culpable. In this respect, age-based separation and differentiation epitomize the preoccupation of modern penality not simply with acts (offenses) but with the identities, minds, and bodies of those classified as offenders (Foucault 1995, pp. 17–27, 170–183, 269; Platt 1977; May 1973).

Regrettably, even radical proposals to abolish youth courts have merely suggested substituting them with unified courts, thereby questioning neither imprisonment generally nor age-segregated incarceration specifically (Ainsworth 1991, 1995; Feld 1997). My argument here, in contrast, is that the solution lies neither in non-segregated incarceration nor in more refined segregation. Only within a carceral logic are these the only imaginable options. Instead of readjusting state violence, a wholesale rethinking of both carcerality and age essentialism is necessary.

Pitfall 4: Harming Youth

Age-segregated incarceration claims to protect youth. However, in associating protection with separation from imprisoned adults, it ends up putting incarcerated youth at risk, in three key respects. First, the conflation of protection with age segregation downplays the risk incarcerated youth face from one another. Perhaps for this reason, among others, there has been relatively little research into youth-on-youth abuse and aggression in prison, as several scholars have noted (Monks et al. 2009, pp. 150–151; Liefaard et al. 2014, p. 6; Klatt et al. 2016, p. 728). To the extent available, self-reported data from carceral facilities for youth in a variety of countries indicates a high level of peer abuse and violence (e.g., Davidson-Arad et al. 2009, pp. 260–261, 267–269 and the sources cited there; Bartollas et al. 1976; Liefaard et al. 2014, pp. 7–9; Klatt et al. 2016, pp. 728, 734). Advocates of age segregation may bemoan this reality but insist that incarceration with adults would expose youth to even greater harm. In actuality, studies comparing the experience of youth incarcerated in youth and adult facilities are scarce (Fagan and Kupchik 2011, p. 38; Ng et al. 2012, pp. 462–463, 466) and are also, at best, inconclusive.

One widely cited study involved interviews with a few dozen youth imprisoned for serious physically violent offenses in the United States. It found that those incarcerated in adult prisons, where there was only partial age segregation, reported higher assault rates than those in youth facilities (Forst et al. 1989). However, a later study with more participants found that youth in adult facilities are better protected from criminal victimization (Fagan and Kupchik 2011, pp. 51–53). According to several other studies, youth are involved in more violence toward other incarcerated people, as well as more disciplinary infractions and assaults on staff, compared with their adult counterparts (McShane and Williams 1989; MacKenzie 1987; Kupchik 2007, p. 248). Similarly, youth facilities in the United Kingdom were recently reported to have higher violence rates than any adult prison (Allison 2014). At the same time, other studies found no significant correlation between people's age and the perpetration of prison violence (Klatt et al. 2016, p. 737).

Where youth and adult facilities do vary in their rates of violence and abuse between incarcerated people, this may stem not from the existence or lack of age segregation, but from other distinguishing features of youth prisons. Such features sometimes include higher staff-per-prisoner ratios, smaller facilities, differences in the offending histories and ages of the incarcerated youth, and a greater professed commitment to treatment and rehabilitation (Fagan and Kupchik 2011, pp. 48–54; Kupchik 2007, pp. 259–263; Bishop 2000, pp. 139–140; Birckhead 2015, p. 59). It is therefore impossible to isolate the effects of age segregation from other factors. And even if this were possible, to generalize about age-segregated incarceration is to make two problematic assumptions: one, an essentialist assumption that all youth (and adults) across time and space are one and the same; the other, a context-insensitive assumption that age segregation would have similar effects in vastly different circumstances.

Second, in associating risk with imprisoned adults, age segregation dangerously mischaracterizes the prison's adult population, in terms of both risks to youth and the available support. Often, as mentioned previously, only a small minority of the incarcerated adults—who at any rate are sometimes held in separate facilities or wings—actually committed physically violent offenses (and many of them have an otherwise nonviolent record). Perhaps conveniently passed over is the risk frequently posed by other adults in prison: the prison staff, whose abuse and violence toward people in criminal custody (youth and adults) have been documented on countless occasions (e.g., Goldson and Muncie 2012, pp. 55–56 and the sources cited there; Miller et al. 2017; Willow 2018). Further, the separation of ostensibly different incarcerated groups fails to take into account the support, solidarity, care, and protection they sometimes offer one another (e.g., Arkles 2009, pp. 527–536 and the sources cited there; Shaylor 1998, pp. 390, 399–400). Such assistance is certainly possible between older and younger inmates (Laws and Lieber forthcoming), including—on the rare occasions that they are incarcerated together—between adults and youth (Viterbo 2012b, pp. 128, 132–143; 2018, pp. 779–782). Unwittingly or not, these various blind spots of age-segregated incarceration place imprisoned populations at greater risk, physically and mentally.

Third, to ensure age segregation, prison staff occasionally resort to harmful practices, such as solitary confinement—some forms of which, incidentally, are also referred to as "segregation." Where incarcerated youth cannot be separated from adults by other means, they have repeatedly been placed in solitary confinement. This has occurred in different parts of the globe, on numerous occasions, and often for long periods of time (UN Special Rapporteur on Torture, 2011, ¶ 66; Viterbo 2012b, p. 127; Birckhead 2015, pp. 4, 20, 37–38, 42, 75 and the sources cited there; Equal Justice Initiative 2017, p. 13). In addition to its grave psychological effects, solitary confinement cuts off the imprisoned person from crucial sources of support and information, and can also facilitate uninterrupted staff abuse (e.g., Arkles 2009, pp. 537–542, 550, 553; Dolovich 2011, pp. 3–4). Thus, in the name of protection, the commitment to age segregation yet again begets greater harm. A similar protective rationale, it is worth noting, has also been used to justify placing incarcerated women and LGBTQI people in solitary confinement (Arkles 2009, pp. 545, 550, 554–555; Dolovich 2011, p. 3; Lamble 2011, p. 244). This, as I pointed out earlier, is not the only troubling parallel between the effects of segregation on youth and other incarcerated groups. Hence, it is identity-based segregation generally that requires dismantling, not solely age segregation.

The harm inflicted on youth is yet another pitfall that age-segregated incarceration shares with other forms of age segregation and differentiation. For example, youth courts—the face of age-segregated adjudication—often deny young defendants important rights that are granted in adult criminal courts (e.g., Feld 2017; Howard League for Penal Reform 2016; Ainsworth 1991). The norm of closing youth hearings is likewise problematic. As critics have observed, closed hearings might shield the youth court from scrutiny more than they protect young people, particularly given the less deleterious alternatives available (e.g., Geis 1957; Trasen 1995). A similarly questionable form of age differentiation, in some countries, is charging youth with "status offenses"—conduct that would not be illegal for adults, such as skipping school and running away (e.g., Coalition for Juvenile Justice 2015). Beyond the youth justice context, the list of examples (such as the separation of school from work) could go on. The harm caused by age-segregated incarceration, then, is but a symptom of a broader problem.

Pitfall 5: Fragmenting Oppressed Communities

A final pitfall of age-segregated incarceration is its use to oppress certain communities by breaking their intergenerational ties. A recent case in point concerns the thousands of noncitizen Palestinians self-identified as political prisoners, including hundreds of youth, whom Israel puts behind bars every year.[4] Over the years, Israel has increasingly sought to fragment Palestinian territory and society. This has recently included segregating Palestinian political prisoners—whose collective endeavors Israel has long decried—based on their regions of residence, as well as cracking down on their study groups and barring them from electing central representatives. Incarcerated Palestinian youth and adults, who until the first decade of the century were mostly held together, are also now systematically separated—a change presented by Israeli authorities both as consistent with international law and in Palestinian youth's "best interests." The Israeli judiciary pushed for age segregation as a means to prevent the exposure of Palestinian youth "to … [the older] prisoners' ideologies" by removing them from "adults who wished to capture [their] … soul." However, Palestinian youth's testimonies and other sources suggest that, prior to their separation, incarcerated adults provided them with invaluable care and support. These adults also represented their concerns to the Israeli prison authorities and, given Israel's frequent denial of family prison visits, could offer the closest substitute for parental care. Moreover, age segregation has left Palestinian youth less protected against the abuse they commonly report suffering at the hands of the Israeli prison and security staff. Human rights organizations, possibly due to their enshrining of age-segregated incarceration, tended to criticize Israel for not separating incarcerated Palestinian youth and mostly started doubting the desirability of such separation only after the fact (Viterbo 2018, pp. 766–785). Broader lessons, it seems, have yet to be learned, judging by criticism recently voiced by the Special Representative of the UN Secretary-General for Children and Armed Conflict: "well-established principles of detention are … [being] overlooked in the context of armed conflict …, [including] children … being held together with adults" (Zerrougui 2016, ¶ 19).

Another contemporary example is to be found in China's north-west Xinjiang region.[5] For decades, the Chinese government has been targeting and closely surveilling Uyghurs and other Muslims in Xinjiang to ensure their loyalty to the state and assimilation into the Han-dominated society. Their private lives have been closely monitored, national expression has been censored, religious activities have been criminalized and persecuted, and, as a complementary measure, Chinese language and culture education has been forcefully promoted (Roberts 2018). In recent years, China has reportedly subjected Xinjiang's Muslim populations to age segregation as well. Hundreds of thousands and possibly even 1.5 million adults, it is estimated, have been preemptively and extrajudicially placed in so-called re-education internment camps. "Re-educating these people," a Chinese official has explained, "is like spraying chemicals on the crops. That is why it is a general re-education, not limited to a few people." Government publications have warned that adults affected by "extremist thought" instill in their children animosity toward non-Muslim groups and Han culture. Having interned such adults, China has removed many of their children and placed them in securitized and centralized education facilities, where it claims they can develop more "open personalities" and improve their Chinese skills. A staff member of one such facility has couched these measures in pedagogical terms: "I tell the children: 'Your parents and you all alike are studying'" (Zenz 2019a, 2019b).

Such use of age-segregated incarceration shares parallels with other forms of generational segregation. Modern child law partly developed to remove young people from perceived problem groups and "civilize" them away from allegedly depraved or unfit parents, often in the name of national interests. Among those thus treated were hundreds of thousands of young Indigenous people in Australia, Canada, and the United States, who were placed in special boarding schools (commonly described by them as prison-like) or put up for adoption. Proponents depicted such segregation as salvaging young Indigenous people from "deleterious influences" and turning them into "honorable, useful, happy citizens." In North America, state authorities also saw generational segregation as a counterinsurgency measure: "It is unlikely," one official argued, "that any Tribe ... would give trouble of a serious nature ... whose members had children completely under Government control" (Viterbo 2012b, pp. 135–138; 2017, pp. 687–688, 701–709, 721–722). Others subjected to similar segregation include Andamanese tribes in British colonial India (Sen 1999, pp. 757–766), the Yenish (often described as "gypsies") in 1970s' Switzerland, "mixed-race" families in both French colonial Morocco and the Dutch East Indies (today's Indonesia), the Inuit in Danish-ruled Greenland in the 1950s, impoverished immigrants in the nineteenth–twentieth-century United States, non-European Jewish immigrants in 1950s' Israel, and Christians in the Ottoman-ruled Balkans. To this could be added other forms of generational segregation in modern times, including child emigration and transnational child adoption programs (Viterbo 2017, pp. 723–728).

Parallels can also be drawn to elements of incarceration other than the separation of incarcerated youth. Specifically, many of the men in prison—who, as I have noted, tend to be overwhelmingly poor, non-white, or noncitizens—are fathers. Incarceration cuts them off from their children while also further impoverishing their families. Thus contextualized, age-segregated incarceration lies at the juncture of two practices—age segregation on the one hand and incarceration on the other—each of which has operated to drive a generational wedge in oppressed populations.

Conclusion

Age-segregated incarceration has established itself as an undisputed social, legal, and human rights norm. Its pitfalls, therefore, have so far largely escaped critical notice, including from youth justice critics. This chapter has brought to light five such interrelated pitfalls.

First, age-segregated incarceration buttresses age essentialism, which boxes people into constrictive and historically specific categories based on dubious assumptions. Second, in attributing greater corrigibility and vulnerability to imprisoned youth, age-segregated incarceration signals that their adult counterparts are less deserving of compassion and leniency. Thus, these separated adults can more easily be denied youth-only protections and treated harshly, with relatively little public outcry. A third pitfall is the legitimation of incarceration. Through age segregation, prison presents itself as humane and effective while also maintaining its punitive fixation with blame. Fourth, in the name of protection, age-segregated incarceration can also harm youth. It downplays the risk posed by their peers and the prison staff, neglects the support they can receive from some imprisoned adults, and has led to harmful practices such as solitary confinement. Finally, age segregation, in and beyond prison, has long served as a means to oppress disempowered communities by severing their intergenerational ties. This occurred, and is still occurring, across different parts of the world.

A more in-depth analysis of these pitfalls exceeds the scope and space constraints of this chapter, as does an exploration of possible alternatives to age-segregated incarceration. I intend to delve into these issues in a forthcoming publication. This chapter is aimed to stimulate further conversations while bringing into dialogue childhood studies, critical prison studies, youth justice, and other ways of thinking. At this stage, suffice it to reiterate that non-segregated imprisonment (incarcerating youth with adults) ought not be the only conceivable alternative. Nor does the solution lie in age-specific penal reforms, more refined separation, or non-carceral age segregation. With the pitfalls of age-segregated incarceration now in plain sight, the need arises for more imaginative alternatives, by moving past essentialism and carcerality. This enterprise is as imperative as it is challenging.

Notes

1. Article 1 of the CRC defines "a child" as "every human being below the age of eighteen years unless under the applicable law applicable to the child, majority is attained earlier." In addition, Article 9 generally prohibits separating a child from her/his parents against her/his will without due legal process; however, where such separation results from detention or imprisonment, all the Article requires (with certain caveats) is to inform the child or the family of the removed child's/parent's whereabouts.
2. Indeed, when imprisoned women are concerned, some countries view incarceration with them as beneficial for girls (e.g., UNICEF 2009, p. 13).
3. At the same time, some child-related laws and policies also enable various forms of harshness toward young people, such as physical chastisement, curfews, and, as discussed later, so-called status offenses.
4. For background information, see Ben-Naftali et al. (2018).
5. Juxtaposing these two parts of the world is not unheard of: Chinese scholar and dissident Wang Lixiong once warned of an "interminable ethnic war" in Xinjiang amounting to a "Palestinization" of the region (Finley 2019).

References

African Charter on the Rights and Welfare of the Child. (1990, entered into force 29 November, 1999). Organization of African Unity Doc. CAB/LEG/24.9/49.

Ainsworth, J. (1991). Re-imagining childhood and reconstructing the legal order: The case for abolishing the juvenile court. *North Carolina Law Review, 69*(4), 1083–1133.

Ainsworth, J. (1995). Youth justice in a unified court: Response to critics of juvenile court abolition. *Boston College Law Review, 36*, 927–951.

Albanian Ministry of Labor, Social Affairs and Equal Opportunities, Terre des hommes, and UNICEF. (2010). *Working protocol for child protection workers*. Retrieved from http://lastradainternational.org/lsidocs/1047_CPW_Protocol_ENG_original.pdf.

Allison, E. (2014). Banging up young offenders in adult jails is a bad idea. *The Guardian*, 11 February. Retrieved from https://www.theguardian.com/society/2014/feb/11/chris-grayling-young-offenders-adult-jails.

Amnesty International. (1997). *Venezuela—The silent cry: Gross human rights violations against children*. Retrieved from https://www.amnesty.org/download/Documents/160000/amr530131997en.pdf.

Amnesty International. (2005). *Nepal: Children caught in conflict*. Retrieved from https://www.amnesty.org/download/Documents/84000/asa310542005en.pdf.

Ananth, A. (2014). The gracious spaces of children's law: Innocence and culpability in the construction of a children's court. *Studies in Law, Politics, and Society, 63*, 89–112.

Ariès, P. (1962). *Centuries of childhood: A social history of family life*. London: Jonathan Cape.

Arkles, G. (2009). Safety and solidarity across gender lines: Rethinking segregation of transgender people in detention. *Temple Political & Civil Rights Law Review, 18*(2), 515–560.

Bartollas, C., Miller, S., & Dinitz, S. (1976). *Juvenile victimization: The institutional paradox*. New York: Halsted Press.

Ben-Naftali, O., Sfard, M., & Viterbo, H. (2018). *The ABC of the OPT: A legal lexicon of the Israeli control over the Occupied Palestinian Territory*. Cambridge and New York: Cambridge University Press.

Bennett, C., & Baird, A. (2006). Anatomical changes in the emerging adult brain: A voxel-based morphometry study. *Human Brain Mapping, 27*, 766–777.

Bernstein, N. (2014). *Burning down the house: The end of juvenile prison*. New York: The New Press.

Bessant, J. (2008). Hard wired for risk: Neurological science, "the adolescent brain" and developmental theory. *Journal of Youth Studies, 11*(3), 347–360.

Birckhead, T. (2015). Children in isolation: The solitary confinement of youth. *Wake Forest Law Review, 50*(1), 1–80.

Bishop, D. (2000). Juvenile offenders in the adult criminal justice system. *Crime and Justice, 27*, 81–168.

Bowman, S. (2018). The kids are alright: Making a case for abolition of the juvenile justice system. *Critical Criminology, 26*(3), 393–405.

Burman, E. (1994). Innocents abroad: Western fantasies of childhood and the iconography of emergencies. *Disasters, 18*(3), 238–253.

Burns Institute for Youth Justice Fairness and Equity. (2016). *Stemming the rising tide: Racial & ethnic disparities in youth incarceration & strategies for change.* Retrieved from https://www.burnsinstitute.org/wp-content/uploads/2016/05/Stemming-the-Rising-Tide_FINAL.pdf.

Campaign for Youth Justice. (2016). *International human rights day: Let's give our youth the human rights they deserve.* Retrieved from http://cfyj.org/2016/item/international-human-rights-day-let-s-give-our-youth-the-human-rights-they-deserve?category_id=257.

Carlton, B., & Russell, E. K. (2018). *Resisting carceral violence: Women's imprisonment and the politics of abolition.* Cham: Palgrave Macmillan.

Carpenter, C. (2006). *Innocent women and children: Gender, norms and the protection of civilians.* London and New York: Routledge.

Chudacoff, H. (1989). *How old are you: Age consciousness in American culture.* Princeton and Oxford: Princeton University Press.

Coalition for Juvenile Justice. (2015). *Status offenses: A national survey.* Retrieved from https://www.juvjustice.org/sites/default/files/resource-files/Status%20Offenses%20-%20A%20National%20Survey%20WEB.pdf.

Convention on the Rights of the Child (CRC). (Adopted 20 November, 1989, entered into force 2 September, 1990). G.A. Res. 44/25, annex, 44 UN GAOR Supp. (No. 49) at 167, UN Doc. A/44/49.

Cox, A. (2014). Brain science and juvenile justice: Questions for policy and practice. In W. T. Church et al. (Eds.), *Juvenile justice sourcebook* (2nd ed., pp. 123–148). Oxford and New York: Oxford University Press.

Cox, A. (2015). *The perils of false distinctions between juveniles and adults in prison.* Retrieved from https://jjie.org/2015/01/14/the-perils-of-false-distinctions-between-juveniles-and-adults-in-prison.

Coyle, A., Heard, C., & Fair, H. (2016). Current trends and practices in the use of imprisonment. *International Review of the Red Cross, 98*(3), 761–781.

Cunningham, H. (2005). *Children and childhood in Western society since 1500* (2nd ed.). London and New York: Routledge.

Davidson-Arad, B., Benbenishty, R., & Golan, M. (2009). Comparison of violence and abuse in juvenile correctional facilities and schools. *Journal of Interpersonal Violence, 24*(2), 259–279.

Davis, A. (2003). *Are prisons obsolete?* New York: Seven Stories.

Dolovich, S. (2011). Strategic segregation in the modern prison. *American Criminal Law Review, 48*(1), 1–110.

Equal Justice Initiative. (2016). *President Obama bans solitary confinement for juveniles in federal prisons.* Retrieved from https://eji.org/news/president-obama-bans-solitary-for-juveniles-in-federal-prisons.

Equal Justice Initiative. (2017). *All children are children: Challenging abusive punishment of juveniles.* Retrieved from https://eji.org/sites/default/files/AllChildrenAreChildren-2017-sm2.pdf.

European Prison Rules, Recommendation No. R (89) 3 of the Committee of Ministers to Member States (June 2006).

Fagan, J., & Kupchik, A. (2011). Juvenile incarceration and the pains of imprisonment. *Duke Forum for Law & Social Change, 3,* 29–61.

Feld, B. C. (1997). Abolish the youth court: Youthfulness, criminal responsibility, and sentencing policy. *The Journal of Criminal Law and Criminology, 88*(1), 68–136.

Feld, B. C. (2017). *The evolution of the juvenile court: Race, politics, and the criminalizing of juvenile justice.* New York: New York University Press.

Finley, J. S. (2019). The Wang Lixiong prophecy: 'Palestinization' in Xinjiang and the consequences of chinese state securitization of religion. *Central Asian Survey, 38*(1), 81–101.

Forst, M., Fagan, J., & Vivona, T. S. (1989). Youth in prisons and training schools: Perceptions and consequences of the treatment-custody dichotomy. *Juvenile and Family Court Journal, 40*(1), 1–14.

Foucault, M. (1995/1975). *Discipline and punish: The birth of the prison.* New York: Vintage Books.

Geis, G. (1957). Publicity and juvenile court proceedings. *Rocky Mountain Law Review, 30*(2), 101–126.

Goldman, E. (1910). Prisons: A social crime and failure. In *Anarchism and other essays* (pp. 115–132). New York: Mother Earth Publishing.

Goldson, B., & Kilkely, U. (2013). International human rights standards and child imprisonment: Potentialities and limitations. *International Journal of Children's Rights, 21*(2), 345–371.

Goldson, B., & Muncie, J. (2012). Towards a global "child friendly" juvenile justice? *International Journal of Law, Crime and Justice, 40,* 47–64.

Hagestad, G. O., & Uhlenberg, P. (2005). The social separation of old and young: A root of ageism. *Journal of Social Issues, 61*(2), 343–360.

Her Majesty's Prison and Probation Service. (2019). *Youth custody report: June.* Retrieved from https://assets.publishing.service.gov.uk/government/uploads/system/uploads/attachment_data/file/823750/youth-custody-report-june-2019.xlsx.

Howard League for Penal Reform. (2016). *They couldn't do it to a grown up: Tagging children without due process.* Retrieved from https://howardleague.org/wp-content/uploads/2016/05/They-couldnt-do-it-to-a-grown-up.pdf.

Hulsman, L. (1991). The abolitionist case: Alternative crime policies. *Israel Law Review, 25*(3–4), 681–709.

Human Rights Watch. (2012). *Egypt: Children on trial.* Retrieved from https://www.hrw.org/news/2012/03/27/egypt-children-trial.

Institut international des droits de l'enfant. (2010). *Children in conflict and in contact with the law*. Retrieved from https://www.childsrights.org/documents/sensibilisation/themes-principaux/juvenile_justice.pdf.

International Covenant on Civil and Political Rights (ICCPR). (Adopted 16 December, 1966, entered into force 23 March, 1976). G.A. Res. 2200A (XXI), 21 UN GAOR Supp. (No. 16) at 52, UN Doc. A/6316, 999 UNT.S. 171.

James, A., Jenks, C., & Prout, A. (1998). *Theorizing childhood*. Cambridge: Polity Press.

Juvenile Justice and Delinquency Prevention Act of 1974, Public Law 93–415, 88 Stat. 1109 (as amended through P.L. 115–385, enacted December 21, 2018) (United States).

Kahn, P. W. (2008). *Sacred violence: Torture, terror, and sovereignty*. Ann Arbor: University of Michigan Press.

Kelly, P. (2012). The brain in the jar: A critique of discourses of adolescent brain development. *Journal of Youth Studies, 15*(7), 944–959.

Kelly, J. (2018). *In another big year for "raise the age" laws, one state now considers all teens as juveniles*. Retrieved from https://chronicleofsocialchange.org/youth-services-insider/juvenile-justice-raise-the-age-vermont-missouri-state-legislation/31430.

Klatt, T., Hagl, S., Bergmann, M. C., & Baier, D. (2016). Violence in youth custody: Risk factors of violent misconduct among inmates of German Young Offender Institutions. *European Journal of Criminology, 13*(6), 727–743.

Kupchik, A. (2007). The correctional experiences of youths in adult and juvenile facilities. *Justice Quarterly, 24*(2), 247–270.

Lamble, S. (2011). Transforming carceral logics: 10 reasons to dismantle the prison industrial complex through queer/trans analysis and action. In N. Smith & E. Stanley (Eds.), *Captive genders: Trans embodiment and the prison industrial complex* (pp. 235–266). Oakland: AK Press.

Laws, B., & Lieber, E. (forthcoming). "King, warrior, magician, lover": Understanding expressions of care among male prisoners. *European Journal of Criminology*.

Lesko, N. (2001). *Act your age! A cultural construction of adolescence*. New York and London: Routledge.

Liefaard, T., Reef, J., &Hazelzet M. (2014) *Report on violence in institutions for juvenile offenders*. Retrieved from https://rm.coe.int/european-committee-on-crime-problems-cdpc-council-for-penological-co-o/16806fb1e8.

MacKenzie, D. L. (1987). Age adjustment in prison: Interactions with attitudes and anxiety. *Criminal Justice and Behavior, 14*(4), 427–447.

Magarey, S. (1978). The invention of juvenile delinquency in early nineteenth-century England. *Labour History, 34*, 11–27.

May, M. (1973). Innocence and experience: The evolution of the concept of juvenile delinquency in the mid-nineteenth century. *Victorian Studies, 17*(1), 7–29.

McShane, M. D., & Williams, F. P. (1989). The prison adjustment of juvenile offenders. *Crime & Delinquency, 35*(2), 254–269.

Mead, M. (1928). *Coming of age in Samoa: A psychological study of primitive youth for Western civilisation*. New York: William Morrow & Co.

Meiners, E. R. (2016). *For the children?: Protecting innocence in a carceral state*. Minneapolis: University of Minnesota Press.

Miller, C. M., et al. (2017). Dark secrets of Florida's juvenile justice system: A Miami Herald investigation. *Miami Herald*, 10 October. Retrieved from http://www.miamiherald.com/news/special-reports/florida-prisons/article176773291.html.

Monks, C. P., et al. (2009). Bullying in different contexts: Commonalities, differences and the role of theory. *Aggression and Violent Behavior, 14*, 146–156.

Montgomery, H. (2008). *An introduction to childhood: Anthropological perspectives on children's lives*. Malden and Oxford: Wiley-Blackwell.

Muncie, J., & Goldson, B. (2012). Youth justice: In a child's best interests? In J. Simon & R. Sparks (Eds.), *The Sage handbook of punishment and society* (pp. 341–355). Los Angeles and London: Sage.

Ng, I. Y. H., et al. (2012). Comparison of correctional services for youth incarcerated in adult and juvenile facilities in Michigan. *The Prison Journal, 92*(4), 460–483.

Nowak, M. et al. (2019). *United Nations global study on children deprived of liberty*. Retrieved from https://omnibook.com/view/e0623280-5656-42f8-9edf-5872f8f08562.

Organization of American States, American Convention on Human Rights ("Pact of San José") (22 November, 1969).

Pilnik, L., & Mistrett, M. (2019). *If not the adult system then where? Alternatives to adult incarceration for youth certified as adults*. Retrieved from http://cfyj.org/images/ALT_INCARCERATION__FINAL.pdf.

Platt, A. M. (1977). *The child savers: The invention of delinquency* (2nd ed.). Chicago and London: University of Chicago Press.

Protocol Additional to the Geneva Conventions of August 12, 1949, and Relating to the Protection of Victims of International Armed Conflicts (Additional Protocol I), Geneva, 1125 UNTS 3 (8 June, 1977).

Roberts, S. R. (2018). The biopolitics of China's "war on terror" and the exclusion of the Uyghurs. *Critical Asian Studies, 50*(2), 232–258.

Rovner, J. (2017). Still increase in racial disparities in juvenile justice. *New York Amsterdam News.*, 19 October. Retrieved from http://amsterdamnews.com/news/2017/oct/19/still-increase-racial-disparities-juvenile-justice.

Save the Children. (2005). *A review of child protection and juvenile justice laws in South Sudan*. Retrieved from https://resourcecentre.savethechildren.net/node/7542/pdf/a_review_of_child_protection_and_juvenile_justice_laws_in_.pdf.

Scottish Institute for Residential Child Care. (2005). *Secure in the knowledge: Perspectives on practice in secure accommodation*. Retrieved from https://www.celcis.org/files/2314/3878/4209/secure-in-the-knowledge-perspectives.pdf.

Sen, S. (1999). Policing the savage: Segregation, labor and state medicine in the Andamans. *The Journal of Asian Studies, 58*(3), 753–773.

Shaylor, C. (1998). It's like living in a black hole: Women of color and solitary confinement in the prison industrial complex. *New England Journal on Criminal and Civil Confinement, 24*(2), 385–416.

Shaylor, C. (2008). Neither kind nor gentle: The perils of "gender responsive justice". In P. Scraton & J. McCulloch (Eds.), *The violence of incarceration* (pp. 145–163). New York and London: Routledge.

Shore, H. (2003). "Inventing" the juvenile delinquent in nineteenth-century Europe. In B. Godfrey, C. Emsley, & G. Dunstall (Eds.), *Comparative histories of crime* (pp. 110–124). Willan: Cullompton.

Siegel, L. J., & Welsh, B. C. (2017). *Juvenile delinquency: Theory, practice, and law* (13th ed.). Boston: Cengage.

SOS Children's Villages—Canada. (2009). *The CRC, child protection, and the law*. Retrieved from https://www.soschildrensvillages.ca/crc-child-protection-and-law.

Spade, D. (2011). Administering gender. In *Normal life: Administrative violence, critical trans politics, and the limits of law* (pp. 137–169). New York: South End Press.

Thai Lawyers for Human Rights. (2017). *Demanding an official explanation regarding detention of a 14-year-old-suspect and military detention must be stopped*. Retrieved from https://www.tlhr2014.com/?p=4302&lang=en.

Trasen, J. L. (1995). Privacy v. public access to juvenile court proceedings: Do closed hearings protect the child or the system? *Boston College Third World Law Journal, 15*(2), 359–384.

UN Children's Fund (UNICEF). (2009). *Regional and international indicators on juvenile justice: Their applicability and relevance in selected countries of Eastern Europe and Central Asia*. Retrieved from https://www1.essex.ac.uk/armedcon/story_id/UNICEF_JJIndicators08.pdf.

UN Committee on the Rights of the Child. (2007). *General comment No. 10: Children's rights in juvenile justice* (44th session, UN Doc. CRC/C/GC/10).

UN Rules for the Protection of Juveniles Deprived of their Liberty (Havana Rules). (Adopted 14 December, 1990). G.A. Res. 45/113, annex, 45 UN GAPR Supp. (no. 49A) at 205, UN Doc. A/45/49.

UN Special Rapporteur on Torture and Other Cruel, Inhuman or Degrading Treatment or Punishment. (2011). *Interim report to the General Assembly* (66th Session, Provisional Agenda Item 69(b), UN Doc. A/66/268).

UN Special Rapporteur on Torture and Other Cruel, Inhuman or Degrading Treatment or Punishment. (2015). *Report to the Human Rights Council* (28th Session, Agenda Item 3, UN Doc. A/HRC/28/68).

UN Standard Minimum Rules for the Administration of Juvenile Justice (Beijing Rules). (Adopted 29 November, 1985). G.A. Res. 40/33, 40 UN GAOR Supp. (No. 53) at 3, UN Doc. A/40/33.

UN Standard Minimum Rules for the Treatment of Prisoners (Nelson Mandela Rules). (Adopted 17 December, 2015). G.A. Res. 70/175, 70 UN GAOR, Agenda Item 106, UN Doc. A/Res/70/175.

Viterbo, H. (2012a). The age of conflict: Rethinking childhood, law, and age through the Israeli-Palestinian case. In M. Freeman (Ed.), *Law and childhood studies—Current legal issues* (Vol. 14, pp. 133–155). Oxford: Oxford University Press.

Viterbo, H. (2012b). *The legal construction of childhood in the Israeli-Palestinian conflict*. Doctoral dissertation, London School of Economics and Political Science, London.

Viterbo, H. (2017). Ties of separation: Analogy and generational segregation in North America, Australia, and Israel/Palestine. *Brooklyn Journal of International Law, 42*(2), 695–759.

Viterbo, H. (2018). Rights as a divide-and-rule mechanism: Lessons from the case of Palestinians in Israeli custody. *Law & Social Inquiry, 43*(3), 764–795.

Washington Post editorial board. (2013). Children, even teenagers, don't belong in adult jails. *Washington Post*, 15 October. Retrieved from https://www.washingtonpost.com/opinions/children-even-teenagers-dont-belong-in-adult-jails/2013/10/15/5561b8fc-32b8-11e3-9c68-1cf643210300_story.html.

Webster, C. M., Sprott, J. B., & Doob, A. N. (2019). The will to change: Lessons from Canada's successful decarceration of youth. *Law and Society Review, 53*(4), 1092–1131.

Willow, C. (2018). Child prisons are beyond reform—It's time to stop jailing young people. *The Guardian*, 3 December. Retrieved from https://www.theguardian.com/society/2018/dec/03/child-prisons-beyond-reform-stop-jailing-young-people.

Zenz, A. (2019a). "Thoroughly reforming them towards a healthy heart attitude": China's political re-education campaign in Xinjiang. *Central Asian Survey, 38*(1), 102–128.

Zenz, A. (2019b). Break their roots: Evidence for China's parent-child separation campaign in Xinjiang. *Journal of Political Risk, 7*(7).

Zerrougui, L. (2016). *Annual report of the Special Representative of the Secretary-General for Children and Armed Conflict* (UN Doc. A/HR/34/44). Retrieved from https://reliefweb.t/sites/reliefweb.int/files/resources/G1643985.pdf.

26

Toward Transformation: The Youth Justice Movement in the United States on Ending the Youth Prison Model

Liz Ryan

Introduction

In this chapter, I will cover a brief history of the youth prison model and delve into advocacy efforts to reform this model and ultimately abolish youth imprisonment. To start, I will first define what I mean by "incarceration" in this chapter. Anytime a youth is deprived of their liberty, that youth is incarcerated. That definition is based on the framework and international standards created by the United Nations' Convention on the Rights of the Child (United Nations 2019). Most youth who are incarcerated throughout the United States (U.S.) are placed in locked facilities that house youth who are accused of delinquent offenses or who are adjudicated delinquent (i.e., similar to a conviction in adult court) in juvenile court.

One of the most harmful, ineffective, and expensive forms of incarceration is the youth prison, the signature feature of nearly every state juvenile justice system in the United States. Throughout this chapter, we intentionally use the word "youth prison" to describe many of the facilities where youth are locked up even though they have been called many names over time, starting with *houses of refuge*, *reform schools* or *reformatories*, then *industrial schools* and

L. Ryan (✉)
Youth First, Washington, DC, USA
e-mail: Liz@YouthFirstInitiative.org

training schools, to an assortment of names today, including *juvenile correctional center, school, institute,* or *development center*. The youth prison model has changed very little. No matter what it has been called over the years or when it was built, youth prisons today are based on the same model of custody, social control, and punishment.

As we approach the 200th anniversary of the establishment of the first youth prison in the U.S. we look back on a long and sordid history of abuse, and it is no surprise that almost from its inception, there have been multiple movements to reform youth prisons. These movements include early reformers such as the Black Child Savers who sought to make the juvenile justice system more equitable for African-American youth (Ward 2012); lawyers who pursued litigation to improve conditions of confinement for incarcerated youth; system leaders and state officials who pushed for reforms; and, more recently, youth who have been court involved and/or incarcerated, their families, and communities, along with direct service providers, youth advocates, and other allies who are seeking to abolish youth prisons entirely.

The Youth First Initiative grew out of this movement and is a national advocacy initiative aiming to accelerate youth justice system transformation through creating and supporting the success of state-based campaigns calling for the end of the punitive youth prison model. Instead, we advocate for investments in effective community-based programs, services, and opportunities for youth. Youth First's theory of change is that high-impact, state-based campaigns in roughly one-third of the U.S. states will move the nation toward a "tipping point," accelerating change and building evidence in favor of youth justice system transformation.

My perspective is informed by my work over the past 20 years to end the inhumane treatment of children in the justice system, including founding the Campaign for Youth Justice, seeking to end the prosecution of youth in adult criminal court. I then went on to create the Youth First Initiative. With well-documented attempts again and again to change youth prisons over nearly two hundred years, I approach the work from an abolitionist frame as I don't believe that youth prisons can be improved, reformed, or fixed. The youth prison model is broken and needs to be dismantled. Until and unless we create the political support to end this flawed approach, the youth prison will continue, likely in a slightly more humane, slightly smaller fashion, even with the weight of research evidence against it and young people who have been directly impacted advocating for its abolishment.

Origins of Youth Prisons

House of Refuge

The first youth prisons in the U.S. were established as "houses of refuge" in northern industrial hubs. In New York City, the Society for the Reformation of Juvenile Delinquents established the first youth prison, the New York House of Refuge, on January 1, 1825 (Bernstein 2014). The New York House of Refuge was built to house up to one thousand children and included orphans, immigrant youth, and other youth in need of supervision (Bernstein 2014). Boston and Philadelphia followed close behind (Kopaczewski 2016).

The early houses of refuge housed youth who were deemed a problem to their communities. They were informal institutions without legal parameters; in other words, youth who had run away from home or were orphaned could be placed there even if they weren't even accused of delinquent offenses. Youth were often required to work long days for no pay in the institution (Pickett 1969).

As the early houses of refuge were created at a time when slavery was still legal, African-American youth were often initially denied access to these institutions (Ward 2012). However inadequate and often harmful the houses of refuge were, they were still a far more preferable option than what most black youth were facing in the adult justice system: prison and the death penalty (Shepherd 1999).

During the 1830s in northern cities, there were efforts to place youth of color in youth prisons (Ward 2012). However, these institutions were segregated, with white and black youth living in separate units or buildings within the overall institution. For example, the New York House of Refuge created a separate section for African-American youth in 1835, a decade after it was founded (Ward 2012).

Reform Schools

Nearly 25 years later, a newer version of the youth prison was created, the "reform school," starting with the Lyman School for Boys in Massachusetts in 1847 (Miller 1998). Although established to be an improved version of the houses of refuge and still an even more humane alternative to adult prisons, the reform schools essentially re-created the very institutions that they were designed to replace: they were similarly large and punitive as houses of refuge (Platt 2009).

Segregation also continued. Some of these institutions were built segregated with separate living units for white and black youth, such as the notorious Arthur Dozier School (also known as the State Industrial School for boys) founded in 1900 in Marianna, Florida (see also Whitehead 2019).

In a number of instances, wholly separate institutions for youth of color were created. For example, after more than a decade of planning (Packard 1841), a new House of Refuge in Philadelphia was created for black youth in 1849 (Kopaczewski 2016). Additional examples include the House of Reformation and Instruction for Colored Boys in 1870 in Cheltenham, Maryland (*The Baltimore Sun*, 1872); the House of the Good Shepherd for Colored Girls in 1892 in Baltimore, Maryland (Jones and Record 2014); the District of Columbia's Reform School for Girls in 1893 (Fletcher 2020); and the Colored Waif's Home in 1906 in New Orleans, Louisiana, an institution where the famous jazz icon Louis Armstrong was sent (Teachout 2009), to name a few (Ryan 2020).

Southern states lagged behind the north in creating these institutions and were slow to permit black youth in as they were mostly handled in adult criminal court and subjected to convict leasing and chain gangs (Ward 2012). California didn't create a reform school until 1889 when it established the State Reform School for Juvenile Offenders, renamed later as the Whittier State School (Chavez-Garcia 2012). But by the end of the 1800s, every state in the U.S. had at least one reform school (Bernstein 2014).

The Juvenile Court

In response to concerns over the treatment of children in houses of refuge and reform schools and to keep children out of adult jails and prisons, Chicago advocates Julia Lathrop and Lucy Flower of the Hull House organization, formed in 1889, pushed for the creation of a new approach: the Juvenile Court (Shepherd 1999). The Hull House women formed a group of advocates, later deemed the "child savers" who advocated for laws that restricted children from harsh labor conditions and required compulsory education. They also fought to establish playgrounds, day care centers, and kindergartens (Platt 2009). As a result of their advocacy efforts, the Illinois legislature approved the Juvenile Court Act in 1899 to place children who were accused of delinquent offenses in the new court. The new court's goals were rehabilitation over punishment, confidentiality, separation of children from adults if they were housed in the same institution, and informal proceedings (Shepherd 1999). The Illinois juvenile court was the first juvenile court in the world

(Meyer 2019). Within a quarter of a century, all U.S. states had a juvenile court (Meyer 2019).

However, despite the juvenile court founders' best intentions, the new juvenile court did not actually challenge the existence of the houses of refuge or reform schools, a seemingly contradictory position given the new court's focus on rehabilitation and individualized justice (Bernstein 2014).

In fact, the new juvenile court assured the central place of youth prisons in the newly created juvenile justice system. Even though the juvenile court founders were concerned about the treatment of children in the houses of refuge and reform schools, the establishment of the juvenile court did not replace these institutions. Rather, the juvenile court arguably built its foundation on them and ensured their continued existence (Nellis 2016) and admissions to these facilities continued to increase (McCarthy et al. 2016).

And while the child savers did not want youth in the adult criminal justice system, they also did not want white youth in the same facilities with youth of color in the newly created juvenile justice system (Nellis 2016). Segregation continued with some facilities keeping youth of color in separate units from white youth or creating wholly separate institutions for youth of color (Ward 2012).

Inequitable treatment of youth continued in these institutions with more educational and apprenticeship opportunities for white youth, longer periods of confinement for youth of color, and less opportunities for youth of color when they were released from the institutions (Ward 2012). California's Whittier School, under the direction of Fred C. Nelles in the 1910s and 1920s, forced some children, particularly children of color who Nelles deemed unintelligent, to undergo forced sterilization even against their parents' objections (Chavez-Garcia 2012).

Under the new juvenile court, girls were treated differently than boys. For example, researcher Mary Odem states, "The juvenile court perpetuated a long-standing gender bias within the criminal justice system, in which women traditionally have been punished for illicit sexual behavior far more harshly than men" (1995, p. 186).

Industrial and Training Schools

As the term "reform school" started to gain a negative reputation, youth prisons were called by other names, such as "industrial schools" or "training schools" (Bernstein 2014). The physical plant of these institutions were not much different than previous versions, but the names were modified to disguise the negative reputation and purpose of the institution.

Youth Correctional Centers

In the 1990s, a short-lived spike in juvenile crime, several high-profile youth crimes, and predictions of a wave of youth "super predators" created a climate that encouraged federal policymakers to dramatically increase the funding for building new youth prisons, renovating existing youth prisons, and expanding the number of youth prison beds through a new crime law, approved by Congress in 1994. At that time, policymakers believed that youth would be safe in youth correctional facilities and that incarceration was the effective response for youth in conflict with the law (Soler et al. 2009). Under the Violent Offender Incarceration and Truth in Sentencing Incentive Grant Program (28 CFR 66.31 (c)), states received tens of millions of dollars (Bureau of Justice Assistance 2012). The U.S. Department of Justice's Bureau of Justice Assistance's final report to Congress on the grant program showed that most states built and expanded juvenile prisons (Bureau of Justice Assistance 2012).

Youth Prisons Today

Signature Features of Youth Prisons

The youth prison model initiated in 1825 and its subsequent variations still embody what we see today. In fact, youth prisons are the signature feature of the juvenile justice system. Former Massachusetts Department of Youth Services Director Jerry Miller effectively sums this up by stating that, "the practice [youth prison] was entrenched fifty years before the creation of juvenile courts," and "from the outset they [juvenile courts] failed to change the pattern of confining juveniles in unspeakable institutions" (Miller 1998, p. 7).

Most youth who are confined in the juvenile justice system today are in facilities of between 50 and 200 beds (Rovner 2015). At least 34 of the nation's largest facilities still in operation today can house more than 200 youth, 19 of which have a design capacity of more than 300, 400, or even 500 beds (Rovner 2015).

There are features of adult prisons that are imitated in youth prisons. To be clear, not every youth prison has all of these features. Youth prisons constructed in the 1990s, some with 1994 crime law federal grant funding, are more apt to have some of the features discussed below (Ryan 2016). These features include the following: (1) Razor wire fence around the perimeter of the prison and sometimes around specific buildings. (2) Concrete or brick buildings that look like adult prisons. (3) Locks everywhere, on cell doors, on hallways, corridors, and wings of the facility, and at the public entrance and exit, and the sally port, where youth enter the facility. (4) Cells with steel doors, sometimes with steel beds and small openings for food or wet cells with a toilet and sink. (5) Isolation or segregation cells, often with no sheets, blankets, or pillows. (6) Hardware that includes handcuffs, shackles, chains, restraints, and restraint chairs. (7) Furniture purchased from correctional catalogs. (8) Dining room tables and seats fastened to the floor with no cushions. (9) Communal bathrooms and showers visible by guards and no privacy. (10) Clothing that consists of prison-like jumpsuits and under garments that are sometimes washed in the general laundry and not returned to the original owner. (11) Generic personal hygiene products purchased (often at a higher cost) from correctional catalogs. Deodorant, body soap, and shampoo are sometimes not available or youth have to buy it themselves, or it is not designed for all skin or hair types. Other products such as body lotion, toothpaste, toothbrushes, and dental floss are sometimes not available at all. (12) Food that is loaded with carbohydrates, grease, and fat with limited access to fresh fruits and vegetables. On occasion, youths' food needs are not provided for, dietary restrictions not accounted for, and almost no culturally relevant and religious holiday food are allowed. Utensils, trays, and cups are all plastic. (13) Glass separates youth from their families and loved ones on visits. (14) Costly phone calls and videoconferencing instead of in-person contact. (15) Security stations with cameras separating staff from youth (Ryan 2016).

Youth and adult correctional agencies sometimes utilize the same architects and construction companies so that youth prisons are built using the same designs as adult prisons and can also be constructed by the same companies (Ryan 2016). There is more flexibility to use the prisons interchangeably if they are similar. Adult-prison-like features in a youth prison seem to fit with the narrative that these are just mini-prisons and that youth are being trained for entrance into the adult criminal justice system and placement in adult prisons.

Racialized Confinement

The juvenile justice system today arguably sustains the features of de facto segregation that were developed during the "Jim Crow" era in the United

States because it is a system where white youth are much more likely to be diverted from the system compared to youth of color. When in the system, white youth are more likely to be placed in alternatives to incarceration (Haywood Burns Institute 2015).

By contrast, youth of color make up the majority of incarcerated youth, comprising nearly 70% of incarcerated youth, according to the latest national data (OJJDP 2019). Black youth are five times more likely to be incarcerated; Native American youth are 3.2 times more likely to be incarcerated; and Latinx youth are two times more likely to be incarcerated than white youth (OJJDP 2019), and these racial and ethnic disparities are increasing (Rovner 2017).

Violence

The abuse of incarcerated youth in the juvenile justice system is well documented in news reports, lawsuits, and studies and by incarcerated youth themselves. Youth face physical abuse, excessive use of force by facility staff, sexual abuse, over-reliance on isolation and restraints, staff on youth violence, and youth on youth violence (see also Egozy and Cox 2017). According to the Federal Bureau of Justice Statistics, one in ten youth in youth prisons have been sexually victimized (Beck 2013). The abuse of incarcerated youth is increasing in the number of states where youth have been abused since 2000, from 22 states to 29 states (Annie E. Casey Foundation 2016). Girls are much more at risk of victimization than boys, especially by sexual assault (Soler et al. 2009).

Federal surveys of incarcerated youth are consistent with these data reports. Surveys showed that 42% of youth were somewhat or very afraid of being physically attacked, 45% said staff used force when they didn't need to, and 30% said staff place youth in solitary confinement or lock them up as discipline (OJJDP 2010).

Horrific Facility Conditions

Incarcerated youth are often subjected to dangerous facility conditions, including physical restraints such as leg irons, chemical restraints, namely pepper spray, and solitary confinement, often referred by correctional staff as "protective custody," "administrative segregation," "seclusion," "isolation," or "room confinement," or by the youth as "the hole" or "the box," among other terms (Ryan 2016). Further, research shows that young people in custody are at high risk of suicide upon entering confinement, and throughout their time there (Annie E. Casey Foundation 2016).

Subpar Education

Incarceration also puts young people further behind in school as education for youth inside of correctional facilities is often not aligned with state curricula or quality standards (Southern Education Foundation 2014). Incarcerated youth are not always able to access courses that would ensure that they can graduate. Youth spend fewer hours in class and are more likely to be taught by uncertified teachers (Korman et al. 2019).

Family Separation

The culture of youth prisons, and the juvenile justice system more generally, functions in a way that excludes the families of young people from engaging in their care. The research shows that family involvement reduces recidivism and that youth thrive best in families (Campaign for Youth Justice 2013). However, geography exacerbates family separation as youth prisons are often geographically located in isolated, rural parts of the state. Under these circumstances, youth have minimal contact with family members and few opportunities to remain engaged with their communities (Justice for Families 2012).

In some states, families are paying for at least some of the daily cost of confinement (Szymanski 2011) and every state permits juvenile courts to impose system costs on youth and their families, and the impact is felt most by youth of color and youth in poverty (Feirman 2016).

Negative Outcomes

By placing youth in correctional settings, research often shows that these placements increase the likelihood that youth will reoffend. For example, recidivism rates following a stay in a youth prison are very high. Within three years of release, around 75% of youth are rearrested and 45–72% are convicted of a new offense (Annie E. Casey Foundation 2011). In some studies, the research demonstrates that incarcerating youth is iatrogenic. In other words, youth are worse off after being incarcerated (Aizer and Doyle 2013; Gatti et al. 2009).

It is well documented that justice system involvement negatively impacts employability and mobility within the job market, especially for youth of color (Center for Law and Social Policy 2016) and incarcerated youth face long-term poor health and mental health outcomes (Barnert et al. 2017).

What the Research Says

However well intentioned the origins of the youth prison or the juvenile court may have been, the youth prison model has arguably become a feeder system, rather than an alternative, to the adult criminal justice system. It is disguised as "rehabilitation" and "treatment" even though it does neither; one study found that youth who spend time in a youth prison are substantially more likely to end up in the adult criminal justice system than (similar) youth were sentenced home on probation (Aizer and Doyle 2013).

While youth incarceration decreased 50% between 2000 and 2015 and 1275 youth facilities have shuttered in the U.S. (Love et al. 2018), almost all states still rely on these costly institutions and the harmful approach they embody. States devote the largest share of their juvenile justice resources to youth prisons at an estimated annual cost of over $5 billion per year (Justice Policy Institute 2014, 2020). If youth prisons were closed and repurposed for non-incarcerative purposes, tens of millions of dollars could be freed up for community-based, non-residential alternatives to youth incarceration, and other youth-serving programs.

With the torrid history of abuse and scandal and the fact that these institutions have poor outcomes for youth, the National Academy of Sciences urges states to stop relying on this model because their analysis found that most youth can be effectively and safely served in their communities (Bonnie et al. 2013).

Movement for Reform

Almost from their beginnings, advocates worked to reform these institutions by improving conditions of confinement for youth. However, at no point was the existence of the youth prison model in jeopardy.

State Investigations and Reports

Early on in the youth prison's lifespan, states undertook investigations, initiated by state legislators and other state officials. For example, in 1876, the Pennsylvania House of Representatives initiated a nine-day investigation into the abuse of children at the Philadelphia House of Refuge. The abuse included lashing children, placing children in solitary confinement, banning play, and sending children to bed without allowing them to eat supper (Kopaczewski 2016).

In Florida, soon after the Florida Industrial School for Boys was established in 1900, there were six state-led investigations in the subsequent 13 years at the facility into abuse of youth at the facility, including whippings, beatings, chaining to walls, shackling, and denial of food and clothing (Kimmerle et al. 2016).

These and other state investigations had little impact on the conditions in the facilities and the treatment of youth in Pennsylvania (Gartner 2019), Florida (Miller and Burch 2017), or elsewhere (Bernstein 2014).

Community-Led Advocacy

In the early 1900s, the Black Child Savers called the juvenile justice system "Jim Crow Juvenile Justice" and argued for equitable treatment for black youth, centering on keeping youth out of adult prisons where they would be exposed to even worse treatment in chain gangs, convict leasing, and the death penalty (Ward 2012). The Black Child Savers were successful at gaining access to youth prisons for black youth but not at ending Jim Crow. From the outset, black youth were segregated into separate and unequal facilities and were subjected to lengthier stays in confinement, less access to educational programs, and limited opportunities upon release (Ward 2012).

Later in the century, in the 1960s, critiques amassed in a number of states from citizen groups such as the Citizens Committee for Children in New York state (Cox 2018). They documented the treatment and conditions children were placed in and issued reports calling for reforms such as the creation of community-based alternatives to incarceration (Cox 2018).

Litigation

Starting in the 1970s, lawyers created legal organizations using litigation to improve conditions of confinement for youth in juvenile (and adult) correctional facilities, such as the Youth Law Center, the National Prison Project of the American Civil Liberties Union, the Juvenile Law Center, and the Prison Law Office of California (McCarthy et al. 2016).

As a result, lawyers filed more than 50 lawsuits on conditions of confinement in youth prisons since 1970 (Annie E. Casey Foundation 2016). This litigation helped to elevate awareness of the egregious conditions youth were exposed to and put substantial pressure on state officials to stop some of the worst abuses such as physical and sexual abuse, chemical and physical restraints, as well as solitary confinement (Bernstein 2014).

In 1980, Congress passed the Civil Rights of Institutionalized Persons Act (CRIPA) to protect the rights of incarcerated people, including youth. The U.S. Department of Justice hired attorneys to focus on the implementation of this law. In the late 1990s, the United States Department of Justice (DOJ) stepped up its actions on improving conditions of confinement in youth prisons and other youth facilities (Bonnie et al. 2013).

Congress hampered litigation by passing the Prison Litigation Reform Act (PLRA) in 1996. The new law made it much more difficult to challenge dangerous practices and conditions in youth prisons (Soler et al. 2009). In some cases, the threat of litigation could force changes in conditions of confinement without having to go to trial (Bonnie et al. 2013). While closure of some youth prisons emerged because litigation raised the profile of the poor conditions in the facility, litigation strategies also arguably reinforced continued reliance on youth prisons as the central approach of the juvenile justice system, using up most of the resources in state budgets for juvenile justice (Bonnie et al. 2013).

Policymakers sometimes responded to the litigation by increasing facility staffing and maintaining institutional funding because the goal of the litigation has been to improve conditions, not to close these institutions (Bonnie et al. 2013). In some cases, the response has been to replace the facility that was the subject of the lawsuit with a new and sometimes larger facility, a situation that occurred in Rhode Island. Litigation was filed in 1971 over poor conditions of youth in the Boys Training School of Rhode Island. After 46 years of litigation, the lawsuit ended with an agreement between the parties to, among other things, construct a new youth prison to meet national standards (ACLU 2017).

State and Local Government-Led Decarceration

In the 1970s when litigation was expanding, another parallel approach emerged in several states: decarceration. The state of Massachusetts was an early pioneer of this new strategy. After a series of studies on the problems at the Massachusetts youth prisons concluded that most youth do not belong in these facilities, and subsequent negative news stories, the state hired Dr. Jerome Miller to run the juvenile justice system (Miller 1998). Initially Miller led with a modest agenda, but after seeing flagrant abuse despite training and support to staff, he changed his mind and decided that youth prisons should be permanently closed and replaced with community-based supports for youth and group home care for youth needing confinement. He overcame political and bureaucratic hurdles to close all seven youth prisons, create alternatives to incarceration, regionalize offices of the Division of Youth Services, remove some kids from state custody altogether and provide group home care for a small number of youth. His strategies included bringing in journalists to see the abysmal conditions, taking incarcerated youth to the state capitol to meet legislators, speaking openly about the brutality inside the institutions, and finally, emptying the institutions which he did not have the authority to close but did anyway (Annie E. Casey Foundation 2012). While his methods were considered unorthodox at the time, they became generally accepted in Massachusetts (Annie E. Casey Foundation 2012) and are viewed now as among the most influential reforms in juvenile justice (Bonnie et al. 2013).

Following in Jerry Miller's footsteps, Peter Edelman, who was appointed in 1975 to run New York's Division for Youth, undertook similar actions to reduce the number of youth in custody and to close some of New York's youth prisons (Cox 2018). Utah took a similar approach during this time as well (Butts and Evans 2011).

Several other states, such as California, Pennsylvania, and Wisconsin incentivized counties to reduce the use of incarceration for young people through fiscal incentives to encourage serving youth in their communities rather than sending youth to youth prisons. Since state governments usually footed 100% of the bill for incarcerating youth in youth prisons, the incentive funding provided a mechanism to keep kids in their communities in community-based programming and a disincentive to send youth to youth prisons. The fiscal incentive strategy was adopted by North Carolina, Ohio, and Oregon in the 1990s and by Michigan, Illinois, and Texas in the 2000s (Butts and Evans 2011).

In the 1990s, the Annie E. Casey Foundation launched the Juvenile Detention Alternatives Initiative (JDAI) to reduce the use of pre-adjudication detention, mainly in counties. Counties led these efforts and included mostly juvenile justice system stakeholders such as judges, juvenile court personnel, detention administrators, prosecutors, and defense lawyers. The initiative has substantially reduced the use of detention and that helped to drain the flow of youth into youth prisons (Annie E. Casey Foundation 2017).

Movement for Reform: Community-Led Decarceration

In the past three decades, formerly incarcerated youth, their families, lawyers, youth advocates, and community members organized campaigns to decarcerate and to shut down select youth prisons in a number of states. Their strategies included policy advocacy, media outreach, coalition building, litigation, and legislative advocacy calling on legislators to engage the following actions:

- National Council on Crime and Delinquency 2014a;
- Remove youth with low-level offenses from youth prisons such as youth with status offenses (e.g., underage drinking);
- Prohibit the incarceration of youth except for youth adjudicated delinquent of the most serious offenses;
- Provide funding streams and incentives to pay for alternatives to incarceration; and
- Require that youth are placed in the least-restrictive environments.

For example, after decades of advocacy and many years of litigation, California advocates achieved the passage of legislation in 2007 to prohibit youth with low-level offenses from being committed to state youth prisons. The bill also allocated substantial resources to the counties to serve youth locally (National Council on Crime and Delinquency 2014b). Advocates sucessfully pressed the state to close eight youth prisons and reduce youth incarceration from more than 10,000 youth in state youth prisons in 1996 to 659 in 2013 (Youth First Initiative 2017). California advocacy strategies focused on documenting horrific facility conditions as well as youths' and families' complaints about those conditions. They shared this information with key legislators to push for legislative hearings, with judges to urge them to use their authority to stop sending youth to youth prisons, and with media outlets to understand the problems with and solutions to youth incarceration (Youth First Initiative 2017).

In the year 2000 in the District of Columbia (Washington DC), a newly formed Mayor's Blue Ribbon Commission on Youth Safety and Juvenile Justice Reform was tasked with examining the strengths and weaknesses of the juvenile justice system and focusing on changes at DC's notorious youth prison, Oak Hill. The prison had been the subject of a lawsuit since 1986 over horrific conditions of confinement and lack of community-based programming for youth.

Washington DC Mayor Tony Williams established a mayoral Blue Ribbon Commission by executive order in 2000. An unorganized group of interested community members started attending commission meetings. They ultimately organized themselves as the Justice for DC Youth Coalition (JDCY) and waged a two-year campaign to inform the commission and move commissioners from leaning toward punitive reforms and toward closing Oak Hill and redirecting the savings toward youth in their communities. The commission's final reports incorporated the coalition's priority recommendations but were then ignored by the mayor and initially by the DC Council. After several more years of concerted advocacy, the DC Council unanimously approved the coalition's legislative proposals and Mayor Williams signed the bills into law in 2004. The new law required the closure of Oak Hill. DC officials finally shuttered Oak Hill in 2009 (Campaign for Youth Justice 2011).

In Louisiana, parents and family members of the youth housed at Tallulah were involved in litigation, led by the Juvenile Justice Project of Louisiana (JJPL), over horrific conditions at the facility. The goals of the litigation were to improve conditions of confinement. However, the families didn't just want improved conditions—they demanded that the facility close for good and that their children come home. Brought together initially as a support group, the families formed Families and Friends of Louisiana's Incarcerated Children (FFLIC) and worked with JJPL to set the goals for and launch the Close Tallulah Now (CTN) campaign (Youth Law Center 2005).

This campaign resulted in the legislature's passage of comprehensive legislation to close Tallulah, reduce youth incarceration, and reinvest the savings in communities in 2003. Tallulah closed in 2004 (Youth First Initiative 2017). After the legislation passed, the campaign used electoral advocacy strategies to ensure that whoever became governor in the upcoming election would stay committed to the legislation and fully implement all of its provisions (Building Blocks for Youth 2005).

Toward Transformation

The movement's advances in the past 20 years have set the stage for the present moment. The current movement has picked up where the previous advocacy left off, building on many of the strategies and drawing on some of the regrets and failures of the earlier generations of advocates (Youth First Initiative 2017).

Bolder Vision

What was envisioned as impossible to achieve even a decade ago is now under consideration. The movement sees the changes that previous generations secured and are now demanding more (Schiraldi 2020). The full abolition of all youth prisons in the country is within sight for several reasons. With the dramatic drop in youth incarceration leaving many facilities substantially under capacity, these events have made it easier for advocates to call into question their very existence. If there are so few children in an institution, why is the institution even needed? Further, much more research exists today about what works with young people in trouble with the law than the past few decades (Soler et al. 2009). That coupled with continued solid public opinion research in favor of closing youth prisons (GBAO Strategies 2019) provides advocates with strong evidence to call for bolder change than in the past, not just improved conditions, reducing the use of incarceration or merely closing one facility. The movement is now challenging the very existence of youth prisons themselves and their advocacy is emboldened with the leadership of current and former youth correctional agency directors (Youth Correctional Leaders for Justice 2019) and prosecutors (Fair and Just Prosecution 2020) who have called for the end of the youth prison model. Twenty years ago, there were a few campaigns that called for the closure of a specific youth prison, such as the Close Tallulah Now campaign, No More Oak Hills campaign, and the Close Cheltenham Now campaign, a campaign to close the notorious Cheltenham youth facility in Maryland that was founded in 1872 as the House of Reformation for Colored Boys (Youth Law Center 2005).

It was unthinkable for these campaigns at that time to call for the closure of all the youth prisons in their state. For example, the Close Tallulah Now campaign made a strategic decision not to advocate for the closing of all youth prisons in Louisiana. Advocates felt it would negatively impact their campaign's credibility and therefore marginalize their campaign and make them less effective (Youth Law Center 2005).

However, campaigns today have bolder goals that have made it more challenging yet more possible to engage a broader constituency. A number of advocates don't want to support a campaign that has limited or mediocre goals; that is, improving conditions of a youth prison or merely reducing the use of incarceration (Oliver 2020). A rally cry like "Close Tallulah Now!" with the Tallulah youth prison as the concrete symbol of all that is wrong with the juvenile justice system is arguably much easier to support than "Reduce Youth Incarceration!" or "Make Tallulah Better!" Even if it will be years before the closure of these facilities is achieved, youth justice advocates, particularly young people who have been impacted by the justice system, have rallied around a bold vision: a vision of a world without incarcerating youth (Youth First Initiative 2019b)

No New Youth Prisons

The movement is now also uncompromising on allowing new but smaller youth prisons (what some call "group homes") to be built. There is a deep division in the youth justice field over abolition, with some juvenile justice agency directors and their allies arguing that smaller youth prisons represent progress (Virginia Department of Juvenile Justice 2020). Others are fighting aggressively against the building of any new youth prisons in any form (Kiefer 2019). Advocates in several jurisdictions have successfully stopped new youth prison construction (Dujardin 2019).

For example, the Virginia Department of Juvenile Justice sought and lost twice in its bid to establish a new youth prison in the Hampton Roads area of Virginia, at the mouth of the Chesapeake Bay, in an area with the state's highest incarceration rate. The RISE for Youth campaign organized against the state, arguing that the state should not devote tens of millions of dollars to build a new youth prison especially when impacted communities don't want it to be built and the state has historically under resourced those communities (Rise for Youth 2017).

Racial Justice

The movement is also front and center in utilizing a racial justice lens in their communications with impacted communities, policymakers, and the media. Previous reform efforts not only didn't lead on racial justice as a lead message in their communications but disguised the messaging on racial and ethnic disparities in poverty and economic language. They did this for fear of upsetting policymakers and turning off would-be allies if they discussed juvenile justice in racial justice terms. Inspired by the Black Lives Matter Movement, the current movement is leading with racial and ethnic disparities as an overarching frame (Youth First Initiative 2019a).

For example, based on an analysis of recent campaigns underway in Virginia and New Jersey, advocates believe the most important elements of a successful campaign are to frame youth justice as a racial justice issue. They seek to ensure that campaigns are housed in organizations that prioritize racial justice and the need to eliminate racial disparities in all communications, leverage relationships with organizations focused on uplifting communities of color to create larger platforms aimed at improving the lives of people of color, identify opportunities where government has failed to address the needs of communities of color and connect those moments to youth justice, invest time and effort in developing leadership of impacted youth supporting them at every stage of the campaign, and work with allies who are willing to step back and support impacted youth and communities' leadership (Youth First Initiative 2019a).

Centering Directly Impacted Youth and Their Families

Organizations like our own, and other youth justice advocacy movements, are centering directly impacted youth, their families, and communities in the work. It seems obvious that people directly impacted by an issue would be at the forefront of the advocacy; that has almost never been the case in the youth justice movement. When youth participate, they are usually asked to tell their personal story, but not invited to put forth recommendations or engage in a meaningful discussion with policymakers (Youth First Initiative 2020).

While not the case in all advocacy efforts, emerging campaigns are putting youth perspectives at the center of what the new youth justice system should be. Campaigns are moving beyond tokenizing youths' participation, that is, inviting youth to tell the story of their experience in the justice system but not participating in policy discussions with decision-makers. In several campaigns, directly impacted youth are leading, with the support of adult allies (Lyons 2020).

For example, in the "Invest in Me Connecticut (CT)" campaign in Connecticut, young people's demands of their policymakers about alternatives to incarceration were drawn from visioning sessions with youth all over the state (Connecticut Juvenile Justice Alliance 2020). The youth participating in this campaign have actively participated in meaningful discussions and provided testimony to the state's Juvenile Justice Planning and Oversight Committee (JJPOC), a joint legislative and executive branch body that convenes all the key policymakers and agencies involved with the juvenile justice system (Connecticut Juvenile Justice Alliance 2019).

Organizing

When impacted communities have engaged in community organizing to build a collective effort toward change, the youth justice system and state and local policymakers have been under intense pressure to respond. For example, the state of New Jersey lost its fight to establish a new youth prison in Newark when the *150 Years Is Enough* campaign organized more than five hundred people to join hands around the outside of the proposed site of a proposed new facility, which was located on the site of the old Pabst Blue Ribbon plant that had been deemed a toxic waste site by the state (Kiefer 2019). After the rally, the Newark mayor withdrew his support of the project (Carter 2019).

Current Challenges

Reform Versus Abolition

Advocates who are working on the issue of youth prisons generally find themselves taking one of two positions: reform the system or abolish it entirely. Reformers believe that prisons will never be eliminated and that strategies must focus on alleviating the harm to the remaining youth who are still incarcerated (Center for Children's Law and Policy 2020). Similar to the early reformers, these advocates focus on fixing the current youth prison model by improving conditions of confinement. This includes efforts to stop solitary confinement of youth and end the use of pepper spray and other chemical restraints, as well as to improve educational and mental health services, and engage in more humane and uniform treatment of youth (Center for Children's Law and Policy 2020).

Other reform-minded advocates, fueled by the premise that most youth don't need incarceration, are working on reducing the use of incarceration for the vast majority of, but not all, youth (Shoenberg 2019). These efforts mainly focus on changing state laws to remove certain categories of youth (e.g., youth adjudicated delinquent of low-level offenses, youth with status offenses, or youth who have committed probation violations) from incarceration altogether. These efforts are focused on reserving incarceration only for youth adjudicated delinquent of the most serious and violent offenses, or reducing the length of stay that youth can be placed in a youth prison (National Council on Crime and Delinquency 2014a).

Abolitionist advocates, assessing the weight of evidence on the ineffectiveness of the youth prison model as a whole, believe that youth prisons cannot be reformed or fixed, and are actively working to fully dismantle the youth prison model and transform the youth justice system so that youth can be supported at home in their communities, rather than through incarceration (Young Women's Freedom Center 2019). While the movement for abolition is gaining traction and can envision the full abolition of youth prisons within the next decade, challenges persist.

Obstacles to Closing Youth Prisons

Even with the staggering amount of research showing how youth prisons don't work, closing youth prisons isn't as simple or as easy as some would acknowledge. The economies of whole towns (many of which are rural) can be wrapped around these facilities. This is especially true since many of the youth prisons today were established more than a century ago and some almost two centuries ago, with some in the same locations and even in the same buildings, and have become like the company town where they are the largest employer in the area and everyone in the community is connected to the facility in one way or another (King et al. 2003).

Labor unions that represent youth prison guards and other staff have put up opposition to youth prison closures. Labor unions are concerned about major reductions in memberships of their unions. They can mobilize quickly to engage their lawmakers to stop the prisons from being shut down (Cox 2018; Ridgeway and Casella 2013).

While the politics of this are challenging, to overcome this, we have considered new strategies to defang opposition by organized labor. To deal with this opposition of job loss and reductions in labor union membership, we have considered the possibility of making an accommodation with the labor unions that represent youth facility staff that exchanges reducing labor jobs in the corrections sector for unionization in community-based nonprofit programs, which nonprofits generally oppose (Capulong 2006). It may also mean bringing in a state's Department of Labor to help with worker dislocation from youth prison closures and by allocating resources in the state's economic development budget to help local economy with their economic transition. This could potentially mute the opposition to youth prison closures as the front line union workers may be able to get other jobs, which is often their priority over organized labor's concerns about their particular membership declines (Ridgeway and Casella 2013).

Some unions publicly state that they want to end mass incarceration (Berkeley 2016). But in practice, it is a different story. Some members oppose facility closures because they believe it impacts their members' jobs, citing concerns that the juvenile justice system will become privatized (Ridgeway and Casella 2013). Journalist and activist James Kilgore sums this up best, "Organized labor can either continue to fight for the narrow job interests of its members or promote the continued mass incarceration of working class people of color" (2013, p. 14).

Repurposing Closed Youth Prisons

Closed and vacant youth prisons remain a major concern. If they are not torn down or repurposed, these facilities could easily be reopened to house youth in the juvenile justice system again or to house other populations, such as adults or immigrant detainees (Egan 2019). The movement to end youth prisons has yet to really tackle this issue, or to collaborate effectively with immigrant rights advocates or allies in the criminal justice reform space.

For example, Virginia's policymakers have discussed reopening the Beaumont youth prison, which had been closed less than a year before as it had stood vacant with no plan to demolish or repurpose it. The facility is currently vacant but that could change on a moment's notice (McFarland 2017). In a similar vein, the Connecticut Juvenile Training School (CJTS) is currently being considered for reopening as other alternatives have not been created to support youth previously removed from the facility. It lies vacant too, with no current plans to repurpose (Kovner 2018). These two empty facilities could end up like Michigan's youth prison which was reopened in May 2019 by the private company, the Geo Group, as a facility for "non-citizen criminal aliens" (Egan 2019).

Repurposing youth prisons needs to be part of the policy decision-making process much earlier in the process when policymakers are discussing the closure of youth prisons. There are numerous examples of repurposed youth prisons that offer policymakers innovative options, such as a juvenile detention center that was repurposed as a teen community center in Apache County,

Arizona. The center provides young people with a space to hang out, a music room, free access to the internet, and other programs (Love et al. 2018).

Ensuring the Reinvestment in Community-Based Programs

Moving the money out of youth prisons and into supporting youth in their communities has proven to be another major hurdle. It is not a given that when a youth prison closes, that there will be reinvestment. This involves a specific, intentional strategy up front that requires engaging with budget and appropriations policymakers, not an area of expertise of youth justice advocates (Impact Justice 2019).

Policymakers appear more willing to invest hundreds of thousands of dollars in incarceration, but not as willing to invest even a fraction of that money in youth in their communities. Moving the money out of incarceration, when that can get political support, is one step. Those funds, however, then can become a free-for-all, with policymakers not necessarily then reinvesting those resources in youth programs (National Council on Crime and Delinquency 2014b). To overcome this, we have found that advocates must maintain a vocal and robust constituency. Otherwise, funds will evaporate or just be funneled back into ineffective approaches that are a poor substitute for community-based programs such as community supervision, electronic monitoring, probation costs, and so on (National Council on Crime and Delinquency 2014b).

Advocates also acknowledge that more funds are needed, beyond what can be taken out of closed youth prisons. And some advocates question the strategy of tying youth prison closures too closely with reinvestment and instead suggest a decoupling of closures with reinvestment so that reinvestment is not contingent on closing a youth prison. Even if these strategies stay connected, other funding sources need to be identified and tapped (Harvell et al. 2019).

With limited investment happening in the youth justice space, there are few examples to promote in advocacy efforts. This has meant that we need to generate new creative ideas such as the California youth justice investment fund. The California legislature signed into law the fund as part of its 2018–2019 budget, allocating $37 million to support youth in staying out of the justice system. It is the first state funded investment specifically dedicated for this purpose in California (Harvell et al. 2019).

Impacted Communities' Perspective

Another major challenge is ensuring that policymakers do not ignore input from communities most impacted by incarceration, especially formerly incarcerated persons. This means expanding the capacity of the campaigns to organize, recruit, and hire more organizers and provide organizing training and support so that impacted communities built their power base and thus can't be ignored by policymakers.

For example, for two years, directly impacted communities, especially children of color and their families, in Wisconsin successfully pressured then Governor Walker to change his strategy from trying to fix the Lincoln Hills youth prison to support its closure. However, when it came time to write the implementing legislation, the governor's office and a small group of mostly white, male legislators wrote the bill without consulting impacted communities. The bill proposed closing Lincoln Hills but also included funding for counties to build new smaller youth prisons all over the state and did not include any resources for community-based programs. This provision served as a poison pill for the legislation, assuring the impacted communities' opposition to the legislation and creating division within the movement as a number of attorneys in the state supported the legislation because of its closure provision (Youth Justice Milwaukee 2018).

Authentic Youth Partnership

Engaging and partnering with youth, especially directly impacted youth, is challenging even when working with strong campaign allies. The movement has a way to go to ensure youth can participate in and take on meaningful leadership roles in the campaigns. An exciting example is San Francisco's Reimagine Justice campaign, a project of the Young Women's Freedom Center, which is being led by young people with previous involvement in the juvenile justice system, including those who have experienced incarceration (Young Women's Freedom Center 2019). This is one of the first successful advocacy campaigns where directly impacted youth are leading the strategy, deciding what policy platform to advance, and driving discussions with policymakers. The campaign has obtained the support of the San Francisco Board of Supervisors to close San Francisco's juvenile hall (i.e., pre-adjudication detention facility) by 2021 (Tucker and Palomino 2019).

Maintaining Momentum

Finally, the ultimate question is whether the movement can maintain its momentum. To fully dismantle the youth prison model, sustained advocacy is crucial to build political power in impacted communities to ensure youth prison closures and reinvestment and, when these do happen, to hold policymakers accountable for effective implementation. To make that happen, more people will be needed who are willing to lead and continue to push back on a deeply entrenched system. It also requires ensuring that there are robust resources for the advocacy needed to overcome the opposition that the movement will face as it seeks to dislodge youth prisons from the landscape. Without that, few advocates will take this on.

Conclusion

With the growing recognition that the youth prison model has been thoroughly discredited by the extensive research as a flawed and harmful approach, the youth justice movement is gaining support and traction on the need for bold change to transform the youth justice system. The movement is creating the pressure on policymakers and, in some jurisdictions, we are seeing youth prison closures. While policymakers are willing to invest more than $100,000 per year to incarcerate a young person (Justice Policy Institute 2014, 2020) they don't show an equal interest in investing even a fraction of these resources to serve youth in their communities. We have yet to create the political will to invest in youth in their communities. To move toward transformation, the movement must be sustained and supported.

References

ACLU. (2017). *Inmates of the Rhode Island Training School for youth v. piccola*. American Civil Liberties Union. Retrieved January 6, 2020, from https://www.aclu.org/cases/inmates-rhode-island-training-school-youth-v-piccola.
Advocacy. (2019). Young women's freedom center. Retrieved September 5, 2019, from https://www.youngwomenfree.org/what-we-do/advocacy.
Aizer, A., & Doyle, J. (2013). Juvenile incarceration, human capital and future crime: Evidence from randomly assigned judges. *Quarterly Journal of Economics, 130*(2), 759–803.

Annie E. Casey Foundation. (2011). *No Place for Kids: The Case for Reducing Juvenile Incarceration.* Baltimore: Annie E. Casey Foundation.

Annie E. Casey Foundation. (2012). *Closing Massachusetts' training schools: Reflections forty years later.* Baltimore: Annie E. Casey Foundation. Retrieved from https://www.aecf.org/resources/closing-massachusetts-training-schools/.

Annie E. Casey Foundation. (2016). *Maltreatment of youth in U.S. juvenile corrections facilities: An update on juvenile correctional facility violence.* Baltimore: Annie E. Casey Foundation.

Annie E. Casey Foundation. (2017). *JDAI at 25: Insights from the annual results reports.* Baltimore: Annie E. Casey Foundation.

Barnert, E., Dudovitz, R., Nelson, B., Coker, R., Biely, C., & Chung, P. (2017). How does incarcerating young people affect their adult health outcomes? *Pediatrics, 139*(2).

Beck, A. (2013). *Sexual victimization in juvenile facilities reported by youth.* Washington, DC: Bureau of Justice Statistics. Retrieved September 5, 2019, from https://www.bjs.gov/index.cfm?ty=pbdetail&iid=4656.

Berkeley, C. (2016). Let's get serious about mass incarceration. *AFL-CIO* [online]. Retrieved September 5, 2019, from https://aflcio.org/2016/4/5/lets-get-serious-about-mass-incarceration.

Bernstein, N. (2014). *Burning down the house: The end of juvenile prison.* New York: The New Press.

Bonnie, R., et al. (2013). *Reforming juvenile justice: A developmental approach.* Washington, DC: The National Academies Press.

Building Blocks for Youth. (2005). *No Turning Back.* Washington, DC.

Bureau of Justice Assistance. (2012). *Report to congress: Violent offender incarceration and truth-in-sentencing incentive formula grant program.* Washington, D.C.

Butts, J., & Evans, D. (2011). *Resolution, reinvestment, and realignment: Three strategies for changing juvenile justice.* New York: Research and Evaluation Center, John Jay College of Criminal Justice, City University of New York.

Campaign for Youth Justice. (2011). *Notorious to notable: The crucial role of the philanthropic community in transforming the juvenile justice system in Washington, D.C.* Washington, DC: Campaign for Youth Justice.

Campaign for Youth Justice. (2013). *Family comes first.* Washington, DC: Campaign for Youth Justice.

Capulong, E. R. (2006). Which side are you on? Unionization in social service nonprofits. *City University of New York Law Review, 9*, 373. https://doi.org/10.31641/clr090209.

Carter, B. (2019). No new jails in my city, despite what you think you heard, N.J. mayor says. *NJ.com*, 19 April [online]. Retrieved September 5, 2019, from https://www.nj.com/essex/2019/04/no-new-jails-in-my-city-despite-what-you-think-you-heard-nj-mayor-says.html.

Center for Children's Law and Policy. *Improving Conditions of Confinement*. Retrieved August 14, 2020, from https://www.cclp.org/improving-conditions-of-confinement/.

Center for Law and Social Policy. (2016). *Realizing youth justice: Advancing education and employment through public policy and investment*. Washington, DC: Center for Law and Social Policy.

Chavez-Garcia, M. (2012). *States of delinquency: Race and science in the making of California's juvenile justice system*. Berkeley, CA: University of California Press.

Connecticut Juvenile Justice Alliance. (2019). *Legislative priorities*. Retrieved September 5, 2019, from https://www.ctjja.org/2019-legislative-priorities.

Connecticut Juvenile Justice Alliance. (2020). *Ending the criminalization of youth one investment at a time*. Retrieved August 14, 2020, from https://static1.squarespace.com/static/5b8413b445776e48dcfec417/t/5ef33ed080c2046beb6c0723/1592999680513/VSP+-+Ending+the+Criminalization+of+Youth%2C+One+Investment+at+a+Time.pdf.

Cox, A. (2018). *Trapped in a vice: The consequences of confinement for young people*. New Brunswick, NJ: Rutgers University Press.

Dujardin, P. (2019). Isle of wight board of supervisors rejects new juvenile jail near Windsor. *The Daily Press*, 18 April [online]. Retrieved August 14, 2020, from https://www.dailypress.com/news/isle-of-wight/dp-nws-windsor-juvenile-jail-20190418-story.html.

Egan, P. (2019). Private company to reopen prison near Baldwin to house 'criminal aliens'. *Detroit Free Press*, 2 May [online]. Retrieved August 14, 2020, from https://www.freep.com/story/news/local/michigan/2019/05/02/baldwin-michigan-prison-criminal-aliens/3653929002/.

Egozy, O., & Cox, A. (2017). Youth facilities and violence: An overview. In P. Sturney (Ed.), *The Wiley handbook of violence and aggression*. Wiley-Blackwell.

Fair and Just Prosecution. (2020). Joint statement by Fair and Just Prosecution and youth correctional leaders for justice on closing youth prisons. Retrieved August 14, 2020, from https://fairandjustprosecution.org/wp-content/uploads/2020/07/Joint-Statement-on-Youth-Prisons-FINAL.pdf.

Feirman, J. (2016). *Debtors' prisons for kids? The high cost of fees and fines in the juvenile justice system*. Juvenile Law Center. Retrieved August 14, 2020, from https://debtorsprison.jlc.org/documents/JLC-Debtors-Prison.pdf.

Fletcher, C. (2020). *The house of the Good Shepherd*. Glover Park History. Retrieved August 14, 2020, from https://gloverparkhistory.com/estates-and-farms/burleith/the-house-of-the-good-shepherd/.

Gartner, L. (2019). Beaten, then silenced: At the oldest U.S. Reform school for boys, leaders of the prestigious Glen Mills Schools in Pennsylvania have hidden a long history of violence. *The Philadelphia Inquirer*, 20 February [online]. Retrieved August 14, 2020, from https://www.inquirer.com/crime/a/glen-mills-schools-pa-abuse-juvenile-investigation-20190220.html.

Gatti, U., Tremblay, R. E., & Vitaro, F. (2009). Iatrogenic effect of juvenile justice. *The Journal of Child Psychology and Psychiatry, 50*, 991–998.

GBAO Strategies. (2019). *New poll results on youth justice reform*.Retrieved September 5, 2019, from https://backend.nokidsinprison.org/wp-content/uploads/2019/03/Youth-First-National-Poll-Memo-March-2019-Final-Version-V2.pdf.

Harvell, S., et al. (2019). *Promoting a new direction for youth justice: Strategies to fund a community-based continuum of care and opportunity*. Washington, DC: Urban Institute.

Haywood Burns Institute. (2015). *Unbalanced Juvenile Justice*. Oakland, CA.

Impact Justice. (2019). *Nothing good happens in there: Closing and repurposing youth detention facilities in California*. Retrieved September 5, 2019, from https://impactjustice.org/resources/nothing-good-happens-in-there-closing-and-repurposing-youth-detention-facilities-in-california/.

Jones, M., & Record, L. (2014). Magdalene laundries: The first prisons for women in the United States. *Journal of the Indiana Academy of the Social Sciences, 17*(1), Article 12. Retrieved from https://digitalcommons.butler.edu/jiass/vol17/iss1/12.

Justice for Families. (2012). *Families unlocking futures: Solutions to the crisis in juvenile justice*. Retrieved from www.justice4families.org/media/Families_Unlocking_FuturesFULLNOEMBARGO.pdf.

Justice Policy Institute. (2014). *Sticker shock*. Washington, DC.

Justice Policy Institute. (2020). *Sticker shock*. Washington, DC.

Kiefer, E. (2019). Teens rally in Newark: 'Build up kids, not prisons: New Jersey should close its youth prisons and reinvest the money in recovery, education and rehabilitation, these students say.' *NJ.com*, 20 May [online]. Retrieved September 5, 2019, from https://patch.com/new-jersey/newarknj/teens-rally-newark-build-kids-not-prisons.

Kilgore, J. (2013). Mass incarceration and working class interests: Which side are the unions on? *Labor Studies Journal, 37*(4), 356–372.

Kimmerle, E., Wells, E., & Antoinette, J. (2016). *Report on the investigation into the deaths and burials of youth at the former Arthur G. Dozier School for boys in Marianna, Florida*. FL Institute for Forensic Anthropology & Applied Sciences, University of South Florida. Retrieved September 5, 2019, from http://mediad.publicbroadcasting.net/p/wusf/files/201601/usf-final-dozier-summary-2016.pdf.

King, R. S., Mauer, M., & Huling, T. (2003). *Big prisons, small towns: Prison economics in rural America*. Washington, DC: The Sentencing Project.

Kopaczewski, J. (2016). *House of refuge*. The Encyclopedia of Greater Philadelphia [online]. Retrieved January 7, 2020, from https://philadelphiaencyclopedia.org/archive/house-of-refuge/.

Korman, T. N., Marchitello, M., & Brand, A. (2019). *Patterns and trends in educational opportunity for students in juvenile justice schools*. Bellweather Education Partners [online]. Retrieved September 5, 2019, from https://bellwethereducation.org/sites/default/files/Patterns%20and%20Trends%20in%20Educational%20

Opportunity%20for%20Students%20in%20Juvenile%20Justice%20Schools_Bellwether.pdf.

Kovner, J. (2018). Connecticut juvenile training school closes. *The Hartford Courant*. 12 April [online]. Retrieved August 14, 2020, from https://www.courant.com/news/connecticut/hc-cjts-closes-20180412-story.html.

Love, H., et al. (2018). *Transforming closed youth prisons*. Washington, DC: Urban Institute.

Lyons, K. (2020). New report on juvenile justice features potential solutions from kids with firsthand experience. *Connecticut Mirror*. 25 June [online]. Retrieved August 14, 2020, from https://ctmirror.org/2020/06/25/new-report-on-juvenile-justice-features-potential-solutions-from-kids-with-firsthand-experience/.

McCarthy, P., Schiraldi, V., & Shark, M. (2016). *The future of youth justice: A community-based alternative to the youth prison model*. Washington, DC: National Institute of Justice.

McFarland, L. (2017). Beaumont Correctional Center in Powhatan closes its' doors. *Richmond Times Dispatch* [online], 22 June. Retrieved August 14, 2020, from https://richmond.com/news/local/central-virginia/powhatan/powhatan-today/beaumont-correctional-in-powhatan-county-closes-its-doors/article_235360fa-57bb-11e7-aabe-27b0eec0a0bb.html.

Meyer, Q. (2019). How Chicago women created the world's first juvenile justice system. *WBEZ 91.5*, 13 May [online]. Retrieved January 5, 2020, from https://www.npr.org/local/309/2019/05/13/722351881/how-chicago-women-created-the-world-s-first-juvenile-justice-system.

Miller, J. (1998). *Last one over the wall: The Massachusetts experiment in closing reform schools* (2nd ed.). Columbus, OH: Ohio State University Press.

Miller, C., & Burch, A. (2017). Florida's juvenile justice system's 'Fight Clubs' exposed. *The Miami Herald*, 10 October [online]. Retrieved September 5, 2019, from https://www.miamiherald.com/news/special-reports/florida-prisons/article177884886.html.

National Council on Crime and Delinquency. (2014a). *Stakeholders' views on the movement to reduce youth incarceration*. Oakland, CA.

National Council on Crime and Delinquency. (2014b). *Using bills & budgets to further reduce youth incarceration*. Oakland, CA.

Nellis, A. (2016). *A return to justice: Rethinking our approach to juveniles in the system*. Lanham, MD: Rowman and Littlefield Publishing Group, Inc.

Odem, M. (1995). *Delinquent daughters: Protecting and policing adolescent female sexuality in the United States, 1885–1920*. Chapel Hill, NC: University of North Carolina Press.

OJJDP. (2010). *Conditions of confinement: Findings from the survey of youth in residential placement* (p. 2010). Washington, DC: Office of Juvenile Justice & Delinquency Prevention.

OJJDP. (2019). *Easy access to the census of juveniles in residential placement*. Washington, DC: Office of Juvenile Justice & Delinquency Prevention [online]. Retrieved September 5, 2019, from https://www.ojjdp.gov/ojstatbb/ezacjrp/.

Oliver, N. (2020). King County's new youth jail and the false promise of 'zero youth detention.' *Crosscut*, 11 February [online]. Retrieved August 14, 2020, from https://crosscut.com/2020/02/king-countys-new-youth-jail-and-false-promise-zero-youth-detention.

Packard, F. A. & African American Pamphlet Collection. (1841). *Report on the practicability and necessity of a house of refuge for coloured juvenile delinquents in Philadelphia*. Philadelphia: Brown, Bicking & Guilbert, Printers. Retrieved from the Library of Congress https://www.loc.gov/item/92838004/.

Pickett, R. S. (1969). *House of refuge: Origins of juvenile reform in New York State, 1815–1857*. Syracuse, NY: Syracuse University Press.

Platt, A. (2009). *The child savers: The invention of delinquency*. New Brunswick, NJ: Rutgers University Press.

Ridgeway, J., & Casella, J. (2013). Big labor's lock 'em up mentality: How otherwise progressive unions stand in the way of a more humane correctional system. *Mother Jones*, 22 February.

RISE for Youth. (2017). *Rise for youth applauds vote against youth prison*. Retrieved January 6, 2020, from https://www.riseforyouth.org/2017/10/13/rise-youth-applauds-vote-youth-prison/.

Rovner, J. (2015). *Declines in youth commitments and facilities in the 21st century*. Washington, DC: The Sentencing Project.

Rovner, J. (2017). *Still increase in racial disparities in juvenile justice*. Washington, DC: The Sentencing Project. Retrieved January 6, 2020, from https://www.sentencingproject.org/news/still-increase-racial-disparities-juvenile-justice/

Ryan, L. (2016). What is a youth prison? *Medium* [online]. Retrieved January 6, 2020, from https://medium.com/@LizRyanYJ/locked-up-b22651d203e1.

Ryan, L. (2020). An historical timeline of youth prisons. *Medium* [online]. Retrieved August 14, 2020, from https://medium.com/@LizRyanYJ/an-historical-timeline-of-youth-prisons-a7e655e46d3.

Schiraldi, V. (2020). *Can we eliminate the youth prisons? (and what should we replace it with?)*. The Square One Project [online]. Retrieved June 17, 2020, from https://squareonejustice.org/wp-content/uploads/2020/06/CJLJ8234-Square-One-Youth-Prisons-Paper-200616-WEB.pdf.

Shepherd, R. (1999). The juvenile court at 100: A look back. *Juvenile Justice*, 6(2), 13–21.

Shoenberg, D. (2019). *How state reform efforts are transforming juvenile justice: Agency leaders share the history and potential of research-driven policy change*. Pew Public Safety Performance Project [online]. Retrieved January 6, 2020, from https://www.pewtrusts.org/en/research-and-analysis/articles/2019/11/26/how-state-reform-efforts-are-transforming-juvenile-justice.

Soler, M., Shoenberg, D., & Schindler, M. (2009). Juvenile justice: Lessons for a new era. *Georgetown Journal on Poverty Law & Policy, XVI*(Symposium Issue 2009), 483.

Southern Education Foundation. (2014). *Just learning*. Atlanta, GA: Southern Education Fund.

Szymanski, L. (2011). *Can parents ever be obligated for the support of their institutionalized delinquent children?* Pittsburgh, PA: National Center for Juvenile Justice.

Teachout, T. (2009). *Pops: A life of Louis Armstrong*. Boston: Houghton Mifflin Harcourt.

The International Prison Congress: Penal and Reformatory Institutions of Maryland. (1872, July 25). ProQuest Historical Newspapers: *The Baltimore Sun*, p. 4.

Tucker, J., & Palomino, J. (2019). In historic move, SF Supervisors vote to close juvenile hall by end of 2021. *The San Francisco Chronicle*, 4 June. Retrieved August 14, 2020, from https://www.sfchronicle.com/bayarea/article/Closure-of-SF-s-juvenile-hall-less-than-one-13936500.php.

United Nations. (2019). *Global study on children deprived of liberty*. New York, NY.

Virginia Department of Juvenile Justice. (2020). *DJJ strategic framework*, 2020. Richmond, VA: Virginia Department of Juvenile Justice. Retrieved August 14, 2020, from http://www.djj.virginia.gov/pages/about-djj/djj-framework.htm.

Ward, G. (2012). *The black child savers: Racial democracy and juvenile justice*. Chicago, IL: University of Chicago Press.

Whitehead, C. (2019). *The nickel boys*. New York: Doubleday.

Youth Correctional Leaders for Justice. (2019). Statement on ending youth prisons. Retrieved January 6, 2020, from https://yclj.org/statement.

Youth First Initiative. (2017). *Breaking down the wall* [online]. Retrieved September 5, 2019, from https://www.nokidsinprison.org/solutions/breaking-down-the-walls.

Youth First Initiative. (2019a). *Racial justice at the core*. Washington, DC: Youth First Initiative.

Youth First Initiative. (2019b). *A united vision for a world without youth prisons*. Washington, DC: Cities United and Youth First Initiative.

Youth First Initiative. (2020). *Covering youth justice*. Washington, DC: Youth First Initiative.

Youth Justice Milwaukee. (2018). WI senate must improve youth prisons bill [online]. Retrieved September 5, 2019, from https://www.youthjusticemke.org/2018/02/28/youth-justice-milwaukee-wi-senate-must-improve-youth-prisons-bill/.

Youth Law Center. (2005). *No turning back* [online]. Retrieved September 5, 2019, from https://www.cclp.org/wp-content/uploads/2016/07/13-ntb_fullreport.pdf.

27

Critical Reflections on Education for Children in Youth Justice Custody

Caroline Lanskey

Introduction

Education is often cited by politicians, policy makers and researchers as having an important role to play in the prevention of crime by children (Farrington and Welsh 2007; Public Health England 2019). It is seen as a means to provide children with the qualifications, skills and capacities they may need for adult life (Ministry of Justice 2013); as a vehicle for moral reform (Learning and Skills Network 2009) and as a useful activity in itself for keeping children away from environments where they might become involved in crime (Bell et al. 2018). A growing body of research in education in youth custodial settings is directed at understanding the impact of the academic, vocational and 'offending behaviour' programmes that are run with such objectives in mind. They investigate the extent to which programmes raise children's skill levels and often also the impact on children's recidivism rates (e.g. Hurry et al. 2005) These evaluations are part of the 'what works' research field in criminology which aspire to identify "how best to educate youth in correctional settings" (Steele et al. 2016, p. 66).

C. Lanskey (✉)
University of Cambridge Institute of Criminology, Cambridge, UK
e-mail: cml29@cam.ac.uk

While such evaluations provide useful insights into the extent to which specific programmes, for example, reading or mathematic courses, are successful in developing particular abilities of children in custody, as a means to establish the 'best' way to educate children in correctional settings, they are limited in three ways: first, they can engage to only a limited extent with the wider societal, political and structural influences on educational provision; second, their programme-oriented focus allows only a partial view of the formal and informal learning that takes place in a secure setting; and, third, they confine normative considerations to the technical efficacy of the programme and do not address broader issues of equity and entitlement in the provision of education for children in secure settings.

In this chapter I argue that alongside such evaluations a larger research agenda needs to be developed which addresses these three limitations. I illustrate these arguments by means of a case-study analysis of educational provision[1] in secure settings in England and Wales which draws from research studies, policies and inspection reports. The chapter is divided into three parts: the first provides some background contextual detail on the system of education in custody in England and Wales and presents fieldwork observations of education in practice which illustrate some key dynamics which shape teaching and learning in secure settings for children. The second part introduces the analytical framework of learning cultures (Hodkinson et al. 2007, 2008) and illustrates how its multi-layered perspective can be applied to an analysis of education in secure settings in England and Wales; the third part discusses normative insights that arise from this holistic perspective on education in secure settings.

Part I: Education for Children in Custody in England and Wales

Political interest in the provision of education for children sentenced to custody in England and Wales has been evident since the middle of the nineteenth century when industrial and reformatory schools for the 'perishing and dangerous classes' were introduced. At the time a group of social campaigners, politicians, prison governors and chaplains argued for a stronger focus on the education of children in custody (comprising religious instruction and

---

[1] The term 'education' is used differently across different settings within the secure estate in England and Wales. In this chapter I use 'education' to refer to the formal programme of teaching and learning within a secure setting for children which can comprise academic, vocational and 'offending behaviour' programmes. This formal provision is contrasted with informal learning that occurs within the setting.

vocational training) for they believed it to be a vehicle for moral reform (e.g. Carpenter 1851). Since the emergence of a distinct youth justice system at the beginning of the twentieth century, various models of youth custody have highlighted their educational or training function: reformatory schools, borstals, approved schools, community homes with education, secure training centres. However policy interests in education for children in custody have at times been sidelined as other reform approaches gained greater favour. Examples include the 'short sharp shock' deterrence-oriented approach of Detention Centres or the medicalised treatment approach of Secure Units (Lanskey 2018). Indeed, a legal entitlement to education for children in custody was not established until the Apprenticeships, Skills, Children and Learning Act in 2009.

In recent years, education for children in custody has again emerged as a core policy interest in England and Wales. In 2013, the Minister of Justice announced that the government intended to "transform" youth custody by "placing education at the heart of detention" (Ministry of Justice 2013). He proposed the establishment of a new purpose-built secure college which would have a fully equipped education facility (Ministry of Justice 2014). This proposal was modified following a further review of the youth justice system, and plans were published to open a secure school instead (Taylor 2016; HM Government 2018). This is due to open in 2022 (Ministry of Justice, 2020).

Currently, the secure estate in England and Wales comprises three types of setting: secure children's homes (SCHs), secure training centres (STCs) and young offender institutions (YOIs). Secure children's homes are for children aged between 10 and 14 years. All are run by local councils, apart from one which is run by a charity (Ofsted 2020a). They accommodate between 8 and 40 children who have been sentenced or remanded to custody and others who are under the care of the local authority for welfare reasons. STCs are run by private companies. They typically hold between 50 and 80 children aged between 10 and 17 years who live in residential units in groups of 5 to 8. YOIs are run by HM Prison Service or are contracted out to private companies. They accommodate young men between the ages of 15 and 21 years who live in 'wings' of between 30 and 60. Under-18s are housed separately from the over-18s. The proposed secure school will be for children aged 12–17 years. It will be managed by a private educational organisation (HM Government 2018).

During 2018–2019 there were on average 860 children under 18 in youth justice custody, 72% sentenced and 28% remanded by the courts. YOIs held 73%, STCs 17% and SCHs 10% of this population. The parameters for educational provision in each of these three settings vary. There are separate legislative frameworks developed for the operation of each (e.g. The Young Offender Institution Rules (2000), The Secure Training Centre Rules (1998) and The Children's Homes (England) Regulations (2015)). The secure school will operate under a new structure as a Secure Academy Trust.

YOIs contract out their education provision, often to further education providers; STCs employ teachers directly as do SCHs if they run education on the premises. Children in SCHs receive between 25 and 30 hours of education a week. In STCs a minimum of 25 hours of education a week is usually required (The Secure Training Centre Rules 1998) although there has recently been an amendment to relax this condition during the coronavirus period (The Secure Training Centre (Coronavirus) (Amendment) Rules 2020). In YOIs, the mandatory requirement for children is 15 hours per week (The Young Offender Institution Rules 2000).

My first observations of education for children in custody were in young offender institutions and secure training centres in 2007/8 during a research evaluation of a training programme for staff in secure settings for children in England and Wales (Lanskey et al. 2008). My initial visits were to a state-run young offender institution (YOI) for young men, most of whom were on remand. Everyone under 16 years of age was required to attend education, 16–18-year-olds could opt for vocational 'workshops' instead, which were not defined as 'education' in these settings. The education wing was a single corridor with rooms to each side. Young men in groups of six or seven were more or less involved in a range of activities, composing music, playing 'hangman', copying down recipes for a practical cookery activity later that week. Some groups were absorbed in activities, others were reluctant to engage. There was a volatility to the atmosphere; petty annoyances between children and between children and staff, something going missing, or a minor show of resistance—leaning back on a chair after being told not to—could quickly turn into something more—a fight, a forceful removal of a young person back to their cell. Few children stayed in the YOI for long and none were studying for the qualifications their peers in school would have been studying for.

The second secure setting I visited was an STC for male and female 'trainees' between the ages of 10 and 17 years. In contrast to the YOI it had more the feel of a residential school than a prison although children's bedrooms were accessed via heavy metal doors, dining room tables and chairs were bolted to the floor, and windows could not be opened. Education was the full-time activity for all children there. It took place in a modern classroom block and there was a broader range of subjects taught than in the YOI. Educational groups were determined by the residential unit a young person was placed on; therefore levels of academic ability ranged within them.

Some activities were richer than others in terms of their learning content: an afternoon could be spent drawing a magic mushroom in a Personal and Social Health Education class or on an outdoor hike as part of a Duke of Edinburgh expedition. Access to educational programmes varied depending on a young person's behaviour, assessed risk level and length of time at the STC. Only a few children were able to continue with the subjects they had been studying in school or were resident long enough to study for the qualifications they might have gained in school. As in the YOI there were moments of volatility—order could disintegrate at the end of the lesson as children ran over desks to the locked classroom door to be let out. Despite the superficially more welfare-oriented appearance of the STC environment, conflict between children and staff was common, and children could be made to comply with pain-inducing force.

At the same time, in both education settings there was much good will amongst staff to help the children in residence. They recognised that children's earlier educational experiences were frequently negative and inconsistent and expressed a desire to work around the limitations of the custodial environment and to make a difference in their lives. In the short term there were opportunities for personal growth—an hour of intensive portrait drawing with a volunteer artist, an animated discussion on politics with the citizenship teacher. Some children, who had had disrupted earlier educational experiences, valued the learning opportunities they received in custody. However, on leaving custody children frequently repeated the familiar experience of educational exclusion—schools or colleges were reluctant to admit them because of their criminal background or because the timing was wrong—term had started and classes were full, or they had missed too much of the curriculum already (Lanskey et al. 2008, see also Office for Standards in Education, Children's Services and Skills (Ofsted) 2010; Lanskey 2014; Smeets 2014).

Such research observations suggested that there was much more to understand about education for children in custody beyond evaluations of individual programmes. They raised questions about the aims and aspirations of education in custodial institutions, about the variability of provision and teaching approaches, about the lack of connection with education in community settings and about what children were actually learning during their time in custody. It was clear that to answer such questions there was a need to look outside as well as within the immediate classroom, and to look at other practices within the secure setting, the structure and management of the secure estate, youth justice sentencing and other educational policies as well as the earlier lives and educational experiences of the children receiving custodial sentences.

Part II: A Multi-layered Cultural Perspective on Education in Custody

Similar observations in a quite different context—that of vocational learning for 16–18-year-olds—have been made by Hodkinson et al. (2007). Their theorisation of learning cultures identifies the multiple layers of influence which need to be taken into consideration in order to understand the practice of education within any environment. Using the metaphor of map scales, they argue that too often theorising on learning is partial and that each scale of investigation results in a different and incomplete perspective of learning. The challenge they suggest is to develop a more holistic analysis of the different fields of influence on learning. Their solution is to combine two theories—a theory of learning cultures which explains how and why situations influence learning and a cultural theory of learning which explains how and why people learn. Learning cultures are presented as a way of understanding the learning context as a social practice constituted by the actions, dispositions and interpretations of the participants (e.g. learners, teachers, residential staff). Cultures are (re)produced by individuals, just as much as individuals are (re)produced by cultures, though 'individuals are differently positioned with regard to shaping and changing a culture' (Hodkinson et al. 2008, p. 34). Learning takes place by means of an individual's 'embodied' (i.e. combined physical, practical, emotional and cognitive) engagement in a learning culture. Hodkinson et al. (2007) found that the dynamics of different fields of influence played out differently in different educational settings, creating variability in learning cultures and in the ways in which individual learners engaged with them.

Hodkinson, Biesta and James's theoretical approach is a particularly helpful heuristic device for thinking about education in custody because it draws analytical attention to the fields of influence (personal, institutional, structural, political and societal) on the secure contexts in which educational programmes are run and on young person's learning experiences (see Fig. 27.1). This multi-layered perspective facilitates a comprehensive understanding of variances and commonalities in the shape and form of education across the secure estate and in the learning experiences of individual children. By this means it lays the groundwork for a deeper analysis of conceptual, contextual and normative issues about education in secure settings than programme evaluation studies on their own can offer.

Fig. 27.1 A multi-layered perspective on education in custody

Fields of Influence on Learning Cultures in Youth Custody

The learning culture framework brings into the frame of analysis both micro and macro influences on the focus and remit of education in secure settings. Hodkinson et al. (2008) suggest that each field of influence interacts with other fields to shape the learning culture in any one setting. To illustrate this point, I present an analysis of the challenges to maintaining continuity in a young person's educational career as a result of the combined influences of criminal justice sentencing policy, the stand-alone and variable structure of educational provision across the secure estate, social representations and attitudes towards children who offend as well as the internal dynamics of the secure setting.

Criminal justice sentencing policy establishes how long a young person will spend in custody and therefore how much education they will receive there.

According to the latest youth justice statistics, children spend on average 90 days in custody (Ministry of Justice and Youth Justice Board 2020). The structure of any custodial sentence imposes a minimum of two breaks on a young person's educational trajectory—the first in the move from a community setting to custody, the second in the move from custody back to the community or, for children serving long sentences, in the move from youth to adult custody. Once in custody a young person may move from one setting to another, which presents further possibilities for disruption given the variation between the different educational settings. Hayden (2008), for example, notes that the short period the majority of children spend in secure children's homes allows little time to complete recognised qualifications. Similarly, an inspection of an STC found that nearly two-thirds of children left without completing their intended qualification as a result of transferring to another secure setting or being released (Ofsted 2020b). The challenge to maintaining continuity is increased further by data sharing agreements between custodial and community educational settings. SCHs and STCs share a data framework with youth offending teams in the community which allows for the transfer of information about a young person's education more straightforwardly than in the YOIs, which use a separate system to record data about the children they hold (Picken et al. 2019).

Hodkinson, Biesta and James's multi-layered learning culture framework also brings into the remit of analysis the influence of the social environment that a young person is released to following their time in custody. A recent criminal justice joint inspection report highlighted the difficulties that many children face in returning to education, employment or training (ETE). They found that of 50 cases they had inspected only 11 children had educational placements immediately on leaving custody, and most of these were provided by the youth offending teams directly (HM Inspectorate of Probation and HM Inspectorate of Prisons 2019). Similarly inspectors have noted low levels of community placements in ETE for children leaving STCs (Ofsted 2019, 2020b). Reasons included a lack of timely support by youth justice workers, limited opportunities for children in community settings, the timing of a child's release which did not coincide with the start of the educational year and a lack of contingency planning if initial plans fell through. It was observed that children were frequently 'fitted into' what was available rather than being found opportunities that aligned with their individual interests (HM Inspectorate of Probation and HM Inspectorate of Prisons 2019, p. 24). Indeed in my research into the educational pathways of young people in the youth justice system (Lanskey 2014), successful re-integration of young people back into community educational settings was often only linked to the individual initiatives of committed professionals who worked around the system. For example, one young man in this study who had been released from custody after the beginning of the new college year was allowed to rejoin his course solely as a consequence of the active efforts of his former college tutor and his youth offending worker. Another example of working around the system to maintain continuity in a young person's educational career was highlighted in an inspection report of a YOI where staff facilitated the return of a young man for one day in order to take a mathematics examination that he had missed due to his early release (HM Inspectorate of Probation and HM Inspectorate of Prisons 2019).

Internal institutional dynamics need also to be considered in order to gain a full picture of the potential for continuity or disruption to a young person's educational experience inside. Attendance rates in education are a common problem in some secure settings. In 2019 an inspection of a YOI found that provision had fallen to a little over eight hours a week per child, and attendance rates stood at 37% (HM Inspectorate of Prisons 2019). Attendance rates in education at STCs have also been found to be low (Ofsted 2019, 2020b). The reasons for low attendance rates can be due both to the setting's management and organisational policies and to young people's resistance to go to education. Risk assessment is one example of how a setting's management approach can impact on attendance rates. In his review of the youth justice system, Charles Taylor asserted that children's educational interests were often secondary to the management of risk processes (Taylor 2016, p. 38). His claims are borne out by inspection reports. For example, the HM Chief Inspector of Prisons' Annual Report for 2018/19 highlighted that 'keep-apart' measures to reduce violence were having a detrimental impact on children's access to education (HM Chief Inspector of Prisons for England and Wales 2018–19). Risk reduction policies can have detrimental educational consequences beyond impeding attendance: another inspection report noted that children missed out on an opportunity to apply for an apprenticeship before leaving custody because it required an online application, and children had no access to the internet in the YOI for security reasons (HM Inspectorate of Probation and HM Inspectorate of Prisons 2019, p. 23).

Many research studies and inspection reports have identified also children's resistance to education across all three types of secure setting (e.g. Andow 2020; Little 2015; Shafi 2019; Ofsted 2020b). Such reports of children's disengagement with education draw attention to the conditions within the secure environment which encourage or discourage children's participation. Rudduck (1997), in her research with children on conditions which encouraged learning, identified the importance of social support and physical and emotional security. Conditions currently found in many YOIs and STCs with high levels of conflict and violence (see Ministry of Justice and Youth Justice Board 2020) in which children feel unsafe, anxious and distressed are thus unlikely to support learning (see also Wood 2006). In contrast children in some SCHs have been found to make good educational progress, prompting the observation that "a violent environment and lack of education is not inevitable when a child is an offender" (Ofsted 2018, p. 18).

Learning Cultures and Informal Learning

In addition to the impact that a secure setting will have on a young person's disposition to participate in formal learning programmes, Hodkinson, Biesta and James's conceptualisation of learning cultures draws attention to the informal learning that takes place in secure settings outside planned educational programmes for "in any situation there are opportunities to learn" (2008, p. 41). Their thinking resonates with Giroux's concept of the 'hidden curriculum': "the myriad of beliefs and values transmitted tacitly through ... social relations and routines" (Giroux 1981, p. 284). An important field of influence therefore to take into consideration in young people's learning from formal education programmes is the hidden curriculum and the extent to which it supports or undermines the objectives of these programmes. Two examples are given below.

The view that prisons are 'schools for crime' is long established. Tonry and Petersilia (1999) refer to the writings of John Howard in the eighteenth century as one of the earliest proponents of this view. Indeed one of the main arguments in favour of establishing reformatory schools for children in the mid-nineteenth century was to prevent them from being 'contaminated' by adults in prisons and developing a more entrenched criminal lifestyle (Hurt 1984). However, research supported by statistics of high recidivism rates of children leaving custody suggests that children in custody influence other children too. For example, Andell and Pitts (2018) suggest that the proliferation of drug distribution networks is partly as a result of interactions in custody between gang-involved youth from different regions within England and Wales.

Children's interactions with staff in custody are also learning situations. In our research evaluation of a training programme for staff in secure settings, we found that staff who demonstrated kindness, empathy and support 'taught' children that they could be trusted. As a result children would seek help from them (Lanskey 2016). However children learned too from the inconsistent behaviours of staff. One young woman in an STC observed that staff were more lenient with children who were badly behaved than with those who were generally well behaved, so the 'lesson' was to behave badly (Lanskey 2016). A setting's approach to discipline and order will communicate values to children too. The practice of pain-inducing restraint of children will, for example, communicate a message that "it is appropriate or permissible in the last resort to enforce one's will or get one's own way by the exercise of violence" (Carr 1992 quoted in Biesta 2010, p. 501). Such informal learning can be as powerful, if not more powerful than the intended learning through the planned education curriculum:

> Prison doesn't make you learn how to be better. It makes you learn how to be sneakier ... not getting caught again. So prison makes people lethal (young man, YOI)
> So I don't see how they can call it a secure training centre 'cos it don't really train you in anything to do with like your attitude towards people or ... the way you treat people (young woman, STC). (Quoted in Lanskey 2016)

Supporting these observations is research by Auty and Liebling (2020) which identifies the relevance of the prison climate for promoting or inhibiting resettlement on release. Gaes and Camp (2009) also found variations in the criminogenic impact of particular prison environments. While these studies are located within adult prisons, it is plausible that similar dynamics exist within the children's secure estate. Education programmes that aim to change offending behaviour may therefore be working in an institutional context that contradicts their messages. In order to understand the impact of individual programmes there is therefore a need to consider the social learning children in custody acquire through the hidden curriculum.

Contextual Complexity

The above examples demonstrate the complexity of the learning context in secure settings in custody as a result of the many different fields of influence and the interactions between them. Hodkinson et al. (2008, p. 44) suggest that this "relational cultural complexity" of learning means that "nothing works for everyone or in all specified situations". Their observation raises questions about the partial and perhaps over-simplified picture of education in secure settings provided by research evaluations of specific programmes. Take, for example, the attempt to link education programmes in custody with re-offending on leaving (see, for example, Steele et al. 2016). Although the acquisition of reading skills from a remedial reading programme may develop a young person's social capital, it is also possible that a young person may become more embedded in criminal activities through their socialisation with others in the secure setting and that they may receive little resettlement support in the community which restricts their opportunities to find an education, training or employment placement on release. Such observations are relevant for understanding why there may be no positive association between a remedial reading course and a young person's re-offending on release.

Thus through Hodkinson, Biesta and James's framework, we gain an appreciation of the complex dynamics of education in secure settings and the complex interweave of structural, socio-political and individual factors that inhibit or enhance a child's educational experiences in custody. Their framework generates insights of relevance for evaluations of individual programmes but also draws attention to system-wide issues that invite broader analysis and commentary on the role of education as a means to achieve criminal justice policy aspirations for a reduction in offending by children and young people.

Part III: Normative Insights

The holistic perspective that a multi-layered analytical framework generates also invites reflection on normative questions about what is desirable and equitable as an educational offering for children sentenced to custody. One set of questions that programme evaluations do not address concerns the values that underpin education in secure settings and their practical consequences. A second and connected set of questions relates to issues of educational equality, access and opportunity for children in custody. These questions engage with wider normative debates about children's rights to education and about social justice.

Questions of Value

Education is a value-laden practice: the aims and practices of education in any society reflect that society's values about what it is desirable for children to learn (Biesta 2010). There is a well-established debate amongst philosophers of education on the aims of education in a liberal democratic society (e.g. Dearden 1975; McLaughlin 2008; White 2003). The development of personal autonomy has been a central focus of these debates and has informed discussions on the development of a national curriculum in England and Wales (White 2003). The philosopher and educator, Bertrand Russell, for example, asserts that:

> The aim of teaching should not be to possess or project ourselves upon the younger generation, nor to teach them dogma, but rather to seek to set them free so that they may—in very truth—create themselves and their opinions and, in time to come, shape their own future and that of the world which will belong no longer to us, but to them. (Russell 1981, p. 37)

Such thinking positions education very differently to the focus on reform and reducing re-offending that has permeated policy discourse on education for children in custody. Peters argues that the concept of reform is more limited than that of education for it implies bringing up children to a standard from which they had lapsed rather than "guiding children towards standards that they never dreamt of" (1966, p. 272). A question that follows from this observation is whether an education system that prioritises reform of children results in less equitable provision for children than one which encourages the development of personal autonomy.

In earlier articles I presented two examples which suggested it might—an inspection framework for secure settings (Lanskey 2011) and a citizenship training programme for children in custody (Lanskey 2010). In the first example education inspection frameworks for custodial settings placed greater weight on the maintenance of behaviour and less weight on the 'aspirations and prior attainment of learners' than the equivalent inspection frameworks in schools (Lanskey 2011, p. 54). In the second example, the teaching notes for a module on 'crime' in a citizenship programme for young people in secure settings gave explicit instructions to challenge learners' attempts to justify a crime, in contrast to the recommended scheme of work for the study of crime in schools which encouraged students to reflect on how crime is defined and to consider whether any crimes should be decriminalised. The more didactic approach of the citizenship programme in custody resonates with Freire's 'banking concept' of education, which aims to 'change the consciousness' of children in order that they can be 'integrated' and 'incorporated' into the healthy society they have 'forsaken' (Freire 2005, p. 74). In contrast the reflective approach to teaching about crime in the schools' programme in its encouragement of independent thinking and critical reflection is more in tune with the liberal democratic aim of developing personal autonomy (Dearden 1975) and children's 'right' to an open future (Feinberg 2007). These are two small examples, but they signal the limitations of an approach to education that is more directed towards containment and control of children than to an aspirational agenda.

A further example of how values play a role in the shaping of education in secure settings is the 'public acceptability test' introduced in 2009 for prison governors deciding what programmes to run in their establishment. The test was introduced following media criticism of a stand-up comedy training programme for prisoners in a maximum security prison. A Prison Service Order (PSO 0050) and subsequent Prison Service Instruction (PSI 38/2010) required governors of any state custodial establishment including YOIs to consider whether any of the programmes they ran, including educational programmes, would "undermine public confidence in the system". The justice secretary at the time was quoted as saying: "Prisons should be places of punishment and reform, and providing educational, training and constructive pursuits is an essential part of this. But the types of courses available—and the manner in which they are delivered—must be appropriate in every prison" (Press Association 2008). His words invite reflection on what is 'appropriate'. To take as an example the art class in a YOI in the fieldwork observations described earlier. This was an additional activity in the education timetable with a member of staff from a local art college. The appropriateness of the afternoon of portrait drawing might be argued in terms of facilitating a young person's desistance from crime: the artistic activity might be viewed as a means to build self-esteem, and hope and a positive outlook on the future (Maruna 2001). The afternoon may serve as a 'turning point' in a young person's life (Laub and Sampson 1993) and contribute to the development of his human and social capital (Farrall 2004), thereby facilitating his capacity to re-integrate into society and to sustain a lifestyle on leaving prison (there are examples of young people who have participated in art programmes in custody and followed a career in art on release). However it is also possible that the young people involved simply spent a pleasurable afternoon learning something new which had no instrumental value in the longer term but which provided a momentary escape from the burdensome experience of being in custody. Would an educational programme that aims to be fun be any less appropriate for young people in custody? It may be argued, given the negative prior experiences of education many children in custody have had (Ministry of Justice and Department of Education 2016), that 'enjoyment' is a particularly important value for education in custodial settings in order to ignite or rekindle an enthusiasm for learning.

The above points illustrate that there is much more to debate about the values that underpin the aims and approach of education for children in custody, how they differ from that of children in mainstream education and whether that difference is justified.

Questions of Equity

It is well documented that many children in custody have had negative experiences of school resulting in lower levels of attainment in comparison to the general school population. For example, a comparative analysis of the academic performance of a cohort of children who committed offences and a matched sample in the school population in England and Wales identified that young people in custody were less likely to have met expected levels of attainment at Key Stage 2 (aged approximately 9/10 years) and at Key Stage 4 (aged approximately 15/16 years) and that they had higher levels of special educational need and higher rates of school exclusion than the general population of children in schools (Ministry of Justice and Department of Education 2016).

As mentioned earlier, until 2009, children in custody in England and Wales had no statutory right to education, and the UK government had been subject to criticism by the United Nations Committee on the Rights of the Child (UNCRC) for this omission (see UNCRC 2008). Subsequent legislation has addressed this issue, but a rights perspective has ongoing relevance for thinking about the provision of education in custody, for example, in 2016 the UNCRC still found that access to education for children in custody was 'insufficient' (UNCRC 2016) and in 2020 the minimum requirements for education in YOIs and STCs were relaxed during a coronavirus period (The Prison and Young Offender Institution (Coronavirus) (Amendment) (No. 2) Rules 2020 and The Secure Training Centre (Coronavirus) (Amendment) Rules 2020). Indeed, during the national lockdown related to the Covid-19 outbreak, HM Chief Inspector of Prisons reported that children in state-run YOIs had received no face-to-face education and were spending 22 hours locked up in their cells (HM Chief Inspector of Prisons 2020). These observations reinforce the importance of an overall view of education within secure settings and of critical scrutiny of system-wide practices.

The multiple barriers to achieving educational equality for children in custody which become visible using Hodkinson, Biesta and James's framework are well documented (e.g. Taylor 2016; Stephenson 2007; Cooper et al. 2007). They illustrate that it matters how education is conceived, managed and delivered for children receiving custodial sentences (in and outside the custodial setting) in order that it might reduce rather than compound their social disadvantage. There are questions to be considered about the range and focus of educational curricula, teaching approaches and inspection frameworks as well as the more general conditions of learning established by the practices and interactions within the secure setting. These issues are particularly important for groups of socially disadvantaged children who are overrepresented within the criminal justice system already such as children from ethnic minorities (Ministry of Justice and Youth Justice Board 2020) and children who are looked after (Laming 2016). Indeed, there is some evidence that these groups receive less educational support than their counterparts in prison. Inspections have found significant differences between the reports of Black Asian and Minority Ethnic children and other children's reports of whether staff encouraged them to attend education training or work (HM Inspectorate of Prisons 2020) and the educational outcomes for looked-after children were found to be particularly poor with none having an educational placement ready for them on release (HM Inspectorate of Probation and HM Inspectorate of Prisons 2019).

Conclusion

In this chapter I have argued for a wider analytical engagement with education in secure settings to supplement the findings of programme evaluations. Evaluation research is important for establishing the impact of particular courses, but there are shortcomings to relying on this body of research for determining how best to educate young people in secure settings because their design limits consideration of the 'bigger picture' of influences that shape custodial learning cultures and children's learning both inside and outside the classroom.

By considering the multiple fields of influence, broader systemic features that enhance or diminish the effectiveness of education are brought clearly into view: the omission of a formal consideration of children's educational careers in sentencing policy; the isolation of education within the youth justice estate from educational settings outside; the fragmented organisation of the youth secure estate in which different secure settings operate different frameworks for the management and delivery of education; the extent to which secure settings actively promote education through their routines and practices and the extent to which young people's learning from hidden curricula supports or contradicts formal educational objectives. Further, by taking into consideration the collective experiences of children in custody and their enthusiasm or resistance to education in general, we get a better understanding of the overall impact of a custodial education; the extent to which it develops children's skills, capacities and enthusiasm for learning; and the extent to which their learning from formal programmes has ongoing relevance for their lives after custody. A wider perspective allows us also to engage with normative questions about the range and remit of education that children receive. It allows a comparison with education in other contexts and provides an opportunity to reflect on similarities and differences and to make judgements about quality of provision and access. It facilitates reflection on the extent to which children's rights to an education are adequately supported.

These two modes of enquiry into education, the technical and the normative, are inextricably linked: overcoming barriers to education may be seen both as a technical challenge and as a moral requirement. However, normative questions reach beyond the conceptual remit of programme evaluations which tend to focus on how to make education most effective within existing settings (e.g. Wexler et al. 2014). In contrast, a normative enquiry might use as a starting point the questions: *Should* we be accommodating education to existing settings? What would be the outcome if instead of placing the provision of education second to justice agenda, justice agenda were placed second to the provision of education?

Biesta asserts that there is a need to move beyond a "what works" approach because "education is a thoroughly moral and political practice, one that needs to be subject to continuous democratic contestation and deliberation" (2007, p. 6). Following Biesta, a final set of questions then is about who is and who should be involved in debates on the development of policy and practice of education in secure settings? Who should decide what is 'appropriate'? Each field of influence in the multi-layered framework discussed in this chapter captures a particular layer of knowledge about education in custody, and that knowledge is held by different actors within the field: education and justice policy makers, leaders of secure establishments, teachers and children. Alford and Head (2017, p. 407) argue that knowledge of complex systems sometimes "receives too much or too little attention because of the way it is framed". We might ask what knowledge receives too much or too little attention in decisions about education in custody? Whose voices are included? Whose are omitted? Whose carry the greatest weight? As researchers involved in the activity of 'democratic underlabouring', the posing of these questions may be viewed as part of the normative task "to supply a constant reminder that there is always more at stake in crime reduction than reducing crime and hence more to evaluation than finding out 'what works'" (Loader and Sparks 2011, p. 127).

References

Alford, J., & Head, B. W. (2017). Wicked and less wicked problems: A typology and a contingency framework. *Policy and Society, 36*(3), 397–413.

Andell, P., & Pitts, J. (2018). The end of the line? The impact of county lines drug distribution on youth crime in a target destination. *Youth & Policy*. Retrieved October 28, 2020, from www.youthandpolicy.org/articles/the-end-of-the-line/.

Andow, C. (2020). The institutional shaping of children's educational experiences in secure custody: A case study of a secure children's home in England. *International Journal of Educational Development, 77*, 102217.

Auty, K. M., & Liebling, A. (2020). Exploring the relationship between prison social climate and reoffending. *Justice Quarterly, 37*(2), 358–381.

Bell, B., Costa, R., & Machin, S. (2018). *Why does education reduce crime?* CEP Discussion Paper No. 1566, August 2018. Retrieved October 28, 2020, from http://cep.lse.ac.uk/pubs/download/dp1566.pdf.

Biesta, G. J. (2007). Why "what works" won't work: Evidence-based practice and the democratic deficit in educational research. *Educational Theory, 57*(1), 1–22.

Biesta, G. J. (2010). Why 'what works' still won't work: From evidence-based education to value-based education. *Studies in Philosophy and Education, 29*(5), 491–503.

Carpenter, M. (1851). *Reformatory schools, for the children of the perishing and dangerous classes, and for juvenile offenders*. London: C. Gilpin.

Cooper, K., Sutherland, A., & Roberts, C. (2007). *Improving education, training and employment opportunities for serious and persistent offenders*. London: Youth Justice Board.

Cope, N. (2000). Drug use in prison: The experience of young offenders. *Drugs: Education, Prevention and Policy, 7*(4), 355–366.

Dearden, R. F. (1975). Autonomy as an educational ideal. In S. C. Brown (Ed.), *Philosophers discuss education* (pp. 3–18). London: Palgrave Macmillan.

Farrall, S. (2004). Social capital and offender reintegration: Making probation desistance focused. In S. Maruna & R. Immarigeon (Eds.), *After crime and punishment: Pathways to offender reintegration* (pp. 57–82). Cullompton, UK: Willan Publishing.

Farrington, D. P., & Welsh, B. C. (2007). *Saving children from a life of crime: Early risk factors and effective interventions*. Oxford: Oxford University Press.

Feinberg, J. (2007). The child's right to an open future. In R. R. Curren (Ed.), *Philosophy of education: An anthology*. Oxford: Blackwell.

Freire, P. (2005). *Pedagogy of the oppressed*. London: Continuum.

Gaes, G. G., & Camp, S. D. (2009). Unintended consequences: Experimental evidence for the criminogenic effect of prison security level placement on post-release recidivism. *Journal of Experimental Criminology, 5*(2), 139–162.

Giroux, H. (1981). Schooling and the myth of objectivity: Stalking the hidden curriculum. *McGill Journal of Education, 17*, 282–304.

Hayden, C. (2008). Education, schooling and young offenders of secondary school age. *Pastoral Care in Education, 26*(1), 23–31.

HM Chief Inspector of Prisons for England and Wales. (2019). *Annual report*. Retrieved August 15, 2020, from https://www.justiceinspectorates.gov.uk/hmi-prisons/wp-content/uploads/sites/4/2019/07/6.5563_HMI-Prisons-AR_2018-19_WEB_FINAL_040719.pdf.

HM Chief Inspector of Prisons for England and Wales. (2020). *Report on short scrutiny visits to Young Offender Institutions holding children*, July 2020. Retrieved August 15, 2020, from www.justiceinspectorates.gov.uk/hmiprisons/wp-content/uploads/sites/4/2020/07/YOI-SSV-2.pdf.

HM Government. (2018). *Secure schools: How to apply guide*. London: HMSO.

HM Inspectorate of Prisons. (2019). *Report on an announced inspection of HMYOI Feltham A Children's Unit (4–19 July 2019)*. Retrieved August 15, 2020, from www.justiceinspectorates.gov.uk/hmiprisons/wp-content/uploads/sites/4/2019/10/Feltham-A-Web-2019.pdf.

HM Inspectorate of Prisons. (2020). *Children in custody 2018–19: An analysis of 12–18-year-olds' perceptions of their experiences in secure training centres and young offender institutions*. Retrieved August 15, 2020, from www.justiceinspectorates.gov.uk/hmiprisons/wp-content/uploads/sites/4/2020/02/Children-in-Custody-2018-19-Web-1.pdf.

HM Inspectorate of Probation and HM Inspectorate of Prisons. (2019). *Youth resettlement – Final report into work in the community: A thematic inspection*. Retrieved August 17, 2020, from https://www.justiceinspectorates.gov.uk/hmiprobation/wp-content/uploads/sites/5/2019/10/Youth-resettlement-%E2%80%93-final-report-into-work-in-the-community-4.pdf.

Hodkinson, P., Biesta, G., & James, D. (2007). Understanding learning cultures. *Educational Review, 59*(4), 415–427.

Hodkinson, P., Biesta, G., & James, D. (2008). Understanding learning culturally: Overcoming the dualism between social and individual views of learning. *Vocations and Learning, 1*(1), 27–47.

Hurry, J., Brazier, L., & Moriarty, V. (2005). Improving the literacy and numeracy skills of children who offend: Can it be done and what are the consequences?'. *Literacy & Numeracy Studies, 14*(2), 47–60.

Hurt, J. (1984). Reformatory and industrial schools before 1933. *History of Education, 13*(1), 45–58.

Laming, L. (2016). *In care, out of trouble: How the life chances of children in care can be transformed by protecting them from unnecessary involvement in the criminal justice system*. London: Prison Reform Trust.

Lanskey, C. (2010). Citizenship education for young people in secure institutions in England and Wales. *Educação, Sociedade & Culturas, 30*, 41–56.

Lanskey, C. (2011). Promise or compromise? Education for children in secure institutions in England'. *Youth Justice Journal, 11*(1), 47–60.

Lanskey, C. (2014). Up or down and out? A systemic analysis of children's educational pathways in the youth justice system in England and Wales. *International Journal of Inclusive Education, 19*(6), 568–582.

Lanskey, C. (2016). Formal and informal learning in custodial settings for children. *Prison Service Journal, 226*, 3–7.

Lanskey, C. (2018). Children's education, youth justice and rehabilitation: An historical overview. In D. Gallard, J. Millington, & K. Evans (Eds.), *Children and their education in secure accommodation*. London: Routledge.

Lanskey, C., Drake, D., Harvey, J., & Liebling, A. (2008). *Training at the edge: Project cascade final report*. Cambridge: Institute of Criminology.

Laub, J. H., & Sampson, R. J. (1993). Turning points in the life course: Why change matters to the study of crime. *Criminology, 31*(3), 301–325.

Learning Skills Network. (2009). *Offender education and citizenship: Post-16 citizenship support programme (Vol. 2009)*. London: Learning and Skills Improvement Service.

Little, R. (2015). Putting education at the heart of custody? The views of children on education in a young offender institution. *British Journal of Community Justice, 13*(2), 27–47.

Loader, I., & Sparks, R. (2011). *Public criminology?* London: Routledge.

Maruna, S. (2001). *Making good: How ex-offenders reform and reclaim their lives*. Washington, DC: American Psychological Association.

McLaughlin, T. H. (2008). Liberalism, education and schooling: Essays by TH McLaughlin. In D. Carr, M. Halstead, & R. Pring (Eds.), *St Andrews Studies in Philosophy and Public Affairs*. Exeter: Imprint Academic.

Ministry of Justice. (2013). *Transforming youth custody. Government consultation paper* CP4/2013. Retrieved August 17, 2020, from https://consult.justice.gov.uk/digital-communications/transforming-youth-custody/supporting_documents/transformingyouthcustody.pdf.

Ministry of Justice. (2014). *Transforming youth custody. Government response to the consultation*. Retrieved March 23, 2020, from https://www.gov.uk/government/consultations/transforming-youth-custody-putting-education-at-the-heart-of-detention.

Ministry of Justice. (2020) A smarter approach to sentencing. Government white paper CP292. Retrieved March 24, 2021 from https://assets.publishing.service.gov.uk/government/uploads/system/uploads/attachment_data/file/918187/a-smarter-approach-to-sentencing.pdf.

Ministry of Justice and Department of Education. (2016). *Understanding the educational background of young offenders Joint experimental statistical report from the Ministry of Justice and Department for Education*. Retrieved March 23, 2020, from https://assets.publishing.service.gov.uk/government/uploads/system/uploads/attachment_data/file/577542/understanding-educational-background-of-young-offenders-full-report.pdf.

Ministry of Justice and Youth Justice Board. (2020). *Youth justice statistics: 2018 to 2019 supplementary tables*. Retrieved August 17, 2020, from https://www.gov.uk/government/statistics/youth-justice-statistics-2018-to-2019.

Ofsted. (2010). *Transition through detention and custody: Arrangements for learning and skills for children in custodial or secure settings*. London: Ofsted. Retrieved October 28, 2020, from https://dera.ioe.ac.uk/106/1/Transition%20through%20detention%20and%20custody.pdf.

Ofsted. (2018). *The annual report of Her Majesty's Chief Inspector of Education, Children's Services and Skills 2016/17*. Retrieved August 17, 2020, from https://assets.publishing.service.gov.uk/government/uploads/system/uploads/attachment_data/file/666871/Ofsted_Annual_Report_2016-17_Accessible.pdf.

Ofsted. (2019). *Oakhill STC annual inspection*. Retrieved August 17, 2020, from https://files.ofsted.gov.uk/v1/file/50081527.

Ofsted. (2020a). *The annual report of Her Majesty's Chief Inspector of Education, Children's Services and Skills 2018/19*. Retrieved August 17, 2020, from https://assets.publishing.service.gov.uk/government/uploads/system/uploads/attachment_data/file/859422/Annual_Report_of_Her_Majesty_s_Chief_Inspector_of_Education__Children_s_Services_and_Skills_201819.pdf.

Ofsted. (2020b). *Rainsbrook STC annual inspection*. Retrieved August 17, 2020, from https://files.ofsted.gov.uk/v1/file/50150183.

Peters, R. S. (1966). *Ethics and education*. London: George Allen and Unwin Ltd.

Petrosino, A., & Lavenberg, J. (2007). Systematic reviews and meta-analyses: Best evidence on what works for criminal justice decision makers. *Western Criminology Review, 8*(1), 1–15.

Picken, N., Baker, K., d'Angelo, C., Fays, C., & Sutherland, A. (2019). *Process evaluation of AssetPlus*. Santa Monica, CA: RAND.

Press Association. (2008). Straw condemns prisoners' stand-up comedy course. *The Guardian*, November 21. Retrieved March 23, 2020, from https://www.theguardian.com/politics/2008/nov/21/jackstraw-prisonsandprobation.

Public Health England. (2019). *Collaborative approaches to preventing offending and re-offending by children (CAPRICORN): Summary*. Retrieved March 23, 2020, from https://www.gov.uk/government/publications/preventing-offending-and-re-offending-by-children/collaborative-approaches-to-preventing-offending-and-re-offending-by-children-capricorn-summary.

Rudduck, J. (1997). Student voices and conditions of learning. In B. Karseth, S. Gudundsdottir, & S. Hopmann (Eds.), *Didaktikk: Tradksjon og fornyelse. Festskrift i anledning professor Bjøg Brandtzæg Gundems 70-års dag*. Oslo: University of Oslo.

Russell, D. (1981). *The tamarisk tree, vol.2, my school and the years of war*. London: Virago.

Shafi, A. A. (2019). The complexity of disengagement with education and learning: A case study of young offenders in a secure custodial setting in England. *Journal of Education for Students Placed at Risk (JESPAR), 24*(4), 323–345.

Smeets, E. (2014). Education in young offender institutions and secure youth care institutions. *Educational Research and Evaluation, 20*(1), 67–80.

Steele, J. L., Bozick, R., & Davis, L. M. (2016). Education for incarcerated juveniles: A meta-analysis. *Journal of Education for Students Placed at Risk (JESPAR), 21*(2), 65–89.

Stephenson, M. (2007). *Young people and offending: Education, youth justice and social inclusion*. Cullompton, UK: Willan Publishing.

Taylor, C. (2016). *Review of the youth justice system in England and Wales*. London: Ministry of Justice.

The Children's Homes (England) Regulations. (2015). (SI 2015/541). Retrieved October 28, 2020, from https://www.legislation.gov.uk/uksi/2015/541/contents/made.

The Secure Training Centre (Coronavirus) (Amendment) Rules. (2020). (SI 2020/664). Retrieved October 28, 2020, from www.legislation.gov.uk/uksi/2020/664/contents/made.

The Secure Training Centre Rules. (1998). (SI 1998/472). Retrieved October 28, 2020, from www.legislation.gov.uk/uksi/1998/472/contents/made.

The Young Offender Institution Rules.(2000). Young Offender Institutions, England and Wales (SI: 2000/3371). Retrieved March 25, 2021, from www.legislation.gov.uk/uksi/2000/3371.

Tonry, M., & Petersilia, J. (1999). American prisons at the beginning of the twenty-first century. *Crime and Justice, 26*, 1–16.

UNCRC. (2008). *Concluding observations: United Kingdom of Great Britain and Northern Ireland*. Retrieved August 19, 2020, from http://www2.ohchr.org/english/bodies/crc/docs/AdvanceVersions/CRC.C.GBR.CO.4.pdf.

UNCRC. (2016). *Committee on the Rights of the Child: Concluding observations on the fifth periodic report of the United Kingdom of Great Britain and Northern Ireland*. Retrieved October 28, 2020, from www.unicef.org.uk/babyfriendly/un-committee-on-the-rights-of-the-child-calls-on-uk-to-protect-breastfeeding/uk-crc-concluding-observations-2016-2/.

Wexler, J., Pyle, N., Flower, A., Williams, J. L., & Cole, H. (2014). A synthesis of academic interventions for incarcerated adolescents. *Review of Educational Research, 84*(1), 3–46.

White, J. (2003). *Rethinking the school curriculum: Values, aims and purposes*. London: Routledge.

Wood, J. J. (2006). Effect of anxiety reduction on children's school performance and social adjustment. *Developmental Psychology, 42*(2), 345–349.

28

Transforming Youth Justice Inside and Out

Vincent Schiraldi and Alexander Schneider

Introduction

We know two very important things about young people, in relation to crime and delinquency: they are fundamentally different from adults—less mature, less culpable, and more prone to aging out of delinquent behavior—and incarcerating them makes the situation worse in several important respects. As approaches to juvenile justice have changed through history, we have learned what does and does not work for young people and have gained an understanding of their development. It is clear to us that the outdated system of punishing young people still used in so many states across the United States (US) needs to change and that the administrators of those systems, alongside advocates, elected officials, and philanthropy, can, and must, be part of that change. Vincent Schiraldi has been one of a number of people pushing for change in youth justice systems. Known nationally in the US as a criminal justice reformer, Schiraldi has turned a career of making government justice systems more community focused into a national movement, one where leaders with decision-making power in government agencies charged with administering justice for young people are working with youth, families, and communities to envision a new path forward and radically shift the youth justice paradigm in the US.

In part, this shift will include the closure of placement facilities for youth, facilities that embody the punitive ethos characteristic of US youth prisons.

V. Schiraldi • A. Schneider (✉)
Columbia University, New York, NY, USA
e-mail: alexander.schneider@columbia.edu

© The Author(s), under exclusive license to Springer Nature Switzerland AG 2021
A. Cox, L. S. Abrams (eds.), *The Palgrave International Handbook of Youth Imprisonment*,
Palgrave Studies in Prisons and Penology, https://doi.org/10.1007/978-3-030-68759-5_28

While it must be part of a larger shift in how our society looks at youth behavior, these youth prisons are often the final vestiges of our outdated approach to youth justice.

The administrators who are in charge of the systems can be champions for this transformation—using their insider knowledge and access to fundamentally change, or even eliminate, the very facilities they run. To examine how this can happen, we first look at what youth justice systems in the United States are like. We highlight studies on the conditions of confinement for young people, Vincent Schiraldi's own career and experience with the system in Washington, District of Columbia (DC), conditions for young people who end up in adult facilities, and also the racial disparities in these systems. In the following sections, we examine how change has come about in specific places—New York and Vermont—by shifting the vision and paradigms at the core of youth justice systems, and we conclude with a hopeful view of the future of youth justice as current and former administrators join this cause.

The Case for Urgent Reform

Currently in the field of juvenile justice, the understanding that young people are different from adults in fundamental ways and should be treated differently, is coming to the fore. However, the justice system strayed from its roots and has yet to fully pivot away from the punitive ethos of the "superpredator era" of the 1990s, when black youth in the United States were seen as irredeemable and handled in the more punitive adult system (DiIulio 1995), and when severe punishment and isolation were deemed the most appropriate responses. Despite important reforms, the conditions for young people who end up in our juvenile justice systems are still often appalling.

Since 2011, the Annie E. Casey Foundation has released two separate reports on institutional conditions in youth prisons. In *No Place for Kids*, Casey found that clear evidence of recurring or systemic maltreatment had been identified in the vast majority of American states since 1970 (Mendel 2011). In nearly half the states, these conditions had been documented in juvenile correctional facilities since 2000, showing abuses still happening at a time when systems were purported to be focused on child development, not punishment. *No Place for Kids* also identified 57 lawsuits in 33 states, the District of Columbia and Puerto Rico since 1970 that resulted in a court-sanctioned remedy in response to allegations of systemic problems with violence, physical or sexual abuse by facility staff, and/or excessive use of isolation or physical restraints.

In 2015, the Casey Foundation updated *No Place for Kids*, revealing that such atrocities were hardly a thing of the past. Evidence of maltreatment was found in Colorado, Georgia, Idaho, Illinois, Iowa, Tennessee, and West Virginia, states where no maltreatment was evident in 2011. Further, the authors found evidence of ongoing violations of constitutional rights of confined youth in seven states—Arkansas, California, Florida, Nevada, New York, Ohio, and Texas—identified originally in *No Place for Kids* (Mendel 2015). Other publications and surveys also found recent evidence of abuse and maltreatment (Beck et al. 2013; Mohr 2008).

The trauma that these systems cause becomes even more evident when talking to people who experienced it firsthand as young people; even older adults who were incarcerated as children talk about the horrors they experienced as if it was yesterday. One man who was able to turn his life around, become a lawyer, and obtain high-level positions in both government and philanthropy spoke about his experience at a Columbia University event and was near tears describing his time at the notorious Rikers Island jail in New York City at age 16.[1] He said that he was immediately recruited into a gang that he joined for his own protection. He was a skinny teenager, and the Rikers Island adolescent unit at that time included youth up to age 21, so he immediately began a workout regime and became particularly violent whenever confronted, quickly earning a reputation for violence. He described witnessing violent incidents, including seeing another youth sliced up with razor blades to within an inch of his life. His "crew," or gang, made up of youth from Brooklyn, "owned" one corner of the dormitory, and the staff put a youth who was not in his gang in one of their bunks. Five youth repeatedly raped the new youth that first night. The man, now approaching age 60, says a day does not go by that he does not think of the atrocities he witnessed while confined in Rikers Island.

Washington, District of Columbia (DC), is just one example that shows how appalling conditions of confinement can be for young people, which we highlight here because of Schiraldi's experience running DC's Department of Youth Rehabilitation Services (DYRS). In the year prior to Schiraldi taking the helm at DYRS, two scathing reports were released detailing the awful conditions in the District's youth prison, Oak Hill. Schiraldi saw firsthand that beatings of children in custody were commonplace, youth stuffed clothing around the toilets to keep out rats and cockroaches, and they were locked up for so long that they often defecated or urinated in their cells. Young people who came in drug free often tested positive for marijuana after 30 days of confinement, suggesting that it was easier to obtain drugs in the facility than on the streets of the District of Columbia (Schiraldi 2015).

In addition to these unsanitary and detrimental conditions, some staff were sexually harassing the young people and one another. One of the corrections officers married a young person shortly after the boy was released from custody. A teacher who had been confined in the facility when she was a teenager confided that a staff member who was still in the department's employ years later had sexually assaulted her. The female staff members widely complained that, if they did not acquiesce to sexual advances by their supervisors, they might find themselves alone and unaided in dangerous situations. Overall Oak Hill was an abusive and traumatic environment for everyone involved, especially for the children placed there.

In 2004 there was enormous pressure on Washington DC's Mayor Anthony Williams to fix what was considered a truly broken juvenile justice system. The system had gone through 19 directors in as many years, and it was clear that hiring people with decades of experience running youth correctional facilities was not working. Instead, the Mayor, under pressure from a law suit and a well-organized advocacy community, created a new cabinet-level agency, the Department of Youth Rehabilitation Services (DYRS), with a legal mandate to close the Oak Hill Youth Center, which was, as we noted previously, a facility notorious for maltreatment, unsanitary conditions, and poor outcomes for the youth (Ryan and Schindler 2011). He hired Vincent Schiraldi, who at the time was openly critical of the system, and was writing opinion-editorial articles critical of the system, including saying that he wouldn't "kennel his dog in DC's juvenile justice system" (Boyes-Watson and Gebo 2018, p. 202).

Schiraldi came to his position within the system after many years working outside of it, although he had begun his career as a house parent in a seven-bed home for boys who had been adjudicated delinquent, run by the New York State Division for Youth. He loved working with the young people and realized how much damage incarceration was doing to them: that work became the foundation for his career and research. While getting a master's degree at Syracuse University, Schiraldi heard a speech by Jerome Miller, a former department head turned non-profit leader who had deinstitutionalized Massachusetts' entire juvenile justice system and later founded the National Center on Institutions and Alternatives (NCIA). After the speech, Schiraldi chased Miller out of the classroom and began to argue with his acerbic description of institutional staff. Miller hired him on the spot to work in his New York office (which later morphed into the Center for Community Alternatives). After that, Schiraldi founded the Center on Juvenile and Criminal Justice in San Francisco, followed by the DC-based Justice Policy Institute, a non-profit think tank "dedicated to reducing the use of incarceration and the justice system by promoting fair and effective policies" (Justice Policy Institute 2019).

Schiraldi had a vision for a system in DC that was vastly—as opposed to incrementally—different from the status quo, and he was transparent with political leaders that change would not be easy. He envisioned a system where most of the youth would be in community-based programs, and much smaller numbers would be locked up, saying "I'm not here to fix [Oak Hill], I'm here to fix a system" (Labbe 2005, p. B2).

While designing and implementing a number of community programs that served as alternatives to incarceration, Schiraldi and his team (almost all of whom came from the non-profit sector outside of government) began to change the actual conditions within the institutions as well. The transparency and involvement of advocates from the community was a key element, as Schiraldi knew that there would be push-back from entrenched institutional interests. He worked closely with parents of incarcerated youth, youth themselves, victims' groups, litigators, counsel, philanthropy and community providers, and advocates to mutually achieve the transformation of that system from a brutal and unconstitutional one that grossly over-incarcerated youth in terrible conditions of confinement, to one that is considered by many to be a model worth emulating (Ryan and Schindler 2011).

As predicted, Schiraldi had several votes of no-confidence from correctional unions. Staff began leaking exaggerated information about incidents within Oak Hill to the press, and suspicions of staff sabotage grew. Those issues could have been the end of his tenure in DC, but because he had come into the position knowing what would happen and had strong backing from the community, both mayors that he worked for stood up for him.

Three years into the job, Schiraldi closed the Oak Hill facility, but the closure was just one element in a wider reform effort. The population of youth placed in locked facilities was halved, and Oak Hill was replaced with a facility less than a third of its size and which looked much more like a school than a traditional prison (Ryan and Schindler 2011).

In Washington, as is the case in the United States more generally, youth of color incarcerated at far higher rates than white youth, and therefore more youth of color are subjected to the abuses found in facilities like Oak Hill. According to the W. Haywood Burns Institute, in 2015, African American, Native American, and Latinx youth in the United States were incarcerated at 5, 3.1, and 1.6 times the rate of white youth, respectively. From 2005 to 2010 while Schiraldi was director, not one white teenager was committed to Washington DC's Department of Youth Rehabilitation Services (W. Haywood Burns 2019).

The situation is even more dangerous for youth incarcerated in adult facilities. While the number of young people who are confined in facilities meant for adults has gone down over the years, from a peak of almost 10,000 in 1999 (Troilo 2018), the Prison Policy Institute reports that there were still more than 4000 youth in adult jails and prisons in 2019 (Sawyer 2019). Youth under the age of 18 who are in adult jails have a mortality rate, while incarcerated, nearly twice that of young adults (18–24-year-olds) in adult jails and nine times higher than youth in the general population (Arya 2018). Youth are much more likely to commit suicide in an adult jail than in juvenile detention. The Bureau of Justice Statistics reported a suicide rate for youth in adult jails of 36 per 100,000 in 2014 (Noonan 2016). In comparison, in 2005 *Corrections Today* reported that suicide rates in juvenile custody were similar to a comparable age group in the general population at 10 per 100,000 (Snyder 2005). The Bureau of Justice Statistics reports that, although less than 1% of those in jail in the US were under age 18, they were victims of 13% of substantiated "inmate-on-inmate" sexual assaults in US jails (Beck et al. 2007).

A Tale of Two Jurisdictions

While these deplorable conditions still exist in youth justice systems around the country, decades of reform and decreasing crime rates have led to the lowest numbers of youth in custody since the 1980s. From the peak of 109,000 incarcerated youth in the 1990s, there are now fewer than 43,580 in custody nationwide (Office of Juvenile Justice and Delinquency Prevention 2019). Between 2002 and 2016, the number of facilities with more than 200 beds declined over 80%, and the number of facilities with more than 100 beds declined by two-thirds (Sickmund 2006; Puzzanchera et al. 2018). These trends are continuing, and many states and jurisdictions are planning for the closures of the last of their archaic facilities and moving their systems into a new era; in states like New York and Vermont, reforms, described below, have led to watershed change for young people.

Bringing New York City Youth Close to Home

The downsizing and/or closure of youth prisons has often emanated from a combination of sophisticated advocacy, reform-minded system administrators, and elected officials willing to experiment with a less punitive approach to youth justice. These officials often take into consideration an understanding of youth brain development and recent studies which show that positive youth development has a greater effect on safety and youth crime than punishment. By looking at New York's youth justice reforms over the past ten years, we can see concrete examples of ways that system insiders, including state agency or department administrators, can close youth prisons and change the landscape of justice for young people. We see here that they can do so by capitalizing on crises, collaborating with advocates and other outsiders instead of negating their work, and ensuring that changes do not mean that children are simply moved to the adult system.

New York is a large state in the northeastern United States and one of many states with major socio-political differences between its largest city and the rest of the state. While New York is the fourth largest state by population, almost half of its residents are in New York City, which is the largest city in the country with more than eight million people (United States Census Bureau 2019).

For much of the 1980s and 1990s, New York followed the national trend of over-incarcerating young people by the thousands, sending them from New York City and other urban centers, to upstate facilities that are located very far from their home communities (Governor Paterson's Task Force 2009). Until 2017, the age of criminal responsibility in New York State, at which everyone is automatically tried as an adult, was 16, and therefore when we discuss youth incarceration trends in New York before 2017, we are only including people aged 15 or younger—16- and 17-year-olds (not to mention youth aged 18–25) were tried as adults and if they were incarcerated would have been in adult facilities. Further discussion of the "raise the age" law and its implementation can be found below. At the height of mass incarceration, in 1997, there were 3800 youth convicted of crimes in juvenile, or family, court annually being sent to nearly three dozen youth prisons scattered throughout New York State (Sickmund et al. 2017). These prisons, run by the State Office of Children and Family Services (OCFS), were primarily in rural areas, and the young people, who were primarily youth of color from urban areas, struggled to maintain connections to their families and communities.

In the early 2000s, a reform movement both nationally and locally in New York was catalyzed by research on adolescent brain development (Steinberg 2009), advocacy, litigation, government leaders, and the philanthropic community. These groups began pushing for deinstitutionalization and improvements to the conditions of confinement for young people.

A number of converging factors became the context for reform in New York, and led to legislation called the "Close to Home" initiative, to move all youth adjudicated in New York City's Family Courts from state custody to smaller and more homelike custody within the city. In addition to sharply declining numbers of youth in the system, there were reports by non-profit organizations and task forces underscoring the inhumane conditions in OCFS facilities (Governor Paterson's Task Force 2009; U.S. Department of Justice 2009; Citizen's Committee for Children 2009). Additionally, the tragic death of a 15-year-old boy held in the Tryon OCFS facility helped to trigger a highly publicized US Department of Justice Civil Rights Division investigation (U.S. Department of Justice 2009).

The reduced numbers of youth in custody also led to the costs per youth mushrooming, since staffing and other fixed costs remained, despite the drops in numbers. The cost of keeping one young person in state custody reached over $250,000 per year by 2011, half of which was borne by counties throughout the state, which paid from their own local budgets (New York State Division of Criminal Justice Services 2012). One study found shockingly high failure rates for New York State's youth justice system, where 71% of boys released from OCFS facilities spent at least some time in adult jail or prison by age 28 (Colman et al. 2009).

The Close to Home Initiative became a reality after New York City Mayor Michael Bloomberg and New York State Governor Andrew Cuomo both toured empty or nearly empty youth prisons that were fully staffed in 2010, and each publicly called for reform (Hammond 2010; City of New York 2010). In 2012, Governor Cuomo signed Close to Home into law (New York City Administration for Children's Services 2019a). Under Close to Home, custody of children adjudicated delinquent (the US juvenile justice system's term for being found guilty) and placed into custody (another term used for being sentenced to incarceration) was transferred from OCFS to the New York City Administration for Children's Services (City of New York 2010).

In 2010, immediately after he left DC's Department of Youth and Family Services (DYRS), Schiraldi was tapped to run New York City's probation department by mayor Michael Bloomberg, overseeing programs and services for all adults and youth placed on community supervision in New York City, which was one of the nation's largest probation departments with, at the time, approximately 25,000 adults and 2500 youth under supervision (NYS Department of Corrections and Community Supervision 2020). Mayor Michael Bloomberg later said that Schiraldi "was an innovative commissioner who was able to turn good ideas into programs that made a real difference" (Harvard Kennedy School 2015). One of those innovative programs was the Neighborhood Opportunity Networks (NeONs), which decentralized probation and parole in New York City and created community centers where people on probation supervision could not only conduct their required appointments nearer to their communities but also receive other services (McGarry et al. 2014). He also expanded the use of check-in kiosks, where certain probation check-ins could be done without waiting to see an officer, which meant that clients did not end up missing work or other appointments due to long wait times, and helping to dramatically reduce revocation rates. After four years running NYC Probation, Schiraldi became a senior advisor to the Mayor's Office of Criminal Justice under Mayor Bill de Blasio (Hawkins 2014). Having been known as a staunch advocate for youth and reform-minded director in Washington DC before moving to New York, Schiraldi's innovative work with the City's probation department added to that reputation and made him an obvious choice to help lead efforts to reform the city's youth justice system through the Close to Home initiative.

Over a year prior to the enactment of Close to Home, in anticipation of its passage, New York City youth justice stakeholders created the Dispositional Reform Steering Committee (DSRC). The DSRC's purpose was to design a comprehensive continuum of residential and non-residential services, revamp policies and practices for youth at disposition, and forecast the number of youth who would be in each type of placement.

A crucial part of the DSRC's planning was based on the idea that jurisdictions around the country had specific policies and practices which could become models as New York reformed its own system. This allowed them to convince key decision-makers that a new model was possible and that many elements did not need to be created from scratch. One example was Wayne County (Detroit), Michigan, which provided an example of how a large metropolitan area could care for its youth locally, instead of sending them to state custody. Ananthakrishnan et al. (2019) described this model in their case study of the New York reforms:

> In 1999, Wayne County (Detroit), Michigan officials found themselves in similar straights as New York City officials, paying for 50 percent of the costs of a state-run youth prison model that was producing brutality, poor outcomes, and high costs. Over a period of more than a decade, Wayne judges, the probation department, and county officials gradually reduced the number of youth in state care from 731 to almost zero.

Aware of this remarkable realignment of state youth corrections in Wayne County, Schiraldi and key probation staff organized a trip with New York City and State officials to Detroit in 2011. A range of high-ranking city and state officials, including the Mayor's and Governor's chief Close to Home negotiators, as well as members of the judiciary, and representatives from

OCFS, prosecution, defense, probation, and youth corrections experienced a full day of presentations and interactions with their Michigan counterparts on site. Although Wayne County's approach occurred administratively, rather than legislatively, and contained elements that New York City did not borrow, seeing how a major city completely took over youth corrections and was able to place incarcerated youth into community programs buoyed the city's realignment efforts and softened some state and advocate resistance to the bold approach.

Despite work put into forecasting the number of youth that the City would need to house, which predicted substantially declining numbers of young people, concerns led to procurement of approximately the same number of beds as there were youth in placements at the time. This decision to ignore forecasting numbers stemmed from concerns expressed by system leaders. One concern was that probation officers would not approve of the new reforms and therefore undermine them by detaining more youth on probation violations, or being less helpful to the youth. Another concern was that judges would see that the new placement options in New York City were more humane and closer to young people's communities, and therefore place more youth out of home than they would have before Close to Home. The City chose to procure beds on a contractual basis with private non-profit organizations, some of which they have terminated as they became unnecessary, and the concerns about buy-in proved unfounded. Instead, juvenile placements in the city dropped far more precipitously than they did outside the city, in jurisdictions which did not enact Close to Home or similar realignment (-68% vs. -20%) (Ananthakrishnan et al. 2019; NY ACS 2019b).

New York City's Close to Home initiative had a diverse group of stakeholders involved in the reform process from the beginning. There was a key shift in philosophy when youth were transferred to city custody, and the priority became keeping them in their communities and providing local services to help them, instead of focusing on punishment and incarceration. That shift could not have happened without buy-in and input from youth, families, advocates, service providers, and system leaders.

There are now fewer than 100 young people in custody in New York City, an 8.6 million-person metropolis, averaging just 16 young people in secure care in 2019 (New York City Administration for Children's Services 2019b). Simultaneously, juvenile crime rates have continued to decline, doing so at an even faster rate in New York City (which Close to Home exclusively affects) than in the rest of the state (-52% vs. -41% between 2012 and 2016) and at a greater rate than they declined in the years preceding Close to Home (-28% between 2008 and 2012, vs. -52% between 2012 and 2016). Close to Home youth also passed 91% of their classes; 82% of them have transitioned to a parent, guardian, or family member; and 91% of youth who transitioned out of Close to Home were enrolled in a community-based program (Ananthakrishnan et al. 2019).

That said, Close to Home remains a work in progress. In 2017, legislation was passed by the city to raise the age that a person is automatically tried as an adult from 16 to 18, over the course of three years. Before the act's passage, New York was one of just a few states still automatically treating 16-year-olds as adults in the criminal justice system. On October 1, 2018, all 16-year-olds detained by the Department of Correction were transferred to the custody of the Administration for Children's Services, and any new cases involving 16-year-olds were handled in family court or the youth part of adult court (New York State Department of Corrections and Community Supervision 2020). The same process occurred for 17-year-olds the following year, on October 1, 2019. As the city and other counties throughout the state absorb 16- and 17-year-olds into their juvenile justice systems, they will continue to have to adapt to meet the needs of these youth and resist the temptation to over-incarcerate this older population.

Raising the Age in Vermont

While New York shows the watershed change that can happen in a huge urban center, and an example that other systems can draw from in its Close to Home initiative, Vermont offers an example of major changes to a youth justice system in a very different setting. Located in the northeastern United States, Vermont is the second smallest state by population, larger only than Wyoming, with just over 600,000 residents (United States Census Bureau 2019). The state is 94% white and mostly rural, with no major metropolitan centers.

In 2018, Vermont became the first state in US history to pass legislation raising the upper age of juvenile court jurisdiction to 19, after having been one of the last states to raise it from 15 to 17 in 2016 (State of Vermont 2016). Other than those accused of the most serious offenses, youth under 20 will be prosecuted in the Family Division of the Superior Court and their supervision and services will be provided by the Department for Children and Families (DCF). The legislation will come into effect in two parts, incorporating 18-year-olds into the youth justice system on July 1, 2020, and 19-year-olds on July 1, 2022.

In an opinion-editorial article co-authored by Vermont Senate Judiciary Chair Dick Sears and Schiraldi, they describe the purpose of the law:

The goal is to increase public safety and the evidence from research indicates that this approach has the potential to be a game-changer in a field in desperate need of innovation. When the law goes into effect, these emerging adults will have access to youth rehabilitation programs and if incarcerated, be confined in youth facilities instead of mingled with adults in prison. Their crimes will be considered confidential, giving them a second chance to make better choices. (Sears and Schiraldi 2018)

This change comes at a time when Vermont has also announced the closure of its last youth prison, Woodside Juvenile Rehabilitation Center, which did not have a single resident at the time of writing (State of Vermont 2019b).

On June 30, 2014, the most recent data available, only 67 people between the ages of 18 and 20 were incarcerated in Vermont (Vermont Department of Corrections 2014). With crime and incarceration both trending down nationally and in Vermont, it stands that the new Raise the Age law is not likely to add significant numbers to the state's already low rate of youth incarceration. With such low numbers, even adding the full number of young people aged 18 and 19 to the juvenile system would not overwhelm it and still allow for younger youth to be in separate areas and given age-appropriate programming.

In a press release, the State of Vermont touted its partnerships with community as a leading factor in their ability to bolster community capacity to a point where "youth with mental health concerns can be treated in the least restrictive setting possible" (State of Vermont 2019a). They pointed to better outcomes for youth through community programming where they can keep ties to their family and other support systems.

Both its Raise the Age reforms and the closure of Woodside, like New York's reforms, included partnerships and collaboration between government agencies and community groups, including events and processes guided by Vincent Schiraldi and the Columbia University Justice Lab. The Vermont DCF convened stakeholder meetings to review and discuss research findings, and DCF leadership participated in site-visits and convenings with other department heads from around the country, hosted by the Justice Lab (State of Vermont Department of Children and Families 2019).

Vermont's youth justice system is a blended model, incorporating both child protection and juvenile services into one agency. The state is embracing the position that children, regardless of their entry point into the system, have needs that are best met by a social service, rather than a punishment, model and that young people do not automatically achieve full maturity at age 18. The transfer of these young people incrementally from Department of

Corrections to Department of Children and Families supervision will enable them to be supported by a system that attempts to understand the unique needs of adolescents, but is also new ground for an agency used to working with younger children. The state reports that currently their caseload is 90% child protection cases and only 10% juvenile services, but that proportion could shift somewhat with the new legislation (Vastine 2018).

Through the combination of these reforms, Vermont is arguably at the cutting edge of youth justice in the United States. While there is a lot of work to be done in implementation, and it remains to be seen what the outcomes will be, other states can take Vermont as a model for eliminating or considerably downsizing incarceration for youth under the age of 20, if not older. While one concern may be that more young people would be involved in the justice system once it includes these older youth, by providing age-appropriate services they can be incorporated into the youth system without it meaning incarceration or increased punishment because youth justice has eschewed incarceration much more rapidly and broadly than the adult system.

Youth Correctional Leaders for Justice

Both New York and Vermont have arguably undergone monumental reforms championed by government officials collaborating with advocates and other stakeholders, to push for community-centered, sustainable change. This insider-outsider approach can be scaled through initiatives like Youth Correctional Leaders for Justice (YCLJ), which mobilizes system leaders to enable youth justice transformation.

YCLJ is a project of the Columbia Justice Lab, which Schiraldi and his co-director Bruce Western originally started as the Program in Criminal Justice at Harvard University after Schiraldi left his position as the probation commissioner in New York, and then the pair moved the project to Columbia University as the Justice Lab. According to its website, "The Justice Lab combines original research, policy development, and community engagement to propel the project of justice reform ... [and] work for a community-centered justice, in which incarceration is no longer used as a solution to problems that are often rooted in poverty and racial inequality" (Justice Lab 2019). The Justice Lab has several projects related to its mission, including its Youth Justice Initiatives (YJI) and Emerging Adult Justice Program (EAJP), which Schiraldi leads. The Youth Justice Initiatives focuses on transforming youth justice across the country, from systems relying on punitive "youth prison" models to community- and family-centered services for young people, including staff dedicated to Youth Correctional Leaders for Justice.

The impetus for YCLJ came after Schiraldi, known as a reformer after the work detailed above, began getting calls from current system administrators across the United States who needed advice or wanted to be part of work being done to change youth justice. After speaking with other former administrators who have championed deinstitutionalization efforts, he realized that others were having the same conversations. YCLJ launched in 2018 with Schiraldi as co-chair alongside Gladys Carrión, the former commissioner of both New York State's Office of Children and Family Services and later New York City's Administration for Children's Services, and with support from the Annie E. Casey and Public Welfare Foundations, as part of the Justice Lab at Columbia University. The project unites current and former youth correctional administrators to build a national movement to shift systems away from the use of punitive sanctions and incarceration and focus instead on a more youth-, family-, and community-oriented vision of youth justice. The group released a statement which noted that "large, punitive youth prisons, often located far from the communities and families of the youth that still exist across the country must be replaced with community-based resources" laying out a series of principles that the group believes youth justice systems should strive to uphold (Columbia Justice Lab 2019). These values, as stated in the group's statement, include:

- Opportunity: All young people matter—including those who have run afoul of the law—and should be treated with love, dignity, and respect. To achieve real and lasting change, we must help them achieve their full potential and become successful, productive citizens, with the power to contribute to society in meaningful ways.
- Understanding: We must recognize and acknowledge that many youth and staff within our systems have experienced trauma, which can have long-lasting impact on their actions. Simultaneously, systems must guide and support both staff and youth through a healing process and help them internalize new skills and approaches for engaging with one another.
- Equity: All youth should have access to the opportunities, networks, resources, and support they need to survive and thrive, based on where they are currently situated and where they see themselves in the future. To do this effectively, we must provide all youth with impartial and just treatment, with a concerted focus on eliminating the many biases that exist in systems, which have been shaped by racism, sexism, and the country's history of oppression.

- Youth, Family, and Community Driven: Youth, families, and communities are experts on what solutions they need to heal and thrive, and must meaningfully participate in decisions and debates that directly impact their well-being. Youth behavior should be viewed in the context of a young person's development, needs, and unique situation.
- Safety: All youth should have the ability to be their authentic selves without the risk of increased physical or emotional harm, and communities should have the resources to be safe places for their residents.
- Accountability: Fair and just systems can and should recognize a young person's humanity, providing a calibrated response to ensure public safety that simultaneously helps young people repair harm and not repeat harmful behaviors. To that end, youth should acknowledge personal responsibility for their actions and appreciate the impact those actions have had on others. Meanwhile, youth justice systems must recognize and validate victims, and be restorative. These systems should also recognize that most court-involved young people are themselves survivors of crime. Given the tremendous power that youth justice systems have to deprive young people of their liberty, it is crucial that we remain vigilant in tracking and sharing how their outcomes adhere to these values.

More than 50 current and former system administrators have signed on to the statement as of the writing of this chapter. The group plans to be a national voice in the field, to work collaboratively with advocates seeking watershed reforms, and to support YCLJ members as they represent the group's vision in local contexts to help systems transform.

This group embodies the notion that youth correctional administrators can be instrumental in closing outdated, prison-like facilities for young people, but must work in partnership with others. Working alongside youth, families, advocates, elected officials, philanthropy, and leaders in other government systems, administrators can close facilities while helping to ensure that the communities the youth come from have the resources they need to help young people thrive.

Conclusion

Youth justice in the United States has come a long way from the depths of the "superpredator era" when 109,000 youth were incarcerated and 250,000 youth were tried as adults. And yet, despite a considerable decline in those numbers, we still have the world's highest rate of youth incarceration and unheard-of rates of trying our young people as, and imprisoning them alongside, adults. Advocates working outside of the government systems are now joining with elected officials and administrators of government agencies in efforts to close youth prisons and create an approach to youth justice which recognizes the cognitive and social needs specific to youth. This combination of advocacy and youth correctional leaders can push US juvenile justice to, and over, a tipping point where youth prisons become a thing of the past, and youth are treated as any of us would want our own children treated if they were before the law.

Note

1. Until 2018, youth ages 16 and 17 were considered adults in New York for criminal justice purposes and, if incarcerated, were confined in adult facilities.

References

Ananthakrishnan, A., Schiraldi, V., & Weissman, M. (2019). *Moving beyond youth prisons: Lessons from New York City's implementation of close to home.* New York, NY: Columbia University Justice Lab.

Arya, N. (2018). *Getting to zero: A 50-state study of strategies to remove youth from adult jails.* Los Angeles, CA: UCLA School of Law.

Beck, A. J., Harrison, P. M., & Adams, D. B. (2007). *Sexual violence reported by correctional authorities, 2006.* Washington, DC: U.S. Department of Justice, Bureau of Justice Statistics. Retrieved September 1, 2020, from https://www.bjs.gov/content/pub/pdf/svrca06.pdf.

Beck, A. J., Cantor, D., Hartge, J., & Smith, T. (2013). *Sexual victimization in juvenile facilities reported by youth, 2012.* Washington, DC: U.S. Department of Justice, Bureau of Justice Statistics. Retrieved September 1, 2020, from https://bjs.gov/content/pub/pdf/svjfry12.pdf.

Boyes-Watson, C., & Gebo, E. (2018). *Youth crime and justice: Learning through the cases.* New York: Rowman & Littlefield.

Citizens' Committee for Children. (2009). *Inside out: Youth experiences inside New York's juvenile placement system.* Retrieved September 1, 2020, from https://www.cccnewyork.org/wp-content/publications/CCCReport.JuvenileJustice.Dec2009.pdf.

City of New York. (2010). *Mayor Bloomberg proposes overhaul of the New York state juvenile justice system to improve public safety, break the cycle of crime and save taxpayers millions.* Retrieved September 1, 2020, from https://www1.nyc.gov/office-of-the-mayor/news/520-10/mayor-bloomberg-proposes-overhaul-the-new-york-state-juvenile-justice-system-improve-public#/2.

Colman, R., Kim, D. H., Mitchell-Herzfeld, S., & Shady, T. (2009). *Long-term consequences of delinquency: Child maltreatment and crime in early adulthood.* Washington, DC: U.S. Department of Justice. Retrieved September 1, 2020, from https://www.ncjrs.gov/pdffiles1/nij/grants/226577.pdf.

Columbia Justice Lab. (2019). *Statement on ending youth prisons.* Retrieved September 1, from http://yclj.org/statement.

DiIulio, J. J., Jr. (1995, November 27). The coming of the superpredators. *The Weekly Standard*, p. 23. Retrieved September 1, 2020, from https://www.washingtonexaminer.com/weekly-standard/the-coming-of-the-super-predators.

Governor David Paterson's Task Force on Transforming Juvenile Justice. (2009). *Charting a new course: A blueprint for transforming juvenile justice in New York State.* New York, NY: Vera Institute. Retrieved September 1, 2020, from http://www.vera.org/download?file=2944/Charting-a-new-course-A-blueprint-for-transformingjuvenile-justice-in-New-York-State.pdf.

Hammond, B. (2010, November 23). Andrew Cuomo tours the belly of the beast: Tryon youth prison is a textbook case of N.Y. dysfunction. *Daily News.* Retrieved September 1, 2020, from https://www.nydailynews.com/opinion/andrew-cuomo-tours-belly-beast-tryon-youth-prison-textbook-case-n-y-dysfunction-article-1.455824.

Harvard Kennedy School. (2015). *Vincent Schiraldi joins program in criminal justice at Harvard Kennedy School.* Retrieved September 1, 2020, from https://www.hks.harvard.edu/announcements/vincent-schiraldi-joins-program-criminal-justice-harvard-kennedy-school.

Hawkins, A. (2014, March 11). De Blasio appoints criminal justice 'dream team'. *Crain's New York Business.* Retrieved September 1, 2020, from https://www.crainsnewyork.com/article/20140311/BLOGS04/140319964/de-blasio-appoints-criminal-justice-dream-team.

Justice Policy Institute. (2019). *About Justice Policy Institute.* Retrieved September 1, 2020, from https://justicepolicy.org.

Labbe, T. (2005, January 5). Juvenile justice expert tapped for D.C. Post. *The Washington Post.* Retrieved September 1, 2020, from https://www.washingtonpost.com/archive/local/2005/01/05/juvenile-justice-expert-tapped-for-dc-post/01b564f9-fc64-4e1f-bcfd-8339801d8078/.

McGarry, P., Yaroni, A., & Addie, S. (2014). *Innovations in NYC Health and human services policy: Adult probation and neighborhood opportunity network initiative.* New York, NY: Vera Institute of Justice. Retrieved September 1, 2020, from https://www.vera.org/downloads/Publications/innovations-in-nyc-health-and-human-services-policy-adult-probation-and-neighborhood-opportunity-network-initiative-neon/legacy_downloads/transition-brief-probation-neon-v2.pdf.

Mendel, R. A. (2011). *No place for kids: The case for reducing juvenile incarceration.* Baltimore, MD: Annie E. Casey Foundation.

Mendel, R. A. (2015). *Maltreatment of youth in U.S. juvenile corrections facilities: An update.* Baltimore, MD: Annie E. Casey Foundation.

Mohr, H. (2008, March 2). *13,000 abuse claims in juvie centers*. The Associated Press. Retrieved September 1, 2020, from https://ylc.org/news/13000-abuse-claims-in-juvie-centers/.

New York City Administration for Children's Services. (2019a). *Non-secure placement and limited-secure placement demographics report to city council: Fiscal year 2019*. Retrieved September 1, 2020, from https://www1.nyc.gov/assets/acs/pdf/data-analysis/2019/LL44CTHDReportFY19.pdf.

New York City Administration for Children's Services. (2019b). *Close to home archived documents 2012*. Retrieved September 1, 2020, from https://www1.nyc.gov/site/acs/about/close-to-home-2012-archived-documents.page.

New York State Department of Corrections and Community Supervision. (2020). *Parolees under community supervision: Beginning 2008*. Retrieved September 1, 2020, from https://data.ny.gov/Public-Safety/Parolees-Under-Community-Supervision-Beginning-200/pmxm-gftz.

New York State Division of Criminal Justice Services. (2012). *Juvenile Justice Advisory Board 2011 annual report*. New York State Division of Criminal Justice Services: Albany, NY.

Noonan, M. (2016). *Mortality in local jails, 2000–2014—Statistical tables*. Washington, DC: U.S. Department of Justice, Bureau of Justice Statistics. Retrieved September 1, 2020, from https://www.bjs.gov/content/pub/pdf/mlj0014st.pdf.

Office of Juvenile Justice and Delinquency Prevention. (2019). *OJJDP statistical briefing book*. Retrieved September 1, 2020, from https://www.ojjdp.gov/ojstatbb/.

Puzzanchera, C., Hockenberry, S., Sladky, T. J., & Kang, W. (2018). *Juvenile residential facility census databook*. Washington, DC: U.S. Department of Justice, Office of Juvenile Justice and Delinquency Prevention. Retrieved September 1, 2020, from https://www.ojjdp.gov/ojstatbb/jrfcdb/.

Ryan, L., & Schindler, M. (2011). *Notorious to notable: The crucial role of the philanthropic community in transforming the juvenile justice system in Washington, D.C.* Washington, DC: Campaign for Youth Justice.

Sawyer, W. (2019). *Youth confinement: The whole pie 2019*. Massachusetts: Prison Policy Initiative. Retrieved September 1, 2020, from https://www.prisonpolicy.org/reports/youth2019.html.

Schiraldi, V. (2015, November 11). What mass incarceration looks like for juveniles. *New York Times*, p. A35. Retrieved September 1, 2020, from https://www.nytimes.com/2015/11/11/opinion/what-mass-incarceration-looks-like-for-juveniles.html.

Sears, D., & Schiraldi, V. (2018). Dick Sears & Vincent Schiraldi: Vermont leads the way on juvenile justice reform. *VT Digger*. Retrieved September 1, 2020, from https://vtdigger.org/2018/07/09/dick-sears-vincent-schiraldi-vermont-leads-way-juvenile-justice-reform/.

Sickmund, M. (2006). *Juvenile residential facility census, 2002: Selected findings*. Washington, DC: U.S. Department of Justice, Office of Juvenile Justice and Delinquency Prevention.

Sickmund, M., Sladky, T.J., Kang, W., and Puzzanchera, C. (2017) Easy Access to the Census of Juveniles in Residential Placement." from http://www.ojjdp.gov/ojstatbb/ezacjrp/.

Snyder, H. (2005, February). Is suicide more common inside or outside of juvenile facilities? *Corrections Today*, p. 84. Retrieved September 1, 2020, from http://www.ncjj.org/PDF/Howardpubs/Research_Notes_2_05.pdf.

State of Vermont Agency of Human Services. (2016). Governor signs law creating more rational juvenile justice policies in Vermont. Retrieved September 1, 2020, from https://dcf.vermont.gov/dcf-blog/governor-signs-law-creating-more-rational-juvenile-justice-policies-vermont.

State of Vermont Agency of Human Services. (2019a). *Woodside Juvenile Rehabilitation Center proposed to close 2020*. Retrieved September 1, 2020, from https://humanservices.vermont.gov/press-release/woodside-juvenile-rehabilitation-center-proposed-close-2020.

State of Vermont Agency of Human Services. (2019b). *Woodside Juvenile Rehabilitation Center Report*. Retrieved September 1, 2020, from https://legislature.vermont.gov/assets/Legislative-Reports/Woodside-legislative-report-4.15.2019.pdf.

State of Vermont Department of Children and Families. (2019). Report on Act 201 implementation plan report & recommendations. Retrieved September 1, 2020, from https://static1.squarespace.com/static/5c6458c07788975dfd586d90/t/5dd2ebfce2b1425d33ae1ef1/1574104062934/Vermont-RTA-DCF-Report-Final_EAJP.pdf.

Steinberg, L. (2009). Should the science of adolescent brain development inform public policy? *American Psychologist, 64*(8), 739.

Troilo, M. (2018). *Locking up youth with adults: An update.* Prison Policy Initiative. Retrieved September 1, 2020, from https://www.prisonpolicy.org/blog/2018/02/27/youth/.

United States Census Bureau. (2019). *QuickFacts Vermont*. Retrieved September 1, 2020, from https://www.census.gov/quickfacts/fact/table/VT/PST045218.

United States Department of Justice. (2009, August 14). *Investigation of the Lansing Residential Center, Louis Gossett, Jr. Residential Center, Tryon Residential Center, and Tryon Girls Center.* Washington, DC: United States Department of Justice. Retrieved September 1, 2020, from https://www.justice.gov/sites/default/files/crt/legacy/2010/12/15/NY_juvenile_facilities_findlet_08-14-2009.pdf.

Vastine, K. (2018, November 1). *Report on the expansion of juvenile jurisdiction*. Vermont Agency of Human Services, Department for Children and Families. Retrieved September 1, 2020, from https://legislature.vermont.gov/assets/Legislative-Reports/Act-201-Report.pdf.

Vermont Department of Corrections. (2014). *Facts and figures FY 2014*. Retrieved September 1, 2020, from http://doc.vermont.gov/about/reports/latest-facts-figures-adobe/view.

W. Haywood Burns Institute for Juvenile Justice Fairness and Equity. (2019). *Unbalanced juvenile justice*. Retrieved September 1, 2020, from http://data.burnsinstitute.org.

Index[1]

A

Abuse/assault
  physical, 4, 248, 268, 357, 574
  sexual, 37, 134n40, 248, 272, 273, 281, 357, 380, 418, 460, 515, 574, 616, 620
  staff in juvenile facilities, 248–249
  youth/peers in facilities, 550
Addiction, 174, 175, 290, 294, 295, 299, 302, 424, 432, 444, 450, 467, 476
Adolescence, 111, 192, 226, 238, 299, 380, 384, 419, 476, 479–497
Advocacy, 11, 42, 276, 448, 504–505, 509, 516, 563, 564, 566, 573, 576–578, 580, 584–586, 618, 620, 621, 630
  legal, 504, 618
  See also Reform
Age, legal meaning, 8
  age of jurisdiction, 132n5, 434, 625
  construction of childhood, 111
  essentialism, 539, 543–546, 549, 554
  minimum age of responsibility, vi, 144
  See also Sentencing; Development; Facility
Assault charges, 310

B

Becker, H., 318
Boys, *see* Gender
Brain development, 226, 238, 621
Brazil, 5, 7, 141–158, 159n8

C

Campbell, A., 317
Child welfare, v, vi, 3, 4, 53, 60, 62, 64, 81, 87, 131, 245, 259, 272, 273, 339, 454
Christianity, 285, 301, 513
Citizen-subjects, 305, 309, 311
Colonialism, 129
Colonisation, 77
Columbia, 7, 617, 627, 628

---

[1] Note: Page numbers followed by 'n' refer to notes.

636 Index

Competing for status, 306
Confinement
  behavioral reaction to, 280
  conditions of, 2, 7, 386, 564, 572, 574, 577, 581, 616, 617, 619, 621
  emotional reaction to, 4, 8
  See also Facilities; Detention; Sentencing
Construction of labor and citizenship, 307
Court
  adult, 10, 88, 120, 121, 124, 167, 563, 625
  criminal, 52, 121, 167, 170, 414, 503, 504, 552, 564, 566
  juvenile, 52, 84, 86, 88–92, 94, 96, 97, 121, 132n5, 143, 167, 170, 206, 267–271, 273, 274, 278–280, 417, 503, 504, 509, 563, 566–568, 571, 576, 625
  See also Sentencing
COVID-19, 7, 19, 20, 607
  See also Isolation
Crime, 2, 4–6, 9, 10, 55, 57, 66, 67, 78, 80, 81, 83–86, 88, 97, 114, 117–126, 128, 129, 132n5, 134n32, 135n54, 142, 144, 146, 156, 159n4, 165–179, 198, 206, 208, 209, 213, 217–219, 229, 230, 245, 289, 311, 324, 329, 339, 345, 380, 382–384, 386, 391, 392, 396, 402, 403, 434, 438, 439, 441, 444, 451, 453, 463, 468, 469, 472–475, 504, 506, 509, 510, 520, 521, 530, 534, 540, 548, 568, 593, 602, 605, 606, 609, 615, 620, 621, 624, 626, 629
  pathways into, 165–179
  See also Delinquency

Cultural inferiority, 307
Curfew, 274, 310, 555n3
Custody, *see* Confinement

D

Delinquency, 7, 80, 107–131, 226, 238, 269, 382, 445, 615
Denmark, 5, 8, 206, 209
Deprivation of liberty, vi, 2, 3, 24, 141–158, 158n1, 158n2, 159n6, 159n7, 497
Desistance
  aging out of crime, 382, 383, 439, 606
  "falling back," 413, 415, 420–422, 428, 433
  role of opportunity, 413, 415, 420–422, 428, 433
Detention, v–vii, 1, 2, 5, 8, 20, 25, 28, 32, 37, 51–55, 57, 59–68, 78, 81–85, 88–90, 98, 113, 114, 117, 141–158, 158n1, 158n2, 186, 200, 243, 244, 261, 273–276, 279, 285–302, 310, 337, 431, 541–543, 553, 555n1, 576, 583, 585, 595, 620
  See also Confinement; Facility
Deterrence, 80, 121, 420, 421
Development, stages
  adolescence/adolescents, 63, 226, 479, 544
  childhood/children, vi, 109, 123, 359, 544, 616
  emerging adulthood, 380, 480, 485
  late adolescence, 480, 485
  young adults, 150, 519
Discourses of meritocracy, 306, 326
Discourses of prostitution, 311, 326
Diversion, v, vi, 8, 78, 84–88, 145, 158
Dominant ideals of womanhood, 308, 324

Drama, 207, 276, 278, 313, 315, 316, 318, 325, 326, 433
Dual transition, 380, 419
Durkheim, 309, 327

E

Education, vi, 8, 11, 26, 40, 55, 65, 80, 91, 93–94, 112, 114, 128, 131, 147, 151, 166, 168, 169, 175, 176, 218, 220, 246, 278–281, 288, 301, 404, 416–419, 432, 510, 517, 518, 520, 544, 548, 553, 566, 571, 593–609
Emotional experience (of confinement)
  boredom, 4, 208
  empathy, 342, 343, 346, 348, 349, 351
  masking, 336
  stress, 4
  vulnerability, 333, 335–337, 342, 349–351
  See also First-person narrative; Pains of imprisonment; Trauma
Emotionality, 306–308, 311, 313–319, 324–326, 329, 360
Emotions, 4, 8, 60, 63, 199, 207, 209, 252–253, 259, 260, 306, 307, 313–316, 318, 319, 323–326, 333–348, 350, 351, 360, 361, 366, 368, 422, 467, 469, 472, 473, 476, 507
Employment, *see* Reentry
Ethnographic research, 309

F

Facilities
  adult facility, 226, 233, 253, 290, 513, 515, 540, 550, 616, 620, 621, 630n1
  detention center, 60, 386

juvenile facility, 3–5, 20, 227, 233, 235, 243–261, 379, 414, 423, 428, 430
  prison, v, 233, 247, 253, 258, 261, 379, 386, 423, 513, 550, 575, 581, 583, 615, 616, 619, 622, 626, 629
  residential placement, 379, 414, 434
  secure
    secure care, 206–210, 212–214, 220n1
    secure school, 27, 28, 595, 596
    secure training center, 27, 28, 603, 607
  segregation by age, 546, 550
  young offender institution, 249, 601
  See also Confinement; Prison
Family, *see* Social relationships
Feld, B., 124, 329, 503, 504, 549, 552
First-person narrative, 438, 495, 509, 521
Fordham, S., 315
Foucault, M., 150, 305, 306, 308, 309, 311, 312, 320, 326, 337, 340, 341, 548, 549

G

Gangs, 107, 123, 131, 134n40, 158, 226–229, 232–236, 238, 274, 288, 317, 357, 386, 425, 442, 445, 453, 511–515, 517, 520, 521, 566, 573, 602, 617
Garfinkel, H., 320, 323
Gender
  boys, 2, 5, 27, 37, 40, 56, 90, 93, 95, 114, 123, 133n19, 188, 194, 209, 210, 212, 214, 215, 217, 233, 248, 253, 254, 256–258, 269, 274, 287, 300, 310, 313–315, 318, 319, 329, 336, 347, 355–370, 466, 495, 565–567, 573, 618, 622

Gender (*Cont.*)
    femininity, policing of, 5, 281, 287, 308, 316, 317, 322, 324, 325, 334
    girls, 4, 5, 80, 90, 93, 114, 118, 122, 123, 209, 247, 250, 267–282, 285–302, 305–329, 356, 357, 417, 441, 451, 452, 455, 466, 493, 555n2, 566, 567
    masculinity/hyper masculinity, 5, 9, 61, 333–351, 355–370, 399, 403, 417, 515
    role expectations, 247, 248
    young men, 5, 9, 26, 52, 56–58, 60–62, 67, 82, 165–179, 217, 225, 227, 229–234, 236–238, 333, 335–337, 339–345, 347, 350, 355–370, 381, 383, 384, 389, 393, 399, 403, 414, 415, 417, 419–425, 427, 429–432, 434n1, 447, 450, 451, 460, 485, 489, 490, 492, 494–497, 514, 519, 595, 596
    young women, 8, 9, 26, 268, 271, 274, 278–282, 290, 383, 437–460, 485, 489, 491, 492, 494–497
    See also Sexuality; Trauma
Gendering processes, 327–329
Gender-segregation, 329
Germany, 7, 8, 165–179
Ghana, 3, 7, 77–98
Girls, *see* Gender
Globalization/globalisation, 77, 78, 97
Group home, 2, 175, 310, 445, 448, 449, 453–456, 575, 579
Group therapy, 275–277, 309, 320, 322, 323, 325, 326, 329, 465

Historical perspective (on juvenile justice), 55, 249, 327
    United States context, 166–167, 246, 249
Horizontal surveillance, 305–329
Human rights
    inconsistencies, 521
    rights framework, 23, 27–35, 39, 84, 531
    in theory and in practice, 23, 67, 540
    United Nations Convention on the Rights of the Child, v, vi, 1, 2, 28, 40, 83, 86, 95, 112, 125, 130, 142, 244, 535n19, 541, 542, 563
    See also Institutional accountability, monitoring; Legal protections; Oversight
Hurtado, A., 308, 312, 324

Identity construction, 317
Immoral selves, 320, 329
Incarceration, 2, 3, 5, 6, 9–11, 20, 24, 55, 56, 61, 90, 97, 123–130, 134n31, 141, 151, 154, 158, 166, 178, 213, 228, 229, 244, 250, 285–290, 292–295, 297, 299–302, 310, 356–358, 363, 364, 367, 369, 379–386, 393, 395–398, 402, 404, 405, 413, 414, 428, 433, 434, 437, 442, 468, 469, 477, 480, 490, 506, 508, 514, 516, 529, 530, 539–555, 563, 568, 570–573, 575–585, 618, 619, 621, 622, 624, 626–629
    legitimacy of, 247, 549
    See also Confinement; Sentencing
India, 7, 107–131, 554
Innocence, 443, 546, 547

Institutional accountability, monitoring, 143, 327
See also Oversight
Institutional power, 306–308, 312, 320, 327
Interviews, 58–60, 67, 85–87, 91, 134n38, 165, 169–171, 173, 176–179, 180n6, 210, 212, 216, 217, 225, 229–232, 234, 235, 237, 250, 251, 254, 270–281, 291, 292, 310, 311, 333, 335, 340–351, 382, 384–386, 389, 390, 394, 396, 402, 414, 418, 420, 421, 438, 439, 442, 443, 446, 448, 450, 452, 458, 460, 480, 482, 484–487, 490–492, 496, 498n3, 498n6, 499n8, 510, 518, 519, 530, 550
Isolation, 40–42, 272, 358, 367, 442, 467, 470, 476, 507, 528, 569, 570, 608, 616

Justice, conceptions of
 community-based justice delivery, 111
 neoliberal, 77
 traditional, 80, 81, 86, 97, 98
 Western, 77
 See also Colonialism; Colonization; Globalization; Historical perspective (on juvenile justice); Restorative justice

Language of meritocracy, 307
Legal protections
 child protective legislation, 272
 discretionary application, 144–147, 151, 154, 155, 158
 legal rights, 35
 See also Advocacy; Human rights; Legal norms
Lived experience, *see* First-person narrative

MacLeod, J., 329
Malawi, 10, 525–534
McCorkel, J.A., 329
Meritocracy, 306, 307, 309, 326
Meritocratic social order, 306, 309
Merit system, 288, 321
Minority, *see* Race
Moralizing therapy, 309
Moral order, 313, 343, 312, 312

Organizational logic, 307, 320, 329
Oversight, 2, 32–34, 36, 250
 See also Institutional accountability, monitoring

Pains of imprisonment, 8, 10, 220, 336, 367, 481, 482, 489
Participant-observations, 310
Personal responsibility (in lieu of systems level-understanding of youth crime), 227, 287, 288, 629
 See also Programming; Religion
Placements, *see* Facilities
Police, v, vi, 4, 56–60, 84–86, 88, 91–94, 98, 119, 130, 134n32, 144, 145, 157, 159n4, 174, 186, 187, 213, 215, 228, 269, 272, 306, 309, 349, 350, 381, 418, 420, 424, 427, 429–432, 442, 445, 447, 453, 455–457, 509, 527–529, 533

Political transition, influence on justice system, 527, 528
Poverty, criminalization of, 53, 151
Prison
  adult prison, 6, 27, 53, 86, 91, 169, 177, 226, 227, 246, 258, 289, 386, 418, 433, 503–521, 528, 550, 565, 568, 569, 573, 603
  youth prison, vi, 7, 9, 10, 19–21, 333–351, 507, 550, 563–586, 615–617, 620–623, 626, 628, 630
  See also Facilities
Probation
  officers, 86, 88, 89, 96, 97, 125, 190, 191, 273–275, 414, 416, 419, 423, 425, 426, 428, 430, 454, 624
  supervision, 433, 445, 584, 622
Programming
  educational, 20, 206, 520, 573, 597, 598, 602, 606
  faith-based, 290 (*see also* Religion)
Prosecution, 52, 64, 65, 84, 88–90, 98, 130, 144, 145, 430, 564, 624
  See also Sentencing
Prostitution, 268, 273, 310–312, 320, 322–324, 326
Protective factors, 55, 58, 59, 66
Puerto Rican gang girls, 317

Race/ethnicity
  African American, 168, 270, 286, 291, 295, 299, 310, 316, 317, 324, 380, 385, 386, 393, 456, 511, 564, 565, 619
  BAME (Black, Asian, & Minority Ethnic), 25
  Black, 25, 186, 189, 193–195, 230, 234, 235, 254–256, 287, 302, 307, 308, 312, 315–317, 324, 379, 381, 391–393, 414, 415, 439, 441, 509, 512, 514, 565, 566, 570, 573, 616
  Latino, 186, 189, 230, 258, 414, 513, 517
  racial disparity, 580, 616
  racism, 2, 6, 286, 415, 544, 546, 628
Racialization in the labor market, 307
Racialized citizen, 313, 326
Ranking of offenses, 320
Reentry
  employment, 403
  reintegration, 5, 433
  See also Desistance; Family
Reform
  advocacy, 563
  decarceration, 2, 244, 548, 576–577
  stakeholders, 623, 624
  systems change, 615–630
Regulating Girls' Emotionality, 313–319
Regulating Women's Sexual Morality, 305, 311–313
Rehabilitation, 9, 84, 89, 91, 93–96, 114, 125, 166, 167, 178, 245, 255, 287, 290, 297, 298, 302, 310, 326, 328, 333, 335, 337, 339, 341, 351n2, 356, 364, 368, 370, 405, 503, 505, 520, 531, 539, 547, 550, 566, 567, 572, 626
Religion
  Christianity, 285, 301, 513
  Hinduism, 107, 131n2
  See also Programming, faith-based
Reproduction of Worker-Citizens, 306–307
Research setting, 309–310

Restorative justice, vi, 10, 52, 54, 55, 57, 65, 84, 86, 145, 147, 158
See also Justice, conceptions of
Risk-taking, 208, 209, 360, 363

S

Safe space, 236–238, 367
Self-policing, 312, 308, 309
Sentencing
    death penalty, 117, 532
    extreme sentencing, 505–507, 520, 521
    indeterminate sentencing, 227
    "JLWOP" (juvenile life without the possibility of parole), 505, 506, 511–513, 516, 517, 521
    juvenile life sentence, 506
    long-term imprisonment, 482
    "LWOP" (life without the possibility of parole), 10, 464, 471, 507, 508
    resentencing, 509, 510, 516, 517, 526, 530
Sexuality
    homophobia, 274, 278
    sexual minority, 274, 278, 280, 281
    See also Gender
Slavery, 308, 324
Social mobility, 321, 323
Social relationships
    family, 382, 385, 386, 389, 394–400, 402–404
    friendship, 469
    peers
        horizontal surveillance, 306, 309, 312, 320, 321, 325, 328, 329
    pro-social relationships, 226
    See also Gangs
Social reproduction, 329

Solitary confinement, vii, 37, 39–42, 276, 508, 540, 547, 551, 555, 570, 573, 574, 581
See also Isolation
Staff, juvenile facility
    abuse, 248–249
    developmental role, 246–247
    "juvenile care workers," 244
    roles, care and control, 248
Stigma, 5, 23, 59, 97, 130, 168, 322, 359, 360
Sweden, 3, 9, 245, 335, 339

T

Theoretical Frameworks, 308–309
Theory of Gendered Organizations, 306
Therapeutic discourses, 415, 305
Therapeutic governance, 305–329
Therapeutic techniques, 322, 325, 327
"Time work," 208, 213, 214, 216, 218
Trauma, 9, 19, 24, 169, 172, 244, 249, 250, 271, 281, 302, 340–342, 350, 351, 355–370, 441, 458, 460, 463–466, 471–473, 475–477, 491, 507, 508, 514, 515, 520, 526, 617, 628

U

United Kingdom (UK), 2, 5, 7, 8, 10, 24, 25, 43, 248, 355, 357, 359, 507, 508, 550, 607
United States (US), vi, 2–10, 19, 20, 28, 43, 55, 121, 142, 143, 151, 165–179, 187, 245, 248, 249, 260, 267, 270, 279–281, 286–289, 355, 357, 358, 379, 482, 503–506, 520, 541, 546, 550, 553, 554, 563, 570, 615, 616, 619–622, 625, 627–630

V

Verbal expressiveness, 314–317, 319
Violence, 1–4, 7, 9, 24, 35, 36, 38, 51–68, 71n13, 80, 84, 114, 116, 122, 123, 129, 130, 146, 155, 169, 228, 232, 235, 237, 238, 248–250, 253, 254, 261, 271, 276, 281, 288, 293–296, 299, 314, 334, 336, 356–360, 362–364, 367, 422, 431–433, 438, 444, 458–460, 466, 467, 476, 477, 482, 508, 512–514, 518–521, 525, 548–550, 601–603, 616, 617
See also Abuse/assault

W

Web of discipline, 308
"What works," 593, 609
Worker-citizen, 306–308, 314, 326, 329

Y

Youth prison model, 563–586, 623, 628

Printed in the United States
by Baker & Taylor Publisher Services